The Princeton Review®

MW00667791

DIGITAL SAT®

PREMIUM PREP

2025 Edition

The Staff of The Princeton Review

PrincetonReview.com

Penguin Random House

The Princeton Review

The Princeton Review
110 East 42nd Street, 7th Floor
New York, NY 10017

Published in the United States by Penguin Random House LLC, New York.

Terms of Service: The Princeton Review Online Companion Tools ("Student Tools") for retail books are available for only the two most recent editions of that book. Student Tools may be activated only once per eligible book purchased for a total of 24 months of access. Activation of Student Tools more than once per book is in direct violation of these Terms of Service and may result in discontinuation of access to Student Tools Services.

ISBN: 978-0-593-51754-3
eBook ISBN: 978-0-593-51755-0
ISSN: 2687-895X

This book is the 2025 edition of Princeton Review SAT Prep. Some material in this book was previously published in Princeton Review PSAT Prep 2024, a trade paperback respectively published by Random House LLC in 2023.

Editor: Laura Rose
Production Editors: Liz Dacey and Wendy Rosen
Production Artist: Deborah Weber

Printed in the United States of America.

10 9 8 7 6 5 4 3 2 1

2025 Edition

The Princeton Review Publishing Team
Rob Franek, Editor-in-Chief
David Soto, Senior Director, Data Operations
Stephen Koch, Senior Manager, Data Operations
Deborah Weber, Director of Production
Jason Ullmeyer, Production Design Manager
Jennifer Chapman, Senior Production Artist
Selena Coppock, Director of Editorial
Orion McBean, Senior Editor
Aaron Riccio, Senior Editor
Meave Shelton, Senior Editor
Chris Chimera, Editor
Patricia Murphy, Editor
Laura Rose, Editor
Isabelle Appleton, Editorial Assistant

Penguin Random House Publishing Team
Tom Russell, VP, Publisher
Alison Stoltzfus, Senior Director, Publishing
Emily Hoffman, Associate Managing Editor
Patty Collins, Executive Director of Production
Mary Ellen Owens, Assistant Director of Production
Alice Rahaeuser, Associate Production Manager
Maggie Gibson, Associate Production Manager
Suzanne Lee, Senior Designer
Eugenia Lo, Publishing Assistant

For customer service, please contact **editorialsupport@review.com**, and be sure to include:

- full title of the book
- ISBN
- page number

Acknowledgments

An SAT course is much more than clever techniques and powerful computer score reports. The reason our results are great is that our teachers care so much about their students. Many teachers have gone out of their way to improve the course, often going so far as to write their own materials, some of which we have incorporated into our course manuals as well as into this book. The list of these teachers could fill this page.

Special thanks to all those who contributed to this year's edition: Kenneth Brenner, Sara Kuperstein, Amy Minster, Scott O'Neal, Brittany Budzon, Tania Capone, Remy Cosse, Stacey Cowap, Jennifer Daniels, Beth Hollingsworth, Adam Keller, Ali Landreau, Aaron Lindh, Christine Lindwall, Jomil London, Sweena Mangal, Sionainn Marcoux, Valerie Meyers, Gabby Peterson, Denise Pollard, Kathy Ruppert, Jess Thomas, Jimmy Williams, and Suzanne Wint.

We are also, as always, very appreciative of the time and attention given to each page by Deborah Weber, Liz Dacey, and Wendy Rosen.

Finally, we would like to thank the people who truly have taught us everything we know about the SAT: our students.

Contents

Foreword

Welcome to *The Princeton Review Digital SAT Prep!* The Digital SAT is not a test of aptitude, how good of a person you are, or how successful you will be in life. The Digital SAT simply tests how well you take the Digital SAT. And performing well on the Digital SAT is a skill, one that can be learned like any other. The Princeton Review was founded more than 40 years ago on this very simple idea, and—as our students' test scores show—our approach is the one that works.

Sure, you want to do well on the Digital SAT, but you don't need to let the test intimidate you. As you prepare, remember two important things that have always been true about the SAT:

- **It doesn't measure the stuff that matters.** It measures neither intelligence nor the depth and breadth of what you're learning in high school. It doesn't predict college grades as well as your high school grades do. Colleges know there is more to you as a student—and as a person—than what you do in a single 2-hour test administered on a random Saturday morning.

- **It underpredicts the college performance of women, minorities, and disadvantaged students.** Historically, women have done better than men in college but worse on the SAT. For a test that is used to help predict performance in college, that's a pretty poor record.

Your preparation for the Digital SAT starts here. We at The Princeton Review spend millions of dollars every year improving our methods and materials so that students are always ready for the Digital SAT, and we'll get you ready too.

However, there is no magic pill: just buying this book isn't going to improve your scores. Solid score improvement takes commitment and effort from you. If you read this book carefully and work through the problems and practice tests included in the book, not only will you be well-versed in the format of the Digital SAT and the concepts it tests, but you will also have a sound overall strategy and a powerful arsenal of test-taking strategies that you can apply to whatever you encounter on test day.

In addition to the comprehensive review in *Digital SAT Prep*, we've included additional practice online, accessible through our website—PrincetonReview.com—to continue helping you to improve your scores. Before doing anything else, be sure to register your book at PrincetonReview.com/prep. When you do, you'll gain access to the Student Tools, which has the most up-to-date information on the Digital SAT, as well as the online practice tests and college admissions resources.

The more you take advantage of the resources we've included in this book and the online Student Tools that go with it, the better you'll do on the test. Read the book carefully and learn our strategies. Take the full-length practice tests under actual timed conditions. Analyze your performance and focus your efforts where you need improvement. Perhaps even study with a friend to stay motivated. Attend a free event at The Princeton Review to learn more about the Digital SAT and how it is used in the college admissions process. Search our website for an event that will take place near you or take place online!

This test is challenging, but you're on the right track. We'll be with you all the way.

Good luck!
The Staff of The Princeton Review

Get More (Free) Content at PrincetonReview.com/prep

As easy as 1·2·3

1 Go to PrincetonReview.com/prep or scan the **QR code** and enter the following ISBN for your book: **9780593517543**

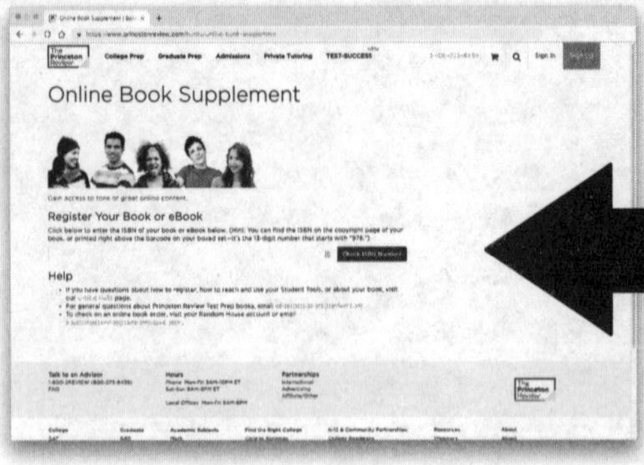

2 Answer a few simple questions to set up an exclusive Princeton Review account. *(If you already have one, you can just log in.)*

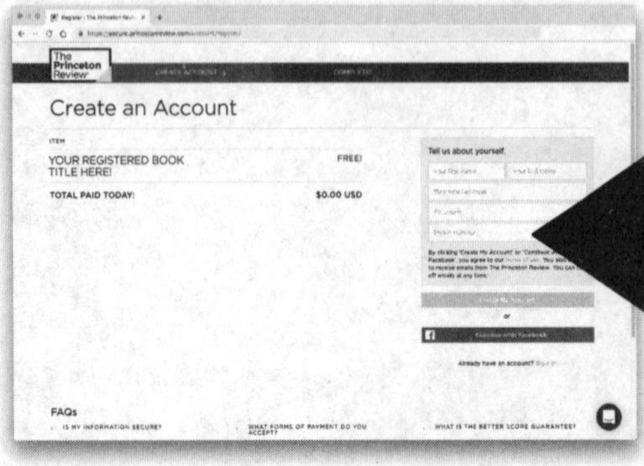

3 Enjoy access to your **FREE** content!

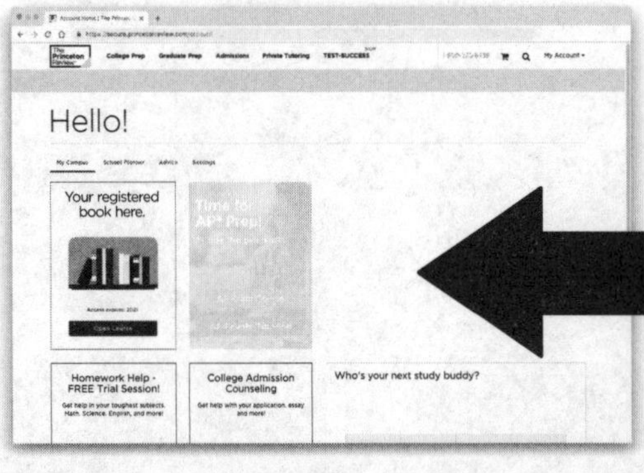

Once you've registered, you can...

- Access three practice Digital SAT exams as well as comprehensive scoring reports
- Check out our comprehensive study guides to help enhance your test prep
- Read our special "SAT Insider" and get valuable advice about the college application process, including tips for writing a great essay and where to apply for financial aid
- Access online flashcards with key Reading and Writing and Math concepts
- Watch video explanations of key in-book questions
- Download extra printable bubble sheets for the in-book tests
- Use our searchable rankings of *The Best 390 Colleges* to find out more information about your dream school
- Check to see if there have been any corrections or updates to this edition
- Get our take on any recent or pending updates to the Digital SAT

LET'S GO MOBILE! Access free, additional resources by downloading the new Princeton Review app at www.princetonreview.com/mobile/apps/highschool or scan the QR Code to the right.

Need to report a potential **content** issue?

Contact **EditorialSupport@review.com** and include:

- full title of the book
- ISBN
- page number

Need to report a **technical** issue?

Contact **TPRStudentTech@review.com** and provide:

- your full name
- email address used to register the book
- full book title and ISBN
- Operating system (Mac/PC) and browser (Chrome, Firefox, Safari, etc.)

Look For These Icons Throughout The Book

- PREMIUM PORTAL
- ONLINE ARTICLES
- ONLINE PRACTICE TESTS
- PROVEN TECHNIQUES
- APPLIED STRATEGIES
- OTHER REFERENCES
- WATCH US CRACK IT
- STUDY BREAK

Part I
Orientation

LET'S GET THIS PARTY STARTED!

You are about to unlock a vast repertoire of powerful strategies that have one and only one purpose: to help you get a better score on the Digital SAT. This book contains the collected wisdom of The Princeton Review, which has spent more than 40 years helping students achieve higher scores on standardized tests. We've devoted millions of dollars and years of our lives to beating the SAT. It's what we do (twisted as it may be), and we want you to benefit from our expertise.

Welcome!
Welcome to the Premium Edition of *Digital SAT Prep.* This edition comes chock-full of awesome online resources, including online Digital SAT practice tests, as well as study guides, college admissions articles, and more. See "Get More (Free) Content" on pages xiv–xv for **step-by-step instructions** for accessing your exclusive Premium tools. Happy test prepping!

WHAT IS THE PRINCETON REVIEW?

The Princeton Review is the leader in test prep. Our goal is to help students everywhere crack the SAT and a bunch of other standardized tests, including the PSAT and the ACT as well as graduate-level exams like the GRE and the GMAT. Starting from humble beginnings in 1981, The Princeton Review is now the nation's largest SAT preparation company. We offer courses in more than 500 locations in 20 different countries, as well as online; we also publish best-selling books, like the one you're holding, and online resources to get students ready for this test.

Our techniques work. We developed them after spending countless hours scrutinizing real SATs, analyzing them with computers, and proving our theories in the classroom.

The Princeton Review Way

This book will show you how to score higher on the Digital SAT by teaching you to:

- extract important information from tricky test questions
- take full advantage of the limited time allowed
- systematically answer questions—even if you don't fully understand them
- avoid the traps that the Digital SAT has laid for you (and use those traps to your advantage)

Study!
If you were getting ready to take a biology test, you'd study biology. If you were preparing for a basketball game, you'd practice basketball. So, if you're preparing for the SAT, you need to study and practice for the SAT. The exam can't test everything you learn in school (in fact, it tests very little), so concentrate on learning what it *does* test.

The test is written and administered by College Board, and they know that our techniques work. For years, the test-writers claimed that the SAT couldn't be coached. But we've proven that view wrong, and they, in turn, have struggled to find ways of changing the SAT so that The Princeton Review won't be able to crack it—in effect, acknowledging what our students have known all along: that our techniques really do work. (In fact, College Board has recently admitted that students can and should prepare for the SAT. So there!) The SAT has remained highly vulnerable to our techniques. And the current version of the SAT is even more susceptible to our methods. Read this book, work through the drills, take the practice tests, and you'll see what we mean.

Chapter 1
The Digital SAT, The Princeton Review, and You

Welcome! Our job is to help you get the best possible score on the Digital SAT. This chapter will tell you what to expect from the Digital SAT as well as some specifics about the test. It will also explain how to make the most of all your Princeton Review materials.

GENERAL INFORMATION ABOUT THE DIGITAL SAT

You may have bought this book because you know nothing about the Digital SAT, or perhaps you took the SAT once and want to raise your score. Either way, it's important to know about the test and the people who write it. Let's take a second to discuss some Digital SAT facts, some of which may surprise you.

What Is Tested on the Digital SAT?

Just because the Digital SAT features math, reading, and writing questions doesn't mean that it reflects what you learned in school. You can ace calculus or write like Shakespeare and still struggle with the SAT. The test-writers claim that the test predicts how well you will do in college by measuring "reasoning ability," but all the Digital SAT really measures is how well you take the Digital SAT. It does *not* reveal how smart—or how good—a person you are.

Wait, *Who* Writes This Test?
You may be surprised to learn that the people who write Digital SAT test questions are NOT necessarily teachers or college professors. The people who write the Digital SAT are professional test-writers, not super-human geniuses, so you can learn to think as they do and beat them at their own game.

Who Writes the Digital SAT?

Even though colleges and universities make wide use of the SAT, they're not the ones who write the test. That's the job of College Board, the organization that creates the tests and decides how they will be administered and used.

The test-writers have been criticized for the SAT over the years. Many educators have argued that the test does not measure the skills you really need for college. In 2005, this led College Board to overhaul the entire test, only to revise it all over again in early 2016. And in January 2022, College Board announced another major change—the shift to a digital, adaptive SAT. The important takeaway here is that the people who write the Digital SAT have made many changes to the test over the years, so understanding the structure of the current exam is your first step to improving on the test.

What's on the Digital SAT?

The Digital SAT is 2 hours and 14 minutes long: 64 minutes for Reading and Writing and 70 minutes for Math.

The test consists of the following sections, in this order:

Key Takeaway
Knowing how the test is structured will help you determine what you need to do to crack it!

- Reading and Writing (RW) (2 modules, each 27 questions in 32 minutes)
  - o All questions in the RW section are multiple-choice.
  - o Two questions in each module are experimental and are not scored.
- A 10-minute break
- Math (2 modules, each 22 questions in 35 minutes)
  - o Most questions in the Math section are multiple-choice.
  - o The rest are "student-produced responses" (fill-ins).
  - o Two questions in each module are experimental and are not scored.

The Math section contains some student-produced-response questions, but all other questions on the exam are multiple-choice. All multiple-choice questions on the Digital SAT have four possible answer choices.

The remaining chapters of this book cover these sections in detail, but here's a brief rundown of what you can expect.

Reading and Writing Section

Previous versions of the SAT had Reading and Writing as separate sections, with several questions attached to each long passage. The Digital SAT combines Reading and Writing. The Reading and Writing (RW) section is 64 minutes long and consists of 2 modules, each with 27 questions that are passage-based and multiple-choice. Each short passage (which College Board calls a "text") or pair of passages (texts) is associated with just one question, and passages may be paired with informational graphics. Some of the selected passages will be from previously published works in the areas of world literature or poetry, but most will be short passages written by College Board and covering topics in history, social studies, and science.

Want More?
For even more practice, check out *SAT Level Up: Verbal* and *SAT Level Up: Math.*

The RW section consists of four parts in order:

1. Craft and Structure (≈28%)
2. Information and Ideas (≈26%)
3. Standard English Conventions (≈26%)
4. Expression of Ideas (≈20%)

The questions in each content area will be arranged by type and, in most cases, in order of difficulty. The first two parts of each module will cover what was previously in the Reading section of the SAT, with questions that require you to justify your selected answer with evidence from the passage and/or graph provided. (This section is not about coming up with anything; it's about finding the correct answer based on the passage.) In the third and fourth parts of each module, there will be questions focused on Writing skills. Instead of asking you to analyze a passage, questions will require you to do things like choose answers with correct punctuation and grammar. Part II of this book will cover each question type in the Reading and Writing section.

Math Section

You will have a total of 70 minutes to complete the Math section, which, as mentioned earlier, is divided into two modules (each with 22 questions in 35 minutes). Most questions are multiple-choice, but there are also a handful of what College Board calls Student-Produced Response questions, which we call fill-ins. For fill-in questions, instead of choosing from four answer choices, you'll have to work through a question and then enter your answer on the screen by typing in the appropriate numbers. We'll discuss this in more detail in Chapter 26. Approximately 11 of the 44 math questions will be fill-ins.

The Math section covers four main content areas, but not in this order:

1. Algebra (≈35%)
2. Advanced Math (≈35%)
3. Problem-Solving and Data Analysis (≈15%)
4. Geometry and Trigonometry (≈15%)

In contrast to the set order of the Reading and Writing topics, each Math module will have questions in each of these content areas scattered throughout but arranged in order of difficulty from the start of the module to the end. Part III of this book covers each of these content areas in depth.

Is My Calculator Allowed?
Not all calculators are permitted by College Board for use on the SAT. To see the full College Board calculator policy, visit satsuite.collegeboard.org/digital/what-to-bring-do/calculator-policy

The Digital SAT has a built-in Desmos calculator that can be used on all Math questions. In addition, students may bring their own approved calculators if they prefer. A calculator will be a game-changer on some questions and completely useless on others, so think about how to use it (or not) as you work through Part III. Practice with the calculator you plan to use on the actual test so you can take full advantage of this tool.

There is one more thing to know about the make-up of the Digital SAT: test-takers do not get the exact same test. In the days of paper-and-pencil SAT tests, the practice of giving students all over the globe the same test form led to issues with test security and possible cheating. With the switch to the Digital SAT, College Board says the testing app will now "assemble" a test for each student that is "unique." So, while all students will see the same concepts, they won't all see the same questions to test those concepts.

Scoring on the Digital SAT

Scores from the Digital SAT will be reported in a matter of days, not weeks as was the case with the paper-and-pencil test. Your score report for the Digital SAT will feature scores for each of the following:

Unlock Premium Content!
Register your book online to unlock Premium online resources, like helpful week-by-week study guides. Plus, use the "SAT Insider" to help navigate college admissions, applications, financial aid, and more.

- **Total Score:**
  The sum of the two section scores (Reading and Writing, Math), ranging from 400 to 1600

- **Section Scores:**
  1. Reading and Writing, ranging from 200 to 800
  2. Math, also ranging from 200 to 800

As previously mentioned, there will be two questions in each module that are experimental. College Board uses these to see how students answer them, but they will not count toward your score. Unfortunately, they are not marked in any way, so make sure to treat all questions as if they will be scored.

On the recent paper-and-pencil versions of the SAT, various subscores and cross-test scores were reported in addition to the section and overall scores. On the Digital SAT, only the scores listed above will be reported. This means that you will not be given any information on how you scored within specific subject areas.

So how do the two modules work together to determine your score in a section? Well, how you score on the first module determines whether you get an Easier or Harder second module. If you are given the Easier second module, you'll find that more of the questions are within your ability to get right, but there will be an upper limit to your score. If you get the Harder second module, you'll have the chance to score higher, but the questions in the module will be more difficult to get right. Of course, if you get enough questions correct in the first module to get the Harder second module, it's likely that the harder questions will be better suited to your abilities.

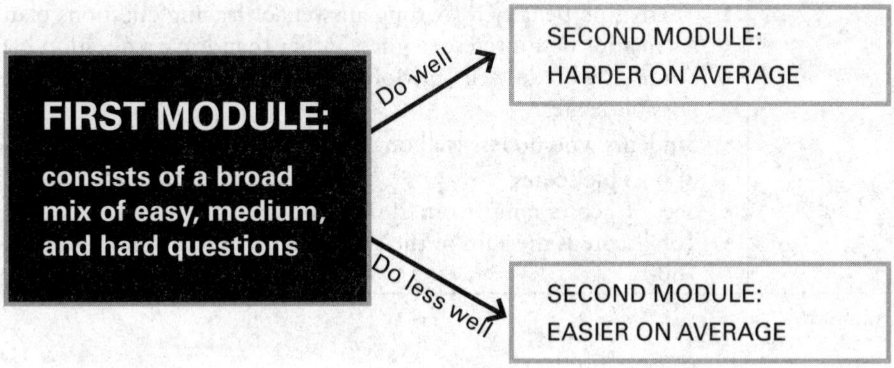

Some questions within a module are also weighted, so doing better on those will increase your score more than doing well on easier, non-weighted questions. As such, your score is determined not only by how many questions you got right but also by how hard those questions were. Although the scoring curve on each Digital SAT may calculate your score slightly differently, you will always have two jobs: understanding which questions can maximize your score and building your stamina to stay sharp through both modules in each section. Throughout this book, we will show you how to do just that.

The following table summarizes the structure and scoring of the Digital SAT.

Category	Digital SAT
Time Overall	134 minutes plus 10-minute break
Components	• Reading and Writing section • Math section
Number of Questions	• Reading and Writing: 54, including 4 experimental questions • Math: 44, including 4 experimental questions
Answer Choices	• Reading and Writing: all multiple-choice with 4 answers per question • Math: 75% multiple-choice with 4 answers per question, 25% student-produced responses
Time by Section	• Reading and Writing: 64 minutes in two 32-minute modules • Math: 70 minutes in two 35-minute modules

Category	Digital SAT
Relationship Between Modules	• Module 1 has a broad mix of levels of difficulty. • Performance on Module 1 determines the difficulty of Module 2. • Students who do well on Module 1 will get a Module 2 that is harder, on average. • Students who do less well on Module 1 will get a Module 2 that is easier, on average.
Scoring	• The score is based on the number of questions correct and the difficulty of those questions. • There is no penalty for wrong answers or leaving questions blank, so it's in your best interest to guess rather than leave a question blank. • Students who do well on Module 1 are put into a higher bracket of possible scores. • Students who do less well on Module 1 are put into a lower bracket of possible scores. • Section scores range from 200 to 800. • Total score is the sum of the section scores and ranges from 400 to 1600.

How Is the Digital SAT Given?

The SAT may be digital, but it is not an online test. You will not be able to take it in the comfort of your own home. It will still be administered at testing centers or schools with testing capabilities. It must be taken on a computer or laptop that has the College Board Bluebook app, which can be downloaded at bluebook.app.collegeboard.org/.

If you do not have your own device, and your school cannot provide one for you, you can request to borrow one from College Board when you register. However, although College Board says that this process will run smoothly for students, that is not a given. It is best to ensure that you have access to a device without relying on College Board, so borrow one from a friend or family member if you must.

Once at the testing center, you will be given a code to access your test in the testing app. The app only needs access to the Internet for a brief period while assembling your test, then you can proceed despite any interruptions in internet connectivity or device power. College Board says that even if your battery dies, your test progress will be saved and no time will be lost, but it is a good idea to have a device that can hold a charge for at least 3 hours.

Practice Makes Progress!
Get comfortable with the Digital SAT by taking at least one of the online tests in your Student Tools. The more online practice tests you take, the more prepared you will be for the actual Digital SAT.

Device Requirements

Here are College Board's device guidelines:

Students can test on Bluebook using Windows laptops or tablets, Mac laptops, iPads, or school-managed Chromebooks. The device must be able to connect to Wi-Fi.

Windows laptops/tablets
- running Windows 10 or later
- have at least 250 MB of free space available

Mac laptops
- running macOS 11.4 or later
- have at least 150 MB of free space available

iPads
- running iPadOS 14–16 or 17.1
- have at least 150 MB of free space available

School-managed Chromebooks
- running Chrome OS 102 or later
- have at least 150 MB of free space available

(Note: The Bluebook app won't run on operating systems before Chrome OS 102. You cannot run Bluebook on a personal Chromebook. Check bluebook.collegeboard.org/students/approved-devices for the most up-to-date information.)

When Is the Digital SAT Given?

The first administration of the Digital SAT was in March 2023 for students outside the United States. The PSAT went digital in the fall of 2023 for all students worldwide. Students in the United States could take the Digital SAT for the first time in March 2024. The full Digital SAT schedule for the school year is posted on the College Board website at collegeboard.org.

The best way to sign up for one of these Digital SAT administrations is by going to satsuite.collegeboard.org/digital and clicking on the link for the test date you want. Try to sign up for the Digital SAT as soon as you know when you want to take the test. If you wait until the last minute to sign up, there may not be any open spots in the testing centers.

Although you may take the Digital SAT any time in your high school career, most students take it for the first time in the spring of their junior year and may retake it in the fall of their senior year. However, the best approach for students is to find a window of about 2–4 months when they have enough time to fully prep leading up to a test administration, while still allowing them to retake it if necessary. In fact, you may have more time to take it between sophomore and junior year or in the fall of junior year.

Stay on Schedule
Find a window of about 2–4 months to fully prep for the Digital SAT. Determine which test administration you are aiming for and leave time to retake the test if necessary. Then sit down and plan a prep schedule that will work for you.

If you require any special accommodation while taking the test (including, but not limited to, extra time or assistance), accommodations.collegeboard.org has information about applying for those accommodations. Make sure to apply early; we recommend applying six months before you plan to take the test.

Your school may also offer a Digital SAT option during the school day. Schools will have the option to offer the test to students over a testing window of several days. If this is an option at your school, the school will register you for the test, but the results can still be used in the college application process.

HOW TO BEGIN

Online Practice Tests
To access the online practice tests in your Student Tools, register your book at PrincetonReview.com/prep.

After this chapter, you will find Practice Test 1 and its answers and explanations. This will act as your "diagnostic" test. We recommend that you take this test before going any further in order to realistically determine the following:

- your approximate starting score
- which question types you're ready for and which you might need to practice
- which content topics you are familiar with and which you will want to carefully review

Scoring Your Practice Tests
Taking your tests online has the added benefit of giving you an immediate estimated score. If you take Tests 1 and 2 in the book, you can use a bubble sheet to record your answers then enter your answers online to get that score. Always check the Student Tools to learn the latest information about scoring for the Digital SAT.

Once you have nailed down your strengths and weaknesses based on this exam, you can focus your test preparation, build a study plan, and be efficient with your time. Use the following steps to make the most of this first "diagnostic" test.

1. **Take a practice test.** To "diagnose" your strengths and weaknesses, take Practice Test 1 starting on page 13 of this book or take it online in your Student Tools. Be sure to do so in one sitting, following the instructions that appear with each section of the test.

2. **Score your test online.** Once you register your book, you can take tests online in the testing app or enter the answers from your in-book practice tests in your online tools. When you do so, you will get a score report that details your performance on a variety of question types. You will also get an approximate score, though the scale for the Digital SAT will change a bit from test to test.

3. **Take stock and make a plan.** With the insights you'll gain from your score report, decide where to start with the content of this book. You may choose to use some parts of this book over others, or you may work through the entire book. The ways in which you use this book will depend on your needs and how much time you have. Now let's look at how to make this determination.

When you enter your practice test answers online, you will get a score report that starts with your Total score, followed by a breakdown of the scores for each section of the test. Below that will be a breakdown of the questions by test section, with a tab for each one. Each question will be represented by a box with a mark to indicate if it was Correct, Incorrect, or Blank. Clicking on the box for a question brings up the explanation for it, which is also found in this book. Additionally, you can see the question category listed as "Concept Tested."

Student Tools
Register your book to access your Student Tools. See pages xiv–xv to find out what's included in your Student Tools and how to register.

To see a section breakdown by concept, you can click the "View by Category" button. Use this view to determine the following:

- question types you are good at, to make sure you can find and correctly answer questions in these categories every time
- question types that have several questions in them but that you struggled with a bit, so you can work to improve your accuracy on these important questions
- question types that were either very difficult for you or had only one or two questions in them. Practice these question types only after you've mastered the others.

After you determine these things for Reading and Writing, you can do the same for Math by clicking on the Math tab of the score report.

Your analysis of your performance on Practice Test 1 will affect how you engage with **Part II** (How to Crack the Reading and Writing Section) and **Part III** (How to Crack the Math Section). Each of these parts is designed to give a comprehensive review of the content tested on the Digital SAT, including the level of detail you need to know and how the content is tested. At the end of each of these chapters, you'll have the opportunity to assess your understanding of the content covered through targeted drills that reflect the types of questions and level of difficulty you'll see on the actual exam. Answers and explanations can be found at the end of each chapter, so use those explanations to continue assessing your skills.

After you have mastered a few key concepts and strategies, take the second practice test (either in the book or online) and analyze it the same way to see where you've improved and where you have more work to do. Continue alternating working through the chapters of this book and taking practice tests in your Student Tools until you feel fully prepared for the Digital SAT.

One important note: In this book, the sample questions are in numerical order within a chapter. The question number does not indicate where you can expect to see a similar question on the test. As we'll show you later, what really matters is your *personal* order of difficulty.

A Final Thought Before You Begin

The Digital SAT does not measure intelligence, nor does it predict your ultimate success or failure as a human being. No matter how high or how low you score on this test initially, and no matter how much you may increase your score through preparation, you should never consider the score you receive on this or any other test a final judgment of your abilities.

Chapter 2
Practice Test 1

The Digital SAT will be administered on a computer or tablet, so it is best if you take your practice tests in the online Student Tools for this book. However, if you are unable to test on a computer or if you have accommodations and will take the official test on paper, you may take the printed version of Test 1 in this book instead. Both sets of instructions are below.

To Test Online:

Register your book according to the instructions on pages xiv–xv. In your Student Tools, you will be able to access the tests associated with this book: both the two printed in this book and the additional online-only tests. Taking these online adaptive tests is a great way to prepare for taking the actual Digital SAT.

The Digital SAT has only two modules in each section, not three like the test printed in this book. The second module you get in each section will be determined by your performance on the first module in that section. The online tests follow this structure, and once you finish the test, you will get an estimated score based on the modules you saw and the questions you got right.

To Test on Paper:

For both RW and Math, the following test contains a standard first module and two options for the second module, one easier and one harder. You should take the appropriate second module based on your performance in the first module, as detailed below, but you can feel free to use the other module for extra practice later.

In order to navigate the practice test in this book, take the following steps. To record your answers, you can either indicate them as described in the directions for print tests included with each module or by entering them onto the answer sheet on pages 75–76.

- ☐ Take Reading and Writing (RW) Module 1, allowing yourself 32 minutes to complete it.
- ☐ Go to the answer key starting on page 78 and determine the number of questions you got correct in RW Module 1.
- ☐ If you get fewer than 15 questions correct, take RW Module 2 – Easier, which starts on page 27. If you get 15 or more questions correct, take RW Module 2 – Harder, which starts on page 38.
- ☐ Whichever RW Module 2 you take, start it immediately and allow yourself 32 minutes to complete it.
- ☐ Take a 10-minute break between RW Module 2 and Math Module 1.
- ☐ Take Math Module 1, allowing yourself 35 minutes to complete it.
- ☐ Go to the answer key starting on page 80 and determine the number of questions you got correct in Math Module 1.
- ☐ If you get fewer than 14 questions correct, take Math Module 2 – Easier, which starts on page 58. If you get 14 or more questions correct, take Math Module 2 – Harder, which starts on page 66.
- ☐ Whichever Math Module you take, start it immediately and allow yourself 35 minutes to complete it.
- ☐ After you finish the test, check your answers to RW Module 2 and Math Module 2.
- ☐ Only after you complete the entire test should you read the explanations for the questions, which start on page 82 and are also available online.
- ☐ Go to your online Student Tools to see the latest information about scoring and to get your estimated score.

SAT Prep Test 1—Reading and Writing
Module 1

Turn to Section 1 of your answer sheet (p. 75) to answer the questions in this section.

DIRECTIONS

The questions in this section address a number of important reading and writing skills. Each question includes one or more passages, which may include a table or graph. Read each passage and question carefully, and then choose the best answer to the question based on the passage(s).

All questions in the section are multiple-choice with four answer choices. Each question has a single best answer.

1 Mark for Review

Despite initial skepticism regarding the feasibility of growing crops on the tops of buildings, Dr. Dickson Despommier has remained ________ in his promotion of vertical farming. In no small part due to Dr. Despommier's persistence and dedication to the cause, cities all over the United States have embraced rooftop gardening as a means of providing fresh produce to urban areas and promoting sustainable agriculture.

Which choice completes the text with the most logical and precise word or phrase?

(A) menacing

(B) subdued

(C) resolute

(D) misunderstood

2 Mark for Review

The fishermen of the coastal village of Kerala, India, ________ traditional fishing methods with modern technology; for example, the fishermen use motorized boats and GPS tracking to increase the efficiency and speed of fishing expeditions while applying age-old knowledge of tides, weathers patterns, and fish migratory patterns that have supported fishing success for centuries.

Which choice completes the text with the most logical and precise word or phrase?

(A) belittle

(B) contemplate

(C) integrate

(D) replace

CONTINUE

3 Mark for Review

Spanning three different storylines set hundreds of years apart, Anthony Doerr's 2021 novel *Cloud Cuckoo Land* depicts the impact of a single story on the lives of three different protagonists living in different time periods. Because the three characters' lives at the center of the story are so ______, each with truncated yet rich and unique life experiences and histories, the reader could not be faulted for wishing each character had been given his or her own novel.

Which choice completes the text with the most logical and precise word or phrase?

Ⓐ meaningless

Ⓑ dynamic

Ⓒ benign

Ⓓ shattered

4 Mark for Review

A study conducted by Monica Gagliano and colleagues found that plants that were exposed to stressors, such as drought or intense heat, were more likely to survive future stressors compared to plants that were not previously exposed to these conditions. This evidence of plant memory challenges the common perception of plants as ______ organisms that simply respond to their environment.

Which choice completes the text with the most logical and precise word or phrase?

Ⓐ courageous

Ⓑ assertive

Ⓒ passive

Ⓓ adaptable

5 Mark for Review

In a 2020 study, Stanford University professor Nicholas Bloom and colleagues were able to demonstrate that working from home can actually increase productivity and work satisfaction, as well as reduce employee turnover rates. Based on this research, many economists have ______ the commonly held belief that remote work leads to decreased productivity.

Which choice completes the text with the most logical and precise word or phrase?

Ⓐ muddied

Ⓑ questioned

Ⓒ usurped

Ⓓ articulated

CONTINUE

6 Mark for Review

The following text is adapted from Laurence Housman's 1916 play, *Bird in Hand*. Professor Braintree, a famous scientist, is examining a series of letters in his study when he is greeted by his secretary, Miss Tuckey.

Miss Tuckey: Good-morning, Sir.

Professor: Miss Tuckey, there is something broken over there, will you please see it removed? And will you kindly make a note to write to Messrs. Spink and Wedge, and say that these new glasses don't suit me—I find them very <u>trying</u> to the—to the eyes. And I must ask you to fetch those proofs which came yesterday. I tried to catch you just now, but you had gone.

As used in the text, what does the word "trying" most nearly mean?

Ⓐ taxing

Ⓑ attempting

Ⓒ soothing

Ⓓ sampling

7 Mark for Review

In 2018, a team of researchers led by Edward Boyden of the Massachusetts Institute of Technology developed a new type of probe that could help researchers better understand the brain. The probe, called "neural dust," is a tiny, wireless sensor that can be implanted directly into the brain to monitor electrical signals. Because the dust is biocompatible, it does not damage brain tissue, and because it is wireless, it can be used to monitor the brain over long periods of time without the need for bulky external equipment.

According to the text, why would neural dust help researchers more than other types of probes?

Ⓐ Because other probes are too small to find once implanted in the brain

Ⓑ Because neural dust can be placed more advantageously than other probes

Ⓒ Because neural dust reduces the amount of monitoring time needed to complete a brain tissue scan

Ⓓ Because the electrical current carried by neural dust is less than that of other probes

CONTINUE

8 Mark for Review

In Māori culture, the Tohunga are revered figures who hold knowledge and wisdom about the history and traditions of their people. They act as healers, navigators, and spiritual leaders, and are responsible for passing on their knowledge to future generations. While modernization has impacted the role of the Tohunga in contemporary society, they remain a crucial source of guidance and guardians of cultural heritage.

What choice best states the main idea of the text?

Ⓐ Contemporary society has less need for the Tohunga.

Ⓑ Despite shifts to their societal function, the Tohunga remain vital to preserving their communities' shared knowledge and traditions.

Ⓒ Although the Tohunga embrace many aspects of society, few welcome technological advancements.

Ⓓ Tohunga traditions are passed down from generation to generation.

9 Mark for Review

The following text is excerpted from Sir Arthur Conan Doyle's 1891 novel *The White Company*. Alleyne is a young monk traveling north from his abbey in Beaulieu, England.

The youth had now journeyed considerably beyond the furthest domains of the Abbey. He was the more surprised therefore when, on coming round a turn in the path, he perceived a man clad in the familiar garb of the order, and seated in a clump of heather by the roadside. Alleyne had known every brother well, but this was a face which was new to him—a face which was very red and puffed, working this way and that, as though the man were sore perplexed in his mind.

Which choice best states the main idea of the text?

Ⓐ Alleyne is less familiar with the man than he is with other members of his order.

Ⓑ Alleyne has become more suspicious of others since his encounter with the man.

Ⓒ Alleyne only trusts men who wear the familiar garb of the order.

Ⓓ Alleyne is perplexed by the behavior of some members of the order.

CONTINUE

10 Mark for Review

The Joy Luck Club is a 1989 novel by Amy Tan. In the novel, Tan suggests that upon smelling fragrant aromas, she felt an intuitive and sometimes unexpected sense of cultural recognition: ______

Which quotation from *The Joy Luck Club* most effectively illustrates the claim?

Ⓐ "We had a feast of warm pork with lettuce, dumplings, tender fish still tasting of lake weeds, red-bean soup with long dumplings, warm sesame-seed cake dotted with watermelon seeds."

Ⓑ "There is so much about my mother I do not understand. And though the food I cook now is not the same as my mother's, when I cook it, when I taste it, I feel a powerful connection to her."

Ⓒ "Ever since I was a child, the smell of that dish stirred me strangely. It carried the flavors of my ancestors, the love and traditions that went into making it."

Ⓓ "Suyaun began to talk about Chinese people who eat dumplings on the last day of the old year and the first day of the new year. She said dumplings were like hopes – little pieces of filling wrapped up in a dough, with the corners twisted tight."

11 Mark for Review

Percentage of Women Serving in Upper and Lower Chamber of Parliament in Five African Countries

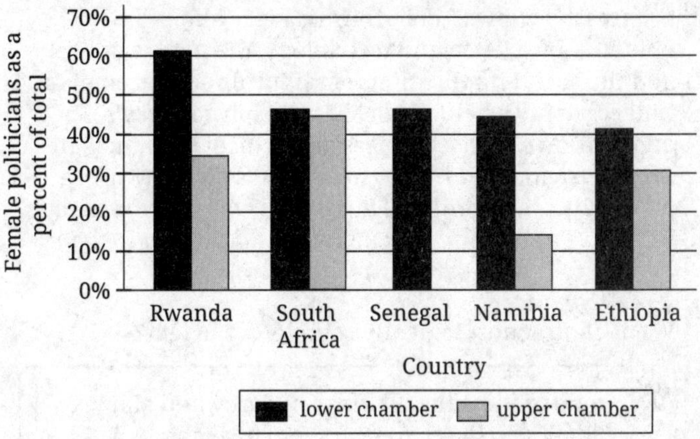

The Inter-Parliamentary Union monitors the percentage of women elected to serve in national parliaments around the world in order to report on the gap between the number of men and women serving in politics. In Africa, the top five countries with the highest number of female politicians are Rwanda, South Africa, Senegal (which only has a lower chamber), Namibia and Ethiopia. In some cases, the percentage of women serving in parliaments was found to be especially prominent; for instance, ______

Which choice most effectively uses data from the graph to complete the example?

Ⓐ a relatively equal percentage of women served in the lower chambers of Rwanda, Senegal, Namibia, and Ethiopia.

Ⓑ most of the members of both chambers of parliament in Ethiopia are women.

Ⓒ approximately equal percentages of women served in the upper and lower chambers in South Africa.

Ⓓ most of the people serving in the lower chamber of parliament in Rwanda are women.

CONTINUE

12 Mark for Review

Literary critics have argued that Mary Shelley's novel *Frankenstein* was deeply influenced by her marriage to Percy Shelley, who was known for his radical and progressive views, including his ideas about the potential of science and technology, the nature of life and the social implications of scientific advancements. Indeed, Percy's beliefs may have inspired Mary's exploration of consequences and ethical dilemmas in *Frankenstein*, but *Frankenstein* stands on its own as a work of literary genius. Thus, those who ascribe Percy's influence as the primary motivation for *Frankenstein* ______

What choice most logically completes the text?

Ⓐ tend to view the writings of Percy and Mary Shelley through too personal of a lens.

Ⓑ neglect the influence of many other individuals on Mary Shelley's writings.

Ⓒ risk oversimplifying the motivating factors for Mary Shelley's novel.

Ⓓ may make incorrect assumptions about Percy and Mary Shelley's relationship.

13 Mark for Review

The purpose of Stonehenge, a famous prehistoric monument, has long been debated by archaeologists. Some historians propose it was an astronomical observatory, but there is no conclusive evidence of this assertion. While certain stone alignments within the structure coincide with celestial events associated with astronomy, Stonehenge's design and construction span different time periods, suggesting shifting scientific, religious, ceremonial, and social functions depending on the era. Our understanding of the true purpose of Stonehenge remains an enigmatic puzzle, suggesting that ______

Which choice most logically completes the text?

Ⓐ Stonehenge likely would not have been used for such diverse purposes had it existed in a less central location.

Ⓑ alterations to structural design affect different types of monuments in different ways.

Ⓒ the development of Stonehenge over multiple eras makes its original function a point of contention for archaeologists and historians.

Ⓓ the design of Stonehenge made it more useful for religious and ceremonial purposes than for astronomy.

CONTINUE

14 Mark for Review

Lisa Fenk and her team at The Rockefeller University used a combination of approaches to understand more precisely how fruit _______ allow for the tracking of visual patterns.

Which choice completes the text so that it conforms to the conventions of Standard English?

Ⓐ flies retinal movements

Ⓑ flies' retinal movement's

Ⓒ flies' retinal movements

Ⓓ fly's retinal movements'

15 Mark for Review

Using commonplace items such as wooden furniture and clothing, Doris _______ created her art installations *Unland: The Orphan's Tunic* and *La Casa Viuda*, memory sculptures that capture the history of her home country Colombia as well as her own personal experiences.

Which choice completes the text so that it conforms to the conventions of Standard English?

Ⓐ Salcedo:

Ⓑ Salcedo—

Ⓒ Salcedo

Ⓓ Salcedo,

16 Mark for Review

The National Day of Listening, started by the national oral history project StoryCorps in 2008, is a day encouraging Americans to record the stories of their loved _______ people interested in participating can access resources and recommendations about the interview process through the StoryCorps website or app.

Which choice completes the text so that it conforms to the conventions of Standard English?

Ⓐ ones,

Ⓑ ones;

Ⓒ ones

Ⓓ ones and

17 Mark for Review

In 1839, English artist Frederick Catherwood joined an expedition to Central America, where he saw over forty sites full of _______ creating detailed drawings and paintings of the ruins, Catherwood helped to reintroduce the Mayan civilization to the Western world.

Which choice completes the text so that it conforms to the conventions of Standard English?

Ⓐ ruins by

Ⓑ ruins, by

Ⓒ ruins. By

Ⓓ ruins and by

CONTINUE

18 Mark for Review

Paleontologist Keyron Hickman-Lewis's analysis of 3.48-billion-year-old rocks, which contain the oldest evidence of life on Earth, from the Dresser Formation in Western Australia ________ scientists analyze rocks that the *Perseverance* rover is collecting on Mars.

Which choice completes the text so that it conforms to the conventions of Standard English?

Ⓐ will help

Ⓑ to have helped

Ⓒ to help

Ⓓ helping

19 Mark for Review

During Japan's Heian period (794–1185), the Heian Palace was located in Heian-kyō, the capital during those years. Within the palace ________ several administration buildings and the living quarters of the emperor.

Which choice completes the text so that it conforms to the conventions of Standard English?

Ⓐ has been

Ⓑ is

Ⓒ was

Ⓓ were

20 Mark for Review

In 1956, American physicists Clyde L. Cowan and Frederick Reines determined that ________ exist by observing the neutrinos' interactions with protons in water.

Which choice completes the text so that it conforms to the conventions of Standard English?

Ⓐ neutrinos—subatomic particles that have no electric charge, very small mass, and a spin of one-half—

Ⓑ neutrinos, subatomic particles that have: no electric charge, very small mass, and a spin of one-half,

Ⓒ neutrinos—subatomic particles—that have no electric charge, very small mass, and a spin of one-half,

Ⓓ neutrinos, subatomic particles that have no electric charge, very small mass, and a spin of one-half

CONTINUE

21 Mark for Review

In 1967, the US Supreme Court ruled that American citizens could not be relieved of their citizenship without their consent in the case *Afroyim v. Rusk.* This case overruled another important case, *Perez v. Brownell*, which mandated the loss of citizenship after voting in an election in another country. ________ *Perez v. Brownell* prompted a discussion about voluntary versus involuntary choices; according to the ruling, citizenship could not be removed for unintentional actions.

Which choice completes the text with the most logical transition?

Ⓐ Actually,

Ⓑ Nevertheless,

Ⓒ Additionally,

Ⓓ For instance,

22 Mark for Review

While researching a topic, a student has taken the following notes:

- Megalodons were ancient sharks that lived between 23 million and 2.6 million years ago.
- In a 2022 study, paleobiologist Catalina Pimiento and colleagues analyzed fossil evidence of the megalodon.
- They hoped to learn more about the megalodon's life, as little is known because very few fossils of the species are available.
- They used rare megalodon fossils and scans of modern great white sharks to create a 3D model of the megalodon, which revealed the shark to be around 50 feet long.
- They also found that the megalodon could swim faster than a great white shark, could travel across multiple oceans, and could have consumed an orca in five bites.

The student wants to present the study and its findings. Which choice most effectively uses relevant information from the notes to accomplish this goal?

Ⓐ In a 2022 study, Catalina Pimiento and colleagues used both records of ancient fossils and scans of modern sharks to determine that the megalodon was around 50 feet long, could travel across multiple oceans, and could consume an orca.

Ⓑ In 2022, Catalina Pimiento and colleagues studied rare megalodon fossils as well as scans of contemporary great white sharks in order to learn more about the megalodon's life.

Ⓒ Megalodon fossils and scans of modern great white sharks were the focus of a 2022 study.

Ⓓ In a 2022 study, Catalina Pimiento and colleagues analyzed fossils of the megalodon, an ancient shark that lived up to 23 million years ago.

CONTINUE

23 Mark for Review

While researching a topic, a student has taken the following notes:

- Franz Joseph Haydn was an Austrian-born classical composer of symphonies and concertos.
- In 1798, he completed the composition *The Creation*, which depicts biblical stories from the Book of Genesis.
- A prominent feature of the composition is that different choral soloists represent Adam and Eve.
- Another prominent feature is tone painting, a technique by which music depicts narrative elements.

The student wants to introduce the composition *The Creation* to an audience already familiar with Franz Joseph Haydn. Which choice most effectively uses relevant information from the notes to accomplish this goal?

(A) *The Creation* was not the only piece written by Austrian-born composer Franz Joseph Haydn.

(B) Franz Joseph Haydn employed the use of both soloists and tone paintings in his work.

(C) In addition to his composition *The Creation*, which was completed in 1798, Austrian-born composer Franz Joseph Haydn produced other symphonies and concertos.

(D) Franz Joseph Haydn's *The Creation* retells biblical stories from the Book of Genesis with choral soloists and tone painting to convey the story.

24 Mark for Review

While researching a topic, a student has taken the following notes:

- There are 118 elements on the periodic table.
- Six elements are classified as the alkaline earth metals.
- One of those elements is beryllium.
- Its chemical symbol is Be.
- Another of those elements is strontium.
- Its chemical symbol is Sr.

The student wants to emphasize a similarity between the two elements. Which choice most effectively uses relevant information from the notes to accomplish this goal?

(A) Beryllium (Be) and strontium (Sr) are different elements.

(B) Among the 118 elements on the periodic table is strontium, which is an alkaline earth metal.

(C) Beryllium's chemical symbol is Be, while strontium's chemical symbol is Sr.

(D) Both beryllium and strontium are classified as alkaline earth metals.

CONTINUE

25 Mark for Review

While researching a topic, a student has taken the following notes:

- Maya Deren was a Ukrainian-born American filmmaker.
- The 1943 experimental short film *Meshes of the Afternoon* was one of her most acclaimed films.
- The film was completely silent and featured no music until 1959, when a score was added.
- The film repeatedly features various shots of the same few objects, including a knife, a key, a flower, and a record spinning on a turntable.
- The film depicts the same events several times from different points of view.

The student wants to introduce Maya Deren and her film *Meshes of the Afternoon* to a new audience. Which choice most effectively uses relevant information from the notes to accomplish this goal?

Ⓐ *Meshes of the Afternoon* was a highly acclaimed experimental short directed by a Ukrainian-born American filmmaker.

Ⓑ In 1943, American filmmaker Maya Deren released one of her most acclaimed films, *Meshes of the Afternoon*, an experimental silent film that features repeated shots of the same objects as well as repeated events shot from different points of view.

Ⓒ Maya Deren directed *Meshes of the Afternoon* in 1943.

Ⓓ *Meshes of the Afternoon*, an acclaimed experimental film, was completely silent and featured repeated shots of a knife, a key, a flower, and a spinning record.

26 Mark for Review

While researching a topic, a student has taken the following notes:

- Agnès Varda was a Belgian-born French director.
- In 2015, she was the first woman to receive an honorary Palme d'Or, the highest prize awarded by the Cannes Film Festival.
- Her film *Cléo from 5 to 7*, one of her most acclaimed and notable works, shows two hours in the life of a pop singer.
- The film mixes documentary and fiction elements, and its events are depicted in real time.

The student wants to introduce *Cléo from 5 to 7* to an audience unfamiliar with the film and its director. Which choice most effectively uses relevant information from the notes to accomplish this goal?

Ⓐ *Cléo from 5 to 7* is a film that mixes documentary with fiction elements and depicts two hours in the life of a pop singer.

Ⓑ Agnès Varda, who directed *Cléo from 5 to 7* and received an honorary Palme d'Or at the Cannes Film Festival, was born in Belgium and then moved to France.

Ⓒ Agnès Varda's film *Cléo from 5 to 7* is highly acclaimed for its portrayal of two hours in the life of a pop singer.

Ⓓ A highly acclaimed film that mixes elements of documentary and fiction, *Cléo from 5 to 7* was directed by Agnès Varda, the first woman to receive an honorary Palme d'Or at the Cannes Film Festival.

CONTINUE

27 Mark for Review

While researching a topic, a student has taken the following notes:

- In 2022, Ruth Peters and colleagues in Australia and the UK studied the relationship between blood pressure and risk of dementia in older age.
- They found that a decrease in blood pressure was correlated with a decrease in dementia risk.
- When systolic blood pressure was 100 millimeters of mercury (mmHg), the risk of dementia was 0.02.
- When systolic blood pressure was 140 mmHg, the risk of dementia was 0.03.
- When systolic blood pressure was 180 mmHg, the risk of dementia was 0.04.

The student wants to summarize the study. Which choice most effectively uses relevant information from the notes to accomplish this goal?

Ⓐ Ruth Peters's 2022 study concerning the relationship between blood pressure and risk of dementia found that as blood pressure increased, the risk of dementia increased.

Ⓑ For a 2022 study, researchers from Australia and the UK gathered data on the blood pressure and risk of dementia in older-age subjects.

Ⓒ Ruth Peters and her colleagues sought to understand the relationship between blood pressure and risk of dementia, so they conducted a study.

Ⓓ Knowing that there was a link between blood pressure and dementia risk, Ruth Peters measured people's risk of dementia, which was as high as 0.04 in some cases.

YIELD

Once you've finished (or run out of time for) this section, use the answer key to determine how many questions you got right. If you got fewer than 15 questions right, move on to Module 2—Easier, otherwise move on to Module 2—Harder.

SAT Prep Test 1—Reading and Writing
Module 2—Easier

Turn to Section 1 of your answer sheet (p. 75) to answer the questions in this section.

DIRECTIONS

The questions in this section address a number of important reading and writing skills. Each question includes one or more passages, which may include a table or graph. Read each passage and question carefully, and then choose the best answer to the question based on the passage(s).

All questions in the section are multiple-choice with four answer choices. Each question has a single best answer.

1 Mark for Review

The electric vehicle market experienced a surge in popularity in the 2010s, with sales increasing from just a few thousand at the start of the decade to more than two million by the end of the decade. As more countries implement policies to reduce carbon emissions, experts ______ that electric vehicle sales will continue to eclipse previous records each year.

Which choice completes the text with the most logical and precise word or phrase?

Ⓐ project

Ⓑ guarantee

Ⓒ reject

Ⓓ deny

2 Mark for Review

According to psychologists, mindfulness—the simple practice of being present and fully engaged in the moment—can improve physical and cognitive function. The ______ of mindfulness have been found to lead to improvements in overall well-being.

Which choice completes the text with the most logical and precise word or phrase?

Ⓐ benefits

Ⓑ drawbacks

Ⓒ basics

Ⓓ physics

CONTINUE

3 Mark for Review

Astrophysicist Kip Thorne received the Nobel Prize in Physics for his work to detect ripples in space-time, confirming one of the last major predictions of Albert Einstein's general theory of relativity. This discovery both ________ our understanding of the universe and provided astronomers with a firmer ground upon which to make further inquiries.

Which choice completes the text with the most logical and precise word or phrase?

Ⓐ confused

Ⓑ clarified

Ⓒ revolutionized

Ⓓ belittled

4 Mark for Review

The Navajo Nation, a sovereign Native American territory occupying parts of Arizona, Utah, and New Mexico, has its own judicial system. The judicial branch consists of different courts, with judges appointed by the Nation president and confirmed by the Navajo Nation Council, and is responsible for protecting the civil rights of Navajo citizens and ________ the established principles of the constitution.

Which choice completes the text with the most logical and precise word or phrase?

Ⓐ copying

Ⓑ maintaining

Ⓒ determining

Ⓓ dismissing

5 Mark for Review

In 2019, an international team of scientists led by Victor Vescovo ________ four new species of gelatinous animals in the Mariana Trench, the deepest point in the world's oceans. This finding gave marine biologists further information regarding the diversity of animals that live and thrive in the extreme ocean depths.

Which choice completes the text with the most logical and precise word or phrase?

Ⓐ reintroduced

Ⓑ discounted

Ⓒ discovered

Ⓓ explored

6 Mark for Review

Psychologist Kurt Gray led a 2019 study demonstrating that human emotions are often ________ animals by the humans observing them. The findings from this study suggest that humans can empathize with a broader diversity of creatures than previously believed.

Which choice completes the text with the most logical and precise word or phrase?

Ⓐ conflated with

Ⓑ demanded of

Ⓒ united with

Ⓓ attributed to

CONTINUE

7 Mark for Review

Female emperor penguins do not care for their own eggs. Instead, after the female lays her egg, she transfers the egg to the male's care. <u>The male emperor penguin uses a fold of skin called a brood pouch to balance the egg on his feet and keep it warm.</u> During the two-month window in which the male penguin cares for the egg amidst often harsh conditions, the female penguin sets out to feed and replenish her energy reserves, thus enabling her to return to the colony and care for the chick once it hatches.

Which choice best describes the function of the underlined sentence in the text as a whole?

Ⓐ It explains how female penguins are able to leave their egg and restore their energy to care for their young.

Ⓑ It introduces a physical feature of male penguins alluded to earlier in the text.

Ⓒ It describes the harsh conditions under which the male penguin cares for the egg.

Ⓓ It offers information about how male penguins carry out the function described in the text.

8 Mark for Review

The following text is adapted from Susan Glaspell's 1917 short story "A Jury of Her Peers." The women in the story, Mrs. Peters and Mrs. Hale, discover an important clue about a murder case with which they have become involved.

> And then again the eyes of the two women met—this time clung together in a look of dawning comprehension, of growing horror. Mrs. Peters looked from the dead bird to the broken door of the cage. Again their eyes met. And just then there was a sound at the outside door. Mrs. Hale slipped the box under the quilt pieces in the basket, and sank into the chair before it. Mrs. Peters stood holding to the table. The county attorney and the sheriff came in from outside.

Which choices best states the main purpose of the text?

Ⓐ To describe the features of the quilt that set it apart from other quilts

Ⓑ To detail the women's sudden realization and reaction to that realization

Ⓒ To demonstrate the women's dislike toward the county attorney

Ⓓ To indicate which possession the women most strongly cherish

CONTINUE

9 Mark for Review

Text 1

It can be argued that there is a sharp disparity between traditional music composition and the use of computer-based technology to compose music. Computer-based programs remove the requirement for certain musical compositional skills, and the program offers shortcuts and features that can help a computer-based "composer" resolve issues within the composition instantaneously.

Text 2

While composing music digitally may seem as if it only requires a few clicks of the mouse, it does not require fewer skills than does traditional music composition. Computer-based composers must know both the foundations of music theory and the intricacies of the programs that they use to create their works. Rather than merely booting up a computer, these composers almost always build their melodies as a traditional composition first, and then transpose the work onto the computer for further editing—in the end, their final products require just as much experimentation as traditional compositions.

Based on the texts, how would the author of Text 2 most likely respond to the claims of the author of Text 1?

Ⓐ By conceding that computer-based composers don't spend time learning the foundations of music theory

Ⓑ By emphasizing that the performance of a musical work is more important than the vehicle used for its creation

Ⓒ By clarifying that it is much easier to produce notes using a traditional instrument than it is using a mouse

Ⓓ By stating that computer-based compositions still require some traditional skills even if the medium of creation is less traditional

10 Mark for Review

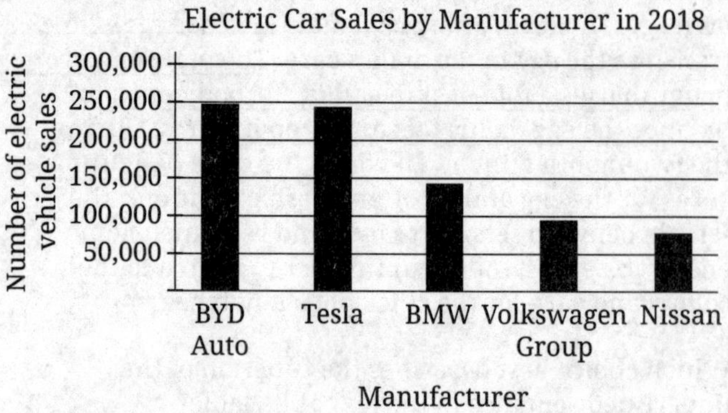

Electric cars are vehicles powered by electricity stored in onboard batteries and offer a clean and efficient alternative to traditional internal combustion engine vehicles. Electric vehicle sales are still a small percentage of total vehicle sales, but each of the five major electric car manufacturers posted strong numbers in 2018. For example, ______

Which choice most effectively uses data from the graph to complete the text?

Ⓐ BYD Auto had more than 250,000 electric vehicle sales.

Ⓑ Nissan had between 50,000 and 100,000 electric vehicle sales.

Ⓒ Tesla had fewer than 200,000 electric vehicle sales.

Ⓓ BMW and Volkswagen Group each had between 100,000 and 150,000 electric vehicle sales.

CONTINUE

11 Mark for Review

"The Set of China" is an 1835 short story by Eliza Leslie. In the story, the narrator describes Mr. Gummage as being an art teacher who actively encourages his students to improve upon the fundamentals that he teaches: ______

Which quotation from "The Set of China" most effectively illustrates the claim?

Ⓐ "Mr. Gummage immediately supplied her with two bristle brushes, and sundry little shallow earthen cups, each containing a modicum of some sort of body color, massicot, flake-white, etc., prepared by himself and charged at a quarter of a dollar apiece, and which he told her she would want when she came to do landscapes and figures."

Ⓑ "All the dark shadows in every part of the picture were done with a mixture of Persian blue and bistre, and of these two colors there was consequently a vast consumption in Mr. Gummage's school."

Ⓒ "Mr. Gummage's style was to put in the sky, water and distances with opaque paints, and the most prominent objects with transparent colors. This was probably the reason that his foregrounds seemed always to be sunk in his backgrounds."

Ⓓ "The model was scarcely considered as a guide, for he continually told his pupils that they must try to excel it; and he helped them to do so by making all his skies deep red fire at the bottom, and dark blue smoke at the top; and exactly reversing the colors on the water, by putting red at the top and the blue at the bottom."

12 Mark for Review

"Stopping by Woods on a Snowy Evening" is a 1923 poem by Robert Frost, which presents a frozen lake on a winter evening while the snow falls. Frost describes his prioritization of personal obligations over admiring the beauty of the winter scene, writing: ______

Which quotation from "Stopping by Woods on a Snowy Evening" most effectively illustrates the claim?

Ⓐ "He will not see me stopping here / To watch his woods fill up with snow"

Ⓑ "The woods are lovely, dark and deep / But I have promises to keep"

Ⓒ "The only other sound's the sweep / Of easy wind and downy flake"

Ⓓ "Between the woods and frozen lake / The darkest evening of the year"

CONTINUE

13 Mark for Review

Number of Citations of Eight Plant Species in Low and High Vegetation Areas

Plant species	Number of citations in Area I	Number of citations in Area II
C. pyramidale	35	46
S. tuberosa	27	45
C. blanctenianus	31	43
M. glaziovi	11	43
Z. joazeiro	30	43
M. urundeuva	27	41
M. tenuiflora	4	40
S. obtusifolium	32	38

Sonaly Silva da Cunha et. al examined two Brazilian semiarid areas to investigate which plant species were collected by agro-pastoralists (people who live in communities centered around livestock and agriculture) during their foraging expeditions. The researchers predicted that if vegetation were uniform across both areas examined, the average number of citations per species would be 30. The agro-pastoralists cited the number of each of eight species found in an area with low vegetation cover (Area I) and an area with high vegetation cover (Area II). Based on these results, the researchers claim that agro-pastoralists living in Area II were able to gather significant quantities of all eight species due to the area's high vegetation cover.

Which choice best describes data from the table that support the researchers' claim?

(A) For all of the different plant species, the number of citations from Area II was higher than the researchers' predicted average.

(B) For all eight plant species, there were fewer than 50 citations from Area II.

(C) The plant species with the lowest number of citations in Area II was *C. pyramidale*.

(D) For *M. glaziovi* and *M. tenuiflora*, the number of citations from Area I was significantly higher than the researchers' predicted average.

14 Mark for Review

"Hieroglyphics" is a 1902 essay by Arthur Machen, a Welsh author and critic. In the essay, Machen addresses the reader as if the two were having a conversation, during which Machen challenges a comparison regarding literary quality that he believes the reader has made: ________

Which quotation from "Hieroglyphics" most effectively illustrates the claim?

(A) "There is no more madness in *that* notion than in the other one—that one has only to print an amusing, interesting, life-like, or pathetic tale to make it into fine literature."

(B) "I am afraid, that in your heart of hearts, you still believe that the 'Odyssey' is fine literature, and that 'Pride and Prejudice' is fine literature, though the 'Odyssey' is 'better' than 'Pride and Prejudice.' It is that 'better' that I want to get out of your head, that monstrous fallacy of comparing Westminster Abbey with the charming old houses in Queen Square."

(C) "Did any cook ever think that he could change a turkey into a bird of paradise by careful attention to the *farse* and the sauce? The farmer might as well expect to breed early phœnixes for Leadenhall Market by the simple process of lighting a bonfire in the farmyard. The young ducks would jump into the blaze, and the transformation would be the work of a second!"

(D) "At least I hope you would see, though, as I told you a few weeks ago, I doubt very much whether many people realise the distinction between the 'Odyssey' and a political pamphlet. The general opinion, I expect, is that both belong to the same class, though the Greek poem is much more 'important' than the pamphlet."

CONTINUE

15 Mark for Review

The Inca Empire existed from the thirteenth to sixteenth century in what is now the Andes Mountains in South America. The high altitude and harsh, dry climate kept the Incans relatively safe from external threats but made farming challenging. So, they created a system of terraces that allowed them to grow crops on the mountainside and practiced preserving their crops by "freeze-drying" the crops in the cold, overnight temperatures. These methods worked well enough to produce enough crops to not only support a large population but also ______

Which choice most logically completes the text?

Ⓐ to store crops despite adverse conditions.

Ⓑ to harvest crops during all times of year.

Ⓒ to prolong the life spans of its citizens.

Ⓓ to protect their crops from snow and freezing temperatures.

16 Mark for Review

In a study of the relationship between sleep and memory consolidation—the process by which memories are embedded in our subconscious after initial acquisition—neuroscientist Matthew Walker and his team measured the brain activity of sleeping participants. They discovered that memory consolidation happens during deep sleep as the brain replays memories and stores them more effectively. They also found that the amount and quality of sleep are vital to memory consolidation. Consequently, an increased amount of high-quality sleep is likely to ______

Which choice most logically completes the text?

Ⓐ decrease an individual's ability to access the subconscious mind.

Ⓑ decrease an individual's ability to achieve deep sleep.

Ⓒ increase an individual's ability to recognize connections between similar memories.

Ⓓ increase an individual's ability to better retain memories.

CONTINUE

17 Mark for Review

Using different parts of his body and incorporating sound effects into his final pieces, sculptor and performance artist Kevin Beasley creates his sculptures ______ found materials (such as clothes) and casting materials (such as resin and foam).

Which choice completes the text so that it conforms to the conventions of Standard English?

Ⓐ with:

Ⓑ with

Ⓒ with,

Ⓓ with—

18 Mark for Review

Abuwtiyuw was an Egyptian royal hunting dog that lived in the Sixth Dynasty and is thought to have been one of the first domesticated animals. A stone depicting gifts donated for the dog's funeral was discovered in 1935, and researchers ______ that these gifts provide evidence that Abuwtiyuw was mummified.

Which choice completes the text so that it conforms to the conventions of Standard English?

Ⓐ to believe

Ⓑ believing

Ⓒ believe

Ⓓ having believed

19 Mark for Review

Journalist Rob Capriccioso founded the publication *Indigenous Wire* to combat the lack of Indigenous representation in the media. He aims to write hard-hitting articles that share the ______ in an authentic and realistic way.

Which choice completes the text so that it conforms to the conventions of Standard English?

Ⓐ experiences' of Native American tribe member's

Ⓑ experience's of Native American tribe members

Ⓒ experience's of Native American tribe members'

Ⓓ experiences of Native American tribe members

20 Mark for Review

Artificial organic dyes, such as phthalocyanines, are used in a wide range of industries, but they are often made using solvents that are harmful to the environment. A team at Aalto University ______ a better method: using solid-state synthesis to minimize the use of dangerous solvents.

Which choice completes the text so that it conforms to the conventions of Standard English?

Ⓐ to recommend

Ⓑ recommends

Ⓒ recommending

Ⓓ having recommended

CONTINUE

21 Mark for Review

Comets, objects made of ice and dust that orbit the Sun, can be visible to the naked eye. Some comets, such as Halley's Comet, can be seen more than once in a ________ others, such as Comet Shoemaker-Levy 9, are visible only once.

Which choice completes the text so that it conforms to the conventions of Standard English?

Ⓐ lifetime, while

Ⓑ lifetime: while

Ⓒ lifetime. While

Ⓓ lifetime; while

22 Mark for Review

The Myriad year clock, one of the Japanese clocks known as *wadokei*, is a universal clock powered by elastic energy. Once the spring inside of it is fully wound, the clock can power ________ for one year without needing another winding.

Which choice completes the text so that it conforms to the conventions of Standard English?

Ⓐ themselves

Ⓑ it

Ⓒ itself

Ⓓ them

23 Mark for Review

May Berenbaum of the University of Illinois's Department of Entomology ________ a research seminar on chemical ecology when she developed an interest in honey and its role in the lives of bees. She later proved that honey contains chemical compounds that help bees resist illness and live longer.

Which choice completes the text so that it conforms to the conventions of Standard English?

Ⓐ was attending

Ⓑ attends

Ⓒ has been attending

Ⓓ will attend

CONTINUE

24 Mark for Review

Sheela Gowda is an Indian artist who creates pieces focused on processes, such as people working everyday jobs. Trained as a painter at the Royal College of Art in London, Gowda expanded into sculpting methods in response to India's shifting political dynamics. She has portrayed Indian political themes in her work. ________ Gowda has incorporated themes of dangerous labor practices and the unfair treatment of women into her pieces.

Which choice completes the text with the most logical transition?

(A) Regardless,

(B) In contrast,

(C) Indeed,

(D) In addition,

25 Mark for Review

Autism is often associated with unique speech patterns, and some of these patterns can be identified reliably throughout different languages. In a study, speech rhythm, or the volume and timing of speech, could identify participants with autism reliably across English- and Cantonese-speaking groups. ________ speech intonation, or the variation of the pitch of speech, could only reliably identify participants with autism in the English-speaking group.

Which choice completes the text with the most logical transition?

(A) In addition,

(B) For example,

(C) By contrast,

(D) Still,

26 Mark for Review

There have been numerous attempts to allow greater input by America voters with regard to participating in a war. A failed amendment to the Constitution was proposed in 1916 that would have mandated a public referendum to declare war, with anyone voting "yes" being required to enlist and serve. ________ another proposal was made in 1935 and again in 1940 to require a public vote to declare war unless the country had been attacked first.

Which choice completes the text with the most logical transition?

(A) Specifically,

(B) Similarly,

(C) For instance,

(D) In sum,

CONTINUE

27 Mark for Review

While researching a topic, a student has taken the following notes:

- Terrance Hayes is an American poet.
- He created the "golden shovel" poetic form in which the last word of each line in the poem forms part or all of an existing poem.
- He was inspired by the work of poet Gwendolyn Brooks.
- His poem "The Golden Shovel" uses the words from Brooks's poem "We Real Cool."
- The "golden shovel" form was named after "The Golden Shovel," the first to use this form.

The student wants to provide an explanation and example of a "golden shovel" poem. Which choice most effectively uses relevant information from the notes to accomplish this goal?

(A) The title of the poem "The Golden Shovel" is also the name of the poetic form poet Terrance Hayes created.

(B) Terrance Hayes, who wrote "The Golden Shovel," created the "golden shovel" poetic form.

(C) Terrance Hayes created the "golden shovel" poetic form, inspired by the work of poet Gwendolyn Brooks, in which the last word of each line forms part or all of an existing poem, as seen in his poem "The Golden Shovel."

(D) The "golden shovel" poetic form, created by American poet Terrance Hayes, was inspired by the work of poet Gwendolyn Brooks.

STOP

If you finish before time is called, you may check your work on this module only.
Do not turn to any other module in the test.

SAT Prep Test 1—Reading and Writing
Module 2—Harder

Turn to Section 1 of your answer sheet (p. 75) to answer the questions in this section.

DIRECTIONS

The questions in this section address a number of important reading and writing skills. Each question includes one or more passages, which may include a table or graph. Read each passage and question carefully, and then choose the best answer to the question based on the passage(s).

All questions in the section are multiple-choice with four answer choices. Each question has a single best answer.

1 Mark for Review

In studying the ability to discern differences in pitch in music, psychologist Diana Deutsch found that native speakers of tonal languages, such as Mandarin or Cantonese, are more apt to recognize pitch differences than native speakers of non-tonal languages, such as English or French, as tonal languages ______ words and phrases using pitch changes, giving speakers of these languages heightened sensitivity.

Which choice completes the text with the most logical and precise word or phrase?

(A) enunciate

(B) suggest

(C) distinguish

(D) camouflage

2 Mark for Review

Groundbreaking research conducted by James Peebles and his team is motivated by their belief that though the importance of the properties of dark matter are widely accepted, there is an ______ the influence of dark matter on the universe that continues to elude the scientific community.

Which choice completes the text with the most logical and precise word or phrase?

(A) acknowledgment of

(B) argument about

(C) understanding of

(D) allegiance to

CONTINUE

3 Mark for Review

Whether the success of a business venture, such as a startup or an established company, can be sustained long-term or is merely temporary is closely related to the concept of credibility and therefore necessitates a comprehensive understanding of the elements that contribute to a business's ability to ______ trust among its potential consumers.

Which choice completes the text with the most logical and precise word or phrase?

Ⓐ invalidate

Ⓑ fortify

Ⓒ demarcate

Ⓓ foster

4 Mark for Review

Psychologist Angela Duckworth's studies found that individuals who possess high levels of perseverance are more likely to ______ their long-term objectives. Through her work, Duckworth found that the ability to sustain high levels of effort is as important as talent or intelligence in determining success.

Which choice completes the text with the most logical and precise word or phrase?

Ⓐ neglect

Ⓑ analyze

Ⓒ recall

Ⓓ attain

5 Mark for Review

The following text is translated from "When Father Brought Home the Lamp," an 1883 short story by Finnish author Juhani Aho. The narrator's father has just decided he will set out on a journey the next morning to acquire a lamp, an item no other family in the village owns.

> And that same evening father brought in from the storehouse the big travelling chest in which grandfather, in his time, had stowed his provisions when he came from Uleaborg, and bade mother fill it with hay and lay a little cotton-wool in the middle of it. <u>We children asked why they put nothing in the box but hay and a little wool in the middle, but she bade us hold our tongues, the whole lot of us.</u> Father was in a better humor, and explained that he was going to bring a lamp from the storekeeper, and that it was of glass, and might be broken to bits if he stumbled or if the sledge bumped too much.

Which choice best states the function of the underlined sentence in the text as a whole?

Ⓐ It describes a point of curiosity regarding an object that the children would like explained.

Ⓑ It demonstrates the conflicting emotions displayed by various members of the family.

Ⓒ It clarifies the loving relationship between the children and their mother.

Ⓓ It examines how the inquisitive nature of children can be encouraged by a parent.

CONTINUE

6 Mark for Review

The following text is from Jane Austen's 1813 novel *Pride and Prejudice*. The narrator is describing Elizabeth's feelings toward Mr. Darcy.

> She began now to comprehend that he was exactly the man who, in disposition and talents, would most suit her. His understanding and temper, though unlike her own, would have answered all her wishes. It was an union that must have been to the advantage of both; by her ease and liveliness, his mind might have been softened, his manners improved; and from his judgement, information, and knowledge of the world, she must have received benefit of greater importance.

Which choice best states the main purpose of the text?

Ⓐ To describe Elizabeth's determination to find a suitable romantic partner

Ⓑ To highlight the benefits of having differing qualities from one's partner

Ⓒ To emphasize Elizabeth's desires in a romantic relationship

Ⓓ To demonstrate that Elizabeth finds her current relationship both enriching and confusing

7 Mark for Review

Novelist Wright Morris, who was also a photographer, complemented his written works with photographs that encapsulated the worlds and characters he created. In his novel *The Home Place* (1948), Morris included a series of photographs throughout the narrative. The images bring to life the people and places Morris described in the text, enhancing the reader's immersion in the story. In that novel, Morris provides perspective on the themes of family, memory, and rural America–ideas that are all reinforced by the imagery contained within the novel.

Which choice best describes the overall structure of the text?

Ⓐ It details the photographs that make up *The Home Place*, then explains how they relate to Morris's convictions.

Ⓑ It makes a claim about Morris, then offers an example that supports that claim.

Ⓒ It describes Morris's impact on the art of storytelling, then discusses Morris's impact on other storytellers.

Ⓓ It notes an artist's unique style, then offers a counterexample of that style.

CONTINUE

8 Mark for Review

Research conducted by neuroscientist Dr. Lisa Feldman Barrett suggests that emotions are based on the way that the brain interprets sensory inputs. Over a period of sixty days in 2004, Barrett and her team asked study participants to self-report their emotional experiences by ranking to what extent they felt base emotions such as anger, anxiety, and happiness. Researchers found that individuals who reported emotional states that accurately correlated with existing data concerning emotional state and heartbeat rhythm typically had lower levels of depression and anxiety compared to those who are less able to report specific emotional states.

Which choice best states the function of the underlined sentence in the overall structure of the text?

Ⓐ To highlight an obstacle the researchers had to overcome to conduct its study

Ⓑ To summarize the findings of a research study

Ⓒ To offer a concrete example that contextualizes the study's findings

Ⓓ To partially explain the method used in a research study

9 Mark for Review

Text 1

Many physicists believe in determinism, which states that reality is strictly physical and everything that happens results from physical forces. But if determinism is taken as fact and not theory, the choices we make become not our own decisions. Some psychologists have offered a somewhat comforting response to this hypothetical loss of free will: if we accept the concept that things are as they must be, we can reduce anxiety in our daily lives.

Text 2

When the philosophy of determinism was first standardized in the twentieth century, it was readily accepted by many within the scientific community. However, science journalist John Horgan argues that the human mind operates differently than the simplified way that scientists prefer their theories. Horgan has compared determinism to a rigid track laid down at the beginning of time but states that the human brain is too complex to accept that it cannot alter that track.

Based on the texts, what would the author of Text 2 most likely say about Text 1's characterization of the psychologists' response regarding determinism?

Ⓐ It is overly critical given the complexity of the human brain referenced by Horgan.

Ⓑ It is logical given that Horgan has offered a comparison that may help individuals accept the theory.

Ⓒ It is overly positive given the comments made about the complexity of the human brain by Horgan.

Ⓓ It is surprising given that Horgan's comments were readily accepted by the scientific community.

CONTINUE

10 Mark for Review

Credited Literary Contributions of Zora Neale Hurston, Nella Larsen, Jessie Redmon Fauset, and Anita Loos

Individual	Years active	Number of credited works published
Zora Neale Hurston	1921–1960	4 novels, 60 short stories, 4 plays
Nella Larsen	1928–1929	2 novels, 5 short stories
Jessie Redmon Fauset	1921–1945	4 novels, 100–200 works as editor
Anita Loos	1910–1970	10 novels, 100–200 short stories, 60 screenplays

Some historians studying African American women literary figures have focused on the early- to mid-1900s, when authors such as Zora Neale Hurston, Nella Larsen, Jessie Redmon Fauset, and Anita Loos were involved in one way or another with numerous literary works. Unfortunately, poor record keeping from this era makes it likely that the numbers of these four authors' contributions to literary canon should not be considered comprehensive; it's entirely possible, for example, that ______

Which choice most effectively uses the data from the table to complete the example?

Ⓐ Zora Neale Hurston wrote exactly 60 short stories and two novels.

Ⓑ Nella Larsen wrote significantly fewer short stories than Zora Neale Hurston, who is credited with 60.

Ⓒ Jessie Redmon Fauset's four credited novels include those written after 1945.

Ⓓ Anita Loos wrote more than 60 screenplays and Nella Larsen wrote more than five short stories.

11 Mark for Review

Researchers Mary Johnson, John Davis, and Robert Smith have studied the effects of exercise on cognitive function in elderly individuals. To effectively conduct these studies, the researchers separated participants aged 65 and older into two groups: one group engaged in a regular exercise program, while the other group remained sedentary. After six months, the exercise group showed significant improvements in memory, attention, and overall cognitive performance compared to the sedentary group. Johnson, Davis, and Smith concluded that regular exercise can have a positive impact on cognitive abilities in older adults.

Which finding, if true, would most directly support Johnson, Davis, and Smith's conclusion?

Ⓐ During periods of activity, elderly adults tend to get more sunshine and fresh air, both of which have a direct correlation to overall cognitive performance.

Ⓑ Overall cognitive performance is easier to ascertain in elderly populations that are physically active than in those that are not.

Ⓒ Cognitive performance in both active and sedentary elderly populations have been found to normalize and be hardly discernible after 12 months of observation.

Ⓓ Active elderly populations have been shown to slow, and sometimes reverse, the effects of aging on cognitive ability, while sedentary elderly populations tend to experience the cognitive effects of aging more rapidly.

CONTINUE

12 Mark for Review

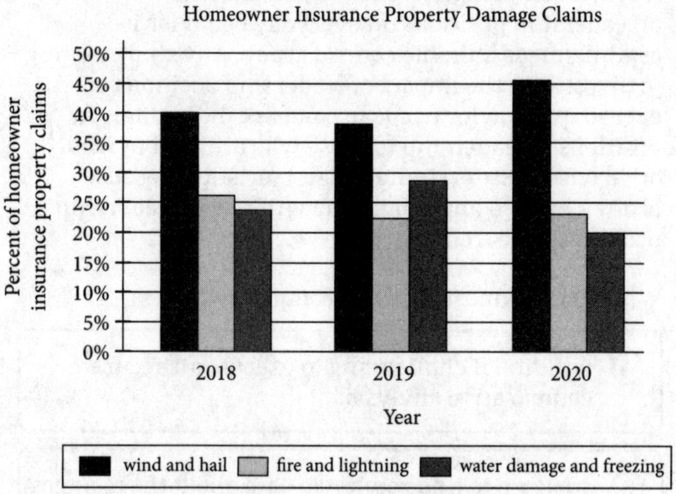

Considering all homeowner's insurance property claims, the Insurance Information Institute assessed the leading causes for property damage claims over a three-year period. According to its report, the Institute determined that the percentage by which different factors caused claims largely fluctuated over the period studied.

Which choice best describes data from the graph that support the Insurance Information Institute's conclusion?

Ⓐ The percentage contribution of water damage and freezing to homeowner's insurance property claims changed every year.

Ⓑ The percentage of homeowner's insurance property claims caused by fire and lightning remained unchanged during the three-year period.

Ⓒ The percentage of homeowner's insurance property claims caused by wind and hail was highest in 2019.

Ⓓ The percentage of homeowner's insurance property claims caused by wind and hail was higher than the percentage for fire and lightning or water damage and freezing in each year.

13 Mark for Review

If *FoxA*, the primary gene that enables some insects to regenerate limbs or even entire bodies, also exists in humans, some biologists have posited that humans may also have the ability to regenerate limbs naturally if stimulated correctly. This concept is also bolstered by evidence that the supplemental genes that interact with *FoxA* during the regeneration process are also found in humans.

Which finding, if true, would most directly weaken the biologists' claim?

Ⓐ The process for determining the genetic makeup of insects is determined to be more effective when used to analyze other types of living organisms.

Ⓑ The genetic makeup of most animal species contains *FoxA*, but when analyzed they contain numerous other genes also found in insects.

Ⓒ A genetically similar species to human beings is revealed to have the same ratio of *FoxA* in its genetic sequence as do insects.

Ⓓ A new study finds that only some of the supplemental genes necessary for aiding *FoxA* in the regeneration process are found in humans.

CONTINUE

14 Mark for Review

While studying art history, Neil MacGregor developed a belief that despite museums' displays of objects from different civilizations, the power of objects to tell stories had not been fully explored. According to a museum expert, during his career as an influential art historian and curator, MacGregor sought to address this issue, not by organizing displays limited to a single culture as was the industry standard, but by presenting the objects as pieces of a larger story, so that people from diverse ethnicities might find the exhibit more accessible.

Which finding, if true, would most directly support the museum expert's claim?

Ⓐ MacGregor organized the exhibition *Living with Gods: People, Places, and Worlds Beyond* not to emphasize a particular religious belief but to demonstrate the diverse spiritual and religious beliefs.

Ⓑ MacGregor curated *Shakespeare: Staging the World* in collaboration with the Royal Shakespeare Company, which explored the historical context during which Shakespeare's plays were written.

Ⓒ As director and curator for the British museum, MacGregor curated *A History of the World In 100 Objects*, which allowed visitors from around the world to explore human history through objects from the museum's collection.

Ⓓ MacGregor's work as curator of the 2015 exhibition *Australia* explored themes such as indigenous heritage, colonization, and environmental challenges in the context of contemporary Australian society.

15 Mark for Review

A central challenge when studying the impact of leadership positions on everyday behavior is establishing a suitable control group. Any study aiming to investigate the impact of leadership positions on everyday behavior needs to compare individuals in positions of leadership to those who are not but who otherwise possess similar characteristics. Because it is often hard to anticipate who will rise to leadership positions, researchers ________

Which choice most logically completes the text?

Ⓐ will find it challenging to execute an accurate comparative analysis.

Ⓑ struggle to find reputable data about the changes in behavior in those who currently hold leadership positions.

Ⓒ can only conduct valid studies on individuals who have recently left leadership positions.

Ⓓ should select a large control group of diverse people.

CONTINUE

16 Mark for Review

Transcribed in the sixteenth century in Classical Quiché by an unknown Mayan scribe, *Popol Vuh* is one of the most significant surviving sources of ancient Mayan culture. The text reflects pre-colonial Mayan beliefs about cosmology, religion, and morality. Nonetheless, some of the passages in *Popol Vuh* included Catholic and European influence, which suggests that the Mayans may have had interactions with those religious and regional groups. Consequently, scholars contend that ______

Which choice most logically completes the text?

Ⓐ any references to beliefs influenced cultural aspects of the Mayan civilization found in the text should be considered distinct from the original Mayan belief.

Ⓑ while most of ancient Mayan culture and traditions predates colonialization, some elements of culture were shaped after contact with European and Catholic ideals.

Ⓒ although the scribe who transcribed *Popol Vuh* was fluent in Classical Quiché, they also had a functional knowledge of European languages.

Ⓓ before colonization, Mayan beliefs about cosmology, religion, and morality were unique to the civilization.

17 Mark for Review

Directed by filmmaker Tony Silver, *Style Wars*, a documentary about New York City street artists, ______ contrasting views on graffiti, including those of the artists themselves, who explain their motivations for creating art that is illegal.

Which choice completes the text so that it conforms to the conventions of Standard English?

Ⓐ present

Ⓑ have presented

Ⓒ are presenting

Ⓓ presents

18 Mark for Review

Unlike all other waterfowl, the black-headed duck does not build a ______ it deposits its eggs into other birds' nests, where they are incubated along with the parents' own eggs. According to biologist John Eadie, the duck's choice of coots for their host nests may be in response to the presence of egg-eating predators, since coots vigorously defend their clutches against predation.

Which choice completes the text so that it conforms to the conventions of Standard English?

Ⓐ nest; instead,

Ⓑ nest, instead;

Ⓒ nest instead,

Ⓓ nest, instead,

CONTINUE

19 Mark for Review

Chemist Stephanie Kwolek ______ tire materials for the DuPont chemical company when she unexpectedly found a new polymer with fibers that aligned themselves parallel to each other, making this polymer exceptionally strong; later trademarked as Kevlar, her discovery is now used in products from phones to body armor.

Which choice completes the text so that it conforms to the conventions of Standard English?

Ⓐ will research

Ⓑ was researching

Ⓒ has been researching

Ⓓ researches

20 Mark for Review

Located on the eastern slopes of the Andes Mountains, the Yungas cloud forests of Bolivia are home to many endemic plants and animals. Herpetologist Teresa Camacho Badani led an expedition into the Yungas to collect specimens of an endangered species of ______ known only from a single individual found in 2009 and nicknamed Romeo, the Sehuencas water frog (*Telmatobius yucarare*) is now being bred in captivity in an effort to restore the population.

Which choice completes the text so that it conforms to the conventions of Standard English?

Ⓐ amphibian previously

Ⓑ amphibian but previously

Ⓒ amphibian. Previously

Ⓓ amphibian, previously

21 Mark for Review

In 2022, a helicopter landed in Palm Springs, California, after completing a pioneering 24-mile ______ by a rechargeable battery and carrying a 50-pound weight (which was added in order to simulate the weight of a transport care system for organ transplants), the fully electric helicopter was copiloted by Martine Rothblatt and Ric Webb.

Which choice completes the text so that it conforms to the conventions of Standard English?

Ⓐ flight, powered

Ⓑ flight and powered

Ⓒ flight powered

Ⓓ flight. Powered

22 Mark for Review

The *Voyager 2* spacecraft was launched by NASA in 1977 in order to take close-up pictures of Uranus and ______ find the furthest extent of the Solar System; and collect data about the interstellar space beyond the Solar System.

Which choice completes the text so that it conforms to the conventions of Standard English?

Ⓐ Neptune, the previously unexplored outer planets;

Ⓑ Neptune the previously unexplored outer planets,

Ⓒ Neptune, the previously unexplored outer planets,

Ⓓ Neptune; the previously unexplored outer planets,

CONTINUE

23 Mark for Review

Ethiopian American artist Julie Mehretu paints by projecting a visual image such as an architectural blueprint or a photograph from a newspaper article onto a canvas and then converting the projection into abstract forms, working in a style that art ______ "a complex dance between abstraction and representation."

Which choice completes the text so that it conforms to the conventions of Standard English?

Ⓐ journalist Maximiliáno Durón, calls,

Ⓑ journalist Maximiliáno Durón calls

Ⓒ journalist, Maximiliáno Durón, calls

Ⓓ journalist, Maximiliáno Durón, calls,

24 Mark for Review

While a local legend credits French cheesemaker Marie Harel with the invention of Camembert cheese, she likely learned the technique from a priest, Abbot Charles-Jean Bonvoust, who passed along the recipe while in hiding during the French Revolution. ______ Harel will likely continue to receive recognition for the cheese, as her descendants created a large-scale cheese factory to mass-produce the variety to share with the rest of the world.

Which choice completes the text with the most logical transition?

Ⓐ Nevertheless

Ⓑ Furthermore,

Ⓒ Indeed,

Ⓓ Consequently,

25 Mark for Review

The Chicxulub crater, located in Mexico, was discovered by Antonio Camargo and Glen Penfield and is believed to be the result of an asteroid impact. Many researchers have found evidence to support the hypothesis that the impact caused the Cretaceous-Paleogene extinction event. ______ the surrounding areas contain shocked quartz that is only formed through high pressure and tektites that are often ejected from meteorites.

Which choice completes the text with the most logical transition?

Ⓐ As a result,

Ⓑ However,

Ⓒ In other words,

Ⓓ Specifically,

CONTINUE

26 Mark for Review

Fingerprinting is often used to settle fraud cases, but a suspect could claim that he or she handled a piece of paper before the fraudulent material was printed on it. By placing a layer of gelatin over a fingerprint and reacting it in a vacuum chamber, the fingerprint will appear "masked" if it was placed before anything was printed on the paper. ______ using this new technique, court cases will have more reliable evidence regarding a suspect's knowledge of the fraud that was committed.

Which choice completes the text with the most logical transition?

(A) Nevertheless,

(B) Thus,

(C) Similarly,

(D) However,

27 Mark for Review

While researching a topic, a student has taken the following notes:

- Researchers have been investigating the effects of sports-related concussions on the brain.
- Biomarkers in the blood indicative of tissue injury were found in participants two weeks following their last injuries.
- Extensive white matter damage deeper in the brain was found in participants six months following their last injuries.
- Many participants had more than one sports-related concussion.

The student wants to make and support a generalization about sports-related concussions. Which choice most effectively uses relevant information from the notes to accomplish this goal?

(A) There are short- and long-term consequences of a sports-related concussion on the brain: two weeks following injury there are biomarkers in the blood indicative of tissue injury, while six months following injury there is damage to the white matter deeper in the brain.

(B) There are many effects of sports-related concussions on the brain, especially in participants with more than one sports-related concussion.

(C) One example of a long-term consequence of sports-related concussions is the damage to white matter deeper in the brain found in participants six months following their last injury.

(D) Many participants had more than one sports-related concussion, and blood biomarkers showed signs of tissue injury two weeks following their sports-related concussions.

STOP

If you finish before time is called, you may check your work on this module only.
Do not turn to any other module in the test.

THIS PAGE LEFT INTENTIONALLY BLANK.

SAT Prep Test 1—Math
Module 1

Turn to Section 2 of your answer sheet (p. 76) to answer the questions in this section.

DIRECTIONS

The questions in this section address a number of important math skills.
Use of a calculator is permitted for all questions.

NOTES

Unless otherwise indicated:

- All variables and expressions represent real numbers.
- Figures provided are drawn to scale.
- All figures lie in a plane.
- The domain of a given function f is the set of all real numbers x for which $f(x)$ is a real number.

REFERENCE

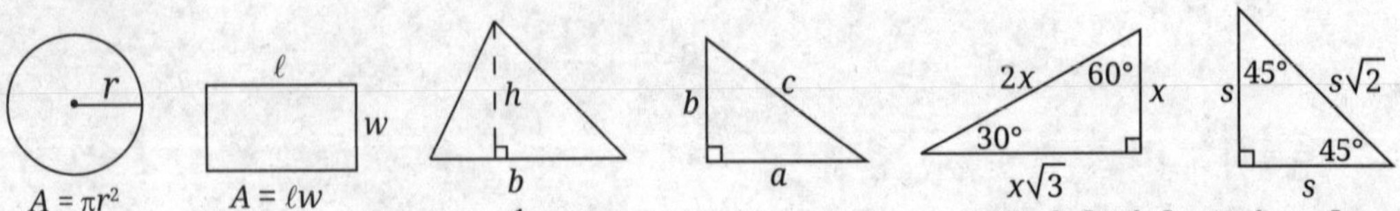

$A = \pi r^2$, $C = 2\pi r$

$A = \ell w$

$A = \frac{1}{2}bh$

$c^2 = a^2 + b^2$

Special Right Triangles

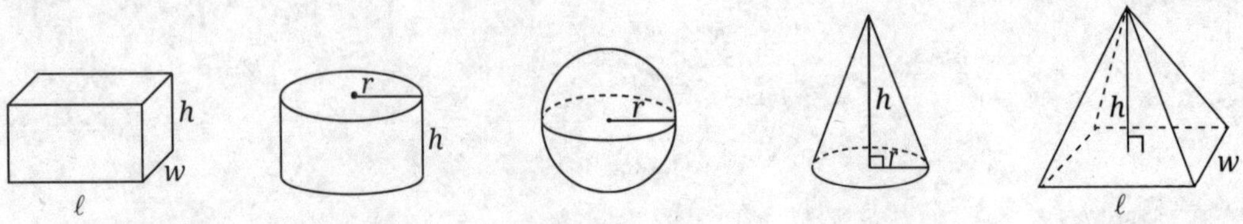

$V = \ell wh$

$V = \pi r^2 h$

$V = \frac{4}{3}\pi r^3$

$V = \frac{1}{3}\pi r^2 h$

$V = \frac{1}{3}\ell wh$

The number of degrees of arc in a circle is 360.
The number of radians of arc in a circle is 2π.
The sum of the measures in degrees of the angles of a triangle is 180.

CONTINUE

For multiple-choice questions, solve each problem, choose the correct answer from the choices provided, and then circle your answer in this book. Circle only one answer for each question. If you change your mind, completely erase the circle. You will not get credit for questions with more than one answer circled or for questions with no answers circled.

For student-produced response questions, solve each problem and write your answer next to or under the question in the test book as described below.

- Once you've written your answer, circle it clearly. You will not receive credit for anything written outside the circle or for any questions with more than one circled answer.
- If you find **more than one correct answer**, write and circle only one answer.
- Your answer can be up to 5 characters for a **positive** answer and up to 6 characters (including the negative sign) for a **negative** answer, but no more.
- If your answer is a **fraction** that is too long (over 5 characters for positive, 6 characters for negative), write the decimal equivalent.
- If your answer is a **decimal** that is too long (over 5 characters for positive, 6 characters for negative), truncate it or round at the fourth digit.
- If your answer is a **mixed number** (such as $3\frac{1}{2}$), write it as an improper fraction (7/2) or its decimal equivalent (3.5).
- Don't enter **symbols** such as a percent sign, comma, or dollar sign in your circled answer.

CONTINUE

1 Mark for Review

Data set S: 2, 3, 8, 8, 11, 24

Data set T: 3, 8, 8, 11, 24

The values in data sets S and T are given. Which of the following is a true statement comparing the means of the two data sets?

Ⓐ There is not enough information to compare the means.

Ⓑ The means of data set S and data set T are equal.

Ⓒ The mean of data set S is less than the mean of data set T.

Ⓓ The mean of data set S is greater than the mean of data set T.

2 Mark for Review

If $x = 8$, what is the value of $30 - x$?

Ⓐ 14

Ⓑ 22

Ⓒ 30

Ⓓ 38

3 Mark for Review

The valve of a water tank remained open for 44 seconds. The water tank contained 7,854 liters of water before the valve was opened and 1,192 liters of water once the valve was closed. Approximately how many liters of water, on average, drained from the tank each second while the valve was open?

Ⓐ 27

Ⓑ 151

Ⓒ 206

Ⓓ 6,662

4 Mark for Review

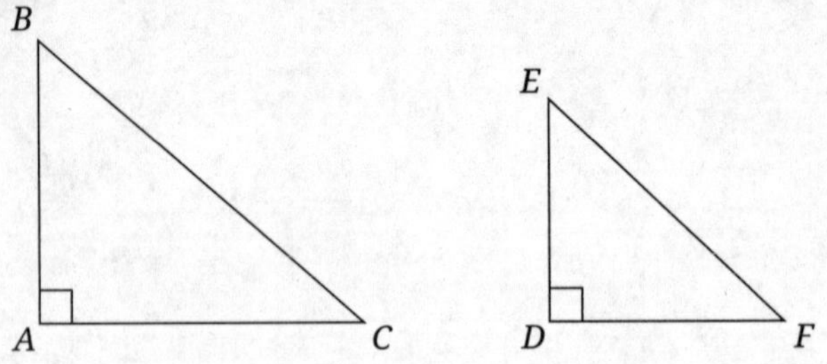

Note: Figures not drawn to scale.

Similar right triangles ABC and DEF are shown, where B corresponds to E. If the measure of angle E is 52°, what is the measure of angle C?

Ⓐ 38°

Ⓑ 52°

Ⓒ 128°

Ⓓ 142°

CONTINUE

5 Mark for Review

Last week, a softball equipment company made \$26,000 from the sale of equally-priced bats and equally-priced gloves. When b is the number of bats sold and g is the number of gloves sold, the equation $500b + 300g = 26{,}000$ represents this situation. The sales price of each glove is how many dollars less than the sales price of each bat?

______

6 Mark for Review

$$8x - y = -17$$
$$-7x = 14$$

The given system of equations has one solution at (x, y). What is the value of $x - y$?

Ⓐ −31

Ⓑ −3

Ⓒ 3

Ⓓ 31

7 Mark for Review

The function $f(d) = 750d + 12{,}000$ models the amount of money, in dollars, that an arts organization has in its account d days after starting a fundraising campaign. Based on this model, how much money, in dollars, did the organization have in its account before starting the fundraising campaign?

Ⓐ 16

Ⓑ 750

Ⓒ 11,250

Ⓓ 12,000

8 Mark for Review

Equilateral triangle T has a perimeter that is one-third the perimeter of equilateral triangle S. If one side of triangle S is 9 inches long, what is the length, in inches, of one side of triangle T?

Ⓐ 3

Ⓑ 9

Ⓒ 12

Ⓓ 27

CONTINUE

9 Mark for Review

If $|7x + 14| = 49$, what is one possible value of $x + 2$?

______

10 Mark for Review

x	$g(x)$
–30	–116
–24	–86
–18	–56
–12	–26
–6	4

Five values of x and their corresponding values of $g(x)$ are shown in the table. The relationship between x and $g(x)$ is linear. If the function g is defined by $g(x) = kx + 34$, what is the value of the constant k?

______

11 Mark for Review

The expression $(-3x^4 + 13) + (-8x^4 - 9)$ is equivalent to $cx^4 + 4$, where c is a constant. What is the value of c?

______

12 Mark for Review

$$\frac{22m}{n} = \frac{2}{3s}$$

The given equation relates the numbers m, n, and s, where n is not equal to 0 and $s > 1$. Which equation correctly expresses m in terms of n and s?

Ⓐ $m = 2n - 66s$

Ⓑ $m = 66ns$

Ⓒ $m = \frac{3ns}{44}$

Ⓓ $m = \frac{2n}{66s}$

13 Mark for Review

A certain ant colony contains 96,000 ants. A disease infects the colony, causing the number of ants to decrease by one-half every 4 days. How many ants remained in the colony 20 days after the infection started?

Ⓐ 3,000

Ⓑ 4,800

Ⓒ 6,000

Ⓓ 24,000

CONTINUE

14 Mark for Review

$$x < 53$$
$$x - 7y < 16$$

When the given system of inequalities is graphed in the xy-plane, one of the solutions is $(39, y)$. Which of the following could be the value of y?

Ⓐ -4

Ⓑ -3

Ⓒ 3

Ⓓ 4

15 Mark for Review

$$\sqrt[9]{s^5t^5}$$

If s and t are positive, which of the following expressions is equivalent to the given expression?

Ⓐ $(st)^{\frac{5}{9}}$

Ⓑ $(st)^{\frac{9}{5}}$

Ⓒ $(st)^{14}$

Ⓓ $(st)^{45}$

16 Mark for Review

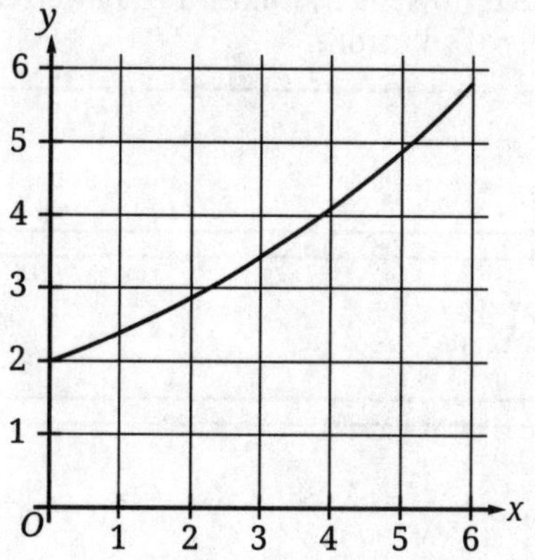

A certain collector's item increased in value every month for the first six months after it was purchased. The graph shows the value, y, in hundreds of dollars, of the item x months after it was purchased, where $0 \le x \le 6$. Which of the following is the best interpretation of the y-intercept of the graph in this context?

Ⓐ The value of the item when it was purchased was \$2.

Ⓑ The value of the item increased by \$200 over the first six months after it was purchased.

Ⓒ The value of the item when it was purchased was \$200.

Ⓓ The value of the item six months after it was purchased was \$2,000.

CONTINUE

17 Mark for Review

Which of the following systems of linear equations has exactly one real solution?

Ⓐ $y = 2$
$y = 4$

Ⓑ $y = 2x$
$y = 2x - 4$

Ⓒ $y = 4x - 4$
$y = 4x + 4$

Ⓓ $y = 4x - 2$
$y = 8x - 4$

18 Mark for Review

The nth term of a sequence is represented by s, and each term after the first term is one-half of the preceding term. If the first term of the sequence is 56, which of the following equations expresses s in terms of n?

Ⓐ $s = \frac{1}{2}(56^{n-1})$

Ⓑ $s = \frac{1}{2}(56^{n})$

Ⓒ $s = 56\left(\frac{1}{2}\right)^{n-1}$

Ⓓ $s = 56\left(\frac{1}{2}\right)^{n}$

19 Mark for Review

In 2023, a certain streaming service decreased its number of movies available by 9% from the number of movies available in 2022. If the number of movies available in 2023 is m times the number of movies available in 2022, what is the value of m?

Ⓐ 0.09

Ⓑ 0.91

Ⓒ 1.09

Ⓓ 1.91

20 Mark for Review

The maximum value of q is 14 more than 7 times the value of r. Which inequality represents the relationship between q and r?

Ⓐ $q \leq 7r + 14$

Ⓑ $q \leq 14r + 7$

Ⓒ $q \geq 7r + 14$

Ⓓ $q \geq 14r + 7$

CONTINUE

21 Mark for Review

The equation $5x + 3y = -8$ represents line l. Line m is obtained by shifting line l up 2 units in the xy-plane. The x-intercept of the graph of line m is (a, b). What is the value of a?

22 Mark for Review

$$AB = 42$$
$$BC = 56$$
$$CA = 70$$

Right triangle ABC is similar to triangle DEF, where A corresponds to D and B corresponds to E. The lengths of the sides of triangle ABC are given. What is the value of $\cos D$?

(A) $\frac{3}{5}$

(B) $\frac{3}{4}$

(C) $\frac{4}{5}$

(D) $\frac{4}{3}$

YIELD

Once you've finished (or run out of time for) this section, use the answer key to determine how many questions you got right. If you got fewer than 14 questions right, move on to Module 2—Easier, otherwise move on to Module 2—Harder.

SAT Prep Test 1—Math

Module 2—Easier

Turn to Section 2 of your answer sheet (p. 76) to answer the questions in this section.

DIRECTIONS

The questions in this section address a number of important math skills.
Use of a calculator is permitted for all questions.

NOTES

Unless otherwise indicated:

- All variables and expressions represent real numbers.
- Figures provided are drawn to scale.
- All figures lie in a plane.
- The domain of a given function *f* is the set of all real numbers *x* for which *f*(*x*) is a real number.

REFERENCE

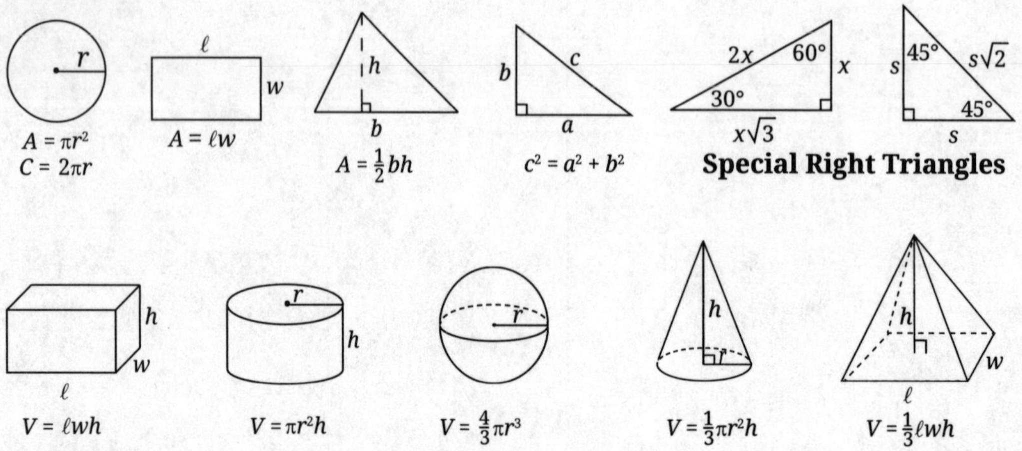

$A = \pi r^2$, $C = 2\pi r$

$A = \ell w$

$A = \frac{1}{2}bh$

$c^2 = a^2 + b^2$

Special Right Triangles

$V = \ell wh$

$V = \pi r^2 h$

$V = \frac{4}{3}\pi r^3$

$V = \frac{1}{3}\pi r^2 h$

$V = \frac{1}{3}\ell wh$

The number of degrees of arc in a circle is 360.
The number of radians of arc in a circle is 2π.
The sum of the measures in degrees of the angles of a triangle is 180.

CONTINUE

For multiple-choice questions, solve each problem, choose the correct answer from the choices provided, and then circle your answer in this book. Circle only one answer for each question. If you change your mind, completely erase the circle. You will not get credit for questions with more than one answer circled or for questions with no answers circled.

For student-produced response questions, solve each problem and write your answer next to or under the question in the test book as described below.

- Once you've written your answer, circle it clearly. You will not receive credit for anything written outside the circle or for any questions with more than one circled answer.
- If you find **more than one correct answer**, write and circle only one answer.
- Your answer can be up to 5 characters for a **positive** answer and up to 6 characters (including the negative sign) for a **negative** answer, but no more.
- If your answer is a **fraction** that is too long (over 5 characters for positive, 6 characters for negative), write the decimal equivalent.
- If your answer is a **decimal** that is too long (over 5 characters for positive, 6 characters for negative), truncate it or round at the fourth digit.
- If your answer is a **mixed number** (such as $3\frac{1}{2}$), write it as an improper fraction (7/2) or its decimal equivalent (3.5).
- Don't enter **symbols** such as a percent sign, comma, or dollar sign in your circled answer.

CONTINUE

1 Mark for Review

An automobile factory makes 1,200 vehicles in 1 day. If the factory operates continuously for 1 week at this rate, how many vehicles will it make?

______

2 Mark for Review

If $10a = 30$, what is the value of $9a$?

Ⓐ 27

Ⓑ 40

Ⓒ 270

Ⓓ 360

3 Mark for Review

Talula baked 340 cookies and gave 20% of them to her neighbors. How many of the cookies did Talula give to her neighbors?

Ⓐ 14

Ⓑ 34

Ⓒ 54

Ⓓ 68

4 Mark for Review

$$h(x) = 11x - 5$$

The function h is defined by the given equation. When $x = 6$, what is the value of $h(x)$?

______

CONTINUE

5 Mark for Review

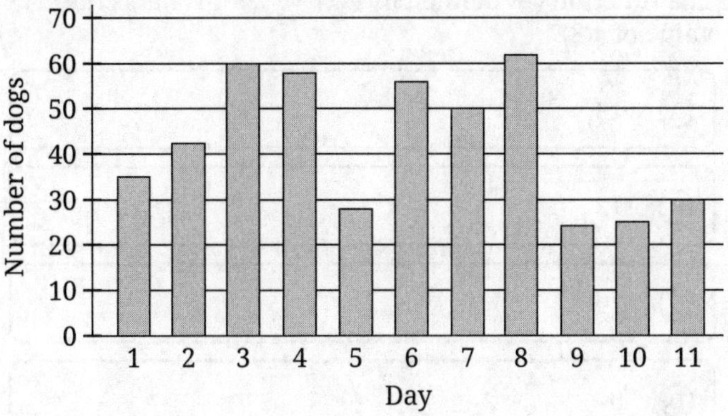

The distribution of 469 dogs that visited a dog park over an 11-day period is shown in the bar graph. How many dogs visited this dog park on day 7?

______

6 Mark for Review

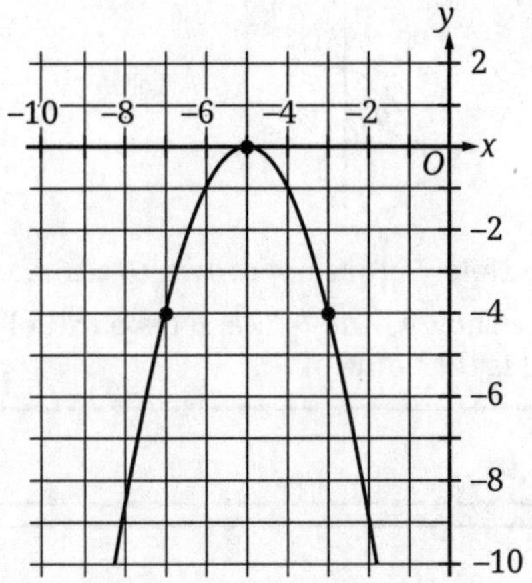

The graph shown intercepts the x-axis at $(x, 0)$. What is the value of x?

______

7 Mark for Review

Which of the following expressions is equivalent to $14a + 7ab^2$?

Ⓐ $2a(7 + 7b^2)$

Ⓑ $7a(2 + b^2)$

Ⓒ $7a(a + 14b)$

Ⓓ $7b(2ab)$

8 Mark for Review

Rectangle A has a length of 80 and a width of 24. What is the perimeter of rectangle A?

______

CONTINUE

9 Mark for Review

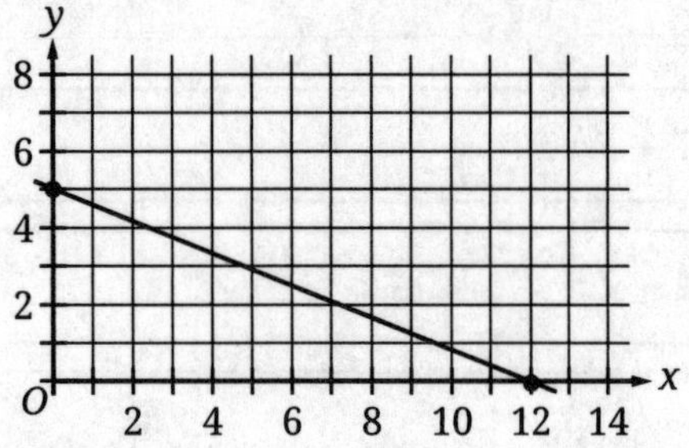

The point with coordinates $(3, n)$ lies on the line shown. What is the value of n?

Ⓐ $\frac{13}{4}$

Ⓑ $\frac{15}{4}$

Ⓒ $\frac{19}{5}$

Ⓓ $\frac{24}{7}$

10 Mark for Review

A magician has a hat with 18 cards inside. The face of each card has a number from 1 to 18 written on it, with a different number on each card. If the magician takes out a single card, what is the probability that the number written on it is <u>not</u> 6?

Ⓐ $\frac{1}{18}$

Ⓑ $\frac{6}{18}$

Ⓒ $\frac{12}{18}$

Ⓓ $\frac{17}{18}$

11 Mark for Review

The function g is defined by $g(x) = -2x^2$. What is the value of $g(3)$?

Ⓐ −18

Ⓑ −12

Ⓒ −10

Ⓓ −6

12 Mark for Review

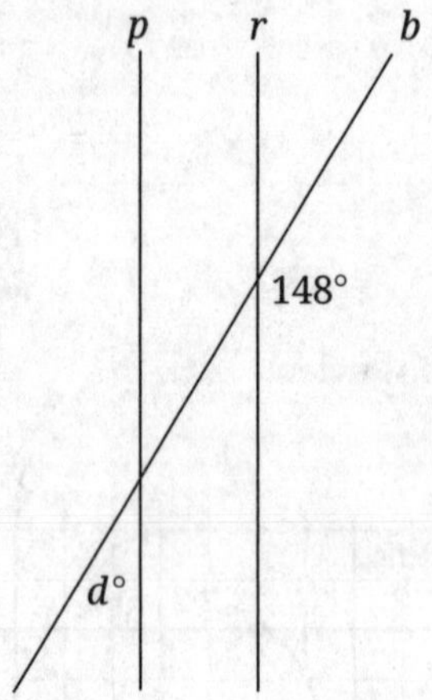

Note: Figure not drawn to scale.

In the figure shown, line b intersects parallel lines p and r. What is the value of d?

Ⓐ 16

Ⓑ 32

Ⓒ 74

Ⓓ 148

CONTINUE

13 Mark for Review

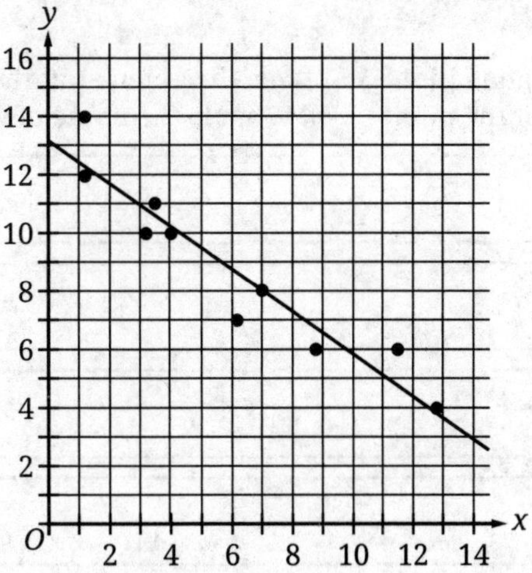

Which of the following equations could define the line of best fit for the scatterplot shown?

Ⓐ $y = -13 - 0.7x$

Ⓑ $y = -13 + 0.7x$

Ⓒ $y = 13 - 0.7x$

Ⓓ $y = 13 + 0.7x$

14 Mark for Review

Data Set R

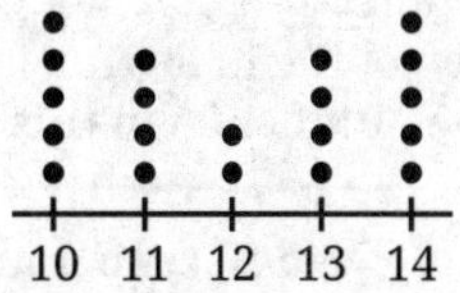

There are 20 values in data set R, represented by the dot plot shown. Data set S is created by subtracting 8 from each of the values in data set R. Which of the following correctly compares the ranges and the means of data sets R and S?

Ⓐ The range of data set S is less than the range of data set R, and the mean of data set S is equal to the mean of data set R.

Ⓑ The range of data set S is less than the range of data set R, and the mean of data set S is less than the mean of data set R.

Ⓒ The range of data set S is equal to the range of data set R, and the mean of data set S is equal to the mean of data set R.

Ⓓ The range of data set S is equal to the range of data set R, and the mean of data set S is less than the mean of data set R.

CONTINUE

15 Mark for Review

During a video game session, a player scored a total of 1,000 points for c cooperative missions and s solo missions. The equation $20c + 25s = 1{,}000$ represents this situation. Which of the following is the best interpretation of the number 25 in this context?

Ⓐ The player completed 25 cooperative missions during this session.

Ⓑ The player scored 25 points for each cooperative mission during this session.

Ⓒ The player completed 25 solo missions during this session.

Ⓓ The player scored 25 points for each solo mission during this session.

16 Mark for Review

$$g(x) = \frac{\sqrt{x}}{2}$$

The function g is defined by the given equation. If $g(x) = 5$, what is the value of x?

Ⓐ 10

Ⓑ 25

Ⓒ 50

Ⓓ 100

17 Mark for Review

$$y = x^2 - 7$$
$$x = -7$$

When graphed in the xy-plane, the given equations intersect at the point (x, y). What is the value of y?

Ⓐ -21

Ⓑ -7

Ⓒ 42

Ⓓ 49

18 Mark for Review

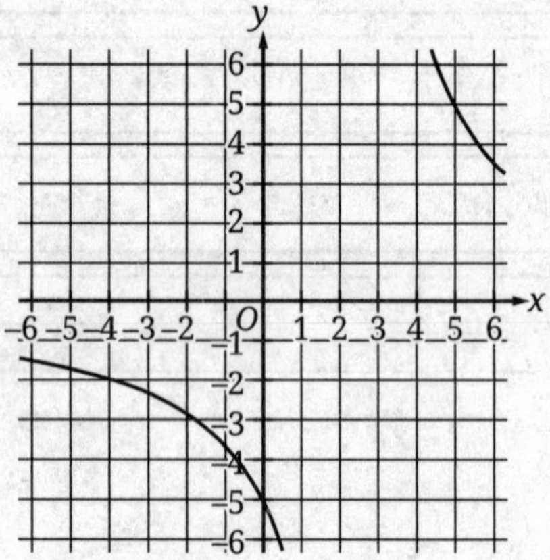

A partial graph of $y = f(x)$ in the xy-plane is shown. Which of the following is the value of $f(0)$?

Ⓐ -5

Ⓑ $-\frac{1}{4}$

Ⓒ 0

Ⓓ 5

CONTINUE

19 Mark for Review

Which of the following equations defines a line in the xy-plane that has a slope of $\frac{1}{6}$ and passes through the point $(12, -7)$?

Ⓐ $y = \frac{x}{6} - 9$

Ⓑ $y = \frac{x}{6} - 7$

Ⓒ $y = -9x + \frac{1}{6}$

Ⓓ $y = 12x - 7$

20 Mark for Review

How many distinct real solutions does the equation $4x^2 - 8x - 5 = 0$ have?

Ⓐ Exactly one

Ⓑ Exactly two

Ⓒ Infinitely many

Ⓓ Zero

21 Mark for Review

A jar contains a total of 37 red and blue tokens used to play a game. The mass of one red token is 90 grams, and the mass of one blue token is 120 grams. If the combined mass of the tokens is 3,810 grams, how many of the tokens in the jar are blue?

Ⓐ 5

Ⓑ 16

Ⓒ 21

Ⓓ 32

22 Mark for Review

Circle R is defined by the equation $(x + 3)^2 + y^2 = 64$. If circle S is the result of shifting the graph of circle R to the right 7 units in the xy-plane, what is the equation of circle S?

Ⓐ $(x + 3)^2 + (y - 7)^2 = 64$

Ⓑ $(x + 3)^2 + (y + 7)^2 = 64$

Ⓒ $(x - 4)^2 + y^2 = 64$

Ⓓ $(x + 10)^2 + y^2 = 64$

STOP

If you finish before time is called, you may check your work on this module only. Do not turn to any other module in the test.

SAT Prep Test 1—Math
Module 2—Harder

Turn to Section 2 of your answer sheet (p. 76) to answer the questions in this section.

DIRECTIONS

The questions in this section address a number of important math skills.
Use of a calculator is permitted for all questions.

NOTES

Unless otherwise indicated:

- All variables and expressions represent real numbers.
- Figures provided are drawn to scale.
- All figures lie in a plane.
- The domain of a given function f is the set of all real numbers x for which $f(x)$ is a real number.

REFERENCE

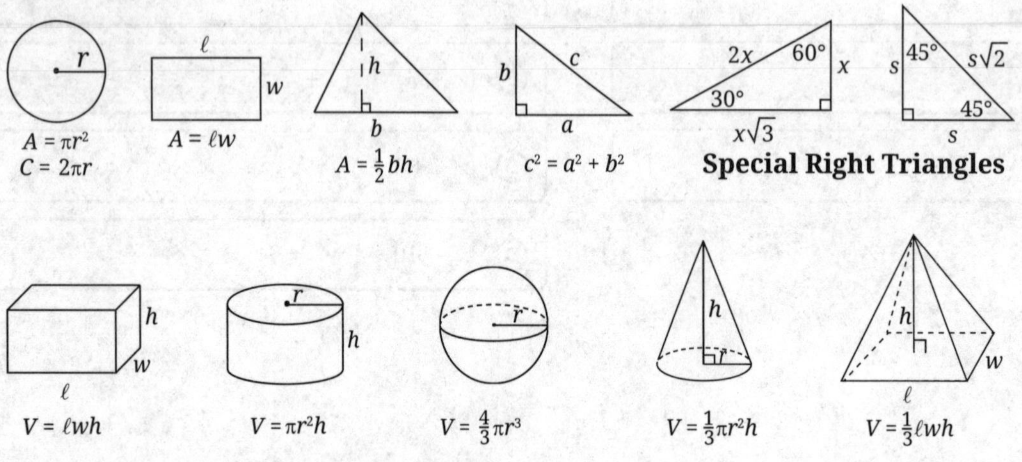

The number of degrees of arc in a circle is 360.
The number of radians of arc in a circle is 2π.
The sum of the measures in degrees of the angles of a triangle is 180.

CONTINUE

For multiple-choice questions, solve each problem, choose the correct answer from the choices provided, and then circle your answer in this book. Circle only one answer for each question. If you change your mind, completely erase the circle. You will not get credit for questions with more than one answer circled or for questions with no answers circled.

For student-produced response questions, solve each problem and write your answer next to or under the question in the test book as described below.

- Once you've written your answer, circle it clearly. You will not receive credit for anything written outside the circle or for any questions with more than one circled answer.
- If you find **more than one correct answer**, write and circle only one answer.
- Your answer can be up to 5 characters for a **positive** answer and up to 6 characters (including the negative sign) for a **negative** answer, but no more.
- If your answer is a **fraction** that is too long (over 5 characters for positive, 6 characters for negative), write the decimal equivalent.
- If your answer is a **decimal** that is too long (over 5 characters for positive, 6 characters for negative), truncate it or round at the fourth digit.
- If your answer is a **mixed number** (such as $3\frac{1}{2}$), write it as an improper fraction (7/2) or its decimal equivalent (3.5).
- Don't enter **symbols** such as a percent sign, comma, or dollar sign in your circled answer.

CONTINUE

1 Mark for Review

A fruit stand sells a total of 200 apples and bananas. The apples are sold in bags of 4 apples per bag, and the bananas are sold in bunches of 6 bananas each. Which of the following equations best represents the number of bags of apples, a, and bunches of bananas, b, that could be sold at the fruit stand?

Ⓐ $(a + b)(4 + 6) = 200$

Ⓑ $(4 + a)(6 + b) = 200$

Ⓒ $4a + 6b = 200$

Ⓓ $6a + 4b = 200$

2 Mark for Review

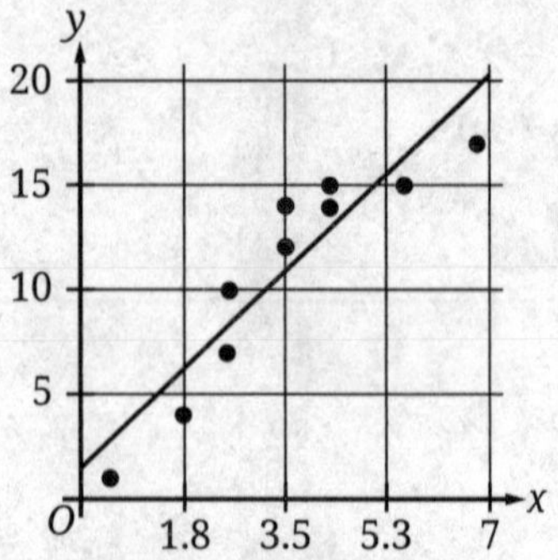

The relationship between two variables, x and y, is shown on the scatterplot, and a line of best fit is also shown. Which of the following equations best represents the line of best fit?

Ⓐ $y = -1.5 - 2.7x$

Ⓑ $y = -1.5 + 2.7x$

Ⓒ $y = 1.5 - 2.7x$

Ⓓ $y = 1.5 + 2.7x$

3 Mark for Review

A random sample of the 120 members of a cycling club was given a survey. The survey asked the cycling club members whether they plan to compete in an upcoming race. Of those surveyed, 45% responded that they do not plan to compete in the upcoming race. Which of the following is the best estimate of the total number of cycling club members who do not plan to compete in the upcoming race, based on the survey?

Ⓐ 45

Ⓑ 54

Ⓒ 66

Ⓓ 120

4 Mark for Review

x	$g(x)$
−1	−11
0	−5
1	−7
2	−17

The table shows four values of x and their corresponding values of $g(x)$ for the quadratic function g. Which of the following equations defines function g?

Ⓐ $g(x) = -x^2 - 4x - 5$

Ⓑ $g(x) = -5x^2 + 3x - 5$

Ⓒ $g(x) = -4x^2 + 2x - 5$

Ⓓ $g(x) = -2x^2 + 4x - 5$

CONTINUE

5 Mark for Review

$$f(x) = \frac{x - 12}{8}$$

The equation given defines function f. If c is a constant, for which value of c does $f(c) = 20$?

Ⓐ 1

Ⓑ 20

Ⓒ 148

Ⓓ 172

6 Mark for Review

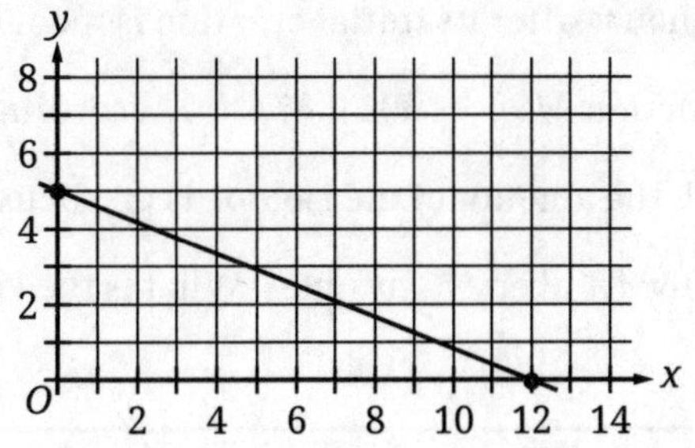

The point with coordinates $(3, n)$ lies on the line shown. What is the value of n?

Ⓐ $\frac{13}{4}$

Ⓑ $\frac{15}{4}$

Ⓒ $\frac{19}{5}$

Ⓓ $\frac{24}{7}$

7 Mark for Review

Line l is graphed in the xy-plane and is defined by $7 + 4y = -16x$. If line m is parallel to line l, what is the slope of line m?

Ⓐ -4

Ⓑ $-\frac{1}{4}$

Ⓒ $\frac{1}{4}$

Ⓓ 4

8 Mark for Review

A concrete block in the shape of a rectangular solid has a mass of 1,690 kilograms. The block has a length of 1.1 meters, a width of 0.8 meters, and a height of 0.8 meters. To the nearest whole number, what is the density, in kilograms per cubic meter, of the concrete block?

Ⓐ 1,082

Ⓑ 1,190

Ⓒ 2,401

Ⓓ 2,641

CONTINUE

9 Mark for Review

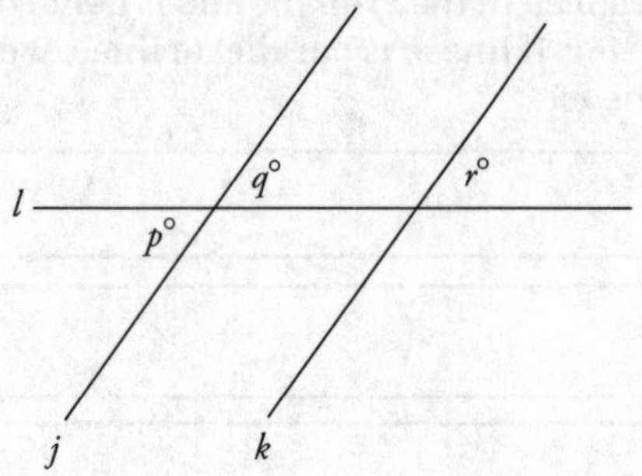

Note: Figure not drawn to scale.

In the figure shown, line l intersects parallel lines j and k. If $q = 10c - 11$ and $r = 15c + 41$, what is the value of p?

Ⓐ 6

Ⓑ 49

Ⓒ 115

Ⓓ 131

10 Mark for Review

$$-7(px + q) = \frac{42}{23}x + \frac{35}{9}$$

The given equation, where p and q are constants, has infinitely many solutions. If $p < 0$, what is the value of q?

11 Mark for Review

During the last business quarter, the number of unique visitors to a small e-commerce website decreased by 25% from its previous average of 620 unique visitors each day. At the start of the upcoming quarter, the website will launch a promotion, and the resulting number of unique visitors per day is projected to be 180% of the number of visitors last quarter. What is the projected average number of unique visitors per day the website will receive during its promotion?

12 Mark for Review

The amount, in micrograms, of a certain radioactive isotope h hours after its initial creation is modeled by the function $M(h) = 302(0.87)^{\left(\frac{4}{5}\right)h}$. According to the model, the amount of the isotope is predicted to decrease by $d\%$ every 75 minutes. What is the value of d?

Ⓐ 0.87

Ⓑ 13

Ⓒ 16.25

Ⓓ 87

CONTINUE

13 Mark for Review

Packages in a warehouse are split into two groups. Group X contains 40 packages, and group Y contains 110 packages. If the mean mass of the packages in group X is 24 kilograms (kg), and the mean mass of the packages in group Y is 9 kg, what is the mean mass, in kg, of all 150 packages?

14 Mark for Review

$$11x^2 - kx + 63$$

The given expression, where k is a constant, can be rewritten as $(px - q)(x - r)$, where p, q, and r are integer constants. Which of the following must be an integer?

Ⓐ $\frac{63}{r}$

Ⓑ $\frac{63}{p}$

Ⓒ $\frac{k}{r}$

Ⓓ $\frac{k}{p}$

15 Mark for Review

The equation $3x^2 - 36x + k = 0$ has exactly two real solutions. If k is a constant and $k < m$, what is the least possible value of m?

16 Mark for Review

Data Set R

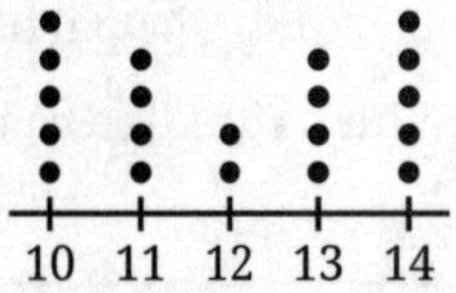

There are 20 values in data set R, represented by the dot plot shown. Data set S is created by subtracting 8 from each of the values in data set R. Which of the following correctly compares the ranges and the means of data sets R and S?

Ⓐ The range of data set S is less than the range of data set R, and the mean of data set S is equal to the mean of data set R.

Ⓑ The range of data set S is less than the range of data set R, and the mean of data set S is less than the mean of data set R.

Ⓒ The range of data set S is equal to the range of data set R, and the mean of data set S is equal to the mean of data set R.

Ⓓ The range of data set S is equal to the range of data set R, and the mean of data set S is less than the mean of data set R.

CONTINUE

17 Mark for Review

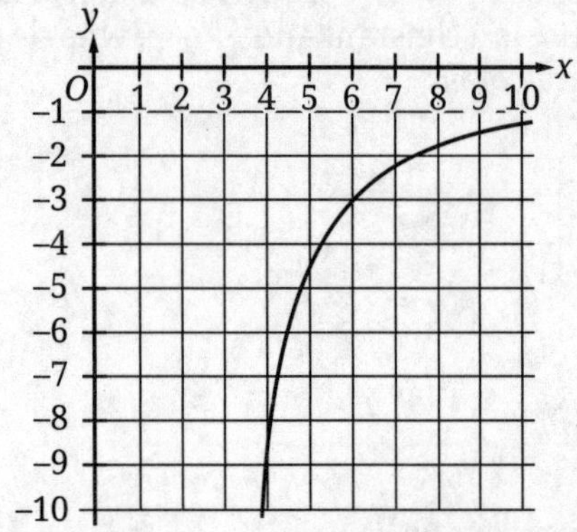

The function g is defined by the equation $g(x) = \frac{c}{x-d}$, where c and d are constants. The partial graph of $y = g(x)$ is shown. Which equation could define function h if $h(x) = g(x - 3)$?

Ⓐ $h(x) = -\frac{9}{x-6}$

Ⓑ $h(x) = -\frac{9}{x-3}$

Ⓒ $h(x) = \frac{-9}{x}$

Ⓓ $h(x) = \frac{-9(x-3)}{x-3}$

18 Mark for Review

$$y = x^2 - 6x - c$$
$$y = 3.5$$

If the given system of equations has exactly one real solution, and c is a negative constant, what is the value of c?

19 Mark for Review

A circle with the equation $x^2 - \frac{1}{2}x + y^2 - \frac{1}{2}y = \frac{7}{8}$ is graphed in the xy-plane. What is the length of the radius of this circle?

20 Mark for Review

In the equation $18x^2 - (18n - m)x - mn = 0$, m and n are positive constants. If the product of the solutions to the given equation is kmn, where k is a constant, what is the value of k?

Ⓐ -18

Ⓑ $-\frac{1}{18}$

Ⓒ $\frac{1}{9}$

Ⓓ 1

CONTINUE

21 Mark for Review

The equation of a parabola is written in the form $y = ax^2 + bx + c$, where a, b, and c are constants. When graphed in the xy-plane, the parabola has vertex $(-1, 4)$ and does not intersect the x-axis. Which of the following could be the value of $a - b - c$?

Ⓐ -5

Ⓑ -4

Ⓒ 0

Ⓓ 4

22 Mark for Review

A rectangular prism has a height of 50 centimeters (cm). The base of the prism is a square and the surface area of the prism is S cm^2. If the prism is divided into two identical rectangular prisms by making a cut parallel to the square base, each resulting prism has a surface area of $\frac{31}{56}S$ cm^2. What is the side length, in cm, of each square base?

Ⓐ 5

Ⓑ 6

Ⓒ 12

Ⓓ 24

STOP

If you finish before time is called, you may check your work on this module only.
Do not turn to any other module in the test.

SAT Prep, 2025 Edition
Practice Test

The Princeton Review

YOUR NAME: ____
(Print) Last First M.I.

SIGNATURE: ______________________________ DATE: ___/___/___

HOME ADDRESS: ____
(Print) Number and Street

____
City State Zip Code

PHONE NO.: ____
(Print)

DATE OF BIRTH: ___/___/___
(Print) Month / Day / Year

For both the Reading and Writing and the Math, be sure to only fill in the bubbles for the version of Module 2 that you took. If you took the Easier Module 2, only fill in the answer in the Easier column. If you took the Harder Module 2, only fill in the answers in the Harder column.

Section 1: Module 1
Reading and Writing

1. (A) (B) (C) (D)
2. (A) (B) (C) (D)
3. (A) (B) (C) (D)
4. (A) (B) (C) (D)
5. (A) (B) (C) (D)
6. (A) (B) (C) (D)
7. (A) (B) (C) (D)
8. (A) (B) (C) (D)
9. (A) (B) (C) (D)
10. (A) (B) (C) (D)
11. (A) (B) (C) (D)
12. (A) (B) (C) (D)
13. (A) (B) (C) (D)
14. (A) (B) (C) (D)
15. (A) (B) (C) (D)
16. (A) (B) (C) (D)
17. (A) (B) (C) (D)
18. (A) (B) (C) (D)
19. (A) (B) (C) (D)
20. (A) (B) (C) (D)
21. (A) (B) (C) (D)
22. (A) (B) (C) (D)
23. (A) (B) (C) (D)
24. (A) (B) (C) (D)
25. (A) (B) (C) (D)
26. (A) (B) (C) (D)
27. (A) (B) (C) (D)

Section 1: Module 2 (Easier)
Reading and Writing

1. (A) (B) (C) (D)
2. (A) (B) (C) (D)
3. (A) (B) (C) (D)
4. (A) (B) (C) (D)
5. (A) (B) (C) (D)
6. (A) (B) (C) (D)
7. (A) (B) (C) (D)
8. (A) (B) (C) (D)
9. (A) (B) (C) (D)
10. (A) (B) (C) (D)
11. (A) (B) (C) (D)
12. (A) (B) (C) (D)
13. (A) (B) (C) (D)
14. (A) (B) (C) (D)
15. (A) (B) (C) (D)
16. (A) (B) (C) (D)
17. (A) (B) (C) (D)
18. (A) (B) (C) (D)
19. (A) (B) (C) (D)
20. (A) (B) (C) (D)
21. (A) (B) (C) (D)
22. (A) (B) (C) (D)
23. (A) (B) (C) (D)
24. (A) (B) (C) (D)
25. (A) (B) (C) (D)
26. (A) (B) (C) (D)
27. (A) (B) (C) (D)

Section 1: Module 2 (Harder)
Reading and Writing

1. (A) (B) (C) (D)
2. (A) (B) (C) (D)
3. (A) (B) (C) (D)
4. (A) (B) (C) (D)
5. (A) (B) (C) (D)
6. (A) (B) (C) (D)
7. (A) (B) (C) (D)
8. (A) (B) (C) (D)
9. (A) (B) (C) (D)
10. (A) (B) (C) (D)
11. (A) (B) (C) (D)
12. (A) (B) (C) (D)
13. (A) (B) (C) (D)
14. (A) (B) (C) (D)
15. (A) (B) (C) (D)
16. (A) (B) (C) (D)
17. (A) (B) (C) (D)
18. (A) (B) (C) (D)
19. (A) (B) (C) (D)
20. (A) (B) (C) (D)
21. (A) (B) (C) (D)
22. (A) (B) (C) (D)
23. (A) (B) (C) (D)
24. (A) (B) (C) (D)
25. (A) (B) (C) (D)
26. (A) (B) (C) (D)
27. (A) (B) (C) (D)

SAT Prep, 2025 Edition
Practice Test

The Princeton Review®

YOUR NAME: ____
(Print) Last First M.I.

SIGNATURE: ______________________________ DATE: ___/___/___

HOME ADDRESS: ____
(Print) Number and Street

____
City State Zip Code

PHONE NO.: ____
(Print)

DATE OF BIRTH: ___/___/___
(Print) Month / Day / Year

!

For both the Reading and Writing and the Math, be sure to only fill in the bubbles for the version of Module 2 that you took. If you took the Easier Module 2, only fill in the answer in the Easier column. If you took the Harder Module 2, only fill in the answers in the Harder column.

Section 2: Module 1 Math	Section 2: Module 2 (Easier) Math	Section 2: Module 2 (Harder) Math
1. (A) (B) (C) (D)	1. ________	1. (A) (B) (C) (D)
2. (A) (B) (C) (D)	2. (A) (B) (C) (D)	2. (A) (B) (C) (D)
3. (A) (B) (C) (D)	3. (A) (B) (C) (D)	3. (A) (B) (C) (D)
4. (A) (B) (C) (D)	4. ________	4. (A) (B) (C) (D)
5. ________	5. ________	5. (A) (B) (C) (D)
6. (A) (B) (C) (D)	6. ________	6. (A) (B) (C) (D)
7. (A) (B) (C) (D)	7. (A) (B) (C) (D)	7. (A) (B) (C) (D)
8. (A) (B) (C) (D)	8. ________	8. (A) (B) (C) (D)
9. ________	9. (A) (B) (C) (D)	9. (A) (B) (C) (D)
10. ________	10. (A) (B) (C) (D)	10. ________
11. ________	11. (A) (B) (C) (D)	11. ________
12. (A) (B) (C) (D)	12. (A) (B) (C) (D)	12. (A) (B) (C) (D)
13. (A) (B) (C) (D)	13. (A) (B) (C) (D)	13. ________
14. (A) (B) (C) (D)	14. (A) (B) (C) (D)	14. (A) (B) (C) (D)
15. (A) (B) (C) (D)	15. (A) (B) (C) (D)	15. ________
16. (A) (B) (C) (D)	16. (A) (B) (C) (D)	16. (A) (B) (C) (D)
17. (A) (B) (C) (D)	17. (A) (B) (C) (D)	17. (A) (B) (C) (D)
18. (A) (B) (C) (D)	18. (A) (B) (C) (D)	18. ________
19. (A) (B) (C) (D)	19. (A) (B) (C) (D)	19. ________
20. (A) (B) (C) (D)	20. (A) (B) (C) (D)	20. (A) (B) (C) (D)
21. ________	21. (A) (B) (C) (D)	21. (A) (B) (C) (D)
22. (A) (B) (C) (D)	22. (A) (B) (C) (D)	22. (A) (B) (C) (D)

Chapter 3
Practice Test 1: Diagnostic Answer Key and Explanations

PRACTICE TEST 1: DIAGNOSTIC ANSWER KEY

Let's take a look at how you did on Practice Test 1. Check your answers and fill in the scorecard below by marking correct answers with a check. Then read the explanations for any questions you got wrong, or you struggled with but got correct. Once you finish working through the scorecard and the explanations, go back to page 10 to review how to make your study plan.

Reading and Writing Comprehension—Module 1

Q #	Ans.	✔	Chap. # Section	Q #	Ans.	✔	Chap. # Section
1	C		**7**, Vocabulary Questions	15	C		**15**, Where Punctuation is Not Needed
2	C		**7**, Vocabulary Questions	16	B		**14**, How to Connect Independent Clauses
3	B		**7**, Vocabulary Questions	17	C		**14**, How to Connect Independent Clauses
4	C		**7**, Vocabulary Questions	18	A		**12**, Verb Forms in Complete Sentences
5	B		**7**, Vocabulary Questions	19	D		**16**, Verbs
6	A		**7**, Vocabulary Questions	20	A		**13**, Extra! Extra! Put Punctuation Around It!
7	B		**8**, Retrieval Questions	21	C		**17**, Transition Questions
8	B		**8**, Main Idea Questions	22	A		**17**, Rhetorical Synthesis Questions
9	A		**8**, Main Idea Questions	23	D		**17**, Rhetorical Synthesis Questions
10	C		**8**, Claims Questions	24	D		**17**, Rhetorical Synthesis Questions
11	D		**8**, Charts Questions	25	B		**17**, Rhetorical Synthesis Questions
12	C		**8**, Conclusions	26	D		**17**, Rhetorical Synthesis Questions
13	C		**8**, Conclusions	27	A		**17**, Rhetorical Synthesis Questions
14	C		**16**, Nouns				

Reading and Writing Comprehension—Module 2: Easier

Q #	Ans.	✔	Chap. # Section	Q #	Ans.	✔	Chap. # Section
1	A		**7**, Vocabulary Questions	15	A		**8**, Conclusions
2	A		**7**, Vocabulary Questions	16	D		**8**, Conclusions
3	B		**7**, Vocabulary Questions	17	B		**15**, Where Punctuation is Not Needed
4	B		**7**, Vocabulary Questions	18	C		**12**, Verb Forms in Complete Sentences
5	C		**7**, Vocabulary Questions	19	D		**16**, Nouns
6	D		**7**, Vocabulary Questions	20	B		**12**, Verb Forms in Complete Sentences
7	D		**7**, Purpose Questions	21	A		**15**, Dependent Clauses
8	B		**7**, Purpose Questions	22	C		**16**, Pronouns
9	D		**7**, Dual Texts Questions	23	A		**16**, Verbs
10	B		**8**, Charts Questions	24	D		**17**, Transition Questions
11	D		**8**, Claims Questions	25	C		**17**, Transition Questions
12	B		**8**, Claims Questions	26	B		**17**, Transition Questions
13	A		**8**, Charts Questions	27	C		**17**, Rhetorical Synthesis Questions
14	B		**8**, Claims Questions				

Reading and Writing Comprehension—Module 2: Harder							
Q #	**Ans.**	**✔**	**Chap. # Section**	**Q #**	**Ans.**	**✔**	**Chap. # Section**
1	A		7, Vocabulary Questions	15	A		**8**, Conclusions
2	C		7, Vocabulary Questions	16	B		**8**, Conclusions
3	D		7, Vocabulary Questions	17	D		**16**, Verbs
4	D		7, Vocabulary Questions	18	A		**14**, Punctuation with Transitions
5	A		7, Purpose Questions	19	B		**16**, Verbs
6	B		7, Purpose Questions	20	C		**14**, How to Connect Independent Clauses
7	B		7, Purpose Questions	21	D		**14**, How to Connect Independent Clauses
8	D		7, Purpose Questions	22	A		**15**, Punctuating Lists
9	C		7, Dual Texts	23	B		**13**, Who or What Are You Talking About?
10	D		**8**, Charts Questions	24	A		**17**, Transition Questions
11	D		**8**, Claims Questions	25	D		**17**, Transition Questions
12	A		**8**, Charts Questions	26	B		**17**, Transition Questions
13	D		**8**, Claims Questions	27	A		**17**, Rhetorical Synthesis Questions
14	C		**8**, Claims Questions				

Math—Module 1							
Q #	Ans.	✔	Chap. # Section	Q #	Ans.	✔	Chap. # Section
1	C		**24**, Averages	12	D		**21**, Fundamentals of Digital SAT Algebra
2	B		**21**, Solving for Expressions	13	A		**21**, Growth and Decay
3	B		**24**, Averages	14	D		**22**, Plugging In the Answers (PITA)
4	A		**25**, Triangles	15	A		**20**, Exponents and Square Roots
5	200		**21**, Digital SAT Algebra: Cracking the System	16	C		**23**, The Coordinate Plane
6	B		**21**, Solving Systems of Equations	17	D		**21**, Solving Systems of Equations
7	D		**23**, Function Fundamentals	18	C		**22**, Plugging In Your Own Numbers
8	A		**25**, Triangles	19	B		**22**, Plugging In Your Own Numbers
9	7 or –7		**21**, When Values are Absolute	20	A		**21**, Writing Your Own Equations
10	5		**23**, Function Fundamentals	21	–0.4 or –2/5		**23**, The Coordinate Plane
11	–11		**21**, Simplifying Expressions	22	A		**25**, Triangles

Math—Module 2: Easier							
Q #	Ans.	✔	Chap. # Section	Q #	Ans.	✔	Chap. # Section
1	8400		**24**, Rates	12	B		**25**, Lines and Angles
2	A		**21**, Solving for Expressions	13	C		**23**, Equations of a Line
3	D		**24**, Percentages	14	D		**24**, Averages, What is a Range?
4	61		**23**, Function Fundamentals	15	D		**22**, Meaning In Context
5	50		**20**, How to Read Charts and Graphs	16	D		**22**, Plugging In the Answers (PITA)
6	–5		**23**, The Coordinate Plane	17	C		**21**, Solving Systems of Equations
7	B		**21**, Simplifying Expressions	18	A		**23**, The Coordinate Plane
8	208		**25**, Rectangles and Squares	19	A		**23**, Equations of a Line
9	B		**23**, The Coordinate Plane	20	B		**21**, Solving Quadratic Equations
10	D		**24**, Probability	21	B		**22**, Plugging In the Answers (PITA)
11	A		**23**, Function Fundamentals	22	C		**23**, Equation of a Circle

Math—Module 2: Harder							
Q #	**Ans.**	**✔**	**Chap. # Section**	**Q #**	**Ans.**	**✔**	**Chap. # Section**
1	C		**21**, Writing Your Own Equations	12	B		**21**, Growth and Decay
2	D		**23**, Equations of a Line	13	13		**24**, Averages
3	B		**24**, Percentages	14	A		**21**, Simplifying Expressions
4	C		**23**, Function Fundamentals	15	108		**21**, Solving Quadratic Equations
5	D		**22**, Plugging In the Answers (PITA)	16	D		**24**, Averages, What is a Range?
6	B		**23**, The Coordinate Plane	17	A		**23**, Graphing Functions
7	A		**23**, Parallel and Perpendicular Lines	18	–50/4 or –12.5		**21**, Solving Quadratic Equations
8	C		**25**, Volume	19	1		**23**, Equation of a Circle
9	B		**25**, Lines and Angles	20	B		**21**, Solving Quadratic Equations
10	–35/63, –5/9, –0.555, –0.556, –.5555, or –.5556		**21**, Fundamentals of Digital SAT Algebra	21	A		**23**, Equations of a Parabola
11	837		**24**, Percentages	22	C		**22**, Plugging In the Answers (PITA)

PRACTICE TEST 1—READING AND WRITING EXPLANATIONS

Module 1

1. **C** This is a Vocabulary question, as it asks for a logical and precise word or phrase to complete the text. The missing word describes Despommier's attitude toward his promotion of vertical farming, so look for and highlight clues in the passage about this attitude. The passage mentions *Despommier's persistence and dedication to the cause*, so a good word to enter into the annotation box would be "determined" or "steadfast."

   - (A), (B), and (D) are wrong because *menacing, subdued*, and *misunderstood* are the **Opposite** tone of "determined," which is positive.
   - (C) is correct because *resolute* (firm) matches "determined."

2. **C** This is a Vocabulary question, as it asks for a logical and precise word or phrase to complete the text. The missing word describes what action the fishermen take toward traditional fishing methods and modern technology, so look for and highlight clues in the passage where both of these ideas show up. The passage states that the fishermen *use motorized boats and GPS tracking...while still applying age-old knowledge of tides, weather patterns, and fish migratory patterns*, so a good phrase to enter into the annotation box would be "use together" or "use both."

   - (A) and (D) are wrong because *belittle* (put down or criticize) and *replace* are the **Opposite** tone and meaning, respectively, of using the traditional fishing methods and modern technology "together."
   - (B) is wrong because *contemplate* (think about) doesn't match "use together."
   - (C) is correct because *integrate* matches "use together."

3. **B** This is a Vocabulary question, as it asks for a logical and precise word or phrase to complete the text. The missing word describes the character's lives, so look for and highlight clues in the passage about their lives. The passage states that each character's story has *truncated yet rich and unique life experiences and histories*, so a good word to enter into the annotation box would be "active" or "interesting."

   - (A) and (D) are wrong because *meaningless* and *shattered* are the **Opposite** tone of "active," which is positive.
   - (B) is correct because *dynamic* matches "active."
   - (C) is wrong because *benign* (nonthreatening) doesn't match "active."

4. **C** This is a Vocabulary question, as it asks for a logical and precise word or phrase to complete the text. The missing word describes the organisms, or plants, so look for and highlight clues in the passage about the plants. The passage states that the common perception is that plants *simply respond to their environment*, so a good phrase to enter into the annotation box would be "not active" or "idle."

- (A), (B), and (D) are wrong because *courageous* (brave), *assertive* (confident), and *adaptable* don't match "not active."
- (C) is correct because *passive* matches "not active."

5. **B** This is a Vocabulary question, as it asks for a logical and precise word or phrase to complete the text. The missing word describes what economists say regarding a commonly held belief, so look for and highlight clues in the passage about this belief. The passage states that *working from home can actually increase productivity and work satisfaction*, which goes against the *commonly held belief that remote work leads to decreased productivity.* Based on this interaction, a good word to enter into the annotation box would be "challenged" or "argued against."

- (A) and (D) are wrong because *muddied* (confused) and *articulated* (expressed) don't match "challenged."
- (B) is correct because *questioned* matches "challenged."
- (C) is wrong because *usurped* (taken over) is the **Opposite** of what happens in the passage—the economists have not taken over the belief as their own; they have a problem with the belief.

6. **A** This is a Vocabulary question, as it asks for what "trying" *most nearly* means in the text. Treat "trying" as if it were a missing or unknown word in the passage. This word describes the effect that the professor's glasses have on his eyes, so look for and highlight clues in the passage about those glasses. The professor states that *these new glasses don't suit me*, so a good word to enter into the annotation box would be "tiring" or "bothersome."

- (A) is correct because *taxing* (exhausting) matches "tiring."
- (B) and (D) are wrong because *attempting* and *sampling* go **Beyond the Text**—each is a common definition for *trying* that does not mean "tiring."
- (C) is wrong because *soothing* is the **Opposite** tone of "tiring," which is negative.

7. **B** This is a Retrieval question, as it asks for a detail *according to the text.* Look for and highlight information in the passage regarding why neural dust would *help researchers more than other types of probes.* The passage states that *Because the dust is biocompatible, it does not damage brain tissue*, and *because it is wireless, it can be used to monitor the brain...without the need for bulky external equipment.* The correct answer should be as consistent as possible with these statements.

- (A) and (D) are wrong because neither the size of *other probes* nor *electrical current* is discussed in the passage, only the size of *neural dust.*

- (B) is correct because it's consistent with the advantages of neural dust stated in the passage.
- (C) is wrong because it's **Recycled Language**—*monitoring*, *time*, and *brain tissue* are misused from different parts of the passage.

8. **B** This is a Main Idea question, as it asks for the *main idea of the text*. Look for and highlight information that can help understand the main idea. The last sentence of the passage states that *While modernization has impacted the role of the Tohunga...they remain a crucial source of guidance and guardians of cultural heritage*. Since the other sentences expand upon these roles, the last sentence serves as a main idea. The correct answer should be as consistent as possible with the last sentence.
    - (A), (C), and (D) are wrong because they each go **Beyond the Text**—the passage doesn't state how *contemporary society* feels about the Tohunga, what the Tohunga think about *technological advancements*, or that *Tohunga traditions are passed down from to generation*. Each of these is a logical but unsupported assumption.
    - (B) is correct because it's consistent with the main idea of the passage—it paraphrases everything that's said in the last sentence of the passage.

9. **A** This is a Main Idea question, as it asks for the *main idea of the text*. Look for and highlight information that can help understand the main idea. The last sentence of the passage states that *Alleyne had known every brother well, but this was a face that was new to him*. Since the other sentences expand upon Alleyne's knowledge of the order or the surprise the new face poses, the last sentence serves as a main idea. The correct answer should be as consistent as possible with the last sentence.
    - (A) is correct because it's consistent with the main idea of the passage—it paraphrases everything that is said in the last sentence of the passage.
    - (B) is wrong because it goes **Beyond the Text**—the passage does not explain if Alleyne became *more* or less *suspicious* of others in the future because of his encounter with the stranger.
    - (C) is wrong because it's **Extreme Language**—it's not stated that Alleyne *only* trusts men who wear the order's outfit.
    - (D) is wrong because it's **Recycled Language**—*perplexed* and *the order* are misused from different parts of the passage.

10. **C** This is a Claims question, as it asks which choice *most effectively illustrates the claim*. Look for and highlight the claim in the passage, which is that *Tan suggests that upon smelling fragrant aromas, she felt an intuitive and sometimes unexpected sense of cultural recognition*. The correct answer should address and be consistent with each aspect of this claim.
    - (A), (B), and (D) are wrong because they're each **Half-Right**—while each answer makes some reference to the character's food or culture, none of them discuss any *aromas*, or smells.

- (C) is correct because it's consistent with the claim—it references both *aromas* and the *sense of cultural recognition.*

11. **D** This is a Charts question, as it asks for *data from the graph* that will *complete the example.* Read the title, key, and variables from the bar graph. Then, read the passage and highlight the claim or argument that references the information from the graph. The last sentence states that *the percentage of women serving in parliaments was found to be especially prominent.* The correct answer should offer accurate information from the graph evidence in support of this claim.

    - (A) and (B) are wrong because they're the **Opposite** of the information presented in the graph—the percentage of women that serve in the lower chambers of Rwanda, Senegal, Namibia, and Ethiopia are not *relatively equal,* and neither of the two chambers in Ethiopia contain more than 50% women.

    - (C) is wrong because it's **Half-Right**—it's consistent with the graph but irrelevant to the claim, as neither chamber in South Africa has a percentage of women at or above 50%, which would be better support of the percentage of women being *prominent,* or notable.

    - (D) is correct because it's consistent with the graph and the claim—since women make up the majority of seats in the lower chamber of Rwanda, that would be an instance of the percentage of women in a parliament being *especially prominent.*

12. **C** This is a Conclusions question, as it asks for what *most logically completes the text.* Look for and highlight the main focus of the passage, which is that *Mary Shelley's novel Frankenstein was deeply influenced by her marriage to Percy Shelley.* Then, highlight the main point made regarding this focus, which is that *Percy's beliefs may have inspired Mary's exploration…but Frankenstein stands on its own as a work of literary genius.* Therefore, *those who ascribe Percy's influence as the primary motivation for Frankenstein* may be focusing too narrowly only one of the novel's influences. The correct answer should be as consistent as possible with this conclusion.

    - (A) is wrong because it's **Extreme Language**—the passage doesn't state that anyone is viewing the Shelley's relationship through *too personal* of a lens.

    - (B) is wrong because no *other individuals* are implied by the passage to have influenced Frankenstein.

    - (C) is correct because it's consistent with the point made in the second sentence that *Frankenstein stands on its own* despite Percy's influence, which implies there was more to the creation of the novel than just Percy's influence.

    - (D) is wrong because it goes **Beyond the Text**—the view *those* from the last sentence would take is only toward *Frankenstein*'s creation, not *Percy and Mary Shelley's relationship* as a whole.

13. **C** This is a Conclusions question, as it asks for what *most logically completes the text.* Look for and highlight the main focus of the passage, which is that *The purpose of Stonehenge...has long been debated by archaeologists.* Then, highlight the main point made regarding this focus, which is *Stonehenge's design and construction span different time periods, suggesting shifting scientific, religious, ceremonial,* and *social functions depending on the era.* Therefore, the debate regarding Stonehenge's original purpose has yet to be resolved. The correct answer should be as consistent as possible with this conclusion.

- (A) and (B) are wrong because they each go **Beyond the Text** for being too specific or too broad of a conclusion—it's not stated in the passage whether Stonehenge exists in a *central location* or not, and only Stonehenge is discussed, not *different types of monuments.*
- (C) is correct because it's consistent with what the highlighted sentences say about the purpose of Stonehenge.
- (D) is wrong because it's **Recycled Language**—the passage mentions *religious* and *ceremonial* purposes as well as *astronomy,* but it never compares which of these purposes is more useful.

14. **C** In this Rules question, apostrophes with nouns are changing in the answer choices. Determine whether each word possesses anything. The flies possess the movements, but the movements don't possess anything. Eliminate any answer that doesn't match this.

- (A) is wrong because *flies* should have an apostrophe.
- (B) and (D) are wrong because *movements* shouldn't be possessive.
- (C) is correct because *flies* is possessive and *movements* is not.

15. **C** In this Rules question, punctuation is changing in the answer choices. The main meaning of the sentence is *Doris Salcedo created her art installations.* The answer choice comes between the subject and the verb, and there is no other punctuation. A single punctuation mark can't separate a subject and a verb, so eliminate answers with punctuation.

- (A), (B), and (D) are wrong because a single punctuation mark can't come between a subject and a verb.
- (C) is correct because no punctuation should be used here.

16. **B** In this Rules question, punctuation is changing in the answer choices. Look for independent clauses. The first part of the sentence says *The National Day of Listening...is a day encouraging Americans to record the stories of their loved ones,* which is an independent clause. The second part says *people interested in participating can access resources and recommendations about the interview process through the StoryCorps website or app,* which is also an independent clause. Eliminate any answer that can't correctly connect two independent clauses.

- (A) is wrong because a comma without a coordinating conjunction (FANBOYS) can't connect two independent clauses.

- (B) is correct because a semicolon can connect two independent clauses.
- (C) is wrong because some type of punctuation is needed in order to connect two independent clauses.
- (D) is wrong because a coordinating conjunction (*and*) without a comma can't link two independent clauses.

17. **C** In this Rules question, punctuation is changing in the answer choices. Look for independent clauses. The first part of the sentence says *Frederick Catherwood joined an expedition to Central America, where he saw over forty sites full of ruins*, which is an independent clause. The second part says *by creating detailed drawings and paintings of the ruins, Catherwood helped to reintroduce the Mayan civilization to the Western world*, which is also an independent clause. Eliminate any answer that can't correctly connect two independent clauses.
    - (A) is wrong because some type of punctuation is needed in order to connect two independent clauses.
    - (B) is wrong because a comma without a coordinating conjunction (FANBOYS) can't connect two independent clauses.
    - (C) is correct because the period makes each independent clause its own sentence, which is fine.
    - (D) is wrong because a coordinating conjunction (*and*) without a comma can't link two independent clauses.

18. **A** In this Rules question, verb forms are changing in the answer choices, so it's testing sentence structure. The subject of the sentence is *analysis*, and there is no main verb, so the answer must provide the main verb. Eliminate any answer that isn't in the correct form to be the main verb.
    - (A) is correct because it's in the right form to be the main verb.
    - (B) and (C) are wrong because a "to" verb can't be the main verb in a sentence.
    - (D) is wrong because an *-ing* verb can't be the main verb in a sentence.

19. **D** In this Rules question, verbs are changing in the answer choices, so it's testing consistency with verbs. Find and highlight the subject, *buildings and the living quarters*, which is plural, so a plural verb is needed. Write an annotation saying "plural." Eliminate any answer that is not plural.
    - (A), (B), and (C) are wrong because they are singular.
    - (D) is correct because it's plural.

20. **A** In this Rules question, punctuation is changing in the answer choices. The main meaning of the sentence is *American physicists determined that neutrinos…exist.* The phrase *subatomic particles that have no electric charge, very small mass, and a spin of one-half* is Extra Information. It should therefore be set off with matching punctuation before and after. Eliminate answers that do not have matching punctuation before and after the Extra Information.

- (A) is correct because it uses a long dash before and after the Extra Information.
- (B) is wrong because there is no reason to use a colon after *have.*
- (C) and (D) are wrong because they don't use matching punctuation both before and after the Extra Information.

21. **C** This is a transition question, so follow the basic approach. Highlight ideas that relate to each other. The preceding sentence states that *This case overruled another important case…which mandated the loss of citizenship,* and this sentence gives additional information about the *important case* from the previous sentence. These ideas agree, so a same-direction transition is needed. Make an annotation that says "agree." Eliminate any answer that doesn't match.

- (A) and (B) are wrong because they are opposite-direction transitions.
- (C) is correct because this sentence provides additional information on the implications of the case.
- (D) is wrong because this sentence isn't an example.

22. **A** This is a Rhetorical Synthesis question, so follow the basic approach. Highlight the goal(s) stated in the question: *present the study and its findings.* Eliminate any answer that doesn't fulfill this purpose.

- (A) is correct because it describes the study and reveals what the scientists determined (the *findings*).
- (B), (C), and (D) are wrong because they don't present the *findings* of the study.

23. **D** This is a Rhetorical Synthesis question, so follow the basic approach. Highlight the goal(s) stated in the question: *introduce the composition The Creation to an audience already familiar with Franz Joseph Haydn.* Eliminate any answer that doesn't *introduce the composition The Creation* in a way that assumes the audience is *familiar with Franz Joseph Haydn.*

- (A), (B), and (C) are wrong because they don't *introduce the composition.*
- (D) is correct because it introduces *the composition The Creation* and doesn't explain the background of Haydn since the audience is familiar with him.

24. **D** This is a Rhetorical Synthesis question, so follow the basic approach. Highlight the goal(s) stated in the question: *emphasize a similarity between the two elements.* Eliminate any answer that doesn't fulfill this purpose.

- (A) and (C) are wrong because they don't mention a *similarity.*
- (B) is wrong because it only mentions strontium.
- (D) is correct because the word *Both* helps to show a *similarity.*

25. **B** This is a Rhetorical Synthesis question, so follow the basic approach. Highlight the goal(s) stated in the question: *introduce Maya Deren and her film Meshes of the Afternoon to a new audience.* Eliminate any answer that doesn't fulfill this purpose.

- (A), (C), and (D) are wrong because they don't *introduce Maya Deren.*
- (B) is correct because it explains who Deren was and describes the film.

26. **D** This is a Rhetorical Synthesis question, so follow the basic approach. Highlight the goal(s) stated in the question: *introduce Cléo from 5 to 7 to an audience unfamiliar with the film and its director.* Eliminate any answer that doesn't fulfill this purpose.

- (A) and (C) are wrong because they don't describe the director, and the audience is unfamiliar with her.
- (B) is wrong because it doesn't *introduce* the film, such as by providing information about it.
- (D) is correct because it describes the film and its director.

27. **A** This is a Rhetorical Synthesis question, so follow the basic approach. Highlight the goal(s) stated in the question: *summarize the study.* Eliminate any answer that doesn't fulfill this purpose.

- (A) is correct because it provides a summary of the study.
- (B) and (C) are wrong because they include only a few details rather than *summarize the study.*
- (D) is wrong because it mentions a specific finding but doesn't *summarize the study.*

Module 2—Easier

1. **A** This is a Vocabulary question, as it asks for a logical and precise word or phrase to complete the text. The missing word describes what experts think about electric vehicle sales, so look for and highlight clues in the passage about electric vehicle sales. The passage mentions that the market *surged in popularity*, and sales increased *from just a few thousand at the start of the decade to more than two million by the end of the decade.* Since the passage does not give any information that suggests this trend will change, a good word to enter into the annotation box would be "predict" or "assume" that sales will continue to increase.

   - (A) is correct because *project* matches "predict."
   - (B) is wrong because *guarantee* is **Extreme Language**—the experts do not say a continued increase will definitely happen.
   - (C) and (D) are wrong because *reject* and *deny* are the **Opposite** of "predict."

2. **A** This is a Vocabulary question, as it asks for a logical and precise word or phrase to complete the text. The missing word describes a characteristic of mindfulness, so look for and highlight clues in the passage about mindfulness. The passage mentions mindfulness *can improve physical and cognitive function* and *lead to improvements in overall well-being*, so a good word to enter into the annotation box would be "advantages" or "positives."

   - (A) is correct because *benefits* match "advantages."
   - (B) is wrong because *drawbacks* are the **Opposite** of "advantages."
   - (C) is wrong because *basics* don't match "advantages."
   - (D) is wrong because *physics* is **Recycled Language**—it misuses *physical* from the passage.

3. **B** This is a Vocabulary question, as it asks for a logical and precise word or phrase to complete the text. The missing word describes how a discovery affected our understanding of the universe, so look for and highlight clues in the passage about the discovery. The passage mentions that Thorne's work confirms one of Einstein's predictions and that it *provided astronomers with a firmer ground*, so a good word to enter into the annotation box would be "improved" or "made clearer."

   - (A) and (D) are wrong because *confused* and *belittled* (put down or insulted) are the **Opposite** tone of "improved," which is positive.
   - (B) is correct because *clarified* matches "improved" or "made clearer."
   - (C) is wrong because *revolutionized* is **Extreme Language**—Thorne's work confirmed something that was already predicted rather than completely changing how we understand the universe.

4. **B** This is a Vocabulary question, as it asks for a logical and precise word or phrase to complete the text. The missing word describes the interaction between the Navajo Nation Council and established principles of the constitution, so look for and highlight clues in the passage about the Council's role. The passage mentions that the Council *is responsible for protecting the civil rights of Navajo citizens*, so a good word to enter into the annotation box would be "protecting" or "upholding."

- (A) is wrong because *copying* doesn't match "protecting."
- (B) is correct because *maintaining* matches "protecting" or "upholding."
- (C) is wrong because *determining* goes **Beyond the Text**—the passage doesn't support that the Council creates or establishes the principles of the constitution, just that it protects what's already there.
- (D) is wrong because *dismissing* is the **Opposite** tone of "protecting," which is positive.

5. **C** This is a Vocabulary question, as it asks for a logical and precise word or phrase to complete the text. The missing word describes the interaction between Vescovo and the four new species of gelatinous animals, so look for and highlight clues in the passage about this interaction. The passage mentions that Vescovo's work was a *finding*, so a good word to enter into the annotation box would be "found" or "documented."

- (A) is wrong because *reintroduced* doesn't match "found."
- (B) is wrong because *discounted* (disregarded) is the **Opposite** of "found."
- (C) is correct because *discovered* matches "found."
- (D) is wrong because exploring something might lead to a finding or discovery but would not be a finding or discovery itself.

6. **D** This is a Vocabulary question, as it asks for a logical and precise word or phrase to complete the text. The missing phrase describes how human emotions might be applied to animals by humans, so look for and highlight clues in the passage about this interaction. The passage mentions that *humans can empathize with a broader diversity of creatures than previously believed*. Since empathy deals with sharing feelings, a good word to enter into the annotation box would be "given to" or "assigned."

- (A) and (C) are wrong because *conflated with* (combined into) and *united with* don't match "given to."
- (B) is wrong because *demanded of* is **Extreme Language**—the passage doesn't state that humans require or force animals to have human emotions.
- (D) is correct because *attributed to* matches "given to."

7. **D** This is a Purpose question, as it asks for the *function of the underlined sentence in the text as a whole.* Read the passage and focus on the sentences before and after the underlined sentence to understand its function. The sentence before states that the female emperor penguin *transfers the egg to the male's care,* and the sentence after continues to explain the male's care of the egg. Therefore, a good function of the underlined sentence to enter into the annotation box would be "explain how male cares for egg."

   - (A) and (C) are wrong because they're both **Right Answer, Wrong Question**—these answers describe the information in the last sentence of the passage rather than the underlined sentence.
   - (B) is wrong because the *physical feature of male penguins* is only first introduced in the underlined sentence, not *earlier in the text.*
   - (D) is correct because it's consistent with the highlighting and annotation.

8. **B** This is a Purpose question, as it asks for the *main purpose of the text.* Read the passage and highlight who or what the passage is focusing on. The passage focuses on *Mrs. Hale and Mrs. Peters* as well as their actions after their eyes met in a look of *dawning comprehension.* Therefore, a good main purpose of the passage to enter into the annotation box would be "describe what women did figuring something out."

   - (A) and (D) are wrong because they each focus on the quilt or a possession, neither of which is the focus of the passage.
   - (B) is correct because it's consistent with the highlighting and annotation.
   - (C) is wrong because it goes **Beyond the Text**—the passage does not offer what the women think of the county attorney.

9. **D** This is a Dual Texts question, which asks how *the author of Text 2* would *respond to the claims of the author of Text 1.* Read Text 1 and highlight the author's claim, which is that *computer-based programs remove the requirement for certain musical compositional skills.* Then, read Text 2 and highlight what Text 2 says about the same topic. The author of Text 2 states that *Computer-based composers must know both the foundations of music theory and the intricacies of the programs that they use to create their works.* The two authors disagree on their shared topic, so enter "Text 2 disagrees with Text 1" into the annotation box.

   - (A) is wrong because it's the **Opposite** of Text 2's point—the author of Text 2 states that computer-based composers do indeed need to know *the foundations of music theory.*
   - (B) is wrong because neither author discusses *performances* or calls those performances *more important.*

- (C) is wrong because it's **Extreme Language**—while the author of Text 2 implies that computer-based composition is not easy, it's never supported that making music with a traditional instrument is *much easier.*

- (D) is correct because it's consistent with the relationship between the passages.

10. **B** This is a Charts question, as it asks for *data from the graph* that will *complete the text.* Read the title, key, and variables from the bar graph. Then, read the passage and highlight the claim or argument that references the information from the graph. The end of the second sentence states that *each of the five major electric car manufacturers posted strong numbers in 2018.* The correct answer should offer accurate information from the graph in support of this claim.

    - (A), (C), and (D) are wrong because they're the **Opposite** of the information in the graph—the numbers in these answers are inconsistent with the values for BYD Auto, Tesla, and Volkswagen.

    - (B) is correct because it's consistent with the graph.

11. **D** This is a Claims question, as it asks which choice *most effectively illustrates the claim.* Look for and highlight the claim in the passage, which is that Mr. Gummage is an *art teacher who actively encourages his students to improve upon the fundamentals that he teaches.* The correct answer should address and be consistent with each aspect of this claim.

    - (A), (B), and (C) are wrong because they're each **Half-Right**—each of these answers expresses some aspect of Mr. Gummage's art style or teaching style, but none of them show him actively encouraging *his students to improve upon the fundamentals.*

    - (D) is correct because it states that Mr. Gummage's model was merely *a guide* and that he *continually told his pupils that they must try to excel it, and he helped them to do so.* All of this is consistent with the highlighted claim.

12. **B** This is a Claims question, as it asks which choice *most effectively illustrates the claim.* Look for and highlight the claim in the passage, which is that *Frost describes his prioritization of personal obligations over admiring the beauty of the winter scene.* The correct answer should address and be consistent with each aspect of this claim.

    - (A), (C), and (D) are wrong because they're each **Half-Right**—each answer describes an aspect of the winter scene but does not state that the speaker is prioritizing his *personal obligations* over any of the scene's aspects.

    - (B) is correct because it's consistent with the claim—it references the beauty of the winter scene, but then clarifies that Frost is focused on the promises he has to keep instead.

13. **A** This is a Charts question, as it asks for *data from the table that supports the researchers' claim.* Read the title and variables from the table. Then, read the passage and highlight the claim that references the information from the table. The last sentence states that *the researchers claim that agro-pastoralists living in Area I were able to gather significant quantities of all eight species due to the area's high vegetation cover.* The correct answer should offer accurate information from the table in support of this claim.

- (A) is correct because it's consistent with the table and highlighting—note that the predicted average in the text was 30, and all citations from Area II are above this number.
- (B) is wrong because it's **Half-Right**—it's consistent with the table, but stating that *there were fewer* citations is the **Opposite** of the claim's point regarding the collection of *significant quantities,* which suggests the correct answer should be discussing the numbers as higher or greater than something, not lower or fewer.
- (C) and (D) are wrong because they're the **Opposite** of the information given in the table—*C. pyramidale* had the highest number of citations from Area II, not the *lowest,* and *M. glaziovi* and *M. tenuiflora*'s citations from Area I were much lower than the predicted average of 30, not *significantly higher.*

14. **B** This is a Claims question, as it asks which choice *most effectively illustrates the claim.* Look for and highlight the claim in the passage, which is that *Machen challenges a comparison regarding literary quality that he believes the reader has made.* The correct answer should address and be consistent with each aspect of this claim.

- (A) and (D) are wrong because they're **Half-Right**—both answers reference a comparison, but neither answer has Machen indicating that he believes the reader has made the comparison. Machen himself makes or addresses the comparisons in these answers without indicating the reader makes them as well.
- (B) is correct because it's consistent with the claim—it both references a comparison and has Machen specifically addressing *you,* the reader, as having made the comparison.
- (C) is wrong because the *cook* and the *farmer* in this answer are not directly compared, nor does Machen state that the reader makes any comparison.

15. **A** This is a Conclusions question, as it asks for what *most logically completes the text.* Look for and highlight the main focus of the passage, which is the *Inca Empire* and the challenges that they faced *farming.* Then, highlight the main point made regarding this focus, which is that *they created a system of terraces that allowed them to grow crops...and practiced preserving their crops.* Since the last sentence already references the first part of this evidence, growing crops, the most likely

conclusion is that the second half of the last sentence will talk about *preserving* crops. The correct answer should be as consistent as possible with this conclusion.

- (A) is correct because it's consistent with what the highlighted sentences say about growing and preserving crops.
- (B) is wrong because *all* is **Extreme Language**—it's not stated by the passage during which periods the Incas harvested crops.
- (C) is wrong because it goes **Beyond the Text**—while it's logical that consistent food sources prolong life spans, there is no evidence for such a connection in the passage.
- (D) is wrong because it's **Recycled Language**—it misuses *freeze* and the concept of *cold* from the third sentence of the passage.

16. **D** This is a Conclusions question, as it asks for what *most logically completes the text.* Look for and highlight the main focus of the passage, which is *the relationship between sleep and memory consolidation.* Then, highlight the main point made regarding this focus, which is that *memory consolidation happens during deep sleep as the brain replays memories and stores them more effectively* and that the *amount and quality of sleep are vital to memory consolidation.* Therefore, the conclusion to the passage should focus on this positive connection between quality and amount of deep sleep and memory consolidation. The correct answer should be as consistent as possible with this conclusion.

- (A) and (B) are wrong because they're each the **Opposite** of the relationship between sleep and memory consolidation stated in the passage—increased sleep should not produce any decreases, or drawbacks.
- (C) is wrong because it's **Half-Right**—while there should be an increase, the passage does not discuss any *connections* between similar memories, just the embedding and storage of memories.
- (D) is correct because it's consistent with what the highlighted sentences say about memory consolidation.

17. **B** In this Rules question, punctuation is changing in the answer choices. The punctuation appears after the preposition *with*, but there shouldn't be punctuation after a preposition, so eliminate answers with punctuation.

- (A), (C), and (D) are wrong because a preposition shouldn't be followed by punctuation.
- (B) is correct because no punctuation should be used here.

18. **C** In this Rules question, verb forms are changing in the answer choices, so it's testing sentence structure. The subject of the sentence is *researchers*, and there is no main verb, so the answer must provide the main verb. Eliminate any answer that isn't in the correct form to be the main verb.

- (A) is wrong because a "to" verb can't be the main verb in a sentence.
- (B) and (D) are wrong because an *-ing* verb can't be the main verb in a sentence.
- (C) is correct because it's in the right form to be the main verb.

19. **D** In this Rules question, apostrophes with nouns are changing in the answer choices. Determine whether each word possesses anything. The members possess the experiences, but the experiences don't possess anything. Eliminate any answer that doesn't match this.

- (A), (B), and (C) are wrong because *experiences* shouldn't be possessive.
- (D) is correct because *experiences* isn't possessive, and *members* shouldn't be possessive either because the word *of* already shows possession.

20. **B** In this Rules question, verb forms are changing in the answer choices, so it's testing sentence structure. The subject of the sentence is *team*, and there is no main verb, so the answer must provide the main verb. Eliminate any answer that isn't in the correct form to be the main verb.

- (A) is wrong because a "to" verb can't be the main verb in a sentence.
- (B) is correct because it's in the right form to be the main verb.
- (C) and (D) are wrong because an *-ing* verb can't be the main verb in a sentence.

21. **A** In this Rules question, punctuation is changing in the answer choices. Look for independent clauses. The first part of the sentence says *Some comets, such as Halley's Comet, can be seen more than once in a lifetime*, which is an independent clause. The second part of the sentence says *while others, such as Comet Shoemaker-Levy 9, are visible only once,* which is a dependent clause. Eliminate any option that doesn't correctly connect an independent + a dependent clause.

- (A) is correct because independent + dependent can be connected with a comma.
- (B), (C), and (D) are wrong because independent + dependent cannot be connected with punctuation other than a comma.

22. **C** In this Rules question, pronouns are changing in the answer choices, so it's testing consistency with pronouns. Find and highlight the word the pronoun refers back to, *the clock,* which is singular, so a singular pronoun is needed. Write an annotation saying "singular." Eliminate any answer that isn't singular or doesn't clearly refer back to *the clock*.

- (A) and (D) are wrong because they are plural.

- (B) is wrong because the word *it* suggests something other than the *clock* being powered, but it's not clear what that would be.
- (C) is correct because *itself* is singular and is consistent with *the clock.*

23. **A** In this Rules question, verbs are changing in the answer choices, so it's testing consistency with verbs. Find and highlight the subject, *May Berenbaum*, which is singular, so a singular verb is needed. All of the answers work with a singular subject, so look for a clue regarding tense. This sentence uses the past tense verb *developed.* Highlight that verb and write an annotation that says "past." Eliminate any answer not in past tense.

    - (A) is correct because it's in past tense, and this specific tense correctly suggests that her interest developed during the seminar.
    - (B) is wrong because it's in present tense.
    - (C) is wrong because it's not in past tense.
    - (D) is wrong because it's in future tense.

24. **D** This is a transition question, so follow the basic approach. Highlight ideas that relate to each other. The preceding sentence says *She has portrayed Indian political themes in her work,* and this sentence provides some additional things Gowda *has incorporated.* These ideas agree, so a same-direction transition is needed. Make an annotation that says "agree." Eliminate any answer that doesn't match.

    - (A) and (B) are wrong because they are opposite-direction transitions.
    - (C) is wrong because *Indeed* would reinforce the previous idea, but this sentence instead includes some additional aspects of Gowda's work.
    - (D) is correct because this sentence provides additional information about Gowda's art.

25. **C** This is a transition question, so follow the basic approach. Highlight ideas that relate to each other. The previous sentence states that *speech rhythm…could identify participants with autism reliably across English- and Cantonese-speaking groups,* and this sentence states that *speech intonation…could only reliably identify participants with autism in the English-speaking group.* These ideas disagree, so an opposite-direction transition is needed. Make an annotation that says "disagree." Eliminate any answer that doesn't match.

    - (A) and (B) are wrong because they are same-direction transitions.
    - (C) is correct because *By contrast* is an opposite-direction transition.
    - (D) is wrong because while *Still* is an opposite-direction transition, it doesn't draw a contrast between two things as is needed here.

26. **B** This is a transition question, so follow the basic approach. Highlight ideas that relate to each other. The preceding sentence says *A failed amendment…was proposed in 1916 that would have mandated a public referendum to declare war,* and this sentence states that *another proposal was made in 1935 and again in 1940 to require a public vote to declare war.* These ideas agree, so a same-direction transition is needed. Make an annotation that says "agree." Eliminate any answer that doesn't match.

   - (A) is wrong because this sentence isn't making the previous information more specific.
   - (B) is correct because this sentence provides a similar proposal from other years.
   - (C) is wrong because this sentence isn't an example of something that came before.
   - (D) is wrong because this sentence isn't a conclusion based on the previous sentence.

27. **C** This is a Rhetorical Synthesis question, so follow the basic approach. Highlight the goal(s) stated in the question: *provide an explanation and example of a "golden shovel" poem.* Eliminate any answer that doesn't fulfill this purpose.

   - (A), (B), and (D) are wrong because they don't *provide an explanation* of what this type of poem is.
   - (C) is correct because it explains what the *poetic form* is and provides an *example.*

Module 2—Harder

1. **A** This is a Vocabulary question, as it asks for a logical and precise word or phrase to complete the text. The missing word describes how tonal languages interact with words and phrases using pitch changes, so look for and highlight clues in the passage about this interaction. The passage mentions that *native speakers of tonal languages…are more apt to recognize pitch differences,* which suggests that these native speakers might interact often with pitch differences in some way. Based on this context, a good word to enter into the annotation box would be "pronounce" or "say."

   - (A) is correct because *enunciate* matches "pronounce."
   - (B) and (D) are wrong because *suggest* and *camouflage* (disguise) don't match "pronounce."
   - (C) is wrong because it goes **Beyond the Text**—while changing the pitch of words most certainly could help *distinguish* (differentiate) one word or phrase from another, the actual goal or function of pitch changing isn't discussed in the passage.

2. **C** This is a Vocabulary question, as it asks for a logical and precise word or phrase to complete the text. The missing phrase describes an aspect of the influence of dark matter, so look for and highlight clues in the passage about dark matter. The passage mentions that *the importance of the properties of dark matter are widely accepted,* but the presence of the word *though* indicates a contrast. Therefore, the thing that *continues to elude the scientific community* should relate to knowledge about

dark matter, so a good word to enter into the annotation box would be "knowledge" or "comprehension."

- (A), (B), and (D) are wrong because *acknowledgment of*, *argument about*, and *allegiance to* (loyalty) don't match "knowledge."
- (C) is correct because *understanding of* matches "knowledge."

3. **D** This is a Vocabulary question, as it asks for a logical and precise word or phrase to complete the text. The missing word describes what a business must do regarding trust, so look for and highlight clues in the passage about businesses and trust. The passage mentions that *the success of a business venture…is closely related to the concept of credibility*, so a good word to enter into the annotation box would be that business needs to "generate" or "build" trust.

   - (A) is wrong because *invalidate* (cancel) is the **Opposite** of what business must do regarding trust.
   - (B) and (C) are wrong because *fortify* (strengthen) and *demarcate* (define) don't match "generate." The passage does not support that trust is already present, as these are only *potential* customers, not existing ones.
   - (D) is correct because *foster* (grow) matches "build."

4. **D** This is a Vocabulary question, as it asks for a logical and precise word or phrase to complete the text. The missing word describes what certain individuals are likely to do regarding long-term objectives, so look for and highlight clues in the passage about these individuals. The passage mentions that these individuals have *high levels of perseverance* and have *the ability to sustain high levels of effort*. Since perseverance and effort are connected with *determining success*, a good word to enter into the annotation box would be "achieve" or "complete."

   - (A) is wrong because *neglect* is the **Opposite** of "achieve."
   - (B) and (C) are wrong because *analyze* and *recall* (remember) don't match "achieve."
   - (D) is correct because *attain* (accomplish) matches "achieve."

5. **A** This is a Purpose question, as it asks for the *function of the underlined sentence in the text as a whole*. Read the passage and focus on the sentences before and after the underlined sentence to understand its function. The sentence before describes the contents of *the big traveling chest*, and the sentence after references the father's explanation as to why the chest contains what it does. Therefore, a good function of the underlined sentence to enter into the annotation box would be "explain what children ask about chest."

   - (A) is correct because it's consistent with the highlighting and annotation.

- (B) and (C) are wrong because they go **Beyond the Text**—each answer makes an assumption about relationship between the children and their mother that isn't supported by the underlined sentence, in which the mother only tells the children to be quiet so the father can explain.
- (D) is wrong because it's the **Opposite** of what happens in the passage—the mother does not encourage the children to be *inquisitive*, or ask questions; she tells them to be quiet.

6. **B** This is a Purpose question, as it asks for the *main purpose of the text.* Read the passage and highlight who or what the passage is focusing on. The passage focuses on *Elizabeth's feelings toward Mr. Darcy*, which are that *It was an union that must have been to the advantage of both.* Therefore, a good main purpose of the passage to enter into the annotation box would be "explain that they benefit from each other."

   - (A) and (C) are wrong because they go **Beyond the Text**—while it's likely that Elizabeth has *determination* and *desires* toward romance, the passage is about one specific relationship rather than a general pursuit and does not state what Elizabeth's desires actually are.
   - (B) is correct because it's consistent with the highlighting and annotation.
   - (D) is wrong because it's **Half-Right**—nothing in the passage supports that Elizabeth finds her current relationship *confusing.*

7. **B** This is a Purpose question, as it asks for the *overall structure of the text.* Read the passage and highlight the connections between ideas in the passage. The first sentence describes the work of *Novelist Wright Morris* and how he *complemented his written works with photographs.* The next three sentences offer a specific example in the novel *The Home Place* and its *perspective on the themes of family, memory*, and *rural America.* Therefore, a good overall structure of the passage to enter into the annotation box would be "introduce Morris's work and give an example."

   - (A) is wrong because it's **Half-Right**—the first half of the answer is accurate, but the passage does not discuss Morris's specific *convictions*, or beliefs, only the themes present in his photographs.
   - (B) is correct because it's consistent with the highlighting and annotation.
   - (C) is wrong because while the passage does discuss Morris's storytelling, it never discusses any *other storytellers.*
   - (D) is wrong because it's **Extreme Language**—Morris's style is never described as *unique*, nor is a *counterexample* offered, just an example.

8. **D** This is a Purpose question, as it asks for the *function of the underlined sentence in the text as a whole.* Read the passage and focus on the sentences before and after the underlined sentence to understand its function. The sentence before states that *emotions are based on the way the brain interprets sensory inputs*, and the sentence after states that individuals who reported their emotions accurately (according to previous data) *had lower levels of depression and anxiety.* Since the sentence before describes a theory and the sentence after describes the results of an experiment meant to test that theory, a good function of the underlined sentence to enter into the annotation box would be "explain setup of experiment."

- (A) and (C) are wrong because the highlighted sentence does not offer an *obstacle* or a *concrete example* related to the study.
- (B) is wrong because it's a **Right Answer, Wrong Question trap**—this answer describes the information in the last sentence of the passage rather than the underlined sentence.
- (D) is correct because it's consistent with the highlighting and annotation.

9. **C** This is a Dual Texts question, which asks for what *the author of Text 2* would *say about Text 1's characterization of the psychologists' response regarding determinism.* Read Text 1 and highlight the author's characterization of the psychologists' response, which is that it's a *somewhat comforting response to this hypothetical loss of free will.* Then, read Text 2 and highlight what Text 2 says about the same topic. The author of Text 2 states that *the human brain is too complex to accept that it cannot alter that track.* The two authors disagree on a human's willingness to accept or be comfortable with determinism, so enter "Text 2 disagrees with Text 1" into the annotation box.

- (A) is wrong because it's the **Opposite** of Text 1's characterization of the response—Text 1 considers the response *somewhat comforting*, not *overly critical.*
- (B) is wrong because it's the **Opposite** of the relationship between the passages—the two authors disagree, and the author of Text 2 believes the human brain would not accept determinism rather than considering it *logical.*
- (C) is correct because it's consistent with the relationship between the passages—the author of Text 2 does not believe that the human brain will find the concept of determinism comforting at all, or even accept it.
- (D) is wrong because it's **Recycled Language**—it's the theory of determinism that was *readily accepted* by many according to the author of Text 2, not *Horgan's comments.*

10. **D** This is a Charts question, as it asks for *data from the table* that will *complete the example.* Read the title and variables from the table. Then, read the passage and highlight the claim or argument that references the information from the table. The end of the second sentence states that *poor record keeping from this era makes it likely that the numbers...should not be considered comprehensive.* In

other words, the authors in the table may have produced more work than the numbers listed. The correct answer should offer accurate information from the graph in support of this claim.

- (A) and (B) are wrong because they're **Half-Right**—they're consistent with the table but the **Opposite** of the claim, which states that the real totals may be greater than they appear.
- (C) is wrong because it's the **Opposite** of what's shown in the table—the claim only indicates that the number of contributions may be wrong, not that any of the authors worked *after* the years listed in the figure.
- (D) is correct because it's consistent with the claim, which states that the authors may have contributed more works than what is shown in the table.

11. **D** This is a Claims question, as it asks which finding *would most directly support Johnson, Davis, and Smith's conclusion*. Look for and highlight the conclusion in the passage, which is that *regular exercise can have a positive impact on cognitive abilities in older adults*. The correct answer should be as consistent as possible with this conclusion.

- (A) is wrong because it goes **Beyond the Text**—while this may be true, the passage's conclusion is only in regard to exercise, not environmental factors such as *sunshine and fresh air* that may result from exercising outdoors.
- (B) is wrong because the conclusion is not about which group it is *easier* to get data for, but about the positive impact of exercise on cognitive abilities.
- (C) is wrong because it's the **Opposite** of the conclusion—if both active and sedentary populations have the same cognitive performance after 12 months, this would weaken the claim that exercise has a *positive impact on cognitive abilities*.
- (D) is correct because it's consistent with the highlighted conclusion—slowing and reversing the effects of aging among active elderly populations would be a *positive impact on cognitive abilities*.

12. **A** This is a Charts question, as it asks for *data from the graph that support the Insurance Information Institute's conclusion*. Read the title, key, and variables from the table. Then, read the passage and highlight the conclusion that references the information from the table. The last sentence states that *the percentage by which different factors caused claims largely fluctuated over the period studied*. The correct answer should offer accurate information from the table in support of this claim.

- (A) is correct because it's consistent with the graph and conclusion—it shows a variable that has *fluctuated* for all three years.
- (B) and (D) are wrong because they're the **Opposite** of the graph or conclusion—the percentage of claims caused by fire and lightning damage did not *remain unchanged* during the period, and (D) points out a consistent trend (that wind and hail was always highest), while the conclusion refers to a fluctuation.

- (C) is wrong because it's not relevant to the conclusion—focusing on a single year (2019) cannot illustrate a fluctuation, which requires at least two different years to be compared.

13. **D** This is a Claims question, as it asks which choice *would most directly weaken the biologists' claim.* Look for and highlight the claim in the passage, which is that *humans may also have the ability to regenerate limbs naturally.* Note that the reason biologists believe humans could do so is that humans have *FoxA* as well as the *supplemental genes that interact with FoxA* to cause regeneration to occur. The correct answer should be as inconsistent as possible with the claim or the evidence, while still staying on the topic of the passage.

    - (A) is wrong because it's not relevant to the claim—the focus of the claim is not on which group of organisms a process is *more effective* for, but if humans have the necessary genes for regeneration.
    - (B) and (C) are wrong because they're the **Opposite** of what the question asks—each would strengthen, not weaken, the claim by displaying similarities in the genetic makeup of animals and humans to that of insects.
    - (D) is correct because it would weaken the claim by suggesting that humans have *only a few of the supplemental genes necessary* for regeneration, not all of them.

14. **C** This is a Claims question, as it asks which choice *would most directly support the museum expert's claim.* Look for and highlight the claim in the passage, which is that *MacGregor sought to address* the *issue...by presenting the objects as pieces of a larger story, so that people from diverse ethnicities might find the exhibit more accessible.* The correct answer should be as consistent as possible with this claim.

    - (A) is wrong because it's **Recycled Language**—the word "diverse" is meant to apply to *ethnicities* rather than *spiritual and religious beliefs*, and the passage does not connect ethnicity to spiritual or religious beliefs, even if such connections may exist in the real world.
    - (B) is wrong because it's not relevant to the claim—there is no connection made in the passage between the works of Shakespeare and *diverse ethnicities.*
    - (C) is correct because it's consistent with each aspect of the highlighted claim.
    - (D) is wrong because it goes **Beyond the Text** with too specific of a focus—the answer only focuses on Australia and therefore does not address *diverse ethnicities.*

15. **A** This is a Conclusions question, as it asks for what *most logically completes the text.* Look for and highlight the main focus of the passage, which is the *impact of leadership positions on everyday behavior.* Then, highlight the main point made regarding this focus, which is that *it is often hard to anticipate who will rise to leadership positions.* Therefore, the conclusion of the passage should discuss how it's difficult to investigate the impact of leadership positions. The correct answer should be as consistent as possible with this conclusion.

- (A) is correct because it's consistent with what the highlighted sentences say about the challenges researchers will face.
- (B) is wrong because it's the **Opposite** of the challenges the passage indicates that researchers will face—the issue will be finding data on those who may become leaders, not data on those who *currently hold leadership positions.*
- (C) is wrong because it's **Extreme Language**—the passage never states that *only* those who recently left leadership positions can be studied.
- (D) is wrong because it goes **Beyond the Text**—while studies always want large control groups, the focus in the passage is on the challenges researchers face, not a general principle of conducting studies.

16. **B** This is a Conclusions question, as it asks for what *most logically completes the text.* Look for and highlight the main focus of the passage, which is that the *Popol Vuh is one of the most significant surviving sources of ancient Mayan culture.* Then, highlight the main point made regarding this focus, which is that while *Popol Vuh* reflects *pre-colonial Mayan beliefs*, some of its passages include *Catholic and European influence.* Therefore, the conclusion to the passage should address these differing aspects of the *Popol Vuh.* The correct answer should be as consistent as possible with this conclusion.

- (A) is wrong because it's the **Opposite** of what's stated in the passage—the *Popol Vuh* contains many of the early Mayan beliefs, so it's text should not be considered *distinct* from the original Mayan belief.
- (B) is correct because it's consistent with what the highlighted sentences say about the *Popol Vuh.*
- (C) is wrong because it's **Recycled Language**—*European* is misused from the second half of the passage.
- (D) is wrong because it's **Extreme Language**—it's not stated whether the Mayan beliefs were *unique* to the civilization or shared by other civilizations.

17. **D** In this Rules question, verbs are changing in the answer choices, so it's testing consistency with verbs. Find and highlight the subject, *Style Wars*, which is singular, as it is *a documentary*, so a singular verb is needed. Write an annotation saying "singular." Eliminate any answer that is not singular.

- (A), (B), and (C) are wrong because they are plural.
- (D) is correct because it's singular.

18. **A** In this Rules question, punctuation with a transition is changing in the answer choices. Look for independent clauses. The first part of the sentence says *Unlike all other waterfowl, the black-headed duck does not build a nest.* There is an option to add *instead* to this independent clause, but it's not contrasting with the previous idea as nothing came before. Eliminate options with *instead* in the first part.

- (A) is correct because it puts *instead* with the second independent clause and puts a semicolon between the independent clauses.
- (B) is wrong because it puts *instead* with the first independent clause.
- (C) and (D) are wrong because the sentence contains two independent clauses, which cannot be connected with commas alone.

19. **B** In this Rules question, verbs are changing in the answer choices, so it's testing consistency with verbs. Find and highlight the subject, *Stephanie Kwolek*, which is singular, so a singular verb is needed. All of the answers work with a singular subject, so look for a clue regarding tense. The same sentence uses past tense verbs: *found* and *aligned*. Highlight those verbs and write an annotation that says "past." Eliminate any answer not in past tense.

- (A) is wrong because it's in future tense.
- (B) is correct because it's in past tense and correctly suggests that Kwolek found the polymer while in the process of doing the research.
- (C) is wrong because it's not in past tense.
- (D) is wrong because it's in present tense.

20. **C** In this Rules question, punctuation is changing in the answer choices. Look for independent clauses. The first part of the sentence says *Herpetologist Teresa Camacho Badani led an expedition…to collect specimens of an endangered species of amphibian*, which is an independent clause. The second part says *previously known only from a single individual…the Sehuencas water frog…is now being bred in captivity in an effort to restore the population*, which is also an independent clause. Eliminate any answer that can't correctly connect two independent clauses.

- (A) is wrong because some type of punctuation is needed in order to connect two independent clauses.

- (B) is wrong because a coordinating conjunction (*but*) without a comma can't connect two independent clauses.
- (C) is correct because the period makes each independent clause its own sentence, which is fine.
- (D) is wrong because a comma without a coordinating conjunction (FANBOYS) can't connect two independent clauses.

21. **D** In this Rules question, punctuation is changing in the answer choices. Look for independent clauses. The first part of the sentence states that *a helicopter landed...after completing a pioneering 24-mile flight,* which is an independent clause. The second part says *powered by a rechargeable battery and carrying a 50-pound weight...the fully electric helicopter was copiloted by Martine Rothblatt and Ric Webb,* which is also an independent clause. Eliminate any answer that can't correctly connect two independent clauses.

    - (A) is wrong because a comma without a coordinating conjunction (FANBOYS) can't connect two independent clauses.
    - (B) is wrong because a coordinating conjunction (*and*) without a comma can't connect two independent clauses.
    - (C) is wrong because some type of punctuation is needed in order to connect two independent clauses.
    - (D) is correct because the period makes each independent clause its own sentence, which is fine.

22. **A** In this Rules question, commas and semicolons are changing in the answer choices. The sentence already contains a semicolon near the end, and the part after this semicolon is not an independent clause, which suggests that the sentence contains a list separated by semicolons. Check the verb at the beginning of each item to see where the semicolons should be placed. The list consists of 1) *take close-up pictures of Uranus and Neptune, the previously unexplored outer planets,* 2) *find the furthest extent of the Solar System*, and 3) *collect data about the interstellar space beyond the Solar System.* Eliminate any answer that doesn't put semicolons between the list items.

    - (A) is correct because it has a semicolon after the first item.
    - (B) and (C) are wrong because they don't have a semicolon after the first item, which ends with *planets.*
    - (D) is wrong because it puts the semicolon after *Neptune*, separating it from *the previously unexplored outer planets*, a description that refers to *Uranus and Neptune.*

23. **B** In this Rules question, punctuation is changing in the answer choices. The punctuation appears near the word *journalist* and the person's name. The word *journalist* is a title for Maximiliáno Durón, so no punctuation should be used. Eliminate answers that use punctuation.

- (A) is wrong because a comma shouldn't be used between the subject *Maximiliáno Durón* and its verb *calls.*
- (B) is correct because titles before names have no punctuation.
- (C) and (D) are wrong because a comma isn't used after a title.

24. **A** This is a transition question, so follow the basic approach. Highlight ideas that relate to each other. The first sentence states that *local legend credits Marie Harel with the invention of Camembert cheese,* though *she likely learned the technique from a priest,* and this sentence states that *Harel will likely continue to receive recognition for the cheese.* These ideas disagree, so an opposite-direction transition is needed. Make an annotation that says "disagree." Eliminate any answer that doesn't match.

- (A) is correct because *Nevertheless* is an opposite-direction transition and correctly implies that despite the fact that Harel may not have completely invented the cheese, she will still be recognized for it.
- (B), (C), and (D) are wrong because they are same-direction transitions.

25. **D** This is a transition question, so follow the basic approach. Highlight ideas that relate to each other. The preceding sentence states that *researchers have found evidence* for the asteroid theory, and this sentence explains that the *shocked quartz* and *tektites* in the areas provide evidence. These ideas agree, so a same-direction transition is needed. Make an annotation that says "agree." Eliminate any answer that doesn't match.

- (A) is wrong because the evidence isn't a result of a hypothesis; a hypothesis is based on evidence.
- (B) is wrong because it's an opposite-direction transition.
- (C) is wrong because this sentence isn't a restatement of the preceding sentence.
- (D) is correct because this sentence specifies what kind of *evidence* has been found.

26. **B** This is a transition question, so follow the basic approach. Highlight ideas that relate to each other. The preceding sentence describes a new fingerprinting technique, and this sentence states that it can provide *more reliable evidence* for *court cases.* These ideas agree, so a same-direction transition is needed. Make an annotation that says "agree." Eliminate any answer that doesn't match.

- (A) and (D) are wrong because they are opposite-direction transitions.
- (B) is correct because this sentence draws a conclusion from the evidence in the previous sentences.

- (C) is wrong because this sentence does not describe a separate thing that is similar to something that was previously described.

27. **A** This is a Rhetorical Synthesis question, so follow the basic approach. Highlight the goal(s) stated in the question: *make and support a generalization about sports-related concussions.* Eliminate any answer that doesn't fulfill this purpose.

    - (A) is correct because *short- and long-term consequences* is a generalization (a broader look at something), and the information after the colon supports this generalization.
    - (B) is wrong because it makes a *generalization* but doesn't *support* it.
    - (C) and (D) are wrong because they give specific details instead of a *generalization.*

PRACTICE TEST 1—MATH EXPLANATIONS

Module 1

1. **C** The question asks for a comparison of the means, or averages, of two data sets. One approach is to ballpark. Both data sets contain the numbers 3, 8, 8, 11, and 24. Data set S contains an additional, smaller number, so its mean will be less, which makes (C) correct. To solve mathematically, use the average formula $T = AN$, in which T is the *Total*, A is the *Average*, and N is the *Number of things*. There are 6 values in data set S, so $N = 6$. Find the *Total* by adding the 6 integers to get $T = 2 + 3 + 8 + 8 + 11 + 24 = 56$. The average formula becomes $56 = (A)6$. Divide both sides of the equation by 6 to get $9.\overline{3} = A$, which means that the mean of data set S is $9.\overline{3}$. Repeat the same steps to find the mean of data set T. There are 5 values in data set T, so $N = 5$. Find the *Total* by adding the 5 integers to get $T = 3 + 8 + 8 + 11 + 24 = 54$. The average formula becomes $54 = (A)(5)$. Divide both sides of the equation by 5 to get $10.8 = A$, which means that the mean of data set T is 10.8. Since $9.\overline{3}$ is less than 10.8, the mean of data set S is less than the mean of data set T. Using either method, the correct answer is (C).

2. **B** The question asks for the value of an expression. Plug in 8 for x in the expression $30 - x$ to get $30 - 8$. Simplify the expression to get $30 - 8 = 22$. The correct answer is (B).

3. **B** The question asks for a value given a specific situation. Since the question includes the word *average*, use the formula $T = AN$, where T is the *Total*, A is the *Average*, and N is the *Number of things*. To find the number of liters of water that drained from the tank, subtract the remaining liters of water from the initial liters of water to get $7{,}854 - 1{,}192 = 6{,}662$ liters of water. Since the question states that 1,192 liters of water remained after the *valve remained open for 44 seconds*, the *Number of things* is 44. The average formula becomes $6{,}662 = (A)(44)$. Divide both sides of the equation by 44 to get $151.4 \approx A$. The correct answer is (B).

4. **A** The question asks for the value of the measure of an angle on a geometric figure. Use the Geometry Basic Approach. Start by redrawing the figures on the scratch paper. The question states that the triangles are similar and that B corresponds to E, and the figure shows that both A and D are right angles, so C must correspond to F. Since angle E has a measure of 52°, angle B also has a measure of 52°. Label this information on the figures. All triangles contain 180°, so the third angle in each triangle has a measure of 180° – 90° – 52° = 38°. Label angles C and F as 38°. The question asks for the measure of angle C, which is 38°. The correct answer is (A).

5. **200** The question asks for a value given a specific situation. Translate the information in bite-sized pieces. One piece of information states that *b is the number of bats sold and g is the number of gloves sold*, and another piece states that the *company made $26,000 from the sale of equally-priced bats and equally-priced gloves.* Since the sum of $500b$ and $300g$ equals the total money made from selling the two types of softball equipment, 500 and 300 must be the cost per bat and the cost per glove, respectively. To find how much less the price of a glove is than the price of a bat, subtract 300 from 500: 500 – 300 = 200. Each glove costs $200 less than each bat. The correct answer is 200.

6. **B** The question asks for the value of an expression given a system of equations. When a Digital SAT question asks for the value of an expression, there is usually a straightforward way to solve for the expression without needing to completely isolate either variable. Try stacking and adding the two equations.

$$\begin{array}{r} 8x - y = -17 \\ +\ (-7x \quad\ = \ \ 14) \\ \hline x - y = \ -3 \end{array}$$

The question asks for the value of $x - y$, so stop here. The correct answer is (B).

7. **D** The question asks for a value based on a function. The question states that d represents the number of days after starting a fundraising campaign and $f(d)$ represents the amount of money in the account d days after starting the campaign. Plug in $d = 0$ to determine how many dollars were in the account before the campaign started. The function becomes $f(0) = 750(0) + 12{,}000$, then $f(0) = 0 + 12{,}000$, and finally $f(0) = 12{,}000$. There was $12,000 in the account before the fundraising campaign started. The correct answer is (D).

8. **A** The question asks for a value given a relationship between two geometric figures. Use the Geometry Basic Approach. Start by drawing two equilateral triangles of different sizes, then label the figure with the given information. The question states that *one side of triangle S is 9 inches long,* so label this on the figure. The perimeter of a geometric shape is the sum of the lengths of its sides, and all three sides in an equilateral triangle are equal, so the perimeter of triangle S is 9 + 9 + 9 = 27 inches. The question states that *equilateral triangle T has a perimeter that is one-third the*

perimeter of equilateral triangle S, so the perimeter of triangle T is $\frac{1}{3}(27) = 9$ inches. Triangle T has three equal sides, so one side of triangle T is $\frac{9}{3} = 3$ inches long. The correct answer is (A).

9. **7 or –7**

The question asks for a possible value of an expression given an equation with an absolute value. With an absolute value, the value inside the absolute value bars can be either positive or negative, so this equation has two possible solutions. To find the solutions, either set $7x + 14$ equal to 49 or set $7x + 14$ equal to –49. The question asks for the value of $x + 2$, which is equivalent to dividing $7x + 14$ by 7. When $7x + 14 = 49$, divide both sides of the equation by 7 to get $x + 2 = 7$. When $7x + 14 = -49$, divide both sides of the equation by 7 to get $x + 2 = -7$. Either 7 or –7 is a possible value of $x + 2$. The correct answer is 7 or –7.

10. **5** The question asks for the value of a constant in a function that represents values given in a table. In function notation, the number inside the parentheses is the *x*-value that goes into the function, or the input, and the value that comes out of the function is the *y*-value, or the output. The table includes five input values and five output values, all of which must work in the equation $g(x) = kx + 34$. Pick any pair of values from the table and plug them into the given equation to solve for k. Plug in $x = -6$ and $g(x) = 4$ to keep the numbers small. The equation of function g becomes $4 = k(-6) + 34$, or $4 = -6k + 34$. Add $6k$ to both sides of the equation to get $6k + 4 = 34$, and then subtract 4 from both sides of the equation to get $6k = 30$. Divide both sides of the equation by 6 to get $k = 5$. The correct answer is 5.

11. **–11** The question asks for a constant in an equivalent expression. The question asks for the value of c, which is multiplied by x^4, so focus on the terms with x^4. Rewrite the first expression with only those terms to get $-3x^4 + (-8x^4)$, which becomes $-11x^4$. Set this equal to the term with x^4 in the second expression to get $-11x^4 = cx^4$, then divide both sides of this equation by x^4 to get $-11 = c$. The correct answer is –11.

12. **D** The question asks for an equation in terms of a specific variable. The question asks about the relationship among variables and there are variables in the answer choices, so one option is to plug in. However, that might get messy with three variables. All of the answer choices have m by itself, so the other option is to solve for m. To isolate m, first cross-multiply to get $(n)(2) = (22m)(3s)$, or $2n = 66ms$. Divide both sides of the resulting equation by $66s$ to get $\frac{2n}{66s} = m$. The correct answer is (D).

13. **A** The question asks for an equation that represents a specific situation. The number of ants is decreasing by a multiple over time, so this question is about exponential decay. Write down the growth and decay formula. When the change is a multiple instead of a percentage, the formula is *final amount* = (*original amount*)(*multiplier*)$^{number\ of\ changes}$. In this case, the *original amount* is 96,000. The question states that the number of ants decreases *by one-half every 4 days*, so the *multiplier* is $\frac{1}{2}$. The question asks for the number of ants *20 days after the infection started*, so the *number of changes* is $\frac{20}{4} = 5$. The formula becomes *final amount* = $96{,}000\left(\frac{1}{2}\right)^5$, or *final amount* = $96{,}000\left(\frac{1}{32}\right)$, and finally *final amount* = 3,000. The correct answer is (A).

14. **D** The question asks for the y-value of a point that satisfies a system of inequalities. The answers contain specific values, so plug in the answers. Rewrite the answer choices on the scratch paper and label them as "y." Start with one of the middle numbers and try (C), 3. The question provides an x-value of 39, which is possible based on the first inequality, so plug $x = 39$ and $y = 3$ into the second inequality. The second inequality becomes $39 - 7(3) < 16$, then $39 - 21 < 16$, and finally $18 < 16$. This is not true, so eliminate (C). The value on the left side of the inequality was close to being less than 16, so try (D), 4, next. Plug $x = 39$ and $y = 4$ into the second inequality to get $39 - 7(4) < 16$, which becomes $39 - 28 < 16$, and then $11 < 16$. This is true, so stop here. The correct answer is (D).

15. **A** The question asks for an equivalent form of an expression. Although there are variables in the answer choices, plugging in on this question would be difficult given all the exponents. Instead, use bite-sized pieces and Process of Elimination to tackle this question. Start by rewriting the expression with fractional exponents. In a fractional exponent, the numerator is the power and the denominator is the root. Taking the 9th root of a value raised to the 5th power can be written using the fractional exponent $\frac{5}{9}$. The expression becomes $s^{\frac{5}{9}}t^{\frac{5}{9}}$, which can also be written as $(st)^{\frac{5}{9}}$. The correct answer is (A).

16. **C** The question asks for the interpretation of a feature of a graph. Start by reading the final question, which asks for the best interpretation of the y-intercept. The y-intercept is the y-value when $x = 0$. The question states that the graph represents the value *of the item x months after it was purchased*, so $x = 0$ means the value at the time it was purchased. Eliminate (B) because it is about a range of months instead of the initial value, and eliminate (D) because it is about the value of the item six months after it was purchased instead of at the time it was purchased. Compare the remaining answer choices. The difference between (A) and (C) is whether the value is \$2 or \$200. Check the units of the y-axis. The question states that y is the value of the item *in hundreds of dollars*, so 2 on the y-axis means the initial value was \$200. The correct answer is (C).

17. **D** The question asks for a system of equations with exactly one real solution. A system of linear equations in two variables has exactly one solution when the y-terms are the same and the x-terms are different or vice versa. Eliminate (A) because it contains two equations of horizontal lines, which are parallel and have no solutions. Eliminate (B) and (C) because the y-terms and the x-terms are the same. Keep (D) because the y-terms are the same and the x-terms are different. Another approach is to enter all four pairs of equations into the built-in calculator and see which pair intersects once. The graphs of the equations in (D) intersect once, so that system of equations has exactly one real solution. Using either method, the correct answer is (D).

18. **C** The question asks for an equation in terms of specific variables. The question asks about the relationship between variables and there are variables in the answer choices, so plug in. The question states that n represents the number of the term of the sequence and that the first term of the sequence is 56. Thus, when $n = 1$, $s = 56$. Plug these values into the answer choices and eliminate any that are not true. Choice (A) becomes $56 = \frac{1}{2}(56)^{1-1}$, or $56 = \frac{1}{2}(56)^0$. Any number raised to the power of zero is 1, so this becomes $56 = \frac{1}{2}(1)$, or $56 = \frac{1}{2}$. This is not true, so eliminate (A). Choice (B) becomes $56 = \frac{1}{2}(56)^1$, or $56 = 28$; eliminate (B). Choice (C) becomes $56 = 56\left(\frac{1}{2}\right)^{1-1}$, or $56 = 56\left(\frac{1}{2}\right)^0$. This becomes $56 = 56(1)$, or $56 = 56$. This is true, so keep (C), but check (D) just in case. Choice (D) becomes $56 = 56\left(\frac{1}{2}\right)^1$, or $56 = 28$; eliminate (D), The correct answer is (C).

19. **B** The question asks for the value of a constant that represents a decrease. The question is about the relationship between values, so plug in. Plug in 100 for the number of movies available in 2022 because 100 works well with percentages. *Percent* means out of 100, so translate 9% as $\frac{9}{100}$. Because the number of movies available decreased by 9% from the starting number of 100, take 9% of 100 and subtract it from 100. The result is $100 - \frac{9}{100}(100) = 100 - 9 = 91$. Thus, the streaming service has 91 movies available in 2023. This is the target value; circle it. Because the number of movies decreased from 100 to 91, (B) is a likely answer. To test it, plug in 0.91 for m. The question states that *the number of movies available in 2023 is m times the number of movies available in 2022*, so multiply the number of movies available in 2022, 100, by 0.91 to get $(100)(0.91) = 91$. This matches the target value for the number of movies available in 2023, so stop here. The correct answer is (B).

20. **A** The question asks for an inequality that represents a given situation. Translate the information in bite-sized pieces and eliminate after each piece. Translate *the maximum value of q* as q is less than or equal to, or $q \leq$. Eliminate (C) and (D) because the inequality sign is the wrong direction. Translate *7 times the value of r* as $7r$. Eliminate (B) because it does not include this term. Choice (A) also correctly translates *14 more than* as + 14. The correct answer is (A).

21. **–0.4 or –2/5**

The question asks for the x-coordinate of the x-intercept of a graph that is a translation of another graph. When a graph is translated, or transformed, up or down, the y-value changes. Start by isolating y. Subtract $5x$ from both sides of the equation to get $3y = -5x - 8$. Divide both sides of the equation by 3 to get $y = -\frac{5}{3}x - \frac{8}{3}$. To translate this graph up 2 units, add 2 to the y-value. The equation of the new graph is $y = -\frac{5}{3}x - \frac{8}{3} + 2$. At this point, the best option is to enter this equation into the built-in calculator, then scroll and zoom as needed to see a gray dot at the x-intercept. Click on the dot to see that the coordinates of the point are (–0.4, 0). The question asks for the x-coordinate of the x-intercept, which is –0.4. It is also possible to solve algebraically by making $y = 0$ in the equation of the new graph and solving for x. This might lead to the decimal form –0.4 or to the fractional form $-\frac{2}{5}$, both of which will be accepted as correct. The correct answer is –0.4 or –2/5.

22. **A** The question asks for the value of a trigonometric function. Use the Geometry Basic Approach. Start by drawing two right triangles that are similar to each other, meaning they have the same proportions but are different sizes. Be certain to match up the corresponding angles that are given in the question, and put the longest side opposite the right angle. The drawing should look something like this:

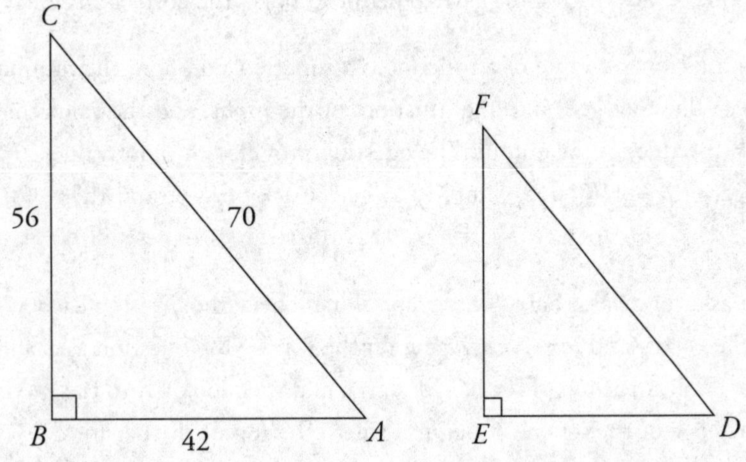

The question asks for the value of cos *D*. Trig functions are proportional, and angle *A* corresponds to angle *D*, so cos *A* = cos *D*. Use SOHCAHTOA to remember the trig functions, and find cos *A*. The CAH part of the acronym defines cosine as $\frac{\text{adjacent}}{\text{hypotenuse}}$. The side adjacent to angle *A* is 42, and the hypotenuse is 70, so $\cos A = \frac{42}{70}$. Since cos *D* = cos *A*, cos *D* is also $\frac{42}{70}$. The numerator and denominator are both multiples of 14, so reduce the fraction to get $\cos D = \frac{3}{5}$. The correct answer is (A).

Module 2—Easier

1. **8400** The question asks for a value given a rate. Begin by reading the question to find information about the rate. The question states that the factory *makes 1,200 vehicles in 1 day*, but asks for the number of vehicles in 1 week. There are 7 days in 1 week, so set up a proportion, being sure to match up the units. The proportion is $\frac{1{,}200 \text{ vehicles}}{1 \text{ day}} = \frac{x \text{ vehicles}}{7 \text{ days}}$. Cross-multiply to get $(1)(x) = (1{,}200)(7)$, which becomes $x = 8{,}400$. Leave out the comma when entering the answer in the fill-in box. The correct answer is 8400.

2. **A** The question asks for the value of an expression based on an equation. There isn't a straightforward way to get from 10*a* to 9*a*, so start by isolating *a*. Divide both sides of the equation by 10 to get *a* = 3. Next, substitute 3 for *a* in the expression 9*a* to get 9(3) = 27. The correct answer is (A).

3. **D** The question asks for a value based on a percentage. Translate the English to math in bite-sized pieces. The question states that Talula *baked 340 cookies and gave 20% of them to her neighbors. Percent* means out of 100, so translate 20% as $\frac{20}{100}$. Translate *of* as times. Thus, 20% of 340 becomes $\frac{20}{100}(340) = 68$ cookies that Talula gave to her neighbors. The correct answer is (D).

4. **61** The question asks for the value of a function. In function notation, the number inside the parentheses is the *x*-value that goes into the function, or the input, and the value that comes out of the function is the *y*-value, or the output. The question provides an input value, so plug *x* = 6 into the function to get $h(6) = 11(6) - 5$. Simplify to get $h(6) = 66 - 5$, and then $h(6) = 61$. The correct answer is 61.

5. **50** The question asks for a value based on a graph. First, check the units on each axis of the bar graph. *Days* are on the *x*-axis, and *number of dogs* is on the *y*-axis. The question asks about day 7, so find 7 on the *x*-axis. Look at the top of the bar for day 7, and then look left to the *y*-axis, using the mouse pointer or the edge of the scratch paper as a ruler. The top of the bar for day 7 is at 50. Thus, 50 dogs visited the dog park on day 7. The correct answer is 50.

6. **–5** The question asks for a value based on a graph. Specifically, the question asks for the value of x at the x-intercept on the graph of a parabola. This is the point at which $y = 0$ and the graph intersects the x-axis. Look on the graph for the point on the parabola at which the y-coordinate equals 0 and the graph touches the x-axis. This point is (–5, 0), so the x-value is –5. The correct answer is –5.

7. **B** The question asks for an equivalent form of an expression. There are variables in the answer choices, so plugging in is an option. However, that might get messy with two variables and exponents, so the other option is to factor. Both 14 and 7 are divisible by 7, and both terms have a, so factor $7a$ out of both terms. Divide $14a$ by $7a$ to get 2, and divide $7ab^2$ by $7a$ to get b^2. The expression becomes $7a(2 + b^2)$. The correct answer is (B).

8. **208** The question asks for a measurement of a geometric figure. Use the Geometry Basic Approach. Start by drawing a rectangle on the scratch paper, then label the figure with the given information. Label one pair of opposite sides as 80 and the other pair of opposite sides as 24. The perimeter of a geometric shape is the sum of the lengths of the sides. Add all four side lengths to get 80 + 24 + 80 + 24 = 208. The correct answer is 208.

9. **B** The question asks for the value of a constant in the coordinates of a point on a line. The constant n represents the y-value when $x = 3$. First, see if any answers can be eliminated by ballparking. Find 3 on the x-axis, and then move up from there to the line, using the mouse pointer or scratch paper as a ruler. Move left from there to the y-axis to see that the y-value is between 3 and 4. Check all four answer choices on a calculator: they are all between 3 and 4, so nothing can be eliminated. Instead, use the two points shown on the graph to find the slope of the line. The points are (0, 5) and (12, 0). Use those two points to calculate the slope of the line using the formula $slope = \frac{y_2 - y_1}{x_2 - x_1}$. The formula becomes $slope = \frac{5 - 0}{0 - 12}$, or $slope = -\frac{5}{12}$. Use the slope formula again, this time with one of the known points and the point that includes n. Use the points (3, n) and (12, 0), and the formula becomes $slope = \frac{n - 0}{3 - 12}$, or $slope = -\frac{n}{9}$. Set this equal to the slope from the first two points to get $-\frac{n}{9} = -\frac{5}{12}$. Cross-multiply to get $(-9)(-5) = (n)(12)$, or $45 = 12n$. Divide both sides of the equation by 12 to get $\frac{45}{12} = n$. Both numbers in the fraction are multiples of 3, so reduce the fraction to get $\frac{15}{4} = n$. The correct answer is (B).

10. **D** The question asks for a probability based on a situation. Probability is defined as $\frac{\text{number of outcomes that give you what you want}}{\text{total number of possible outcomes}}$. Read carefully to find the numbers that make up the probability. The question states that there are *18 cards*, so that is the total number of possible outcomes. Each card has a different number, so out of the 18 cards, 1 of them has a 6 written

on it. Thus, there are $18 - 1 = 17$ cards that do not have a 6 written on them, and the number of outcomes that give you what you want is 17. Therefore, the probability that a single card does not have a 6 written on it in $\frac{17}{18}$. The correct answer is (D).

11. **A** The question asks for the value of a function. In function notation, the number inside the parentheses is the x-value that goes into the function, or the input, and the value that comes out of the function is the y-value, or the output. The question provides an input value, so plug $x = 3$ into the function to get $g(3) = -2(3)^2$. Simplify to get $g(3) = -2(9)$, and then $g(3) = -18$. The correct answer is (A).

12. **B** The question asks for the value of an angle on a figure. Use the Geometry Basic Approach. Redraw the figure on the scratch paper, and add the labels. When a line intersects two parallel lines, two kinds of angles are created: big and small. All the small angles are equal to each other, all the big angles are equal to each other, and any small angle plus any big angle = 180°. The angle marked $d°$ is a small angle, and the angle marked 148° is a big angle. Thus, $d + 148 = 180$. Subtract 148 from both sides of the equation to get $d = 32$. The correct answer is (B).

13. **C** The question asks for an equation that represents a graph. One approach is to enter the equation from each answer choice into the built-in graphing calculator and see which graph looks most like the line of best fit of the scatterplot. Another approach is to compare features of the graph to the answer choices. The equations in the answer choices are all close to the form $y = mx + b$, in which m is the slope and b is the y-intercept, except the mx and b terms are reversed. The y-intercept is the y-coordinate of the point where $x = 0$, which is between 12 and 14 on this graph. Eliminate (A) and (B) because they have negative y-intercepts. Compare the remaining answer choices. The difference between (C) and (D) is the sign of the slope. The line of best fit descends from left to right, so it has a negative slope. Eliminate (D) because it has a positive slope. Using either method, the correct answer is (C).

14. **D** The question asks which answer correctly compares the data represented by a dot plot to the data from a related data set. Range is easy to calculate, if necessary, so start there. Subtracting 8 from each value will not change the range because the greatest value and the least value will both decrease by 8, which means the difference between them will be the same in data set S as it is in data set R. Eliminate (A) and (B) because they say that the ranges are different, not equal. Mean is a measure of center, and the center will change when the values change. Subtracting 8 from every value will make the mean less, so the mean of data set S is less than the mean of data set R. Eliminate (C) because it says that the two means are equal. The correct answer is (D).

15. **D** The question asks for the interpretation of a number in context. Start by reading the final question, which asks for the meaning of the number 25. Then label the parts of the equation with the information given. The question states that c represents cooperative missions and s represents solo missions. The number 25 is multiplied by s, so it must have something to do with solo missions. Eliminate (A) and (B) because they are about cooperative missions, not solo missions. Since s

already represents the number of solo missions, 25 cannot represent the same thing; eliminate (C), so (D) must be correct. The question also states that 1,000 is the total points scored, so it makes sense that the two coefficients on the left side of the equation represent numbers of points per mission. Because 25 is multiplied by s, it represents the number of points per solo mission. The correct answer is (D).

16. **D** The question asks for the value of a function. In function notation, the number inside the parentheses is the x-value that goes into the function, or the input, and the value that comes out of the function is the y-value, or the output. The question provides an output value of 5, and the answers have numbers that could represent the x-value, so plug in the answers. Start with one of the middle numbers and try (B), 25. Plug 25 into the function for x to get $g(25) = \frac{\sqrt{25}}{2}$, which becomes $g(25) = \frac{5}{2}$, and then $g(25) = 2.5$. This does not match the output value given in the question, so eliminate (B). The result was too small, so also eliminate (A). Another perfect square is likely to result in an integer output, so try (D), 100, next. Plug 100 into the function for x to get $g(100) = \frac{\sqrt{100}}{2}$, which becomes $g(100) = \frac{10}{2}$, and then $g(100) = 5$. This matches the output value given in the question, so stop here. The correct answer is (D).

17. **C** The question asks for the value of a variable in a system of equations. The second equation gives the value of x, so plug in –7 for x in the first equation to get $y = (-7)^2 - 7$. Simplify the right side of the equation—keeping in mind that a negative number squared becomes positive—to get $y = 49 - 7$, and then $y = 42$. The correct answer is (C).

18. **A** The question asks for the value of a function. In function notation, $y = f(x)$. The number inside the parentheses is the x-value that goes into the function, or the input, and the value that comes out of the function is the y-value, or the output. The question asks for the value of $f(0)$, which means $x = 0$ and the question is asking for the y-intercept. Find $x = 0$ on the graph and move straight down to see that the graph crosses the y-axis at (0, –5). When $x = 0$, $y = -5$. The correct answer is (A).

19. **A** The question asks for the equation of a line. All of the answer choices are linear equations in slope-intercept form, $y = mx + b$, where m is the slope and b is the y-intercept. The question states that the graph *has a slope of* $\frac{1}{6}$. Therefore, $m = \frac{1}{6}$. Eliminate (C) and (D) because they have the wrong slope. The question also states that the line *passes through the point* (12, –7), so plug $x = 12$ and $y = -7$ into the remaining two answer choices. Choice (A) becomes $-7 = \frac{12}{6} - 9$, then $-7 = 2 -$

9, and finally –7 = –7. This is true, so keep (A), but check (B) just in case. Choice (B) becomes $-7 = \frac{12}{6} - 7$, then –7 = 2 – 7, and finally –7 = –5. This is not true; eliminate (B). The correct answer is (A).

20. **B** The question asks for the number of solutions to a quadratic equation. One method is to use the built-in graphing calculator. Enter the equation without the "= 0" part to see a parabola, and then scroll and zoom to see how many times, if any, the parabola intersects the *x*-axis. There are two points of intersection, at (–0.5, 0) and (2.5, 0), so there are exactly two real solutions, and the answer is (B). To determine the number of solutions algebraically, use the discriminant. The discriminant is the part of the quadratic formula under the square root sign and is written as $D = b^2 - 4ac$. When the discriminant is positive, the quadratic has exactly two real solutions; when the discriminant is 0, the quadratic has exactly one real solution; and when the discriminant is negative, the quadratic has no real solutions. The quadratic is given in standard form, $ax^2 + bx + c = 0$, so $a = 4$, $b = -8$, and $c = -5$. The discriminant is $D = (-8)^2 - 4(4)(-5)$, which becomes $D = 64 + 80$, and then $D = 144$. This is positive, so there are exactly two real solutions. Using either method, the correct answer is (B).

21. **B** The question asks for a value given a specific situation. Since the question asks for a specific value and the answers contain numbers in increasing order, plug in the answers. Rewrite the answer choices on the scratch paper and label them as "# of blue tokens." Next, start with a number in the middle and try (B), 16. The question states that the *jar contains a total of 37 red and blue tokens*. If there are 16 blue tokens, there are 37 – 16 = 21 red tokens. The question also states that *the mass of one red token is 90 grams*, so 21 red tokens have a mass of (21)(90) = 1,890 grams. The question also states that *the mass of one blue token is 120 grams*, so 16 blue tokens have a mass of (16)(120) = 1,920 grams. Add the total grams of the red and blue tokens to get 1,890 + 1,920 = 3,810 grams. This matches the combined mass given in the question, so stop here. The correct answer is (B).

22. **C** The question asks for the equation of a circle that has been shifted in the *xy*-plane. The equation of a circle in standard form is $(x - h)^2 + (y - k)^2 = r^2$, where (h, k) is the center and r is the radius. Shifting a circle to the right 7 units does not change the radius, and all the equations in the answer choices are equal to 64, so focus on the center. Moving a circle left or right does not change the *y*-value. Eliminate (A) and (B) because the $(y - k)^2$ portion of the equation is different. To move a circle left or right, change the *x*-value. In circle R, $(x - h) = (x + 3)$, so $-h = 3$ and $h = -3$. Since the *x*-value of the center of circle R is –3, the *x*-coordinate of the center of circle S, which is shifted to the right 7 units, is –3 + 7 = 4. Thus, the value of h in circle S is 4. The term $(x - 4)^2$ must appear in the correct answer, so eliminate (D). To check, enter the equation of circle R and the equation in (C) for circle S into the built-in graphing calculator, and confirm that circle S is 7 units to the right of circle R. The correct answer is (C).

Module 2—Harder

1. **C** The question asks for an equation that represents a specific situation. Translate the information in bite-sized pieces and eliminate after each piece. One piece of information says that *apples are sold in bags of 4 apples per bag, and bananas are sold in bunches of 6 bananas each.* Since the number of bags of apples is represented by a and the number of bunches of bananas is represented by b, the correct equation must include the terms $4a$ and $6b$. Eliminate (B) and (D) because they do not contain these terms. When (A) is expanded, it includes those two terms but also includes $6a$ and $4b$, which do not match the information in the question; eliminate (A). The correct answer is (C).

2. **D** The question asks for an equation that represents a graph. One approach is to enter the equation from each answer choice into the built-in graphing calculator and see which graph looks most like the line of best fit of the scatterplot. Another approach is to compare features of the graph to the answer choices. The equations in the answer choices are all close to the form $y = mx + b$, in which m is the slope and b is the y-intercept, except the mx and b terms are reversed. The y-intercept is the y-coordinate of the point where $x = 0$, which is between 1 and 2 on this graph. Eliminate (A) and (B) because they have negative y-intercepts. Compare the remaining answer choices. The difference between (C) and (D) is the sign of the slope. The line of best fit goes up from left to right, so it has a positive slope. Eliminate (C) because it has a negative slope. Using either method, the correct answer is (D).

3. **B** The question asks for a value based on survey data. Since 45% of the respondents do not plan to compete in the upcoming race, apply that percentage to all 120 members of the cycling club. *Percent* means out of 100, so translate 45% as $\frac{45}{100}$. Taking the percent of a number translates to multiplication, so 45% of 120 becomes $\frac{45}{100}(200)$. Use scratch paper or a calculator to do the math to get that 54 members of the cycling club do not plan to compete in the upcoming race. The correct answer is (B).

4. **C** The question asks for the function that represents values given in a table. In function notation, the number inside the parentheses is the x-value that goes into the function, or the input, and the value that comes out of the function is the y-value, or the output. The table includes four pairs of input and output values, and the correct equation must work for every pair of values. Plug in values from the table and eliminate functions that don't work. Because 0 and 1 are likely to make more than one answer work, try the first row of the table and plug $x = -1$ and $f(x) = -11$ into the answer choices. Choice (A) becomes $-11 = -(-1)^2 - 4(-1) - 5$. Simplify to get $-11 = -1 + 4 - 5$, and then $-11 = -2$. This is not true, so eliminate (A). Choice (B) becomes $-11 = -5(-1)^2 + 3(-1) - 5$. Simplify to get $-11 = -5 - 3 - 5$, and then $-11 = -13$; eliminate (B). Choice (C) becomes $-11 = -4(-1)^2 + 2(-1) - 5$. Simplify to get $-11 = -4 - 2 - 5$, and then $-11 = -11$. This is true, so keep (C), but check (D) just in case. Choice (D) becomes $-11 = -2(-1)^2 + 4(-1) - 5$. Simplify to get $-11 = -2 - 4 - 5$, and then $-11 = -11$. This is also true, so try another pair of values.

Try the last row of the table and plug $x = 2$ and $f(x) = -17$ into the remaining answer choices. Choice (C) becomes $-17 = -4(2)^2 + 2(2) - 5$. Simplify to get $-17 = -4(4) + 4 - 5$, then $-17 = -16 + 4 - 5$, and finally $-17 = -17$. Keep (C) and check (D). Choice (D) becomes $-17 = -2(2)^2 + 4(2) - 5$. Simplify to get $-17 = -2(4) + 8 - 5$, then $-17 = -8 + 8 - 5$, and finally $-17 = -5$; eliminate (D). The correct answer is (C).

5. **D** The question asks for a value given a function. In function notation, the number inside the parentheses is the *x*-value that goes into the function, or the input, and the value that comes out of the function is the *y*-value, or the output. The question provides an output value of 20, and the answers have numbers that could represent the *x*-value, so plug in the answers. Rewrite the answers on the scratch paper and label them as "*c*." Start with one of the middle numbers and try (B), 20. Plug 20 into the function for *x* to get $f(20) = \frac{20 - 12}{8}$, which becomes $f(20) = \frac{8}{8}$, and then $f(20) = 1$. This does not match the output value of 20 given in the question, so eliminate (B). The result was too small, so also eliminate (A), and try (C), 148, next. Plug 148 into the function for *x* to get $f(148) = \frac{148 - 12}{8}$, which becomes $f(148) = \frac{136}{8}$, and then $f(148) = 17$. Eliminate (C). Only (D) remains, so it must be correct. The output value for (C) was closer to 20 but still too small, so it makes sense that a larger number is needed. The correct answer is (D).

6. **B** The question asks for the value of a constant in the coordinates of a point on a line. The constant *n* represents the *y*-value when $x = 3$. First, see if any answers can be eliminated by ballparking. Find 3 on the *x*-axis, and then move up from there to the line, using the mouse pointer or scratch paper as a ruler. Move left from there to the *y*-axis to see that the *y*-value is between 3 and 4. Check all four answer choices on a calculator: they are all between 3 and 4, so nothing can be eliminated. Instead, use the two points shown on the graph to find the slope of the line. The points are (0, 5) and (12, 0). Use those two points to calculate the slope of the line using the formula $slope = \frac{y_2 - y_1}{x_2 - x_1}$. The formula becomes $slope = \frac{5 - 0}{0 - 12}$, or $slope = -\frac{5}{12}$. Use the slope formula again, this time with one of the known points and the point that includes *n*. Use the points (3, *n*) and (12, 0), and the formula becomes $slope = \frac{n - 0}{3 - 12}$, or $slope = -\frac{n}{9}$. Set this equal to the slope from the first two points to get $-\frac{n}{9} = -\frac{5}{12}$. Cross-multiply to get $(-9)(-5) = (n)(12)$, or $45 = 12n$. Divide both sides of the equation by 12 to get $\frac{45}{12} = n$. Both numbers in the fraction are multiples of 3, so reduce the fraction to get $\frac{15}{4} = n$. The correct answer is (B).

7. **A** The question asks for the slope of a line. The question states that line m is perpendicular to line l, which means they have equal slopes. The question gives the equation of line l, so find the slope of that line. First, convert the equation of line l into slope-intercept form, $y = mx + b$, in which m is the slope and b is the y-intercept. Subtract 7 from both sides of the equation to get $4y = -16x - 7$. Divide both sides of the equation by 4 to get $y = -4x - \frac{7}{4}$. The slope of line l is thus –4. It is also possible to convert the equation of line l into standard form by adding $16x$ to both sides of the equation and subtracting 7 from both sides of the equation to get $16x + 4y = -7$. In standard form, $Ax + By = C$, the slope is $-\frac{A}{B}$. In this case, $A = 16$ and $B = 4$, so the slope of line l is $-\frac{16}{4} = -4$. Using either form of a linear equation, the slope of line l is –4. Since line m is parallel and has the same slope, the slope of line m is also –4. The correct answer is (A).

8. **C** The question asks for the density of a rectangular solid. Use the Geometry Basic Approach. Start by drawing a rectangular solid on the scratch paper as best as possible, and then label the length, width, and height as 1.1, 0.8, and 0.8, respectively. Other information about the concrete block is given, so use the units to determine what to do next. The question asks for the density in kilograms per cubic meter, and the question gives the mass in kilograms, so look for a way to find a value in cubic meters. Since the side lengths are in meters, the volume will be in cubic meters. Write down the formula for the volume of a rectangular solid or prism, either from memory or after looking it up on the reference sheet. The formula is $V = lwh$. Plug in the side lengths given in the question to get $V = (1.1)(0.8)(0.8)$, or $V = 0.704$ cubic meters. The mass in kilograms divided by the volume in cubic meters equals the density in kilograms per cubic meter. This happens to be the formula for density, which can be written as $D = \frac{m}{V}$. Plug in the known values to get $D = \frac{1{,}690}{0.704}$. Divide the fraction on the right side of the equation to get $D \approx 2{,}400.57$. The nearest whole number is 2,401. The correct answer is (C).

9. **B** The question asks for the value of an angle on a figure. Use the Geometry Basic Approach. Redraw the figure on the scratch paper, and add the labels. When a line intersects two parallel lines, two kinds of angles are created: big and small. All the small angles are equal to each other, all the big angles are equal to each other, and any small angle plus any big angle = 180°. Angle q is a small angle, and angle r is a big angle, so they add up to 180. Since $q = 10c - 11$ and $r = 15c + 41$, add

those expressions together and set them equal to 180. The equation becomes $(10c - 11) + (15c + 41) = 180$. Combine like terms on the left side of the equation to get $25c + 30 = 180$. Subtract 30 from both sides of the equation to get $25c = 150$. Divide both sides of the equation by 25 to get $c = 6$. Be careful: the question asks for the value of p, which is a small angle. Plug $c = 6$ into the equation for the other small angle, q, to get $q = 10(6) - 11$, which becomes $q = 60 - 11$, and then $q = 49$. Because p and q are both small angles, p is also 49. The correct answer is (B).

10. **–35/63, –5/9, –0.555 –0.556, –.5555, or –.5556**

The question asks for a value given an equation. A linear equation has infinitely many solutions when the x-terms are the same and the constants are the same. The question asks for the value of q, which is not part of an x-term, so focus on the constants and ignore the x-terms. Distribute on the left side of the equation to get $-7q = \frac{35}{9}$. Divide both sides of this equation by –7 to get $q = \frac{35}{(9)(-7)}$, or $q = -\frac{35}{63}$. When the answer is negative, there is space in the fill-in box for six characters, including the negative sign. This fraction fits, so there is no need to reduce it, although the reduced form will also be accepted as correct. Decimal forms, such as –0.555 or –.5556, will also be accepted. The correct answer is $-\frac{35}{63}$ and equivalent forms.

11. **837** The question asks for a new value after two changes to an initial value. Start by finding the number of unique visitors after the initial 25% decrease. Translate 25% as $\frac{25}{100}$ and multiply by the previous average of 620 unique visitors each day to get $\frac{25}{100}(620) = 155$. The number of unique visitors decreased by 25%, so the new number is $620 - 155 = 465$ unique visitors each day. Next, find 180% of this new number. Translate 180% as $\frac{180}{100}$ and multiply it by 465 to get $\frac{180}{100}(465) = 837$ unique visitors each day during the promotion. The correct answer is 837.

12. **B** The question asks for the value of a percent decrease given a function that represents a specific situation. The value of the function is decreasing by a certain percent, so this question is about exponential decay. Write down the growth and decay formula: *final amount* = (*original amount*)$(1 \pm rate)^{number\ of\ changes}$. The *number of changes* is given in terms of hours, but the question asks about the increase *every 75 minutes*. There are 60 minutes in 1 hour, so set up a proportion: $\frac{60 \text{ minutes}}{1 \text{ hour}} = \frac{75 \text{ minutes}}{h \text{ hours}}$. Cross-multiply to get $(1)(75) = (60)(h)$, or $75 = 60h$. Divide both sides of the equation by 60 to get $\frac{75}{60} = h$. Reduce the fraction to get $\frac{5}{4} = h$. Now, plug in

$\frac{5}{4}$ for h in the function to get $M(h) = 302(0.87)^{\left(\frac{4}{5}\right)\left(\frac{5}{4}\right)}$, which becomes $M(h) = 302(0.87)^1$. The amount of the isotope is decreasing once, so $0.87 = 1 - rate$. Add *rate* to both sides of the equation to get $rate + 0.87 = 1$, and then subtract 0.87 from both sides of the equation to get $rate = 0.13$. The question asks for $d\%$, which is the rate as a percentage, so multiply 0.13 by 100 to get 13%. The correct answer is (B).

13. **13** The question asks for the mean, or average, of a data set. For averages, use the formula $T = AN$, in which T is the *Total*, A is the *Average*, and N is the *Number of things*. First, apply this formula to group X, in which there are 40 packages with a mean, or average, mass of 24 kg. In group X, $N = 40$ and $A = 24$. The average formula becomes $T = (40)(24)$, or $T = 960$ kg. Now do the same for group Y, in which there are 110 packages with a mean, or average, mass of 9 kg. In group Y, $N = 110$ and $A = 9$. The average formula becomes $T = (110)(9)$, or $T = 990$ kg. Now calculate the average of all 150 packages. The number of packages combined is given as 150, and the total of the masses of all of the packages is $960 + 990 = 1{,}950$ kg. Therefore, $N = 150$ and $T = 1{,}950$. The average formula becomes $1{,}950 = (A)(150)$. Divide both sides of the equation by 150 to get $13 = A$. The correct answer is 13.

14. **A** The question asks for an expression that must be an integer. The question provides a quadratic in both standard form, which is $ax^2 + bx + c$, and factored form, which is $a(x - m)(x - n)$. Use FOIL to expand the factored form quadratic into standard form: $(px - q)(x - r) = px^2 - prx - qx + qr$. Combine the middle terms to get $px^2 - (pr + q)x + qr$. Now set this equal to the standard form expression, $11x^2 - kx + 63$, and match up terms. It might make things clearer to write the two expressions above each other:

$$11x^2 - kx + 63$$

$$px^2 - (pr + q)x + qr$$

Therefore, $p = 11$, $(pr + q) = k$, and $qr = 63$. Examine the answer choices to see if any answers can be eliminated quickly. Eliminate (B) because $p = 11$ and $\frac{63}{11}$ is not an integer. Since $qr = 63$, $q = \frac{63}{r}$. The question states that q is an integer, so any value that is equivalent to q will also be an integer. Thus, $\frac{63}{r}$ must be an integer. The correct answer is (A).

15. **108** The question asks for the least possible value that is greater than a constant in a quadratic equation. To determine when a quadratic equation has exactly two real solutions, use the discriminant. The discriminant is the part of the quadratic formula under the square root sign and is written as $D = b^2 - 4ac$. When the discriminant is positive, the quadratic has exactly two real solutions; when the discriminant is 0, the quadratic has exactly one real solution; and when the discriminant is negative, the quadratic has no real solutions. Thus, the discriminant of this quadratic must

equal a positive number. Since the quadratic is in standard form, which is $ax^2 + bx + c = 0$, $a = 3$, $b = -36$, and $c = k$. Plug these into the discriminant formula to get $D = (-36)^2 - 4(3)(k)$, or $D = 1{,}296 - 12k$. The discriminant must be greater than 0, so $1{,}296 - 12k > 0$. Add $12k$ to both sides of this inequality to get $1{,}296 > 12k$, then divide both sides of the inequality by 12 to get $108 > k$, or $k < 108$. If $k < 108$ and $k < m$, the value of m can be greater than or equal to 108, or $m \geq 108$. The correct answer is 108.

16. **D** The question asks which answer correctly compares the data represented by a dot plot to the data from a related data set. Range is easy to calculate, if necessary, so start there. Subtracting 8 from each value will not change the range because the greatest value and the least value will both decrease by 8, which means the difference between them will be the same in data set S as it is in data set R. Eliminate (A) and (B) because they say that the ranges are different, not equal. Mean is a measure of center, and the center will change when the values change. Subtracting 8 from every value will make the mean less, so the mean of data set S is less than the mean of data set R. Eliminate (C) because it says that the two means are equal. The correct answer is (D).

17. **A** The question asks for the equation that defines a function. The question asks about function h, which is transformed, or translated, from the graph of function h. When a graph is transformed, subtracting inside the parentheses shifts the graph to the right. Since $h(x) = g(x - 3)$, the graph of function h is shifted 3 units to the right of the graph of function g. The graph of function g contains a point at $(6, -3)$, so the graph of function h must include a point 3 units to the right at $(9, -3)$. In function notation, $h(x) = y$, so $x = 9$ and $h(x) = -3$. Plug these values into the answer choices and eliminate any answer that doesn't work. Choice (A) becomes $-3 = \frac{-9}{9-6}$, then $-3 = \frac{-9}{3}$, and finally $-3 = -3$. This is true, so keep (A), but check the remaining answers just in case. Choice (B) becomes $-3 = \frac{-9}{9-3}$, then $-3 = \frac{-9}{6}$, and finally $-3 = -\frac{3}{2}$. This is not true, so eliminate (B). Choice (C) becomes $-3 = \frac{-9}{9}$, or $-3 = -1$; eliminate (C). Choice (D) becomes $-3 = \frac{-9(9-3)}{9-3}$, then $-3 = \frac{-9(6)}{6}$, and finally $-3 = -9$; eliminate (D). The correct answer is (A).

18. $-\frac{50}{4}$ **or −12.5**

The question asks for the value of a constant in a system of equations. The equations are both equal to y, so set them equal to each other. The new equation becomes $x^2 - 6x - c = 3.5$. Put the quadratic in standard form, which is $ax^2 + bx + c = 0$, by setting one side equal to 0. Subtract 3.5 from both sides of the equation to get $x^2 - 6x - c - 3.5 = 0$. The question states that *the system has exactly one real solution*, so use the discriminant. The discriminant is the part of the quadratic formula under the square root sign, and it can be written as $D = b^2 - 4ac$. When the discriminant is positive, the quadratic has exactly two real solutions; when the discriminant is 0, the quadratic has exactly one real solution; and when the discriminant is negative, the quadratic has no real solutions. In this case, the quadratic has exactly one real solution, so the discriminant must equal 0.

In this equation, the constant c is part of the c term in the discriminant, so be careful not to confuse the constant c in the original equation with the c in the discriminant. With the equation in standard form, $a = 1$, $b = -6$, and $c = -c - 3.5$. Plug these values into the discriminant formula and set it equal to 0 to get $(-6)^2 - 4(1)(-c - 3.5) = 0$. Simplify the left side of the equation to get $36 + 4c + 14 = 0$, and then $50 + 4c = 0$. Subtract 50 from both sides of the equation to get $4c = -50$, and then divide both sides of the equation by 4 to get $c = -\frac{50}{4}$. This fraction fits in the fill-in box, so there is no need to reduce it, although the reduced form, $-\frac{25}{2}$, will also be accepted as correct. The decimal form, −12.5, will also be accepted. The correct answer is $-\frac{50}{4}$ and equivalent forms.

19. **1** The question asks for the radius of a circle given the equation of the graph in the xy-plane. The equation of a circle in standard form is $(x - h)^2 + (y - k)^2 = r^2$, where (h, k) is the center and r is the radius. However, the equation of this circle is not in standard form, so look for another way to find the radius. One method is to complete the square for both terms in order to put the equation in standard form. A much simpler approach is to enter the equation into the built-in graphing calculator. Zoom in to see that there are several gray dots on the graph, which can be seen if they disappear by clicking on the equation or on the circle itself. Four of the gray dots are where the circle intercepts the x- and y-axes. Click on the other two dots, which are at the top and bottom of the circle and form the diameter. The points are (0.25, −0.75) and (0.25, 1.25). They have the same x-coordinate, so the distance between the two points, or the diameter, is the difference between the y-coordinates: $1.25 - (-0.75) = 2$. Be careful: the diameter of the circle is 2, but the question asks for the radius. The radius of a circle is half of the diameter, so the radius is 1. The correct answer is 1.

20. **B** The question asks for the value of a constant that is part of the product of the solutions to a quadratic equation. It takes a lot of algebra to answer this question, but a shortcut is to recall that, when a quadratic is in standard form, $ax^2 + bx + c$, the product of the solutions is $\frac{c}{a}$. In the given quadratic, $a = 18$ and $c = -mn$, so the product of the solutions is $\frac{-mn}{18}$. The question states that the product of the solutions is kmn, so set the two ways to represent the product of the solutions equal to each other to get $\frac{-mn}{18} = kmn$. Multiply both sides of the equation by 18 to get $-mn = 18kmn$, then divide both sides of the equation by mn to get $-1 = 18k$. Finally, divide both sides of the equation by 18 to get $-\frac{1}{18} = k$. The correct answer is (B).

21. **A** The question asks for the value of an expression with three constants in a quadratic equation. The question states that the vertex of the parabola is at (–1, 4), and that the parabola does not intersect the x-axis. Since the y-coordinate of the vertex is positive and the parabola does not intersect the x-axis, the parabola must open upwards. The vertex of a parabola is expressed as (h, k). Use this information to rewrite the parabola in vertex form, which is $y = a(x - h)^2 + k$. Plug in the values for h and k from the vertex to get $y = a(x + 1)^2 + 4$. Expand $(x + 1)^2$ using FOIL to get $y = a(x^2 + 2x + 1) + 4$. Next, distribute the a to get $y = ax^2 + 2ax + a + 4$. Finally, since this vertex form of the parabola is equal to the given standard form of the same parabola, set them equal to each other: $ax^2 + 2ax + a + 4 = ax^2 + bx + c$. Write the two equations above each other to see the matching terms more clearly:

$$ax^2 + 2ax + a + 4$$

$$ax^2 + bx + c$$

Given this, the ax^2 terms cancel, $2a = b$ and $a + 4 = c$. Thus, $a - b - c$ becomes $a - 2a - (a + 4)$. Combine like terms to get $-2a - 4$.

Since the parabola opens upwards, the value of a must be positive. Since the question asks for a specific value, and the answers contain numbers in increasing order, plug in the answers. Rewrite the answer choices on the scratch paper and label them as "$-2a - 4$." Next, start with a number in the middle and try (B), –4. The equation becomes $-2a - 4 = -4$. Add $2a$ to both sides of the equation to get $-4 = 2a - 4$, and then add 4 to both sides of the equation to get $0 = 2a$. Finally, divide both sides of the equation by 2 to get $0 = a$. This is not positive, so eliminate (B). The result was close to being a negative number, so try (A), –5, next. The equation becomes $-2a - 4 = -5$. Add $2a$ to both sides of the equation to get $-4 = 2a - 5$, and then add 5 to both sides of the equation to get $1 = 2a$. Finally, divide both sides of the equation by 2 to get $\frac{1}{2} = a$. This is positive, so stop here. The correct answer is (A).

22. **C** The question asks for a measurement of a geometric figure. Use the Geometry Basic Approach. Because the surface area of a 3-dimensional figure is the sum of the areas of its faces, draw three rectangles of different sizes to represent the faces of the rectangular solid. Label the height of 50 on two of the rectangles. Since the question asks for a specific value and the answers contain numbers in increasing order, plug in the answers. Rewrite the answer choices on the scratch paper and label them as "*side length of base.*" Next, start with a number in the middle and try (B), 6. Label the remaining sides lengths of the rectangles as 6. The figures should now look something like this:

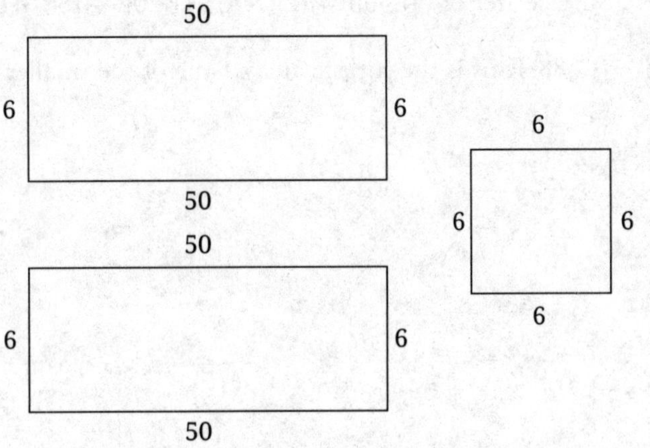

Use the formula for the area of a rectangle, $A = lw$, to find the area of each face. One 6×50 face has an area of 300, and one 6×6 face has an area of 36. There are 4 faces with an area of 300 and 2 faces with an area of 36 for a surface area of $(4)(300) + (2)(36) = 1,200 + 72 = 1,272$. Thus, $S = 1,272$.

If the two prisms were cut into two identical prisms parallel to the square base, the resulting shapes would each be a shorter rectangular prism with a height of $\frac{50}{2} = 25$ and a square base with a side length of 6. Perform the same calculations to find the surface area of one of the smaller prisms. One 6×25 face has an area of 150, and one 6×6 face has an area of 36. There are 4 faces with an area of 150 and 2 faces with an area of 36 for a surface area of $(4)(150) + (2)(36) = 600 + 72 = 672$. The question states that *each resulting prism has a surface area of* $\frac{31}{56}S$, so plug in 1,272 for S. The result is $\frac{31}{56}(1,272) \approx 704$. This does not match the surface area of one of the smaller prisms, so eliminate (B).

It might be difficult to determine whether a larger or smaller number is needed, so pick a direction and try (C), 12. The dimensions of the original single prism are now 50 × 12 × 12. There are four faces with an area of (50)(12) = 600 and two faces with an area of (12)(12) = 144 for a surface area of (4)(600) + (2)(144) = 2,400 + 288 = 2,688. The dimensions of one of the smaller prisms are now 25 × 12 × 12. There are four faces with an area of (25)(12) = 300 and two faces with an area of (12)(12) = 144 for a surface area of (4)(300) + (2)(144) = 1,200 + 188 = 1,488. Plug in 2,688 for S to get $\frac{31}{56}(2{,}688) = 1{,}488$. This is the surface area of one of the smaller prisms, so stop here. The correct answer is (C).

Chapter 4
Cracking the Digital SAT: Basic Principles

The first step to cracking the Digital SAT is knowing how best to approach the test. The Digital SAT is not like many of the tests you've taken in school, so you need to learn to look at it in a different way. This chapter provides and explains test-taking strategies that will immediately improve your score before you spend time working on the actual test content. Make sure you fully understand these concepts before moving on to Part II. Good luck!

BASIC PRINCIPLES OF CRACKING THE TEST

What College Board Does Well

The folks at College Board have been writing standardized tests for a long time. Even though the test format is new for the Digital SAT, the concepts tested are the same, so the test-writers still know how students will approach the questions. They know how you'll attempt certain questions, what sort of mistakes you'll probably make, and even what answer you'll be most likely to pick. Freaky, isn't it?

However, this strength is also a weakness. Because the test is standardized, the Digital SAT asks the same types of questions over and over again. Sure, the numbers or the words might change, but the basics don't. With enough practice, you can learn to think like the test-writers. But try to use your powers for good, okay?

The Digital SAT Isn't School

Our job isn't to teach you math or English—leave that to your super smart school teachers. Instead, we're going to teach you what the Digital SAT is and how to crack it. You'll soon see that the Digital SAT involves a very different skill set from the one you use in school.

Be warned that some of the approaches we're going to show you may seem counterintuitive or unnatural. Some of these strategies may be very different from the way you learned to approach similar questions in school, but trust us! Try tackling the questions using our techniques, and keep practicing until they become easier. When you do this, you'll see a real improvement in your score.

TAKE THE EASY TEST FIRST

Within a section, each question counts toward your score. There will inevitably be questions you are great at and questions you don't like. The beauty of the Digital SAT is that you can answer questions in any order you like. The question you can nail in 25 seconds may be worth just as much as the question that will torture you for minutes on end. Why should you spend 4 or 5 minutes on one question when you can answer two or three questions that are easier for you in the same amount of time? To maximize your score, leave the questions you don't like for last. That way, if you do run out of time, at least you've gotten a chance to answer all the questions that you find easiest.

You can think of this as taking the easy test first. Skip early and skip often. Doing so will result in two passes through an individual module. On the first pass, cherry-pick. Answer the questions you like. Get all of those easy points in the bank before time starts running short. Nearly everyone at some point starts to feel the pressure of the clock as time starts running low. This is often when mistakes happen. Leave those difficult, time-consuming questions for the end of the test. If you run out of time or make some mistakes at that point, it won't matter as much because these are questions that you are less likely to get right anyway. Focus your time where you feel confident you are likely to score points.

Embrace Your POOD

When you take the easy test first, you are using your POOD, or **Personal Order of Difficulty**. The Digital SAT will put questions in rough order of difficulty by content domain on the Reading and Writing section and overall on the Math section. But this Order of Difficulty (OOD) is only what College Board thinks about the question levels, not how you will do on them. And different people do well on different types of questions. We believe it is essential that you identify the questions that you find easy or hard and that you work the test in a way most suitable to your goals and strengths. The way this works may differ in the Reading and Writing section and the Math section, but we'll give you the tools to establish your POOD.

Mark and Move On

On your first pass through a section, you will likely see questions that strike you as too hard or too time-consuming. If you think they are worth coming back to in the second pass, use the Mark for Review tool to add a little flag next to the question. Then keep on moving until you find a question that better suits your POOD.

Sometimes, though, a question that seems easy at first may turn out to be more troublesome than it appeared. If you get stuck on a question, don't keep working on it. Mark it and move on to do more questions. Only once you've conquered all the questions in your POOD should you come back and retry a question. Often, given some distance from the question, you can come back to it with fresh eyes and get the right answer. If you encounter more trouble, though, move on again. Find another question in the module to distract your brain whenever you get stuck.

You can see the marked questions at a glance both at the end of the module and by opening the module overview at any time. This will allow you to quickly find the ones you want to work on after you've done all the questions you know you can do quickly and accurately.

As you see a question on the screen, the testing app tells you where you are in the module. The question navigation bar is a black bar at the bottom of the screen. Clicking it opens the Review tool, which gives you an overview of the module that will look something like this.

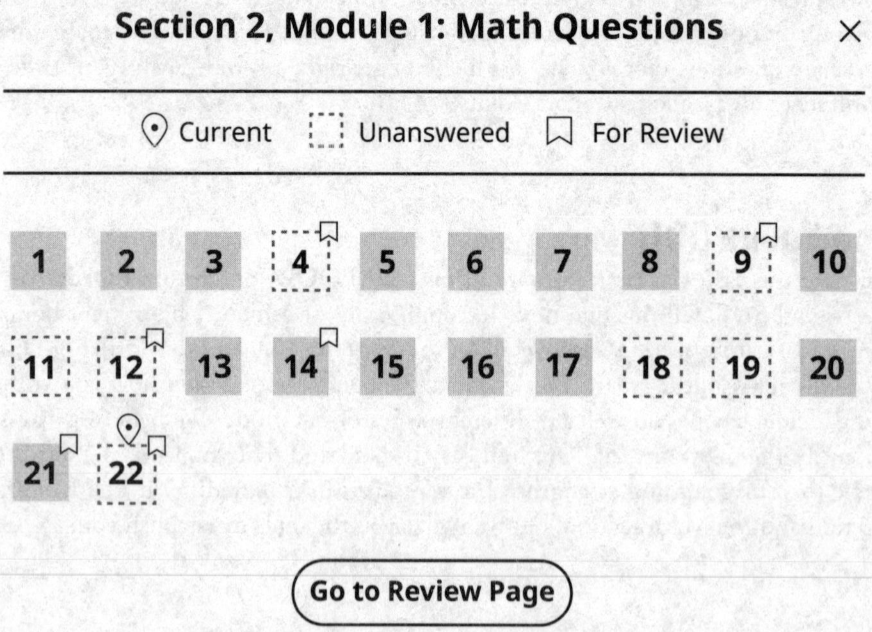

Navigating around a section is easy from here. Simply click on a question, and you will go directly to that question. This opens up a whole new realm of strategic opportunities for the savvy test-taker. It also allows you to quickly see any questions that remain unanswered in the final minutes so that you can enter answers for them.

Let's say the example above is your section. At this point, you have seen all 22 questions in the module. Questions 11, 18, and 19 are unanswered and haven't been marked. These are questions that you likely skipped because they looked very difficult and/or time-consuming, and you should do them only at the very end if there is any time left. Then, there are 5 marked questions, some of which have been answered. You might have marked these because you got an answer but weren't sure it was right or because you started the question but then got stuck. After you've taken the easy test, you should go back to the marked questions and attempt to get as many of them right as you can, starting with the easiest ones or the ones that are closest to being finished. Remember to unmark a question once you've finalized your answer.

Keep an eye on the timer. When there is a minute left, go back to any of your unanswered questions and enter a guess, even a random one if necessary.

Navigating the Test Modules

- In your first pass, only do questions that you think you can do quickly and accurately.
- If you start a question and get stuck, mark it and move on.
- If you think a question is a good one to do later, mark it to easily find it again.
- If you see a question that looks tough but may be in your POOD, leave it blank.
- If you see a question that you know you *never* want to tackle, fill in an answer and move on.
- In your second pass, do the marked questions that seem most suited to your POOD. Then do any unanswered questions you think are worth trying.
- If you decide to skip any questions in the second pass, fill in an answer and move on.
- In the last minute or two, use the Review tool to ensure that every question has been answered.

Just be careful when using the Review Page instead of accessing the overview from the question navigation bar. If you are on that page and click Next, it will end the module. You will not be asked if you are sure you want to submit your answers and move on. So, make sure to only click Next from the Review Page if all your answers have been entered.

Guessing on the Digital SAT

You may be wondering why we're telling you to enter answers to some questions you haven't even fully read. No matter how much you practice, you still may run into a question that you don't know how to answer no matter how many times you look at it. Or, you may look at a question with an incredibly long or difficult-looking passage and decide it's not worth your time and energy.

No Wrong-Answer Penalty!
You will NOT be penalized on the Digital SAT for any wrong answers. This means you should always guess rather than leaving a question blank, even if this means choosing an answer at random.

When you confront a question like this, try to eliminate any answer choice you can, but make sure to guess. There is no penalty for incorrect answers on the Digital SAT. As a result, it's better to guess than it is to leave a question blank. At least by guessing, you stand a chance at getting lucky and guessing correctly.

So, what should you guess? It doesn't really matter! There is a roughly equal distribution of answers on each test, so just click on one of the answers and keep going.

Pace Yourself

By now, we've talked a lot about skipping some questions. You may think you need to work to answer every question to get a good score on the Digital SAT. The truth is, rushing through to try to do every question can lead to careless mistakes, causing you to lose points. You are much better off focusing your attention fully on the questions in your POOD and only answering the harder or more time-consuming ones after you've built up those easier points. As you improve, you can aim to answer more questions in each module and guess on fewer. Unless you're currently scoring in the 700+ range on the two sections, you shouldn't be working all the questions.

Slow down, score more. You're not scored on *how many questions you do.*
You're scored on *how many questions you answer correctly.*
Doing fewer questions can mean more correct answers overall!

Now that you know how to navigate the modules to find questions in your POOD, let's talk about some strategies to use on the questions as you work through them.

CRACKING MULTIPLE-CHOICE QUESTIONS

What is the capital of Azerbaijan?

Give up?

Unless you spend your spare time studying an atlas or live in that region of the world, you may not know Azerbaijan's capital. If this question came up on a test, you'd have to skip it, wouldn't you? Well, maybe not. To find out if you can figure out the answer anyway, let's turn this question into a multiple-choice question—just like the majority of questions you'll find on the Digital SAT.

1 Mark for Review

What is the capital of Azerbaijan?

(A) Washington, D.C.

(B) Paris

(C) London

(D) Baku

The question doesn't seem that hard anymore, does it? Of course, we made our example extremely easy. (By the way, there won't actually be any questions about geography on the Digital SAT.) But you'd be surprised by how many people give up on Digital SAT questions that aren't much more difficult than this one just because they don't know the correct answer right off the top of their heads. "Capital of Azerbaijan? Oh, no! I've never heard of Azerbaijan!"

These students don't stop to think that they might be able to find the correct answer simply by eliminating all of the answer choices they know are wrong.

You Already Know Almost All of the Answers

All but a handful of the questions on the Digital SAT are multiple-choice questions, and every multiple-choice question has four answer choices. One of those choices, and only one, will be the correct answer to the question. You don't have to come up with the answer from scratch. You just have to identify it.

How will you do that?

Look for the Wrong Answers Instead of the Right Ones

Why? Because wrong answers are usually easier to find than the right ones. After all, there are more of them! Remember the question about Azerbaijan? Even though you didn't know the answer off the top of your head, you easily figured it out by eliminating the three obviously incorrect choices.

You looked for wrong answers first.

In other words, you used Process of Elimination, which we'll call POE for short. This is an extremely important concept, one we'll come back to again and again. It's one of the keys to improving your Digital SAT score. When you finish reading this book, you will be able to use POE to answer many questions that you may not understand.

The great artist Michelangelo once said that when he looked at a block of marble, he could see a statue inside. All he had to do to make a sculpture was to chip away everything that wasn't part of it. You should approach difficult multiple-choice questions on the Digital SAT in the same way, by "chipping away" the answers that are not correct. By first eliminating the most obviously incorrect choices on difficult questions, you will be able to focus your attention on the few choices that remain.

PROCESS OF ELIMINATION (POE)

There won't be many questions on the Digital SAT in which incorrect choices will be as easy to eliminate as they were on the Azerbaijan question. But if you read this book carefully, you'll learn how to eliminate at least one choice on almost any Digital SAT multiple-choice question, if not two or even three choices.

What good is it to eliminate just one or two choices on a four-choice Digital SAT question?

Plenty. In fact, for most students, it's an important key to earning higher scores. For every answer that you confidently eliminate, you increase the odds of selecting the correct answer, even on harder questions. Here's another example:

2 Mark for Review

What is the capital of Qatar?

Ⓐ Paris

Ⓑ Dukhan

Ⓒ Tokyo

Ⓓ Doha

On this question, you'll almost certainly be able to eliminate two of the four choices by using POE. That means you're still not sure of the answer. You know that the capital of Qatar has to be either Doha or Dukhan, but you don't know which. So just pick one and move on! You've already improved your chances of getting it right from 25% to 50%.

The Answer Eliminator Tool

The Digital SAT Bluebook app has a great tool to help you keep track of your POE. It is called the Answer Eliminator, and it crosses off answers for you right on the screen. To use it, click the box on the right side of the gray bar that has "ABC" with a slash through the letters. A new set of letters will appear to the right of each answer, and clicking on one crosses off the corresponding answer.

Here is what our Qatar question would look like after eliminating (A) and (C).

2 Mark for Review

What is the capital of Qatar?

~~(A) Paris~~

(B) Dukhan

~~(C) Tokyo~~

(D) Doha

This tool is a great way to keep track of your thoughts on each answer and see which ones remain after using POE. And if you decide to mark this question to come back to it, your eliminated answers will still be crossed off when you return.

Try It Out!
When you take a practice test in your online Student Tools, use that opportunity to try out all the tools. Being familiar and comfortable with these tools on test day will give you a real leg up, as you won't have to waste time during the test getting used to them.

The Annotate Tool

But what if you want to remember something specific about the question or the remaining answers? In the Reading and Writing section, there is a tool for that as well. If you highlight some text on the screen, you can then click the Annotate button to add a notation to that text. Again, this will be saved as you move through the module, so it will still be there if you come back to a question. We'll give you more advice in the coming chapters on how to make use of this great tool.

However, there are some limitations to the Annotate tool. You cannot annotate text on figures or from the answer choices, so you would have to leave yourself a note on the question stem or the passage text. Also, this tool is not available in the Math section at all.

Scratch Paper

This brings us to the final tool that may help you stay organized on the Digital SAT. When you arrive at the testing center, you will be given three pages of scratch paper to use. If you find that you have trouble making annotations in the Reading and Writing section or you have calculations to do in the Math section, your scratch paper is there for you.

While you can use the Answer Eliminator tool to cross off answers you know are wrong, you may need a more sophisticated way to track what you think of certain answers to narrow down choices. In those cases, write the question number and answer letters on your scratch paper and use the following notations to help you make the best possible guess.

✔ Put a check mark next to an answer that seems correct.

~ Put a squiggle next to an answer that seems like it could work but you're not sure.

? Put a question mark next to an answer you don't understand.

~~A~~ Cross out the letter of any answer choice you KNOW is wrong.

You can always come up with your own system. Just make sure you are consistent. Do your best to keep your scratch paper neat and organized. If you do come back to a question later, you want to be able to easily find your work. We'll give you more tips for using your scratch paper in the following lessons.

Double-Check

By now, you have learned strategies for navigating the modules of the Digital SAT and for dealing with the questions as you work them. You've also seen a bit of information about the tools at your disposal and how to use them. All these things should help you get an answer to the questions you work on, but get in the habit of double-checking before you click on your final answer choice. You probably won't have time to go back to a question that you have already finished, so it's best to ensure that you've answered as you intend to the first time.

The only way to reliably avoid careless errors is to adopt habits that make them less likely to occur. Always check to see that you've transcribed information correctly to your scratch paper. Always read the problem carefully and note any important parts that you might forget later. Always check your calculations. And always read the question one last time before selecting your answer. By training yourself to avoid careless errors, you will increase your score.

Summary

- Take the easy test first. Work carefully on questions you know how to do to make sure you get them right.
- Use the Mark for Review tool to flag questions you want to come back to later.
- There are bound to be at least a few questions you simply don't get to or ones on which you find it difficult to eliminate even one answer choice. When this happens, just enter an answer and move on.
- There's no guessing penalty on the Digital SAT, so it's best to guess rather than leave a question blank.
- When you don't know the right answer to a multiple-choice question, look for wrong answers instead. They're usually easier to find.
- When you find a wrong answer, use the Answer Eliminator tool to cross it off on the screen. In other words, use Process of Elimination, or POE.
- Use the Annotate tool to leave notes for yourself on Reading and Writing questions as needed.
- Use your scratch paper for more complex POE or other notations and calculations. Keep your work neat and organized, with a question number next to every note.
- Get into the habit of double-checking your work to avoid careless errors as much as possible.
- Make the test your own. When you can work the test to suit your strengths (and use our strategies to overcome any weaknesses), you'll be on your way to a higher score.

Part II
How to Crack the Reading and Writing Section

Chapter 5
Reading and Writing Introduction

Now that you've learned some general strategies for the Digital SAT and taken and analyzed your first test, it is time to dive into some content chapters. This chapter will introduce you to the Reading and Writing (RW) section of the Digital SAT.

FIND YOUR STRENGTHS AND WEAKNESSES

As you may recall from the Introduction, your Digital SAT is going to have two Reading and Writing modules, each consisting of 27 questions. Of those 54 total verbal questions, 25–33 will be Reading questions and 19–31 will be Writing questions. You'll have 32 minutes for each module, which gives you a little more than a minute for each question.

While College Board combines the topics of Reading and Writing into the same section, you may have recognized that they really represent two different sets of skills. The Reading questions ask you to either answer a question about a passage you have read (such as what its main idea is or why the author included a certain piece of information) or choose an answer that completes the passage based on the inferences that can be made. On the other hand, the Writing questions will ask you to choose the best construction of a sentence based on such aspects as punctuation, grammar, and style. These questions will also ask you to connect ideas with transitions or to fit certain rhetorical goals.

This distinction is important because you may find that you are stronger at Reading or stronger at Writing. Recognizing your strengths and weaknesses will help you follow POOD most effectively, and as you practice it will allow you to identify what areas you need to focus on during your study time.

READING, RULES, AND RHETORIC QUESTIONS

We think you'll find it most helpful to think of each Reading and Writing module as having three parts, displayed visually below.

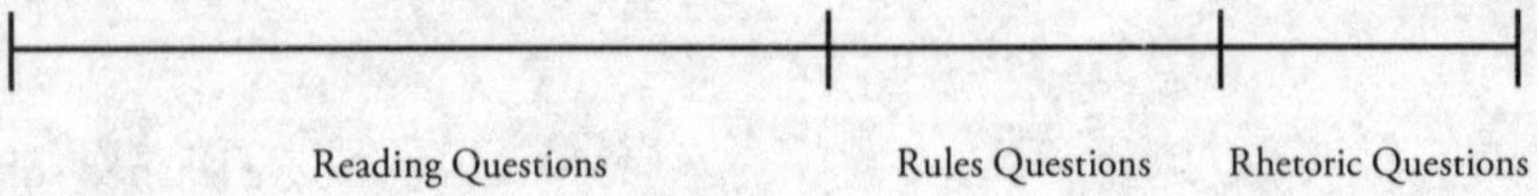

Reading actually has two parts according to College Board, but there isn't a strong difference in the types of questions you'll see in both parts, so we don't think you need to notice when the section switches.

This is the same order and rough proportion of questions you will see in each module. If you are stronger or faster at Writing questions, you may find that it makes more sense for you to start about halfway through the section where those questions start. Of course, if Reading questions are easier for you, it's fine to start at the beginning of the module. Either way, it's helpful to be able to recognize these three categories of questions so that you'll notice when the module switches from one to the next and be able to apply the right set of steps to each question type. Let's take a look at the characteristics of each category.

Reading Questions

Any question with text in the form of a poem or a work of fiction is going to be in the Reading portion. The same is true for dual texts (which have a Text 1 and a Text 2), passages that involve graphs, and questions that ask you to fill in the blank with the most appropriate word. The rest of the Reading questions will generally ask you for the meaning or purpose of some or all of the passage.

Rules Questions

The questions that College Board calls Standard English Conventions can be more simply called Rules questions. It should be easy to spot when the module switches from Reading questions to Rules questions. That's because all Rules questions ask the same thing: *Which choice completes the text so that it conforms to the conventions of Standard English?* Only Rules questions ask this, so if you're planning to start with the Rules questions, you can skip to about the middle of the section and click ahead until you see the first one with that question. It's worth noting that Rules questions will be some of the fastest ones for many students, as you typically only need to read a single sentence and will be tested on basic punctuation and grammar rules rather than comprehension.

Rhetoric Questions

Once again, it should be easy to spot when the Rules questions end. That's because the rest of the questions, Rhetoric questions, will not ask the standard question you saw above for Rules questions. If you want to start with these questions, go about three-quarters of the way into the section and continue until you stop seeing the questions about the conventions of Standard English. Furthermore, Rhetoric questions come in only two formats. The first involves transition words and the second has bullet points instead of a passage. So, these should be relatively easy to identify by looking for those two unique attributes, but you will learn more about these distinctions in later chapters.

As you prepare for the Digital SAT, try to identify which of these three categories makes sense for you to begin with. It's best to start with the category in which you will be able to get the questions right quickly and easily.

START WITH THE QUESTION

As you saw earlier in this introduction, it's the question, rather than the passage, that will give you a clue as to what category of question you are dealing with. Once you've established that, you'll be able to execute the appropriate strategy for that specific type of question. To that end, we've developed a basic approach for all Reading and Writing questions:

Reading and Writing Basic Approach

1. Read the question.
2. Identify the question type.
3. Follow the basic approach for that question type.

As we discussed earlier, you are free (and encouraged!) to start with the types of questions at which you excel and to leave for last the ones you struggle with most or that you expect to take the most time. For each question, skip over the passage initially and go straight to the question. That will help you to confirm whether it is a Reading question, Rules question, or Rhetoric question. In some cases, such as with most Reading questions, reading the question first will also give you an idea of what you need to find in the passage, which will allow you to do double duty as you read: you can already start to look out for what the question will be asking you about as you read the passage.

In the chapters that follow, we'll show you our basic approach for each type of question that we expect you to see on the Reading and Writing section. Once you have learned and practiced these approaches, you'll know exactly what to do once you identify the type of question you are looking at. It's worth noting that we have put the verbal chapters in the same order that we expect the questions to be in for both modules of the Reading and Writing section, so you can use them as a guide for approximately where each question type will appear. Let's dive in!

Chapter 6
The Reading Questions

Reading questions will account for just over half of the 54 Reading and Writing questions and will always appear before the Writing questions in each of the two RW modules. The Reading questions will ask you to perform many different, and of course highly enjoyable, tasks, including selecting the best vocabulary word to fill in a blank, understanding the function of a portion of the passage, comparing two passages, finding the main idea of a passage, determining which answer would best support an argument, and completing the passage based on data from tables and graphs. Each passage will range from 25 to 150 words and be accompanied by just a single question, so efficiency will be of the essence. The purpose of this chapter is to introduce you to how the Reading and Writing Basic Approach can be adapted to each of the Reading question types. This will help you streamline how you take the test and keep you focused on what information you need in order to get as many points as you can. Not many people would call the Reading questions overly fun, but this chapter will teach you how to take control of the section and handle it on your own terms.

SAT READING: CRACKING THE PASSAGES

You read every day. From street signs to text messages to the back of the cereal box, you spend a good part of your day recognizing written words. So, this test should be pretty easy, right?

Unfortunately, reading on the Digital SAT is different from reading in real life. In real life, you read *passively*. Your eyes go over the words, the words go into your brain, and some stick and some don't. On the Digital SAT, you have to read *actively*, which means trying to find specific information to answer specific questions. Once you've found the information you need, you have to understand what it's actually saying.

Reading on the Digital SAT is also very different from the reading you do in school. In English class, you are often asked to give your own opinion and support it with evidence from a passage. You might have to explain how Scout Finch and Boo Radley in *To Kill a Mockingbird* are, metaphorically speaking, mockingbirds. Or you might be asked to explain who is actually responsible for the tragedies in *Romeo and Juliet.* On the Digital SAT, however, there is no opinion. You don't have the opportunity to justify why your answer is the right one. That means there is only *one* right answer, and your job is to find it. It's the weirdest scavenger hunt ever.

Let's start with the instructions for the Reading and Writing (RW) module.

DIRECTIONS

The questions in this section address a number of important reading and writing skills. Each question includes one or more passages, which may include a table or graph. Read each passage and question carefully, and then choose the best answer to the question based on the passage(s).

All questions in the section are multiple-choice with four answer choices. Each question has a single best answer.

Great news! This is an open-book test. Notice the directions say *based on the passage(s).* This means that you are NOT being tested on whether you have read, studied, and become an expert on African folklore, *The Great Gatsby*, or your biology textbook. All the test-writers care about is whether or not you can read a passage and understand it well enough to correctly answer a question about it. Unlike the Math modules and the Writing questions, there are no formulas to memorize or comma rules to learn for the Reading questions. You just need to know how to approach the passage(s), questions, and answer choices in a way that maximizes your accuracy and efficiency. It's all about the text of the passage!

Your Mission:

Identify what you are being asked to do for each question and locate the answer or support in the passage as efficiently as possible.

POOD and the Reading Questions

You will get one question with its passage (or, occasionally, with two passages) on screen at a time. While it's tempting to do the questions in the order they appear, you will sometimes be confronted with a question or passage that seems difficult or confusing to you for one reason or another. In that situation, skip the question for now or mark and move on if you already started working on it and think you'll be able to get it later. You can always come back to any questions you skipped or marked later after you've tackled every question you knew how to do for certain. In short, the sooner you move on from a frustrating, difficult question, the more time you have to slow down and get many other questions correct.

Consider the following:

- **Question Type:** Throughout the Reading chapters, you'll learn how to identify the different types of questions and you'll learn the order they come in. Determine which ones will be fastest and easiest for you, and start with those. If you're not sure what question types will be easiest for you, pay attention to how you do on the various question types as you do the practice tests and drills in this book.

- **Literature:** Fictional passages will contain a blurb that will, at minimum, introduce the author and title. This will help you quickly decide whether or not to do these passages. You'll also spot poems quickly, and your strengths and weaknesses will tell you when to do those.

- **Topic:** You may be able to tell from glancing at the passage whether it is about science, history, the arts, or another topic area. If you have significant topic-based strengths and weaknesses, use that knowledge to decide your POOD.

Don't forget: On any questions that you skip, always fill in a guess!

The Reading Question Types

There are eight different question types on the Reading portion of the RW module, and the good news is that they will always appear in the same set order. Chapters 7 and 8 will teach you the eight question types in depth, but for now, even just knowing their names gives you some insight as to what you'll be looking for or dealing with on each question.

The Eight Reading Question Types

1. Vocabulary	5. Main Idea
2. Purpose	6. Claims
3. Dual Texts	7. Charts
4. Retrieval	8. Conclusions

Soon enough, you'll be an expert on all of these, but for now, let's learn the basic approach you'll use regardless of question type.

Not every question type shows up on every RW module, but you need to prepare for all of them. You won't know which ones will be excluded from your module, and types that don't appear on your first RW module will very likely appear on your second one!

Basic Approach for Reading Questions

1. **Read the Question.** As with all Reading and Writing questions, you need to first understand what you are being asked to do before you dive into any passage.

2. **Identify the Question Type.** Each question has a phrase that indicates a very specific task that you are being asked to accomplish for that question. This also affects how you will adapt the rest of the approach and is a chance to apply your POOD: you may want to mark question types you'd rather deal with later or just fill in answers on question types you'd rather not tackle at all.

3. **Read the Passage(s).** Read the passage(s) thoroughly, keeping the question task in mind. Remember: you are looking for an answer to the question, or at the very least, evidence that can help answer the question. You don't need to memorize, or even understand, every detail!

4. **Highlight What Can Help (and Annotate If Needed).** Within the passage, you'll want to highlight a phrase or sentence that can help answer the question. It could be a direct answer to the question or a piece of information that the question wants you to do something with. On certain question types, such as Vocabulary or Purpose, you'll also make an annotation that will help you nail the correct answer.

5. **Use POE.** Eliminate anything that isn't consistent with what you highlighted and/or annotated. Don't necessarily try to find the right answer immediately, because there is a good chance you won't see anything that you like (and an answer that you like immediately may be a trap). If you can eliminate answers that you know are wrong, though, you'll be closer to the right answer. If you can't eliminate three answers with your highlights and annotation, use the POE criteria (which we'll talk about later in this chapter).

"Where the Money Is"
A reporter once asked notorious thief Willie Sutton why he robbed banks. Legend has it that his answer was, "Because that's where the money is." While reading comprehension is much safer and more productive than larceny, the same principle applies. Concentrate on the questions and answer choices because that's where the points are. The passage is just a place for the test-writers to stash facts and details. You'll find them when you need to.

STEPS OF THE BASIC APPROACH

You might be surprised to see that we don't recommend reading the passage until Step 3 of the Basic Approach. This is part of what we call *active reading*, an essential skill for standardized passages. You shouldn't read the passage until you know exactly what you are trying to find. Said another way, you want to know your destination before you start the journey.

On the following page is a sample passage and question stem for a Purpose question, one of the eight question types we mentioned previously. We've removed the four answer choices so you can focus on learning the steps one piece at a time, but have no fear: you'll deal with them soon enough. Skip over the passage for now and go right into Applying the Steps.

The following text is adapted from J.M. Barrie's 1911 short story "The Inconsiderate Waiter." The narrator, an upper-class gentleman, is describing his waiter, William, at a dining club that the gentleman frequents.

Until William forced his affairs upon me that was all I did know of the private life of waiters, though I have been in the club for twenty years. I was even unaware whether they slept downstairs or had their own homes; nor had I the interest to inquire of other members, nor they the knowledge to inform me. I hold that this sort of people should be fed and clothed and given airing and wives and children, and I subscribe yearly, I believe for these purposes; but to come into closer relation with waiters is bad form; they are club fittings, and William should have kept his distress to himself, or taken it away and patched it up like a rent in one of the chairs.

1 Mark for Review

Which choice best states the main purpose of the text?

APPLYING THE STEPS

STEP 1 Step 1: Read the Question

It may be tempting to dive right into the passage, but if you do so, you are not *reading actively.* Remember that *active* reading requires that you read with a purpose: you need to know what you are looking for in the passage before you read it. Also, slow down and read the task carefully. Each Reading question gives an incredibly specific task, and it's dangerous to assume they all simply want some detail from the passage. Lastly, it's from this step that you will be able to identify the question type, which affects how you are going to adapt the rest of the approach.

Reading Basic Approach
1. Read the Question.

Which choice best states the main purpose of the text?

STEP 2

Step 2: Identify the Question Type

Each Reading question has a word, phrase, or series of phrases that indicates which type of question it is. Each question type has several different formats in which it can be asked, so familiarizing yourself with those formats through these chapters is critical to making you an ace identifier.

For instance, the question above clearly asks for the *main purpose* of the text. If a question says *purpose, overall structure,* or *function,* it's what we call a Purpose question. Once you have finished working through the Purpose Questions lesson, you'll be able to apply the appropriate strategy for this question type. For now, all you need to know is that if a question is asking for a *main purpose,* it's asking why the author wrote the passage.

Reading Basic Approach
1. Read the Question.
2. Identify the Question Type.

The important thing to understand is that answers to Purpose questions, as with all question types, must come—you guessed it—from the passage itself. So, on to the next step!

> **Step 2 and POOD:** Identifying the question type is your first opportunity to use your POOD: if this question type has caused you difficulty in the past, consider Marking for Review or entering a random guess.

STEP 3

Step 3: Read the Passage(s)

With the exception of one question type which we will see a bit later, all Digital SAT question types have exactly one passage attached to each question. If the passage is sourced from an existing novel, short story, or poem, it will have a citation preceding it like the one we see in our example:

> The following text is adapted from J.M. Barrie's 1911 short story "The Inconsiderate Waiter." The narrator, an upper-class gentleman, is describing his waiter, William, at a dining club that the gentleman frequents.

Reading Basic Approach
1. Read the Question.
2. Identify the Question Type.
3. Read the Passage(s).

Start by reading this citation, or blurb, if there is one. It will identify the type of literature you're dealing with and exactly how old it is. Also, College Board will usually provide a sentence of descriptive information because the writers are well aware they are throwing you into the deep end of the unfamiliar story pool. You can use this to gain a small piece of insight before tackling a sometimes-dense piece of literature.

Step 3 and POOD: This is your second opportunity to apply your POOD. If there is a blurb and it references a particularly complex work or old poem that you'll be reading, this could be the right time to mark and move on or even guess with very little time lost.

Then, it's time to read the passage itself. But remember that you want to be an *active* reader. You are not reading the passage for pleasure or because the Digital SAT is so, so fun. You are reading only because it's necessary in order to accomplish the specific task of determining, in this case, *why the author wrote the text,* which means you are looking for both the topic the author wants to discuss and any feelings or motivations the author has regarding that topic.

> Until William forced his affairs upon me that was all I did know of the private life of waiters, though I have been in the club for twenty years. I was even unaware whether they slept downstairs or had their own homes; nor had I the interest to inquire of other members, nor they the knowledge to inform me. I hold that this sort of people should be fed and clothed and given airing and wives and children, and I subscribe yearly, I believe for these purposes; but to come into closer relation with waiters is bad form; they are club fittings, and William should have kept his distress to himself, or taken it away and patched it up like a rent in one of the chairs.

Step 3 and POOD, revisited: This is your third opportunity to apply your POOD. If you are reading the passage and your eyes start to glaze over, you find yourself rereading one particular sentence because it's so involved, or the passage is simply confusing to you, it may be time to mark and move on.

STEP 4 Step 4: Highlight What Can Help (and Annotate If Needed)

As you read the passage, you want to be reading with both your eyes and your mouse. Keep your cursor near the passage or even use it to guide your eyes. The instant you find something that either answers the question directly or helps answer the question, highlight it and click the "Annotate" button in the top-right corner of your screen. In this case, you should identify that the main idea of the passage was to discuss the narrator's changing knowledge of his waiter William's life.

Reading Basic Approach
1. Read the Question.
2. Identify the Question Type.
3. Read the Passage(s).
4. Highlight What Can Help (and Annotate If Needed).

> Until William forced his affairs upon me that was all I did know of the private life of waiters, though I have been in the club for twenty years. I was even unaware whether they slept downstairs or had their own homes; nor had I the interest to inquire of other members, nor they the knowledge to inform me. I hold that this sort of people should be fed and clothed and given airing and wives and children, and I subscribe yearly, I believe for these purposes; but to come into closer relation with waiters is bad form; they are club fittings, and William should have kept his distress to himself, or taken it away and patched it up like a rent in one of the chairs.

This isn't the complete story, however. The narrator here does not just want to inform us of what he used to know about waiters' lives and what he knows now. You also need to highlight any attitude the narrator displays towards this main idea.

> Until William forced his affairs upon me that was all I did know of the private life of waiters, though I have been in the club for twenty years. I was even unaware whether they slept downstairs or had their own homes; nor had I the interest to inquire of other members, nor they the knowledge to inform me. I hold that this sort of people should be fed and clothed and given airing and wives and children, and I subscribe yearly, I believe for these purposes; but to come into closer relation with waiters is bad form; they are club fittings, and William should have kept his distress to himself, or taken it away and patched it up like a rent in one of the chairs.

The negative words *forced, bad form,* and *distress* indicate that the narrator is not at all pleased to know more about his waiter than he did before.

Since you wouldn't actually spend time removing previous highlighting, the final passage looks something like this:

> Until William forced his affairs upon me that was all I did know of the private life of waiters, though I have been in the club for twenty years. I was even unaware whether they slept downstairs or had their own homes; nor had I the interest to inquire of other members, nor they the knowledge to inform me. I hold that this sort of people should be fed and clothed and given airing and wives and children, and I subscribe yearly, I believe for these purposes; but to come into closer relation with waiters is bad form; they are club fittings, and William should have kept his distress to himself, or taken it away and patched it up like a rent in one of the chairs.

Not every question requires this much highlighting, and more than one sentence may point to the main idea of a passage or attitude of an author. You only need to find one of each to handle a Purpose question like this one.

Now, it's time to annotate. Not every question type requires an annotation, but on Purpose questions, it's helpful. Since authors rarely state their purpose directly, it's a great idea to jot down a summary of the main idea and attitude once you've found them. A good purpose annotation for this passage would be:

Highlight Color: ◯ **Underline style:** U

"knows more about waiter now – unhappy about it"

Save **Cancel**

Note how annotations should not be elaborate or particularly long—you don't want to spend too much time effectively rewriting the passage. You want a quick summary that you can compare the answers to in the next step. Nothing you typed in the box is new—it's a direct summary of what you highlighted in the passage.

> **Step 4 and POOD:** Unlike with the other steps, failing to find evidence in a question isn't necessarily a reason to mark and move on. If you understand the passage well but cannot settle on the right evidence in an efficient manner, consider going to the answers and using POE.

STEP 5

Step 5: Use POE

Once you have your highlighting and, for this question type, your annotation, it's time to head to the answers. When looking at the answers, remember to constantly ask this question.

> Is this answer consistent with my highlighting and annotation?
> Yes, no, maybe, or no idea?

Reading Basic Approach

1. Read the Question.
2. Identify the Question Type.
3. Read the Passage(s).
4. Highlight What Can Help (and Annotate If Needed).
5. Use POE.

It's not a matter of an answer sounding good or you liking an answer. Nor is it a good idea to ask whether the answer "matches the passage": while the ideas between passage and answer will agree, the words will often be very different, as the person who wrote the passage and the person who wrote the question and answers may not be the same person and may not write the same way. You took the time in

Steps 2–4 to figure out what you were being asked and to find an answer to that question: use the tool you created for yourself and don't undersell your own abilities right at the end of the task. Let's see those answers one at a time.

Ⓐ To define a distinction between William and the other waiters at the dining club

Is this answer consistent with your highlighting and annotation? No, it's not. The words "William," "waiters," and "dining club" are all what we called **Recycled Language**—these words are grabbed directly from the passage and thrown into an answer but not used the same way the passage used them. These answers may trap students who only seek to match words on the Digital SAT.

In this case, no *distinction* between William and the other waiters at the dining club is given in the passage. It may be tempting to say that because the narrator knows something about William that he would rather not know, that's a distinction. However, the passage would need to actually say that William is different from other waiters somehow—you should not need to apply outside steps of logic to make connections between the passage and the answer choice.

At this point, we'd strike out (A) using the Answer Eliminator tool and move on to the next answer.

Ⓑ To examine the type of service that the narrator most highly values

Is this answer consistent with your highlighting and annotation? No, it's not. All you know from the passage is that the narrator wants waiters to wait on him and doesn't want to know about their private lives. The passage offers no indication as to what type of service the narrator *most highly values*, which is what we call **Extreme Language**. These traps typically include a word or phrase beyond what the passage can support.

Believe it or not, *most highly values* can be eliminated for another reason! Valuing something is a positive emotion; it means we hold an idea or person in certain esteem and are grateful for it. However, the emotions you highlighted in the passage (*forced, distress, bad form*) were entirely negative. So, the emotions presented in (B) are the **Opposite** of those in the passage. Answers may express a conflicting attitude, tone, or meaning to the passage, and often a single one of those opposite words is enough to eliminate an answer.

At this point, we'd strike out (B) using the Answer Eliminator and move on to the next answer.

Ⓒ To demonstrate the narrator's disappointment with the dining club for hiring William

Is this answer consistent with your highlighting and annotation? No, it's not. Some answers can start so well and go so, so wrong. This answer is **Half-Right:** the narrator is 100% disappointed by something…but his disappointment is not directed at *the dining club for hiring William.* Because exams like the Digital SAT are stressful, it's easy to read part of an answer and be tempted to just choose it so you can move on. Force yourself to read all the way to the end of the answer, because that's where the trap in a **Half-Right** answer will often lie.

Half-Right answers usually rely on one of the other traps to make up the flawed half of the answer. In this case, this answer could be seen as **Recycled Language** or **Beyond the Text.** In fact, these traps often appear together in the same answer. The words *dining club* and *William* both appear in the passage, but William's *hiring* is never mentioned in the passage. Yet, the answer seems tempting because it's very logical to assume that the narrator *is* upset about William's hiring: after all, he certainly believes he now knows things about William that he really shouldn't know about his waiter. Again, you would need textual support for that conclusion, and you don't have it.

At this point, you'd strike out (C) using the Answer Eliminator and move on to the next answer. You still need to evaluate (D) even if it's the only answer remaining and not simply choose it because it's the last answer standing. An answer on the Digital SAT is correct only because it's supported by the passage, so (D) must be treated the same as the other answers. We'll discuss POE in greater detail later in these chapters.

Ⓓ To express the narrator's strong emotions towards professional boundaries

Is this answer consistent with your highlighting and annotation? Yes, it's fairly consistent. The narrator believes it is *bad form* to *come into closer relation with waiters* and that William *should have kept his distress to himself.* This is fairly consistent with our annotation box as well, which stated, "knows more about waiter now – unhappy about it." Notice how the answer doesn't use the same words as the passage nor does it use the same words as our annotation—it almost never will. However, it does express all of the correct ideas. The narrator does indeed have strong emotions towards professional boundaries and feels that they have been crossed with what the narrator now knows about William's private life. Even if this is not how you would personally phrase the passage's main purpose, this answer is fully supported by the passage and shouldn't be eliminated.

You keep this answer in play. Since all three of the other answers are crossed out and (D) remains because it is supported by the passage, you can now confidently click on (D) as the answer.

(A) ~~To define a distinction between William and the other waiters at the dining club~~

(B) ~~To examine the type of service that the narrator most highly values~~

(C) ~~To demonstrate the narrator's disappointment with the dining club for hiring William~~

(D) **To express the narrator's strong emotions towards professional boundaries**

The point of the highlighting and annotation isn't to confirm or justify any particular answer—it's to eliminate the three answers with clear flaws and leave the correct, supported answer in play until the end of the POE process.

POE CRITERIA

On many questions, you'll be able to eliminate three of the four answers simply by using your highlights and annotation. On more difficult questions, however, you'll get rid of one or two answer choices, and then you'll need to consider the remaining answers a little more carefully. If you've narrowed it down to two answer choices and they both seem to make sense, you're probably down to the right answer and a trap answer. Luckily, we know some common traps that the test-writers use, and they include the following:

- **Opposite:** These answer choices use a single word or phrase that make the answer convey a tone, viewpoint, or meaning not intended by the author. This can include a word such as *not* in the answer or a negative vocabulary word when the tone of the passage was positive.

- **Extreme Language**: These answers look just about perfect except for a word or phrase that goes too far beyond what the passage can support. This also includes answers that could be called insulting or offensive to a person or a group.

- **Recycled Language:** These answer choices repeat exact words and phrases from the passage but put the words together to say something that the passage didn't actually say. They often establish relationships between the words and phrases that do not exist in the passage.

- **Right Answer, Wrong Question:** These answer choices are true based on the passage, but they don't answer the question that was asked. For example, they might state *what* the author said when the question was asking *why* the author said it.

- **Beyond the Text:** These answers might initially look good because they make sense or seem logical based on outside reasoning, but they lack support within the passage itself.

- **Half-Right:** These answers address part of but not the entire question task. They can also have one half of the answer address the question perfectly and the other half contain at least one of the traps mentioned previously.

Being aware of these traps will help you spot them on the Digital SAT and therefore avoid them. In the previous question, (A) contained **Recycled Language**, (B) contained **Extreme Language** and an emotion **Opposite** of the narrator's emotion in the passage, and (C) was **Half-Right**, with language in the second half of the answer that could be called **Recycled Language** or a **Beyond the Text** trap.

Keep in mind that not every answer fits perfectly into a trap category—sometimes an answer is simply not supported by the passage or wasn't mentioned by the author. The best time to apply these criteria, as we said before, is when you're down to two or three answers after you've compared each answer to what you highlighted and annotated.

Summary

- The Reading questions on the Digital SAT make up approximately 50 percent of your RW section score.
- Reading questions are presented in order of question type and then in order of difficulty within the question type. Don't be afraid to skip a hard question, and don't worry if you can't answer every question.
- Use your POOD to pick up the points you can get, and don't forget to fill in answers on the rest!
- The Reading questions are open-book questions! Use that to your advantage by focusing only on the evidence within the passage that is key to answering the questions.
- Highlight the answer in the passage and annotate if necessary before you look at the answer choices.
- Use POE to eliminate answers that are not consistent with the answer you found in the passage.
- If you have more than one answer left after you eliminate the ones that do not match the passage, compare the remaining answer choices and decide whether any of them are trap answers:
    - Opposite
    - Extreme Language
    - Recycled Language
    - Right Answer, Wrong Question
    - Beyond the Text
    - Half-Right

Chapter 7
Reading Question Types 1–3: Craft and Structure

In this chapter, we'll take a look at the first three question types you will see on the Reading and Writing section. Each of the question types in this chapter focuses on the construction of the passage itself: the correct vocabulary word for a sentence, the purpose or function of the passage, or how two different passages regarding the same topic interact with each other. For each type, we'll show how the Basic Approach can be adapted to maximize your score.

VOCABULARY QUESTIONS

The first group of questions you will see will ask you to choose an appropriate vocabulary word to fill in a blank or determine what the meaning of a word is in the context of the paragraph that the word is in. The Digital SAT tests a blend of common words with multiple meanings and slightly more advanced vocabulary words on harder questions, but the important thing to remember is that the *context* of the sentence(s) surrounding the word will provide a clue that you can highlight. This will allow you to annotate, or write down, your own word for the blank, which will help you with POE. Let's see how to adapt the Basic Approach for Vocabulary questions.

1. **Read the Question.**

2. **Identify the Question Type.** If you see "most logical or precise word or phrase" or "most nearly mean(s)," you have a Vocabulary question that is asking you what word would best fill a blank or define a word in context.

3. **Read the Passage.** As you read, focus particularly on the sentence containing the blank or word itself—your clue for the next step will often come from that sentence.

4. **Highlight What Can Help and Annotate.** Within the passage, you'll want to highlight a phrase or sentence that provides a clue for the type of word that can go in the blank (or, if a word is already present, what word could replace it). Then, based on the clue, you'll want to write down your *own* word in your annotation box.

5. **Use POE.** The most common traps on a Vocabulary question are **Beyond the Text** (common definitions of the original word or words that seem logical based on other parts of the passage), **Extreme Language** (words that go too far in the positive or negative direction), and **Opposite** (words that convey the opposite tone of the one used by the author or a character). You'll see these as we work through some examples.

Kuei-Chih Lee's landscape artistry can best be described as ________: his large-format installations make use of raw materials collected on-site in order to blend his created work with the natural environment.

1 Mark for Review

Which choice completes the text with the most logical and precise word or phrase?

Ⓐ beautiful

Ⓑ harmonious

Ⓒ jarring

Ⓓ acclaimed

Here's How to Crack It

As you **Read the Question**, you can also **Identify the Question Type** as Vocabulary when you see the phrase "most logical and precise word or phrase." The vast majority of Vocabulary questions are phrased identically to the question you see above (we'll see the less common format in just a bit). So, you now know that you need a word to fit in the blank.

Next up, you **Read the Passage.** Most Vocabulary passages tend to be on the shorter side (25–50 words), but they can be longer, especially if they are quoting a literature source. As you read, you'll want to understand what type of word should go where your blank is—in this case, you're looking for some adjective to describe Lee's artistry.

Then, it's time to **Highlight** a clue in the passage that can help you understand what should go in the blank. The blank describes Lee's artistry, and the passage elsewhere states that Lee uses *raw materials collected on-site in order to blend his created work with the natural environment.* Based on this, a good word to write in your **Annotation** box to describe Lee's style of art would be "blended" or "merged."

Lastly, it's time to **Use POE.** Let's consider these answers one at a time.

Choice (A) should be eliminated because *beautiful* is a **Beyond the Text** trap answer. While both artistry and the natural environment are often beautiful, the passage here would need to describe them as so, and it does not! You should always eliminate answers that can only be supported by outside knowledge or assumptions but not by the passage itself.

Choice (B) should be kept because *harmonious* is a good synonym for "blended" or "merged." Your word may not be a direct synonym for the correct answer, but as long as it's along the same lines of meaning, it will do the job of eliminating most of the wrong answers and leaving you, hopefully, with just one answer remaining.

Choice (C) should be eliminated because *jarring* is the **Opposite** meaning of "blended." The passage never states that Lee's final productions look disjointed or disconnected in any way.

Choice (D) should be eliminated because the passage never describes Lee or his work as *acclaimed.* This is a **Beyond the Text** trap as it's logical to assume an artist is well-known or highly regarded, but looking back at the passage, there isn't a single word that describes Lee's popularity or renown.

With three answers eliminated and only (B) remaining, select (B) and congratulate yourself on a job well done!

By the way, it's pretty reasonable to have had (A), (D), or even (C) still remaining after the initial POE pass, so that's where we'd start asking, "Which of my remaining answers is a trap?" On harder questions, answers may also survive that first pass because you are unsure of what the word means, which means that word becomes a **Greatest Hits** word for you. More information about the **Greatest Hits** can be found in Chapter 9!

Vocabulary (The Second Format)

Some questions that test vocabulary won't have a blank. Instead, the question will ask what a word or phrase in the passage "most nearly mean(s)." The Basic Approach for Vocabulary works equally well even if a word is provided instead of a blank—you'll highlight a clue in the passage and then write down your own word, treating the word given as if it weren't there. Do not give in to the temptation to simply pick an answer without following all of the steps—**Beyond the Text** traps are even more prevalent when a word is already included, as College Board will create one or more answers that are common definitions of the indicated word but don't fit the context. Writing down your own word is the most foolproof, stress-free way of not falling for those traps!

The following text is adapted from Thomas Love Peacock's 1818 novel *Nightmare Abbey.* Marionetta, a young woman, is reflecting on her relationship with a young man named Scythrop.

> Scythrop grew every day more reserved, mysterious, and distrait; and gradually lengthened the duration of his diurnal seclusions in his tower. Marionetta thought she perceived in all this very manifest symptoms of a warm love cooling.

2 Mark for Review

As used in the text, what does the word "reserved" most nearly mean?

Ⓐ Agreeable

Ⓑ Observant

Ⓒ Withdrawn

Ⓓ Hostile

Here's How to Crack It

As you **Read the Question**, you can also **Identify the Question Type** as Vocabulary when you see the phrase "most nearly mean(s)." While this format is less common, it can be handled the exact same way as the other Vocabulary questions. Treat the word *reserved* as if it were a blank and follow the same Vocabulary Basic Approach.

Next up, you **Read the Passage.** As you read, you'll want to understand what type of word should go in the "blank." You're looking for some adjective that describes Scythrop.

Then, it's time to **Highlight** a clue in the passage that helps you understand what word should go in the "blank" you created. Scythrop is already described as *mysterious* and is said to have *gradually lengthened the duration of his diurnal seclusions in the tower.* Marionetta also describes this behavior as *symptoms of a warm love cooling.* All of these clues suggest that a good phrase to **Annotate** would be "less available" or "not around as much." Sometimes, a single perfect word for the blank won't immediately come to you, so using a phrase is perfectly acceptable!

Lastly, it's time to **Use POE**, which should always be part of your test-taking vocabulary.

Choice (A) should be eliminated because it's the **Opposite** tone of "less available." *Agreeable* would describe Scythrop positively, but "less available" is a more negative idea.

Choice (B) should be eliminated because *observant* is a **Right Answer, Wrong Question** trap. Marionetta could be described as observant, as she *perceived* and drew conclusions from Scythrop's behavior, but the question is looking for a description of Scythrop, not Marionetta.

Choice (C) should be kept because it's a good synonym for "less available" or "not around as much."

Choice (D) should be eliminated because it's **Extreme Language**. Nothing in the passage suggests that Scythrop has become *hostile* to Marionetta or anyone else around him, just that he's spending more time alone.

With three answers eliminated and only (C) remaining, you select (C) and hope Marionetta and Scythrop can work things out, but we've got more Digital SAT business to attend to.

The Vocabulary Bottom Line: You MUST write down your own word in the annotation box. It's the best way to avoid falling for traps!

Studying Vocabulary

Vocabulary is one of the most common Reading question types on the Digital SAT—it's not uncommon for it to make up 4–8 of the Reading questions you see within each module. This is important for a few reasons. First of all, that's a significant number of points for your Reading and Writing (RW) score considering there are only 27 questions in each RW module. Second, this is one of the few spots where College Board's order of difficulty is helpful. Recall that questions increase in difficulty as they go on, so you'll notice the words and passages get slightly more difficult as you go, especially if you have 7–8 Vocabulary questions. As your score increases, you'll likely start encountering the harder second RW module, so you'll need some word knowledge to keep things moving along swimmingly. While there are many ways to study vocab, we've provided three of them below and encourage you to use all three of them, especially if you are pursuing the highest possible score.

Method 1: Use the Greatest Hits in Chapter 9 of this book. In Chapter 9, you'll find a list of the 60 most common words we've seen on past exams, along with the primary textbook definition for each. These words are not meant to be a complete list, as College Board uses a large variety of words on the Digital SAT. However, the words on the list provide a great starting point for sharpening your vocabulary skills as you explore the Digital SAT more deeply.

Generally, you don't want to add difficult words from poems or literature sources to your Greatest Hits (such as *distrait, diurnal,* or *manifest* from the previous question). These passages may feature antiquated or difficult words, and since these passages aren't written by College Board, such words are not likely to appear outside of the individual passages in which you see them.

Method 2: Create Your Own Greatest Hits. Throughout these chapters, you'll come across words in the passage and answers that you may not know, and sometimes this will even happen on non-Vocabulary questions. Create a physical or digital document to track these words. Whenever you encounter a word you're unfamiliar with on a practice Digital SAT question, add it to the list, along with a definition for how it was used on that question, and, optionally, a mnemonic device to help you remember that word. For example, the word *paucity,* which means scarcity or a lack of something, could be remembered by thinking of a *pauper,* or beggar.

Method 3: Read One Challenging Article/Short Story Per Day. Publications such as *Forbes*, *National Geographic*, *The Economist*, and *The New Yorker* typically publish articles with reading levels equal to and, in many cases, higher than those of the Digital SAT's passages. Additionally, many Digital SAT passages are excerpts from novels, poems, and short stories written in the 1800s and early 1900s. The *Century Past Free Online Library* is a great website to find such passages.

By reading one such article or story per day as often as your schedule allows, you'll not only be exposed to difficult words that are often understandable through context, but you'll also train yourself to better sort through some of the more sophisticated Digital SAT passages as you look for the correct evidence to answer the question.

PURPOSE QUESTIONS

The next question type will ask you why the author wrote the passage or how a sentence functions in the passage. The Digital SAT doesn't require any outside reasoning on these questions either, as it's not really possible to know why any author does anything without asking them! Instead, Purpose questions are looking for the *most likely, best supported* reason that the passage or sentence was written or included. You may see just one of these questions or several of them, but in all cases, remember that the key is finding the evidence!

1. **Read the Question.**

2. **Identify the Question Type.** If you see the words *purpose, function*, or *structure* in the question stem, you have a Purpose question that is asking you why the passage was written, why a sentence was included, or how the passage is organized, respectively.

3. **Read the Passage.** As you read, focus particularly on sentence structure. Typically, each sentence within a passage has a role within the paragraph. Understanding what each sentence does and how each sentence connects to the ones before and after it is key to the following step.

4. **Highlight What Can Help and Annotate.**

   - If a question asks for the "main purpose" of the passage, there is a main claim the author is making somewhere in the passage—each sentence will in some way contribute to this claim. You want to find and highlight this claim!
   - If a question asks for the "function" of a sentence, the sentences before and after the indicated sentence will reference ideas that the sentence in question interacts with. Highlighting ideas that persist across the sentence before, the sentence itself, and/or the sentence after will help you understand those connections.
   - If a question asks for the "overall structure" of the passage, it's looking for a combination of the first two bullets. You're still looking for the main claim the author is making, but you want to examine each sentence to see how that claim is supported. Look in particular to highlight words that show some type of chronology, comparison, or contrast between ideas.
   - No matter what the prompt is, make sure to **Annotate!** Write down a simple description of WHY or HOW the author wrote the passage or included a sentence. A good tip is to write down both the topic of the passage and any attitude the author seems to express towards that topic.

5. **Use POE.** The most common traps on a Purpose question will be answers that use **Recycled Language** (repeating words verbatim from the passage but using those words differently from the passage), **Right Answer, Wrong Question** traps (answers that are supported by the passage but only describe the content of the passage and not the author's purpose in writing it), and **Opposites** (answers that express the opposite purpose or tone from what the author is trying to do).

In 1978, British biochemist Sir Philip Cohen was experimenting with a type of enzyme to understand how calcium activated that enzyme. He noticed a faint blue smear occurring at the bottom of the gel used in his experiments but had assumed it to be of little importance. After hearing another scientist's lecture, Cohen realized that calmodulin, a calcium-binding protein, was the source of the blue smear. His next experiments confirmed that calmodulin still appeared in his gels even after the gels had been boiled and was therefore heat stable. He correctly concluded that calmodulin mediated the activity of calcium within the enzyme.

3 Mark for Review

Which choice best states the main purpose of the text?

(A) To explain how misunderstood calmodulin is

(B) To describe Cohen's realization regarding calmodulin

(C) To illustrate how calcium-binding proteins function

(D) To place emphasis on the importance of calcium within enzymes

Here's How to Crack It

As you **Read the Question**, you can also **Identify the Question Type** as Purpose when you see the phrase "main purpose." Yes, it's sometimes that straightforward. You know that you want to understand the main point the author is making in this passage.

Next up, you **Read the Passage.** Remember—you're not reading because it's fun. You are *actively* looking for the main purpose of the passage. In general, there are three purposes that most authors will seek to fulfill: **inform**, **persuade/argue**, or **entertain** (the last of these, as we're sure you'll agree, is pretty rare on the Digital SAT).

Then, it's time to **Highlight** evidence that can help you understand the author's main purpose. The author focuses mainly on two ideas: *British biochemist Sir Philip Cohen* and his connection to the protein *calmodulin.* The critical statement to highlight that connects both of these ideas is *Cohen realized that calmodulin, a calcium-binding protein, was the source of the blue smear.* The passage goes on to **inform** the reader of the relevance of this discovery to Cohen's experiments. Write in your **Annotation** box that the purpose of the passage is to "explain link between Cohen and calmodulin," or whatever shorthand or abbreviation makes sense to you.

It's time to use **POE.** Let's be *purpose*ful as we compare these answers to our annotation.

Choice (A) should be eliminated because it is **Extreme Language:** just because Cohen himself didn't immediately recognize the blue smear does not mean that calmodulin is *misunderstood* by anyone to any notable extent.

Choice (B) should be kept because it's fairly consistent with the highlighting and annotation—this is exactly what the author does, just with different words from those used in the passage, as we've come to expect.

Choice (C) should be eliminated because it's **Half-Right:** you do learn a little about the role that one calcium-binding protein, calmodulin, performs, but the answer doesn't mention Cohen whatsoever. Too much of the passage focuses on Cohen and his work for him to not be part of the correct answer regarding the *main purpose* of the passage.

Choice (D) should be eliminated because it's **Recycled Language**, borrowing the phrase from *calcium within enzymes* almost verbatim from the end of the passage. The answer focuses neither on Cohen nor calmodulin, so it should be eliminated fairly quickly if you highlighted and annotated.

With three answers eliminated and only (B) remaining, you select (B) and thank Sir Cohen for his tireless efforts as you continue your own efforts to master this exam.

Purpose (Sentence Function)

The same approach can be used when a question asks how a sentence functions in the passage. Generally, if you focus on the sentences before and/or after the indicated sentence, you'll be able to highlight connections between ideas that keep the sentences flowing logically. From this logical flow, you'll be able to annotate the role that the indicated sentence performs.

The following text is from Alexandre Dumas's 1850 novel *The Black Tulip*. Cornelius, the main character, is in jail and is guarded by a turnkey, an older word for jailer.

> Cornelius saw nothing but the golden brocade cap, tipped with lace, such as the Frisian girls wore; he heard nothing but some one whispering into the ear of the turnkey. But the latter put his heavy keys into the white hand which was stretched out to receive them, and, descending some steps, sat down on the staircase which was thus guarded above by himself, and below by the dog. The head-dress turned round, and Cornelius beheld the face of Rosa, blanched with grief, and her beautiful eyes streaming with tears.

4 Mark for Review

Which choice best describes the function of the underlined sentence in the text as a whole?

(A) It details the outcome of a conversation mentioned in the previous sentence.

(B) It describes the specifics of the construction of the jailhouse.

(C) It explains that an individual is debating his obligations to duty.

(D) It introduces a claim that the following sentence further explains.

Watch Us Crack It
Check out the Video Walk-throughs in your online Student Tools to see and hear a Princeton Review teacher work through, step-by-step, this and other questions from this book.

Here's How to Crack It

As you **Read the Question**, you can also **Identify the Question Type** as Purpose when you see the phrase "function." Typically, the question will ask for the function either of an underlined sentence or of a numbered sentence in the passage, such as the second or third sentence.

Next up, you **Read the Passage.** Pay specific attention to not just the sentence itself, but the sentences before and after. The ideas that repeat among these three sentences form the core of what you should highlight in the next step.

So, it's time to **Highlight** ideas that help you understand the sentence's function. The sentence before states that *Cornelius heard nothing but some one whispering into the ear of the turnkey.* In the underlined sentence, the turnkey *put his heavy keys into the white hand* of whoever was whispering to him and then went to go sit down. In the sentence after, the person who whispered *turned round* and was revealed to be Rosa, someone who is clearly saddened by Cornelius's situation in jail. With this, you can **Annotate** the function of the sentence: "explain what happens after whisper."

It's time to **Use POE** and eliminate some dys*function*al answers.

Choice (A) should be kept because it's fairly consistent with your highlighting and annotation. It describes exactly what happens as a result of Rosa's whisper into the turnkey's, or guard's, ear.

Choice (B) should be eliminated because it's a **Right Answer, Wrong Question.** You do learn a little bit about the layout of this particular floor of the jail cell when the staircase is described, but based on the sentences before and after, this isn't the focus of the passage as the other two sentences don't expand on this idea.

Choice (C) should be eliminated because there is no mention of any *debate* that the guard is having. This answer is a **Beyond the Text** trap because you would hope a jail guard would probably heavily debate handing his keys to someone, but no mention of any such debate appears in the passage.

Choice (D) should be eliminated because it's **Half-Right**: the following sentence does indeed further explain the action from the underlined sentence. However, the underlined sentence doesn't make any actual *claim* or state any argument—it merely describes the action in the story.

With three answers eliminated and only (A) remaining, select (A) and hope the guard keeps his job after his questionable lack of judgment.

You can also be asked for the overall structure of the passage. Don't panic! You are still being asked for the purpose of the passage as a whole. Once you write down what the purpose is, the correct answer will describe what the author did in the passage to accomplish that goal. An example of one of these questions is included in the Reading Drill chapter.

The Purpose Bottom Line: You MUST remember that the question is looking for the *most supported* reason the author wrote something—the author will likely not directly state "this is why I wrote this" in the story.

DUAL TEXTS QUESTIONS

The next question type will offer you two passages rather than one and ask how someone from the second passage would respond to an idea, person, or group from the first passage. These can seem intimidating at first, but all you are looking for is a single idea mentioned in the first passage that is commented upon by the second. It will be pretty obvious when you are faced with a Dual Texts question (after all, there will be two passages!), so we'll modify the Basic Approach slightly to handle this unique question type.

Remember POOD: you typically only get one Dual Texts question (if any) on each module, so if you're concerned about the question being confusing or time-consuming, enter an answer and move on!

1. **Read and Understand the Question.** The presence of two passages will make it clear that this is a Dual Texts question, but it's still critical to make sure exactly who or what you should be focusing on in each passage.

2. **Read Text 1 and highlight the idea or viewpoint referenced in the question.** As you read, remember that there was a specific hypothesis, statement, or claim that was referenced by the question. For Text 1, you pretty much just need to find and highlight that idea.

3. **Read Text 2 and highlight the main idea or viewpoint towards the same information from Text 1.** Text 2 will typically feature an individual or group conducting an experiment or responding to the claim from Text 1 in some way. They could confirm the claim from Text 1, contradict it, or expand on it. Finding and highlighting the line or sentence in which Text 2 comments on the same idea that you highlighted from Text 1 is critical to understanding the connection between the passages.

4. **Write the relationship between the passages down in your Annotation box.** As stated before, this will typically be an agreement, disagreement, or explanation. More complex connections are possible, but it's a fair bet that the second passage will have one of those three reactions to the claim from the first!

5. **Use POE and eliminate answers that are inconsistent with one or both passages.** The most common trap answers on Dual Texts questions are **Opposites** (answers that take the opposite viewpoint that Text 2 expresses, such as agreeing with Text 1 when Text 2 actually disagrees) and **Extreme Language** (answers that take a stated opinion or claim further than the relevant passage can support).

Watch Us Crack It
Check out the Video Walk-throughs in your online Student Tools to watch a Princeton Review teacher work through this question step-by-step.

Text 1

Anxiety has long been considered a critical area of focus for those involved in both psychological analysis and behavior management. The traditional treatment for anxiety has been prescription medication. But what about situations when medication is ineffective or ill-advised? Psychologists continue to explore possible alternative treatments for anxiety to this day.

Text 2

Professor Spike W.S. Lee and his team have demonstrated a possible link between self-cleansing and anxiety reduction. They conducted a study of 1,150 adults and showed each of them one of three different videos: how to properly wash hands, how to properly peel an egg, and how to properly draw a circle. The subjects were then all exposed to a series of situations meant to induce anxiety. Those individuals who had seen the handwashing video demonstrated consistently lower levels of anxiety than those who had seen either of the other two videos.

5 Mark for Review

Based on the texts, how would Lee and his team (Text 2) most likely respond to the "traditional treatment" discussed in Text 1?

(A) By noting that it may not be the only possible treatment by which an individual may reduce anxiety

(B) By claiming that those who prescribe medication for anxiety completely ignore the emotional benefits of frequent handwashing

(C) By stating that his team's findings help establish handwashing as an alternative treatment to prescribed medication

(D) By calling for other psychologists to focus their own efforts on how handwashing frequency increases with exposure to instructional videos

Here's How to Crack It

First, **Read and Understand the Question**. You need to first find what Text 1 says about the *traditional treatment* and then find HOW *Lee and his team* respond to it.

Next up, you **Read Text 1** and look for what it says about the *traditional treatment.* You can highlight that Text 1 states that *the traditional treatment for anxiety has been prescription medication.* Then, you need to **Read Text 2** and find Lee and his team's reply to this idea. The opening sentence of the passage states that Lee and his team *have demonstrated a possible link between self-cleansing and behavior management.* The passage goes on to say that *those who had seen the handwashing video demonstrated consistently lower levels of anxiety than those who had seen either of the other two videos.* These lines don't address prescription medication directly, but instead offer a different way someone may possibly reduce anxiety.

So, that becomes what you **Annotate**: write "Text 2 offers other possible method" in the annotation box. As with Purpose questions, try to keep these annotations short and sweet so you avoid straying too far from what the passage states—you are merely writing down exactly what Lee and his team did and nothing further.

Lastly, it's time to **Use POE.** One text, Dual Texts? It doesn't matter: three of the four answers won't be consistent with the claim and response that you **Highlighted** and **Annotated.**

Choice (A) should be kept because it's fairly consistent with our highlighting and annotation. Lee and his team do suggest an alternative *possible treatment* for reducing anxiety rather than *prescription medication.*

Choice (B) should be eliminated because it's **Extreme Language.** While Text 1 doesn't mention handwashing as a treatment for anxiety, the phrase *completely ignores* goes too far—there is no evidence that those who prescribe medication don't consider handwashing to be emotionally beneficial.

Choice (C) should be eliminated because it's also **Extreme Language.** Lee's findings don't *establish* handwashing as an *alternative treatment* to prescribed medication. All Lee and his team's findings do is offer some evidence that self-cleansing, or at least watching videos about handwashing, may reduce anxiety levels. Much more work would need to be done for handwashing to be *established* as a true alternative. Keep an eye out for words like *established* or *proved*—these words often go too far even if they are not as obviously extreme as words like *completely* or *only.*

Choice (D) should be eliminated because it's **Recycled Language**. *Handwashing* and *videos* are taken directly from the passage, but the words around them are not supported. Nowhere in Text 2 do Lee and his team call *for other psychologists* to do anything. As logical as it is that Lee and his team may want other scientists to investigate this possible alternative treatment method, the passage never includes any such call to action (making this also a **Beyond the Text** trap).

With three answers eliminated and only (A) remaining, you select (A) and have taken a crucial step towards reducing your own anxiety on Dual Texts questions.

The Dual Texts Bottom Line: Keep the question in mind—if you remember that both passages will address the same claim or idea in some way and find that claim referenced both times, that's a major accomplishment.

Summary

- Always come up with your own word and phrase on Vocabulary questions and write it down in the annotation box before looking at the answer choices.
- Study vocabulary by using the Greatest Hits in Chapter 9, creating your own Greatest Hits, and reading challenging articles or older short stories, excerpts from novels, and poems.
- Make sure you are consistently finding the main claim the author makes in the passage for Purpose questions.
- Identify the claim/idea/hypothesis that both passages reference on Dual Texts questions. That is the best way to identify the link between the two passages.
- For all three of these question types, **annotation is critical.** Make sure you've written down a word, purpose, or relationship in the Annotation box to help you apply POE.
- Don't forget POOD and guessing. If the words in a Vocabulary question are too confusing or a Purpose or Dual Texts question looks too dense or time-consuming, consider marking the question for review. Make sure to enter an answer on questions you are not sure you'll make it back to.

Chapter 8
Reading Question Types 4–8: Information and Ideas

In this chapter, we'll take a look at the final five Reading question types you will see on the Reading and Writing section. Each of the question types in this chapter focuses on the information presented in the passage (or chart, as you'll see). These questions can ask you to find relevant information, find a main idea, find or support a claim, work with data in a table or graph, or choose a concluding sentence for the passage. For each type, we'll show how the Basic Approach can be adapted to maximize your score.

RETRIEVAL QUESTIONS

After Dual Texts, the next group of questions will switch up the focus of the Reading section. Two types of questions will be mixed together: Retrieval questions and Main Idea questions. Retrieval questions ask what the passage says that would be an answer to the question—you won't need to determine why the author included the information or how someone else would respond to it. On Retrieval questions, you'll often be able to go right to POE once you highlight the answer in the passage. With that in mind, let's examine the Basic Approach for Retrieval questions.

1. **Read the Question.**

2. **Identify the Question Type.** If you see the words *according to the text* or *based on the text* in the question stem, you have a Retrieval question that is asking you WHAT the passage said. The question could ask for many different types of details, such as why or how something happens, but these details will be something you can definitively find in the passage each time.

3. **Read the Passage.** As you read, focus on the person, place, or thing referenced in the question. You are looking for some detail about that person, place, or thing that will answer the question.

4. **Highlight What Can Help.** This is one of the most straightforward question types—you want to highlight what the passage actually offers as an answer to the question. Bear in mind that straightforward doesn't necessarily mean easy—you'll still need to read carefully and avoid highlighting details irrelevant to the question task.

5. **Use POE.** The most common traps on a Retrieval question will be answers that use **Recycled Language** (repeating words verbatim from the passage but using those words differently from the passage), **Beyond the Text** trap answers based on making outside assumptions not supported by the passage, and **Extreme Language** answers that go beyond what the passage states.

The following is adapted from George Eliot's 1871 novel *Middlemarch*. The author is describing Dorothea Brooke, one of the central characters in the novel.

It had now entered Dorothea's mind that Mr. Casaubon might wish to make her his wife, and the idea that he would do so touched her with a sort of reverential gratitude. How good of him—nay, it would be almost as if a winged messenger had suddenly stood beside her path and held out his hand towards her! For a long while she had been oppressed by the indefiniteness which hung in her mind, like a thick summer haze, over all her desire to make her life greatly effective.

1 Mark for Review

According to the text, what is true about Dorothea?

Ⓐ She is skeptical of Mr. Casaubon's career as a messenger.

Ⓑ She wants to know Mr. Casaubon's feelings towards summer.

Ⓒ She is enthused by the prospect of marriage to a particular individual.

Ⓓ She prefers marriage over other types of relationships.

Here's How to Crack It

As you **Read the Question**, you can also **Identify the Question Type** as Retrieval when you see the phrase *according to the text.*

Next up, you **Read the Passage.** As you read, have your mouse ready to highlight what the passage actually says about Dorothea.

The very first sentence, which you should **Highlight**, says that *it had now entered Dorothea's mind that Mr. Casaubon might wish to make her his wife, and the idea that he would do so touched her with a sort of reverential gratitude.* The next two sentences pretty much double down on having Dorothea ponder how much better her life will be if she becomes Mr. Casaubon's wife. Simply stated, the best answer will be as consistent as possible with that opening sentence, and the three wrong answers will have some flaw that makes them inconsistent.

It's time to **Use POE.** Three of these four answers won't be consistent with what we retrieved from the passage.

Choice (A) should be eliminated for multiple reasons. First, *skeptical* is the **Opposite** tone of *reverential gratitude,* which is positive. Second, *messenger* is **Recycled Language**—the passage doesn't state that Mr. Casaubon's career is that of a messenger. Instead, it uses *winged messenger* as part of a description for *how good* Dorothea believes Mr. Casaubon's proposal of marriage would be for her.

Choice (B) should be eliminated because it's also **Recycled Language**. *Thick summer haze* is used in the passage to describe Dorothea's negative mental state before realizing that Mr. Casaubon might propose and has nothing to do with Mr. Casaubon's *feelings towards summer* as a season.

Choice (C) should be kept because it's consistent with the positive emotions towards the proposal that you highlighted in the opening sentence.

Choice (D) should be eliminated because it is a **Beyond the Text** trap answer. Dorothea is certainly excited by the prospect of marriage, but the passage doesn't give any information regarding any other types of relationships Dorothea might be considering and which type of relationship would be her preference.

With three answers eliminated and only (C) remaining, select (C) and hope that Dorothea and Mr. Casaubon experience a long, happy life together. Or, just move on to the next question type.

The Retrieval Bottom Line: *According to the text* or *based on the text* means that the passage needs to provide the answer to the question. Don't overthink or try to make deductions from what you read. Compare the answer you find in the passage directly to the four answer choices and use POE.

MAIN IDEA QUESTIONS

Mixed in with the Retrieval questions, Main Idea questions also ask what the author said. The difference is that Main Idea questions are looking for the single sentence or idea that is the main focus of the passage rather than a detail about a character or thing. This should be the sentence or idea that all of the other sentences and ideas are connected to. Many times, this will be the first or last sentence of the paragraph, but College Board can place the main idea anywhere. As you read, ask yourself, "Which sentence do all of the other sentences build onto or build off of?"

1. **Read the Question.**

2. **Identify the Question Type.** If you see the words *main idea* in the question stem, you have a Main Idea question that is asking for the central idea of the passage. This can be explicitly stated in a single sentence, but it can also be a summary of the statements made in the passage, especially if the author is describing an experiment or telling a chronological story.

3. **Read the Passage.** As you read, focus on the person, place, or thing that is the central idea of the passage. This should be an idea that each sentence describes or expands upon in some way.

4. **Highlight What Can Help**. This is another one of the more straightforward question types—you want to highlight the topic on which the passage focuses the most. Make sure you're not putting too much emphasis on a single detail. For instance, the author may describe a work from a famous environmentalist in one line, but if the rest of the lines don't expand on that work but rather describe the environmentalist's entire career, the work is not the main idea. Instead, the main idea would be the environmentalist's career as a whole.

5. **Use POE.** The most common traps on a Main Idea question are **Right Answer, Wrong Question** (answers that focus on an accurate detail that is not the main focus of the other sentences as we described in Step 4), **Recycled Language** (repeated words that are used differently in the answer than in the passage), and **Beyond the Text** answers (conclusions that seem logical but are not ideas supported directly by the passage itself).

Fire photography, the practice of taking photographs of firefighting operations, has numerous applications in both occupational safety and criminal investigation. Fire photographers can also work with fire departments directly. Despite their numerous job prospects, all fire photographers must first and foremost undergo rigorous safety training before setting foot into the field.

2 Mark for Review

Which choice best states the main idea of the text?

(A) Advanced cameras can now take pictures from a much safer distance than fire photographers can.

(B) Although there are numerous possible career paths for fire photographers, they must prioritize safety given the nature of their jobs.

(C) While there are many possible career paths, most fire photographers prefer working directly with fire departments.

(D) Fire photographers have been charged with documenting fires for a century.

Here's How to Crack It

As you **Read the Question**, you can also **Identify the Question Type** as Main Idea when you see the phrase "main idea."

Next up, you **Read the Passage.** As you read, ask yourself what person, place, or thing is discussed in each sentence. Every single sentence here is about *fire photography* in one way or another.

The last sentence, which you should **Highlight**, says that *Despite their numerous job prospects, all fire photographers must first and foremost undergo rigorous safety training.* Notice how this not only captures the multiple career opportunities of fire photographers that the other two sentences mention but also adds a detail about how *all fire photographers…must undergo rigorous safety training,* regardless of career choice.

Once more, it's time to **Use POE.** Compare the answers to the main idea you found in the passage.

Choice (A) should be eliminated because it's a **Beyond the Text** trap answer: as likely as it is that technology has reduced the need for fire photographers to put themselves in harm's way in some cases, the passage makes no mention of any *advanced cameras.*

Choice (B) should be kept because it's consistent with our highlighting. As you've seen several times in these chapters, it paraphrases the passage rather than repeats it directly, but the meanings of both our highlighted sentence and (B) are identical, or at least very close.

Choice (C) should be eliminated because it's **Half-Right:** *numerous career paths* is consistent with our highlighting, but the second half of the answer contains **Recycled** and **Extreme Language**. *Fire photographers, fire departments,* and *directly* are taken verbatim from the passage, but it's never stated that *most* fire photographers *prefer working with fire departments directly.*

Choice (D) should be eliminated because it is a **Beyond the Text** trap answer. While it sounds logical that fire photographers have been doing their jobs for as long as photographical equipment became portable enough to go out into the field, the passage offers no statement on how long fire photographers have been doing their jobs.

With three answers eliminated and only (B) remaining, you select (B) and have successfully doused the fires of uncertainty regarding Main Idea questions.

> The Main Idea Bottom Line: Search for and highlight the person, place, or thing that each sentence seems to be discussing or describing. While Main Idea questions are different from Purpose questions, both are concerned with finding the main focus or topic of the passage. Avoid latching onto a single detail as a main idea.

CLAIMS QUESTIONS

The next question type asks which answer would best illustrate, support, or weaken a claim made by the author or someone in the passage. Note that these questions are often interspersed with the next question type, **Charts,** but luckily, the skills you need for these two question types are similar. As with Retrieval and Main Idea questions, your main job here will be to identify the claim made by the author in the passage without any regard to the structure or purpose of the passage. However, you'll need to perform the exact task required by the question and keep a razor-sharp eye as you use POE: it only takes one word or phrase to make an answer do the opposite of what was intended!

1. **Read the Question.** As you read the question, pay special attention to whether you'll be *illustrating, supporting,* or *weakening* some idea from the passage.

2. **Identify the Question Type.** There are a few different ways College Board can ask a Claims question, but most commonly, you'll see language in the question looking for something to *illustrate*, *support*, or *weaken* someone's *claim*, *hypothesis*, *argument*, or *prediction.* These questions can also reference a *quotation* from the passage that accomplishes a goal. When this happens, the passage will be quite short, but the answers will be longer to compensate.

3. **Read the Passage.** As you read, focus on finding the claim or argument referenced by the question. In a longer passage, this claim is likely to be part of the passage's main idea. In a shorter passage asking about a quotation that illustrates the claim, the claim itself will precede the colon and the blank in the question stem.

4. **Highlight What Can Help**. Your only job here is to highlight the claim, theory, argument, etc., referenced by the question stem, regardless of whether you need to illustrate it, strengthen it, or weaken it.

5. **Use POE.** The most common traps on a Claims question are **Half-Right** answers that only address part of the claim from the question and **Opposite** answers that would weaken when they are supposed to support the claim and vice versa. On longer Claim passages, you'll also see answers include **Extreme Language** or make **Beyond the Text** assumptions that are unsupported by the passage.

"A Dry Spell" is a 1905 short story by Einar H. Kvaran. In the story, the narrator and his companions wait out an ongoing rain torrent in a store where they work as clerks. In his musings, the narrator expresses a desire for the presence of individuals that he formerly considered an annoyance: ________

3 Mark for Review

Which quotation from the narrator's musings best illustrates the claim?

Ⓐ "We sat there and smoked, staring vacantly at the half-empty shelves, and all but shivering in the damp room."

Ⓑ "We made clever comments to the effect that the farmers were now getting plenty of moisture for the hay-fields, and that it would be a pity if rain should set in now, right at the beginning of the haying season."

Ⓒ "We were tired of the store—indeed, I should like to know who would have enjoyed it."

Ⓓ "We had often cursed their lengthy visits, but now that they had hired themselves out during the haymaking, we suddenly realized that they had often been entertaining."

Here's How to Crack It

As you **Read the Question**, notice that it is specifically looking for a quotation, so scrutinizing the answers will be key. You can **Identify the Question Type** as Claims by the phrase *illustrates the claim.*

Next up, **Read the Passage.** As you read, remember that if the Claims question has a blank at the end of it, the claim will typically be right before it, as is the case here.

Sure enough, you want to **Highlight** the claim that the quotations from the answers should illustrate. In this case, *the narrator expresses a desire for the presence of individuals that he formerly considered an annoyance.* The correct quotation should mention a group that the narrator formerly didn't want around but now does.

Lastly, it's time to **Use POE.** Quotations in Claims questions will be among the longer answer choices you'll need to deal with, so double down on how carefully you read.

Choice (A) should be eliminated because it doesn't mention any group besides the group of people inside the store, of which the narrator is one. You are looking for a group the narrator now wishes was there but is not.

Choice (B) should be eliminated because it is **Half-Right:** while it references a group that the narrator and his fellow clerks make fun of, the answer never includes any mention of a *desire for the presence* of those individuals now. Make sure to read all the way to the end of each quotation and make sure it does every job stated in the claim!

Choice (C) should be eliminated because, like (A), there is no mention of any group besides the narrator's. Furthermore, the negative emotions presented are towards the store, and not any other group of people.

Choice (D) should be kept because it's consistent with the claim. *We had often cursed their lengthy visits* could support *annoyance* at whoever *they* are, and the narrator and his group stating that they *suddenly realized that they had often been entertaining* supports that the presence of this group may be welcome during the dreary storm the narrator and his group are experiencing. Notice that the quotation doesn't directly state that the narrator necessarily wants this group here at this moment, but out of the four options, it *best illustrates* the claim, rather than directly restating or proving it.

With three answers eliminated and only (D) remaining, you select (D) and clear yet another Digital SAT storm cloud.

The Claims Bottom Line: Focus on finding the claim and what the question asks you to do to it. Remember that the answers to a *support* or *weaken* question do NOT need to be supported by the passage but rather, if true, would *best* support or weaken the claim in the passage.

CHARTS QUESTIONS

As mentioned before, Charts questions are interspersed with Claims questions, though you won't necessarily see both in the same module. Like Claims questions, Charts questions will ask you to illustrate, support, or weaken some claim. The biggest difference between the types is that here you'll be reading some information from a table or graph in addition to the passage. As with Dual Texts, it will be pretty clear when you are asked a Charts question, so we'll once again modify the Reading Basic Approach slightly to make sure you catch everything needed to earn these points!

1. **Read and understand the question.** As with Claims questions, make sure you understand whether you're being asked to *illustrate*, *support*, or *weaken* a statement from the passage.

2. **Read the title, key/legend, variables, and units in the chart.** Orienting yourself to the graph before you are influenced by the passage or answers will ensure you don't jump to any conclusions and are able to efficiently process the chart again once you're starting to use POE.

3. **Read the passage and look for the same information you saw in the chart.** Much of the passage will describe the setup or background to the data in the chart. What you're actually looking for is when the author references the same variables or values as in the chart and makes some statement regarding them.

4. **Highlight the claim or conclusion made regarding that same information.** Once you've found the claim in question, highlight it. Often, it will appear towards the end of the passage. Also, if a summary of the passage is more helpful to you than a long-winded claim, don't forget about your Annotation box and write a note to yourself if it is helpful.

5. **Use POE.** The most common trap answer on Charts questions is **Right Answer, Wrong Question.** Most of the answers to the question are accurate representations of the information from the chart but fail to address the claim that they are supposed to be illustrating, supporting, or weakening. These answers can focus on the wrong variable entirely or only focus on one variable when they need to focus on two. Answers can also be **Half-Right** for only addressing some of the claim, especially if the author names multiple conditions in their statement. Lastly, wrong answers can offer the **Opposite** relationship of the one proposed by the passage, especially in the case of needing to support or weaken a claim.

Nutritional Information for Skim Cow's Milk and Unsweetened Oat Milk Based on a 1 Cup Serving

Milk type	Skim cow's milk	Unsweetened oat milk
Calories	90	90
Fat (g)	0	1.5
Sodium (mg)	130	120
Sugars (g)	12	4

In the field of nutrition, skim cow's milk and unsweetened oat milk are two popular substitutions for whole milk, which can be too high in fat and cholesterol for some individuals. Each whole milk substitute goes through different processes that affect its final nutritional value. For instance, unsweetened oat milk is made by straining a blend of rolled oats (which have less sugar than cow's milk) and water. A scientist theorized that because skim milk is whole milk that has been run through a centrifuge to separate out all of the fat droplets, it would likely have less fat content but higher sugar content than would unsweetened oat milk.

4 Mark for Review

Which choice most effectively uses data from the table that support the scientist's hypothesis?

Ⓐ The skim cow's milk has higher sugar content than fat content, but it also contains more sodium than does unsweetened oat milk.

Ⓑ Both the skim cow's milk and the unsweetened oat milk's sodium contents were over 100 milligrams per cup.

Ⓒ The skim cow's milk and unsweetened oat milk both contain 90 calories in an average 1 cup serving.

Ⓓ The unsweetened oat milk has lower sugar content but higher fat content than does the skim cow's milk.

Here's How to Crack It

As you **Read and understand the question**, note that the question asks you to *support* the scientist's hypothesis using *data from the table.*

Next up, **Read the title, key/legend, variables, and units from the table or graph.** Not every chart has all of this (this two-way table has no key or legend), but you want to understand as much as you can. This chart shows *Nutritional Information for Skim cow's milk* and *Unsweetened oat milk*, and it shows *Fat* and *Sugars* in grams and *Sodium* in milligrams. You head into the passage fully expecting the scientist to make some claim about one or more of these terms.

As you **Read the passage and look for the same information**, notice that most of the passage simply offers some background to the data. While this must be read in case the theory or claim has multiple aspects to it, keep pushing your eyes forward and find the *scientist's hypothesis* regarding the information from the table.

Highlight that the *scientist theorized that because* ***skim milk*** *is whole milk that has been run through a centrifuge to separate out all of the fat droplets, it would likely have* ***less fat content but higher sugar content*** *than* ***unsweetened oat milk***. The bolded segment at the end is the actual piece of the theory that references the information from the table, so you know this is the sentence to focus on.

You know what's coming: it's time to **Use POE.** Consider these answers one at a time and compare them to the table AND what you highlighted.

Choice (A) should be eliminated because while it's consistent with the table, it does not address the claim. The claim focuses on the differing fat and sugar contents of skim cow's milk and unsweetened oat milk, while (A) only focuses on the fat and sugar content in skim cow's milk. Additionally, sodium is not relevant to the claim.

When doing POE, remember that the answer needs to reference the terms mentioned in the claim. Since the claim deals exclusively with fat and sugar content, (B) and (C) can be eliminated immediately for referencing sodium and calories, respectively.

Choice (B) should be eliminated because it is **Right Answer, Wrong Question.** The answer is perfectly consistent with the chart but isn't at all referencing the highlighted claim, which asks you to focus on differing *fat* and *sugar content* for the two milks, not *sodium content.*

Choice (C) should be eliminated because it is also **Right Answer, Wrong Question.** It's completely true based on the chart, but the claim offers no link between *calories* and how calorie count would affect differences in *fat content* and *sugar content* for the two milks.

Choice (D) should be kept because it's consistent with the table AND the claim. Unsweetened oat milk has *lower sugar content* (4 grams to unsweetened cow's milk's 12 grams) *but higher fat content* (1.5 grams to skim cow's milk's 0 grams). A correct answer won't always repeat the claim exactly but will offer a statement consistent with the claim.

With three answers eliminated and only (D) remaining, you select (D) and wonder why you must work your way through charts about milk on the Digital SAT instead of just enjoying some cereal.

The Charts Bottom Line: The correct answer to a Charts question needs to be consistent with both the chart AND the passage. There can (and usually will) be several answers consistent with the chart, but only one will also be consistent with the stated claim in the passage.

CONCLUSIONS

The last question type is very similar to the Claims question type that you saw earlier: it will ask you to complete the passage. However, rather than asking you to potentially *illustrate, support,* or *weaken* some claim, Conclusions questions are always asking you the same thing: which of the four answers is a logical conclusion based on all of the other sentences given in the passage? You just need to read for the main claim made or investigated by the author and choose a conclusion that is logically consistent with both the claim and anything the author includes or discovers in relation to the claim. This sounds thrilling, we know, so let's see how the Basic Approach can help you.

1. **Read the Question.**

2. **Identify the Question Type.** If a question says *Which choice most logically completes the text*, you know that you have a Conclusions question. Almost every Conclusions question is phrased this way, though we have also seen "Which choice best describes X as presented by the text?" Either way, you're being asked to include a logical summary or final statement consistent with everything described in the passage.

3. **Read the Passage.** Here, the central claim or statement made by the author or group is likely to be followed up by some additional data or information. This information could support or contradict the original claim, but either way, you'll need to read the entire passage to make sure you catch those wrinkles in the story!

4. **Highlight What Can Help.** There are two helpful things to highlight on Conclusions questions: the claim itself and, as mentioned, the additional data or information that sheds more light, for better or worse, on the claim. Similarly, if the question instead asks you to describe someone or something, you'll want to catch each major point made about that person or thing, as the correct answer should be a summary that captures all of the main points made by the passage.

5. **Use POE.** The most common trap answer on Conclusions questions is **Recycled Language**, as College Board is counting on you to only look for matching words but not matching ideas. You'll also see **Right Answer, Wrong Question**, as wrong answers can focus on a single detail from the passage rather than serve as a conclusion to the entire passage. Lastly, you'll see **Beyond the Text** trap answers, as logical or real-world conclusions that are not supported by the passage can really seem justified unless you double down on your highlighting and remember that you are here to eliminate answers, not justify them!

Western honeybees (*Apis mellifera)* are social insects that live inside rigid colonial nests made from wax, which can make it difficult to observe bee behavior within the colony. Bees typically form colonies with thousands to tens of thousands of bees, the weight of which would seem to place immense strain on the nest structure. Using an X-ray machine, researchers at CU Boulder have observed that swarms of *A. mellifera* inside the nest will form pyramids of bees, with larger numbers of bees at the base of the pyramid and fewer bees in each level as you move up the swarm. These researchers therefore imply that ______

5 Mark for Review

Which choice most logically completes the text?

Ⓐ the pyramids formed by *A. mellifera* swarms may reduce strain on the nest structure.

Ⓑ any individual *A. mellifera* bee can be in danger of suffocation by the rest of the bee swarm.

Ⓒ improving the numbers of *A. mellifera* requires Western intervention.

Ⓓ colonial nests enable *A. mellifera* to produce high quantities of wax.

Here's How to Crack It

As you **Read the Question,** you can also **Identify the Question Type** as a Conclusions question because it asks you to *logically complete the text.*

As you **Read the Passage,** be on the lookout for some claim or statement regarding the main focus of the passage. The main focus here is the *Western honeybee.*

Highlight that the *weight* of the bee colony *would seem to place immense strain on the nest structure.* This statement is very much like a claim—even though it's more fact than opinion or argument, it's still a topic that the passage will explore further. Later, also **Highlight** that *swarms of A. mellifera inside the nest will form pyramids of bees, with larger numbers of bees at the base of the pyramid and fewer bees in each level as one moves up the pyramid.* The correct answer will be consistent with both the statement made in the passage and the observations highlighted by the researchers towards the end.

As always, the conclusion of these steps is to **Use POE.** Three of the four answers won't be consistent with all of that highlighting.

Choice (A) should be kept because it's consistent with both items you highlighted. Notice how, very importantly, the answer says *may* reduce the strain rather than *will* reduce the strain. The passage doesn't support that there is a definitive connection between the two, but the answer's use of the word *may* allows you to keep it and continue using POE.

Choice (B) should be eliminated because it is a **Beyond the Text** trap answer. As logical as it is to assume that *any individual* bee could be in *danger of suffocation* given the quantity of bees, the author never mentions *suffocation* or anything like it in the passage.

Choice (C) should be eliminated because it contains **Recycled Language.** *Western* is used in the passage as part of the name of the bee species, not as an identifier for a region of the world, and the bee's numbers are not stated to be in need of *intervention.*

Choice (D) should be eliminated because it also contains **Recycled Language.** The passage states that the *colonial nests* are made ***from*** *wax,* not that the *colonial nests enable* the bees to produce *high quantities* ***of*** *wax.* Even if this were true in the real world, this answer ignores the central question and observation regarding the strain placed on the nest and the pyramid structure that the bees form.

With three answers eliminated and only (A) remaining, you select (A) and tell the Digital SAT to mind its own beeswax.

The Conclusions Bottom Line: The correct answer on a Conclusions question MUST take into account all of the information presented in the passage. These questions, therefore, can require more highlighting than other question types. Above all else, eliminate answers that aren't consistent with that highlighting and don't look to justify answers—look to eliminate them!

Summary

- You should **Annotate** whenever a summary or paraphrase of the passage would be helpful when using POE.
- Retrieval questions require you to look for what the author said about a topic or why something occurred in the story.
- Main Idea questions require you to look for the central person and/or idea that the author focuses on in each sentence.
- Claims questions are interspersed with Charts questions and ask you to illustrate, support, or weaken some claim in the passage.
- Charts questions are interspersed with Claims questions and ask you to select data from a table or graph that illustrates, supports, or weakens a claim.
- Conclusions questions always come last and ask for a concluding sentence to a series of ideas or a summary of the passage's main points.
- Don't forget POOD and guessing. If a chart looks intimidating or a passage is so dense that it's hard to find a claim to strengthen or weaken, enter an answer and move on!

Chapter 9
Advanced Reading Skills

In this chapter, we'll run through four different areas of the exam that you can focus on to further improve your score. Keep in mind that if you're following the Basic Approach and adapting it to the eight question types we discussed in the last two chapters, that should be enough to earn you a good chunk of the points that you may have been missing. However, sometimes difficult vocabulary, appealing trap answers, dense poetry, and complicated sentence structure can really affect your ability to find correct answers within the passage and use POE. This chapter seeks to offer a solution to each of those issues to keep your score and spirits improving.

1 month
Know

VOCABULARY: PLAYING THE GREATEST HITS

As we discussed back in Chapter 7, Vocabulary is one of the most frequent of the eight question types, which means that you'll likely be able to notice the difficulty increase (unlike with other question types that may have only 1 or 2 questions in an RW module). Similarly, should you do well enough on RW Module 1 to get the harder RW Module 2, you'll notice more difficult vocabulary words. In Chapter 7, we mentioned that creating a Greatest Hits list is a great way to start familiarizing yourself with words that you've seen and want to remember for next time. Here, we'll do our part as well: below is a list of words we've seen show up frequently on official SAT exams or released College Board products.

Sort of know
3-4 a day

> Spending 5–10 minutes a day EVERY DAY on our Greatest Hits, your own Greatest Hits, or a combination of both is the best way to improve your vocabulary and potentially boost your RW score!

N-C 1 or 2 a day
(no clue)

Word	Part of Speech	Definition
adhere	**verb**	to believe in and follow the practices of

Example: It can be difficult to *adhere* to a workout regimen without coaching and discipline.

advocate	**verb**	to publicly recommend or support

Example: Upon his appointment, the new vice president of the company promised to *advocate* for increased vacation time for all employees.

allude	**verb**	to suggest or call attention to indirectly; to hint at

Example: I didn't mean to *allude* to your past breakup when discussing celebrity romances that ended badly.

ambivalence	**noun**	the state of having mixed feelings or contradictory ideas about something or someone

Example: Understandably, Jillian struggled with *ambivalence* regarding the group project: she loved working with her friends but felt that the work was never divided evenly.

analogous	**adjective**	comparable in certain respects, typically in a way which makes clearer the nature of the things compared

Example: The rocking of a ship against the waves has been described by some as *analogous* to the ups and downs of a rollercoaster ride.

Word	Part of Speech	Definition
anecdote	**noun**	a short amusing or interesting story about a real incident or person

Example: Our professor opened the semester with a number of humorous *anecdotes* about excuses he has heard from students who missed class.

apprehensive	**adjective**	anxious or fearful that something bad or unpleasant will happen

Example: Lauren was *apprehensive* about her upcoming violin recital: she had practiced enough but had never performed in front of more than four or five people.

arbitrary	**adjective**	based on random choice or personal whim, rather than any reason or system

Example: The town's enforcement of parking rules felt *arbitrary*, as some days the rules would be strictly enforced and other days it seemed impossible to get a ticket no matter how severe the infraction.

assert	**verb**	to state a fact or belief confidently and forcefully

Example: After listening to the rest of the board members shout over each other, Dominic felt the need to *assert* that this time could have been better spent offering practical solutions to the issue.

bias	**noun**	prejudice in favor of or against one thing, person, or group compared with another, usually in a way considered to be unfair

Example: Though she promised to be free of *bias*, it became evident very quickly that my mom preferred a dog over a cat as a potential pet.

brevity	**noun**	concise and exact use of words in writing or speech

Example: Sabrina's notes were known for their *brevity*, as entire concepts were often summed up into a small series of words and phrases.

buttress	**verb**	to increase the strength of or justification for; to reinforce

Example: The commissioner has promised to train 30 new recruits by the end of the year in order to *buttress* the police force as the city's borders expand.

Word	Part of Speech	Definition
concede	**verb**	to admit that something is true or valid after first denying or resisting it

Example: After an intense debate, I was forced to *concede* that my opponent had a strong argument regarding the need for district-wide budget reallocation.

consensus	**noun**	a general agreement

Example: With everyone wanting a different cuisine, the group of friends found it nearly impossible to come to a *consensus*.

corroborate	**verb**	to confirm or give support to (a statement, theory, or finding)

Example: The thief claimed to have an alibi at the time of the crime but could not produce any friend or family to *corroborate* his story.

decisive	**adjective**	settling an issue; producing a definite result

Example: Megan scored a *decisive* victory for her field hockey team, netting four goals in just the first half of the game.

deference	**noun**	humble submission and respect

Example: The student spoke with *deference* to his master when discussing the proper application of a mixed martial arts technique.

degrade	**verb**	to treat or regard (someone) with contempt or disrespect

Example: The harsh note taped to the bulletin board in the employee breakroom was clearly meant to *degrade* those who were not clocking back in from breaks on time.

denounce	**verb**	to publicly declare to be wrong or evil

Example: The principal was expected to *denounce* graphic T-shirts as unacceptable school attire, but she surprised everyone when she stated that she considered them to be an important part of self-expression.

dispute	**noun**	a disagreement, argument, or debate

Example: A handshake, or verbal, agreement between employer and employee can lead to a *dispute* when one party does not follow through and there is no written documentation to resolve the matter.

Word	Part of Speech	Definition
divergent	**adjective**	tending to be different or develop in different directions

Example: Due to the unclear instructions, students took *divergent* paths in their papers, with some arguing multiple perspectives and some switching topics altogether.

dormant	**adjective**	having normal physical functions suspended or slowed down for a period of time; in or as if in a deep sleep

Example: Though the volcano once erupted randomly and violently for decades, it now lies *dormant* and is a popular tourist attraction.

eloquent	**adjective**	fluent or persuasive in speaking or writing

Example: Shakespeare's sonnets are considered some of the most *eloquent* poems in British literature.

evoke	**verb**	to bring or recall to the conscious mind

Example: A country's national anthem is meant to *evoke* feelings of pride in its citizens.

exert	**verb**	to make a physical or mental effort

Example: Math Olympiad competitors *exert* a tremendous amount of mental energy solving calculations while under a time limit.

explicit	**adjective**	stated clearly and in detail, leaving no room for confusion or doubt

Example: The teacher's classroom rules were *explicit*; they were written on a poster right above her desk.

imminent	**adjective**	about to happen

Example: The decreasing temperatures and darkening skies mean that a rainstorm is *imminent.*

impede	**verb**	to delay or prevent (someone or something) by obstructing; to hinder

Example: The city council attempted to *impede* the fast-food restaurant's efforts to install a drive-thru window.

Word	Part of Speech	Definition
implicit	**adjective**	implied but not plainly expressed

Example: The group had seen Sara's terrified reactions to horror movies and had an *implicit* understanding not to choose that genre for movie night.

Word	Part of Speech	Definition
impose	**verb**	to take advantage of someone by demanding attention or commitment

Example: The mayor has decided to *impose* a curfew upon residents of his town.

Word	Part of Speech	Definition
indifference	**noun**	lack of interest, concern, or sympathy

Example: Sam responded to the discussion of a road trip with *indifference,* as he would have been equally happy staying home.

Word	Part of Speech	Definition
inevitable	**adjective**	certain to happen; unavoidable

Example: Once the school mandated a dress code, it was *inevitable* that the students would test the limits of what they could get away with.

Word	Part of Speech	Definition
invoke	**verb**	to cite or appeal to (someone or something) as an authority for an action or in support of an argument

Example: The police captain's son would often *invoke* his father's name to get himself out of trouble.

Word	Part of Speech	Definition
ironic	**adjective**	happening in the opposite way from what is expected and typically causing amusement because of this

Example: It is *ironic* that the tech support company's website was listed as down for maintenance.

Word	Part of Speech	Definition
novel	**adjective**	new or unusual in an interesting way

Example: *Novel* ideas, such as Galileo's model for the Earth revolving around the Sun, usually take time to be accepted by those comfortable with traditional views.

Word	Part of Speech	Definition
obscure	**adjective**	not discovered or known about; uncertain

Example: John's pop culture references were so remarkably *obscure* that his friends could go for hours without knowing a single actor or movie he mentioned.

Word	**Part of Speech**	**Definition**
obsolete	**adjective**	no longer produced or used; out of date

Example: Zara was dismayed to learn her phone was considered *obsolete* just one year after she purchased it.

oppressive	**adjective**	unjustly inflicting hardship and constraint; weighing heavily on the mind or spirits

Example: The heat of the jungle was so *oppressive* that the expedition team took breaks twice as often as planned.

pervasive	**adjective**	spreading widely throughout an area or a group of people, especially in an unpleasant way

Example: The aging boat had holes in its hull and a *pervasive* smell of rotting wood.

prevalence	**noun**	the fact or condition of being prevalent; commonness

Example: The *prevalence* of transfer students on college football teams has made roster adjustments a year-round endeavor.

prominent	**adjective**	important; famous

Example: One of the most *prominent* American presidents, George Washington, is often noted as having set numerous presidential precedents.

provoke	**verb**	to stimulate or give rise to a reaction or emotion, typically a strong or unwelcome one in someone

Example: I knew I couldn't let Anthony *provoke* me into an argument again, as he often did.

reciprocate	**verb**	to respond to (a gesture or action) by making a corresponding one

Example: Jennifer was so touched by the Christmas gift she received from Isabelle that she made plans to *reciprocate* as soon as she could get to the mall.

reconcile	**verb**	to restore friendly relations between

Example: William texted Caleb an apology as a means to *reconcile* following their recent disagreement.

Word	Part of Speech	Definition
refute	**verb**	to prove (a statement or theory) to be wrong or false; disprove

Example: Scientists often publish papers meant to *refute* theories that they have disproven through experimentation.

renounce	**verb**	to formally declare one's abandonment of (a claim, right, or possession)

Example: In a shocking move, the king has decided to *renounce* his right to the throne, sending the country into a panic.

repression	**noun**	the restraint, prevention, or inhibition of a feeling, quality, etc.

Example: When citizens of a nation endure long periods of political *repression*, it can lead to verbal or physical altercations throughout that country.

retain	**verb**	to continue to have (something); keep possession of

Example: In an effort to *retain* her position as class president, Cynthia put up flyers asking for students' votes in the upcoming election.

skeptical	**adjective**	not easily convinced; having doubts or reservations

Example: Bryce was *skeptical* of his order's estimated arrival date: past orders from the same company had taken a week longer than advertised.

speculate	**verb**	to form a theory or conjecture about a subject without firm evidence

Example: The lawyer refused to *speculate* on the outcome of the trial, but she was hopeful that her client would be found innocent.

substantiate	**verb**	to provide evidence to support or prove the truth of

Example: The researcher ran a series of experiments hoping to *substantiate* her theory of engine mechanics before presenting it to her supervisor for review.

subtle	**adjective**	so delicate or precise as to be difficult to analyze or describe

Example: A slight cough from a friend can be a *subtle* indication that the friend wishes to depart from a social situation in which they feel uncomfortable.

Word	Part of Speech	Definition
supplement	**noun**	something that completes or enhances something else when added to it

Example: Milk is often considered the perfect *supplement* to cereal, though other liquids have become popular choices in recent years.

tenuous	**adjective**	very weak or slight

Example: With just seconds to go in the game, the team clung to a *tenuous* one-point lead.

undermine	**verb**	to lessen the effectiveness, power, or ability of

Example: Michael practically ran on his way to school, worried that a mark of tardy would *undermine* his perfect attendance record.

underscore	**verb**	to emphasize or draw attention to

Example: Margaux came to her presentation with a series of handouts for her colleagues, hoping this would *underscore* the amount of work she had put into her project.

unobtrusive	**adjective**	not conspicuous or attracting attention

Example: Garbage cans at Disney World are painted to be as *unobtrusive* as possible, often blending into their surroundings.

validate	**verb**	to check or prove the validity or accuracy of (something)

Example: The clerk refused to *validate* my license, noting that it expired one month ago.

verisimilitude	**noun**	the appearance of being true or real

Example: Despite being a work of fiction, the movie possessed such authentic characters and believable dialogue that critics praised it for its *verisimilitude.*

viable	**adjective**	capable of working successfully; feasible

Example: The hiring supervisor was pleased to find that so many *viable* candidates had applied for the position.

DOWN TO TWO (OR MORE): MASTERING POE

Sometimes, even when you find an amazing piece of evidence to highlight, you'll still have two (or more) appealing answers that have survived the initial POE process. Other times, the passage is difficult enough that you aren't able to pin down that one piece of evidence or aren't able to make an annotation. In these cases, all hope is not lost. Remember that every question has three wrong answers and that most, though not all, of these answers are traps. Understanding trap answers and *actively* looking for traps can earn you points at these critical moments!

As a reminder, here's the Process of Elimination criteria you saw in Chapter 6:

- **Opposite:** These answer choices have a single word or phrase that make the answer convey a tone, viewpoint, or meaning not intended by the author. This can include a word such as "not" in the answer or a negative vocabulary word when the tone of the passage was positive.

- **Extreme Language:** These answers look just about perfect except for a word or phrase that goes too far beyond what the passage can support.

- **Recycled Language:** These answer choices repeat exact words and phrases from the passage but put the words together to say something that the passage didn't actually say. They often establish relationships between the words and phrases that do not exist in the passage.

- **Right Answer, Wrong Question:** These answer choices are true based on the passage, but they don't answer the question asked. They can also state *what* the author said when the question was asking *why* the author said it.

- **Beyond the Text:** These answers might initially look good because they make sense or seem logical based on outside reasoning, but they lack support within the passage itself.

- **Half-Right:** These answers address part but not all of the question task. They can also have one half of the answer address the question perfectly and the other half contain at least one of the traps mentioned previously.

> The most critical question to ask if two or more answers remain once you've compared every answer to what you found in the passage is "Which answer is the trap?" This turns your focus away from justification and back to active Process of Elimination!

In the following exercises, you'll see that we've eliminated at least one answer already based on highlighting, annotating, or an answer being so completely inconsistent with the topic of the passage that it's no longer even worth displaying here.

Try to determine the remaining trap answer, or answers, on your own, then read through the explanation below in order to understand the most efficient way to use POE when two or more answers remain.

The following text is from Jane Austen's 1818 novel *Northanger Abbey.* Catherine Morland, the main character, has recently been invited to spend the next six weeks on vacation in Bath, England.

> In addition to what has been already said of Catherine Morland's personal and mental endowments, when about to be launched into all the difficulties and dangers of a six weeks' residence in Bath, it may be stated, for the reader's more certain information, lest the following pages should otherwise fail of giving any idea of what her character is meant to be, that her heart was affectionate; her disposition cheerful and open, without conceit or affectation of any kind—her manners just removed from the awkwardness and shyness of a girl; her person pleasing, and, when in good looks, pretty—and her mind about as ignorant and uninformed as the female mind at seventeen usually is.

1 Mark for Review

Which choice best states the main purpose of the text?

Ⓐ To establish that Catherine is as naïve as expected of one her age

Ⓑ To describe Catherine's personality and level of maturity prior to her trip

Ⓒ ~~To convey Catherine's disapproval towards the family that will host her in Bath~~

Ⓓ ~~To explain the difficulties and dangers that Catherine will face in Bath~~

Which answer is the trap? The trap answer to this Purpose question is (A).

Why? This trap answer is **Right Answer, Wrong Question.** It's completely supported by the final sentence of the passage, which states *and her mind about as ignorant and uninformed as the female mind at seventeen usually is.* The problem is that the question asks for the *main purpose* of the passage, and the rest of the passage doesn't discuss Catherine's naiveté at all!

So, which answer must be correct? By Process of Elimination, the correct answer is (B).

Why? Careful **highlighting** would show that the passage describes *Catherine Morland's mental and personal endowments,* that *her heart was affectionate, her disposition cheerful and open, without conceit or affectation,* and *her person pleasing,* which are all just as important to the description as the naiveté from the last lines you saw earlier. A good **annotation** for the answer here would have been "describe how Catherine acts and thinks," which is fairly consistent with (B).

Artificial sweeteners offer an appealing alternative to sugar, but they may carry unintended consequences for the body because of their effect on the gut microbiome. It has been demonstrated that the bacteria that make up the gut microbiome affect glucose tolerance and appetite. Researchers at the Weizmann Institute of Science claim that the consumption of artificial sweeteners such as sucralose can lower glucose tolerance and increase appetite in humans. The researchers conducted a study comparing the glucose tolerance and appetite levels of people who had been fed sucralose against a control group who was not fed sucralose.

2 Mark for Review

Which finding from the researchers' study, if true, would most directly support their hypothesis?

(A) Both the individuals who consumed sucralose and the control group had much higher glucose tolerance levels at the conclusion of the study.

(B) At the conclusion of the study, individuals who consumed sucralose had lower glucose tolerance levels but also decreased appetite levels compared to the control group.

(C) Individuals who consumed sucralose had lower glucose tolerance levels and increased appetite levels at the conclusion of the study compared to the control group.

(D) When individuals who consumed sucralose were interviewed, they were found to also have consumed large quantities of water, which is known to decrease appetite.

Which answer is the trap? The trap answer to this Claims question is (B).

Why? This trap answer is **Half-Right.** It looks incredibly solid, except for the very end when it mentions that the sucralose group had *decreased appetite levels compared to the control group*, while the passage states that sucralose should *increase appetite.* Most of the time, Half-Right answers will contain one of the other traps; in this case, the very end of the answer contains information that is the **Opposite** of what's presented in the passage.

So, which answer must be correct? By Process of Elimination, the correct answer is (C).

Why? This answer is consistent with the researchers' claim from the passage, which should be **highlighted** when taking the test: *sucralose can lower glucose tolerance and increase appetite in humans.* Therefore, the group taking sucralose should present *lower glucose tolerance levels and increased appetite levels compared to the control group*, as (C) states.

Even if you eliminate just a single answer, or even no answers at all, through your highlighting and annotating, you can still efficiently use POE by comparing the answers to what you can see in the passage!

Barefoot running, the act of running without footwear, has increased in popularity since the year 2000, with exercise enthusiasts looking to reduce the repetitive stress injuries caused by padded running footwear. However, the practice dates back thousands of years, with some long-established Latin American and African groups utilizing barefoot running even up to the present day despite the availability of modern footwear in those regions. This suggests that before the year 2000, ______

3 Mark for Review

Which choice most logically completes the text?

(A) certain practitioners of barefoot running in different regions of the world may have already discovered the benefits of the practice.

(B) barefoot running has made exercise more accessible to those who cannot afford expensive footwear.

(C) barefoot running will soon surpass other methods of exercise as awareness of its benefits becomes more prevalent.

(D) ~~footwear manufacturers could increase profits if they created region-specific running shoe designs.~~

Which answer is a trap? The first trap answer to this Conclusions question is (B).

Why? This trap answer is a **Beyond the Text** trap. Anytime you look at an answer and say, "Well, this is true" or "This makes sense," you want to remind yourself that what makes an answer correct on the Digital SAT is that it is supported by the passage and that it answers the question. As logical as it is to assume that increased awareness of the benefits of barefoot running may decrease the barrier to exercise created by expensive footwear, the author never mentions anything regarding *expensive footwear* in the passage. If an answer is something you could only support if you had a chance to argue about it with someone, it's probably a wrong answer.

Which remaining answer is also a trap? The second trap answer is (C).

Why? This answer is a type of **Extreme Language** trap. While it may not contain words like *only* or *most* which are more concretely extreme words, it still takes an opinion or claim made in the passage too far. The opening sentence states that *barefoot running...has increased in popularity*, but that doesn't mean that barefoot running will *surpass other methods of exercise* as (C) states. The passage would need to state this bold prediction and not just offer a piece of evidence that may support such a prediction as if it were part of a much longer, much more detailed argument.

Answers that say something *will* happen are almost certainly wrong because they are Extreme Language. People can predict what is *likely to* happen, or what *may* happen, but no one can say what *will* happen.

So, which answer must be correct? By Process of Elimination, the correct answer is (A).

Why? This answer is consistent with the passage. In the opening line, the passage states that *barefoot running…has increased in popularity since the year 2000.* However, *the practice dates back thousands of years* for certain *Latin American and African groups*, who are described as still using the practice up to the present day *despite the availability of modern footwear in those regions.* This means that those Latin American and African groups have chosen to continue barefoot running even with the option to acquire modern footwear. While you can't know for sure that this means they *discovered* the *benefits* of barefoot running before the year 2000, the phrase *may have* is just loose enough to be supported by the passage. Remember, one more time, that the right answer for Conclusions questions will not always be directly stated or proven by the passage—it will be the *best supported* of the four answers.

POETRY: KEEPING YOUR COOL

Occasionally (likely no more than two times per module), your source passage on a literature-based question will be a poem or poetry excerpt. This is no reason to panic: College Board isn't expecting you to be a Poet Laureate or the next Shakespeare. Understand that poems still make claims and tell stories just as prose does, only the language follows a meter and/or rhyme scheme. Poetry often shows up on Claims questions, but we have seen it on Purpose, Retrieval, and Main Idea questions as well.

Before we dive into some poetry-based Digital SAT questions, let's see some common phrases as they appear in poetry and what those mean in modern English.

Poetic Contraction or Abbreviation	Modern English Word(s)
'tis	it is
'twas	it was
o'er	over
ne'er	never
ere	before
e'en	even
o'	of
an'	and

This may clear up some confusion, but the other key to understanding poetry is that poets often use more comparative literary devices than other writers do, most often comparing the person or thing that is the focus to some element from the natural or supernatural world. While you won't be asked to identify literary devices as part of a question, know that poems on the Digital SAT often use analogies, metaphors, and similes to enhance the impact of their language. The distinctions among these don't matter that much, as long as you understand that all of them are used to describe ideas by comparing them to other ideas.

- Example of an analogy: *Pain is our fire alarm. The sharpness of the alarm alerts us to an issue.*
- Example of a metaphor: *Our car sailed gracefully through the sea of traffic as we navigated the rough waters of the interstate with a captain's precision.*
- Example of a simile: *He's got a heart as warm as solid ice and a smile as pleasing as spoiled milk.*

The following text is from Archibald Lampman's 1899 poem "The Mystery of a Year." In this poem, the speaker is describing a woman whom he has known for some time.

A little while, a year agone,
  I knew her for a romping child,
A dimple and a glance that shone
  With idle mischief when she smiled.

To-day she passed me in the press,
  And turning with a quick surprise
I wondered at her stateliness,
  I wondered at her altered eyes.

4 Mark for Review

Which choice best states the main idea of the text?

Ⓐ The speaker is reminiscing about a past romantic relationship with a woman.

Ⓑ The speaker is astonished at the changes within a certain individual.

Ⓒ The speaker is an expert in observing subtle changes in others.

Ⓓ The speaker uses intricate and complex thought processes to impress those around him.

Watch Us Crack It
Watch the step-by-step video explanation of how to answer this question in your Student Tools.

Here's How to Crack It

As you **Read the Question,** you can also **Identify the Question Type** as a Main Idea question when you see *main idea* in the question stem—we know, it's quite revolutionary!

As you **Read the Passage,** focus on the person, place, or thing the lines chiefly focus on.

The main focus of the passage is the woman the narrator is describing. **Highlight** *A little while, a year agone, I knew her for a romping child.* This indicates what the narrator thought of the woman in the past (he thought of her as a child). Also **Highlight** *To-Day she passed me in the press, And turning with a quick surprise, I wondered at her stateliness.* This indicates what the narrator thinks of her now (he is surprised by her growth and now thinks of her as a woman). You may wish to make an **annotation** to the effect of "girl narrator knew has changed" in your annotation box.

It's time to use **POE.** Only one of these answers will be consistent with the main idea we found, poetry or not.

Choice (A) should be eliminated because there is no mention of a *romantic relationship* in the passage. It would be a **Beyond the Text** trap to assume there needs to be any romance between the narrator and the woman.

Choice (B) should be kept because while *astonished* is a fairly strong word, the mention of *surprise* and *wondered* within the passage are enough to keep this answer in play for now, and the narrator certainly notices *changes within a certain individual,* the woman.

Choice (C) should be eliminated because it is the **Opposite** of what the passage states. These are not *subtle* changes in the girl; they are quite stark, or obvious, changes. Additionally, the passage doesn't support that the narrator is an *expert* in noticing changes.

Choice (D) should be eliminated because it is a **Beyond the Text** trap and a fairly **Extreme** logical leap as well. One might assume *intricate and complex thought processes* to be part of poetry in general, but the narrator's thoughts are not described in the passage. Also, the passage doesn't state that the narrator uses these thoughts to *impress* anyone around him.

With three answers eliminated and only (B) remaining, you select (B) and celebrate the not-so-subtle positive changes in your own Digital SAT performance.

"A Ballad of Evesham" is a 1933 poem by Francis T. Palgrave. The poem demonstrates a character's ignorance of a deception created by his enemy.

______

5 Mark for Review

Which quotation from the poem most effectively illustrates the claim?

Ⓐ "Earl Simon on the Abbey tower / In summer sunshine stood, / While helm and lance o'er Greenhill heights / Come glinting through the wood."

Ⓑ "'My son!' he cried, 'I know his flag / Amongst a thousand glancing':— / Fond father! no!—'tis Edward stern / In royal strength advancing."

Ⓒ "The Prince fell on him like a hawk / At Al'ster yester-eve, / And flaunts his captured banner now / And flaunts but to deceive:—"

Ⓓ "—Look round! for Mortimer is by, / And guards the rearward river:— / The hour that parted sire and son / Has parted them for ever!"

Here's How to Crack It

As you **Read the Question,** you can also **Identify the Question Type** as a Claims question when you see *illustrates the claim* in the question stem.

As you **Read the Passage,** which is quite short, you can **Highlight** the claim you are meant to illustrate: *a character's ignorance of a deception created by his enemy.*

Once again, it's time to **Use POE.** Keep in mind that the right answer must address the entire claim, not just part of it.

Choice (A) should be eliminated because the answer only describes *Earl Simon* and what he observes approaching his tower. The answer doesn't indicate anyone who has fallen for any type of deception.

Choice (B) should be kept because the first half of the answer has a character (*he*) believe the approaching figure is his *son* because he sees his son's *flag.* However, another character in the second half of the answer, presumably another son of the Earl's since he cries out *"Fond father,"* warns the first person that the approaching individual is *Edward,* who is *advancing* his forces towards the tower.

Choice (C) should be eliminated because it is **Half-Right:** it more thoroughly explains the *deception* carried out by Edward, which makes the answer quite appealing. However, recall that the right answer here must also mention *a character's ignorance,* and in these lines, no one has fallen for the ruse as the character did in (B).

Choice (D) should be eliminated because it doesn't mention the deception by Edward nor the Earl's ignorance of that deception.

With three answers eliminated and only (B) remaining, you select (B) and won't be deceived by the Digital SAT's own clever tricks.

SENTENCE FUNCTION: UNDERSTANDING WHY SENTENCES ARE INCLUDED

Since you only have approximately 1 minute and 11 seconds per question, spending large amounts of time understanding the structure of each passage isn't practical. However, learning to understand the roles that sentences can perform will help you on Purpose, Dual Texts, Main Idea, Claims, and Conclusions question, as each of these question types tends to require you to find a main idea and/or the most likely reason the author would have included something. If you're finding it difficult to navigate a passage but can determine which role each sentence is performing, this can help you zero in on the one or two sentences you need in order to capture that main idea or understand the link between ideas. **Keep in mind that these sentence functions are much more common in non-literature passages (such as science) than in literature passages.**

The most common functions a sentence can perform on the Digital SAT are as follows:

Background: This sentence provides context or information regarding a topic that the author feels is necessary for the reader to understand before any arguments are made. Background sentences are usually factual in nature and often occur at the start of a story.

Claim: This sentence contains the author's, an individual's, or a group's main argument, theory, or opinion. A critical feature of a claim is that it is something that can be disagreed with and needs to be supported by evidence.

Objection: This sentence is a special type of claim in which someone in the passage argues against a claim, theory, or opinion made by someone else in the passage. It often includes words such as *but* or *however.*

Evidence: This sentence usually contains lots of details and is used to support Claims or Objections. While most evidence occurs after a claim or objection, it can also come before if the author has chosen to build up to their claim.

Consider the following passage:

> With the initial growth of suburban communities in the mid-twentieth century, residential pools went from the domain of only the wealthiest individuals to attainable amenities for those with more modest incomes. However, this boon came with predictably negative consequences for local wildlife near these communities. Improper drainage of water in pools and spas used for personal recreation has led to widespread contamination that can cause immense environmental damage and even kill plant and animal life. A group of researchers has posited that proper drainage of pool water can help to reverse the damage done to suburban environments. In a survey conducted on soil surrounding residential pools in various American suburbs, the researchers found the toxicity of soil surrounding pools in which the owner had followed the manufacturer's drainage instructions to be 46% lower than the toxicity levels of soil surrounding pools for which the instructions had been followed improperly.

This example is among the longest passages you'd ever see on the Digital SAT but actually only comprises five sentences, each with one of the four main sentence functions. For each sentence, try to determine which function the sentence is performing before looking at our explanation on the next page.

> With the initial growth of suburban communities in the mid-twentieth century, residential pools went from the domain of only the wealthiest individuals to attainable amenities for those with more modest incomes.

How would you categorize Sentence 1: background, claim, objection, or evidence?

Sentence 1 gives **background information.** It states the historical context that helps the reader understand how residential pools became more prevalent, which contributes to the problem discussed in the passage. If you're looking for a claim or a main idea, you know to keep pushing your eyes forward to the next sentence.

> However, this boon came with predictably negative consequences for local wildlife near these communities.

How would you categorize Sentence 2: background, claim, objection, or evidence?

Sentence 2 provides an **objection**. Note the presence of the word *However* at the start of the sentence. It may seem odd that an author can object to background information, but it's a very common way for authors to generate interest in their topic and call attention to an issue that has arisen from a prior decision. You now know that the author believes the prevalence of residential pools has been negative, so answers that express a positive attitude towards residential pools can be eliminated.

> Improper drainage of water in pools and spas used for personal recreation has led to widespread contamination that can cause immense environmental damage and even kill plant and animal life.

How would you categorize Sentence 3: background, claim, objection, or evidence?

Sentence 3 is **evidence.** Authors shouldn't make claims or objections without backing them up. Here, the author needed to explain exactly how an increase in residential pools has harmed the environment. Make sure to read evidence carefully but not to over-analyze it. Unless you're dealing with a Retrieval question, you want to know why the evidence is there rather than deeply comprehend every last word in the evidence.

> A group of researchers has posited that proper drainage of pool water can help to reverse the damage done to suburban environments.

How would you categorize Sentence 4: background, claim, objection, or evidence?

Sentence 4 is a **claim.** Words such as *believe, posit,* or *hypothesize* are dead giveaways that a claim or opinion is being stated in the passage. This is often the key thing you are looking for on Dual Texts, Main Idea, Claims, and Charts questions, and it's helpful as part of the answer to Purpose questions as well. This is why reading the question carefully matters so much: does the question ask you to work with the researchers' claim from this sentence, or the author's view from sentence 2? You could easily see a Right Answer, Wrong Question trap that focuses on the wrong claim entirely.

In a survey conducted on soil surrounding residential pools in various American suburbs, the researchers found the toxicity of soil surrounding pools in which the owner had followed the manufacturer's drainage instructions to be 46% lower than the toxicity levels of soil surrounding pools for which the instructions had been followed improperly.

How would you categorize Sentence 5: background, claim, objection, or evidence?

Sentence 5 is **evidence.** As with the objection in sentence 2, the passage should offer some data that either supports or refutes the claim made previously. In this case, the data here supports that proper drainage would help reduce environmental damage, as the researchers claimed. You already know that this evidence supports the researchers' claim, so answers that contradict the researchers' claim can be eliminated right away.

Summary

- Studying the Vocabulary Greatest Hits 5–10 minutes a day is a straightforward but powerful way to help your RW score. You should study a blend of your own Greatest Hits discussed in Chapter 7 and the one included in this chapter.
- When down to two (or more) answers after comparing the answers to your highlighting and annotation, the critical question to ask is "Which of the remaining answers is a trap?" Aim to find a reason each answer is wrong, not justify an answer that you want to pick but that isn't fully supported.
- As a reminder, the six trap answers are:
    - Opposite
    - Extreme Language
    - Recycled Language
    - Right Answer, Wrong Question
    - Beyond the Text
    - Half-Right
- On poetry questions, keep your cool—just because the lines follow a meter and rhyme doesn't mean you can't still find claims and statements. Be aware of poetic contractions and how poets use analogies, similes, and metaphors.
- In non-literature passages, most sentences serve as background information, a claim, an objection, or evidence. Understanding the role of each sentence can help you find the right information needed to answer your question even if you aren't exactly sure what's happening in the passage overall.
- Don't forget your POOD! It may be worth marking or even entering a random guess on a tough Vocabulary question, a tricky poem, a dense paragraph, or if you've simply spent too long debating two answers. There will be plenty of other questions in the module to use these skills on!

Chapter 10 Comprehensive Reading Drill

Use your new reading comprehension and test-taking skills on the following drill, which features at least one of each of the eight question types. Remember to read *actively* and use the Reading Basic Approach for all 11 examples.

Comprehensive Reading Drill

Answers can be found starting on page 222.

1 Mark for Review

While most fiction writers edit their stories and re-write them when faced with challenging narrative obstacles, Argentine author César Aira ________ the traditional revision process, choosing instead to construct creative solutions to tricky narrative problems rather than simply cut anything that he has already written.

Which choice completes the text with the most logical and precise word or phrase?

Ⓐ allows

Ⓑ avoids

Ⓒ embraces

Ⓓ integrates

2 Mark for Review

While Navajo musician Klee Benally is perhaps best known for his role as lead vocalist and guitarist for the band Blackfire, he is also a documentary filmmaker and activist. One of his films, *The Snowball Effect,* cautioned against the possible ________ impact of a proposed ski resort on sacred tribal lands in Arizona.

Which choice completes the text with the most logical and precise word or phrase?

Ⓐ aesthetic

Ⓑ detrimental

Ⓒ economic

Ⓓ restorative

3 Mark for Review

The following text is from Anne Virginia Culbertson's 1904 short story "How Mr. Terrapin Lost His Beard."

> The "cook-house" stood at some little distance from the "big house," and every evening after supper it was full of light and noise and laughter. The light came from the fire on the huge hearth, above which hung the crane and the great iron pots which Eliza, the cook, declared were indispensable in the practice of her art. To be sure, there was a cook-stove, but 'Liza was wedded to old ways and maintained there was nothing "stove cooked" that could hope to rival the rich and nutty flavor of ash cake, or greens "b'iled slow an' long over de ha'th, wid a piece er bacon in de pot."

As used in the text, what does the word "practice" most nearly mean?

Ⓐ Amusement

Ⓑ Recital

Ⓒ Execution

Ⓓ Appraisal

4 Mark for Review

Invented in 1775, Scheele's green ($CuHAsO_3$) is an acidic copper arsenite that creates a vivid emerald-green pigment and is dangerous to humans. Used in wallpaper and candles in Victorian-era England, the arsenite was completely phased out by the late 1800s, as the public gained knowledge of how toxic its vapors were. However, after the turn of the century, Scheele's green reappeared as an effective insecticide and, controversially, as a food dye to create bright green candy.

Which choice best describes the overall structure of the text?

Ⓐ It describes an invention and then gives specific reasons for its continued use.

Ⓑ It describes a hypothesis concerning a compound and then contradicts that hypothesis.

Ⓒ It introduces a product and then discusses both the uses and the dangers associated with that product.

Ⓓ It explains the initial purpose of an invention and then questions the ethics behind that invention.

5 Mark for Review

Text 1

Binge-watching, or viewing multiple episodes of a show at once, became popular with the widespread availability of internet streaming services in the early twenty-first century. Clinical psychologist Dr. John Mayer explains that binge-watching can serve as a form of stress relief for viewers. According to Dr. Mayer, the experience of disconnecting from the real world through an extended viewing session triggers the release of dopamine, a chemical, from the brain, which leads to feelings of relaxation and pleasure.

Text 2

Clinical psychologist Dr. Renee Carr warns that any activity that produces dopamine can potentially be dangerous if an individual engages in the behavior too frequently and becomes dependent on the desirable feelings it produces. She notes that while dopamine is not addictive in and of itself, a form of addiction can take hold whenever an individual develops a need for any activity, including binge-watching, no matter how harmless that activity might seem.

Based on the texts, how would Dr. Renee Carr (Text 2) most likely respond to Dr. John Mayer's observations (Text 1)?

Ⓐ She would argue that binge-watching can have very different effects on people depending on the subject matter being viewed.

Ⓑ She would point out that the long-term effects of binge-watching will be negative for streaming companies as well.

Ⓒ She would suggest that Dr. Mayer compare the dopamine effects of binge-watching to the dopamine effects experienced as the result of engaging in other kinds of pleasurable activities.

Ⓓ She would suggest that frequent binge-watching may not have an entirely positive effect upon an individual.

6 Mark for Review

The following text is from the 1914 short story "A Mother" by James Joyce. Mrs. Kearney, the mother of local pianist Kathleen Kearney, is being discussed.

> She had been educated in a high-class convent, where she had learned French and music. As she was naturally pale and unbending in manner she made few friends at school. When she came to the age of marriage she was sent out to many houses where her playing and ivory manners were much admired. She sat amid the chilly circle of her accomplishments, waiting for some suitor to brave it and offer her a brilliant life. But the young men whom she met were ordinary and she gave them no encouragement, trying to console her romantic desires by eating a great deal of Turkish Delight in secret.

According to the text, what is true about Mrs. Kearney?

Ⓐ Mrs. Kearney had certain standards regarding a potential husband.

Ⓑ Mrs. Kearney's desperation to marry was obvious to those around her.

Ⓒ Mrs. Kearney was criticized for treating potential suitors rudely.

Ⓓ Mrs. Kearney sometimes disapproved of the behavior of her would-be suitors.

7 Mark for Review

In one of their numerous studies on invasive species, researcher Satu Ramula and her team in Finland planted a mixture of North American and Finnish garden lupines (*lupinus polyphyllus*) into Finnish soil to examine the impact of soil microbiota (bacteria that live in a plant's root system) on the plant's growth and development. One crop was planted into nutrient-poor soil that contained microbiota from local lupine populations, while the other crop was planted into nutrient-poor soil that contained no microbiota. Regardless of the country of origin, the crop of garden lupines in the soil containing microbiota not only grew much larger than the other crop's lupines, but also secreted a much stronger scent that is a natural deterrent to snails, the garden lupine's most common predator.

Which choice best states the main idea of the text?

Ⓐ It discusses the study by Ramula and her team to examine one possible reason that garden lupines are able to grow and thrive.

Ⓑ It details the study by Ramula and her team to critique other researchers for ignoring the impact of soil microbiota on garden lupines.

Ⓒ It argues that the effects of soil microbiota on garden lupines are often difficult to observe, as was the case with Ramula and her team's study.

Ⓓ It explains a significant threat to the environment caused by garden lupines that the study by Ramula and her team attempted to address.

8 Mark for Review

Approximate Appearance Percentage for Three Blood Types in Four Regions

Region	O+	A+	B+
Asia	37%	28%	25%
Americas	55%	28%	9%
Africa	47%	27%	17%
Oceania	42%	33%	11%

Blood is critical to the function of the human body, as it delivers nutrients to vital organs, exchanges carbon dioxide and oxygen, and moves white blood cells through the circulatory system to fight infections. Blood is often categorized by one of eight blood types, which are referred to first by a letter or letter combination (A, B, AB, or O) and then a positive or negative marker (such as O+ or AB–). Researcher Anshool Deshmukh compiled blood type data from thousands of individuals and reorganized the data by region to better understand the distribution of the blood types O+, A+, and B+ by region. His research shows that type O+ blood has the highest frequency of occurrence in all four regions researched, while type B+ blood in turn has the lowest frequency of occurrence. For example, whereas the approximate appearance percentage for type O+ blood in Asia was 37%, the approximate appearance percentage for ________

Which choice most effectively uses data from the table to complete the example?

Ⓐ type O+ blood in the Americas was 55%.

Ⓑ type B+ blood in Africa was 17%.

Ⓒ type O+ blood in Oceania was 42%.

Ⓓ type B+ blood in Asia was 25%.

9 Mark for Review

"John G." is a 1918 short story by Katherine Mayo. In the story, the narrator describes a horse named John G. as dependable and well-behaved: ______

Which quotation from "John G." most effectively illustrates the claim?

Ⓐ "In the time that goes to saddling a horse, the detail rode into the storm, First Sergeant Price on John G., leading."

Ⓑ "Delicately, nervously, John G. set his feet, step by step, till he had reached the centre of the second plank."

Ⓒ "John G., on that diluvian night, was twenty-two years old, and still every whit as clean-limbed, alert, and plucky as his salad days had seen him."

Ⓓ "And John G. is a gentleman and a soldier, every inch of him. Horse-show judges have affixed their seal to the self-evident fact by the sign of the blue ribbon, but the best proof lies in the personal knowledge of "A" Troop, soundly built on twelve years' brotherhood."

10 Mark for Review

Obedience Rates After Training for 3 Behaviors in Dogs, by Reinforcement Schedule

Behavior	Fixed ratio (FR)	Variable ratio (VR)	Fixed interval (FI)	Variable interval (VI)
Sitting on command	90%	71%	65%	60%
Fetching on command	86%	66%	54%	46%
Remaining quiet on command	78%	64%	63%	53%

Behavior modification through positive reinforcement, which is essentially the rewarding of desired behavior, can occur by means of four different reinforcement schedules: a fixed ratio (FR) schedule rewards behavior after a specific number of responses, a fixed interval (FI) schedule rewards behavior after a specific amount of time, a variable ratio (VR) schedule rewards behavior after a varying number of responses, and a variable interval (VI) schedule rewards behavior after a varying amount of time. An animal trainer compiled data that indicate that dogs will exhibit higher rates of obedience for a given behavior, such as sitting or fetching, when trained on a ratio schedule than when trained on an interval schedule for that same behavior. For example, whereas the average obedience rate for sitting after training on a VR schedule is 71%, the average obedience rate for ______

Which choice most effectively uses data from the table to complete the example?

Ⓐ fetching after a VR schedule is 66%.

Ⓑ sitting after an FR schedule is 90%.

Ⓒ fetching after a VI schedule is 46%.

Ⓓ sitting after a VI schedule is 60%.

11 Mark for Review

Clostridium botulinum (*C. botulinum*) is a spore-forming food-borne bacterium that releases a highly dangerous neurotoxin, often causing serious illness or death. Boiling food for 10 minutes will kill *C. botulinum* in the unlikely event that it is present, but this will also destroy many beneficial vitamins and minerals. Since *C. botulinum* is almost exclusively found in home-canned goods, some experts recommend eating only commercially-produced cans of food, consequently ______

Which choice most logically completes the text?

Ⓐ avoiding the ingestion of *C. botulinum* without losing healthful nutrients.

Ⓑ making *C. botulinum* more vulnerable to the effects of boiling.

Ⓒ maximizing the many health benefits of *C. botulinum*.

Ⓓ enabling safe consumption of food tainted with *C. botulinum*.

COMPREHENSIVE READING DRILL ANSWERS AND EXPLANATIONS

1. **B** This is a Vocabulary question, as it's asking for a word that *completes the text with the most logical word or phrase.* Read the passage and highlight what can help fill in the blank. The passage states that *most fiction writers edit their stories and re-write them,* but the transition word *While* sets up a contrast, meaning that Aira does not edit his stories and re-write them as other writers do. Based on this, a good phrase to enter into the annotation box would be that Aira "stays away from" the traditional revision process.

    - (A), (C), and (D) are wrong because they are the **Opposite** of "stays away from" in some way—they all deal with some form of acceptance or joining together.
    - (B) is correct because *avoids* matches "stays away from."

2. **B** This is a Vocabulary question, as it's asking for a word that *completes the text with the most logical word or phrase.* Read the passage and highlight what can help to fill in the blank. The *impact* that the blank is describing is something that Benally *cautioned against,* so a good word for our annotation box would be "negative" or "harmful."

    - (A) and (C) are wrong because *aesthetic* and *economic* don't match with "negative."
    - (B) is correct because *detrimental* matches with "negative."
    - (D) is wrong because *restorative* is a positive word, which is the **Opposite** of "negative."

3. **C** This is a Vocabulary question, as it's asking for what a word *most nearly* means. Read the passage as if *practice* were not there and highlight what can help to fill in a word in its place. *Eliza, the cook, declared* that *the crane and the great iron pots* were *indispensable* to her. This most logically means that she must use them to cook (which is her "art"), so write "act of doing" in the annotation box.

    - (A), (B), and (D) are wrong because *amusement, recital,* and *appraisal* don't match with "act of doing."
    - (C) is correct because *execution* matches with "act of doing."

4. **C** This is a Purpose question, as it asks for the *overall structure of the text.* Read the passage and highlight what can help understand the order of ideas within the passage. The first sentence introduces *Scheele's green* and notes that it is *dangerous to humans.* The second sentence states that Scheele's green was *Used in wallpaper and candles* but stopped being used when *the public gained knowledge of how toxic its vapors were.* The last sentence discusses Scheele's green used as an *insecticide* and a *food dye.* A good overall structure to enter into the annotation box would be "Scheele's green—the good and the bad."

- (A) is wrong because the passage never gives any *specific reasons* as to why Scheele's green kept getting used, just what it was used for.
- (B) is wrong because the passage never mentions any *hypothesis.*
- (C) is correct because it's consistent with the highlighting and annotation.
- (D) is wrong because it's **Half-Right:** the passage implies that Scheele's green is first *Used for wallpaper and candles,* but the passage does not later question the *ethics* behind the invention of Scheele's green.

5. **D** This is a Dual Texts question, as it asks how *Dr. Renee Carr* would *mostly likely respond to Dr. John Mayer's observations.* Read Text 1 and highlight Dr. John Mayer's observations, which are that *binge-watching...triggers the release of dopamine, a chemical, from the brain, which leads to feelings of relaxation and pleasure.* Read Text 2 and highlight what Dr. Renee Carr says about the same topic. She *warns that any activity that produces dopamine can potentially be dangerous* and that *a form of addiction can take hold.* Therefore, a good reply from Dr. Carr to enter into the annotation box would be "warn against too much dopamine."

- (A) is wrong because Text 2 never mentions the *subject matter being viewed* or why it would be important to the argument.
- (B) is wrong because Text 2 never mentions *streaming companies.*
- (C) is wrong because Text 2 never mentions *other kinds of pleasurable activities,* nor does Text 2 directly advise Dr. Mayer from Text 1 to compare anything.
- (D) is correct because it's consistent with the highlighting and annotation: *may not have an entirely positive effect* is the same as suggesting there may be negative effects.

6. **A** This is a Retrieval question, as it says *According to the text.* Since the entire passage is about Mrs. Kearney and it may be difficult to highlight a single correct answer in the passage, first read the passage and then compare the answer choices to the passage directly.

- (A) is correct because the third sentence states that Mrs. Kearney was *waiting for some suitor to brave it and offer her a brilliant life*, but the fourth sentence states that *the young men whom she met were ordinary and she gave them no encouragement.* This implies that Mrs. Kearney would not just accept any man as a husband.
- (B) is wrong because it's the **Opposite** of what is stated in the third and fourth sentences.
- (C) is wrong because the passage never states that anyone *criticized* Mrs. Kearney or that she was rude.
- (D) is wrong because the passage never states that Mrs. Kearney disapproved of her suitors' *behavior*—only that she found them *ordinary.*

7. **A** This is a Main Idea question, as it says *main idea.* Read the passage and highlight the main phrases or lines that all of the other sentences seem to support. The author first states that Ramula and her team wanted *to examine the impact of soil microbiota* on the *growth and development* of *garden lupines.* Later in the passage, it's stated that the *crop of garden lupines in the soil containing microbiota not only grew much larger than the other crop's lupines, but also secreted a much stronger scent that is a natural deterrent to snails,* which are a predator of the garden lupines. This piece of evidence demonstrates the effect that Ramula and her team wanted to examine, so the correct answer should be consistent with both of these sentences.

- (A) is correct because it is consistent with the aim and outcome of Ramula and her team's study as described in the passage.
- (B) is wrong because no *other researchers* besides Ramula and her team are mentioned in the passage, nor does the author of the passage *critique* anyone.
- (C) is wrong because it is the **Opposite** of the passage: Ramula and her team don't seem to have any difficulty observing the *effects of soil microbiota on garden lupines.*
- (D) is wrong because it is a **Beyond the Text** trap answer: while *invasive species* normally do pose *environmental threats,* no threat from the garden lupines is mentioned in the passage.

8. **D** This is a Charts question as it asks about *data from the table.* The table displays the distribution percentages of three different blood types over four different regions. Read the passage and highlight the claim or statement referencing as many of these ideas as possible. The second to last sentence states *His research shows that type O+ blood has the highest frequency of occurrence in all four regions researched, while type B+ blood in turn has the lowest frequency of occurrence.* The next sentence, which is meant to be an example of this claim, starts by mentioning that *the approximate appearance percentage for type O+ blood in Asia was 37%.* To complete this example, the correct answer must reference the other blood type from the claim, B+, and the same region to properly compare the frequencies of the two blood types.

- (A), (B), and (C) are wrong because each references the wrong region: to complete the example, they should mention the same region, Asia, which is in the first half of the example. Choices (A) and (C) could also be eliminated for referencing the wrong blood type, O+, when that blood type has already been included in the first half of the example.

- (D) is correct because it is consistent with the claim and the table by completing the example, providing a statistic from the table that shows that *B+ blood* has the *lowest frequency of occurrence* in Asia.

9. **D** This is a Claims question, as it asks for a quotation that would *most effectively illustrate the claim.* Read the passage and highlight the claim, which is that *the narrator describes a horse named John G. as dependable and well-behaved.* The correct answer will be as consistent as possible with this claim.

- (A), (B), and (C) are wrong because they do not describe John G. as *dependable and well-behaved*, even if they list other positive qualities about him.

- (D) is correct because the quotation calls John G. *a gentleman and a soldier* and states that John G.'s reputation is *soundly built on twelve years' brotherhood.*

10. **D** This is a Charts question, as it asks for *data from the table* to *complete an example.* Read the title and variables in the table. Then, read the passage and highlight the claim and example being made in the passage. The animal trainer compiled data that indicates that *dogs will exhibit higher rates of obedience for a given behavior…when trained on a ratio schedule than when trained on an interval schedule for that same behavior.* The example begins with *the average obedience rate for sitting after training on a VR schedule is 71%.* The correct answer will complete this example while remaining consistent with the claim as well as the table.

- (A) and (C) are wrong because *fetching* is the wrong behavior—the claim states that the comparison needs to be for *the same behavior,* and the example uses *sitting,* not *fetching.*
- (B) is wrong because the claim compares a *ratio schedule* (which is already in the example) to an *interval schedule,* but *FR* stands for *fixed ratio,* making it another ratio schedule.
- (D) is correct because it's consistent with the highlighting and table: it has both the right behavior, *sitting,* and an *interval schedule,* VI, or variable interval.

11. **A** This is a Conclusions question, as it asks for an answer that *most logically completes the text.* Read the passage and highlight the main ideas. The first sentence states that *Clostridium botulinum…releases a highly dangerous neurotoxin.* The second sentence states that *Boiling food for 10 minutes will kill C. botulinum,* but this will also *destroy many beneficial vitamins and minerals.* The last sentence states that *C. botulinum is almost exclusively found in home-canned goods, so some experts recommend eating only commercially-produced cans of food.* Connecting these points together, if unlike home-canned goods, commercially-produced cans of foods are less likely to have *C. botulinum,* they are also less likely to require boiling for 10 minutes, which will avoid the potential loss of beneficial vitamins and minerals.

- (A) is correct because it's consistent with the highlighting and the flow of ideas within the passage.
- (B) is wrong because it's **Recycled Language**, misusing *boiling* from a different part of the passage.
- (C) is wrong because it's the **Opposite** of the passage: *C. botulinum* is *highly dangerous.* It does not have *many health benefits.*
- (D) is wrong because it's also the **Opposite** of the passage: commercially-produced cans are extremely unlikely to have *C. botulinum* in the first place.

Chapter 11 Introduction to Rules Questions

You can expect your test to contain 11–19 questions in a category that College Board calls Standard English Conventions. We simply call these Rules questions, as they test grammar and punctuation rules. In the next five chapters, you'll learn all the rules you need to know in order to ace these questions.

LEARN THE RULES AND FOLLOW THEM

Rules questions cover lots of different topics: punctuation, subject-verb agreement, pronouns and nouns, verb tense, sentence construction, apostrophes, and more. However, College Board does not categorize these topics separately from one another, as all of the Rules questions will appear in order of difficulty, with the topics mixed up. That means that, unlike every other portion of the Reading and Writing section, the Rules part does not group the questions by topic or type. Remember, you can identify Rules questions by their common question:

> Which choice completes the text so that it conforms to the conventions of Standard English?

What's tricky about Rules questions is there's no way to know which rule is being tested by reading the passage. In fact, it may be difficult to understand the passage because some of the words that should be in a sentence have been replaced by a blank. What's a savvy student to do?

Rules Questions Basic Approach

1. Look at the answers to see what's changing and determine the topic.
2. Apply the rules associated with that topic.
3. Use Process of Elimination.

Following the Reading and Writing basic approach that we went over earlier, you should always be looking at the question to determine where you are in the section and what category of question you're dealing with. Once you find the standard question for Rules, look at the answer choices to see what's changing. That will allow you to figure out what the question is testing you on.

If all the words stay the same but punctuation changes, you know you're being tested on punctuation rules. If each answer choice contains the same verb but in a different tense, that's your cue to think about tense—and ignore anything else you might like to change in the sentence, as it's not being tested on that question. You may not even need to read all of the sentences in the passage if some of them don't pertain to what's being tested.

As you work through the chapters in the Rules section of this book, you may find that some categories of questions come more naturally to you. Perhaps you had a teacher who drilled subject-verb agreement into you or you don't have difficulty deciding between a semicolon and a comma. Or, perhaps you find that a topic that was previously challenging or unfamiliar now makes perfect sense after working through our lessons and exercises. Whatever the case may be, if you identify any topics that you tend to do well on, as well as any questions that you know you tend to struggle with, remember to follow your Personal Order of Difficulty. Even though the Rules questions are intended to follow a rough order of difficulty, the mix of topics means that you may find it benefits you to skip around and do the ones you find easier first.

TOOLS FOR RULES

Remember, if you decide to skip around within the Rules section, you'll be able to use the Mark for Review tool if you come across a question that probably does fall within your POOD but that you don't want to do right that second. Likewise, mark a question if you are stuck between two options or if you think you'd benefit from looking at the question a second time after a few minutes. Sometimes, an answer choice might sound perfectly fine, but when you read it again a little later you instantly spot an error.

Digital Tools
Remember, the online practice tests give you the opportunity to try out all the tools. Being familiar and comfortable with these tools on test day will give you a real leg up, as you won't have to waste time during the test getting used to them.

The Highlight and Annotate tools will also be extremely helpful on Rules questions. As you'll soon learn, consistency is key on grammar topics. Highlighting the words that the blank needs to be consistent with will help you to avoid making mistakes. You can also make annotations to remind yourself what type of word you're looking for (such as singular or plural).

Lastly, Process of Elimination using the Answer Eliminator tool will be extremely helpful on this portion of the test. You won't necessarily know what you are looking for in the answers to these questions, so eliminating answers that don't work will lead you to the one answer that does.

In the Writing chapters of this book, we don't mention using scratch paper, as we think the online tools are sufficient for our strategies. That being said, we always encourage students to find techniques that work for them. If you find that scratch paper is helpful for you on this section, go right ahead and use it to your heart's content. Just make sure your work is neat and organized, so you can come back to a question later if you need to.

In the following lessons, you'll learn all the rules that you need to apply when you see each topic appear in the answer choices. But first, try this exercise to practice identifying what's changing in the answers and therefore what the question is testing.

WHAT'S CHANGING IN THE ANSWERS EXERCISE

1 Mark for Review

Ⓐ babies' favorite bottles

Ⓑ baby's favorite bottle's

Ⓒ babies' favorite bottles'

Ⓓ baby's favorite bottles

What's changing in the answer choices? ______________________

What is this question testing? ______________________

2 Mark for Review

Ⓐ have done

Ⓑ has done

Ⓒ were doing

Ⓓ do

What's changing in the answer choices? ______________________

What is this question testing? ______________________

3 Mark for Review

Ⓐ standing; with

Ⓑ standing. With

Ⓒ standing, with

Ⓓ standing with

What's changing in the answer choices? ______________________

What is this question testing? ______________________

4 Mark for Review

Ⓐ their

Ⓑ they're

Ⓒ it's

Ⓓ its

What's changing in the answer choices? ______________________

What is this question testing? ______________________

5 Mark for Review

Ⓐ approaches

Ⓑ had approached

Ⓒ was approaching

Ⓓ approached

What's changing in the answer choices? ______________________

What is this question testing? ______________________

6 Mark for Review

Ⓐ today's experience of culture is largely shaped by dime novels.

Ⓑ we experience culture the way we do because of dime novels.

Ⓒ dime novels have shaped the way we experience culture today.

Ⓓ the shape of dime novels influences cultural experiences.

What's changing in the answer choices? ______________________

What is this question testing? ______________________

ANSWERS TO WHAT'S CHANGING IN THE ANSWERS EXERCISE

1. Apostrophes with nouns; plural versus possessive nouns
2. Verbs; verb tense and/or number
3. Punctuation; how to connect clauses
4. Apostrophes with pronouns; pronoun agreement and possessive pronouns versus contractions
5. Verbs; verb tense and/or number
6. Subjects of the phrases; modifiers

Chapter 12
Rules Questions: Complete Sentences

Even though the Rules questions cover a variety of topics related to punctuation, grammar, and style, they all ultimately test you on how to properly construct a sentence. So, in this chapter we're going to start at the very beginning with how to write a basic sentence.

WHAT DOES A SENTENCE NEED?

At its most basic, a sentence needs a **subject** and a **verb**. Here are some examples with the subjects circled and the verbs underlined:

> Throughout the Writing portion of the book, you'll see a ✓ or an ✗ next to many of the example sentences so that you can easily tell whether they are correctly or incorrectly written.

The dog eats. ✓

Malia will sing. ✓

Snow was falling. ✓

Not all verbs can work in this structure, however. For example, a word like *give* or *want* requires an **object**, which is a word that in these examples would tell what someone gives or wants. It wouldn't make sense to say *Jackson wants,* would it? Here are two of the same examples but with objects added and put in boxes:

> You may remember learning about direct versus indirect objects in school, but this distinction isn't important for the Digital SAT.

The dog eats peanut butter. ✓

Malia will sing the national anthem. ✓

An object typically follows a verb, and it answers the question *What does the dog eat?* or *What will Malia sing?*, for example.

As you already know, a sentence must end in a period. The exceptions are questions, which end in question marks, and exclamations or commands, which can end with exclamation marks. Exclamation marks aren't tested on the Digital SAT, but questions occasionally are, so let's take a look at question construction.

QUESTION OR STATEMENT?

A topic that is occasionally tested on the Digital SAT is questions versus statements. The question will ask you to determine whether the blank should be a question or a statement. These ones can be pretty easy as long as you know the difference between questions and statements. A **statement** provides information. A **question** asks for information. Let's see an example.

Gammalsvenskby is a small Ukrainian village that experienced a mass migration of Swedes from Estonia around 1780. Historians wonder whether the mass migration was a punishment forced upon these people or ______

1 Mark for Review

Which choice completes the text so that it conforms to the conventions of Standard English?

Ⓐ did it provide positive opportunities for them?

Ⓑ a choice that provided positive opportunities for them.

Ⓒ a choice that provided positive opportunities for them?

Ⓓ did it provide positive opportunities for them.

Here's How to Crack It

First, recognize based on the question that this is a Rules question, so look at the answers to see what's changing. Two answers end in question marks and two end in periods, so this is testing questions versus statements. Look at the passage to determine whether it's intended to be a question or a statement. The sentence starts with *Historians wonder*, so it's providing information and is therefore a statement, not a question. Eliminate (A) and (C). Next, determine which wording is correct. In a question, the verb comes first, and a two-word verb (like *did provide*) is split—just like (D). This shouldn't be a question, so (D) isn't phrased correctly. Thus, the correct answer is (B).

VERB FORMS IN COMPLETE SENTENCES

You saw earlier how every sentence needs a subject and a verb. Let's take a closer look at what those subjects and verbs can look like. A subject is usually a noun or pronoun: *dog, tree, Mya, they, swimming.* You might be thinking, "Hold on—I thought *swimming* was a verb!" Of course, it can be a verb in some contexts (*She is swimming*), but an *-ing* verb can also function as a noun. See the following example:

When an *-ing* verb functions as a noun, it's known as a gerund. But you don't need to know this term for the Digital SAT.

Swimming is my favorite sport. ✓

The word *swimming* in this context refers to an act or a *sport*, so it functions as a noun and is the subject of this sentence. So, subjects can be nouns, pronouns, or *-ing* verbs.

What about the verb in a sentence? As you know, a verb can come in different tenses—think *danced* versus *dances* versus *will dance.* But verbs can also come in different forms, such as *dances, dancing,* and *to dance.* Not all of these can be "the verb" in a sentence, so it's important to know which verbs can and can't be. Now that we've established that a sentence must contain a subject and a verb, we're going to call that verb the "main verb." A sentence can have other verbs in it within different phrases or clauses, but it must have a main verb to go along with the subject. Here's the rule to know for the Digital SAT:

An *-ing* or "to" verb cannot be the main verb in a sentence.

Let's see some examples.

He dances after school on Fridays. ✓

He dancing after school on Fridays. ✗

He to dance after school on Fridays. ✗

Now that you've seen these examples, you can probably tell that you intuitively knew this rule, as the second and third sentences should sound really wrong. However, it won't always be this obvious on the Digital SAT. Let's see an example.

American inventor Otis Boykin's mother died of heart failure when Boykin was a year old. He earned many patents for electronic control devices, including for artificial cardiac pacemakers. These pacemakers ______ electrical impulses to regulate a patient's heartbeat.

2 Mark for Review

Which choice completes the text so that it conforms to the conventions of Standard English?

Ⓐ having used

Ⓑ using

Ⓒ use

Ⓓ to use

Here's How to Crack It

Start by identifying the category: Rules. Then, look at the answers to see what's changing. Since there is a "to" verb and an *-ing* verb, the question is testing verb forms. Start by identifying the subject: *pacemakers.* Then, look to see whether the sentence contains a main verb to go with this subject. There is no verb in the sentence other than *to regulate,* which can't be the main verb since it's in the "to" form. Thus, the blank must contain the main verb. Eliminate (A), (B), and (D) because neither an *-ing* verb nor a "to" verb can be the main verb in a sentence—they would not produce a complete sentence. Therefore, the correct answer is (C).

When this topic is tested, you will almost always see a "to" verb (known as the infinitive) and at least one *-ing* verb in the answer choices. That's how you can spot that the question is not testing you on tense but rather on complete sentences. When should you use the "to" form or the *-ing* verb? Here are some examples:

> Always check whether the sentence already has a main verb. If it does not, then the blank needs to provide the main verb. The "to" or *-ing* form can only be correct if the sentence already has a main verb.

*I want **to ride** on the roller coaster.* ✓

*They are on a mission **to find** double-stick tape.* ✓

*Emma wore her lucky sweater on test day, **thinking** it would give her an edge.* ✓

As you can see, the "to" verb is not the main verb in the example sentences. In some cases, it follows the main verb idiomatically (meaning, as a set phrase), such as *want to, need to, have to, like to,* or *choose to.* In other cases, it's used with a noun, such as *a mission to, a hope to, a wish to, courage to,* or *tendency to.* An *-ing* verb can be used within a separate phrase or clause that describes someone or something. In the example above, *thinking* isn't the main verb in the sentence, but it begins a phrase that describes *Emma* (she is *thinking*).

It's worth noting that an *-ing* verb can be part of the main verb in a sentence. Here are some examples:

He is jogging in the park. ✓

The competitors were preparing their notes. ✓

In these examples, there is another verb that is allowed to function as the main verb—*is* and *were*, respectively. Remember, if you see the *-ing* word by itself, it can't be the main verb in the sentence.

A sentence can also have two or more verbs that either apply to the same subject or are part of a list:

The athletes are running laps, lifting weights, and studying technique. ✓

*The job consists of **filing** papers, **taking** phone calls, and **assisting** clients.* ✓

As you can see from these correct examples, the verbs must be in the same form when they are applied to the same subject or are part of a list. Here are some incorrect examples:

The athletes are running, lift weights, and to study techniques. ✗

*The job consists of **filing** papers, **to take** phone calls, and **assists** clients.* ✗

Let's see how this could be tested on the Digital SAT.

Researchers were surprised to find white spruce trees growing in the Alaskan tundra. The spread of white spruce trees is part of Arctic greening, a phenomenon in which vegetation moves farther north as the region warms. White spruce seeds can travel long distances and ______ areas with little competition, leading to their rapid population increase.

3 Mark for Review

Which choice completes the text so that it conforms to the conventions of Standard English?

Ⓐ accessed

Ⓑ accessing

Ⓒ access

Ⓓ accesses

Here's How to Crack It

Identify the category based on the question: Rules. Next, look at the answers to see what's changing: verb forms. When verbs are changing in the answer choices, always locate the subject of the sentence. Here, it's *white spruce seeds*. The sentence contains a verb for the subject, *can travel*, but notice that after that is the word *and*. There's no second subject after *and*, so the underlined portion must be another verb that goes with the same subject. Since the first verb is *can travel*, the underlined portion must be in the same form as *travel*. Eliminate (A), (B), and (D) because they aren't in the same form as *travel*. Choice (C) is in the correct form: with this answer, the sentence says *White spruce seeds can travel...and access...*which is consistent. The correct answer is (C).

Complete Sentences Drill

Answers can be found starting on page 242.

Time: 6 minutes

1 Mark for Review

The Bumblebee Conservation Trust's BeeWalk project is a citizen science project where volunteers collect information about bumblebees. Researchers combine the citizen science data with land cover data to learn where bumblebees live. If the particular types of habitats bumblebees live in are identified, ________ That is the question that researchers like Dr. Penelope Whitehorn are trying to answer.

Which choice completes the text so that it conforms to the conventions of Standard English?

Ⓐ conservation efforts could be more directed and successful?

Ⓑ conservation efforts could be more directed and successful.

Ⓒ could conservation efforts be more directed and successful?

Ⓓ could conservation efforts be more directed and successful.

2 Mark for Review

Egyptologist Howard Carter led the excavations that discovered the tomb of the pharaoh Tutankhamun in 1922. At this time, the Egyptians had recently gained some independence from the British. The timings of the discovery and these political changes led many to wonder ________

Which choice completes the text so that it conforms to the conventions of Standard English?

Ⓐ whether the Egyptians or the British should control access to the tomb?

Ⓑ should the Egyptians or the British control access to the tomb?

Ⓒ the Egyptians or the British to control access to the tomb.

Ⓓ whether the Egyptians or the British should control access to the tomb.

3 Mark for Review

The idea of the Great American Novel, a novel that considers the national character and essence of the United States, dates from the 1800s. In the early 1900s, many ________ that the idea of the Great American Novel was out of date, but since the 1920s, this concept has re-emerged among literary circles.

Which choice completes the text so that it conforms to the conventions of Standard English?

(A) believed

(B) believing

(C) to believe

(D) having believed

4 Mark for Review

As one of the highest-ranking women working for the government in her time, Mary Margaret O'Reilly served as the Assistant Director of the United States Bureau of the Mint from 1924 through 1938. When her mandatory retirement came due in 1935, President Franklin D. Roosevelt felt she was too valuable and ________ adjustments to allow her to serve for three additional years.

Which choice completes the text so that it conforms to the conventions of Standard English?

(A) having made

(B) making

(C) to make

(D) made

5 Mark for Review

Ada Yonath is a crystallographer from Israel who focused on the structure of ribosomes. She identified the mechanisms surrounding how antibiotics attack ribosomes and then ________ the Nobel Prize in Chemistry, alongside Thomas A. Steitz and Venkatraman Ramakrishnan.

Which choice completes the text so that it conforms to the conventions of Standard English?

(A) receives

(B) will receive

(C) receive

(D) received

COMPLETE SENTENCES DRILL ANSWERS AND EXPLANATIONS

1. **C** In this Rules question, periods and question marks are changing in the answer choices, so it's testing questions versus statements. The following sentence states that *researchers like Dr. Penelope Whitehorn are trying to answer* a *question*, so the preceding sentence should be a question. Eliminate answers that aren't correctly written as questions.
   - (A) is wrong because it has a question mark but is written as a statement.
   - (B) and (D) are wrong because they are statements.
   - (C) is correct because it's correctly written as a question.

2. **D** In this Rules question, periods and question marks are changing in the answer choices, so it's testing questions versus statements. The beginning of the sentence provides a statement that says *The timings of the discovery and these political changes led many to wonder*, so the second part of the sentence should be a statement. Eliminate answers that aren't correctly written as statements.
   - (A) and (B) are wrong because they are questions.
   - (C) is wrong because, although it is a statement, it makes the sentence incomplete.
   - (D) is correct because it's correctly written as a statement that makes the sentence complete.

3. **A** In this Rules question, verb forms are changing in the answer choices, so it's testing sentence structure. In this case, the blank represents the main verb for the subject *many.* If the main verb is in the wrong form, the sentence won't be complete. Eliminate any answer that does not produce a complete sentence.
   - (A) is correct because it's in the right form to make a complete sentence.
   - (B) and (D) are wrong because an *-ing* verb can't be the main verb in a sentence.
   - (C) is wrong because a "to" verb can't be the main verb in a sentence.

4. **D** In this Rules question, verb forms are changing in the answer choices, so it's testing sentence structure. In this case, the blank represents a second main verb for the subject President Franklin D. Roosevelt. If the main verb is in the wrong form, the sentence won't be complete. Eliminate any answer that does not produce a complete sentence.
   - (A) and (B) are wrong because an *-ing* verb can't be the main verb in a sentence.
   - (C) is wrong because a "to" verb can't be the main verb in a sentence.
   - (D) is correct because it's in the right form to make a complete sentence.

5. **D** In this Rules question, verbs are changing in the answer choices, so it's testing consistency with verbs. In this case, the verb is part of a list of two things that Yonath accomplished, the first of which is *She identified*. Highlight the word *identified*, which the verb in the answer should be consistent with. Eliminate any answer that isn't consistent with *identified*.

- (A), (B), and (C) are wrong because *receives*, *will receive*, and *receive* aren't consistent with *identified*.
- (D) is correct because *received* is in the same tense and form as *identified*.

Summary

- A complete sentence must have a subject and a verb.
- Statements provide information, while questions ask for information.
- Neither an *-ing* verb nor a "to" verb can be the main verb in a sentence.
- Two verbs that apply to the same subject must be in the same form.

Chapter 13 Rules Questions: Describing Phrases

A writer is not always satisfied with a basic sentence like the ones we showed you in the last chapter. In this chapter, we'll take a look at common ways to include additional information in a sentence. Some of these pieces of information require commas, while others don't. In this chapter, you'll learn about Specifying and Extra Information and how to identify and correctly punctuate them.

WHO OR WHAT ARE YOU TALKING ABOUT?

We'll begin with the information that should not have commas separating it from other parts of the sentence. Here's our first example:

> *Mae Jemison became interested in space in part because of Lieutenant Uhura.* ✓

This is a complete sentence, but it's not a great topic sentence. That's because it doesn't actually introduce who we're talking about. If you don't know who Mae Jemison or Lieutenant Uhura is, you may be wondering why we bothered to tell you this. So, let's add some additional details to make this sentence more meaningful:

> ***Astronaut** Mae Jemison became interested in space in part because of* **Star Trek *character*** *Lieutenant Uhura.* ✓

This sentence makes a lot more sense, doesn't it? Digital SAT passages will not assume that you are familiar with the often obscure people and events they are describing, so you'll typically see titles and labels that appear before a person's name, a book title, or any other noun that needs to be explained. As you can see, these titles function like adjectives to describe the noun, so there is no punctuation used between the title and the name.

> Labels that precede a person's name, a book title, or any other potentially unfamiliar noun are never followed by a comma.

Let's see an example of how this can be tested on the Digital SAT.

The understanding of cancer genomics was greatly expanded by ______ Bert Vogelstein, a doctor whose research on colorectal cancer has led to identifying numerous genes associated with cancer and new tools to diagnose cancer earlier.

1 Mark for Review

Which choice completes the text so that it conforms to the conventions of Standard English?

Ⓐ scientist,

Ⓑ scientist;

Ⓒ scientist:

Ⓓ scientist

Here's How to Crack It

First identify the category: Rules. In that case, look at the answers to see what's changing. The punctuation is changing, so the question is testing punctuation rules. The word *scientist* comes before a person's name. Is Bert Vogelstein a scientist? Yes, he's *a doctor* who has done *research*. Thus, the word *scientist* is a title that precedes Vogelstein's name. Remember, there's no need for punctuation in that case. Eliminate (A), (B), and (C). The correct answer is (D).

There are other kinds of phrases that are important enough in the sentence that they don't get commas. We call these phrases **Specifying Information**. Here's an example:

*The person **who sold me my bike** offered to give me a discount.* ✓

*The person, **who sold me my bike,** offered to give me a discount.* ✗

By separating the phrase from the sentence with commas, the second example implies that this information isn't essential to the sentence's meaning—as you'll learn later on, information that could be removed without affecting the sentence's meaning should be surrounded by commas, dashes, or parentheses. But if we remove the phrase, it says *The person offered to give me a discount.* Which person? While this is a complete sentence without the phrase, it's not clear who we are talking about. So, the phrase shouldn't be separated by punctuation. It specifies which person we are talking about. Here are some more examples of information coming after a noun that doesn't get commas:

*The paper airplane **that travels farthest** will be the winner.* ✓

*The dog **sniffing the fence** is mine.* ✓

*That bakery offers discounts for anyone **who has taken a bus tour**.* ✓

*The backpack **on the floor** isn't hers.* ✓

*The girl **whose book I borrowed** told me not to write in it.* ✓

In all of these examples, the phrase that comes after the noun or pronoun specifies *which* person or thing we're talking about. Which paper airplane? The one that travels farthest. Which dog? The one sniffing the fence. Which anyone (okay, that doesn't work grammatically, but you could say "Which people")? Those who have taken a bus tour. Which backpack? The one on the floor. Which girl? The one whose book I borrowed. All of this Specifying Information is used to specify which person or thing is being discussed.

As you can see from the examples above, Specifying Information can come in different forms. To make things a bit easier, we'll give you a couple of rules that will help with some of the questions that test this topic.

Specifying Information Rules

1. Phrases that begin with "that" are always Specifying and never get commas around them.
2. Prepositional phrases are usually Specifying and don't get commas unless they appear at the beginning of the sentence.

Let's take a closer look at that second rule. First, we need to define a **prepositional phrase**, which starts with the definition of **preposition**. A preposition is a small, directional word such as *in*, *of*, *for*, *by*, *with*, *on*, or *to*. So, a prepositional phrase is a phrase that begins with a preposition, such as *in the house*, *of my friends*, *for you*, or *by the tree*. Here's an example of how that works with commas:

Squirrels were playing ***at the top of the tree.*** ✓

At the top of the tree, *squirrels were playing.* ✓

Squirrels ***at the top of the tree*** *were playing.* ✓

The prepositional phrase here is *at the top of the tree* (actually, it's two prepositional phrases put together: *at the top* and *of the tree*). When it comes later in the sentence, this phrase is Specifying and isn't separated from the sentence with commas. However, when the prepositional phrase comes at the beginning of the sentence, it is followed by a comma. Without the comma, the sentence could be a bit confusing because it has *tree* and *squirrels* right in a row. If you read the sentence this way (*At the top of the tree squirrels were playing*), it's easy to miss where the prepositional phrase ends and where the rest of the sentence begins. For that reason, (see what we did there?) prepositional phrases are usually followed by commas when they come at the beginning of the sentence, and they usually do not have commas when they come elsewhere.

Although this is a "usually" rule, it's not likely that College Board would test you on this in a way that isn't obvious. That's because this is one of the few comma rules that is actually reflected in how we speak. You would likely put a small pause after the prepositional phrase in the second example above, but you probably wouldn't have any pause in the other two examples. This will help you know when to use a comma in this context.

EXTRA! EXTRA! PUT PUNCTUATION AROUND IT!

We saw earlier that titles that precede a name never have commas. The exception to this rule is if the description contains the word "a" or "an." Here's an example:

> ***An astronaut,*** *Mae Jemison became interested in space in part because of* Star Trek *character Lieutenant Uhura.* ✓

A description with "a" or "an" can go before or after the person's name, but it must always be separated from the name by commas. In that case, we call it **Extra Information**. Let's see some examples.

> *Mae Jemison,* ***an astronaut,*** *became interested in space in part because of Lieutenant Uhura,* ***a* Star Trek *character*.** ✓

> *Mae Jemison* **(*an astronaut*)** *became interested in space in part because of Lieutenant Uhura,* ***a* Star Trek *character*.** ✓

> *Mae Jemison,* ***an astronaut,*** *became interested in space in part because of Lieutenant Uhura—****a* Star Trek *character*.** ✓

All of these examples are correctly punctuated. Both of the names in the sentence refer to specific people, so the information that follows the names can be removed without changing the meaning of the sentence. In that case, it's Extra Information, and it needs to be separated from the rest of the sentence using two commas, two parentheses, or two dashes. (Note that if the Extra Information comes at the beginning or end of the sentence, as in the case of *a Star Trek character* above, it only needs a single punctuation mark to separate it.)

Let's compare two sentences that are punctuated differently to understand what they mean:

> ***An astronaut,*** *Mae Jemison became interested in space in part because of* Star Trek *character Lieutenant Uhura.* ✓

> *An astronaut,* ***Mae Jemison,*** *became interested in space in part because of* Star Trek *character Lieutenant Uhura.* ✓

In the first sentence, *Mae Jemison* is the subject, and *an astronaut* is simply giving her a description. In the second sentence, *An astronaut* is actually the subject. Since *Mae Jemison* is separated with commas, it's Extra Information, which means that it could be removed from the sentence. This suggests that in the second example the point is that there was an astronaut whose interest in space was spurred in part by the *Star Trek* character, but her name isn't important to the author's point. The first example could be used if the author is telling us about Jemison. If the author is telling us about Lieutenant Uhura or *Star Trek*, however, the second example could be perfectly fine, as the author only wants us to know that an astronaut was inspired—who it was isn't important.

The fact that we just showed you an example of the same sentence with and without a comma may seem concerning, but don't worry. College Board will never give you two answer choices that can both work. You would not see both of these sentences in the answer choices since they could both be logical.

Another way to think of the phrase *An astronaut* in the first example above is that it is a describing phrase. We saw how describing phrases beginning with "a" or "an" are followed by a comma. We can call this a noun phrase because the "a" or "an" always comes before a noun.

There are many other kinds of describing phrases that get commas around them because they are Extra Information. Let's see another version of a noun phrase as well as some examples of other types of describing phrases.

A noun phrase: *Summer, **my favorite time of year,** is when I go to camp.* ✓

A phrase beginning with an *-ing* verb: ***Having stayed up all night playing video games,*** *Isaiah was not surprised that he felt terrible the next day.* ✓

A phrase beginning with an *-ed* verb or an irregular past participle (such as forgotten, known, begun, hidden, or kept): ***Located in Maryland,*** *Baltimore has a rich history.* ✓

A phrase beginning with *which, who, whom,* or *whose* or that contains a preposition + one of those words (such as *of whom* or *in which*): *Summer, **which is my favorite time of year,** is when I go to camp.* ✓

A clause with a "to be" verb removed: *Ella timidly blew into the trumpet, **the sound barely audible.*** ✓

A definition or alternative term starting with *or*: *The humerus, **or funny bone,** is an arm bone that runs from one's shoulder to one's elbow.* ✓

In some cases, a describing phrase can come either before or after the person or thing it's describing. Here are some examples, which you can compare to the previous ones:

*Isaiah, **having stayed up all night playing video games,** was not surprised that he felt terrible the next day.* ✓

*Baltimore, **located in Maryland,** has a rich history.* ✓

My favorite time of year, *summer is when I go to camp.* ✓

Remember, most of these types of describing phrases can be either Specifying or Extra Information. For example, phrases with *who* are sometimes needed in order to specify which person is being discussed. You'll need to try removing the phrase from the sentence to see whether it's needed in order to specify who or what is being discussed. If it's not needed, it's Extra.

Lastly, note that transitions such as *however*, *in addition*, *moreover*, or *therefore* are always followed by a comma if they come at the beginning of a sentence, and they are surrounded by commas if they appear in the middle. These transitions are considered Extra Information because the sentence still works without them.

Let's see some examples of how the Specifying vs. Extra Information topic can be tested on the Digital SAT.

To measure the flow of pitch (highly viscous liquids which appear solid, such as asphalt), scientists use what is known as a pitch drop experiment. In this ______ a funnel filled with pitch allows the pitch to drop into a container below. In most pitch drop experiments, a single drop falls approximately once every ten years.

2 Mark for Review

Which choice completes the text so that it conforms to the conventions of Standard English?

Ⓐ experiment, the most famous of which was started in 1927 at the University of Queensland,

Ⓑ experiment, the most famous of which was started in 1927 at the University of Queensland

Ⓒ experiment the most famous of which was started in 1927 at the University of Queensland,

Ⓓ experiment the most famous of which was started in 1927 at the University of Queensland

Here's How to Crack It

Start by identifying the category, which is Rules, as evidenced by the question. As per the strategy, look to the answers to see what's changing: all the words are the same, but the commas change, and they seem to be surrounding the phrase *the most famous of which was started in 1927 at the University of Queensland*. If this is Extra Information, it does need commas before and after the phrase. To test, try removing the phrase from the sentence. Then it reads *In this experiment, a funnel filled with pitch allows the pitch to drop into a container below.* This is perfectly fine, so the phrase is Extra Information and thus needs punctuation before and after. Eliminate (B), (C), and (D) because they don't have a comma both before and after. The correct answer is (A).

In his writings, Vietnamese American poet and novelist Ocean Vuong combines the folkloric traditions and oral storytelling of Vietnam and experimentation with the English language to explore trauma and identity. His poetry collection ______ contains numerous poems about the Vietnam War and its effects, while his novel *On Earth We're Briefly Gorgeous* is written as a letter from a son to his mother and explores both personal and colonial histories.

3 Mark for Review

Which choice completes the text so that it conforms to the conventions of Standard English?

Ⓐ *Night Sky with Exit Wounds:*

Ⓑ *Night Sky with Exit Wounds*

Ⓒ *Night Sky with Exit Wounds,*

Ⓓ *Night Sky with Exit Wounds—*

Here's How to Crack It

The question lets you know that this is a Rules question, and the answers reveal that it's testing punctuation. Start from the beginning of the sentence: it says *His poetry collection*, and the part after gives the name of the collection. This is a good clue that the question is testing Specifying versus Extra Information. If the phrase is Specifying, it will not have any punctuation around it, but if it's Extra, it will need matching punctuation before and after. Notice that the part before the blank doesn't have any punctuation, though. This proves that the phrase is Specifying, as there's no way to put any punctuation before the phrase. Therefore, you can eliminate all of the answers with punctuation: (A), (C), and (D). The correct answer is (B).

A jazz cellist and composer known for her unique sounds and blend of musical ______ Tomeka Reid founded the Chicago Jazz String Summit in 2013 and continued to organize it as an annual event.

4 Mark for Review

Which choice completes the text so that it conforms to the conventions of Standard English?

Ⓐ traditions,

Ⓑ traditions;

Ⓒ traditions:

Ⓓ traditions

Here's How to Crack It

Look at the question to determine that the category is Rules, and look at the answers to determine that the topic is punctuation. Start at the beginning of the sentence: it says *A jazz cellist and composer known for her unique sounds and blend of musical traditions* and then gives a person's name. This is a describing phrase beginning with "A." According to the rule, these phrases should always get commas around them, as they are Extra Information. Eliminate (B), (C), and (D) as they don't have a comma after the phrase. The correct answer is (A).

If you feel a little iffy about this Extra versus Specifying Information idea, it's worth keeping in mind that while there are gray areas with this rule, those ambiguities aren't tested on the Digital SAT. On the test, it should be obvious whether the information is Extra or not if they give you the option of no punctuation versus matching punctuation before and after.

Extra Information Rules

1. Extra Information can come before or after the noun or pronoun it's describing.
2. Extra Information can be removed and produce a sentence with the same meaning, just a little less detail. It's not needed for specifying which person or thing you're talking about.
3. Extra Information must always have commas, dashes, or parentheses both before and after the phrase.
4. If you're not sure whether the information is Extra or Specifying, try removing it from the sentence. If it is Extra, its removal will not affect your understanding of who or what the sentence is about.

SPECIFYING VS. EXTRA INFORMATION EXERCISE

Determine whether each bolded phrase is Specifying or Extra Information. If it is Specifying, put a checkmark because no punctuation is needed. If it is Extra, add commas where they are needed. Answers are on page 256.

1. Composer and librettist Stephen Sondheim **who studied with Oscar Hammerstein and Milton Babbitt** was known for his creative wordplay and tightly constructed musical ideas.

2. The person **who composed "Dies Irae"** is unknown.

3. **Intending to finish my homework before school** I set my alarm earlier than usual.

4. Intending **to do well** is not enough to succeed.

5. Senegal **a country in Africa** is the westernmost country in Africa, Europe, or Asia.

6. The tortoise **that lives in our backyard** hibernates during the winter.

7. Some careers **such as medicine and law** require education beyond a bachelor's degree.

8. The chance for rain tomorrow **according to the weather station** is high.

9. My favorite book **kept away from me as punishment** was returned by my parents.

10. **British engineer** George Stephenson was known for his contributions to the improvement of railways.

A final topic that is occasionally tested on the Digital SAT is how to properly construct the describing phrases we went over earlier. Here's an example.

Rachel Fuller Brown, a chemist, and Elizabeth Lee Hazen, a microbiologist, started working together to research fungi and bacteria. At the time, antibiotics would kill all bacteria, allowing fungus to grow out of control and cause diseases. Brown and Hazen began their project in 1948 and eventually created a drug called Nystatin, the first antifungal ______ cures fungal infections in humans.

5 Mark for Review

Which choice completes the text so that it conforms to the conventions of Standard English?

(A) antibiotic, that

(B) antibiotic

(C) antibiotic that

(D) antibiotic,

Watch Us Crack It
Watch the step-by-step video explanation of how to answer this question in your Student Tools.

Here's How to Crack It

Start by looking at the question to determine that it's in the Rules category. Next, look at the answers to see what's changing. In this case, it's commas and the word *that.* This is a good clue that the question is testing the construction of describing phrases. Read from the beginning of the sentence: *Brown and Hazen began their project in 1948 and eventually created a drug called Nystatin* is already a complete sentence, also known as an independent clause. Then it's followed by a comma and a description of the drug.

Start with the options that don't contain *that*, (B) and (D). With (B), the second part of the sentence would say *the first antifungal antibiotic cures fungal infections in humans.* This is an independent clause, and it's not correct to link two independent clauses with only a comma (we'll talk much more about this in the next chapter). Thus, eliminate (B). Next, look at (D). In this answer choice, *the first antifungal antibiotic* is Extra Information since it's separated with commas. So, if this is Extra, try reading the sentence without the phrase. It reads *...eventually created a drug called Nystatin cures fungal infections in humans.* The verb *cures* does not have a subject here—if it's referring to *Nystatin*, there would need to be a word such as *which* to refer back to Nystatin. This isn't a complete sentence with the extra verb, so eliminate (D).

Now that we recognize that *that* is needed, the hard part is finished. This is because we know that phrases beginning with *that* are always Specifying and don't get commas. So, eliminate (A). The correct answer is (C). This correctly completes the describing phrase.

ANSWERS TO SPECIFYING VS. EXTRA INFORMATION EXERCISE

1. Extra—put commas before and after the bolded phrase
2. Specifying—correct as written
3. Extra—put a comma after the bolded phrase
4. Specifying—correct as written
5. Extra—put commas before and after the bolded phrase
6. Specifying—correct as written
7. Extra—put commas before and after the bolded phrase
8. Extra—put commas before and after the bolded phrase
9. Extra—put commas before and after the bolded phrase
10. Specifying—correct as written

Describing Phrases Drill

Answers can be found starting on page 259.

Time: 7 minutes

1 Mark for Review

In 1965, farm workers participated in a labor strike against grape growers to protest exploitation of farm workers. The five-year strike was the first time many common strike tactics were used—boycotts, community organization, nonviolent resistance, and ______ and ultimately resulted in a victory for the farm workers.

Which choice completes the text so that it conforms to the conventions of Standard English?

Ⓐ marches

Ⓑ marches—

Ⓒ marches;

Ⓓ marches,

2 Mark for Review

Israeli poet and ______ has used his studies of ancient religions in his works *The Song of Tahira*, an epic about a fictional society's religion and customs, and *The Kingdom*, a novel about the life of King David.

Which choice completes the text so that it conforms to the conventions of Standard English?

Ⓐ novelist, Amir Or

Ⓑ novelist Amir Or

Ⓒ novelist, Amir Or,

Ⓓ novelist Amir Or,

3 Mark for Review

Ultrasound technology utilizes a form of sound waves and is used in medicine to generate images of areas of the human body. John J. ______ as the father of medical ultrasound, helped develop the technology with a focus on imaging cancerous cells.

Which choice completes the text so that it conforms to the conventions of Standard English?

Ⓐ Wild, known

Ⓑ Wild known

Ⓒ Wild—known

Ⓓ Wild (known

4 Mark for Review

By activating multiple pathways in the brain at once, scientists hope to treat neurological disorders. For example, ______ may be able to be treated by simultaneously stimulating brain cells devoted to hearing and brain cells devoted to pain.

Which choice completes the text so that it conforms to the conventions of Standard English?

Ⓐ tinnitus, or ringing in the ears

Ⓑ tinnitus, or ringing in the ears,

Ⓒ tinnitus or ringing in the ears,

Ⓓ tinnitus or ringing in the ears

5 Mark for Review

Gronk, born Glugio Nicandro, is a Chicano ______ shows his work not only in galleries but also in public spaces, going so far as to distribute flyers featuring his work at bus stops.

Which choice completes the text so that it conforms to the conventions of Standard English?

Ⓐ artist,

Ⓑ artist

Ⓒ artist, which

Ⓓ artist who

6 Mark for Review

Maki Kawai is a chemist from Japan who invented spatially selective single-molecule spectroscopy. She combined two forms of spectroscopy into this new ______ led to the detection of a novel reaction pathway on the superficial level of titanium dioxide.

Which choice completes the text so that it conforms to the conventions of Standard English?

Ⓐ method

Ⓑ method, which

Ⓒ method, that

Ⓓ method,

DESCRIBING PHRASES DRILL ANSWERS AND EXPLANATIONS

1. **B** In this Rules question, punctuation is changing in the answer choices. The first part of the sentence says *The five-year strike was the first time many common strike tactics were used—boycotts, community organization, nonviolent resistance, and marches*, which contains a dash. A pair of dashes can be used to indicate Extra Information. If the phrase *boycotts, community organization, nonviolent resistance, and marches* is Extra Information, it does need dashes before and after the phrase. To test, try removing the phrase from the sentence. Then it reads *The five-year strike was the first time many common strike tactics were used and ultimately resulted in a victory for the farm workers*. This is perfectly fine, so the phrase is Extra Information and thus needs matching punctuation before and after. Eliminate answers that do not have a dash.

    - (A) is wrong because it doesn't have punctuation after the Extra Information.
    - (B) is correct because it has a dash after the Extra Information, which matches the dash before the Extra Information.
    - (C) and (D) are wrong because they don't use a dash after the Extra Information.

2. **B** In this Rules question, punctuation is changing in the answer choices. The first part of the sentence says *Israeli poet and novelist Amir Or*. The word *novelist* is a title for *Amir Or*, so no punctuation should be used between *novelist* and *Amir Or*. The verb (*has used*) comes right after this. A single punctuation mark can't separate a subject and a verb. Eliminate answers that use punctuation.

    - (A) and (C) are wrong because there should be no punctuation between *novelist* and *Amir*, since it's a title.
    - (B) is correct because no punctuation should be used here.
    - (D) is wrong because a single punctuation mark can't come between a subject and a verb.

3. **A** In this Rules question, punctuation is changing in the answer choices. The first part of the sentence says *John J. Wild*, which is the subject. The phrase after the subject, *known as the father of medical ultrasound*, ends with a comma, which indicates it may be Extra Information. To test, try removing the phrase from the sentence. Then it reads *John J. Wild helped develop the technology with a focus on imaging cancerous cells*. This is perfectly fine, so the phrase is Extra Information and thus needs matching punctuation before and after. Eliminate answers that do not have a comma.

    - (A) is correct because it has a comma before the Extra Information.
    - (B), (C), and (D) are wrong because they don't separate the Extra Information with a comma before the phrase to match the one after.

4. **B** In this Rules question, punctuation is changing in the answer choices. The first part of the sentence says *For example, tinnitus.* In the answer choices, commas appear around the phrase *or ringing in the ears,* indicating that it may be Extra Information. To test, try removing the phrase from the sentence. Then it reads *For example, tinnitus may be able to be treated by simultaneously stimulating brain cells devoted to hearing and brain cells devoted to pain.* This is perfectly fine, so the phrase is Extra Information and thus needs matching punctuation before and after. Eliminate answers that do not have commas before and after the Extra Information.

- (A) and (C) are wrong because they only have one comma, not a pair, around the Extra Information.
- (B) is correct because it has commas before and after the Extra Information.
- (D) is wrong because it doesn't separate the Extra Information with two commas.

5. **D** In this Rules question, commas and the words *which* and *who* are changing in the answers, which suggests that the question is testing the construction of describing phrases. The first part of the sentence says *Gronk, born Glugio Nicandro, is a Chicano artist,* which is an independent clause. The second part of the sentence says *shows his work not only in galleries but also in public spaces, going so far as to distribute flyers featuring his work at bus stops,* which is a describing phrase and needs to be properly constructed. Eliminate any answer that doesn't properly construct the describing phrase.

- (A) and (B) are wrong because the describing phrase needs a subject for the verb *shows.*
- (C) is wrong because *which* cannot be used with people.
- (D) is correct because *who* is used with people and is the subject of the verb *shows.*

6. **B** In this Rules question, commas and the words *which* and *that* are changing in the answers, which suggests that the question is testing the construction of describing phrases. The first part of the sentence says *She combined two forms of spectroscopy into this new method,* which is an independent clause. The second part of the sentence says *led to the detection of a novel reaction pathway on the superficial level of titanium dioxide.* The second part of the sentence is a describing phrase and needs to be properly constructed. Eliminate any answer that doesn't properly construct the describing phrase.

- (A) and (D) are wrong because *led* is missing a subject.
- (B) is correct because *which* is the subject of *led* and properly constructs a describing phrase.
- (C) is wrong because a phrase starting with "that" is Specifying and never follows a comma.

Summary

- Specifying Information is needed in order to tell *which* person or thing the sentence is discussing.
- Specifying Information should never be separated from the rest of the sentence with punctuation. If it were removed, the meaning of the sentence would change and become unclear or nonsensical.
- Extra Information can be removed from the sentence without affecting the sentence's meaning.
- Extra Information must be separated from the sentence with commas, dashes, or parentheses both before and after, unless it appears at the beginning or end of the sentence.
- If you're not sure whether something is Specifying or Extra Information, try removing it from the sentence to see whether the meaning is affected.
- Use clues in the part of the sentence before and/or after the blank. If the phrase already has or does not have punctuation before or after it, then the blank simply needs to match.

Chapter 14
Rules Questions: Linking Independent Clauses

Now that you have learned how to construct a complete sentence, the next step is to see how two complete sentences, also known as independent clauses, can be combined. You'll also learn the various ways that they should never be combined so that you can eliminate the answers that make those mistakes.

HOW TO CONNECT INDEPENDENT CLAUSES

We've seen how a complete sentence is constructed. Of course, it's also possible to put two complete sentences together—in this case, we'll refer to the individual sentences as **independent clauses**. An independent clause is something that could stand alone as a sentence—that's why it's called independent! Next, we're going to look at how to put two independent clauses together in the same sentence. Let's take a look at a few different types of punctuation marks and how they are used.

Semicolons

A semicolon is a punctuation mark that functions like a period; it is used between two ideas that could be their own separate sentences. See how we did that? Anytime you see a semicolon in the answer choices, look to see whether you have two independent clauses, or ask yourself whether a period could be used there. If a period can be used, then a semicolon can be used. (There is an exception to this rule that involves lists, which will be covered in the next chapter.)

Commas

A comma can *never* link two independent clauses. A sentence that does this creates an error called a comma splice or a run-on sentence. A comma can be used with two independent clauses if there is a **coordinating conjunction**, also known as **FANBOYS**: **F**or, **A**nd, **N**or, **B**ut, **O**r, **Y**et, **S**o. Earlier, we saw examples similar to this:

He brushed his teeth and went to bed. ✓

This sentence has a single subject and two verbs that go along with the one subject. What if we add a subject for the second verb? Then we'd have two independent clauses, and we'd need to put a comma before the coordinating conjunction. Here's how that looks:

He brushed his teeth, and he went to bed. ✓

Both of these sentences are perfectly fine. It simply depends on what you wish to write. When it comes to the Digital SAT, you'll need to know this rule:

> You must put a comma before a coordinating conjunction (FANBOYS) if there are independent clauses both before and after the conjunction.
>
> **FANBOYS**:
> **F**or
> **A**nd
> **N**or
> **B**ut
> **O**r
> **Y**et
> **S**o

Here are some examples of incorrect ways to write this sentence, at least when it comes to the Digital SAT.

He brushed his teeth, he went to bed. ✗

He brushed his teeth and he went to bed. ✗

These sentences might seem okay for casual writing, but when it comes to the rules that are tested on the Digital SAT, it's very important to remember that a comma by itself can never come in between two independent clauses, nor can the FANBOYS word on its own.

Colons and Dashes

Using a colon is a great way to make writing more concise. Here's an example:

For the test, we need to bring three items, which are a pencil, a calculator, and a ruler. ✓

For the test, we need to bring three items: a pencil, a calculator, and a ruler. ✓

A colon tells you that what comes after is going to elaborate on or explain what came before. In this case, it tells us that the *three items* are going to follow the colon. Here, we used a list after the colon, which you may be comfortable with. But colons can come before an explanation or a definition as well. Here's an example:

English punctuation is not always easy: there are often several possible ways to punctuate a sentence. ✓

In this case, the part after the colon is another independent clause, and it explains the first part—why punctuation *is not always easy.* You might be thinking that you would punctuate this sentence differently. If so, that's perfectly fine. Here are a few other ways this could be written:

English punctuation is not always easy. There are often several possible ways to punctuate a sentence. ✓

English punctuation is not always easy; there are often several possible ways to punctuate a sentence. ✓

English punctuation is not always easy—there are often several possible ways to punctuate a sentence. ✓

English punctuation is not always easy, for there are often several possible ways to punctuate a sentence. ✓

English punctuation is not always easy because there are often several possible ways to punctuate a sentence. ✓

Since we have two independent clauses, we could use either a semicolon or a period—remember that they are interchangeable in this context. We can also use a dash, which suggests the same thing a colon does and can be used the same way. It's also possible to add a coordinating conjunction (in this case, we used *for*) with a comma, since we have two independent clauses. Lastly, you could add a **subordinating conjunction** such as *because* to connect the ideas, which we will talk more about in the next chapter. It's important to keep in mind that College Board will *never* give you more than one answer that could be correct. You won't be asked to choose between two punctuation marks that both work in a given context.

It's worth noting that there is an incorrect way students might like to write sentences using colons. Here's an example:

My favorite colors are: silver, pink, and yellow. ✗

Here's how that should be written:

My favorite colors are silver, pink, and yellow. ✓

There's no need for a colon here. As we saw above, the part after the colon does not have to be an independent clause. However, when it comes to the Digital SAT, the part before the colon does need to be an independent clause. Therefore, another way to write that example is as follows:

I have three favorite colors: silver, pink, and yellow. ✓

A colon or a single dash can only come after an independent clause.

Let's put all of those rules together.

Two independent clauses can be joined with...	**Two independent clauses can NEVER be joined with...**
• A semicolon, anytime (**;**) • A comma plus an appropriate coordinating conjunction (**FANBOYS**) • A colon or a dash, if the second part of the sentence explains the first in some way (**:** or **—**)	• A comma without a coordinating conjunction • A coordinating conjunction without a comma • No punctuation to separate the independent clauses

Now that we have seen the different ways to connect independent clauses, let's try a few Digital SAT-style questions to put it all together.

American folk musician Mike Seeger came from a family of ______ parents, Ruth Crawford Seeger and Charles Louis Seeger, Jr., were composers and ethnomusicologists, and his half-brother Pete Seeger was also a folk singer.

1 Mark for Review

Which choice completes the text so that it conforms to the conventions of Standard English?

Ⓐ musicians, his

Ⓑ musicians, his,

Ⓒ musicians his

Ⓓ musicians; his

Here's How to Crack It

Start by looking at the question to identify the question type: Rules. Next, look at the answer to see what's changing and determine what the question is testing. The punctuation after *musicians* is changing, so look for independent clauses. Start at the beginning of the sentence: *American folk musician Mike Seeger came from a family of musicians.* That's an independent clause. Take a look at the rest of the passage, including the first word in the answer choices: *His parents, Ruth Crawford Seeger and Charles Louis Seeger, Jr., were composers and ethnomusicologists, and his half-brother Pete Seeger was also a folk singer.* This is also an independent clause, so eliminate any answers that contain punctuation that creates a run-on sentence.

Eliminate (A), (B), and (C) because a comma without a coordinating conjunction and no punctuation at all are not correct ways to combine two independent clauses; they each create a run-on sentence. Choice (D) has a semicolon, which is an appropriate way to link two independent clauses. The correct answer is (D).

Physicist Edward Witten is known for his rigorous use of mathematics in his research. He was the first physicist to earn the Fields Medal from the International Mathematical Union. Witten earned his professional reputation as a ______ he was originally interested in politics, publishing articles in *The New Republic* and *The Nation* and working on George McGovern's presidential campaign.

2 Mark for Review

Which choice completes the text so that it conforms to the conventions of Standard English?

Ⓐ scientist, but

Ⓑ scientist,

Ⓒ scientist but

Ⓓ scientist

Here's How to Crack It

Look at the question to see that this is in the Rules category, so check what's changing in the answers: commas with a coordinating conjunction. Look for independent clauses. The first part of the sentence says *Witten earned his professional reputation as a scientist*. That's an independent clause. Read the rest of the sentence as it is: *he was originally interested in politics, publishing articles in The New Republic and The Nation and working on George McGovern's presidential campaign.* This is also an independent clause. We know that a comma by itself or no punctuation at all can never go in between two independent clauses; that would create a run-on sentence. Eliminate (B) and (D).

Since there are two independent clauses, you can connect them with a coordinating conjunction if you use a comma as well. That knowledge allows you to eliminate (C), which has the coordinating conjunction but not the comma, which isn't okay when you have two independent clauses. The correct answer is (A).

Fordlandia is a district located in Brazil on the Tapajós river that was founded in 1928 to serve as a hub of ______ the goal was for the 10,000 inhabitants to generate rubber for the Ford Motor Company to use when making automobiles.

3 Mark for Review

Which choice completes the text so that it conforms to the conventions of Standard English?

Ⓐ industry while

Ⓑ industry

Ⓒ industry,

Ⓓ industry:

Here's How to Crack It

Identify that this is a Rules question, and then go to the answers to see that it's testing punctuation. Read from the beginning of the sentence and look for independent clauses. The first part says *Fordlandia is a district located in Brazil on the Tapajós river that was founded in 1928 to serve as a hub of industry*, which is an independent clause. Read the second part of the sentence without the word *while* in (A): *the goal was for the 10,000 inhabitants to generate rubber for the Ford Motor Company to use when making automobiles*. This is also an independent clause, so eliminate (B) and (C) because two independent clauses must be separated by some punctuation other than a comma alone.

Keep (D) because a colon can come after an independent clause if the second part of the sentence elaborates on the first. In this case, the second independent clause explains how the district would be a *hub of industry*, so the colon is appropriate. Consider (A) next. The word *while* isn't the appropriate connector in this case; *while* is used either to show a contrast, which isn't appropriate here, or to express two events happening at the same time, which also isn't the link between the clauses. Eliminate (A). The correct answer is (D).

PUNCTUATION WITH TRANSITIONS

A final, trickier way that College Board likes to test you on connecting independent clauses is to make you determine where the punctuation goes based on which part of the sentence gets a transition, which is a word or phrase such as *however*, *for example*, or *in addition* that shows the reader what direction the ideas are going to move in. Take a look at the next example.

Researchers at the University of Edinburgh have discovered a link between learning a musical instrument as a child and improved cognitive skills later in ______ emeritus Ian Deary warns that this effect was small and that it is difficult to prove that learning an instrument causes greater mental abilities.

4 Mark for Review

Which choice completes the text so that it conforms to the conventions of Standard English?

Ⓐ life. However, professor

Ⓑ life, however. Professor

Ⓒ life, however, professor

Ⓓ life, however: professor

Here's How to Crack It

Use the question to identify the category, Rules, and then the answers to determine the topic, punctuation. Notice that two options have periods—(A) and (B)—but one has the period before the transition (*however*), and one has the period after. This means that in addition to punctuation, you're being tested on whether the transition belongs with the first or the second part of the sentence. Start by reading the first part, which says *Researchers at the University of Edinburgh have discovered a link between learning a musical instrument as a child and improved cognitive skills later in life*. This is an independent clause, but is it contrasting with something that came before? No, because there is nothing before. Thus, *however*, shouldn't go with the first part of the sentence, and (B), (C), and (D) can be eliminated.

To confirm, read the second part of the sentence: *professor emeritus Ian Deary warns that this effect was small and that it is difficult to prove that learning an instrument causes greater mental abilities.* This is also an independent clause, and it does provide a contrast—the first clause says there is *a link* between two things, but the second part *warns* that the *effect was small* and *difficult to prove.* Thus, it is appropriate for the contrast word to be in the second idea. The correct answer is (A).

As you saw in the last example, it's important to keep an eye out for questions in which the transition can go with one part of the sentence or the other. When you see this being tested, you will need to look back at the previous sentence, if there is one.

Linking Independent Clauses Drill

Answers can be found starting on page 274.

Time: 10 minutes

1 Mark for Review

José Barreiro is a Cuban-American novelist who serves as an advocate for Indigenous culture and history for native communities in Guatemala, Cuba, and ______ Barreiro works with the Smithsonian Institution to ensure that the communities are recognized respectfully and accurately.

Which choice completes the text so that it conforms to the conventions of Standard English?

Ⓐ Peru

Ⓑ Peru,

Ⓒ Peru and

Ⓓ Peru.

2 Mark for Review

There are many proteins that control the cell cycle and when cells grow and divide. Sir Paul Maxime Nurse discovered one of these proteins in yeast ______ he was awarded the Nobel Prize in Physiology or Medicine alongside Leland Hartwell and Tim Hunt for identifying a similar protein in human cells.

Which choice completes the text so that it conforms to the conventions of Standard English?

Ⓐ cells and

Ⓑ cells, and

Ⓒ cells

Ⓓ cells,

3 Mark for Review

Since many of his works are sardonic, some of Chinese author Yan Lianke's stories have been viewed as controversial. Many of his works question reality and utilize twisted and complex ______ these personas often display apprehension and concern about the living conditions in China.

Which choice completes the text so that it conforms to the conventions of Standard English?

- (A) characters and
- (B) characters
- (C) characters;
- (D) characters,

4 Mark for Review

Jenny Tung is an evolutionary anthropologist who studies the connections between genomics, health, and social experiences in different populations of primates and monkeys. While studying a population of Kenyan baboons, she found several factors that led to significantly shorter life ______ environmental conditions, such as droughts, isolation from other baboons, and lower social status within the community.

Which choice completes the text so that it conforms to the conventions of Standard English?

- (A) spans:
- (B) spans
- (C) spans;
- (D) spans,

5 Mark for Review

In 1984, Romanian poet and politician Ana Blandiana wrote her first protest poem against her country's communist ______ "Totul," which contrasted the government's official statements about life in Romania with her and others' lived experiences.

Which choice completes the text so that it conforms to the conventions of Standard English?

- (A) government:
- (B) government;
- (C) government
- (D) government.

6 Mark for Review

The oldest known surviving film is *Roundhay Garden Scene*, a short silent piece filmed by a French artist. The film has been preserved in multiple ______ it was copied onto glass plates from the original negative, and it was printed on 35 mm film.

Which choice completes the text so that it conforms to the conventions of Standard English?

- (A) forms
- (B) forms:
- (C) forms, for example
- (D) forms,

7 Mark for Review

Scientist Margaret S. Collins was the first African American female entomologist and was known as the "Termite Lady." Starting in the 1970s, she began researching termites for the Smithsonian's National Museum of Natural ______ in 1989, she discovered a new species of termite called *Neotermes luykxi* with her colleague David Nickle.

Which choice completes the text so that it conforms to the conventions of Standard English?

Ⓐ History, then,

Ⓑ History,

Ⓒ History;

Ⓓ History then,

8 Mark for Review

In languages, classifiers are used to describe a noun, such as how "cups" describes "coffee" in the phrase "three cups of coffee." Unlike English, which only sometimes uses classifiers, Chinese languages use classifiers very frequently. Often, the specific classifier used is based on some quality of the ______ objects such as tables and paper use "zhāng," whereas long, thin objects such as sticks and pens use "tiáo."

Which choice completes the text so that it conforms to the conventions of Standard English?

Ⓐ noun, for example, flat

Ⓑ noun, for example. Flat

Ⓒ noun. For example, flat

Ⓓ noun for example flat

LINKING INDEPENDENT CLAUSES DRILL ANSWERS AND EXPLANATIONS

1. **D** In this Rules question, punctuation is changing in the answer choices. The first part of the sentence says *José Barreiro is a Cuban-American novelist who serves as an advocate for Indigenous culture and history for native communities in Guatemala, Cuba, and Peru*, which is an independent clause. The second part says *Barreiro works with the Smithsonian Institution to ensure that the communities are recognized respectfully and accurately*, which is also an independent clause. Eliminate any answer that can't correctly connect two independent clauses.
   - (A) is wrong because it creates a run-on sentence.
   - (B) and (C) are wrong because neither a comma alone nor a coordinating conjunction (FANBOYS) alone can connect two independent clauses.
   - (D) is correct because two independent clauses can be two separate sentences.
2. **B** In this Rules question, punctuation is changing in the answer choices. The first part of the sentence says *Sir Paul Maxime Nurse discovered one of these proteins in yeast cells*, which is an independent clause. The second part says *he was awarded the Nobel Prize in Physiology or Medicine alongside Leland Hartwell and Tim Hunt for identifying a similar protein in human cells*, which is also an independent clause. Eliminate any answer that can't correctly connect two independent clauses.
   - (A) and (D) are wrong because neither a comma alone nor a coordinating conjunction (FANBOYS) alone can connect two independent clauses.
   - (B) is correct because a comma + a coordinating conjunction (FANBOYS) can connect two independent clauses.
   - (C) is wrong because it creates a run-on sentence.
3. **C** In this Rules question, punctuation is changing in the answer choices. The first part of the sentence says *Many of his works question reality and utilize twisted and complex characters*, which is an independent clause. The second part says *these personas often display apprehension and concern about the living conditions in China*, which is also an independent clause. Eliminate any answer that can't correctly connect two independent clauses.
   - (A) and (D) are wrong because neither a comma alone nor a coordinating conjunction (FANBOYS) alone can connect two independent clauses.
   - (B) is wrong because it creates a run-on sentence.
   - (C) is correct because a semicolon can connect two independent clauses.

4. **A** In this Rules question, punctuation is changing in the answer choices. Look for independent clauses. The first part of the sentence says *While studying a population of Kenyan baboons, she found several factors that led to significantly shorter life spans*, which is an independent clause. The second part of the sentence says *environmental conditions, such as droughts, isolation from other baboons, and lower social status within the community*, which is a list of the *factors*. Eliminate any option that doesn't correctly connect an independent clause with a list.

- (A) is correct because a colon is appropriate to connect an independent clause and a list.
- (B) and (D) are wrong because they don't make it clear that the second part lists the *factors*.
- (C) is wrong because a semicolon can only link two independent clauses.

5. **A** In this Rules question, punctuation is changing in the answer choices. Look for independent clauses. The first part of the sentence says *In 1984, Romanian poet and politician Ana Blandiana wrote her first protest poem against her country's communist government*, which is an independent clause. The second part of the sentence says *"Totul," which contrasted the government's official statements about life in Romania with her and others' lived experiences*, which is not an independent clause and tells what the *poem* was. Eliminate any option that doesn't correctly connect the independent clause with the explanation of the poem.

- (A) is correct because a colon is used when the first part is an independent clause and the second provides an explanation or definition.
- (B) is wrong because a semicolon can only link two independent clauses.
- (C) is wrong because the lack of punctuation doesn't make it clear that the second part gives the name and description of the poem.
- (D) is wrong because the second part isn't an independent clause and can't stand on its own.

6. **B** In this Rules question, punctuation is changing in the answer choices. Look for independent clauses. The first part of the sentence says *The film has been preserved in multiple forms*, which is an independent clause. The second part of the sentence says *it was copied onto glass plates from the original negative, and it was printed on 35 mm film*, which is also an independent clause. Eliminate any answer that can't correctly connect two independent clauses.

- (A) is wrong because it creates a run-on sentence.
- (B) is correct because a colon can connect two independent clauses, and the second part explains the first.
- (C) and (D) are wrong because a comma without a coordinating conjunction (FANBOYS) can't connect two independent clauses.

7. **C** In this Rules question, punctuation is changing in the answer choices. Look for independent clauses. The first part of the sentence says *Starting in the 1970s, she began researching termites for the Smithsonian's National Museum of Natural History*, which is an independent clause. The second part says *in 1989, she discovered a new species of termite called Neotermes luykxi with her colleague David Nickle*, which is also an independent clause. Some of the answers include *then* with the second part of the sentence, which does not change whether or not the second part is an independent clause. Eliminate any answer that can't correctly connect two independent clauses.

   - (A), (B), and (D) are wrong because a comma without a coordinating conjunction (FANBOYS) can't connect two independent clauses.
   - (C) is correct because a semicolon can connect two independent clauses.

8. **C** In this Rules question, punctuation with a transition is changing in the answer choices. Look for independent clauses. The first part of the sentence says *Often, the specific classifier used is based on some quality of the noun*. There is an option to add *for example* to this independent clause, but it's not an example of something. Eliminate options with *for example* in the first part.

   - (A) and (D) are wrong because the clauses before and after *for example* are independent and can't be linked without punctuation or with a comma alone.
   - (B) is wrong because it puts *for example* with the first independent clause.
   - (C) is correct because *for example* is part of the second independent clause.

Summary

- An independent clause can stand on its own as a complete sentence.
- Two independent clauses can be put together in the same sentence using a semicolon.
- Two independent clauses can also be connected with a comma + an appropriate coordinating conjunction (FANBOYS—For, And, Nor, But, Or, Yet, So).
- A colon or a dash can be used when the second part of the sentence elaborates on the first. In this case, the first part of the sentence must be an independent clause, but the second part doesn't have to be.
- Two independent clauses can never be connected with a comma alone, a coordinating conjunction alone, or no punctuation at all.
- When transitions and punctuation are changing, determine whether the transition belongs with the first or the second part of the sentence.

Chapter 15
Rules Questions: Dependent Clauses, Lists, and No Punctuation

There are a few more punctuation-related topics that you are likely to see on the Digital SAT. In this chapter, you'll learn about dependent clauses and how to connect them to independent clauses, how to answer questions that involve complicated lists, and when no punctuation is needed at all.

DEPENDENT CLAUSES

You already know that an independent clause can stand on its own to be a sentence. Thus, a **dependent clause** can't be its own sentence. It "depends" on an independent clause to make a complete sentence. We've already seen examples involving the Independent Clause + Independent Clause combination and the different ways they can be joined. In this chapter, we'll see how a dependent clause can be joined with an independent clause. But first, let's recognize what a dependent clause looks like.

Knowing that an independent clause requires a subject and a verb, you might think that a dependent clause doesn't have one of these things. But actually, a dependent clause still has a subject and a verb. What usually makes a clause dependent is that it starts with a **subordinating word** (or phrase). Let's break down that term: *sub-* means "below," right? So, a subordinating word moves a clause to a lower level: in other words, it takes a clause from being independent to being dependent. Let's see some examples.

Independent: *they wanted to watch a movie*

Dependent: ***because*** *they wanted to watch a movie*

Dependent: ***since*** *they wanted to watch a movie*

Dependent: ***that*** *they wanted to watch a movie*

Dependent: ***if*** *they wanted to watch a movie*

Dependent: ***though*** *they wanted to watch a movie*

Dependent: ***when*** *they wanted to watch a movie*

Try the following drill to practice identifying independent and dependent clauses.

INDEPENDENT VS. DEPENDENT CLAUSES EXERCISE

Circle whether each clause is independent or dependent. Answers are on page 289.

1.	they sang	Independent / Dependent
2.	until he pays her back for lunch	Independent / Dependent
3.	where I put my socks	Independent / Dependent
4.	as soon as I was elected captain of my team	Independent / Dependent
5.	singing my friends' favorite songs is one of my favorite activities	Independent / Dependent
6.	snow fell overnight in my neighborhood	Independent / Dependent
7.	that you will be supporting me	Independent / Dependent
8.	if she walks	Independent / Dependent
9.	they will wash the dishes and take out the garbage	Independent / Dependent
10.	if I decided to have dinner and play games with my roommate	Independent / Dependent

There are two ways to connect an independent clause and a dependent clause: Independent + Dependent or Dependent + Independent. In either case, the only punctuation that is allowed is a comma. Usually the Independent + Dependent combination will not have a comma, but the Dependent + Independent one will, though this is not a strict rule. Let's take a look at some correctly punctuated examples.

***Because** it was raining, I brought my umbrella.* ✓

*I brought my umbrella **because** it was raining.* ✓

***Even though** the weather was cold, I didn't wear my heavy jacket.* ✓

*I didn't wear my heavy jacket **even though** the weather was cold.* ✓

***If** you're ready, we can leave the house now.* ✓

*We can leave the house now **if** you're ready.* ✓

***While** dogs need care more frequently, cats can be left alone for several days.* ✓

*Cats can be left alone for several days, **while** dogs need care more frequently.* ✓

From the last example, you can see that a comma can sometimes be used when the dependent clause comes second. This would typically happen when there is a contrast or when the author wants to put a greater pause or separation between the ideas. That being said, remember that College Board won't test you on anything that is a gray area. Chances are, if you were to see a sentence like the last one above, there wouldn't be an option without a comma before *while*, since both ways could be acceptable.

Let's see a couple of examples of how this topic can be tested.

There were two volcanic eruptions that occurred in the U.S. during the 20th century. Lassen Peak erupted in 1915 and destroyed an area to the northeast of the ______ the eruption of Mount St. Helens in 1980 was a much more devastating event.

1 Mark for Review

Which choice completes the text so that it conforms to the conventions of Standard English?

Ⓐ peak. Though

Ⓑ peak: though

Ⓒ peak, though

Ⓓ peak; though

Here's How to Crack It

Use the question to identify the category, which is Rules. Then, look at the answer choices to see what's changing: punctuation. Start from the beginning of the sentence: *Lassen Peak erupted in 1915 and destroyed an area to the northeast of the peak.* That's an independent clause. The second part of the sentence reads *though the eruption of Mount St. Helens in 1980 was a much more devastating event.* This is a dependent clause since it begins with the subordinating word *though.* We know that the independent + dependent combination can only be connected with either a comma or no punctuation at all, so eliminate (A), (B), and (D). The correct answer is (C).

Remember, a period and a semicolon function the same way. Chances are, if you see both of them in the answer choices with no changes in wording, both answers are wrong.

Known for his headless, life-size sculptural figures, British-Nigerian artist Yinka Shonibare often uses so-called "African" fabric in his work. He has stated that he actually likes that this material is not authentically ______ it symbolizes how culture is artificially constructed.

2 Mark for Review

Which choice completes the text so that it conforms to the conventions of Standard English?

(A) African because

(B) African; because

(C) African: because

(D) African. Because

Here's How to Crack It

Look at the question to determine that this is a Rules question. Next, look at the answers to see that punctuation is changing. Start from the beginning of the sentence: *He has stated that he actually likes that this material is not authentically African* is an independent clause. The second part, *because it symbolizes how culture is artificially constructed,* is a dependent clause since it starts with the subordinating conjunction *because.* The independent + dependent combination can only be connected with either a comma or no punctuation at all, so eliminate (B), (C), and (D). The correct answer is (A).

An independent clause and a dependent clause (in either order) can be joined with...	**An independent clause and a dependent clause (in either order) can NEVER be joined with...**
• A comma (,) • No punctuation at all	• A period (.) • A semicolon (;) • A colon (:) • A coordinating conjunction (**FANBOYS**) • A dash, unless the dependent clause is Extra Info (—)

PUNCTUATING LISTS

As you probably remember from school, anytime you write a sentence that has a list of three or more things, you must put commas in between the items. Let's see some examples:

> *Do you prefer pumpkin pie, pecan pie, or apple pie?* ✓

> *The professor's day consisted of teaching classes to undergraduate students, meeting with graduate student mentees, and editing an article for publication in a research journal.* ✓

When it comes to the Digital SAT, and most of the time in real life, a list should always have *and* or *or* before the final item in the list. Many publications, such as newspapers, don't bother putting a comma before the *and* or *or* in order to save space (much like how newspaper headlines leave out some words), although many style guides call for this comma to always be used. Since this is a disputed rule in punctuation, it isn't tested on the Digital SAT. The Digital SAT will put a comma before the *and* or *or* in the correct answer, but you won't be given an option without that comma that doesn't make some other mistake.

Let's see an example of how this could be tested.

L. Frank is an activist for Indigenous languages and art. One of her primary publications included a book called *First Families: Photographic History of California Indians*, which featured pictures of a traditional canoe being ______ and an expedition being completed along the coast of California.

3 Mark for Review

Which choice completes the text so that it conforms to the conventions of Standard English?

Ⓐ sailed a man performing a traditional funerary dance

Ⓑ sailed, a man performing a traditional funerary dance,

Ⓒ sailed a man performing a traditional funerary dance,

Ⓓ sailed, a man, performing a traditional funerary dance

Here's How to Crack It

Start by using the question to identify that this falls into the Rules category. Then, look to see what's changing in the answers: commas. Read the sentence to determine how commas are being tested. The sentence explains what the book *featured* and contains the word *and* towards the end, so look for a list. In a list, all of the items must be in the same form. The first item after *pictures* is *a traditional canoe*, and the last item after *and* is *an expedition*, both of which are nouns, so the second item should start with a noun. The second and third words, *a man*, represent a noun, so try putting the comma before that to form the list. In this case, the list would consist of 1) *a traditional canoe being sailed*, 2) *a man performing a traditional funerary dance*, and 3) *an expedition being completed along the coast of California*. This makes sense because those are all in the same form and all are things that could be pictures.

Now that we've established that this question has a list of three or more things, we can use the rule that such a list must have commas in between. Eliminate (A) and (C) because they don't have a comma after *sailed*. Eliminate (D) because there is no reason to put a comma after *man*. The correct answer is (B).

The key is to notice when the sentence contains a list. In the example above, the word *and* appears in the original sentence, and the answer choices include some words that together aren't logical: *sailed a man*. This suggests that there is some need for punctuation, which can help you realize that the sentence contains a list.

There is also a more complicated, more unusual way that the Digital SAT may construct lists in a passage. Take a look at the following example.

> *The committee members are Alex, a parent, Taylor, a teacher, and Ali, a community member.*

Can you spot what's a little confusing about that list? It's unclear whether the committee has three people on it (the ones with the names) or more people, some of whose names aren't given. In this case, the intention is to provide the names and titles of the three committee members. We can make that clearer by doing this:

> *The committee members are Alex, a parent; Taylor, a teacher; and Ali, a community member.* ✓

In this case, semicolons are used to visually separate the items in the list so that each item can have commas within it if needed. Earlier, we saw how semicolons function just like periods. This example illustrates the one exception: semicolons can separate a complicated list that includes commas within one or more of the list items. If you see multiple semicolons in the original sentence and the answers, that's a good sign that the question is testing this topic.

Let's see an example.

Throat singing is a technique that uses a guttural (as opposed to the more common chest or head) voice and produces a sound that is often perceived as including multiple pitches from one person. Throat singing is a feature of many musical traditions, including *Canto a* ______ Buddhist chant, practiced in some monasteries in India and Tibet; and Inuit throat singing, used as a contest between two people in northern Canada.

4 Mark for Review

Which choice completes the text so that it conforms to the conventions of Standard English?

Ⓐ *tenóre*; a style of quartet singing from Sardinia, Italy,

Ⓑ *tenóre*, a style of quartet singing from Sardinia, Italy,

Ⓒ *tenóre*, a style of quartet singing from Sardinia, Italy;

Ⓓ *tenóre*; a style of quartet singing from Sardinia, Italy;

Here's How to Crack It

Start by looking at the question to determine that this is in the Rules category. Then, look at the answer choices to see what's changing, which reveals that the question is testing commas and semicolons. Remember, there are two uses for a semicolon. It can work like a period to connect two independent clauses, or it can separate a complicated list that has commas within the items. Read the sentence to see which of those it has. Notice that the sentence already contains a semicolon near the end, but the part after the semicolon (*and Inuit throat singing, used as a contest between two people in northern Canada*) isn't an independent clause. Since the only other use of a semicolon is to connect independent clauses, this sentence must have a list separated with semicolons.

Use the third example to determine the structure of each item: Musical tradition, Comma, Use. Now, return to the first item in the list. After the musical tradition *Canto a tenóre*, there should be a comma in order to follow the pattern of the third item. Eliminate (A) and (D). The next place the punctuation changes is after *Italy*. This is the end of the first item, as the next thing is *Buddhist chant*, which is the second singing style. So, there must be a semicolon after *Italy* to separate it from the next item in the list. Eliminate (B). The correct answer is (C).

WHERE PUNCTUATION IS NOT NEEDED

Now you have learned about all of the different types of punctuation and when they should be used (besides apostrophes, which are coming up soon). It's equally important to know when they should *not* be used. You might think that when College Board is asking you about punctuation, it's because the sentence needs some type of punctuation. However, sometimes the sentence doesn't need any punctuation at all. Let's see an example.

American physicist and educator Edward Alexander ______ the first African American to earn a Ph.D. in the United States, writing his dissertation in physics on the refractive indices of various glasses.

5 Mark for Review

Which choice completes the text so that it conforms to the conventions of Standard English?

(A) Bouchet, was

(B) Bouchet was

(C) Bouchet: was

(D) Bouchet. Was

Here's How to Crack It

Identify the category, Rules, based on the question. Then, notice that punctuation is changing in the answer choices. Start at the beginning of the sentence: *American physicist and educator Edward Alexander Bouchet*. This has given us the subject but not the verb. We can't separate the subject and verb with a single punctuation mark, since they are the most crucial components of the sentence, so eliminate (A), (C), and (D). No punctuation should be used, so the correct answer is (B).

We know that was pretty obvious since we basically implied that the correct answer wouldn't have punctuation. But let's go over a few rules related to this "no punctuation" topic.

"No Punctuation" Rules

1. Don't put punctuation where there is Specifying Information.
2. Never put a single punctuation mark in between a subject and its verb.
3. Don't put punctuation after a preposition.

Above all else, don't use punctuation unless you have a reason to do so.

We've already discussed Rule #1 above, so let's take a look at the second rule.

Astronaut Mae Jemison became interested in space in part because of Lieutenant Uhura, a Star Trek *character.* ✓

Mae Jemison, an astronaut, became interested in space in part because of Lieutenant Uhura, a Star Trek *character.* ✓

Here are some of our sentences from earlier. The subject is *Mae Jemison* and the verb is *became.* It is fine to put an Extra phrase in between the subject and verb as long as it has matching punctuation on both sides, in this case commas. However, what you can never do is put a *single* comma in between the subject and the verb (the same is true for any other punctuation mark). Here are some incorrect examples:

Astronaut Mae Jemison, became interested in space in part because of Lieutenant Uhura, a Star Trek *character.* ✗

Astronaut Mae Jemison: became interested in space in part because of Lieutenant Uhura, a Star Trek *character.* ✗

Astronaut Mae Jemison—became interested in space in part because of Lieutenant Uhura, a Star Trek *character.* ✗

Sometimes there is more distance between the subject and the verb. Still, make sure there isn't a single punctuation mark between them. Here is another incorrect example:

The sandwich I wanted to order, was no longer available. ✗

The subject is *sandwich* and the verb is *was*. This example puts a single comma in between, so it's wrong. No punctuation should be used here.

Finally, let's take a look at the third place that punctuation should not be used—after a preposition. Here are some incorrect examples:

The fundraising contest offered rewards of: giftcards, headphones, and sneakers. ✗

You should try to listen to the new album with—an open mind. ✗

Once again, no punctuation should be used other than the commas in the list in the first sentence above. College Board particularly likes to test this rule when there is a list. It helps to remember that while you might be tempted to use a colon when there is a list, the colon can only follow an independent clause, which won't be the case after a preposition.

ANSWERS TO INDEPENDENT VS. DEPENDENT CLAUSES EXERCISE

1. Independent
2. Dependent
3. Dependent
4. Dependent
5. Independent
6. Independent
7. Dependent
8. Dependent
9. Independent
10. Dependent

Dependent Clauses, Lists, and No Punctuation Drill

Answers can be found starting on page 292.

Time: 8 minutes

1 Mark for Review

Stephen Pile's *The Book of Heroic Failures* describes a variety of instances of individual and group deficiency. For example, the chapter "Off Work" describes *English as She Is Spoke*, a guide to English conversation for Portuguese speakers. However, the phrases included in this book are typically inaccurate or ______ its author, Pedro Carolino, did not speak English and instead relied on two translation books: a Portuguese-to-French and a French-to-English.

Which choice completes the text so that it conforms to the conventions of Standard English?

Ⓐ unidiomatic because

Ⓑ unidiomatic,

Ⓒ unidiomatic. Because

Ⓓ unidiomatic: because

2 Mark for Review

Throughout his life, Indian musician Ram Narayan brought attention to the instrument *sarangi* ______ playing major music festivals as a solo artist, recording albums, and eventually touring internationally.

Which choice completes the text so that it conforms to the conventions of Standard English?

Ⓐ by:

Ⓑ by—

Ⓒ by,

Ⓓ by

3 Mark for Review

As suggested by the research of Lisa Espinosa of the Emotion Lab at the Karolinska Institute, the reason that people may have intrusive memories with neutral ______ is that the neutral content was paired with a negative experience in the past, such as seeing a picture of an umbrella while receiving a mild electric shock.

Which choice completes the text so that it conforms to the conventions of Standard English?

Ⓐ content

Ⓑ content;

Ⓒ content:

Ⓓ content,

4 Mark for Review

Diane E. Benson is a creative writer and actress from Alaska who also ran for governor. She first ventured into politics in ______ she ran for office alongside Desa Jacobson, representing the first two Native women to share a ticket together.

Which choice completes the text so that it conforms to the conventions of Standard English?

Ⓐ 2002, when

Ⓑ 2002,

Ⓒ 2002; when

Ⓓ 2002

5 Mark for Review

Scientists have discovered that the area of the human brain responsible for self-serving choices is separate from the area that is responsible for altruistic choices. The hope is that this research will help scientists discover the motivation behind philanthropic behaviors, for instance, donating to charities, such as animal ______ such as recycling plastic and other materials; and helping strangers with tasks, such as holding the door for someone to walk through.

Which choice completes the text so that it conforms to the conventions of Standard English?

Ⓐ shelters; adopting environmental habits,

Ⓑ shelters, adopting environmental habits;

Ⓒ shelters, adopting environmental habits,

Ⓓ shelters; adopting environmental habits;

6 Mark for Review

The chemical composition of Jupiter's atmosphere is relatively well-known due to the observations made by the Galileo atmospheric probe in 1995. The ratios of helium to hydrogen and phosphorus to hydrogen in Jupiter's atmosphere are relatively close to the same ratios for the Sun. However, for other elements, Jupiter's atmosphere has a much greater abundance: the ratio of nitrogen to hydrogen in Jupiter is about 3.5 times as great as that of the Sun; carbon to ______ and krypton to hydrogen, 2.7 times as great.

Which choice completes the text so that it conforms to the conventions of Standard English?

Ⓐ hydrogen 2.9 times as great;

Ⓑ hydrogen 2.9 times as great,

Ⓒ hydrogen, 2.9 times as great,

Ⓓ hydrogen, 2.9 times as great;

DEPENDENT CLAUSES, LISTS, AND NO PUNCTUATION DRILL ANSWERS AND EXPLANATIONS

1. **A** In this Rules question, punctuation is changing in the answer choices. Look for independent clauses. The first part of the sentence says *However, the phrases included in this book are typically inaccurate or unidiomatic*, which is an independent clause. The second part of the sentence says *because its author, Pedro Carolino, did not speak English and instead relied on two translation books: a Portuguese-to-French and a French-to-English*, which is a dependent clause. Eliminate any option that doesn't correctly connect an independent + a dependent clause.

    - (A) is correct because independent + dependent can be connected with no punctuation.
    - (B) is wrong because eliminating *because* changes the second clause to an independent clause, and independent + independent can't be connected with a comma alone.
    - (C) is wrong because a dependent clause can't stand alone as a sentence.
    - (D) is wrong because independent + dependent cannot be connected with punctuation other than a comma.

2. **D** In this Rules question, punctuation is changing in the answer choices. Look for independent clauses. The first part of the sentence says *Throughout his life, Indian musician Ram Narayan brought attention to the instrument sarangi by*, which ends with a preposition. There should not be punctuation after a preposition, so eliminate answers with punctuation.

    - (A), (B), and (C) are wrong because punctuation cannot come after a preposition.
    - (D) is correct because no punctuation should be used here.

3. **A** In this Rules question, punctuation is changing in the answer choices. The first part of the sentence says *the reason that people may have intrusive memories with neutral content is that*, and it contains the subject-verb pair *reason* and *is*. There should not be a single punctuation mark between the subject and verb, so eliminate answers with punctuation.

    - (A) is correct because no punctuation should be used here.
    - (B), (C), and (D) are wrong because a single punctuation mark cannot come between a subject and a verb.

4. **A** In this Rules question, punctuation is changing in the answer choices. The first part of the sentence says *She first ventured into politics in 2002,* which is an independent clause. The second part of the sentence says *she ran for office alongside Desa Jacobson,* which is an independent clause; however, with the addition of *when,* it becomes a dependent clause: *when she ran for office alongside Desa Jacobson.* Eliminate any option that doesn't correctly connect the two clauses.

   - (A) is correct because independent + dependent can be connected with a comma.
   - (B) and (D) are wrong because without *when* the second clause is independent, and independent + independent cannot be connected with a comma by itself or no punctuation.
   - (C) is wrong because independent + dependent cannot be connected with a semicolon.

5. **A** In this Rules question, commas are changing in the answer choices. The sentence already contains a semicolon near the end, and the part after it is not an independent clause, which suggests that the sentence contains a list separated by semicolons. Use the third example to determine the structure of each item: Philanthropic behavior, Comma, Example. Make an annotation of this pattern and eliminate any answer that doesn't follow it.

   - (A) is correct because it follows the pattern of the third item.
   - (B) and (C) are wrong because they don't have a semicolon after the second item.
   - (D) is wrong because a comma, not a semicolon, should follow the philanthropic behavior.

6. **D** In this Rules question, commas are changing in the answer choices. The sentence already contains a semicolon near the end, and the part after it is not an independent clause, which suggests that the sentence contains a list separated by semicolons. Use the third example to determine the structure of each item: Elements, Comma, Comparison. Make an annotation of this pattern and eliminate any answer that doesn't follow it.

   - (A) and (B) are wrong because there is no comma between the elements and the comparison.
   - (C) is wrong because it doesn't have a semicolon after the second item.
   - (D) is correct because it follows the pattern of the third item.

Summary

- A dependent clause has a subject and a verb but begins with a subordinating word.
- A dependent clause can be connected to an independent clause in either order. In some cases a comma is used, and in other cases no punctuation is used.
- No other punctuation besides a comma can come between an independent and a dependent clause in either order.
- In a list of three or more things, there must be commas in between the items and before the word *and* or *or* before the last item.
- If one or more items in the list has a comma within it, the list will be separated by semicolons.
- Establish the pattern of a list by looking at a complete item in the passage.
- Never put a single punctuation mark between a subject and a verb.
- Don't use punctuation unless there is a reason to do so.

Chapter 16 Rules Questions: Grammar

The Rules category covers both punctuation and grammar. In this chapter, we'll look at the remaining topics (verbs, pronouns, nouns, and modifiers) and see how the Digital SAT tests consistency in these subject areas.

GRAMMAR AND CONSISTENCY

Now that you have learned everything there is to know about sentence construction on the Digital SAT, it's time to move on to the other component of the Rules questions: grammar. Don't worry, there are far fewer rules to know when it comes to this topic. In fact, we're going to boil it down to a single word: **Consistency**. All of the rules we are going to go over in this chapter tie back to Consistency. This means, for example, your verbs are consistent with each other in tense, your pronouns are consistent with the nouns they're replacing, and your describing phrases are consistent with the people or things they're describing. Let's take a look at the specific topics to which Consistency applies.

VERBS

You already learned a great deal about verbs in the sentence structure portion of this book. For instance, you learned that only certain types of verbs can be the main verb in a sentence (that is, not *-ing* verbs or "to" verbs), and you also learned that multiple verbs that are part of a list within a sentence must be in the same form. There are two additional, major ways that verbs are tested on the Digital SAT. The first one is **subject-verb agreement**.

You already know that every sentence must have a subject and a verb. Once we stop thinking about structure, though, we can take things a step further: the subject and verb must *agree*. As we know, subjects are usually nouns, and nouns can be either singular or plural. As it turns out, verbs can also be singular or plural. So, if your subject is singular, then your verb needs to be singular as well, and vice versa. Even if you haven't thought about this much, it's something you do every day when you speak or write. Let's see some examples.

The assignment is due on Friday. ✓

The assignments are due on Friday. ✓

In the first example, both the subject and the verb are singular. In the second example, both are plural. If we try to mix that up, your ear will probably tell you that it's wrong:

The assignment are due on Friday. ✗

The assignments is due on Friday. ✗

Of course, it would be great if the Digital SAT would give you sentences as simple as these. You'd have no trouble with such an obvious question (and once in a while you may get lucky with one of those on your test). Unfortunately, and probably to no one's surprise, College Board has some tricks to make subject-verb agreement a little more challenging. Let's see an example.

Susan Sontag was an American writer and activist who wrote extensively throughout her life. One of her many focuses ______ photography; in her book of essays, *On Photography*, she wrote about how photography influences people's relationship to the world.

1 Mark for Review

Which choice completes the text so that it conforms to the conventions of Standard English?

(A) have been

(B) are

(C) was

(D) were

Watch Us Crack It
Watch the step-by-step video explanation of how to answer this question in your Student Tools.

Here's How to Crack It

Start by looking at the question to determine that this falls into the Rules category. Next, look at the answers to see that verbs are changing, so the question is testing consistency with verbs. Start by identifying and highlighting the subject. Although the word *focuses* comes right before the blank, be careful. The sentence is not saying that "her focuses were/are photography" (which doesn't really make sense anyway since photography is only one thing). It's describing photography as *one* of her focuses. So, the subject is *One*, which is singular. Highlight this word and write an annotation saying "singular." In order to be consistent, you need to use a singular verb. Choices (A), *have been*; (B), *are*; and (D), *were*, are all plural. Eliminate them and the correct answer is (C), which is singular.

Most students would look at the answers on a question like the one above and assume that the question is testing verb tense. As it turns out, you didn't need to worry about the tense at all. You could have spent a long time deciding whether you needed past or present tense and even trying to choose between two different options in similar tenses.

To save time, always find the subject before worrying about tense. We can't promise this will always be the case, but most of the time, if not all the time, College Board does not test tense at the same time as testing number (which is the term for singular vs. plural). This means that once you recognize that the question is testing number, you don't need to think about tense. You only need to find the subject and eliminate the answers that don't match.

Of course, in order to answer these questions correctly, you need to know the difference between singular and plural subjects and verbs. Let's see what those look like.

Singular subjects	Plural subjects
• Most nouns that don't end in *-s* (dog, book, teacher, airplane, approval, bravery, person) • Nouns that end in *-s* but refer to only one thing (boss, dress, bus, gas, glass, happiness, success) • *-ing* verbs (swimming, running, watching, dancing) • Collective nouns (team, group, family, army) • Singular pronouns (she, he, it, this, each, everybody, anyone, nothing, everywhere)	• Nouns that end in *-s* where the version without the *-s* or *-es* is singular (dogs, books, teachers, airplanes, teams, groups, families, bosses, dresses, buses, gases, glasses) • Irregular plurals that don't end in *-s* (children, mice, teeth, men, women, people, deer) • Plural pronouns (we, they, these, those, both, many) • Two or more things joined with *and* (my parents and I, Hallie and Amelia)

Like we said earlier, a lot of this will probably be intuitive. For instance, students often think the word *team* must be plural because a team must include more than one person. However, these same students would never say "The team are"—they say "The team is." So, they do know the word is singular because they match it correctly with *is*. In fact, this is the strategy we recommend when you're not sure whether a word is singular or plural:

> If you're not sure whether the subject of a sentence is singular or plural, try putting "is" and "are" after the word. If it matches with "is," it's singular. If it matches with "are," it's plural.

Another aspect of this topic that can be tricky is determining whether a verb is singular or plural. You might assume a verb like "wants" is plural because it ends in *-s*. While we know that nouns ending in *-s* are usually plural, this isn't the case for verbs. In fact, it's usually the opposite. You would say "it wants" or "they want." Here's our trick for testing whether a verb is singular or plural:

> If you're not sure whether a verb is singular or plural, try putting "it" and "they" before the verb. If it matches with "it," it's singular. If it matches with "they," it's plural.

The hardest part about subject-verb agreement on the Digital SAT actually isn't determining whether the subject or verb is singular or plural, especially once you know the strategies we just mentioned. The part students have the most difficulty with is finding the subject. In the previous chapters, we circled the subjects and underlined the verbs in the example sentences. You may have noticed that the subject almost always comes before the verb. This is where things get tricky: the subject is likely going to be before the verb, but it may not be *right* before the verb.

In Question 1 from this chapter, that was the case: the phrase *of her many focuses* separated the subject (*one*) from the verb (*was*). Let's take a closer look at that phrase. It starts with the word *of*, which you should remember as being a preposition, and therefore this is a prepositional phrase. Putting one or more prepositional phrases in between the subject and the verb is one of the most common ways the Digital SAT likes to try to trick you on subject-verb agreement questions. Let's see some examples.

The words ***of the poem*** *were strange and hard to understand.* ✓

Animals ***in the wild*** *spend their days looking for food.* ✓

The hall ***of mirrors*** *makes people bump into the walls.* ✓

Swimming ***in the lake while wearing shoes*** *is a bad idea.* ✓

In the examples above, College Board wants you to think that the word directly before the verb is the subject. Then you would say "poem was," "wild spends," "mirrors make," and "shoes are," respectively, and get all four questions wrong. This is why it's so important to correctly locate the subject.

There are other ways to separate the subject and the verb besides prepositional phrases:

Sewing ***your own clothes*** *has become more expensive than buying clothes.* ✓

A bicycle ***that has three wheels*** *is actually called a tricycle.* ✓

The person ***watering the plants*** *lives over there.* ✓

Prairie dogs, ***which live in North America,*** *have elaborate societies.* ✓

Once again, College Board would want you to think "clothes have," "wheels are," "plants live," and "North America has," respectively. But we're sure you wouldn't make that mistake now that you have learned subject-verb agreement! Just in case, though, try out the following drill to ensure that you can correctly find the subject for a given verb in a sentence.

SUBJECTS AND VERBS EXERCISE

Circle the subject of each underlined verb. Watch out for describing phrases between the subject and the verb. Answers are on page 311.

1. The collection of books, magazines, and movies available at the library covers a broad range of topics.

2. Fishes living in the lake include bass, crappie, and muskellunge.

3. Even if one may be embarrassed, dancing with your friends at a party is very fun.

4. Members of the jury have a serious responsibility to consider all the facts when deciding a case.

5. The jury, after deliberating in private, decides which side has won.

6. The United States has a history of success in international sports competitions.

7. Making one's bed in the morning starts the day on the right foot.

8. A passport and a plane ticket are necessary in order to travel to another continent.

9. Games developed by Gary Gygax, such as *Chainmail* and *Dungeons and Dragons*, are among the most popular games played today.

10. In algebra, letters towards the end of the alphabet, such as *x*, *y*, and *z*, usually represent variables.

We mentioned earlier that questions that look like they are testing tense may actually be testing number. Of course, sometimes the question is testing tense. Let's see an example.

Broadcast stations, such as radio and television stations, are identified by their unique call signs. In the U.S., stations west of the Mississippi River use *K* as the first letter of their call signs. Those east of the Mississippi River ______ *W*.

2 Mark for Review

Which choice completes the text so that it conforms to the conventions of Standard English?

(A) will use

(B) have used

(C) were using

(D) use

Here's How to Crack It

Start by looking at the question, which reveals that the topic here is Rules. In that case, consult the answers to see what's being tested. Verbs are changing in the answer choices, so the question is testing consistency with verbs. Start by finding the subject, which is *Those.* Highlight this word, which is plural, so try putting a plural word such as "They" before each answer choice. "They will use," "They have used," "They were using," and "They use" all work, so there isn't an issue of subject-verb agreement.

Consider tense next, as the answers are in different tenses. The previous two sentences use present tense verbs: *are* and *use.* Highlight those verbs. In order to be consistent, this sentence should also be in present tense. Write an annotation that says "present tense." Eliminate (A), which is future tense, (B), which isn't exactly present tense, and (C), which is past tense. Choice (D) is in present tense, so it's the correct answer. It's consistent with *are* and *use* in the previous sentence, as there is no indication of a shift in tense.

You might be thinking that the last question seemed pretty easy. It's usually not too hard to choose among past, present, and future tenses. But what about the different variations of those tenses? Let's see another example.

The National Raisin Reserve was created in the U.S. after World War II. The reserve allowed the government to take a portion of raisins produced by farmers, thus limiting supply and increasing the price. A U.S. Supreme Court case ______ the reserve in 2015.

3 Mark for Review

Which choice completes the text so that it conforms to the conventions of Standard English?

Ⓐ ends

Ⓑ has ended

Ⓒ will end

Ⓓ ended

Here's How to Crack It

Use the question to identify that this falls under the Rules category. Then, look at the answers to see that verbs are changing, so it's testing consistency with verbs. In that case, you need to check first for subject-verb agreement. Locate and highlight the subject, which is *U.S. Supreme Court case.* That's singular, but all of the answers work with "it," so the question isn't testing number.

Next, consider tense. Highlight the phrase *in 2015*, which indicates that this event happened in the past. Make an annotation that says "past tense." Eliminate (A) because it's present tense. Keep (B) because it could refer to something in the past. Eliminate (C) because it's future tense. Keep (D) because it's past tense.

Compare (B) and (D). The verb *has ended* should be used when referring to the present. If something *has ended* it means that by this point (now) it is over. However, the sentence does not go up to the present; it refers to an event that occurred *in 2015*. So, eliminate (B). Choice (D) is the only one in regular past tense, which is what we need here to refer to an event that occurred at a specific time in the past. The correct answer is (D).

Present Perfect vs. Past Perfect

The two tenses that students tend to have the most trouble with on the Digital SAT are present perfect and past perfect. Of course, you don't need to know these terms for the test. Let's take a look at some examples:

Past: *I went to the museum in 2017.*

Present perfect: *I have been to the museum before.*

Present perfect: *I have been to the museum several times.*

Past perfect: *I had been to the museum before the new wing opened.*

Past tense, or simple past tense, is used for an event that occurred at some time in the past. The first example occurred *in 2017.*

Present perfect always uses the helping verb *has* (singular) or *have* (plural). This tense implies something that happened at an indefinite time (*before*) or multiple times (*several times*) and suggests that it could happen again. In the two present perfect examples, the implication is that this person could go to the museum again.

Past perfect always uses the helping verb *had*. This tense suggests that something happened before something else that was also in the past. In our example, sometime in the past *the new wing opened*. Even before that, *I had been to the museum*. We use *had* to show that going to the museum happened before the other past tense verb.

Try the following drill to test your proficiency in verb tense.

VERB TENSE EXERCISE

Circle the correct tense based on the clue in each sentence. Answers are on page 311.

1. They *study* / *studied* / *have studied* every night this week.
2. Next year, after her birthday, she *visits* / *visited* / *will visit* her cousins.
3. Today, I *am* / *was* / *will be* ready to perform for my school.
4. I *was* / *am* / *had been* working on my project every day before it was finished.
5. Yesterday, he *goes* / *went* / *will go* to the park to watch birds.
6. The team *went* / *had gone* / *has gone* to the state championship last year.

When you see verbs changing in the answer choices...

1. If there is a "to" form and/or an *-ing* form, check for a complete sentence.
2. Otherwise, find the subject and eliminate any answers that aren't consistent in number (singular/plural) with the subject.
3. If needed, check tense. Look for other verbs in the sentence or surrounding sentences, as well as time-change clues.

PRONOUNS

Let's start with the basics: What is a pronoun? A pronoun is a word that stands in for a noun. It would sound very repetitive and annoying to say, "Sara brought Sara's book to show Sara's grandma," wouldn't it? Instead, we would say "Sara brought *her* book to show *her* grandma." The pronoun *her* in this sentence refers back to Sara. Here are the personal pronouns in English:

	Singular	Plural
First person	I	We
Second person	You	You
Third person	He/she/it	They

While understanding first, second, and third person isn't crucial for success on the Digital SAT, it is important to understand which pronouns are singular and which are plural, especially for the most commonly tested ones—*it* and *they*. A lot of times students think that the difference between these pronouns is that *it* is for objects and *they* is for people. But if we think about that a little more, we'll realize that idea isn't true. Here's an example to illustrate:

The markers are on the table.

They are on the table.

In real life, some individuals prefer to use "they" as a personal pronoun. When it comes to the Digital SAT, however, "they" is always plural.

We can use the word *they* to talk about a bunch of markers, right? So, *they* can be used for people and objects. The real difference between these two is that *they* is plural and *it* is singular. This can be difficult to remember because there are many places in real life that we use *they* when we are not referring to something plural. For example, let's say you went to the drugstore looking for your favorite brand of toothpaste and couldn't find it. It sounds perfectly natural to tell your family, "They were out of the toothpaste!" Who's *they*? The store? A store is really an "it," so you would want to say, "It was out of the toothpaste." Of course, we're well aware that that sentence sounds ridiculous. This just goes to show you that spoken English and written English are different.

Remember, your goal here is to ace the Digital SAT. You don't necessarily need to follow these grammar rules when you speak, text, or write emails, but you do need to know them if you want to get the Writing questions correct on the Digital SAT.

Let's see an example of how this could be tested.

A carillon is a type of percussion instrument consisting of a keyboard and bells. The clappers of the bells are connected to the keyboard. To be classified as a carillon, the instrument must have at least 23 bells; if not, _______ considered a chime.

4 Mark for Review

Which choice completes the text so that it conforms to the conventions of Standard English?

(A) it is

(B) they are

(C) those are

(D) one is

Here's How to Crack It

First, look at the question to identify the category: Rules. Then, look to see that pronouns are changing in the answer choices, so it's testing consistency of pronouns. In that case, look for and highlight the noun that the pronoun refers back to, which is *the instrument* in the earlier part of the sentence. That's singular, so a singular pronoun is needed. Eliminate (B) and (C) because they are both plural.

While *one* is singular, it cannot refer back to *the instrument*, as that is a specific noun. We'll show you the correct use of *one* in a minute, but for now, eliminate (D). Choice (A) is singular and is appropriate to refer back to *the instrument*, so it's the correct answer.

It's important to keep in mind that the Digital SAT tests *it* versus *they* the vast majority of the time when pronouns are tested. You will never be asked to use a pronoun for a person who hasn't already been referred to using a pronoun. For example, if you were given a passage in which a person was referred to as "she," then College Board could ask you to choose a pronoun later on that would be consistent, such as *she*, *her*, or *herself*. But you will not be asked to fill in a pronoun for a person if one has not already been given.

Just Say No

On the Digital SAT, each question has to have four answer choices. However, sometimes College Board just wants to test *it* versus *they* or *them*. The writers still have to put in two more answer choices, so they will give you some weird pronoun options to round out the four choices. Let's take a look at when and why to eliminate them.

- The pronoun *you* is almost certainly going to be wrong, as College Board almost never writes passages that refer to the reader. Only use *you* if the passage has already used a form of this pronoun elsewhere in the passage. The same is true for *we*.
- The pronoun *one* by itself usually refers to a person (*One shouldn't wear wet socks*). It can refer back to a noun (*Mateo had a popsicle, but I didn't want one*), but only if that noun is nonspecific. It can't stand in for a noun introduced with "the." Neither of these situations is very likely to show up on the Digital SAT.
- The pronouns *this*, *those*, or *these* are also not likely to be correct. They are typically not going to be specific enough if they are not followed by a noun (*this idea*, *those paintings*, *these books*).

Pronouns and Apostrophes

The other common way pronouns are tested is with apostrophes. There are only two simple rules to know:

> Apostrophes on pronouns represent contractions.
>
> Possessive pronouns don't get apostrophes.

Let's try an example question.

The slow loris, a type of primate that lives in rainforests in South and Southeast Asia, is threatened by both habitat loss and the wildlife trade. The popularity of the slow loris as an exotic pet is due to ______ large eyes, which people view as charming.

5 Mark for Review

Which choice completes the text so that it conforms to the conventions of Standard English?

A) its

B) they're

C) their

D) it's

Here's How to Crack It

The question reveals that this is a Rules question. Look at the answers to see that pronouns and apostrophes are changing, so this question is testing possessive pronouns versus contractions as well as pronoun consistency. Start with the consistency part and highlight the word the pronoun refers back to. Whose *large eyes*? They belong to *the slow loris*. Highlight this phrase, which is singular. Eliminate (B) and (C) because they are both plural.

Next, consider whether a contraction is needed. Choice (D) means "it is," which isn't correct here ("it is large eyes"). Eliminate (D). Choice (A), *its*, is the possessive form of *it*, which is appropriate because *the slow loris* is an *it*, and it possesses the *large eyes*. Therefore, (A) is correct.

A contraction is a shorter way of saying two words. The apostrophe stands in for the letter or letters that have been removed. Here are some common contractions and their meanings:

It's	It is / It has
They're	They are
You're	You are
Who's	Who is / Who has

Here are some common possessive pronouns and their meanings:

Its	Belonging to it
Their	Belonging to them
Your	Belonging to you
Whose	Belonging to whom

College Board loves to test *its/it's* and *their/they're*, as in the previous example. In fact, those are the only pronouns you're likely to see tested with apostrophes. As long as you remember these simple rules, you'll get those questions right every time.

When you see pronouns changing in the answer choices...

1. Look for and highlight the noun or pronoun that the blank refers back to.
2. Eliminate any answers that are not consistent with the noun or pronoun in terms of singular versus plural.
3. If apostrophes are changing, determine whether a contraction or a possessive pronoun is needed and use POE accordingly.

NOUNS

We just saw how apostrophes are tested with pronouns. Another apostrophe topic relates to nouns. Let's see an example.

N. K. Jemisin is an award-winning American science fiction and fantasy writer. The three books in her series *The Broken Earth Trilogy* each won a Hugo Award for Best Novel, making her the first author to win this award for each book in a trilogy and the first to win Best Novel awards for three consecutive years. Her ______ include environmental crises and social inequalities.

6 Mark for Review

Which choice completes the text so that it conforms to the conventions of Standard English?

(A) books' subjects

(B) books subjects

(C) books' subjects'

(D) books subjects'

Here's How to Crack It

Start by using the question to identify that this falls under the Rules category. Then, look at the answers to see what's changing: noun apostrophes. An apostrophe on a noun shows possession, so start with the first noun and consider whether it's possessing something. Does something belong to the *books*? Yes, it's the *subjects* of the books. So, there should be an apostrophe on *books*. Eliminate (B) and (D) because they don't have an apostrophe on that word.

Next, determine whether the *subjects* possess anything. The word after subjects is *include*, which is a verb, so it can't be possessed. Therefore, *subjects* shouldn't have an apostrophe. It's plural, not possessive. Eliminate (C). The correct answer is (A).

Unlike pronouns, nouns use apostrophes to show possession. For a singular noun, simply add an apostrophe + *s* to make the noun possessive. Here are some examples:

a hat's logo

the story's meaning

the dress's sleeves

As we saw earlier, most nouns take on an *-s* when they become plural. For most plural possessives, make the original noun plural by adding *-s* or *-es* and then add the apostrophe after. Here are some plural possessives:

hats' logos

the stories' meanings

the dresses' sleeves

For irregular plurals that don't end in *-s*, make the word plural and then add the apostrophe + *s*:

a woman's coat → *women's coats*

my tooth's root → *my teeth's roots*

the person's letter → *the people's letter*

When you see apostrophes on nouns changing in the answer choices…

1. Determine whether the first word is possessing anything. If not, eliminate options with apostrophes on that word.
2. Determine whether any additional words are possessing anything. Remember that a possessive noun must be followed by something that can be possessed (i.e., another noun).
3. Use POE.

It's possible but rare to have two words in a row with apostrophes. A noun can only have an apostrophe if the next word is a noun—in other words, it must be something that can be possessed.

MODIFIERS

Earlier in this book, you saw how describing phrases, such as noun phrases or those beginning with an *-ing* or *-ed* verb, are usually separated from the rest of the sentence with commas. Describing phrases, also known as modifiers, can also be tested in terms of wording, not just punctuation.

Consider the following sentence:

Made with organic oils and plant butters, Noah sold out of his natural soaps at the craft fair. ✗

Do you spot the error? While you might understand that the soap is *made with organic oils and plant butters*, the way the sentence is written, *Noah* is the one made with these ingredients, which sounds ridiculous once you realize it.

This grammar error is called a misplaced modifier. According to this rule, a describing phrase or "modifier" (in this case, *Made with organic oils and plant butters*) needs to come as close as possible to the thing it's describing. Here are two ways the sentence above could be rewritten.

> *Made with organic oils and plant butters, Noah's natural soaps sold out at the craft fair.* ✓
>
> *Noah sold out of his natural soaps, made with organic oils and plant butters, at the craft fair.* ✓

As you can see, the sentence can be rewritten so that the thing being described comes right before or after the modifying phrase.

Let's see an example of how this could be tested on the Digital SAT.

Starting in 2008, over 50 U.S. embassies across 38 countries installed air monitors and regularly posted social media updates about the air quality at those locations. Studying the impact of these posts, ______

7 Mark for Review

Which choice completes the text so that it conforms to the conventions of Standard English?

Ⓐ researchers' findings were a reduction in fine particulate concentration levels in those locations.

Ⓑ researchers found a reduction in fine particulate concentration levels in those locations.

Ⓒ a reduction in fine particulate concentration levels in those locations was found by researchers.

Ⓓ there was a reduction in fine particulate concentration levels in those locations, according to researchers.

Here's How to Crack It

Begin by looking at the question, which reveals that this is a Rules question. Then, look at the answers to see what's changing. The answer choices seem to be starting with different subjects, which is a good clue that the sentence may be testing consistency with a modifier. Start at the beginning of the sentence to see if there is a modifying phrase. It starts with *Studying the impact of these posts*, which is a modifier as it would describe the person doing the studying. Highlight this phrase.

Next, look at the beginning of each answer choice to see whether it refers to someone who studies something. Eliminate (A) because it says *researchers' findings*, not *researchers*. The *findings* can't be *studying* something. Keep (B) because *researchers* could study something. Eliminate (C) because *a reduction* can't study something. Eliminate (D) because *there was* doesn't refer to anything specific that would be studying something. Thus, (B) is the correct answer.

When this topic is tested on the Digital SAT, College Board will usually put the blank after the describing phrase. That means all you have to do is look at the first few words of each answer choice to see whether that's the person or thing that could be described by the modifier.

ANSWERS TO SUBJECTS AND VERBS EXERCISE

1. collection
2. Fishes
3. dancing
4. Members
5. jury
6. United States
7. Making (or Making one's bed)
8. A passport and a plane ticket
9. Games
10. letters

ANSWERS TO VERB TENSE EXERCISE

1. have studied (clue – *every night this week*)
2. will visit (clue – *Next year*)
3. am (clue – *Today*)
4. had been (clue – *before it was finished*)
5. went (clue – *Yesterday*)
6. went (clue – *last year*)

Grammar Drill

Answers can be found starting on page 315.

Time: 12 minutes

1 Mark for Review

Several dwarf planets, including Pluto, _______ found in the Kuiper Belt, a region of space beyond Neptune's orbit. The Kuiper Belt contains many remnants from the solar system's early history and was first explored in 2015 by NASA's New Horizons mission.

Which choice completes the text so that it conforms to the conventions of Standard English?

Ⓐ has been

Ⓑ are

Ⓒ is

Ⓓ was

2 Mark for Review

In 1991, American biologists Linda B. Buck and Richard Axel published a landmark paper on the olfactory system. The paper detailed the discovery of the location of odor receptors in the nose and led to a more comprehensive understanding of how humans smell. In 2004, _______ received the Nobel Prize in Physiology or Medicine for that research.

Which choice completes the text so that it conforms to the conventions of Standard English?

Ⓐ we

Ⓑ one

Ⓒ they

Ⓓ some

3 Mark for Review

Clifford Possum Tjapaltjarri is one of the most recognized and well-known Australian artists despite some confusion over the details of his life and the exact date of his death. His works are often predicted to raise large amounts at auctions and are often purchased by Australian galleries. The ______ may have been supported by the Australian government to avoid sending such important works internationally.

Which choice completes the text so that it conforms to the conventions of Standard English?

(A) galleries' purchases

(B) galleries' purchase's

(C) galleries purchases

(D) galleries purchase's

4 Mark for Review

Oglala Lakota poet, writer, and activist Layli Long Soldier published her first small poetry book, *Chromosomory*, in 2010, and her first full-length volume of poetry, *Whereas*, in 2017. The poems in *Whereas* ______ the historical experience of native tribes in the U.S. as well as Soldier's personal experiences and relationships.

Which choice completes the text so that it conforms to the conventions of Standard English?

(A) explores

(B) has explored

(C) is exploring

(D) explore

5 Mark for Review

"Kilroy was here" is a meme that gained popularity in graffiti art during World War II. The origin of the meme is debated, but some theories claim that German intelligence agents found the meme on American weaponry and therefore ______ Kilroy was a high-level American spy.

Which choice completes the text so that it conforms to the conventions of Standard English?

(A) had believed

(B) believed

(C) would believe

(D) were believing

6 Mark for Review

Cockatoos in Australia are experts at opening trash bins. The white bird can grab the lid of the bin with ______ beak and push toward the hinge until the lid flips open. People have used various tools, such as bricks or rubber bands, to keep the bins closed, yet the birds are undeterred by these obstacles.

Which choice completes the text so that it conforms to the conventions of Standard English?

(A) their

(B) they're

(C) its

(D) it's

7 Mark for Review

In 1977, Emily Kame Kngwarreye, an Aboriginal Australian artist, learned an art technique from Indonesia called batik. Wanting to support other women interested in creating their own art, she founded the Utopia Women's Batik Group with other Aboriginal artists in 1978. The Utopia Women's Batik Group provided a space where the development of ______ was supported.

Which choice completes the text so that it conforms to the conventions of Standard English?

Ⓐ artists' individual styles'

Ⓑ artist's individual styles

Ⓒ artists individual styles

Ⓓ artists' individual styles

8 Mark for Review

Kim Hyesoon is a poet from South Korea who currently teaches creative writing at an art institute in Seoul. Hoping to align with South Korea's strong movement of female poets in the 1990s, ______ and rose to fame as an author of numerous works.

Which choice completes the text so that it conforms to the conventions of Standard English?

Ⓐ the works written by Hyesoon used imagery and experimental language

Ⓑ Hyesoon used imagery and experimental language to create her pieces

Ⓒ numerous works written by Hyesoon used imagery and experimental language

Ⓓ there was a poet, Hyesoon, who used imagery and experimental language

9 Mark for Review

Researchers found that some streaked shearwaters, a type of seabird, survive typhoons by flying into the storms. When stuck between land and a typhoon, the birds will fly toward the eye of the storm, potentially reducing ______ risk of crashing into land or hitting debris.

Which choice completes the text so that it conforms to the conventions of Standard English?

Ⓐ its

Ⓑ their

Ⓒ it's

Ⓓ they're

10 Mark for Review

NASA originally equipped astronauts with pencils to write in space, as ballpoint pens wouldn't work without gravity; however, pencils could smear, break, or catch fire. NASA eventually abandoned its own development of a space pen due to costs. However, a private company, the Fischer Pen Company, was working on its own space pen. Developed by Paul Fischer, ______

Which choice completes the text so that it conforms to the conventions of Standard English?

Ⓐ the Fischer Space Pen's testing and approval by NASA led to its use in Project Apollo.

Ⓑ Project Apollo used the Fischer Space Pen after it was tested and approved by NASA.

Ⓒ NASA tested and approved the Fischer Space Pen for use in Project Apollo.

Ⓓ the Fischer Space Pen was tested and approved by NASA for use in Project Apollo.

GRAMMAR DRILL ANSWERS AND EXPLANATIONS

1. **B** In this Rules question, verbs are changing in the answer choices, so it's testing consistency with verbs. Find and highlight the subject, *dwarf planets*, which is plural, so a plural verb is needed. Write an annotation saying "plural." Eliminate any answer that is not plural.

    - (A), (C), and (D) are wrong because they are singular.
    - (B) is correct because it's plural.

2. **C** In this Rules question, pronouns are changing in the answer choices, so it's testing consistency with pronouns. Find and highlight the phrase the pronoun refers back to, *Linda B. Buck and Richard Axel*, which is plural, so a plural pronoun is needed. Write an annotation saying "plural." Eliminate any answer that isn't consistent with *Linda B. Buck and Richard Axel.*

    - (A) is wrong because *we* is not consistent with *Linda B. Buck and Richard Axel.*
    - (B) is wrong because *one* is singular.
    - (C) is correct because *they* is plural and is consistent with *Linda B. Buck and Richard Axel.*
    - (D) is wrong because *some* doesn't refer back to a specific thing.

3. **A** In this Rules question, apostrophes with nouns are changing in the answer choices. Determine whether each word possesses anything. The *galleries* possess the *purchases*, but the *purchases* don't possess anything. Eliminate any answer that doesn't match this.

    - (A) is correct because *galleries* is possessive and *purchases* is not.
    - (B) is wrong because *purchases* should be plural, not possessive.
    - (C) and (D) are wrong because *galleries* should have an apostrophe, as it is possessive.

4. **D** In this Rules question, verbs are changing in the answer choices, so it's testing consistency with verbs. Find and highlight the subject, *poems*, which is plural, so a plural verb is needed. Write an annotation saying "plural." Eliminate any answer that is not plural.

    - (A), (B), and (C) are wrong because they are singular.
    - (D) is correct because it's plural.

5. **B** In this Rules question, verbs are changing in the answer choices, so it's testing consistency with verbs. Find and highlight the subject, *German intelligence agents*, which is plural, so a plural verb is needed. All of the answers work with a plural subject, so look for a clue regarding tense. The previous part of the sentence uses a past tense verb: *found*. Highlight that verb, which is past tense, so write an annotation that says "past." Eliminate any answer not in past tense.

    - (A) is wrong because *had* is used when two events occur in the past and one event is earlier.
    - (B) is correct because it's past tense.
    - (C) and (D) are wrong because *would believe* and *were believing* aren't consistent with *found*.

6. **C** In this Rules question, pronouns and apostrophes are changing in the answer choices, so it's testing consistency with pronouns. Find and highlight the word or phrase that the pronoun refers back to: *The white bird*, which is singular, so in order to be consistent, a singular pronoun is needed. Write an annotation saying "singular." Eliminate any answer that isn't consistent with *bird* or is incorrectly punctuated.

    - (A) and (B) are wrong because *they* is plural.
    - (C) is correct because it is singular and possessive.
    - (D) is wrong because it means "it is."

7. **D** In this Rules question, apostrophes with nouns are changing in the answer choices. Determine whether each word possesses anything. The *artists* possess the *individual styles*, but the *individual styles* don't possess anything. Eliminate any answer that doesn't match this.

    - (A) is wrong because *styles* shouldn't be possessive.
    - (B) is wrong because *artist's* is used for one artist, but the passage discusses *Aboriginal artists*.
    - (C) is wrong because *artists* should have an apostrophe, since it is possessive.
    - (D) is correct because *artists* is plural and possessive, and *individual styles* is plural but not possessive.

8. **B** In this Rules question, the subjects of the answers are changing, which suggests it may be testing modifiers. Look for and highlight a modifying phrase: *Hoping to align with South Korea's strong movement of female poets in the 1990s*. Whoever is *Hoping* needs to come immediately after the comma. Eliminate any answer that doesn't start with someone who can hope.

    - (A) and (C) are wrong because *works* can't hope.
    - (B) is correct because *Hyesoon* can hope.
    - (D) is wrong because *there was* can't hope.

9. **B** In this Rules question, pronouns and apostrophes are changing in the answer choices, so it's testing consistency with pronouns. Find and highlight the word that the pronoun refers back to: *birds*. This word is plural, so in order to be consistent, a plural pronoun is needed. Eliminate any answer that isn't consistent with *birds* or is incorrectly punctuated.

- (A) and (C) are wrong because *it* is singular.
- (B) is correct because it is plural and possessive.
- (D) is wrong because it means "they are."

10. **D** In this Rules question, the subjects of the answers are changing, which suggests it may be testing modifiers. Look for and highlight a modifying phrase: *Developed by Paul Fischer*. Whatever was *Developed by Paul Fischer* needs to come immediately after the comma. Eliminate any answer that doesn't start with whatever was developed by Paul Fischer.

- (A) is wrong because *testing and approval* were done *by NASA*, not Paul Fischer.
- (B) is wrong because it was the *Fischer Space Pen*, not *Project Apollo*, that was developed by *Paul Fischer*.
- (C) is wrong because *NASA* was not developed *by Paul Fischer*.
- (D) is correct because *the Fischer Space Pen* was developed *by Paul Fischer*.

Summary

- When verbs are changing in the answer choices, find the subject, determine whether it is singular or plural, and eliminate any answers that aren't consistent. If there are still multiple answers remaining, look for clues to determine what tense is needed.
- When pronouns are changing in the answer choices, find the noun or other pronoun that the blank refers back to and determine whether it's singular or plural. Eliminate answers that aren't consistent.
- Apostrophes on pronouns represent contractions. Possessive pronouns don't have apostrophes.
- Apostrophes on nouns show possession. Nouns that are plural but not possessive don't get apostrophes.
- When the subjects of the answers are changing, look for a modifier. Eliminate answers that begin with something that couldn't logically be described by the modifier.

Chapter 17 Rhetoric Questions

This chapter covers the final category of questions on the Reading and Writing section: Rhetoric questions, which are based on the content of the ideas rather than rules or the structure of the sentences.

The last portion of each Reading and Writing module will include two types of questions: Transitions and Rhetorical Synthesis, in that order. We call these Rhetoric questions because they relate to the purpose or quality of the writing. These questions will not test your understanding of the rule-based punctuation and grammar topics. In fact, for these questions, all four answer choices will be or will produce complete sentences that are grammatically correct. Instead, you will need to consider the *content* of the writing and how the answers fulfill certain meaning-related or rhetorical goals. Let's take a look at the first type of question in this category.

TRANSITION QUESTIONS

Transition questions will be easy to spot. Let's look at an example.

Cynthia Leitich Smith is a member of the Muscogee Nation and a prolific author of books for children and young adults. She has written over a dozen books. _______ she is the author-curator of a Native-focused imprint, called Heartdrum, at the publishing company HarperCollins.

1 Mark for Review

Which choice completes the text with the most logical transition?

Ⓐ On the other hand,

Ⓑ Still,

Ⓒ Eventually,

Ⓓ Additionally,

Like the question above, all transition questions will ask you the same question: *Which choice completes the text with the most logical transition?* As soon as you see that question, you'll know you're dealing with a transition question. Let's take a look at the basic approach for transition questions and apply it to this problem.

Transition Questions Basic Approach

1. Read the passage and highlight any ideas that support or contradict each other.
2. Make an annotation indicating whether the ideas surrounding the blank agree or disagree.
3. Eliminate any answers that go the wrong direction. Then, use POE on any remaining options.

Here's How to Crack It

Highlight anything that is the same in the sentence with the blank and the sentences before or after. The first sentence states that Leitich Smith is *a prolific author*. The second sentence supports this by saying *She has written over a dozen books*. Then, this sentence says *she is the author-curator* at a publishing company. Highlight all of these phrases. These ideas agree, so make an annotation that says "agree." Then, eliminate any opposite-direction transitions since we need a same-direction transition here. Eliminate (A) and (B), which would both indicate a contrast.

Now, compare the remaining answers. *Eventually* is used when something is expected to happen in the future or did happen after a period of time. However, this sentence is in present tense, so *eventually* isn't consistent. Eliminate (C). This sentence builds on the previous idea, so *additionally* is an appropriate transition. Therefore, (see what we did there?) the correct answer is (D).

Let's try another example.

Camille Henrot's installation *The Pale Fox* is a collection of objects that at first glance appears to be random. For example, a sculpture of Buddha props up a copy of a modern magazine. There is an organization, ______ that is revealed as the audience spends time in the space.

2 Mark for Review

Which choice completes the text with the most logical transition?

Ⓐ likewise,

Ⓑ specifically,

Ⓒ though,

Ⓓ rather,

Here's How to Crack It

Start by highlighting ideas that relate to each other. The first sentence says that the collection *at first glance appears to be random*. The third sentence says *There is an organization*. These ideas disagree, so write that in an annotation. Next, eliminate any same-direction transitions: (A) and (B). Compare (C) and (D). *Though* works well, so keep (C). While *rather* is an opposite-direction transition, it means something more like "instead," so it doesn't fit correctly in this sentence. The correct answer is (C).

Let's try one more.

Sandra Welner, a medical professor, wanted to make medical care more accessible for patients with disabilities. ______ she invented an examination table that could be lowered for easier access to and from a wheelchair and called it the Universally Accessible Examination Table.

3 Mark for Review

Which choice completes the text with the most logical transition?

(A) To that end,

(B) Additionally,

(C) Not surprisingly,

(D) Rather,

Here's How to Crack It

First, highlight any phrases that draw a connection. The first sentence states that Welner *wanted to make medical care more accessible for patients with disabilities*. The second sentence says she *invented* the *Universally Accessible Examination Table*. These ideas agree, so make an annotation saying "agree" and eliminate any opposite-direction transitions. In this case, (D) can be eliminated.

Next, consider the link between the highlighted phrases. The first sentence states Welner's goal, while the second sentence states what she did. Use POE. Choice (A) is a good match because an *end* is a goal, and this transition essentially means "with that goal in mind." Keep (A). Eliminate (B) because *additionally* is used to add on to the previous point, but this would suggest that the sentences are two separate things, when instead the second sentence explains what she did in pursuit of her goal. Eliminate (C) because there is no evidence that her invention was *not surprising*; one could be surprised or not that she was able to accomplish her goal. The correct answer is (A).

RHETORICAL SYNTHESIS QUESTIONS

Now, let's move on to the other type of question in the Rhetoric category, the one that will appear at the very end of each verbal module: Rhetorical Synthesis. The word *synthesize* means "put together," so these questions are asking you to put together two or more bullet points in order to fulfill a certain rhetorical goal. Let's see an example.

While researching a topic, a student has taken the following notes:

- Robin Wall Kimmerer is a writer, educator, and scientist working in the field of biocultural restoration.
- She is also a member of the Citizen Potawatomi Nation.
- Her first book, *Gathering Moss*, published in 2003, contained a series of essays about mosses that mixed scientific writing and personal reflection together.
- In her second book, *Braiding Sweetgrass*, Kimmerer's writing weaves together different types of knowledge: the Western scientific tradition, Traditional Ecological Knowledge, and lessons that plants themselves can teach.

4 Mark for Review

The student wants to emphasize a similarity between the two books Kimmerer wrote. Which choice most effectively uses relevant information from the notes to accomplish this goal?

Ⓐ *Gathering Moss* is about moss, and *Braiding Sweetgrass* is about lessons from plants.

Ⓑ *Gathering Moss* and *Braiding Sweetgrass* both include scientific writing.

Ⓒ *Gathering Moss* combines science and personal reflection, while *Braiding Sweetgrass* combines three different types of knowledge.

Ⓓ Published in 2003, *Gathering Moss* was written by Robin Wall Kimmerer, who has worked in the field of biocultural restoration.

Watch Us Crack It
Watch the step-by-step video explanation of how to answer this question in your Student Tools.

Here's How to Crack It

First, identify the type of question. Rhetorical Synthesis questions are extremely easy to identify: they are the only question type to use bullet points instead of text in the form of a paragraph. Then, like with all Reading and Writing questions, determine what the question is asking. Rhetorical Synthesis questions always contain the same question: *Which choice most effectively uses relevant information from the notes to accomplish this goal?* The key part to notice is *this goal*. You MUST read the sentence before the question to determine what the goal is.

Here, the stated goal is to *emphasize a similarity between the two books*. Now, your impulse might be to read the bullet points and identify a similarity. However, we've found that you probably don't need to do this. Instead, highlight the task or tasks of the question and then go straight to the answer choices and eliminate anything that doesn't completely fulfill the task. In this case, highlight *similarity* and *two books*. Any answer that does not mention *two books* or draw a comparison can be eliminated. Let's go to POE.

Choice (A) mentions the two books, and *moss* and *plants* are somewhat similar, so keep (A). Choice (B) mentions the two books and uses the word *both* to state a similarity. Keep (B). Choice (C) mentions both books, but the word *while* and the types of content in the books indicate a contrast, not a *similarity*. Eliminate (C). Choice (D) only mentions one of the books, so eliminate it because the question asked about *two books*.

Finally, compare (A) and (B). Choice (A) does not clearly state that this is a similarity between the two; it merely presents information about the content of both books. Eliminate (A). On the other hand, (B) clearly states that there is a similarity between the two books: they both contain *scientific writing*. Therefore, the correct answer is (B).

Of course, we can also confirm that this information is in the bullet points: the third bullet point states that *Gathering Moss* contains *scientific writing*, and the fourth bullet point mentions that the *Western scientific tradition* is part of the book's content, which clearly indicates that *scientific writing* is a component of the book.

Here's the basic approach for these questions:

Rhetorical Synthesis Basic Approach

1. Read the question and highlight each goal that is mentioned.
2. Eliminate any answer choice that does not completely fulfill the goal or goals.
3. Read the bullet points to confirm the answer if needed.

It's very unlikely that you will see an answer choice that is inconsistent with what is stated in the bullet points. That is, you won't see the kind of wrong answers that you will see on the Reading questions—ones that could be arrived at through misreading or making assumptions. Instead, the wrong answers will simply not completely fulfill the goal or goals stated in the question. This is why you can save yourself some time by not reading the bullet points first; you generally won't need to prove that the information is supported. It's also worth remembering that these questions do NOT test you on punctuation, grammar, style, being concise, or any other Rules topics. Focus on the content of the sentence in each answer choice and how well it does or does not fulfill the goal or goals.

Let's try another one.

While researching a topic, a student has taken the following notes:

- Large animals known as megafauna have substantial impacts on their environments.
- However, many native megafauna are extinct, so their effects on the ecosystem are unknown.
- Bison are a type of megafauna that used to be dominant in the United States.
- Reintroducing bison to their native environments doubled plant diversity.
- The presence of cattle, a domesticated megafauna, in the same environments produced a significantly lower increase in plant diversity.

5 Mark for Review

The student wants to present one impact that native megafauna have on their environments. Which choice most effectively uses relevant information from the notes to accomplish this goal?

Ⓐ Bison, a type of native megafauna, doubled plant diversity in their native environments.

Ⓑ Bison and cattle are two types of megafauna that live in the United States.

Ⓒ Although many native megafauna are extinct, bison were reintroduced to their native environment.

Ⓓ Native and domesticated megafauna can have impacts on their environments.

Here's How to Crack It

Once you've established that you're dealing with a Rhetorical Synthesis question, highlight the goal or goals in the question. Here, you should highlight *one impact that native megafauna have on their environments*. The correct answer should relate to *native megafauna* and a specific environmental *impact*. Move on to POE.

Choice (A) mentions *a type of native megafauna* and describes an environmental *impact* (*doubled plant diversity*), so keep (A). Choice (B) mentions *megafauna*, but there's no environmental impact. Eliminate (B). Choice (C) mentions *native megafauna* but does not mention the *impact* of reintroducing bison; eliminate it. Choice (D) mentions *impacts* but does not *present one impact*; it's not specific about what that impact might be. Eliminate (D). The correct answer is (A).

Let's try one more.

While researching a topic, a student has taken the following notes:

- R. Murray Schafer was a Canadian composer, writer, and environmentalist.
- Schafer created many soundscapes during his career.
- Soundscapes are the sounds that arise from a location.
- Soundscapes include animal sounds, natural sounds such as weather, and human-created sounds.
- Schafer wrote *The Tuning of the World* and *The Soundscape,* which are books on soundscapes.

6 Mark for Review

The student wants to introduce soundscapes to an audience familiar with Schafer. Which choice most effectively uses relevant information from the notes to accomplish this goal?

(A) Canadian composer, writer, and environmentalist R. Murray Schafer created and wrote about the collections of animal sounds, natural sounds such as weather, and human-created sounds known as soundscapes.

(B) *The Tuning of the World* and *The Soundscape* were written by R. Murray Schafer, a Canadian composer, writer, and environmentalist.

(C) R. Murray Schafer, a Canadian composer, writer, and environmentalist, created many soundscapes during his career.

(D) Schafer wrote about and created soundscapes, which are sounds that arise from a location, including animal sounds, natural sounds such as weather, and human-created sounds.

Here's How to Crack It

Identify that this is a Rhetorical Synthesis question, and then highlight the goal or goals in the question. In this case, you should highlight *introduce soundscapes* and *audience familiar with Schafer.* It's common for Rhetorical Synthesis questions to specify whether the audience is familiar or unfamiliar with something. If the audience is unfamiliar, the answer should explain who or what the person or thing is, while if the audience is familiar, the answer should not. Let's go to POE.

Eliminate (A) because it describes Schafer—the audience is *familiar* with Schafer, so he should not be introduced. Eliminate (B) and (C) for the same reason. No description of Schafer is needed if the audience is familiar with him. Check (D). This answer does not describe Schafer, but it does *introduce soundscapes* by defining what they are. Therefore, this answer fulfills all parts of the question. The correct answer is (D).

Conclusion

While the term Rhetoric might have sounded scary initially, we hope you're feeling more confident now that you know how to approach the two types of questions in this category. Remember, you choose the order of questions—practice Rhetoric questions on the following drill and use the results to help determine when to attempt them.

Rhetoric Drill

Answers can be found starting on page 333.

Time: 14 minutes

1 Mark for Review

People who are interested in reducing food waste are using banana peels in unique ways. ______ banana peels can be dried and ground into flour and used in baking. Researchers found that baking cookies with banana peel flour led to more healthful cookies.

Which choice completes the text with the most logical transition?

Ⓐ For instance,

Ⓑ Fortunately,

Ⓒ Still,

Ⓓ Moreover,

2 Mark for Review

During the Apollo 14 mission in 1971, astronaut Stu Roosa carried 500 tree seeds into lunar orbit. Once back on Earth, the seeds were germinated and the majority of the trees were successfully planted around the world. The locations of the moon trees were not recorded, ______ until a renewed interest in them in 1996 led to the creation of a database of the rediscovered moon trees and their locations.

Which choice completes the text with the most logical transition?

Ⓐ moreover,

Ⓑ for instance,

Ⓒ still,

Ⓓ however,

3 Mark for Review

Emmett Chappelle, a scientist who started working with NASA in the 1960s, discovered a way to detect extraterrestrial life. He found that mixing two chemicals found in fireflies, insects known for their bioluminescence, with adenosine triphosphate (ATP) produces light. ATP is present in all living organisms. ______ the presence of life can be confirmed if light is produced when the two firefly chemicals are applied to a sample.

Which choice completes the text with the most logical transition?

(A) Still,

(B) Therefore,

(C) Nevertheless,

(D) Though,

4 Mark for Review

Larissa Behrendt's novel *After Story* tells the tale of Indigenous lawyer Jasmine and her mother Della as they take a literary tour of England. During their tour, a girl disappears, echoing the disappearance of Jasmine's older sister twenty-five years earlier. ______ Jasmine reexamines her past, and family secrets come to light.

Which choice completes the text with the most logical transition?

(A) Consequently,

(B) In conclusion,

(C) Similarly,

(D) Despite this,

5 Mark for Review

Although street art is sometimes treated as commonplace graffiti or vandalism, Bright Tetteh Ackwerh has used the medium to represent his satirical views on religious and political issues in Ghana. ______ his goal is to provoke spirited conversation about these topics after people view his works.

Which choice completes the text with the most logical transition?

(A) As a rule,

(B) Conversely,

(C) Accordingly,

(D) Subsequently,

6 Mark for Review

While researching a topic, a student has taken the following notes:

- Ferrofluid is a liquid created when magnetic nanoparticles are dissolved in a solvent.
- The shape of ferrofluid can be manipulated by magnetic fields.
- Sachiko Kodama is a Japanese artist who makes liquid sculptures with ferrofluid.
- Her sculptures include *Pulsate* and *Protrude, Flow.*

The student wants to introduce Sachiko Kodama and what her sculptures are made of. Which choice most effectively uses relevant information from the notes to accomplish this goal?

Ⓐ *Pulsate* and *Protrude, Flow* by Sachiko Kodama are made with ferrofluid, a type of liquid created when magnetic nanoparticles are dissolved in a solvent.

Ⓑ Sachiko Kodama is a Japanese artist who uses magnetic fields to change the shape of ferrofluid to create her sculptures.

Ⓒ Sachiko Kodama's ferrofluid sculptures include *Pulsate* and *Protrude, Flow.*

Ⓓ Ferrofluid is a magnetic liquid that can be manipulated into sculptures.

7 Mark for Review

While researching a topic, a student has taken the following notes:

- Emmanuelle Charpentier, born in 1968, is a French scientist who studies microbiology, biochemistry, and genetics.
- Jennifer Doudna, born in 1964, is an American biochemist who studies biochemistry and molecular biology.
- Charpentier and Doudna met in 2011.
- They worked together and discovered that CRISPR-Cas9 technology could be used for genome editing in 2012.
- In 2020, they were both awarded the Nobel Prize in Chemistry.

The student wants to emphasize the results of Charpentier's and Doudna's working relationship. Which choice most effectively uses relevant information from the notes to accomplish this goal?

Ⓐ Charpentier and Doudna both study biochemistry.

Ⓑ Charpentier and Doudna met in 2011 and were awarded the Nobel Prize in 2020.

Ⓒ Charpentier and Doudna discovered how to use CRISPR-Cas9 for genome editing and were awarded the Nobel Prize in 2020.

Ⓓ Charpentier studies genetics, and Doudna studies molecular biology.

8 Mark for Review

While researching a topic, a student has taken the following notes:

- Kolkata, also known as Calcutta, is in eastern India.
- The Kolkata Metro System was initially planned in the 1920s but construction didn't start until the 1970s.
- The Kolkata Metro System is a rapid transit system featuring two train lines.
- The Blue Line runs north-south, opened in 1984, and is 31.36 km long.
- The Green Line runs east-west, opened in 2020, and is 9.1 km long.

The student wants to compare the dates of opening and lengths of the lines of the Kolkata Metro System to an audience familiar with the Kolkata Metro System. Which choice most effectively uses relevant information from the notes to accomplish this goal?

Ⓐ The Kolkata Metro System opened its second line—the 9.1 km-long Green Line—in 2020.

Ⓑ The 31.36-km-long Blue Line opened in 1984, whereas the 9.1-km-long Green Line opened in 2020.

Ⓒ The Kolkata Metro System, which began construction in the 1970s, includes the 31.36-km-long Blue Line, which opened in 1984, and the 9.1 km-long Green Line, which opened in 2020.

Ⓓ Kolkata, also known as Calcutta, is located in eastern India and began construction on the Kolkata Metro System in the 1970s.

9 Mark for Review

While researching a topic, a student has taken the following notes:

- Various vertebrate species, including honeybees, have the ability to judge numbers.
- Researchers were curious about whether bees organize numbers spatially from left to right, from smallest to largest.
- Humans organize numbers spatially from left to right, from smallest to largest.
- Martin Giurfa and his team trained bees to connect specific numbers with a sucrose reward.
- The bees organized the numbers from left to right based on magnitude.

The student wants to emphasize the aim of the research study. Which choice most effectively uses relevant information from the notes to accomplish this goal?

Ⓐ The bees in the study by Martin Giurfa and his team were trained with sucrose rewards.

Ⓑ Martin Giurfa and his team wanted to see whether bees organize numbers spatially from left to right, similar to how humans organize numbers.

Ⓒ Various vertebrate species, such as humans and honeybees, organize numbers spatially from left to right.

Ⓓ Martin Giurfa and his team found that bees did organize numbers in a similar way to how humans do.

10 Mark for Review

While researching a topic, a student has taken the following notes:

- Wolffram's red salt is an inorganic compound.
- Inorganic chemists in the 20th century were interested in Wolffram's red salt because it has a deep red color but its components are colorless.
- In 1935, inorganic chemists H. D. K. Drew and H. J. Tress hypothesized that the red color was due to the presence of platinum (3+) ions.
- In 1936, inorganic chemist K. A. Jensen proved that Wolffram's red salt did not have platinum (3+) ions.
- In 1956, inorganic chemists Yamada Shoichiro and Tsuchida Ryutaro discovered that the red color was due to chains of platinum (2+) and platinum (4+) ions.

The student wants to emphasize a similarity among the research to an audience familiar with Wolffram's red salt. Which choice most effectively uses relevant information from the notes to accomplish this goal?

Ⓐ 20th-century research into Wolffram's red salt, a deep red inorganic compound made up of colorless components, focused on the presence of various platinum ions.

Ⓑ While Drew and Tress hypothesized that Wolffram's red salt was red due to platinum (3+) ions, Jensen proved that Wolffram's red salt did not have platinum (3+) ions.

Ⓒ 20th-century hypotheses and research into the color of Wolffram's red salt focused on the presence of various platinum ions.

Ⓓ Wolffram's red salt is not deep red due to the presence of platinum (3+) ions, as Drew and Tress hypothesized, but rather due to chains of platinum (2+) and platinum (4+) ions, as discovered by Shoichiro and Ryutaro.

RHETORIC DRILL ANSWERS AND EXPLANATIONS

1. **A** This is a transition question, so follow the basic approach. Highlight ideas that relate to each other. The first sentence says *using banana peels in unique ways*, and the second sentence says *banana peels can be dried and ground into flour and used in baking.* These ideas agree, so a same-direction transition is needed. Make an annotation that says "same." Eliminate any answer that doesn't match.
    - (A) is correct because it is a same-direction transition, and the second sentence is an example of the first.
    - (B) is wrong because the second sentence is an example, not a new idea.
    - (C) is wrong because it is an opposite-direction transition.
    - (D) is wrong because the second sentence is an example, not an additional point.

2. **D** This is a transition question, so follow the basic approach. Highlight ideas that relate to each other. The first part of the sentence says *The locations of the moon trees were not recorded*, and the second part of the sentence says *until a renewed interest...led to the creation of a database of the rediscovered moon trees and their locations.* These ideas disagree, so an opposite-direction transition is needed. Make an annotation that says "opposite." Eliminate any answer that doesn't match.
    - (A) and (B) are wrong because they are same-direction transitions.
    - (C) is wrong because *still* suggests that the second part of the sentence is happening despite the first part of the sentence.
    - (D) is correct because *however* is an opposite-direction transition.

3. **B** This is a transition question, so follow the basic approach. Highlight ideas that relate to each other. The first sentence mentions *a way to detect extraterrestrial life.* The third sentence says *ATP is present in all living organisms*, and the final sentence says *the presence of life can be confirmed....* These ideas agree, so a same-direction transition is needed. Make an annotation that says "same." Eliminate any answer that doesn't match.
    - (A), (C), and (D) are wrong because they are opposite-direction transitions.
    - (B) is correct because *Therefore* is a same-direction transition, and the last sentence provides a conclusion.

4. **A** This is a transition question, so follow the basic approach. Highlight ideas that relate to each other. The previous sentence says *echoing the disappearance of Jasmine's older sister twenty-five years earlier*, and this sentence says *Jasmine reexamines her past, and family secrets come to light*. These ideas agree, so a same-direction transition is needed. Make an annotation that says "same." Eliminate any answer that doesn't match.

- (A) is correct because it is a same-direction transition, and the reexamination is a result of what happens on the tour.
- (B) is wrong because this sentence does not summarize the previous one.
- (C) is wrong because there is no *similar* reexamination in the previous sentence.
- (D) is wrong because it is an opposite-direction transition.

5. **C** This is a transition question, so follow the basic approach. Highlight ideas that relate to each other. The first sentence says *Bright Tetteh Ackwerh has used [street art] to represent his satirical views*, and the second sentence says *his goal is to provoke spirited conversation about these topics*. These ideas agree, so a same-direction transition is needed. Make an annotation that says "same." Eliminate any answer that doesn't match.

- (A) is wrong because the second sentence is not a rule of the first sentence.
- (B) is wrong because it is an opposite-direction transition.
- (C) is correct because it is a same-direction transition, and the second sentence goes along with the idea in the first.
- (D) is wrong because the second sentence is not an event that follows the first sentence.

6. **B** This is a Rhetorical Synthesis question, so follow the basic approach. Highlight the goal(s) stated in the question: *introduce Sachiko Kodama and what her sculptures are made of.* Eliminate any answer that doesn't *introduce Sachiko Kodama* and describe *what her sculptures are made of.*

- (A) and (D) are wrong because they don't *introduce Sachiko Kodama.*
- (B) is correct because it introduces Kodama and says she uses *ferrofluid to create her sculptures.*
- (C) is wrong because it doesn't describe what Kodama's *sculptures are made of.*

7. **C** This is a Rhetorical Synthesis question, so follow the basic approach. Highlight the goal(s) stated in the question: *emphasize the results of Charpentier's and Doudna's working relationship*. Eliminate any answer that doesn't *emphasize the results* of their *relationship*.

- (A) and (D) are wrong because they don't describe the *results of Charpentier's and Doudna's working relationship*.
- (B) is wrong because it doesn't clearly describe what *the relationship* was between Charpentier and Doudna.
- (C) is correct because it describes what Charpentier and Doudna worked on together and the *result* of this work.

8. **B** This is a Rhetorical Synthesis question, so follow the basic approach. Highlight the goal(s) stated in the question: *compare the dates of opening and lengths of the lines of the Kolkata Metro System to an audience familiar with the Kolkata Metro System*. Eliminate any answer that doesn't *compare the dates of opening and lengths of the lines* and assume that the audience is *familiar with the Kolkata Metro System*.

- (A) and (D) are wrong because they don't provide a comparison between multiple *lines*.
- (B) is correct because it makes a comparison of the *dates of opening and lengths of the lines* and doesn't introduce the Metro System, since the audience is familiar.
- (C) is wrong because it explains the *Kolkata Metro System*, but the audience is already familiar.

9. **B** This is a Rhetorical Synthesis question, so follow the basic approach. Highlight the goal(s) stated in the question: *emphasize the aim of the research study*. Eliminate any answer that doesn't *emphasize the aim of the research study*.

- (A), (C), and (D) are wrong because they don't mention the *aim*, or what the scientists were trying to do.
- (B) is correct because describes the *aim of the research study* by saying *wanted to see*.

10. **C** This is a Rhetorical Synthesis question, so follow the basic approach. Highlight the goal(s) stated in the question: *emphasize a similarity among the research to an audience familiar with Wolffram's red salt*. Eliminate any answer that doesn't *emphasize a similarity* and assume that the audience is *familiar with Wolffram's red salt*.

- (A) is wrong because it explains what *Wolffram's red salt* is, but the audience is familiar.
- (B) and (D) are wrong because they don't *emphasize a similarity among the research*.
- (C) is correct because it emphasizes *a similarity among the research* (the focus) and doesn't explain *Wolffram's red salt*, since the audience is familiar.

Summary

- For transition questions, look at the previous sentence(s) for a clue that relates to something in the sentence with the blank. Highlight any clues.
- Determine whether the ideas agree or disagree, and write a note indicating which direction the answer should go.
- Eliminate answers that go the wrong direction, and then use POE with the remaining answers.
- For Rhetorical Synthesis questions, highlight the goal(s) stated in the question.
- Eliminate answers that don't completely fulfill the goal or goals.
- Read the bullet points if needed.

Part III
How to Crack the Math Section

Chapter 18
Math Introduction

As you learned in Chapter 4, the Digital SAT isn't your typical school test. This goes for the Math section of the Digital SAT as well as the Reading and Writing section. This chapter will give you an overview of the Math section, show you what kind of math to expect, talk about applying the test-taking strategies you learned in Chapter 4 to the Math section, and introduce you to the only questions on the Digital SAT that are not multiple-choice.

THE MATH BREAKDOWN

The Math section of the Digital SAT is split into two modules. Each module contains 22 questions, of which 16 or 17 are multiple-choice questions and the rest are student-produced response questions (SPR), meaning that you fill in your own answer instead of choosing from four answers. Questions on the second module are, on average, easier or harder based on your performance on the first module. Each module has two "pre-test" questions that do not count towards your score, but they are not identified, so treat every question as if it counts.

No Need to Know
Here are a few things you won't need to know to answer Digital SAT Math questions: calculus, logarithms, and matrices. Essentially, the Digital SAT tests a whole lot of algebra and some arithmetic, statistics, and geometry.

The Math section is further broken down by question type and content area, as described below. Unlike the Verbal section, the question types and content areas do not go in any predictable order. Everything is mixed together, so you could see a trig question, then a word problem about averages, then a question about the vertex of a parabola. We'll cover these topics and many more in the next several chapters, so you'll be ready for all of it.

Question Type Breakdown	
70% Problem Solving	15–16 questions per module
30% Word Problems	6–7 questions per module
Content Breakdown	
35% Algebra	7–8 questions per module
35% Advanced Math	7–8 questions per module
15% Problem-Solving & Data Analysis	3–4 questions per module
15% Geometry and Trigonometry	3–4 questions per module

Fill-In Questions

Approximately 25% of the questions on the Math section of the Digital SAT are what College Board calls Student-Produced Response questions, or SPRs. These are the only questions on the test that are not multiple-choice. Instead of selecting the correct answer from among several choices, you will have to find the answer on your own and type it into a box. We call these fill-ins because you fill in your answer. The fill-in questions cover the same math topics as the multiple-choice questions do, and they fit within the order of difficulty of the module. The fill-in format has special characteristics, and we'll tell you more about them in Chapter 26.

You Don't Have to Finish

We've all been taught in school that when you take a test, you have to finish it. If you answered only two-thirds of the questions on a high school math test, you probably wouldn't get a very good grade. But as we've already seen, the Digital SAT is not at all like the tests you take in school. Most students don't know about the difference, so they make the mistake of trying to work all of the questions on both Math modules of the Digital SAT.

Quick Note
Remember, this is not a math test in school! It is not scored on the same scale your math teacher uses. You don't need to get all the questions right to get an above-average score.

Because they have only a limited amount of time to answer all the questions, most students rush through the questions they think are easy in order to get to the harder ones as soon as possible. At first, it seems reasonable to save more time for the more challenging questions, but think about it this way. When students rush through a Math section, they're actually spending too little time on the easier questions (which they have a good chance of getting right), just so they can spend more time on the harder questions (which they have less chance of getting right). Does this make sense? Of course not.

Here is the secret: on the Math section, you don't have to answer every question in each module. In fact, unless you are aiming for a top score, you should intentionally skip some harder questions. Most students can raise their Math scores by concentrating on correctly answering all of the questions that they think are easy or medium difficulty. In other words…

Slow Down!

Most students do considerably better on the Math section when they slow down and spend less time worrying about the more complex questions (and more time working carefully on the more straightforward ones). Haste causes careless errors, and careless errors can ruin your score. In most cases, you can actually raise your score by answering fewer questions. That doesn't sound like a bad idea, does it? If you're shooting for an 800, you'll have to answer every question correctly. But if your target is 550, you should ignore the hardest questions in each module and use your limited time wisely.

POOD and the Math Section

The questions in both modules of the Digital SAT Math section are arranged in a loose order of difficulty. The earlier questions are generally easier and the last few are harder, but the level of difficulty may jump around a little. Furthermore, the second module might start with a question that feels much easier than the last question of the first module. Assessing the difficulty of a question is also complicated by the fact that in College Board's view, "hard" on the Digital SAT means that a higher percentage of students tend to get it wrong, often due to careless errors or lack of time.

The two experimental questions in each module can also alter the order of difficulty. If you encounter a question that seems surprisingly easy or surprisingly hard based on the questions before and after, use your POOD to decide whether to do it, mark it for later, or enter a guess.

Because difficulty levels can go up and down a bit, don't worry too much about how hard the test-writers think a question is. Focus instead on the questions that are easiest for you, and do your best to get those right—no matter where they appear—before moving on to the tougher ones. So which will be the easy ones for you? It is *personal* order of difficulty, but here are some things to consider:

- **Math knowledge:** Do you know the topic cold? Do you see exactly how to start solving it? Then the question is worth attempting, but read and work carefully!
- **SAT knowledge:** Is there a Princeton Review technique from this book that would be perfect for this question? Now is the time to put your skills to use.
- **Self-knowledge:** Do your eyes glaze over halfway through a word problem? Do you think, "More like trigoNOmetry" when you see a trig question? Then come back to that question later or just pick a random answer to select.
- **Take the first bite:** A great way to decide whether a question deserves your time is to think about Bite-Sized Pieces. If you know immediately how to start a question, there's a good chance you'll be able to finish it and get it right.

Don't forget: Fill in answers for questions you decide to skip, use the Mark for Review tool to mark questions to come back to later, and enter an answer for every question.

USING THE ONLINE TOOLS AND SCRATCH PAPER

Online Tools

Several of the built-in features of the Digital SAT will be useful on the Math section.

- Mark for Review tool to mark questions to come back to later
- Built-in calculator, which can be accessed at any time
- Reference sheet with common geometry formulas, which can be accessed at any time
- The Annotate tool is NOT available on the Math section, so you will not be able to underline or highlight parts of the question.

Scratch Paper

The proctor at the test center will hand out three sheets of scratch paper, and you can use your own pen or pencil. Plan ahead about how to use the scratch paper in combination with what's on the screen.

Use the Tools Effectively!

Online Tools	**Scratch Paper**
Eliminate wrong answers	Rewrite key parts of the question
Work steps on the calculator	Write out every calculation
Look up geometry formulas	Redraw geometric figures and label them
	Rewrite answer choices as needed

Here's a question from your first practice test with an image of the testing app screen on the left and scratch paper on the right. On a question like this, use your scratch paper to rewrite parts of the question and translate them into math, and then use the Answer Eliminator tool to cross out answers that don't match that piece. Always include the question number next to your work on the scratch paper to keep yourself organized.

16

Stella had 211 invitations to send for an event. She has already sent 43 invitations and will send them all if she sends 24 each day for the next d days. Which of the following equations represents this situation?

~~(A) $24d - 43 = 211$~~ Undo

(B) $24d + 43 = 211$ (B)

~~(C) $43d - 24 = 211$~~ Undo

~~(D) $43d + 24 = 211$~~ Undo

16)

24 a day for d days
24d

add to 43 sent,
not subtract

Calculators

Calculators are permitted on every Math question on the Digital SAT. In addition, the testing app includes a built-in calculator with many, many features. Practice with the built-in calculator or the one you're planning to bring with you. We'll tell you more about calculators as we go along.

The Princeton Review Approach

We're going to give you the tools you need in order to handle the easier questions on the Digital SAT Math section, along with several great techniques to help you crack some of the more difficult ones. But you must concentrate first on getting the easier questions correct. Don't worry about the questions you find difficult on the Math section until you've learned to work carefully and accurately on the easier questions.

When it does come time to look at some of the harder questions, use Process of Elimination to help you avoid trap answers and to narrow down your choices if you have to guess. You will learn to use POE to improve your odds of finding the answer by getting rid of answer choices that can't possibly be correct.

Generally speaking, each chapter in this section begins with the basics and then gradually moves into more advanced principles and techniques. If you find yourself getting lost toward the end of the chapter, don't worry. Concentrate your efforts on principles that are easier to understand but that you still need to master.

Chapter 19
Digital SAT Math: The Big Picture

In this chapter, you'll see a few ways you can eliminate bad answer choices, avoid traps, improve your odds of answering correctly if you have to guess, and maximize your Math score. You'll also learn how to best make use of the built-in calculator, should you choose to use it instead of bringing your own.

THE BIG PICTURE AND IMPORTANT STRATEGIES

The Reading and Writing section of this book describes various ways to eliminate wrong answers. That idea comes into play on the Digital SAT Math section, as well. There are also ways to break down math questions and avoid trap answers. This chapter provides an overview of the strategies you should know in order to maximize your Math score.

BALLPARKING STRATEGY

One way to eliminate answers on the Math section is by looking for ones that are the wrong size, or that are not "in the ballpark." We call this strategy **Ballparking.** Although you can use your calculator on the following question, you can also eliminate one answer without doing any calculations.

1 Mark for Review

In a garden, the corn on the north edge of the garden is 30% shorter than that on the south edge. If the corn on the south edge of the garden is 50 inches tall, how tall is the corn on the north edge of the garden, in inches?

Ⓐ 30

Ⓑ 33

Ⓒ 35

Ⓓ 65

Here's How to Crack It

The question asks for the height of the corn on the north edge of the garden and states that the corn there is shorter than the corn on the south edge, which is 50 inches tall. You are asked to find the height of the corn on the north edge, so the correct answer must be less than 50. Eliminate (D), which is too high. Often, one or more of the bad answers on these questions is the result you would get if you applied the percentage to the wrong value. To find the right answer, take 30% of 50 by multiplying 0.3 by 50 to get 15; then subtract that from 50. The corn on the north edge is 35 inches tall. The correct answer is (C).

READ THE FINAL QUESTION STRATEGY

It's a bad idea to assume you know what a question is going to ask you to do. Make sure to always read the final question *before* starting to work on the question. Write key words or the entire final question on the scratch paper. Then, try to ballpark before you solve.

2 Mark for Review

If $16x - 2 = 30$, what is the value of $8x - 4$?

Ⓐ 12

Ⓑ 15

Ⓒ 16

Ⓓ 28

Here's How to Crack It

The question asks for the value of an expression, but don't just dive in and solve for the variable. First, see if you can eliminate answers by Ballparking, which can also work on algebra questions. To go from $16x$ to $8x$, you would just divide by 2. Dividing 30 by 2 gives you 15, so 28 is way too big. Eliminate it. The correct answer is not likely to be 15, either, because that ignores the –2 and the –4 in the question.

To solve this one, add 2 to each side of the equation to get $16x = 32$. Divide both sides by 2, which gives you $8x = 16$. But don't stop there! The final question asks for $8x - 4$, so (C) is a trap answer. You have to take the last step and subtract 4 from both sides to find that $8x - 4 = 12$. The correct answer is (A).

RTFQ:
Read
The
Final
Question

Get started faster and avoid trap answers by reading and rewriting the actual question being asked.

BITE-SIZED PIECES STRATEGY

When dealing with complicated math questions, take it one little piece at a time. We call this strategy **Bite-Sized Pieces.** If you try to do more than one step at a time, especially if you do it in your head, you are likely to make mistakes or fall for trap answers. After each step, take a look at the answer choices and determine whether you can eliminate any.

Try the following question.

3 Mark for Review

A paper airplane is thrown horizontally from the top of a hill. It travels in a straight line, and as it moves forward, it also descends. The plane moves horizontally at 9 feet per second while descending one foot for every 3 feet traveled horizontally. After 5 seconds of travel, how many feet has the plane descended from the height at which it was thrown?

(A) 3

(B) 10

(C) 15

(D) 20

Here's How to Crack It

The question asks how many feet the plane has descended after 5 seconds. There are a few things going on here. The plane is traveling horizontally, and it is also descending. Start by figuring out how far it travels horizontally. It moves in that direction at 9 feet per second for 5 seconds, so it moves horizontally $9 \times 5 = 45$ feet. It descends 1 foot for every 3 traveled horizontally. If it goes 45 feet horizontally, it will descend more than 3 feet, so eliminate (A). Now figure out how many "3 feet" are in 45 feet—for each one of them, the plane will descend 1 foot. Since $45 \div 3 = 15$, the plane descends 15 feet. The correct answer is (C).

Bite-Sized Pieces: Do one small, manageable piece at a time and keep writing things down.

You may also have noticed that all the numbers in the question are odd. This makes it unlikely that the answer would be 10 or 20, which are even. If you see things like that, use them as opportunities to eliminate.

Here's another example.

4 Mark for Review

$$(5ck^2 + 5c^2 - 2c^2k) - (ck^2 + 2c^2k + 5c^2)$$

Which of the following is equivalent to the expression above?

Ⓐ $4ck^2$

Ⓑ $4ck^2 - 4c^2k$

Ⓒ $5c^2k^4 - 10c^4k$

Ⓓ $8c^2k^3 + 7c^2k - 5c^2$

Here's How to Crack It

The question asks for an expression that is equivalent to the difference of two polynomials. In math class, your teacher would want you to combine all like terms and show your work, but this isn't math class. Start with one tiny piece of this intimidating question. The first set of parentheses starts with a term containing ck^2. Check the second set of parentheses for the same combination of variables and exponents. The first term there matches, so the first step to take is $5ck^2 - ck^2 = 4ck^2$. There are no other terms with ck^2, so the correct answer must contain $4ck^2$. Eliminate (C) and (D). Now you have a fifty-fifty chance of getting it right, so you can guess and go, *or* you can do one more step to determine whether the answer is (A) or (B). The difference between the two answers is the $-4c^2k$ term, so focus on the terms in the expression that contain c^2k. In the first set of parentheses, you have $-2c^2k$, and then you subtract the $2c^2k$ term in the second set of parentheses to get $-2c^2k - 2c^2k = -4c^2k$. The correct answer is (B).

WORD PROBLEMS

The two strategies we just showed you—RTFQ and Bite-Sized Pieces—are a large part of the approach to word problems on the Digital SAT. The test-writers will try to make things difficult to understand by making a story out of the math. To make sure you have the best shot at reaching the correct answer quickly and accurately, follow this basic approach.

Word Problem Basic Approach

1. **Read the Final Question (RTFQ)**—Understand the actual question being asked. Write down key words.
2. **Let the answers point the way**—Use the answer type to help determine how to start working on the question.
3. **Work in bite-sized pieces**—Find one piece to start with, then work piece-by-piece until the final question has been answered.
4. **Use POE**—Check to see whether any answers can be eliminated after each bite-sized piece.

This approach can be helpful on questions that are "just" math, but they are vital on word problems. Here are some details about the word problem basic approach.

RTFQ—The final question will start with something like *Which of the following, What is,* or *How many.* Find the final question (it's usually at the end) and write down key words. If the question asks for the value of a variable or the measure of an angle, write down which variable or which angle. If it asks for a specific part of a graph or a word problem, write down which part. Terms and units, such as *median, positive, minutes,* or *miles,* also go on the scratch paper.

Let the answers point the way—On multiple-choice questions, the answer type often gives a clue about how to approach the question. Do the answers have numbers? variables? equations? graphs? a bunch of words? Use that information to get started.

Work in bite-sized pieces—Rather than trying to plan the entire question up front, just get started. Work the question one bite-sized piece at a time, reading more along the way and making notes on the scratch paper. The final question and the answer types usually reveal the best approach. If it's not obvious, either mark the question to come back to later or enter a guess.

Use POE—On some questions, it's possible to eliminate answers along the way while working in bite-sized pieces. If the question asks about an equation representing a situation, for example, an answer that gets any piece of the equation wrong can be eliminated. Eliminate answers that don't work when you plug them in, answers that are clearly too big, too small, or have the wrong sign, and answers that contradict information given in the question.

THE CALCULATOR

You are allowed to use a calculator on every question in the Math section, although it doesn't help on every question. You have two calculator options:

- Use the built-in Desmos calculator within the testing app.
- Bring your own approved scientific or graphing calculator.

Whether you use the built-in calculator or your own, practice, practice, practice! A calculator can make some questions much easier to answer and will save you time on other questions. To practice with the built-in calculator, download the Bluebook app or just use the free version on the Desmos website.

Calculator Guide

Head to your Student Tools to read our Guide for the built-in calculator. There you will find basic information about opening and using the calculator, details about how to use the keypads and advanced functions, and instructions for getting the most out of the graphing calculator. This Guide also includes a number of questions from your first practice test with detailed instructions and screenshots to show you how to solve them using the built-in calculator.

Even if you are planning to use your own calculator, this Guide might help you think of ways to use it that you hadn't considered before.

Call on the Calculator
Practice using the built-in calculator in your Student Tools or your own throughout your test preparation. Use it for example questions in this book, use it while taking practice tests, and use it any time you're doing practice questions for the Digital SAT.

Personal Calculator

If you have a good calculator that you are familiar with and like using, you may take it with you and use it on the test. Make sure that your calculator is either a scientific or a graphing calculator and can perform the order of operations correctly. To test your calculator, try the following problem, typing it in exactly as written without hitting the ENTER or "=" key until the end: $3 + 4 \times 6 =$. The calculator should give you 27. If it gives you 42, it's not a good calculator to use.

If you do decide to use your own graphing calculator, keep in mind that it *cannot* have a QWERTY-style keyboard (like the TI-95). Most of the graphing calculators have typing capabilities, but because they don't have typewriter-style keyboards, they are perfectly legal. To see the full College Board calculator policy, visit satsuite.collegeboard.org/digital/what-to-bring-do/calculator-policy.

Also, you *cannot* use the calculator on your phone. In fact, on test day, you will have to turn your phone off and put it away.

The only danger in using a calculator on the Digital SAT is that you may be tempted to use it in situations in which it won't help you. Some students believe that their calculator will solve many difficulties they have with math. This type of thinking may even occasionally cause students to miss a question they might have otherwise answered correctly on their own.

Remember that your calculator is only as smart as you are. But if you practice and use a little caution, you will find that your calculator will help you a great deal.

What a Calculator Is Good at Doing

Here's a list of some of the things a calculator is good for on the Digital SAT:

- arithmetic
- decimals
- fractions
- square roots
- percentages
- graphs (if it is a graphing calculator)

We'll discuss the calculator's role in most of these areas in the next few chapters.

Calculator Arithmetic

Calculators Don't Think for You
A calculator crunches numbers and often saves you a great deal of time and effort, but it is not a substitute for your problem-solving skills.

Adding, subtracting, multiplying, and dividing integers and decimals is easy on a calculator. But, you need to be careful when you key in the numbers. A calculator will give you an incorrect answer to an arithmetic calculation if you press the wrong keys.

The main thing to remember about a calculator is that it can't help you find the answer to a question you don't understand. If you wouldn't know how to solve a particular problem using pencil and paper, you won't know how to solve it using a calculator either. Your calculator will help you, but it won't take the place of a solid understanding of basic Digital SAT mathematics.

Use Your Paper First

Write Things Down
You have scratch paper, so make the most of it. Keep track of your progress through each question by writing down each step.

When you decide to use a calculator to help answer a question, the first step should be to set up the problem or equation on paper; this will keep you from getting lost or confused. This is especially important when solving the problem involves a number of separate steps. The basic idea is to use the scratch paper to make a plan, and then use your calculator to execute it.

Working on paper first will also give you a record of what you have done if you change your mind, run into trouble, or lose your place. If you suddenly find that you need to try a different approach to a question, you may not have to go all the way back to the beginning. This will also make it easier for you to check your work, if you have time to do so.

Don't use the memory function on your calculator (if it has one). Because you can use your scratch paper, you don't need to juggle numbers within the calculator itself. Instead of storing the result of a calculation in the calculator, write it on your scratch paper, clear your calculator, and move to the next step of the question. A calculator's memory is fleeting; scratch paper is forever.

Order of Operations

In the next chapter, we will discuss the proper order of operations for solving equations that require several operations to be performed. Be sure you understand this information, because it applies to calculators as much as it does to pencil-and-paper computations. You may remember PEMDAS from school. PEMDAS is the order of operations. You'll learn more about it and see how questions on the Digital SAT require you to know the order of operations. You must always perform calculations in the proper order.

Fractions

Most scientific calculators have buttons that will automatically simplify fractions or convert fractions from decimals. (For instance, on the TI-81, TI-83, and TI-84, hitting "Math" and then selecting the first option, "Answer → Fraction," will give you the last answer calculated as a fraction in the lowest terms.) Find out if your calculator has this function! If it does, you can use it to simplify messy fractions. This function is also very useful when you get an answer as a decimal, but the answer choices given are all fractions.

The Digital SAT Calculator Guide has details about working with fractions, along with other types of math and graphs. Pull up the Guide in your Student Tools and become an expert!

Batteries

Change the batteries on your calculator a week before the Digital SAT so that you know your calculator won't run out of power halfway through the test. You can also take extra batteries with you, just in case. Although it isn't very likely that the batteries will run out on your calculator on the day of the test, it could happen—so you want to be prepared.

Final Words on the Calculator

Remember that the test-writers are trying to test your ability to use your calculator wisely. As such, they have purposely created many questions in which the calculator is worthless. So be sure to read the final question—there may be some serious surprises in there. Practice your math skills *and* your calculator skills so you have options about how you solve questions.

Summary

- Look for ways to eliminate answer choices that are too big or too small. Ballparking can help you find the right answer without extensive calculations, avoid trap answers, and improve your chances of getting the question right even if you have to guess.
- Use the built-in tools as much as possible. The most useful ones on the Math section are the Calculator, Reference Sheet, and Answer Eliminator tool.
- Use your scratch paper constantly: number the work for each question, write down key words from the final question, redraw geometric figures, and write down every step of math. Even if you use a calculator, it's worth setting up the math on your scratch paper to stay organized and avoid mistakes.
- Utilize the Word Problem Basic Approach: Read the Final Question (RTFQ), Let the Answers Point the Way, Work in Bite-Sized Pieces, and use Process of Elimination (POE).
- Practice with the calculator you plan to use for the test: either the built-in Desmos calculator or your personal scientific or graphing calculator.
- If you are going to use the built-in calculator, read the Digital SAT Calculator Guide in your Student Tools to maximize its effectiveness.
- If you are going to use your own calculator, make sure it is on the approved list and has fresh batteries.
- Set up the question on the scratch paper before entering anything into a calculator. By doing so, you will eliminate the possibility of getting lost or confused.
- A calculator can't help you find the answer to a question you don't understand. Be sure to use your calculator as a tool, not a crutch.
- Whether you are using a calculator or not, you must always perform calculations in the proper order (PEMDAS).

Chapter 20
Fun with Fundamentals

We'll show you which mathematical concepts are most important to know for the Digital SAT. However, this book relies on your knowledge of basic math concepts. If you're a little rusty, this chapter is for you. Read on for a quick review of the math fundamentals you'll need to know.

THE BUILDING BLOCKS

As you go through this book, you might discover that you're having trouble with stuff you thought you already knew—like fractions or square roots. If this happens, it's probably a good idea to review the fundamentals. That's where this chapter comes in. Our drills and examples will refresh your memory if you've gotten rusty. Always keep in mind that the math tested on the Digital SAT is different from the math taught in school. If you want to raise your score, don't waste time studying math that the Digital SAT never tests.

Keep in mind that calculators are allowed on every question in both Math modules. You can use the built-in calculator available to you in the testing app, and you can also bring your own. A calculator can perform many basic math operations for you, such as working with fractions and converting between fractions and decimals. However, a calculator only does exactly what you tell it to do, so read carefully and write things down rather than relying on a calculator too much. Learn the content in this chapter, but also practice with the calculator you plan to use on test day. Your brain, pencil, and calculator all work together to get questions right efficiently.

Let's talk first about what you should expect to see on the test.

The Instructions

Both of the Math modules on the Digital SAT begin with the same set of instructions. The clock starts right away, so you want to know the instructions cold before you go in. That way, you can click Close and start working right away. If you forget something about the instructions while you're working on the test, click the Directions button in the upper left corner. We've reprinted the instructions below. Be sure to familiarize yourself with them ahead of time.

The questions in this section address a number of important math skills.

Use of a calculator is permitted for all questions. A reference sheet, calculator, and these directions can be accessed throughout the test.

Unless otherwise indicated:

- All variables and expressions represent real numbers.
- Figures provided are drawn to scale.
- All figures lie in a plane.
- The domain of a given function *f* is the set of all real numbers *x* for which *f*(*x*) is a real number.

For **multiple-choice questions**, solve each problem and choose the correct answer from the choices provided. Each multiple-choice question has a single correct answer.

For **student-produced response questions,** solve each problem and enter your answer as described below.

- If you find **more than one correct answer**, enter only one answer.
- You can enter up to 5 characters for a **positive** answer and up to 6 characters (including the negative sign) for a **negative** answer.
- If your answer is a **fraction** that doesn't fit in the provided space, enter the decimal equivalent.
- If your answer is a **decimal** that doesn't fit in the provided space, enter it by truncating or rounding at the fourth digit.
- If your answer is a **mixed number** (such as $3\frac{1}{2}$), enter it as an improper fraction (7/2) or its decimal equivalent (3.5).
- Don't enter **symbols** such as a percent sign, comma, or dollar sign.

Examples

Answer	Acceptable ways to enter answer	Unacceptable: will NOT receive credit
3.5	3.5 3.50 7/2	31/2 3 1/2
$\frac{2}{3}$	2/3 .6666 .6667 0.666 0.667	0.66 .66 0.67 .67
$-\frac{1}{3}$	–1/3 –.3333 –0.333	–.33 –0.33

The instructions have a lot to say about the fill-in questions. Don't worry: we'll show you everything you need to know about that question format in Chapter 26.

Standard Symbols

The following standard symbols are used frequently on the Digital SAT:

Formulas and Definitions
Go to your online Student Tools for a complete list of the math terms and formulas that you'll need to know for the Digital SAT.

SYMBOL	MEANING
$=$	is equal to
$\neq$	is not equal to
$<$	is less than
$>$	is greater than
$\leq$	is less than or equal to
$\geq$	is greater than or equal to

THE SIX ARITHMETIC OPERATIONS

There are only six arithmetic operations that you will ever need to perform on the Digital SAT:

1. Addition $(3 + 3)$
2. Subtraction $(3 - 3)$
3. Multiplication $(3 \times 3$ or $3 \cdot 3)$
4. Division $(3 \div 3$ or $3/3)$
5. Raising to a power (3^3)
6. Finding a root $(\sqrt{9}$ and $\sqrt[3]{8})$

If you're like most students, you probably haven't paid much serious attention to these topics since junior high school. You'll need to learn about them again if you want to do well on the Digital SAT. By the time you take the test, using them should be automatic. All the arithmetic concepts are fairly basic, but you'll have to know them cold. You'll also have to know when and how to use your calculator, which will be quite helpful.

What Do You Get?

You should know the following arithmetic terms:

- The result of addition is a *sum* or *total.*
- The result of subtraction is a *difference.*
- The result of multiplication is a *product.*
- The result of division is a *quotient.*
- In the expression 5^2, the 2 is called an *exponent.*

ORDER OF OPERATIONS

The Six Operations Must Be Performed in the Proper Order

Very often, solving an equation on the Digital SAT will require you to perform several different operations, one after another. These operations must be performed in the proper order. In general, the questions are written in such a way that you won't have trouble deciding what comes first. In cases in which you are uncertain, you need to remember only the following sentence:

Please **E**xcuse **M**y **D**ear **A**unt **S**ally;
she walks from *left* to *right.*

That's **PEMDAS**, for short. It stands for **P**arentheses, **E**xponents, **M**ultiplication, **D**ivision, **A**ddition, and **S**ubtraction. First, do any calculations inside the parentheses; then take care of the exponents; then perform all multiplication and division, from *left* to *right,* followed by addition and subtraction, from *left* to *right.*

Do It Yourself
The Digital SAT's built-in calculator follows the order of operations. It will also rewrite division into fractions—pretty neat! However, as with all calculators, the built-in calculator will only calculate *exactly* what you put in. Furthermore, if you decide to use your own calculator, be sure to practice and use parentheses whenever necessary. Write out the steps on your scratch paper first to avoid entry errors.

The following exercise will help you learn the order in which to perform the six operations. First, set up the equations on paper. Then, use your calculator for the arithmetic. Make sure you perform the operations in the correct order.

Exercise 1

Solve each of the following problems by performing the indicated operations in the proper order. Answers can be found on page 385.

1. $107 + (109 - 107) =$ 109
2. $(7 \times 5) + 3 =$ 38
3. $6 - 3(6 - 3) =$ -3
4. $2 \times [7 - (6 \div 3)] =$ 10
5. $10 - (9 - 8 - 6) =$ 15

2[7-2]

Whichever Comes First

For addition and subtraction, solve from left to right. The same is true of multiplication and division. And remember: if you don't solve in order from left to right, you could end up with the wrong answer!

Example:

$24 \div 4 \times 6 = 24 \div 24 = 1$ wrong

$24 \div 4 \times 6 = 6 \times 6 = 36$ right

Parentheses Can Help You Solve Equations

Using parentheses to regroup information in arithmetic problems can be very helpful. In order to do this, you need to understand a basic law that you have probably forgotten since the days when you last took arithmetic—the **Distributive Law.** You don't need to remember the name of the law, but you do need to know how to use it to help you solve problems.

The Distributive Law

If you're multiplying the sum of two numbers by a third number, you can multiply each number in your sum individually. This comes in handy when you have to multiply the sum of two variables.

If a question gives you information in "factored form"—$a(b + c)$—then you should distribute the first variable before you do anything else. If you are given information that has already been distributed—$(ab + ac)$—then you should factor out the common term, putting the information back in factored form. Very often on the Digital SAT, simply doing this will enable you to spot the answer.

Here are some examples:

Distributive: $6(53) + 6(47) = 6(53 + 47) = 6(100) = 600$

Multiplication first: $6(53) + 6(47) = 318 + 282 = 600$

You get the same answer each way, so why get involved with complicated arithmetic? If you use the Distributive Law for this problem, you don't even need to use your calculator.

The exercise below illustrates the Distributive Law.

Exercise 2

Rewrite each problem by either distributing or factoring and then solve. (Hint: For questions 1, 2, 4, and 5, try factoring.) Questions 3, 4, and 5 have no numbers in them; therefore, they can't be solved with a calculator. Answers can be found on page 385.

1. $(6 \times 57) + (6 \times 13) =$ 420
2. $51(48) + 51(50) + 51(52) =$ 7659
3. $a(b + c - d) =$ ab + ac − ad
4. $xy - xz =$ x(y − z)
5. $abc + xyc =$ c(ab + xy)

FRACTIONS

A Fraction Is Just Another Way of Expressing Division

The expression $\frac{x}{y}$ is exactly the same thing as $x \div y$. The expression $\frac{1}{2}$ means nothing more than $1 \div 2$. In the fraction $\frac{x}{y}$, x is known as the **numerator,** and y is known as the **denominator.**

Fractions and Calculators

It can be tempting to try to directly enter the information from the question into the calculator. The writers of the Digital SAT know this, so they write questions that will lead you to errors if you do so. Always start by writing out what you need to calculate on your scratch paper; only afterwards should you move to use the calculator.

On the Digital SAT's built-in calculator, fractions will appear as fractions. You can use arrow keys or a mouse to navigate between the numerator and denominator of a fraction.

The results will be given as a decimal. To get the results as a fraction, click the button next to the entry box that looks like this:

Adding and Subtracting Fractions with the Same Denominator

To add two or more fractions that all have the same denominator, simply add the numerators and put the sum over the common denominator. Consider the following example:

$$\frac{1}{100}+\frac{4}{100}=\frac{1+4}{100}=\frac{5}{100}$$

Subtraction works exactly the same way:

$$\frac{4}{100}-\frac{1}{100}=\frac{4-1}{100}=\frac{3}{100}$$

Call on the Calculator

Whether you are adding, subtracting, multiplying, or dividing fractions, a calculator can make it a snap. Keep the following things in mind:

1. Practice with whichever calculator you plan to use on test day.
2. Follow the order of operations and use parentheses to make sure the calculator does exactly what you want.
3. Learn the rules anyway. You might need them if, for example, the fractions include variables.

Adding and Subtracting Fractions with Different Denominators

In school you were taught to add and subtract fractions with different denominators by finding the common denominator. To do this, you have to multiply each fraction by a number that makes all the denominators the same. Most students find this process annoying.

Fortunately, we have an approach to adding and subtracting fractions with different denominators that simplifies the entire process. Use the example below as a model. Just multiply in the direction of each arrow, and then either add or subtract across the numerator. Lastly, multiply across the denominator.

$$\frac{1}{3}+\frac{1}{2}=$$

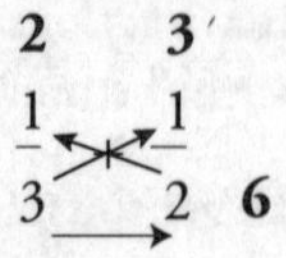

$$\frac{2+3}{6}=\frac{5}{6}$$

We call this procedure the **Bowtie** because the arrows make it look like a bowtie. Use the Bowtie to add or subtract any pair of fractions without thinking about the common denominator, just by following the steps above.

Multiplying All Fractions

Multiplying fractions is easy. Just multiply across the numerator; then multiply across the denominator.

Here's an example.

$$\frac{4}{5}\times\frac{5}{6}=\frac{20}{30}$$

When you multiply fractions, all you are really doing is performing one multiplication problem on top of another.

You should never multiply two fractions before looking to see if you can reduce either or both. If you reduce first, your final answer will be in the form that the test-writers are looking for. Here's another way to express this rule: *Simplify before you multiply.*

$$\frac{63}{6} \times \frac{48}{7} = \frac{\overset{9}{\cancel{63}}}{6} \times \frac{48}{\underset{1}{\cancel{7}}} = \frac{\overset{9}{\cancel{63}}}{\underset{1}{\cancel{6}}} \times \frac{\overset{8}{\cancel{48}}}{\underset{1}{\cancel{7}}} =$$

$$\frac{9}{1} \times \frac{8}{1}$$

$$\frac{72}{1} = 72$$

Dividing All Fractions

To divide one fraction by another, flip over (or take the reciprocal of) the second fraction and multiply.

Here's an example.

$$\frac{2}{3} \div \frac{4}{3} =$$

$$\frac{2}{3} \times \frac{3}{4} = \frac{6}{12} = \frac{1}{2}$$

Be careful not to cancel or reduce until after you flip the second fraction. You can even do the same thing with fractions whose numerators and/or denominators are fractions. These problems look quite frightening, but they're actually easy if you keep your cool.

Just Flip It
Dividing by a fraction is the same thing as multiplying by the reciprocal of that fraction. So just flip over the fraction you are dividing by and multiply instead.

Here's an example.

$$\frac{4}{\frac{4}{3}} =$$

$$\frac{4}{1} \div \frac{4}{3} =$$

$$\frac{4}{1} \times \frac{3}{4} =$$

$$\frac{\cancel{4}}{1} \times \frac{3}{\cancel{4}} =$$

$$\frac{3}{1} = 3$$

Reducing Fractions

When you add or multiply fractions, you will very often end up with a big fraction that is hard to work with. You can almost always reduce such a fraction into one that is easier to handle.

Start Small
It is not easy to see that 26 and 286 have a common factor of 13, but it's pretty clear that they're both divisible by 2. So start from there.

To reduce a fraction, divide both the numerator and the denominator by the largest number that is a factor of both. For example, to reduce $\frac{12}{60}$, divide both the numerator and the denominator by 12, which is the largest number that is a factor of both. Dividing 12 by 12 yields 1; dividing 60 by 12 yields 5. The reduced fraction is $\frac{1}{5}$.

If you can't immediately find the largest number that is a factor of both, find any number that is a factor of both and divide both the numerator and denominator by that number. Your calculations will take a little longer, but you'll end up in the same place. In the previous example, even if you don't see that 12 is a factor of both 12 and 60, you can no doubt see that 6 is a factor of both. Dividing numerator and denominator by 6 yields $\frac{2}{10}$. Now divide both numbers by 2. Doing so yields $\frac{1}{5}$. Once again, you have arrived at the answer.

Reducing fractions can be pretty easy on a calculator. Using the built-in calculator, click the button to the left of the entry field that toggles between fractions and decimals. When in fraction mode, the result will appear in its most reduced form. Take a look at the same fraction in decimal mode and fraction mode:

Converting Mixed Numbers to Fractions

A **mixed number** is a number such as $2\frac{3}{4}$. It is the sum of an integer and a fraction. When you see mixed numbers on the Digital SAT, you should usually convert them to ordinary fractions.

Here's a quick and easy way to convert mixed numbers.

- Multiply the integer by the denominator.
- Add this product to the numerator.
- Place this sum over the denominator.

For practice, let's convert $2\frac{3}{4}$ to a fraction. Multiply 2 (the integer part of the mixed number) by 4 (the denominator). That gives you 8. Add that to the 3 (the numerator) to get 11. Place 11 over 4 to get $\frac{11}{4}$.

The mixed number $2\frac{3}{4}$ is exactly the same as the fraction $\frac{11}{4}$. We converted the mixed number to a fraction because fractions are easier to work with than mixed numbers.

Just Don't Mix
For some reason, the test-writers think it's okay to give you mixed numbers as answer choices. On fill-in questions, however, if you use a mixed number, you won't get credit. You can see why. In your fill-in box, $3\,^1\!/_4$ will look like $\frac{31}{4}$. See Chapter 26 for more about fill-in questions.

Exercise 3

Try converting the following mixed numbers to fractions. Answers can be found on page 385.

1. $8\frac{1}{3}$

2. $2\frac{3}{7}$

3. $5\frac{4}{9}$

4. $2\frac{1}{2}$

5. $6\frac{2}{3}$

Fractions Behave in Peculiar Ways

Fractions don't always behave the way you might want them to. For example, because 4 is obviously greater than 2, it's easy to forget that $\frac{1}{4}$ is less than $\frac{1}{2}$. It's particularly confusing when the numerator is something other than 1. For example, $\frac{2}{7}$ is less than $\frac{2}{5}$. Finally, you should keep in mind that when you multiply one fraction by another, you'll get a fraction that is smaller than either of the first two. Study the following example:

$$\frac{1}{2} \times \frac{1}{4} = \frac{1}{8}$$

$$\frac{1}{8} < \frac{1}{2}$$

$$\frac{1}{8} < \frac{1}{4}$$

A Final Word About Fractions and Calculators

Throughout this section, we've given you some hints about using a calculator to work with fractions. The built-in calculator or your own can be a tremendous help if you know how to use it properly. Make sure you practice with the calculator you plan to use on test day so that working fractions on it becomes second nature before the test.

Exercise 4

Work these examples with the techniques you've read about in this chapter so far. Then work them again using a calculator. If you have any problems, go back and review the information just outlined. Answers can be found on page 385.

1. Reduce $\frac{18}{6}$. ____________________

2. Convert $6\frac{1}{5}$ to an improper fraction. ____________________

3. $2\frac{1}{3} - 3\frac{3}{5} =$ ____________________

4. $\frac{5}{18} \times \frac{6}{25} =$ ____________________

5. $\frac{3}{4} \div \frac{7}{8} =$ ______________________________

6. $\frac{\frac{2}{5}}{5} =$ ______________________________

7. $\frac{\frac{1}{3}}{\frac{3}{4}} =$ ______________________________

DECIMALS

A Decimal Is Just Another Way of Expressing a Fraction

Fractions can be expressed as decimals. To find a fraction's decimal equivalent, simply divide the numerator by the denominator. (You can do this easily with a calculator.)

$$\frac{3}{5} =$$

$$3 \div 5 = 0.6$$

Adding, Subtracting, Multiplying, and Dividing Decimals

Manipulating decimals is easy with a calculator. Simply punch in the numbers—being especially careful to get the decimal point in the right place every single time—and read the result from the display. A calculator makes these operations easy. In fact, working with decimals is one area on the Digital SAT in which your calculator will prevent you from making careless errors. You won't have to line up decimal points or remember what happens when you divide. The calculator will keep track of everything for you, as long as you punch in the correct numbers to begin with. Just be sure to practice carefully before test day.

Exercise 5

Calculate each of the answers to the following questions on paper with your pencil, rounding any awkward numbers to make the math easier to handle. Sometimes, estimating the answer is all you need to do to answer a multiple-choice question. Then use a calculator to find the exact answer. Answers can be found on page 385.

1. $0.43 \times 0.87 =$ ______________

2. $\dfrac{43 + 0.731}{0.03} =$ ______________

3. $3.72 \div 0.02 =$ ______________

4. $0.71 - 3.6 =$ ______________

EXPONENTS AND SQUARE ROOTS

Exponents Are a Kind of Shorthand

Many numbers are the product of the same value multiplied over and over again. For example, $32 = 2 \times 2 \times 2 \times 2 \times 2$. Another way to write this would be $32 = 2^5$, or "thirty-two equals two to the fifth power." The little number, or **exponent,** denotes the number of times that 2 is to be used as a factor. In the same way, $10^3 = 10 \times 10 \times 10$, or 1,000, or "ten to the third power," or "ten cubed." In this example, the 10 is called the **base** and the 3 is called the **exponent.** (You won't need to know these terms on the Digital SAT, but you will need to know them in order to understand our explanations.)

Warning #1
The rules for multiplying and dividing exponents do not apply to addition or subtraction:
$2^2 + 2^3 = 12$
$(2 \times 2) + (2 \times 2 \times 2) = 12$
It does not equal 2^5 or 32.

Multiplying Numbers with Exponents

To multiply two numbers with the same base, simply add the exponents. For example, $2^3 \times 2^5 = 2^{3+5} = 2^8$.

Dividing Numbers with Exponents

To divide two numbers with the same base, simply subtract the exponents. For example, $\frac{2^5}{2^3} = 2^{5-3} = 2^2$.

Raising a Power to a Power

When you raise a power to a power, you multiply the exponents. For example, $(2^3)^4 = 2^{3\times 4} = 2^{12}$.

MADSPM

To remember the exponent rules, all you need to do is remember the acronym **MADSPM**. Here's what it stands for:

- **M**ultiply → **A**dd
- **D**ivide → **S**ubtract
- **P**ower → **M**ultiply

Whenever you see an exponent question, you should think MADSPM. The three MADSPM rules are the only rules that apply to exponent operations.

Here's a typical Digital SAT exponent question.

Warning #2
Parentheses are very important with exponents because you must remember to distribute powers to everything within them.

For example, $(3x)^2 = 9x^2$, not $3x^2$. Similarly, $\left(\frac{3}{2}\right)^2 = \frac{3^2}{2^2}$, not $\frac{9}{2}$. But the Distributive Law applies only when you multiply or divide: $(x+y)^2 = x^2 + 2xy + y^2$, not $x^2 + y^2$.

1 Mark for Review

For the equations $\frac{a^x}{a^y} = a^{10}$ and $(a^y)^3 = a^x$, if $a > 1$, what is the value of x?

Ⓐ 5

Ⓑ 10

Ⓒ 15

Ⓓ 20

Here's How to Crack It

The question asks for the value of x, but it looks pretty intimidating with all those variables. In fact, you might be about to cry "POOD" and go on to the next question. That might not be a bad idea, but before you skip the question, pull out those MADSPM rules.

For the first equation, you can use the Divide-Subtract Rule: $\frac{a^x}{a^y} = a^{x-y} = a^{10}$. In other words, the first equation tells you that $x - y = 10$.

For the second equation, you can use the Power-Multiply Rule: $\left(a^y\right)^3 = a^{3y} = a^x$. So, that means that $3y = x$.

Now, it's time to substitute: $x - y = 3y - y = 10$. So, $2y = 10$ and $y = 5$. Be careful, though! Don't choose (A). That's the value of y, but the question wants to know the value of x. Since $x = 3y$, $x = 3(5) = 15$. The correct answer is (C).

Exponents and Your Calculator

The built-in calculator has both an a^2 button (for squaring a value) and an a^b button (for other exponents). As with fractions, the built-in calculator shows you the operations in the same way you'd write them out on paper.

You could also do this question by using Plugging In the Answers, or PITA, which will be discussed in more detail later in this book. Of course, you still need to know the MADSPM rules to do the question that way.

The Peculiar Behavior of Exponents

Raising a number to a power can have quite peculiar and unexpected results, depending on what sort of number you start out with. Here are some examples.

See the Trap

The test-writers may hope you won't know these strange facts about exponents and throw them in as trap answers. Knowing the peculiar behavior of exponents will help you avoid these tricky pitfalls in a question.

- If you square or cube a number greater than 1, it becomes larger.
  For example, $2^3 = 8$.
- If you square or cube a positive fraction smaller than one, it becomes smaller.
  For example, $\left(\frac{1}{2}\right)^3 = \frac{1}{8}$.
- A negative number raised to an even power becomes positive.
  For example, $(-2)^2 = 4$.
- A negative number raised to an odd power remains negative.
  For example, $(-2)^3 = -8$.

You should also have a feel for relative sizes of exponential numbers without calculating them. For example, 2^{10} is much larger than 10^2 ($2^{10} = 1{,}024$; $10^2 = 100$). To take another example, 2^5 is twice as large as 2^4, even though 5 seems only a bit larger than 4.

Square Roots

The radical sign ($\sqrt{\ }$) indicates the **square root** of a number. For example, $\sqrt{25} = 5$. Note that square roots cannot be negative. If the test-writers want you to think about a negative solution, they won't use the radical sign; instead they'll say $x^2 = 25$ because then $x = 5$ or $x = -5$.

The Only Rules You Need to Know

Here are the only rules regarding square roots that you need to know for the Digital SAT.

1. $\sqrt{x}\sqrt{y} = \sqrt{xy}$. For example, $\sqrt{3}\sqrt{12} = \sqrt{36} = 6$.

2. $\sqrt{\frac{x}{y}} = \frac{\sqrt{x}}{\sqrt{y}}$. For example, $\sqrt{\frac{5}{4}} = \frac{\sqrt{5}}{\sqrt{4}} = \frac{\sqrt{5}}{2}$.

3. $\sqrt{x}$ = positive root only. For example, $\sqrt{16} = 4$.

Note that rule 1 works in reverse: $\sqrt{50} = \sqrt{25} \times \sqrt{2} = 5\sqrt{2}$. This is really a kind of factoring. You are using rule 1 to factor a large, clumsy radical into numbers that are easier to work with. Rule 2 works in reverse as well. $\sqrt{75}$ divided by $\sqrt{3}$ looks complicated, but $\sqrt{\frac{75}{3}} = \sqrt{25} = 5$. And remember that radicals are just fractional exponents, so the same rules of distribution apply. We'll get to fractional exponents below.

Careless Errors

The Digital SAT will try to confuse you with the behavior of roots. Remember that the square root of a number between 0 and 1 is *larger* than the original number. For example, $\sqrt{\frac{1}{4}} = \frac{1}{2}$, and $\frac{1}{2} > \frac{1}{4}$.

Negative and Fractional Exponents

So far we've dealt with only positive integers for exponents, but they can be negative integers as well as fractions. The same concepts and rules apply, but the numbers just look a little weirder. Keep these concepts in mind:

- Negative exponents are a fancy way of writing reciprocals:

$$x^{-n} = \frac{1}{x^n}$$

- Fractional exponents are a fancy way of taking roots and powers:

$$x^{\frac{y}{z}} = \sqrt[z]{x^y}$$

Roots and the Calculator

The Digital SAT's built-in calculator has a button for square roots right on the main ABC keypad. The calculator can do other roots, but College Board has hidden that function. Click the "funcs" button and scroll all the way down to the "NUMBER THEORY" section. There you'll find the $\sqrt[n]{\ }$ button. As with other functions on the built-in calculator, both radicals will look the same as they would if you wrote them out yourself on paper.

If you don't want to scroll through a menu, you can also use fractional exponents using the a^b button to do roots other than square roots, as well.

Here's an example.

2 Mark for Review

If $x > 0$, which of the following is equivalent to $\sqrt{x^3}$?

I. $x + x^{\frac{1}{2}}$

II. $\left(x^{\frac{1}{2}}\right)^3$

III. $\left(x^2\right)\left(x^{-\frac{1}{2}}\right)$

Ⓐ None

Ⓑ I and II only

Ⓒ II and III only

Ⓓ I, II, and III

Here's How to Crack It

The question asks for an equivalent form of a root and gives three expressions with exponents, so it really tests your knowledge of exponents. First, convert $\sqrt{x^3}$ into an exponent to more easily compare it to the choices in the Roman numeral statements. (Plus, exponents are easier to work with because they have those nice MADSPM rules.) According to the definition of a fractional exponent, $\sqrt{x^3} = x^{\frac{3}{2}}$. You want the items in the Roman numerals to equal $x^{\frac{3}{2}}$.

Now, it's time to start working with the Roman numerals. In (I), the test-writers are trying to be tricky. (There's a surprise.) There's no exponent rule for adding exponent expressions with like bases. So, $x + x^{\frac{1}{2}}$ does *not* equal $x^{\frac{3}{2}}$. (If you want to be sure, you could try a number for x: if $x = 4$, then $\sqrt{4^3} = 8$, but $4 + 4^{\frac{1}{2}} = 4 + 2 = 6$.) So, cross off any answer that includes (I): (B) and (D) are gone.

Now, since you are down to either (A) or (C), all you really need to do is try either (II) or (III). If either one works, the answer is (C). Try (II). Use the Power-Multiply Rule: $\left(x^{\frac{1}{2}}\right)^3 = x^{\left(\frac{1}{2}\right)(3)} = x^{\frac{3}{2}}$. Since (II) works, (C) is the correct answer.

Notice that you didn't even need to check (III). Using POE on a Roman numeral question often means that you won't need to check all of the Roman numerals.

HOW TO READ CHARTS AND GRAPHS

Another basic math skill you will need for the Digital SAT is the ability to interpret data from charts, graphs, tables, and more. This section will cover the basics of reading these figures. How to answer questions related to charts and other figures in detail will be discussed in Chapter 24.

What's Up with All of These Figures?

The Digital SAT includes charts, graphs, and tables throughout the test to present data for students to analyze. College Board believes this will better reflect what students learn in school and what they need to understand in the real world. Questions will typically include real-life scenarios, such as finance and business situations, social science issues, and scientific matters.

Since you'll be seeing graphics throughout the test, let's look at the types you may encounter and the skills you'll need to work with to analyze charts and graphs.

Types of Graphs

The Scatterplot

A **scatterplot** is a graph with distinct data points, each representing one piece of information. On the scatterplot below, each dot represents the number of televisions sold at a certain price point.

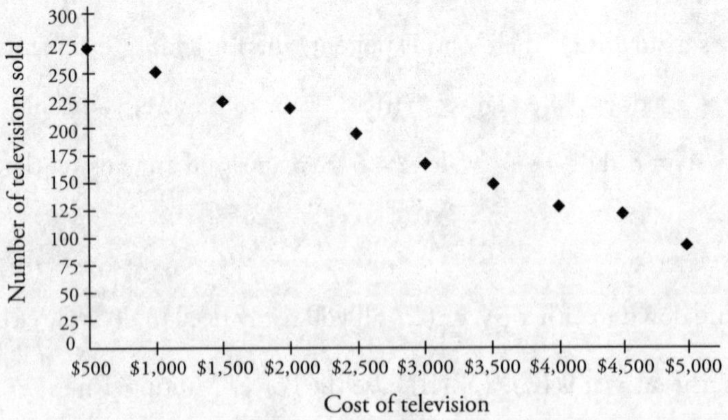

Here's How to Read It

To find the cost of a television when 225 televisions are sold, start at 225 on the vertical axis and look to the right until you hit a data point. Use the edge of your scratch paper as a ruler or, if you have a steady hand, drag the mouse pointer. Once you hit a point, visualize (again using your scratch paper or the mouse pointer to help) a straight line down from the point to the horizontal axis and read the number the line hits, which should be $1,500. To determine the number of televisions sold when they cost a certain amount, reverse the steps—start at the bottom, look up until you hit a point, and then look left until you intersect the vertical axis.

Now try a question based on that scatterplot.

3 Mark for Review

A certain store sells televisions ranging in price from $500 to $5,000 in increments of $500. The scatterplot graph shows the total number of televisions sold at each price during the last 12 months. Approximately how much more revenue did the store collect from the televisions it sold priced at $3,500 than it did from the televisions it sold priced at $1,000?

Ⓐ $175,000

Ⓑ $250,000

Ⓒ $275,000

Ⓓ $350,000

Here's How to Crack It

The question asks for the difference in revenue from selling televisions at two different prices. The revenue is the *cost of television* × *number of televisions sold*. You need the information from the graph only for the television that costs $3,500 and for the television that costs $1,000 in order to determine how much more revenue the $3,500 television produced. There were 150 of the $3,500 televisions sold, for a revenue of $525,000. There were 250 of the $1,000 televisions sold, for a revenue of $250,000. The difference between the two is $525,000 – $250,000 = $275,000. The correct answer is (C).

A scatterplot may also include a **line of best fit.** This is the line that best represents the data.

The Line Graph

A **line graph** is similar to a scatterplot in that it shows different data points that relate the two variables. The difference with a line graph, though, is that the points have been connected to create a continuous line.

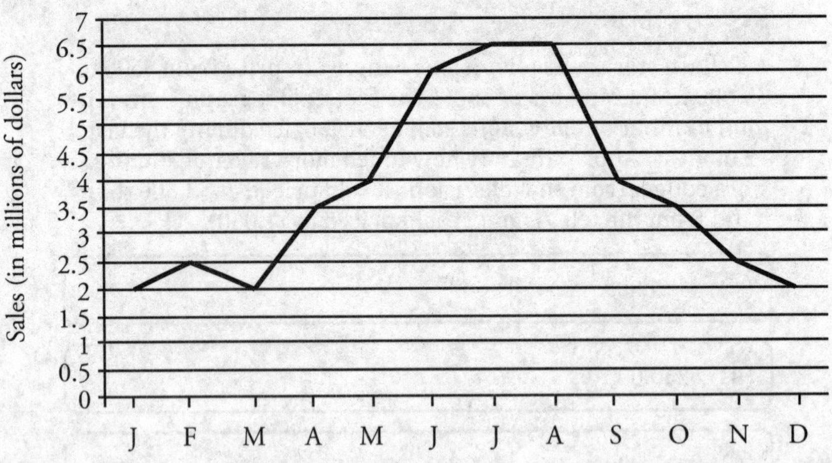

Here's How to Read It

Reading a line graph is very similar to reading a scatterplot. Start at the axis that represents the data given, and use scratch paper or the mouse pointer to visualize a straight line up or to the right until you intersect the graph line. Then move left or down until you hit the other axis. For example, in February, indicated by an F on the horizontal axis, there were $2.5 million in sales. Be sure to notice the units on each axis. If February sales were only $2.50, rather than $2.5 million, then this company wouldn't be doing very well!

Let's look at a question about this line graph.

4 Mark for Review

The forecasted monthly sales of sunscreen are presented in the line graph. For which period are the forecasted monthly sales figures strictly decreasing and then strictly increasing?

(A) January to March

(B) February to April

(C) June to August

(D) September to November

Here's How to Crack It

The question asks for a period during which the forecasted sales are decreasing and then increasing. Look up the values for each period in question and use Process of Elimination to get rid of those that don't fit. For (A), January sales are forecasted to be \$2 million, February \$2.5 million, and March \$2 million. This is an increase followed by a decrease, not the other way around, so eliminate (A). For (B), you already know sales decreased from February to March, so check for a following increase in April. The figure for April is \$3.5 million, which is an increase over the March figure. The correct answer is (B).

The Bar Graph (or Histogram)

Instead of showing a variety of different data points, a **bar graph** shows the number of items that belong to a particular category. If the variable at the bottom is given in ranges instead of distinct items, the graph is called a **histogram,** but you read it the same way.

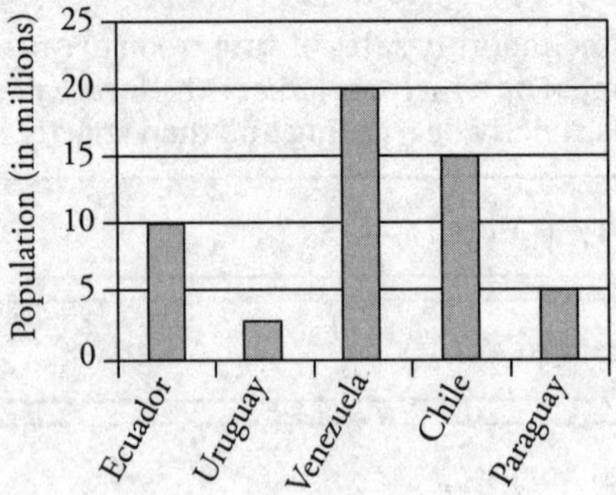

Here's How to Read It

The height of each bar corresponds to a value on the vertical axis. In this case, the bar above Chile hits the line that intersects with 15 on the vertical axis, so there are 15 million people in Chile. Again, watch the units to make sure you know what the numbers on the axes represent. On this graph, horizontal lines are drawn at 5-unit intervals, making the graph easier to read. If these lines do not appear on a bar graph, use your scratch paper to determine the height of a given bar.

Here's an example of a bar graph question, which is based on the Populations of Countries graph above.

5 Mark for Review

The populations of five countries are shown in the bar graph. If population density is defined as $\frac{\text{population}}{\text{area}}$, and the area of Paraguay is 400,000 square kilometers, what is the population density of Paraguay, in people per square kilometer?

Ⓐ 0.08

Ⓑ 0.8

Ⓒ 1.25

Ⓓ 12.5

Here's How to Crack It

The question asks for the population density of Paraguay. Start by determining the population of Paraguay. The bar hits right at the horizontal line for 5, which is in millions, so there are 5 million people in Paraguay. Now use the definition of population density in the question.

$$\frac{\text{population}}{\text{area}} = \frac{5{,}000{,}000}{400{,}000}$$

Be very careful with the number of zeroes you put in the fraction—the answer choices are pairs that vary by a factor of 10, meaning the test-writers expect you to miss a zero. The answer must be greater than 1, since your numerator is bigger than your denominator, so eliminate (A) and (B). Choice (C) also seems too small, but check the math on your calculator (carefully). You should get 12.5 people per square kilometer. The correct answer is (D).

The Two-Way Table

A **two-way table** is another way to represent data without actually graphing it. Instead of having the variables represented on the vertical and horizontal axes, the data will be arranged in rows and columns. The top row will give the headings for each column, and the left-most column will give the headings for each row. The numbers in each box indicate the data for the category represented by the row and the column the box is in. This two-way table, for example, shows computer production arranged by days of the week and shift times.

	Morning Shift	Afternoon Shift
Monday	200	375
Tuesday	245	330
Wednesday	255	340
Thursday	250	315
Friday	225	360

Here's How to Read It

If you want to find the number of computers produced on Tuesday morning, you can start in the Morning Shift column and look down until you find the number in the row that says Tuesday, or you can start in the row for Tuesday and look to the right until you find the Morning Shift column. Either way, the result is 245. Some tables will give you totals in the bottom row and/or the right-most column, but sometimes you will need to find the totals yourself by adding up all the numbers in each row or in each column. More complicated tables will have more categories listed in rows and/or columns, or the tables may even contain extraneous information.

Give this one a try.

6 Mark for Review

	Morning Shift	Afternoon Shift
Monday	200	375
Tuesday	245	330
Wednesday	255	340
Thursday	250	315
Friday	225	360

Computer production at a factory occurs during two shifts, as shown in the chart above. If computers are produced only during the morning and afternoon shifts, on which of the following pairs of days is the greatest total number of computers produced?

Ⓐ Monday and Thursday

Ⓑ Tuesday and Thursday

Ⓒ Wednesday and Friday

Ⓓ Tuesday and Friday

Here's How to Crack It

The question asks for the pair of days on which the greatest number of computers was produced. This is a perfect calculator question. Just add the Morning Shift and the Afternoon Shift for each day to see which total is the greatest. Write each day and total on your scratch paper, so you don't have to keep track of it all in your head. Monday is 200 + 375 = 575, Tuesday is 245 + 330 = 575, Wednesday is 255 + 340 = 595, Thursday is 250 + 315 = 565, and Friday is 225 + 360 = 585. According to these calculations, Wednesday and Friday have the two greatest totals, so the greatest number of computers is produced on those two days together. The correct answer is (C).

Figure Facts

Every time you encounter a figure or graphic on the Digital SAT, you should make sure you understand how to read it by checking the following:

- What are the variables for each axis or the headings for the table?
- What units are used for each variable?
- Are there any key pieces of information (numbers, for example) in the legend of the chart that you should note?
- What type of relationship is shown by the data in the chart? For instance, if the chart includes curves that show an upward slope, then the graph shows a **positive association,** while curves that show a downward slope show a **negative association.**
- You can use the edge of your scratch paper as a ruler to help you make sure you are locating the correct data in the graph. The mouse pointer on the screen can also help, as long as you trust yourself to move it in a straight line.

Surveys on the Digital SAT

Some Digital SAT math questions will appear to be about data, but there's no figure and the question has a lot of words about survey results. These questions are usually about a biased sample, meaning that the group doing the survey asked people who are likely to already be in favor of or opposed to the issue, but then drew a conclusion about a larger group. For example, we couldn't survey people who read this book to ask whether they read the final question and take bite-sized pieces and then assume that everyone who takes the Digital SAT does the same thing.

The best way to perform a survey is to ask a random sample rather than asking a group that's probably already picked a side. Questions about surveys might include numbers, and there's a chance that there is a problem with the sample size, meaning the survey asked too few people to get an accurate result. But usually the number is a distraction, so focus on using POE and crossing out answers that don't fit the information given in the question.

Fundamentals Drill

Work these questions using the skills you've learned so far. Be sure to use a calculator when necessary to avoid careless calculation errors. Don't forget, though, that using it may slow you down when doing the math on paper would be faster. Answers and explanations can be found starting on page 386.

1 Mark for Review

If 7 times a number is 84, what is 4 times the number?

Ⓐ 16

Ⓑ 28

Ⓒ 48

Ⓓ 56

2 Mark for Review

If $3x = 12$, what is the value of $\frac{24}{x}$?

Ⓐ $\frac{1}{6}$

Ⓑ $\frac{2}{3}$

Ⓒ 4

Ⓓ 6

3 Mark for Review

Which of the following represents the statement "the sum of the squares of x and y is equal to the square root of the difference of x and y"?

Ⓐ $x^2 + y^2 = \sqrt{x - y}$

Ⓑ $x^2 - y^2 = \sqrt{x + y}$

Ⓒ $(x + y)^2 = \sqrt{x} - \sqrt{y}$

Ⓓ $\sqrt{x + y} = (x - y)^2$

4 Mark for Review

If $a = -2$, then $a + a^2 - a^3 + a^4 - a^5 =$

5 Mark for Review

Which of the following graphs shows a strong positive association between x and y?

Ⓐ
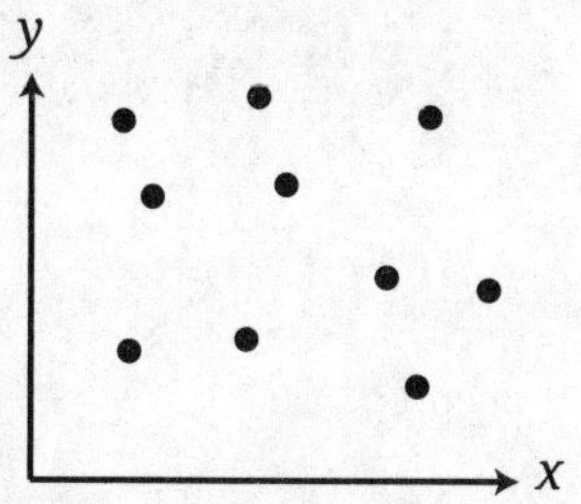

Ⓑ
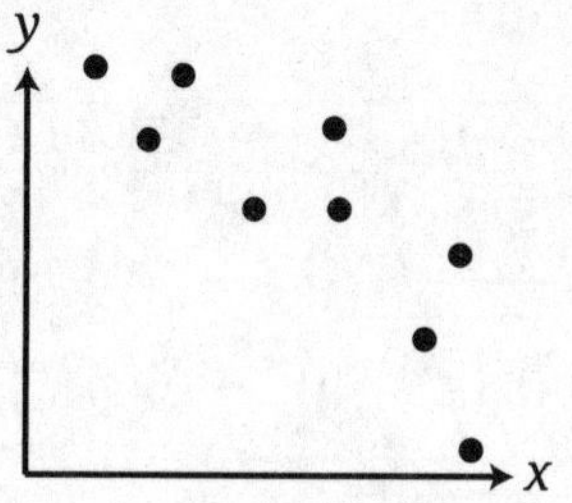

Ⓒ
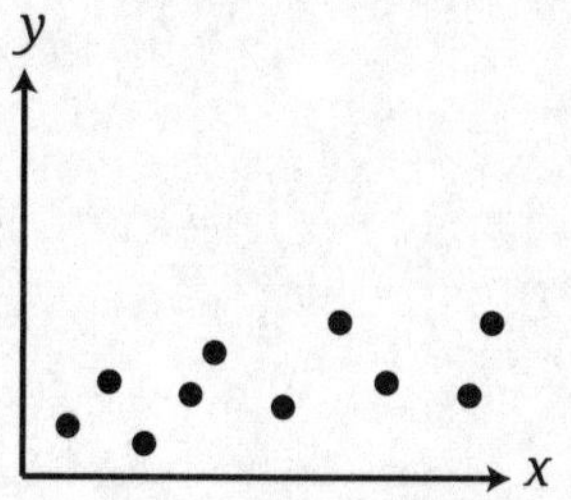

Ⓓ
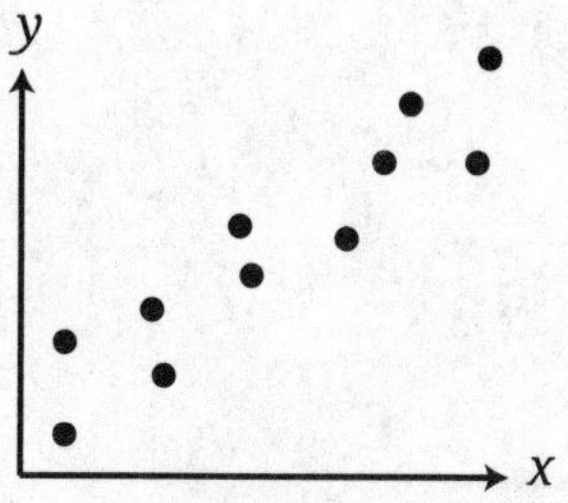

6 Mark for Review

If $9^{-2} = \left(\frac{1}{3}\right)^x$, what is the value of x?

Ⓐ 1

Ⓑ 2

Ⓒ 4

Ⓓ 6

7 Mark for Review

If $\sqrt{x} + 22 = 38$, what is the value of x?

Ⓐ 4

Ⓑ 16

Ⓒ 32

Ⓓ 256

8 Mark for Review

$$\frac{1}{8}+\frac{1}{10}=\frac{a}{b}$$

In the equation above, if a and b are positive integers and $\frac{a}{b}$ is in its simplest reduced form, what is the value of a?

Ⓐ 2

Ⓑ 9

Ⓒ 18

Ⓓ 40

9 Mark for Review

If $4^x \cdot n^2 = 4^{x+1} \cdot n$ and x and n are both positive integers, what is the value of n?

Answers to Chapter Exercises

Exercise 1

1. 109
2. 38
3. –3
4. 10
5. 15

Exercise 2

1. $6(57 + 13) = 6 \times 70 = 420$
2. $51(48 + 50 + 52) = 51(150) = 7{,}650$
3. $ab + ac - ad$
4. $x(y - z)$
5. $c(ab + xy)$

Exercise 3

1. $\frac{25}{3}$
2. $\frac{17}{7}$
3. $\frac{49}{9}$
4. $\frac{5}{2}$
5. $\frac{20}{3}$

Exercise 4

1. 3
2. $\frac{31}{5}$
3. $-\frac{19}{15}$
4. $\frac{1}{15}$
5. $\frac{6}{7}$
6. $\frac{2}{25}$
7. $\frac{4}{9}$

Exercise 5

	Estimated Answer	Calculator Answer
1.	$0.4 \times 0.9 = 0.36$	0.3741
2.	$44 \div 0.03 = 1{,}466$	1,457.7
3.	$3.7 \div 0.02 = 185$	186
4.	$0.7 - 3.6 = -2.9$	–2.89

FUNDAMENTALS DRILL ANSWERS AND EXPLANATIONS

1. **C** The question asks for the value of 4 times an unknown number. Translate the English into math, calling the number *n*, to get $7n = 84$. Divide both sides by 7 to get $n = 12$. Finally, $4n = 4(12) = 48$. The correct answer is (C).

2. **D** The question asks for the value of $\frac{24}{x}$. First, solve for *x*. Divide both sides of the equation by 3, and you get $x = 4$. Then divide 24 by 4, which gives you 6. The correct answer is (D).

3. **A** The question asks for an algebraic expression. Translate the English into math by taking it one phrase at a time. "Sum" means you will add two things. The "squares of *x* and *y*" means to square *x* and square *y*, or x^2 and y^2. Add these to get $x^2 + y^2$. Cross out any choice that does not have $x^2 + y^2$ as the first part of the equation. Eliminate (B), (C), and (D). The correct answer is (A).

4. **58** The question asks for the value of an expression for a certain value of the variable. Plug in the number given for *a* in the expression to find the value: $-2 + (-2)^2 - (-2)^3 + (-2)^4 - (-2)^5$. Remember PEMDAS, the order of operations. The first thing to do here is deal with the **E**xponents, then take care of the **A**ddition and **S**ubtraction: $-2 + 4 - (-8) + 16 - (-32)$, which simplifies to $-2 + 4 + 8 + 16 + 32 = 58$. The correct answer is 58.

5. **D** The question asks for the graph that shows a strong positive association between *x* and *y*. A "strong positive association" means that as one variable increases, the other one increases. This will be shown as a line that angles through the graph from the lower left to the upper right. These scatterplots don't have any lines of best fit drawn on them, so imagine the line that would go through most of the points on each graph. In (A), the points are all over the place, so no line of best fit can even be drawn. Eliminate (A). In (B), the line that hits most of the points would go from the upper left to the lower right. This is a negative association, not a positive one, so eliminate (B). In (C), the line would go straight across, parallel to the *x*-axis. This is not a positive association, so eliminate (C). The correct answer is (D).

6. **C** The question asks for the value of *x* in an equation with exponents. A negative exponent means to take the reciprocal and apply the positive exponent. So $9^{-2} = \left(\frac{1}{9}\right)^2 = \frac{1}{81}$. Now find what power of $\frac{1}{3}$ equals $\frac{1}{81}$. Because $3^4 = 81$, $\left(\frac{1}{3}\right)^4 = \frac{1}{81}$, and *x* must be 4. The correct answer is (C).

7. **D** The question asks for the value of *x*. To solve this equation, get $\sqrt{x}$ by itself by subtracting 22 from both sides. The result is $\sqrt{x} = 16$, so square both sides: $(\sqrt{x})^2 = 16^2$, so $x = 256$. The correct answer is (D).

8. **B** The question asks for the value of a in an equation with fractions. The lowest number that both 8 and 10 are factors of is 40. Convert the fractions to a denominator of 40: $\frac{5}{40} + \frac{4}{40} = \frac{9}{40}$. There is no factor that 9 and 40 have in common, so the fraction cannot be reduced. The number in place of a in $\frac{a}{b}$ is 9. Be careful not to choose (D), which contains the value of b. The correct answer is (B).

9. **4** The question asks for the value of n. First, simplify the equation $4^x \cdot n^2 = 4^{x+1} \cdot n$ by dividing both sides by n to get $4^x \cdot n = 4^{x+1}$, and then try an easy number for x. If $x = 2$, then $4^2 \cdot n = 4^{2+1}$. Since $16n = 4^3$, $16n = 64$ and $n = 4$. The correct answer is 4.

Summary

- There are only six arithmetic operations tested on the Digital SAT: addition, subtraction, multiplication, division, exponents, and square roots.
- These operations must be performed in the proper order (PEMDAS), beginning with operations inside parentheses.
- Apply the Distributive Law whenever possible. This is often enough to find the answer.
- A fraction is just another way of expressing division.
- You must know how to add, subtract, multiply, and divide fractions. Don't forget that you can also use your calculator or the built-in calculator on all questions.
- If any questions involving large or confusing fractions appear, try to reduce the fractions first. Before you multiply two fractions, for example, see if it's possible to reduce either or both of the fractions.
- If you know how to work out fractions on your calculator or the built-in calculator, use it to help you with questions that involve fractions. If you intend to use your calculator for fractions, be sure to practice. You should also know how to work with fractions the old-fashioned way with paper and pencil.
- A decimal is just another way of expressing a fraction.
- Use your calculator or the built-in calculator to add, subtract, multiply, and divide decimals.
- Exponents are a kind of shorthand for expressing numbers that are the product of the same factor multiplied over and over again.
- To multiply two exponential expressions with the same base, add the exponents.
- To divide two exponential expressions with the same base, subtract the exponents.
- To raise one exponential expression to another power, multiply the exponents.

- To remember the exponent rules, think MADSPM.
- When you raise a positive number greater than 1 to a power greater than 1, the result is larger. When you raise a positive fraction less than 1 to an exponent greater than 1, the result is smaller. A negative number raised to an even power becomes positive. A negative number raised to an odd power remains negative.
- When you're asked for the square root of any number, $\sqrt{x}$, you're being asked for the positive root only.
- Here are the only rules regarding square roots that you need to know for the Digital SAT:

$$\sqrt{x} \times \sqrt{y} = \sqrt{xy}$$

$$\sqrt{\frac{x}{y}} = \frac{\sqrt{x}}{\sqrt{y}}$$

- The rule for fractional exponents is this:

$$x^{\frac{y}{z}} = \sqrt[z]{x^y}$$

- The rule for negative exponents is this:

$$x^{-n} = \frac{1}{x^n}$$

- When you encounter questions with charts, carefully check the chart for important information. Remember that you can use your scratch paper or the mouse pointer to help yourself locate the information.

Chapter 21
Algebra: Cracking the System

In the last chapter, we reviewed some fundamental math concepts featured on the Digital SAT. Many questions raise the difficulty by replacing numbers with variables, or letters that stand for unknown quantities. This chapter covers multiple ways to answer algebra questions, while the next chapter provides some ways to turn algebra questions back into arithmetic.

DIGITAL SAT ALGEBRA: CRACKING THE SYSTEM

The Digital SAT generally tests algebra concepts that you most likely learned in eighth or ninth grade. So, you are probably pretty familiar with the level of algebra on the test. However, the test-writers are fairly adept at wording algebra questions in a way that is confusing or distracting in order to make the questions more difficult than the mathematical concepts that are being tested.

In this way, the Digital SAT Math section is not only a test of your math skills, but also, and possibly even more important to your score improvement, your reading skills. It is imperative that you read the questions carefully and translate the words in the question into mathematical symbols.

ENGLISH	MATH EQUIVALENTS
is, are, were, did, does, costs	=
what (or any unknown value)	*any variable* (x, y, n)
more, sum	+
less, difference	–
of, times, product	× (*multiply*)
ratio, quotient, out of, per	÷

A Little Terminology

Here are some words that you will need to know to understand the explanations in this chapter. These words may even show up in the text of a question, so make sure you are familiar with them.

Term: An equation is like a sentence, and a **term** is the equivalent of a word. It can be just a number, just a variable, or a number multiplied by a variable. For example, 18, $-2x$, and $5y$ are the terms in the equation $18 - 2x = 5y$.

Expression: If an equation is like a sentence, then an **expression** is like a phrase or a clause. An expression is a combination of terms and mathematical operations with no equals or inequality sign. For example, $9 \times 2 + 3x$ is an expression.

Polynomial: A **polynomial** is any expression containing two or more terms. Binomials and trinomials are both examples of polynomials. Binomials have two terms, and trinomials have three terms.

FUNDAMENTALS OF DIGITAL SAT ALGEBRA

Many questions on the Digital SAT require you to work with variables and equations. In your math classes, you probably learned to solve equations by "solving for *x*" or "solving for *y*." To do this, you isolate *x* or *y* on one side of the equals sign and put everything else on the other side. The good thing about equations is that to isolate the variable you can do anything you want to them—add, subtract, multiply, divide, square—provided you perform the same operation to both sides of the equation.

Thus, the golden rule of equations:

> Whatever you do to the terms on one side of the equals sign, you must do to the terms on the other side of it as well.

Let's look at a simple example of this rule, without the distraction of answer choices.

Problem: If $2x - 15 = 35$, what is the value of x?

Solution: The question asks for the value of x, so you want to isolate the variable. First, add 15 to each side of the equation. Now you have the following:

$$2x = 50$$

Divide each side of the equation by 2. Thus, x equals 25.

The skills for algebraic manipulation work just as well for more complex equations. The following question is another example of the way the Digital SAT may ask you to manipulate equations. Don't panic when you see a question like this; just use the skills you already have and work carefully so you don't make an avoidable mistake in your algebra.

Find the Math
Word problems on the Digital SAT are full of, well, words. To stay focused on the math, always read the final question, work in bite-sized pieces, and use your scratch paper to write down important information. If there are words that don't help you work the problem—such as the explanation of the variables in this question—ignore them.

1 Mark for Review

The wave velocity of a vibrating string can be determined using the formula $v = \sqrt{\frac{T}{\frac{m}{L}}}$, where T is the tension of the string, m is the mass of the string, and L is the length of the string. Which of the following expresses the length of the string in terms of v, T, and m?

Ⓐ $L = \frac{T}{v^2m}$

Ⓑ $L = \frac{v^2m}{T}$

Ⓒ $L = v\sqrt{\frac{m}{t}}$

Ⓓ $L = \sqrt{\frac{T}{vm}}$

Here's How to Crack It

The question asks for an equation that expresses the length of a string, which is represented by L, so the goal is to get L by itself. Anything you do to one side of the equation, you must also do to the other side of the equation. Start by squaring both sides of the equation to get rid of the square root on the right side.

The equation becomes

$$v^2 = \frac{T}{\frac{m}{L}}$$

Next, multiply both sides by $\frac{m}{L}$ to get the fraction out of the denominator.

$$\frac{v^2m}{L} = T$$

To finish isolating L, multiple both sides by L to get

$$v^2m = TL$$

Now divide both sides by T to get L by itself.

$$\frac{v^2m}{T} = L$$

The correct answer is (B).

SOLVING RADICAL EQUATIONS

Radical equations are just what the name suggests: an equation with a radical ($\sqrt{\ }$) in it. Not to worry, just remember to get rid of the radical first by raising both sides to that power.

Here's an example.

2 Mark for Review

If $7\sqrt{x} - 24 = 11$, what is the value of x?

Ⓐ $\sqrt{5}$

Ⓑ $\sqrt{7}$

Ⓒ 5

Ⓓ 25

Here's How to Crack It

The question asks for the value of x, so start by adding 24 to both sides to get $7\sqrt{x} = 35$. Now, divide both sides by 7 to find that $\sqrt{x} = 5$. Finally, square both sides to find that $x = 25$. The correct answer is (D).

SOLVING RATIONAL EQUATIONS

The built-in calculator or a calculator you bring with you can help on a lot of algebra questions. However, there are times when you will need to solve an equation algebraically by hand. Even when the calculator might help, you may find it more efficient to use your mathematical skills to answer a question. When a question asks you to solve for an expression, algebraic manipulation will often be the best way to answer the question.

Here's an example.

3 Mark for Review

If $\frac{18}{r+10} = \frac{3}{r}$, what is the value of $\frac{r}{3}$?

Ⓐ $\frac{2}{3}$

Ⓑ $\frac{3}{2}$

Ⓒ 2

Ⓓ 3

Here's How to Crack It

The question asks for the value of $\frac{r}{3}$. Cross-multiply to get $18r = 3(r + 10)$ or $18r = 3r + 30$. Subtracting $3r$ from both sides gives you $15r = 30$, so $r = 2$. Finally, $\frac{r}{3} = \frac{2}{3}$. The correct answer is (A).

Extraneous Solutions

Sometimes solving an equation with a rational or radical expression makes funny things happen. Look at the following example.

4 Mark for Review

$$\sqrt{t + 4} = t - 2$$

Which of the following contains all possible solutions to the equation above?

Ⓐ 0, 5

Ⓑ 0, 4, 5

Ⓒ 0

Ⓓ 5

Extra Answers
Any time you are solving for a variable, make sure your solutions actually work. If they do not, they are *extraneous*, or extra.

Here's How to Crack It

The question asks for the solution set to the equation, so solve it for *t*. Start by squaring both sides of the equation to get rid of the radical. The equation becomes

$$t + 4 = (t - 2)^2$$

Use FOIL (First, Outer, Inner, Last) to multiply the right side of the equation to get $t^2 - 2t - 2t + 4$ or $t^2 - 4t + 4$. Now the equation is

$$t + 4 = t^2 - 4t + 4$$

FOIL:
First
Outer
Inner
Last

Subtract *t* and 4 from both sides to get

$$0 = t^2 - 5t$$

The right side factors to $t(t - 5)$, so $t = 0$ or 5. Eliminate (B), since 4 is not a solution at all, extraneous or otherwise. Now plug 0 and 5 back into the original equation to see if they work. If both do, the answer is (A). If one of them does not, that one is an extraneous solution.

$\underline{t = 0}$	$\underline{t = 5}$
$\sqrt{0+4} = 0-2$	$\sqrt{5+4} = 5-2$
$\sqrt{4} = -2$	$\sqrt{9} = 3$
$2 \neq -2$	$3 = 3$

Since the equation is false when $t = 0$, eliminate (A) and (C). The correct answer is (D).

SOLVING FOR EXPRESSIONS

Some algebra questions on the Digital SAT ask you to find the value of an expression rather than the value of a variable. In most cases, you can find the value of the expression without finding the value of the variable.

5 Mark for Review

If $4x + 2 = 4$, what is the value $4x - 6$?

Ⓐ −6

Ⓑ −4

Ⓒ 4

Ⓓ 8

Here's How to Crack It

The question asks for the value of an expression. This is where reading the final question (RTFQ) can save time. Since the question doesn't ask for the value of x, there may be a shortcut. The term $4x$ is in both expressions, so instead of solving for x, you can solve for $4x$. Subtract 2 from both sides of $4x + 2 = 4$ to get $4x = 2$. Now, plug $4x = 2$ into $4x - 6$ to get $(2) - 6 = -4$. The correct answer is (B).

This approach will save you time—provided that you see it quickly. So, while you practice, you should train yourself to look for these sorts of direct solutions whenever you are asked to solve for the value of an expression.

Here's another example.

6 Mark for Review

If $\sqrt{5} = x - 2$, what is the value of $(x-2)^2$?

Ⓐ $\sqrt{5}$

Ⓑ $\sqrt{7}$

Ⓒ 5

Ⓓ 25

Here's How to Crack It

The question asks for the value of an expression. If you were to attempt the math class way, you'd find that $x = \sqrt{5} + 2$ and then you would have to substitute that into the provided expression. There's got to be an easier way!

The question is much easier if you read the final question and look for a direct solution. Then, you notice that all the question wants you to do is to square the expression on the right of the equals sign. Well, if you square the expression on the right, then you'd better square the expression on the left too. Therefore, $(\sqrt{5})^2 = 5 = (x-2)^2$, and the correct answer is (C). That was pretty painless by comparison.

SOLVING SYSTEMS OF EQUATIONS

Some Digital SAT questions will give you two or more equations involving two or more variables and ask for the value of an expression or one of the variables. These questions are very similar to the questions containing one variable. The test-writers would like you to spend extra time trying to solve for the value of each variable, but that is not always necessary.

Here's an example of this type of question as a fill-in. We'll look at fill-ins in more detail in Chapter 26.

Watch Us Crack It
Check out the Video Walk-throughs in your online Student Tools to watch a Princeton Review teacher work through this question step-by-step.

7 Mark for Review

If $4x + y = 14$ and $3x + 2y = 13$, what is the value of $x - y =$?

Here's How to Crack It

The question asks for the value of an expression. You've been given two equations here. But read the final question: instead of being asked to solve for a variable (x or y), you've been asked to solve for $x - y$. Why? Because there must be a direct solution.

Rather than solving for one variable and then substituting it to solve for the other variable, see if there's a faster way. Try stacking the two equations on top of each other and then adding or subtracting the two equations. There's a good chance that this shortcut will take you right to the answer. Let's try it.

Adding the two equations gives you this:

$$\begin{array}{r} 4x + y = 14 \\ +\ 3x + 2y = 13 \\ \hline 7x + 3y = 27 \end{array}$$

Unfortunately, that doesn't get you anywhere, so try subtracting:

$$\begin{array}{r} 4x + y = 14 \\ -(3x + 2y = 13) \end{array}$$

When you subtract equations, just change the signs of the second equation and add. So the equation above becomes

$$\begin{array}{r} 4x + y = 14 \\ +(-3x - 2y = -13) \\ \hline x - y = 1 \end{array}$$

The value of $(x - y)$ is precisely what you are looking for. The correct answer is 1.

Solving for Variables in Systems of Equations

Shortcuts are awesome, so take them whenever you can on the Digital SAT. But occasionally, you won't have the option of using a shortcut with a system of equations, so knowing how to solve for a variable is crucial.

Here's an example.

8 Mark for Review

If $3x + 2y = 17$ and $5x - 4y = 21$, what is the value of y?

Here's How to Crack It

The question asks for the value of y. Look for the most direct way to get there. In this case, the stack and solve method doesn't give you an immediate answer:

IF YOU ADD:	IF YOU SUBTRACT:
$3x + 2y = 17$	$3x + 2y = 17$
$+ \underline{5x - 4y = 21}$	$+ \underline{(-5x + 4y = -21)}$
$8x - 2y = 38$	$-2x + 6y = -4$

Neither of these methods gives you the value of y. The best way to approach this question is to try to eliminate one variable. To do this, multiply one or both of the equations by a number that will cause the other variable to have a coefficient of 0 when the equations are added or subtracted.

Since the question is asking you to solve for y, try to make the x terms disappear. You want to make the coefficient of x zero so you can quickly find the value of y.

Use the coefficient of x in the second equation, 5, to multiply the first equation:

$$5(3x + 2y) = 5(17)$$
$$15x + 10y = 85$$

Then use the original coefficient of x in the first equation to multiply the second equation:

$$3(5x - 4y) = 3(21)$$
$$15x - 12y = 63$$

Now stack your equations and subtract (or flip the signs and add, which is less likely to lead to a mistake).

$$\begin{array}{r} 15x + 10y = \ \ 85 \\ \underline{+\ (-15x + 12y = -63)} \\ 0x \ + 22y = \ \ 22 \end{array}$$

Simplify your equation and you have your answer.

$$22y = 22$$
$$y = 1$$

Number of Solutions to a System of Equations

Some Digital SAT Math questions won't even ask you to solve for the solution(s) to a system of equations: they'll simply ask you how many solutions there are. A solution to a system is a point of intersection when the system is graphed, so the graphing calculator can help on these. If you know the rules of when two linear equations have zero, one, or infinitely many solutions, you can use that knowledge and a little algebra to answer the question.

Here's an example that can be solved algebraically or with a calculator.

9 Mark for Review

Which of the following systems of equations has an infinite number of solutions?

Ⓐ $x = -5$
$y = 10$

Ⓑ $x = 10y$
$y = 10x$

Ⓒ $y = -4x - 10$
$y = -4x - 15$

Ⓓ $y = \frac{1}{2}x + 5$
$4y = 2x + 20$

Here's How to Crack It

The question asks which system of equations has infinitely many solutions. A system of linear equations has infinitely many solutions when the two equations are identical. That means both equations represent the same line, so there are infinitely many points of intersection. The two equations in (A) do not represent the same line, so eliminate (A). The equations in (B) look similar, but rearrange them to check. Plug $y = 10x$ into the first equation to get $x = 10(10x)$, which becomes $x = 100x$. The only possible value of x is 0. Do the same thing with the second equation: substitute $x = 10y$ to get $y = 10(10y)$, which becomes $y = 100y$. The only possible value of y is 0. Thus, the two lines intersect only once, at (0, 0), not infinitely many times. Eliminate (B). The equations in (C) have the same y-term and the same x-term, but different constants. This means the lines defined by the equations are parallel and have zero solutions. Eliminate (C). The equations in (D) don't look the same, but do a little algebra to make them look similar. Make the y-terms the same by multiplying the first equation by 4 to get $4y = 2x + 20$. It's the same equation! That means the two equations describe the same line, and the system has infinitely many solutions.

The other way to answer a question like this is to use a graphing calculator. To use the built-in calculator, test one answer at a time by entering each equation in an entry field and looking in the graphing area to see what the graphs look like. Graphing the equations in (A) shows two perpendicular lines that intersect once; eliminate (A). Graphing the equations in (B) shows two lines that intersect once at the origin; eliminate (B). Graphing the equations in (C) shows two parallel lines that never intersect; eliminate (C). Graphing the equations in (D) shows only one line. Click the equations one after another to see the line change color. This confirms that the exact same line was graphed twice, so the two equations have infinitely many solutions.

Using either algebra or the calculator, the correct answer is (D).

SOLVING INEQUALITIES

In an equation, one side equals the other. In an **inequality,** one side does not equal the other. The following symbols are used in inequalities:

SYMBOL	MEANING
$>$	is greater than
$<$	is less than
$\geq$	is greater than or equal to; at least
$\leq$	is less than or equal to; no more than

Hungry Gator
Think of the inequality sign as the mouth of a hungry alligator. The alligator eats the bigger number.

Solving inequalities is pretty similar to solving equations. You can collect like terms, and you can simplify by performing the same operation to both sides. All you have to remember is that if you multiply or divide both sides of an inequality by a negative number, the direction of the inequality symbol changes.

For example, here's a simple inequality:

$$x > y$$

Now, just as you can with an equation, you can multiply both sides of this inequality by the same number. But if the number you multiply by is negative, you have to change the direction of the symbol in the result. For example, if you multiply both sides of the inequality above by –2, you end up with the following:

$$-2x < -2y$$

When you multiply or divide an inequality by a negative number, you must reverse the inequality sign.

Here's an example of how an inequality question may be framed on the test.

10 Mark for Review

If $-3x + 6 \geq 18$, which of the following must be true?

(A) $x \leq -4$

(B) $x \leq 8$

(C) $x \geq -4$

(D) $x \geq -8$

Here's How to Crack It

The question asks for a true statement based on the inequality, and the answers are all possible values of x. Isolate the x by simplifying the inequality as you would with any equation:

$$-3x + 6 \geq 18$$
$$-3x \geq 12$$

Remember to change the direction of the inequality sign!

$$x \leq -4$$

The correct answer is (A).

WRITING YOUR OWN EQUATIONS

Sometimes you'll be asked to take a word problem and create one or more equations or inequalities from that information. In general, you will not be asked to solve these equations/inequalities, so if you are able to locate and translate the information in the question, you have a good shot at getting the correct answer. Always start with the most straightforward piece of information. What is the most straightforward piece of information? Well, that's up to you to decide. Consider the following question.

11 Mark for Review

Max uses a humidifier in his son's bedroom. The humidifier must be filled with 0.5 gallons of water before it starts running, and it has to be refilled with 0.07 gallons of water each week. Which of the following equations models the total gallons of water, g, needed to run the humidifier for w weeks?

Ⓐ $g = 0.07 + 0.5w$

Ⓑ $g = 0.07(0.5 + w)$

Ⓒ $g = 0.5(0.07 + w)$

Ⓓ $g = 0.5 + 0.07w$

When to translate

Start translating words into math in bite-sized pieces when you see the following:

- The question asks what "models" or "represents" a situation.
- The answers contain one or more equations or inequalities.

Here's How to Crack It

The question asks for an equation that models a situation. Find a straightforward piece of information, translate it into math, and eliminate answers that don't match. One piece of information is that the *humidifier must be filled with 0.5 gallons of water before it starts running.* If 0.5 is the starting value and not something that is added every week, it should not be multiplied by anything. Only (D) has 0.5 by itself, so it's the right answer.

What if you started with a different piece of information? The other piece of information is that the humidifier *has to be refilled with 0.07 gallons of water each week.* The question also states that w represents weeks. The number of gallons added each week must be multiplied by the number of weeks, which translates to $0.07w$. Eliminate (A) and (C) because they do not include this term, even after distributing. Although (B) includes the term $0.07w$ after you distribute, the other term becomes 0.035. This does not match any of the information in the question, so eliminate (B). Only (D) is left.

It doesn't matter which piece of information you start with. Just be sure to eliminate after each piece. In this case, either piece alone was enough to eliminate 3 answers, so the remaining answer is right. The correct answer is (D).

Sometimes you will need more than one bite-sized piece in order to eliminate all but one answer. This will often happen when the answers have systems of equations or inequalities rather than a single equation or inequality.

Here's one of those.

12 Mark for Review

A tailor is ordering red and blue ribbon to use when creating a set of dresses. The tailor wants to include at least 200 meters of ribbon in her order, and she will order no more than 3 times as much blue ribbon as red ribbon. Each spool of red ribbon contains 22.86 meters, and each spool of blue ribbon contains 18.29 meters. If r and b are nonnegative integers and represent the number of spools of red and blue ribbon, respectively, that the tailor will order, which of the inequalities below best represents this scenario?

Ⓐ $22.86r + 18.29b \geq 200$
$3b \leq r$

Ⓑ $22.86r + 54.87b \geq 200$
$3b \leq r$

Ⓒ $22.86r + 18.29b \geq 200$
$b \leq 3r$

Ⓓ $22.86r + 54.87b \geq 200$
$b \leq 3r$

Here's How to Crack It

The question asks for a system of inequalities that describes the situation. Start with the most straightforward piece of information and translate it into math. In this case, the most straightforward information is about the total meters of ribbon, 200 meters. However, all of the answers include ≥ 200, so look for something else. The answers also all include $22.86r$ for the red ribbon, so work with the blue ribbon. The question states that *each spool of blue ribbon contains 18.29 meters* and that b represents the number of spools of blue ribbon. Therefore, the equation should include $18.29b$. Eliminate (B) and (D) because they have the wrong number multiplied by b.

Next, look at the relationship between the blue and red ribbon. The question states that *she will order no more than 3 times as much blue ribbon as red ribbon.* The phrase *no more than* is indicated by the symbol $\leq$, and the amount of blue ribbon is being compared to 3 times the amount of red ribbon. The correct inequality to depict this information is $b \leq 3r$. Eliminate (A). The correct answer is (C).

SIMPLIFYING EXPRESSIONS

If a question contains an expression that can be factored, it is very likely that you will need to factor it to solve the question. So, you should always be on the lookout for opportunities to factor. For example, if a question contains the expression $2x + 2y$, you should see if factoring it to produce the expression $2(x + y)$ will help you to solve the problem.

If a question contains an expression that is already factored, you should consider using the Distributive Law to expand it. For example, if a question contains the expression $2(x + y)$, you should see if expanding it to $2x + 2y$ will help.

Something to Hide
Because factoring or expanding is usually the key to finding the answer on such questions, learn to recognize expressions that could be either factored or expanded. This will earn you more points. The test-writers will try to hide the answer by factoring or expanding the result.

Here are five examples that we've worked out:

1. $4x + 24 = 4(x) + 4(6) = 4(x + 6)$

2. $\frac{10x-60}{2} = \frac{10(x)-10(6)}{2} = \frac{10(x-6)}{2} = 5(x-6) = 5x-30$

3. $\frac{x+y}{y} = \frac{x}{y} + \frac{y}{y} = \frac{x}{y} + 1$

4. $2(x + y) + 3(x + y) = (2 + 3)(x + y) = 5(x + y)$

5. $p(r + s) + q(r + s) = (p + q)(r + s)$

Here's how this might be tested on the Digital SAT.

13 Mark for Review

Which of the following is equivalent to $\frac{a^2}{b} + a$?

Ⓐ $a\left(\frac{a}{b}+1\right)$

Ⓑ $a\left(\frac{a}{b}+a\right)$

Ⓒ $a^2 + ab$

Ⓓ $a^2\left(\frac{1}{b}+1\right)$

Here's How to Crack It

The question asks for an equivalent form of an expression. Two of the answers have a factored, so try factoring a first. Rewrite each term as a times something else:

$$a\left(\frac{a}{b}\right) + a(1)$$

Then factor a out of both terms:

$$a\left(\frac{a}{b} + 1\right)$$

This matches (A), which is the correct answer. You can check by distributing a in (A) to confirm that it returns the expression to its original form.

Don't be tempted by (C). It looks plausible because both terms from the original expression have been multiplied by b. However, you cannot multiply an expression by a value other than 1. That only works with equations because then you multiply both sides by the same value. Choice (C) is a trap answer based on not remembering the difference between an expression and an equation. The correct answer is (A).

Multiplying Binomials

Multiplying binomials is easy. Just be sure to use **FOIL** (First, Outer, Inner, Last).

$$(x + 2)(x + 4) = (x + 2)(x + 4)$$

$$= (x \times x) + (x \times 4) + (2 \times x) + (2 \times 4)$$

FIRST OUTER INNER LAST

$$= x^2 + 4x + 2x + 8$$

$$= x^2 + 6x + 8$$

Combine Like Terms First

When manipulating long, complicated algebraic expressions, combine all like terms before doing anything else. In other words, if one of the terms is $5x$ and another is $-3x$, simply combine them into $2x$. Then you won't have as many terms to work with. Here's an example:

$$(3x^2 + 3x + 4) + (2 - x) - (6 + 2x) =$$
$$3x^2 + 3x + 4 + 2 - x - 6 - 2x =$$
$$3x^2 + (3x - x - 2x) + (4 + 2 - 6) =$$
$$3x^2$$

TERMinology

Remember: A **term** is a number, variable, or a number *and* variable that are combined by multiplication or division. Consider the expression $6x + 10 - y$. In this expression, $6x$, 10, and y are all terms. $6x + 10$, however, is not a term. It is two terms added together, which makes it an *expression.*

SOLVING QUADRATIC EQUATIONS

To solve quadratic equations, remember everything you've learned so far: look for direct solutions and either factor or expand when possible.

Here's an example.

14 Mark for Review

If $(x - 3)^2 = (x + 2)^2$, what is the value of x?

Here's How to Crack It

The question asks for the value of x. Expand both sides of the equation using FOIL:

$$(x - 3)(x - 3) = (x + 2)(x + 2)$$
$$x^2 - 6x + 9 = x^2 + 4x + 4$$

Now you can simplify. Eliminate the x^2 terms because they are on both sides of the equals sign. Now you have $-6x + 9 = 4x + 4$, which simplifies to

$$-10x = -5$$
$$x = \frac{1}{2}$$

Factoring Quadratics

To solve a quadratic, you might also have to factor the equation. Factoring a quadratic basically involves doing a reverse form of FOIL.

For example, suppose you needed to know the factors of $x^2 + 7x + 12$. Here's what you would do:

1. Write down 2 sets of parentheses and put an x in each one because the product of the first terms is x^2.

$$x^2 + 7x + 12 = (x \quad)(x \quad)$$

2. Look at the number at the end of the expression you are trying to factor. Write down its factors. In this case, the factors of 12 are 1 and 12, 2 and 6, and 3 and 4.

3. To determine which set of factors to put into the parentheses, look at the coefficient of the middle term of the quadratic expression. In this case, the coefficient is 7. So, the correct factors will also either add or subtract to get 7. The only factors that work are 3 and 4. Write these factors in the parentheses.

$$x^2 + 7x + 12 = (x \_\_ 3)(x \_\_ 4)$$

Factoring
When factoring an equation like $x^2 + bx + c$, think "**A.M.**" Find two numbers that **A**dd up to the middle term (b) and **M**ultiply to give the last term (c).

4. Finally, determine the signs for the factors. To get a positive 12, the 3 and the 4 are either both positive or both negative. But, since 7 is also positive, the signs must both be positive.

$$x^2 + 7x + 12 = (x + 3)(x + 4)$$

You can always check that you have factored correctly by using FOIL on the factors to see if you get the original quadratic expression.

To find the solutions on paper, you would set each factor equal to zero and solve for x. This becomes $x + 3 = 0$ and $x + 4 = 0$, so $x = -3$ or -4.

The built-in graphing calculator or your own calculator can also quickly provide the solutions to a quadratic. We'll show you how to do it on the built-in calculator. If you're planning to use your own, make sure you know how to do this.

Open the built-in calculator, then enter the quadratic into the first entry field. Let's use the same one as above and enter $x^2 + 7x + 12$.

The graph shows three grey dots. One is the vertex, and the other two are the solutions, or x-intercepts. Hover over or click on one of the x-intercept dots to see the x-value for that point, and write it down. You can scroll and zoom to make it easier to see. Do the same for the other x-intercept dot.

The calculator will look like this on the screen:

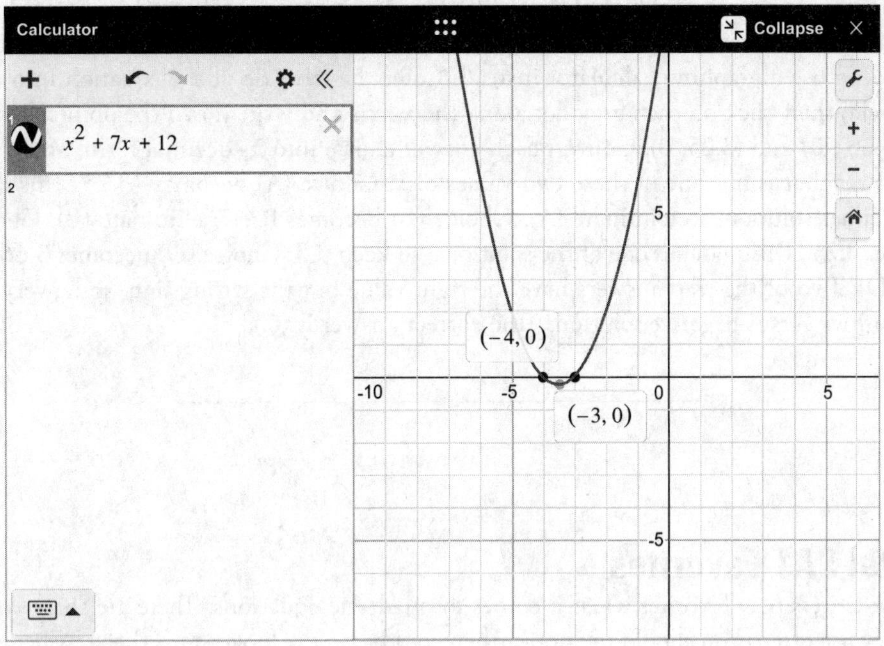

The two points are (–4, 0) and (–3, 0), so the solutions to the quadratic are $x = -4$ and $x = -3$.

It's best to enter only the expression and *not* include "= 0" when you enter a quadratic in the built-in graphing calculator. Try entering $x^2 + 7x + 12 = 0$, and the resulting graph is two parallel lines at $x = -4$ and $x = -3$. This still shows the solutions, but it isn't as easy to interpret as the graph of the parabola.

Try a Digital SAT question that is much easier to solve using a graphing calculator.

15 Mark for Review

For the equation $12x^2 + 5x - 143 = 0$, what is one possible value of x?

Ⓐ $-\frac{13}{4}$

Ⓑ $\frac{5}{12}$

Ⓒ $\frac{13}{4}$

Ⓓ $\frac{11}{3}$

Here's How to Crack It

The question asks for a possible value of x in a quadratic equation. The values of x are also the solutions to the equation. This quadratic would not be fun to factor, even with the quadratic formula, so use a graphing calculator instead. Enter the left side of the equation into the first entry field, then click on each gray dot along the x-axis and write down the points. The points are (–3.667, 0) and (3.25, 0). Convert each answer choice into its decimal form, and eliminate any answer that is not one of these two values of x. Choice (A) becomes –3.25. This does not match either solution, so eliminate (A). Choice (B) becomes 0.417; eliminate (B). Choice (C) becomes 3.25. This matches one of the solutions, so keep (C). Choice (D) becomes 3.667; eliminate (D). Two of the trap answers have the right value but the wrong sign, so be very careful with positive versus negative solutions. The correct answer is (C).

Digital SAT Favorites

The test-writers play favorites when it comes to quadratic equations. There are three equations that they use often. You should memorize these and be on the lookout for them. Whenever you see a quadratic that contains two variables, it is frequently one of these three.

$$(x + y)(x - y) = x^2 - y^2$$

$$(x + y)^2 = x^2 + 2xy + y^2$$

$$(x - y)^2 = x^2 - 2xy + y^2$$

Here's an example of how these equations will likely be tested on the Digital SAT.

16 Mark for Review

If $2x - 3y = 5$, what is the value of $4x^2 - 12xy + 9y^2$?

Ⓐ $\sqrt{5}$

Ⓑ 12

Ⓒ 25

Ⓓ 100

Here's How to Crack It

The question asks for the value of an expression. Since the expression seems kind of random, see if there is a way to get from the given equation to the expression.

In this case, work with $2x - 3y = 5$. If you square the left side of the equation, you get

$$(2x - 3y)^2 = 4x^2 - 12xy + 9y^2$$

That's precisely the expression for which you need to find the value. It's also the third of the equations from the box on the preceding page. Now, since you squared the left side, all you need to do is square the 5 on the right side of the equation to discover that the expression equals 25. The correct answer is (C).

Did you notice that this question was just another version of being asked to solve for the value of an expression rather than for a variable? Quadratics are one of the test-writers' favorite ways to do that.

Solving Quadratics Set to Zero

Before factoring most quadratics, you need to set the equation equal to zero. Why? Well, if $ab = 0$, what do you know about a and b? At least one of them must equal 0, right? That's the key fact you need in order to solve most quadratics.

Here's an example.

17 Mark for Review

If $3 - \frac{3}{x} = x + 7$, and $x \neq 0$, which of the following is a possible value for x?

(A) −7

(B) −1

(C) 1

(D) 3

Here's How to Crack It

The question asks for a possible value of x. Here, the test-writers have tried to hide that the equation is actually a quadratic. Start by multiplying both sides of the equation by x to get rid of the fraction.

$$x\left(3-\frac{3}{x}\right)=x(x+7)$$

$$3x - 3 = x^2 + 7x$$

Rearrange the terms to set the quadratic equal to 0. You'll get $x^2 + 4x + 3 = 0$. Now it's time to factor:

$$x^2 + 4x + 3 = (x + 1)(x + 3) = 0$$

At least one of the factors must equal 0. If $x + 1 = 0$, then $x = -1$. If $x + 3 = 0$, then $x = -3$. Only one of these values appears in the answer choices. The correct answer is (B).

The Quadratic Formula

In addition to asking you to solve easily factorable quadratics, the test-writers would also like to see you demonstrate your understanding of the quadratic formula. We know what you're thinking: "Not that thing *again!* Can't I just solve it with a graphing calculator?" Why yes, yes you can. However, once in a while there's a question that requires knowledge of the quadratic formula. Let's review it so you're prepared.

For a quadratic equation in the form $y = ax^2 + bx + c$, the quadratic formula is

$$x=\frac{-b\pm\sqrt{b^2-4ac}}{2a}$$

To find the roots of a quadratic, or the points where $y = 0$, simply plug your values for a, b, and c into the quadratic formula.

Here's an example:

$$7x^2 - 5x - 17 = 0$$

So $a = 7$, $b = -5$, and $c = -17$. Plugging the constants into the quadratic equation, you get

$$x = \frac{5 \pm \sqrt{(-5)^2 - 4(7)(-17)}}{2(7)}$$

$$x = \frac{5 \pm \sqrt{25 + 476}}{14}$$

$$x = \frac{5 \pm \sqrt{501}}{14}$$

$$x = \frac{5}{14} + \frac{\sqrt{501}}{14} \text{ and } x = \frac{5}{14} - \frac{\sqrt{501}}{14}$$

The Signs, They Are a Changin'
The quadratic formula works for quadratics in the form $y = ax^2 + bx + c$. There is only addition in that form, so be careful when your quadratic has negative signs in it.

Let's put your quadratic skills to work with a question you may see on the Digital SAT.

18 Mark for Review

What is the product of all the solutions to the equation $3z^2 - 12z + 6 = 0$?

Ⓐ $\sqrt{2}$

Ⓑ 2

Ⓒ 4

Ⓓ $4\sqrt{2}$

Here's How to Crack It

The question asks for the product of the solutions to a quadratic. The radicals in the answer choices are a clue that the quadratic may be hard to factor. Simplify the equation first by dividing both sides by 3 to get

$$z^2 - 4z + 2 = 0$$

To find the solutions using the quadratic formula $x = \frac{-b \pm \sqrt{b^2 - 4ac}}{2a}$, you would do the following:

Call on the calculator

Don't forget that a graphing calculator is a fast way to find the solutions to a quadratic. To answer this question using the built-in graphing calculator, enter the left side of the quadratic, find the values of the two *x*-intercepts, and multiply them.

$$x = \frac{-(-4) \pm \sqrt{(-4)^2 - 4(1)(2)}}{2(1)}$$

$$x = \frac{4 \pm \sqrt{16 - 8}}{2} = \frac{4 \pm \sqrt{8}}{2}$$

$$x = \frac{4 \pm \sqrt{4 \times 2}}{2} = \frac{4 \pm 2\sqrt{2}}{2}$$

$$x = 2 \pm \sqrt{2}$$

So $x = 2 + \sqrt{2}$ *or* $2 - \sqrt{2}$. "Product" means to multiply, so use FOIL to multiply $\left(2 + \sqrt{2}\right) \times \left(2 - \sqrt{2}\right)$ to get $4 - 2\sqrt{2} + 2\sqrt{2} - \left(\sqrt{2}\right)^2 = 4 - 2 = 2$. The correct answer is (B).

The Root of the Problems

Sometimes you'll be asked to solve for the sum or the product of the roots of a quadratic equation. You can use the quadratic formula and then add or multiply the results, but it's quicker to just memorize these two expressions.

sum of the roots: $-\frac{b}{a}$ product of the roots: $\frac{c}{a}$

Wow, that was a lot of work! Wouldn't it be great if there were a shortcut? Actually, there is! When a quadratic is in the form $y = ax^2 + bx + c$, the product of the roots is equal to the value of c divided by the value of a. In this case, that's $6 \div 3 = 2$! It's the same answer for a lot less work. (See the inset "The Root of the Problems" for this and another handy trick—they're worth memorizing.)

Number of Solutions to a Quadratic Equation

There is one more useful thing that can be determined from just a piece of the quadratic formula. The part under the root symbol in the formula is called the *discriminant*. The value of the discriminant can tell you the number of roots the quadratic has.

The discriminant, D, of a quadratic in the standard form $ax^2 + bx + c = 0$ is $b^2 - 4ac$.

- If the discriminant is positive, the quadratic has 2 real solutions.
- If the discriminant equals 0, the quadratic has 1 real solution.
- If the discriminant is negative, the quadratic has no real solutions.

You saw earlier in this chapter how a question might ask about the number of solutions to a system of linear equations. When you see a similar question about a single quadratic, see if you can graph it or use the discriminant.

Take a look at a typical question.

19 Mark for Review

If the equation $12x = k - 4x^2$ has exactly one real solution, what is the value of the constant k?

Watch Us Crack It
Check out the Video Walk-throughs in your online Student Tools to watch a Princeton Review teacher work through this question step-by-step.

Here's How to Crack It

The question asks for the value of a constant in a quadratic equation. When a quadratic has exactly one real solution, the discriminant equals 0. First, put the quadratic in standard form, which is $ax^2 + bx + c$. Add $4x^2$ to both sides of the equation to get $4x^2 + 12x = k$, and then subtract k from both sides of the equation to get $4x^2 + 12x - k = 0$. Now that the quadratic is in standard form, $a = 4$, $b = 12$, and $c = -k$. Plug the values for a, b, and c into the discriminant, $D = b^2 - 4ac$, and set it equal to 0 to get $12^2 - (4)(4)(-k) = 0$. Simplify the left side of the equation to get $144 + 16k = 0$. Subtract $16k$ from both sides of the equation to get $144 = -16k$. Divide both sides of the equation by -16 to get $-9 = k$. The correct answer is -9.

GROWTH AND DECAY

There's one more equation with an exponent that's tested frequently on the Digital SAT: the **growth and decay** formula. Real-world examples include population growth, radioactive decay, and compound interest, to name a few. The growth or decay can be a percent or a multiple, which changes what's inside the parentheses.

When the growth or decay rate is a percent of the total population:

$$\textit{final amount} = \textit{original amount}\ (1 \pm \textit{rate})^{\textit{number of changes}}$$

When the growth or decay is a multiple of the total population:

$$\textit{final amount} = \textit{original amount}\ (\textit{multiplier})^{\textit{number of changes}}$$

Let's see how this formula can make quick work of an otherwise tedious question.

20 Mark for Review

Becca deposits $100 into a bank account that earns an annual interest rate of 4%. If she does not make any additional deposits and makes no withdrawals, how long will it take her, in years, to increase the value of her account by at least 60%?

(A) 12

(B) 15

(C) 25

(D) 30

Here's How to Crack It

The question asks for the number of years it will take for Becca's account to reach a certain value. You could add 4% to the account over and over again until you get to the desired amount, but that would take a long time. Knowing the formula will make it a lot easier. First, set up the equation with the things you know. The original amount is 100, and the rate is 4%, or 0.04.

The account is increasing, so you add the rate, and you can put in "years" for the number of changes. The formula becomes

$$final\ amount = 100(1 + 0.04)^{years}$$

Now you need to figure out what you want the final amount to be. Translate the English to math: the value of her account (100) will increase (+) by 60 percent (0.6) of the current value (×100). This becomes 100 + (0.6)(100) = 100 + 60 = 160. Now the formula is

$$160 = 100(1.04)^{years}$$

The answer choices represent the number of years Becca keeps her money in the account. Now you are all set to easily plug in the answers. Start with (B), so *years* = 15. Is $100(1.04)^{15}$ = 160? Use your calculator to check, making sure to follow PEMDAS rules and do the exponent before you multiply by 100. The result is \$180.09. That is a bit too much money, so the answer will likely be (A), but let's just check it. $100(1.04)^{12}$ = \$160.10, which is at least \$160. The correct answer is (A).

Here's an example of growth with a multiplier instead of a rate.

21 Mark for Review

An invasive species was discovered to have a population of 2,100 individuals after 10 years of uninhibited growth. The equation $P = G(3)^{\frac{t}{10}}$ gives the number of individuals in the population, where t is the number of years after the uninhibited growth began, P is the current number of individuals in the population, and G is the number of individuals in the population when the uninhibited growth began. What is the value of G?

Ⓐ 30

Ⓑ 700

Ⓒ 2,100

Ⓓ 6,300

Here's How to Crack It

The question asks for a value in an equation. The equation is in the form of the growth and decay formula, and recognizing that leads to the next step. Label each piece of the formula and fill in the number given for each piece. The question states that P *is the current number of individuals in the population*, and that the invasive species had *a population of 2,100 individuals*, so $P = 2{,}100$. The question also states that 2,100 was the final amount *after 10 years of uninhibited growth*, and that *t is the number of years after the uninhibited growth began*, so $t = 10$. Plug those values into the formula and solve for G: $2{,}100 = G(3)^{\frac{10}{10}}$. Simplify the right side of the equation to get $2{,}100 = G(3)^1$, and then $2{,}100 = 3G$. Divide both sides of the equation by 3 to get $700 = G$. The correct answer is (B).

WHEN VALUES ARE ABSOLUTE

Absolute value is a measure of the distance between a number and 0. Since distances are always positive, the absolute value of a number is also always positive. The absolute value of a number is written as $|x|$.

When solving for the value of a variable inside the absolute value bars, it is important to remember that the variable could be either positive or negative. For example, if $|x| = 2$, then $x = 2$ or $x = -2$, as both 2 and –2 are a distance of 2 from 0.

Here's an example.

Digital SAT Smoke and Mirrors

When you're asked to solve an equation involving an absolute value, it is very likely that the correct answer will involve the negative result. Why? Because the test-writers know that you are less likely to think about the negative result! Another way to avoid mistakes is to do all the math inside the absolute value symbols first, and then make the result positive.

22 Mark for Review

Which of the following is the value of $|y + z|$ if y and z are the solutions to the equation $|-4x - 2| = 6$?

Ⓐ –3

Ⓑ –2

Ⓒ 1

Ⓓ 3

Here's How to Crack It

The question asks for the value of an expression with an absolute value given an equation with an absolute value. Start with the equation and find the two solutions. Remember that the expression inside the absolute value symbols could be positive or negative and will still yield a positive result. Set that expression, $-4x - 2$, equal to 6 and -6, and solve for the two solutions.

$$-4x - 2 = 6 \qquad\qquad -4x - 2 = -6$$
$$-4x = 8 \qquad \textbf{and} \qquad -4x = -4$$
$$x = -2 \qquad\qquad x = 1$$

Thus, the solutions y and z are -2 and 1. There's no way to know which is y and which is z, but it doesn't matter. Replace the variables in the expression $|y + z|$ with those values in either order, and calculate the result.

$$|-2 + 1| = |-1| = 1$$

If you're curious, try the other order for y and z to see that, because of the absolute value, it still works.

$$|1 + (-2)| = |1 - 2| = |-1| = 1$$

In either case the result is 1. The correct answer is (C).

Algebra Drill

Work these questions without your calculator using the skills you've learned so far. Answers and explanations can be found starting on page 425.

1 Mark for Review

For the inequality $3 > 9x - 3$, which of the following is a possible value of x?

Ⓐ 0

Ⓑ $\frac{2}{3}$

Ⓒ 3

Ⓓ 6

2 Mark for Review

For the equation $\sqrt{mx - 5} = x + 3$, the value of m is -3. Which of the following contains all possible solutions to the equation?

Ⓐ -3, 3

Ⓑ -2

Ⓒ -2, -7

Ⓓ 3, 6

3 Mark for Review

The equation $\frac{ac}{20} = \frac{3d}{z}$ expresses the relationship among a, c, d, and z. Which of the following equations expresses z in terms of a, c and d?

Ⓐ $z = \frac{60d}{ac}$

Ⓑ $z = \frac{ac}{60d}$

Ⓒ $z = \frac{3ac}{20}$

Ⓓ $z = \frac{20ac}{3d}$

4 Mark for Review

A student spends $4\frac{1}{2}$ hours each day working on history and science assignments. It takes the student $\frac{1}{4}$ of an hour to complete a history assignment and $\frac{1}{2}$ of an hour to complete a science assignment. Which of the following equations represents the number of history assignments, h, and science assignments, s, the student can complete each day?

Ⓐ $\left(h + \frac{1}{2}\right)\left(s + \frac{1}{4}\right) = \frac{9}{2}$

Ⓑ $\left(\frac{1}{2} + \frac{1}{4}\right)(h + s) = \frac{9}{2}$

Ⓒ $\frac{1}{4}h + \frac{1}{2}s = \frac{9}{2}$

Ⓓ $\frac{1}{2}h + \frac{1}{4}s = \frac{9}{2}$

5 Mark for Review

If $x + 6 > 0$ and $1 - 2x > -1$, which of the following values of x is NOT a solution?

Ⓐ -6

Ⓑ -4

Ⓒ 0

Ⓓ $\frac{1}{2}$

6 Mark for Review

If $\frac{2x}{x^2+1} = \frac{2}{x+2}$, what is the value of x?

Ⓐ $-\frac{1}{4}$

Ⓑ $\frac{1}{2}$

Ⓒ 0

Ⓓ 2

7 Mark for Review

If the product of x and y is 76, and x is twice the square of y, which of the following pairs of equations could be used to determine the values of x and y?

Ⓐ $xy = 76$
$x = 2y^2$

Ⓑ $xy = 76$
$x = (2y)^2$

Ⓒ $x + y = 76$
$x = 4y^2$

Ⓓ $xy = 76$
$x = 2y$

8 Mark for Review

A tadpole that has just hatched from an egg weighs t grams. The equation $y = t(3)^w$ displays the weight y, in grams, of the tadpole w weeks after it hatches. If the tadpole reaches a weight of 9.72 grams at 5 weeks after hatching, what is the value of t?

9 Mark for Review

How many solutions exist to the equation $|x| = |2x - 1|$?

Ⓐ 0

Ⓑ 1

Ⓒ 2

Ⓓ 3

10 Mark for Review

The sum of three numbers, a, b, and c, is 400. One of the numbers, a, is 40 percent less than the sum of b and c. What is the value of $b + c$?

Ⓐ 40

Ⓑ 60

Ⓒ 150

Ⓓ 250

ALGEBRA DRILL ANSWERS AND EXPLANATIONS

1. **A** The question asks for a value in an inequality. To begin to isolate *x*, add 3 to both sides of the equation to get $6 > 9x$. Divide both sides of the equation by 9 to get $\frac{6}{9} > x$. Because 9 is positive, it is not necessary to flip the inequality sign. Reduce the fraction to get $\frac{2}{3} > x$. Only (A) is less than $\frac{2}{3}$. The correct answer is (A).

2. **B** The question asks for all possible solutions to an equation. Since the question gives the value of *m*, the first step is to plug that value into the original equation to get $\sqrt{-3x-5} = x+3$. Now square both sides of the equation to remove the square root: $\left(\sqrt{-3x-5}\right)^2 = (x+3)^2$ or $-3x - 5 = x^2 + 6x + 9$. Now combine like terms. If you combine the terms on the right side of the equation, you can avoid having a negative x^2 term. The equation becomes $0 = x^2 + 9x + 14$. Factor the quadratic to find the roots: $0 = (x + 2)(x + 7)$. The possible solutions to the quadratic are –2 and –7. Don't forget to plug these numbers back into the original equation to check for extraneous solutions. Begin by checking $x = -2$. When you do this, you get $\sqrt{(-3)(-2)-5} = (-2) + 3$, or $\sqrt{6-5} = 1$, or $\sqrt{1} = 1$, which is true. Now, check $x = -7$. Set it up as $\sqrt{(-3)(-7)-5} = (-7) + 3$, and start simplifying to get $\sqrt{21-5} = -4$. You can technically stop simplifying here, as there is a negative number on the right-hand side of the equals sign. Remember, when taking a square root with a radical provided, it will yield the positive root only. So –7 cannot be part of the solution set. Be very careful of (C), which is a trap answer. The correct answer is (B).

3. **A** The question asks for an equation in terms of a specific variable. To begin to isolate *z*, cross-multiply to get $(20)(3d) = (ac)(z)$, which becomes $60d = (ac)(z)$. Divide both sides of the equation by *ac* to get $\frac{60d}{ac} = z$. The correct answer is (A).

4. **C** The question asks for an equation that represents a specific situation. Translate the information in bite-sized pieces and eliminate after each piece. All of the answer choices equal $\frac{9}{2}$, which represents the $4\frac{1}{2}$ hours each day the student spends on both types of assignment. The left side of the equation must add up to that total time. One piece of information says that it *takes the student* $\frac{1}{4}$ *of an hour to complete a history assignment*, and another piece says that *h* represents the number of history assignments. The total time spent on history assignments can be represented by $\frac{1}{4}h$. Eliminate (D) because it multiplies *h* by $\frac{1}{2}$ instead of by $\frac{1}{4}$. Choice (A) includes the term $\frac{1}{4}h$ after FOILing, but it also includes *hs*. There is no reason to multiply the number of history

assignments by the number of science assignments, so eliminate (A). Choice (B) includes the term $\frac{1}{2}h$ after FOILing, but h should only be multiplied by $\frac{1}{4}$. Eliminate (B). Choice (C) also correctly multiplies the time per science assignment by the number of science assignments to get $\frac{1}{2}s$. The correct answer is (C).

5. **A** The question asks for the value of x that is not a solution. Solve the first inequality by subtracting 6 from each side so that $x > -6$. You are looking for values that won't work for x, and x cannot equal -6. Therefore, the answer must be (A). Just to be sure, solve the next inequality by subtracting 1 from each side to get $-2x > -2$. Divide by -2, remembering to switch the sign because you are dividing by a negative number to get $x < 1$. The values in (B), (C), and (D) fit this requirement as well, so they are values for x and not the correct answer. The correct answer is (A).

6. **B** The question asks for the value of x. To solve this equation, use cross-multiplication to get $(2x)(x + 2) = (x^2 + 1)(2)$. Expand the equation to get $2x^2 + 4x = 2x^2 + 2$. Once you combine like terms, the result is $2x^2 - 2x^2 + 4x = 2$ or $4x = 2$. Solve for x by dividing both sides by 4 to get $x = \frac{1}{2}$. The correct answer is (B).

7. **A** The question asks for a pair of equations to represent the situation. Translate each statement, piece by piece. The first part tells you that "the product of x and y is 76." Since *product* means multiplication, the first equation must be $xy = 76$, so you can eliminate (C). The second part says that "x is twice the square of y," which translates to $x = 2y^2$, so eliminate (B) and (D), and (A) is the only choice left. Notice that only the y needs to be squared, which is why (B) is wrong. The second equation for (B) would be written as "the square of twice y," which is not what the question states. The correct answer is (A).

8. **0.04** The question asks for a value given a specific situation. The weight of the tadpole is increasing by a multiple over time, so write down the growth and decay formula. That formula is *final amount* = (*original amount*)(*multiplier*)$^{number\ of\ changes}$. The equation in the question already shows that 3 is the *multiplier*. The question states that *the tadpole reaches a weight of 9.72 grams at 5 weeks after hatching*, so 9.72 is the *final amount* and 5 is the *number of changes*. Plug in these values and solve for t. The equation becomes $9.72 = t(3)^5$. Start with the exponent on the right side of the equation to get $9.72 = t(243)$. Divide both sides of the equation by 243 to get $0.04 = t$. The correct answer is 0.04, which can also be entered in the fill-in box as .04 or a fractional equivalent.

9. **C** The question asks for the number of solutions to an equation. If $|x| = |2x - 1|$, either $x = 2x - 1$ or $-x = 2x - 1$. The solutions to these equations are 1 and $\frac{1}{3}$, respectively. However, the only thing you need to recognize is that the equation has two different solutions. Another option is making a quick graph on a calculator, which will show you that there are two solutions and what those solutions are. Either way, the correct answer is (C).

10. **D** The question asks for the value of $b + c$. This is a system of equations question in disguise. First, locate a piece of information in this question that you can work with. "The sum of three numbers, a, b, and c, is 400," seems very straightforward. Write the equation $a + b + c = 400$. Now the question tells you that "one of the numbers, a, is 40 percent less than the sum of b and c." Translate this piece by piece to get $a = (1 - 0.4)(b + c)$, or $a = 0.6(b + c)$. Distribute the 0.6 to get $a = 0.6b + 0.6c$. Arrange these variables so they line up with those in the first equation as $a - 0.6b - 0.6c = 0$. To solve for $b + c$, stack the equations and multiply the second equation by −1:

$$a + b + c = 400$$
$$-1(a - 0.6b - 0.6c) = 0(-1)$$

Now solve:

$$\begin{array}{r} a + \quad b + \quad c = 400 \\ \underline{-a + 0.6b + 0.6c = 0} \\ 1.6b + 1.6c = 400 \end{array}$$

Simplify by dividing both sides by 1.6 to get $b + c = 250$. The correct answer is (D).

Summary

- Don't "solve for *x*" or "solve for *y*" unless you absolutely have to. (Don't worry; your math teacher won't find out.) Instead, look for direct solutions to Digital SAT questions. Math section questions rarely require time-consuming computations or endless fiddling with big numbers. There's almost always a trick—if you can spot it.
- If a question contains an expression that can be factored, factor it. If it contains an expression that already has been factored, multiply it out.
- To solve systems of equations, simply add or subtract the equations. If you don't have the answer, look for multiples of your solutions. When the question asks for a single variable and addition and subtraction don't work, try to make something disappear. Multiply the equations to make the coefficient(s) of the variable(s) you don't want go to zero when the equations are added or subtracted.
- If a question asks for the number of solutions, the graphing calculator can help, but it's also useful to know the rules.
    - Two linear equations have *no solution* when they have the same coefficient on the variable but different constants. This makes the lines parallel.
    - Two linear equations have *exactly one solution* when a single (x, y) point is a solution to both equations. The two lines intersect once.
    - Two linear equations have *infinitely many solutions* when they have the same coefficient on the variable and the same constants. This makes them the same line.
- Some Digital SAT questions require algebraic manipulation. Use tricks when you can, but if you have to manipulate the equation, take your time and work carefully to avoid unnecessary mistakes. You don't get partial credit for getting the question mostly correct.
- When working with inequalities, don't forget to flip the sign when you multiply and divide by negative numbers.
- When asked to create an equation, start with the most straightforward piece of information. You can also use the equations in the answer choices to help you narrow down the possibilities for your equation. Eliminate any answers in which an equation doesn't match your equation.

- o When a question asks for an extraneous solution, first solve the equation, and then plug the answers back into the equation. If the equation is not true when solved with the solution, then that solution is extraneous.

- o When solving quadratic equations, you may need to use FOIL or factor to get the equation into the easiest form for the question task. Don't forget about the common equations that the test-writers use when writing questions about quadratics.

- o To solve for the roots of a quadratic equation, set it equal to zero by moving all the terms to the left side of the equation, then factor and solve, or use the quadratic formula:

$$x = \frac{-b \pm \sqrt{b^2 - 4ac}}{2a}$$

When solving for the sum or product of the roots, you can also use these formulas:

- sum of the roots: $-\frac{b}{a}$
- product of the roots: $\frac{c}{a}$

- o The discriminant of a quadratic in the form $ax^2 + bx + c = 0$ is the value of $b^2 - 4ac$. If this value is positive, there are 2 real roots; if it is 0, there is 1 real root; if it is negative, there are no real roots. A graphing calculator can also help with questions about the number of solutions to a quadratic equation.

- o When a question is about exponential growth or decay, use the following formula:

$$\textit{final amount} = (\textit{original amount})(1 \pm \textit{rate})^{\text{number of changes}}$$

If the change is by a multiple instead of a rate, use the same formula with *multiplier* inside the parentheses.

- o The absolute value of a number is its distance from zero; distances are always positive. When working inside the | |, remember to consider both the positive and the negative values of the expression. Also remember that | | work like ( ); you need to complete all the operations inside the | | before you can make the value positive.

Chapter 22
Other Digital SAT Algebra Strategies

Now that you're familiar with the basics of algebra, it's time to learn how to avoid using algebra on the Digital SAT. Yes, you read that correctly. Algebra questions on the Digital SAT are filled with traps carefully laid by the test-writers, so you need to know how to work around them. This chapter gives you the strategies you need in order to turn tricky algebra questions into simple arithmetic.

PRINCETON REVIEW ALGEBRA—AKA HOW TO AVOID ALGEBRA ON THE DIGITAL SAT

Now that you've reviewed some basic algebra, it's time to find out when and how NOT to use it on the Digital SAT. The Digital SAT is not your math class at school, and all that matters is the correct answer. So we're going to show you how to avoid doing algebra on the Digital SAT whenever possible. Even if you love algebra, using it all the time on the Digital SAT can actually hurt your score, and we don't want that.

We know it's difficult to come to terms with this. But if you use only algebra on the Digital SAT, you're doing exactly what the test-writers want you to do. You see, when the test-writers design the questions on the Digital SAT, they expect the students to use algebra to solve them. Many Digital SAT problems have built-in traps meant to take advantage of common mistakes that students make when using algebra. But if you don't use algebra, there's no way you can fall into those traps.

Your Best Friend
Plugging In allows you to use your calculator on many of the algebra questions that show up on the Digital SAT.

Plus, when you avoid algebra, you add one other powerful tool to your tool belt: you can use the built-in calculator or your own! Calculators can help with algebra, but they're designed first and foremost for arithmetic. Our goal, then, is to turn algebra on the Digital SAT into arithmetic. We do that using techniques we call Plugging In and Plugging In the Answers (PITA).

PLUGGING IN THE ANSWERS (PITA)

Algebra uses letters to stand for numbers. You don't go to the grocery store to buy x eggs or y gallons of milk. Most people think about math in terms of numbers, not letters that stand for numbers.

You should think in terms of numbers on the Digital SAT as much as possible. On many Digital SAT algebra questions, even very difficult ones, you will be able to find the correct answer without using any algebra at all. You will do this by working backward from the answer choices instead of trying to solve the problem using your standard math-class methods.

Plugging In the Answers is a useful technique for solving word problems in which the answer choices are all numbers. Using this powerful technique can solve many algebra problems on the Digital SAT simply and quickly.

In algebra class at school, you solve word problems by using equations. Then, you check your solution by plugging in your answer to see if it works. Why not skip the equations entirely by simply checking the four possible solutions on the multiple-choice questions? One of these is the correct answer. You don't have to do any algebra, you will seldom have to try more than two choices, and you will never have to try all four. Use PITA for questions that ask for a specific amount.

Here's an example of using PITA instead of writing equations.

1 Mark for Review

On a certain assignment, student X takes 20 seconds per grammar question and 35 seconds per punctuation question. On the same assignment, student Y takes 30 seconds per grammar question and 55 seconds per punctuation question. It takes 310 seconds for student X to complete the assignment and 480 seconds for student Y to complete the assignment. If those are the only two types of questions on the assignment, how many punctuation questions are on the assignment?

(A) 5

(B) 6

(C) 7

(D) 8

Here's How to Crack It

The question asks for a value given a specific situation. Sure, you could make up some variables, translate words into equations, and use skills from the previous chapter to solve the system of equations, but that's what you would do in math class at school. On the Digital SAT, **there's a better way**. Notice that the question asks for a single, specific value: the number of punctuation questions on the assignment. Each answer choice also has a single, specific value. One of those values has to be the answer to the question, so start with the answers and plug them into the question.

Representation
Make sure you know what the numbers in the answer choices represent. Be sure to label them!

Before you plug in an answer, make sure you know what the answers represent. The question asks for the number of punctuation questions, so rewrite the answers on your scratch paper and label them "# of punct Qs" or something similar.

Now it's time to start working the steps of the problem. But first, notice that the answer choices are in numerically ascending order. The test-writers like to keep their questions organized, so they will always put the answers in order on this kind of question. You can use that to your advantage by starting with one of the middle answer choices. If it ends up being too big or small, you should be able to eliminate more than one answer. If the first answer you plug in happens to work, you can just stop there. Try (B) first.

Look at (B) and ask yourself, "If the number of punctuation questions is 6, what's the next thing I can figure out?" In this case, you could figure out how much time each student spends on punctuation questions. The question states that student X takes *35 seconds per punctuation question*, so student X will take (6)(35) = 210 seconds to finish the punctuation questions. It takes student X a total of 310 seconds to complete the assignment, so that leaves 310 – 210 = 100 seconds for the grammar questions. The question also states that *student X takes 20 seconds per grammar question*, so there are $\frac{100}{20} = 5$ grammar questions.

Next, do the same thing for student Y, who takes 55 seconds per punctuation question. If there are 6 punctuation questions, that's (6)(55) = 330 seconds. Student Y takes 480 seconds to complete the assignment, so that leaves 480 – 330 = 150 seconds for the grammar questions. The question states that *student Y takes 30 seconds per grammar question*, so there are $\frac{150}{30} = 5$ grammar questions.

Take a look at the numbers on your scratch paper. Did both students complete 6 punctuation questions? Yes, because that's the number you plugged in. Did both students complete 5 grammar questions? Yes, they did. Are you done? Yes, you are!

If you had started with a different number, somewhere along the way the math wouldn't have worked. You would end up with a fractional number of questions, or the two students wouldn't have the same number of each question type. When that happens, cross out the answer and try another one. In some cases, you'll be able to tell whether the number you tried was too big or too small, which helps you eliminate more answers and choose which one to try next. That's not necessary here because the first number you tried worked. The correct answer is (B).

Here are the steps for solving a problem using the PITA approach:

To solve a problem by plugging in the answers:

1. Rewrite the answer choices on your scratch paper and label them.
2. Starting with one of the middle answer choices, work the steps of the problem.
3. Look for something in the question that tells you what must happen for the answer to be correct.
4. When you find the correct answer, STOP.

You've seen how PITA gets you through a word problem quickly, efficiently, and accurately. But the technique also works on questions that aren't word problems but still ask for a specific value and have numbers in the answer choices. Here's an example.

2 Mark for Review

$$2x + y = 6$$
$$7x + 2y = 27$$

The system of equations above is satisfied by which of the following ordered pairs (x, y)?

Ⓐ (–5, 4)

Ⓑ (4, –2)

Ⓒ (5, 4)

Ⓓ (5, –4)

Which Way?
Sometimes, it's hard to tell if you need a larger number or a smaller number if the first answer you tried didn't work. Don't fret. Just pick a direction and go! Spend your time trying answers rather than worrying about going in the wrong direction.

Here's How to Crack It

The question asks for the coordinates of the point that satisfies the system of equations. When you feel the urge to do a whole lot of algebra, it is a good time to check whether it would be possible to just plug in the answers instead. In this case, trying your answer choices will be not only effective but also incredibly fast.

Start by rewriting the answer choices on your scratch paper and labeling them "(x, y)." It doesn't seem like you will be able to tell whether to move up or down this time, as the ordered pairs don't really have an ascending or descending order, but start in the middle anyway. Even if you end up trying three of the four, you will be saving time by plugging in the answers instead of solving.

Starting with (B) gives you 4 for x and –2 for y. Try that out in the first equation: $2(4) + (-2) = 6$. That matches the first equation, so this is a possibility. Try it out in the second equation: $7(4) + 2(-2) = 24$. That does not match the second equation, so you can eliminate (B).

Try out (C) next. If $x = 5$ and $y = 4$, then $2(5) + 4 = 14$, and you wanted it to be 6, so you can eliminate this answer choice as well.

Move on to (D). That would give you $2(5) + (-4) = 6$. So far so good! Try the second equation to see if this choice satisfies both: $7(5) + 2(-4) = 27$. This works, so the correct answer is (D).

You may recall that we covered questions like this in the last chapter. It is important to know how to solve these, in case a question like this comes up on a fill-in question. When you have answers available to you, though, don't be afraid to use them!

One last thing about PITA: here's how to determine whether you should use this approach to solve a problem.

Three ways to know that it's time for PITA:

1. There are numbers in the answer choices.
2. The question asks for a specific amount. Look for phrases like "the number of," "what was," or "how many."
3. You have the urge to write an algebraic equation to solve the problem.

Here's an example of using PITA instead of writing equations.

3 Mark for Review

A bakery sold exactly 85% of the cupcakes it baked on Tuesday. Which of the following could be the total number of cupcakes baked on Tuesday?

(A) 130

(B) 140

(C) 145

(D) 150

Here's How to Crack It

The question asks for a possible total number of cupcakes. Is your first reaction that there isn't nearly enough information here to start on this question? That makes it a great opportunity to plug in the answers! Start with one of the middle answer choices and test it out. Sometimes, even if you can't see how a question works ahead of time, it starts to make a lot more sense once you plug real numbers into it.

Choice (C) is 145, but 145 what? Read the question very carefully. The question asks for the total number of cupcakes baked on Tuesday, so rewrite the answer choices and label them "Total."

Next, work your way through the problem. If 145 is the total number of cupcakes baked on Tuesday, the number the bakery sold on Tuesday is 85% of 145, or 123.25. Have you ever bought 0.25 cupcakes at a bakery? It would be really weird for a bakery to sell fractions of cupcakes, so this answer could not be the total number baked on Tuesday.

In this particular question, it is hard to tell whether you should try bigger or smaller numbers next, but you have learned two things from your first attempt: you can get rid of (C), and the correct answer will be the one that gives you a whole number of cupcakes. Instead of spending time trying to predict which direction to go for the answer, just get to work on the other answer choices.

Try (B) next. If the bakery baked 140 cupcakes on Tuesday, it sold 85% of 140, or 119. Is there anything wrong with selling 119 cupcakes? No! Since the bakery sold only whole cupcakes, the correct answer is (B).

Here's another example of how PITA turns algebra into arithmetic.

4 Mark for Review

For what value of x is $|2x + 3| + 5 = 0$?

Ⓐ −4

Ⓑ 0

Ⓒ 4

Ⓓ There is no such value of x.

Here's How to Crack It

The question asks for the value of x. Although we covered it in the last chapter, solving algebraically on an absolute value question can be treacherous. There are so many ways to go wrong with those signs! Luckily, this absolute value question comes complete with answer choices, so we can simply plug in the answers to get a solution. As always, start by rewriting the answer choices on your scratch paper and labeling them. In this case, the label is simply "x."

Start with (C). When you put 4 in for x, you get $|2(4) + 3| + 5 = 0$, or $16 = 0$. This is clearly not true, so cross off (C) and move on to (B). If x is 0, then the original equation becomes $|2(0) + 3| + 5 = 0$ or $8 = 0$, so you can eliminate (B) as well. Next, try (A): $|2(-4) + 3| + 5 = 0$ could be rewritten as $|-8 + 3| + 5 = 0$, or $|-5| + 5 = 0$. As long as you remember that the absolute value of a number is always positive, it is clear that this gives you $5 + 5 = 0$. Since this is also clearly untrue, eliminate (A). Apparently, there is no such value of x! The correct answer is (D).

SOLVING RATIONAL EQUATIONS

A rational equation is basically an equation in which one (or more) of the terms is a fractional one. Rational equations look scary, but there are very simple ways of solving them. All in all, the test-writers can't get too messy here, so they will keep the math nice and tidy. Try the following question.

5 Mark for Review

$$x - 3 = \frac{5}{x - 3}$$

Which of the following is a possible value of $x - 3$ in the equation above?

Ⓐ $\sqrt{5}$

Ⓑ 5

Ⓒ $3 + \sqrt{5}$

Ⓓ 25

Watch Us Crack It
Watch the step-by-step video explanation of how to answer this question in your Student Tools.

Here's How to Crack It

The question asks for a possible value of (x –3) in an equation with fractions and binomials. You could use your skills with quadratics from the last chapter, but it's much simpler to use PITA! After all, there are numbers in the answers and the question asks for a specific value, so it sure looks like a PITA question. This approach will also avoid the issue of extraneous solutions.

Follow the PITA approach: start by rewriting the answers on your scratch paper and labeling them as "$x - 3$" and then start with one of the middle answer choices. The value in (C) looks complicated, so start with (B), 5. When $x - 3 = 5$, the equation becomes

$$5 = \frac{5}{5} \text{ or } 5 = 1$$

This is not true, so eliminate (B). Plugging in 25 would make the fraction too small, so ballpark out (D). Try the next simplest answer, (A). When $x - 3 = \sqrt{5}$, the equation becomes

$$\sqrt{5} = \frac{5}{\sqrt{5}}$$

Multiply both sides by $\sqrt{5}$ to get 5 = 5, or use a calculator to find out that the two sides are equal. This makes the equation accurate, so $\sqrt{5}$ is a possible value of $x - 3$. The correct answer is (A).

PLUGGING IN YOUR OWN NUMBERS

Plugging In the Answers enables you to find the answer to questions whose answer choices are all numbers. What about questions that have answer choices containing variables? On these questions, you will usually be able to find the answer by plugging in your own numbers.

Plugging In is easy. It has three steps:

1. Pick numbers for the variables in the question.
2. Use your numbers to find an answer to the questions. Circle your answer.
3. Plug your number(s) for the variable(s) into the answer choices and eliminate choices that don't equal the answer you found in Step 2.

The Basics of Plugging In Your Own Numbers

This sort of Plugging In is simple to understand. Here's an example.

6 Mark for Review

Which of the following is equivalent to $\frac{3}{5} + \frac{y}{1-2y}$?

(A) $\frac{3+y}{6-2y}$

(B) $\frac{3-y}{5-10y}$

(C) $\frac{2y}{5-10y}$

(D) $\frac{3y}{5-10y}$

Here's How to Crack It

The question asks for an equivalent form of an expression. Rather than do complicated algebra, try plugging in. First, pick a number for *y*. Pick something easy to work with, like 2. On your scratch paper, write $y = 2$ so you won't forget. Then plug in 2 everywhere there's a *y* in the expression to get $\frac{3}{5}+\frac{2}{1-2(2)}$, which becomes $\frac{3}{5}+\frac{2}{1-4}$, then $\frac{3}{5}+\frac{2}{-3}$, and then $\frac{3}{5}-\frac{2}{3}$. Either find a common denominator and subtract the fractions by hand to get $\frac{9}{15}-\frac{10}{15}=-\frac{1}{15}$ or use a calculator to get the decimal equivalent of $-0.0\overline{6}$. In either form, this is your target value. Write it on the scratch paper and circle it.

Next, plug $y = 2$ into the answer choices and eliminate ones that do not equal the target value. Rewrite the answers one at a time with 2 in place of *y*.

A) $\frac{3+2}{6-2(2)}=\frac{5}{6-4}=\frac{5}{2}$ Not the target; eliminate!

B) $\frac{3-2}{5-10(2)}=\frac{1}{5-20}=\frac{1}{-15}=-\frac{1}{15}$ Matches the target; keep but check the rest just in case.

C) $\frac{2(2)}{5-10(2)}=\frac{4}{5-20}=\frac{4}{-15}=-\frac{4}{15}$ Not the target; eliminate!

D) $\frac{3(2)}{5-10(2)}=\frac{6}{5-20}=\frac{6}{-15}=-\frac{6}{15}$ Not the target; eliminate!

Only (B) matches the target value, so it's the correct answer.

Here's another example.

7 Mark for Review

During a special sale at a furniture store, Erica bought a floor lamp at a 10% discount. She paid a total of t dollars, which included the discounted price of the floor lamp and a 6% sales tax on the discounted price. In terms of t, what was the original price of the floor lamp?

Ⓐ $\frac{t}{0.96}$

Ⓑ $(0.9)(1.06)t$

Ⓒ $\frac{t}{(0.9)(1.06)}$

Ⓓ $0.96t$

Get Real
Trying to imagine how numbers behave in the abstract is a waste of time. So, if the question says that Tina is x years old, why not plug in your own age? That's real enough. You don't have to change your name to Tina.

Here's How to Crack It

The question asks for an expression to represent the situation. This could be a pretty tricky algebra question, but if you read the question carefully and plug in easy numbers, it will be a breeze.

Start at the beginning. When Erica bought that floor lamp on sale, what did you really wish you knew? It would be very helpful to start this problem knowing the original price of the floor lamp. So, start plugging in there. Plug in a number that you know how to take a percentage of, like 100. Write down "original = 100" and move on to the next step of the problem. Erica got a 10% discount, so take 10% of the original price. That means she got a \$10 discount, and the discounted price of her floor lamp was \$90. Write that down and move on to the sales tax. If you read carefully, it is clear that the sales tax is 6% of the discounted price. So, you need to take 6% of the \$90 discounted price, or \$5.40. To get her total, add the \$5.40 of tax to the \$90 for the discounted floor lamp, and you get \$95.40. This is where the careful reading comes in. The variable t in this question is supposed to be the total amount she paid, so make sure that you label this "t = \$95.40."

Next, read the last sentence of the question again to be sure you know which of the answers is your target answer. The question asks for the original price of the floor lamp, so circle the number you plugged in for the original price. Your target answer is 100.

On to the answer choices! When you put $95.40 in for t in (A), you get 99.375. This is not your target answer, so you can eliminate (A). Choice (B) gives you 91.0116, so that will not work either. Plugging $95.40 into (C) yields the target of 100, so hang on to it while you check (D) just in case. When you plug $95.40 into (D), you get 91.584. Since that does not match your target, you can eliminate (D). The correct answer is (C).

Which Numbers?

Although you can plug in any number, you can make your life much easier by plugging in "good" numbers—numbers that are simple to work with or that make the problem easier to manipulate. Picking a small number, such as 2, will usually make finding the answer easier. If the question asks for a percentage, plug in 100. If the question has to do with minutes, try 30 or 120.

Except in special cases, you should avoid plugging in 0 and 1; these numbers have weird properties. Using them may allow you to eliminate only one or two choices at a time. You should also avoid plugging in any number that appears in the question or in any of the answer choices. Using those numbers could make more than one answer match your target. If more than one answer choice matches your target, plug in a new number and check those answer choices. You may have to plug in more than once to eliminate all three incorrect answers.

Be Good
"Good" numbers make a problem less confusing by simplifying the arithmetic. This is your chance to make the Digital SAT easier for you.

Many times you'll find that there is an advantage to picking a particular number, even a very large one, because it makes solving the problem more straightforward.

Here's an example.

8 Mark for Review

If 60 equally priced downloads cost x dollars, then how much do 9 downloads cost?

(A) $\frac{20}{3x}$

(B) $\frac{20x}{3}$

(C) $60x + 9$

(D) $\frac{3x}{20}$

Here's How to Crack It

The question asks for the cost of 9 downloads. Since the question is asking you to arrive at a number (how much 9 downloads cost) in terms of variable *x*, try plugging in. Should you plug in 2 for *x*? You could, but plugging in 120 would make the math easier. After all, if 60 downloads cost a total of \$120, then each download costs \$2. Write $x = 120$ on your scratch paper.

If each download costs \$2, then 9 downloads cost \$18. Write an 18 and circle it. You are looking for the answer choice that works out to 18 when you plug in \$120 for *x*. Try each choice:

A) $\frac{20}{3(120)} \neq 18$

B) $\frac{20(120)}{3} \neq 18$

C) $60(120) + 9 \neq 18$

D) $\frac{3(120)}{20} = 18$

That last one matches the target answer, so the correct answer is (D).

Let's try another example.

Watch Us Crack It
Watch the step-by-step video explanation of how to answer this question in your Student Tools.

9 Mark for Review

A watch loses x minutes every y hours. At this rate, how many <u>hours</u> will the watch lose in one week?

Ⓐ $7xy$

Ⓑ $\frac{5y}{2x}$

Ⓒ $\frac{14y}{5x}$

Ⓓ $\frac{14x}{5y}$

Here's How to Crack It

The question asks for the number of hours lost in one week and gives information about minutes. This is an extremely difficult question for students who try to solve it using math-class algebra. You'll be able to find the answer easily, though, if you plug in carefully.

What numbers should you plug in? As always, you can plug in anything. However, if you think just a little bit before choosing the numbers, you can make the question easier to understand. There are three units of time—minutes, hours, and weeks—and that's a big part of the reason this question is hard to understand. If you choose units of time that are easy to think about, you'll make the question easier to handle.

Start by choosing a value for x, which represents the number of minutes that the watch loses. You might be tempted to choose $x = 60$ and that would make the math pretty easy. However, it's usually not a good idea to choose a conversion factor such as 60, the conversion factor between minutes and hours, for plugging in. When a question deals with time, 30 is usually a safer choice to avoid having multiple answers work the first time you plug in. So, write down $x = 30$.

Next, you need a number for y, which represents the number of hours. Again, you might be tempted to use $y = 24$, but that's the conversion factor between hours and days. Therefore, $y = 12$ is a safer choice. Write down $y = 12$.

Now, it's time to solve the problem to come up with a target. If the watch loses 30 minutes every 12 hours, then it loses 60 minutes every 24 hours. Put another way, the watch loses an hour each day. In one week, the watch will lose 7 hours. That's your target, so be sure to circle it.

Now, you just need to check the answer choices to see which one gives you 7 when $x = 30$ and $y = 12$.

A) $7xy = 7(30)(12)$ = Something too big! Cross it off.

B) $\frac{5y}{2x} = \frac{5(12)}{2(30)} = \frac{60}{60} = 1$. Also wrong.

C) $\frac{14y}{5x} = \frac{14(12)}{5(30)} = \frac{168}{150} = \frac{28}{25}$. Cross it off.

D) $\frac{14x}{5y} = \frac{14(30)}{5(12)} = \frac{420}{60} = 7$. Choose it!

The correct answer is (D).

MEANING IN CONTEXT

Some questions, instead of asking you to come up with an equation, just want you to recognize what a part of the equation stands for. These questions will look like algebra, with variables and equations, but they're often more about reading carefully, working in bite-sized pieces, and using your pencil.

First things first, though, you want to think about your POOD. Do these questions make sense to you, or are they a little confusing? Do you usually get them right quickly, or do they take up too much time? You can always use the Mark for Review tool to flag a meaning in context question to come back to later after you get some easier, quicker questions right.

If the question does fit your POOD, read carefully, write down labels for the parts of the equation, and use POE to get rid of any answer choices that don't match your labels.

Here's an example.

10 Mark for Review

There are m boxes of red marbles and n boxes of blue marbles in a crate, and the crate contains a total of 204 marbles. If this situation is represented by the equation $12m + 7n = 204$, what does the number 12 most likely represent?

(A) The total number of red marbles

(B) The total number of blue marbles

(C) The number of red marbles in each box

(D) The number of blue marbles in each box

Here's How to Crack It

The question asks for the meaning of a value in context. Start by reading the final question, which asks for the meaning of the number 12. Then label the parts of the equation with the information given. The question states that *there are m boxes of red marbles*, so label m as "# of boxes of red marbles." Similarly, label n as "# of boxes of blue marbles." The question also states that *the crate contains a total of 204 marbles*, so label 204 as "total # of marbles." The equation is now labeled as follows:

12(# of boxes of red marbles) + 7(# of boxes of blue marbles) = (total # of marbles)

Next, use Process of Elimination to get rid of answer choices that are not consistent with the labels. Since 12 is multiplied by the number of boxes of red marbles, it has something to do with the red marbles. Eliminate (B) and (D) because they refer to blue marbles. Since 12 is multiplied by the number of boxes of red marbles, it must represent a value per box, not a total value. Keep (C) because it is consistent with this information, and eliminate (A) because it refers to a total number. The correct answer is (C).

If labeling the equation isn't enough to eliminate three answers, try plugging in! This will help clarify what's going on in confusing equations or show the relationship between two parts of an equation.

Let's try a meaning in context question that uses plugging in.

11 Mark for Review

$$n = 1{,}273 - 4p$$

The equation above was used by the cafeteria in a large public high school to model the relationship between the number of slices of pizza, n, sold daily and the price of a slice of pizza, p, in dollars. What does the number 4 represent in this equation?

(A) For every $4 the price of pizza decreases, the cafeteria sells 1 more slice of pizza.

(B) For every dollar the price of pizza decreases, the cafeteria sells 4 more slices of pizza.

(C) For every $4 the price of pizza increases, the cafeteria sells 1 more slice of pizza.

(D) For every dollar the price of pizza increases, the cafeteria sells 4 more slices of pizza.

Here's How to Crack It

The question asks for the meaning of the number 4 in the context of the situation. First, read the question very carefully, and label the variables on your scratch paper. You know that p is the price of pizza, and n is the number of slices, so you can add that information to the equation. If you can, eliminate answer choices that don't make sense. But what if you can't eliminate anything, or you can eliminate only an answer choice or two?

Even with everything labeled, this equation is difficult to decode, so it's time to plug in! Try a few of your own numbers in the equation, and you will get a much better understanding of what is happening.

Try it out with $p = 2$. When you put 2 in for p, $n = 1{,}273 - 4(2)$ or 1,265.

So, when $p = 2$, $n = 1{,}265$. In other words, at $2 a slice, the cafeteria sells 1,265 slices.

When $p = 3$, $n = 1{,}261$, so at $3 a slice, the cafeteria sells 1,261 slices.

When $p = 4$, $n = 1{,}257$, so at $4 a slice, the cafeteria sells 1,257 slices.

Now, use POE. First of all, is the cafeteria selling more pizza as the price goes up? No, as the price of pizza goes up, the cafeteria sells fewer slices of pizza. That means you can eliminate (C) and (D).

Choice (A) says that for every $4 the price goes down, the cafeteria sells 1 more slice of pizza. Does your plugging in back that up? No. The cafeteria sells 8 more slices of pizza when the price drops from $4 to $2, so it will sell 16 more slices of pizza when the price drops by $4, and (A) is no good.

Now take a look at (B). Does the cafeteria sell 4 more slices of pizza for every dollar the price drops? Yes! The correct answer is (B).

Here are the steps for solving meaning in context questions. The first three steps are often enough, but plug in when they aren't.

Meaning in Context

1. Read the question carefully. Make sure you know which part of the equation you are being asked to identify.
2. Use your scratch paper to rewrite the equation, replacing the parts of the equation you can identify with labels.
3. Eliminate any answer choices that clearly describe the wrong part of the equation, or go against what you have labeled.
4. Plug in! Use your own numbers to start seeing what is happening in the equation.
5. Use POE again, using the information you learned from plugging in real numbers, until you can get it down to one answer choice. Or get it down to as few choices as you can, and guess.

Let's look at a slightly different one now.

12 Mark for Review

$$7x + y = 133$$

Jeffrey has set a monthly budget for purchasing frozen blended mocha drinks from his local coffee shop. The equation above can be used to model the amount of his budget, y, in dollars, that remains after buying coffee for x days in a month. What does it mean that (19, 0) is a solution to this equation?

Ⓐ Jeffrey starts the month with a budget of \$19.

Ⓑ Jeffrey spends \$19 on coffee every day.

Ⓒ It takes 19 days for Jeffrey to drink 133 cups of coffee.

Ⓓ It takes 19 days for Jeffrey to run out of money in his budget for purchasing coffee.

Here's How to Crack It

The question asks about a point that is the solution to an equation in the context of the situation. Start by labeling the x and the y in the equation to keep track of what they stand for. Use your scratch paper to replace x with "days" and y with "budget." So 7 × days + budget = 133. Hmm, still not very clear, is it? One way to approach this is to plug in the point. If x = days = 19 when y = budget = 0, then Jeffrey will have no budget left after 19 days. This matches (D).

If you have trouble seeing this, you can use the answer choices to help you plug in. If (A) is true, the budget at the start of the month, when days = 0, is $19. Plug these values into the equation to see if it is true. Is 7 × 0 + 19 = 133? Not at all, so eliminate (A). If (B) is true, Jeffrey drinks a lot of coffee! Try some numbers and see if it works. For $x = 1$, the equation becomes $7(1) + y = 133$ or $y = 126$, and for $x = 2$, it is $7(2) + y = 133$ or $y = 119$. The difference in y, the budget remaining, is 126 – 119 = 7, so that's not $19 per day. Eliminate (B) so only (C) and (D) remain. These both have 19 for the number of days, and the point (19, 0) would indicate that 19 is the x-value, or days. If you saw that right away—great! That would allow you to skip right to testing (C) and (D).

For (C), you can plug in 19 for days in the equation to get 7 × 19 + budget = 133, or budget = 0. Does that tell you how many cups of coffee Jeffrey drank? You have no information about the cost of a single cup of coffee, so the answer can't be (C). It does tell you, however, that after 19 days, Jeffrey has no budget left. The correct answer is (D).

You might have noticed that the equation in this question could have been graphed in the *xy*-plane, which could help you visualize the situation. Some Digital SAT questions ask about the meaning of a piece of a linear graph, so keep the meaning in context approach in mind when you get to the Functions and Graphs chapter.

Other Digital SAT Algebra Strategies Drill

Work these algebra questions using Plugging In or PITA. Answers and explanations can be found starting on page 454.

1 Mark for Review

The length of a certain rectangle is twice the width. If the area of the rectangle is 128, what is the length of the rectangle?

Ⓐ 4

Ⓑ 8

Ⓒ 16

Ⓓ $21\frac{1}{3}$

2 Mark for Review

If $xy < 0$, which of the following must be true?

I. $x + y = 0$

II. $2y - 2x < 0$

III. $x^2 + y^2 > 0$

Ⓐ I only

Ⓑ III only

Ⓒ I and III

Ⓓ II and III

3 Mark for Review

If $\frac{\sqrt{x}}{2} = 2\sqrt{2}$, what is the value of x?

Ⓐ 4

Ⓑ 16

Ⓒ $16\sqrt{2}$

Ⓓ 32

4 Mark for Review

$$\sqrt{2x - k} = 3 - x$$

If $k = 3$, which of the following contains all possible solutions to the equation above?

Ⓐ −2

Ⓑ 2

Ⓒ 2 and 6

Ⓓ 6

5 Mark for Review

If Alex can fold 12 napkins in x minutes, how many napkins can he fold in y hours?

Ⓐ $\frac{720}{xy}$

Ⓑ $\frac{xy}{720}$

Ⓒ $\frac{720y}{x}$

Ⓓ $\frac{720x}{y}$

6 Mark for Review

Nails are sold in 8-ounce and 20-ounce boxes. If 50 boxes of nails were sold and the total weight of the nails sold was less than 600 ounces, what is the greatest possible number of 20-ounce boxes that could have been sold?

Ⓐ 16

Ⓑ 17

Ⓒ 25

Ⓓ 33

7 Mark for Review

In a certain school, 55% of the students sing in the choir. Of those who do not sing in the choir, 80% play in the band. If all students at the school participate in exactly one musical activity, what percentage of the students in the school participate in a musical activity other than singing in the choir or playing in the band?

Ⓐ 9%

Ⓑ 11%

Ⓒ 36%

Ⓓ 44%

8 Mark for Review

The equation $ax^2 - 12x + 12 = 0$ has exactly one solution for which of the following values of constant a?

Ⓐ -3

Ⓑ -2

Ⓒ 2

Ⓓ 3

9 Mark for Review

A gas station sells regular gasoline for \$2.39 per gallon and premium gasoline for \$2.79 per gallon. If the gas station sold a total of 550 gallons of both types of gasoline in one day for a total of \$1,344.50, how many gallons of premium gasoline were sold?

Ⓐ 25

Ⓑ 75

Ⓒ 175

Ⓓ 475

10 Mark for Review

On a test, all right answers are worth the same number of points and all wrong answers are worth the same number of points. The equation $25C - 20W = 400$ represents the number of right answers, C, and wrong answers, W, a student had on a test when the student earned a total of 400 points. The point value of a right answer is how much more than the point value of a wrong answer?

Ⓐ 20

Ⓑ 25

Ⓒ 45

Ⓓ 80

OTHER DIGITAL SAT ALGEBRA STRATEGIES DRILL ANSWERS AND EXPLANATIONS

1. **C** The question asks for the length of the rectangle. This is a specific value, and there are numbers in the answer choices, so plug in the answers. If you start with (B), the length is 8, and the width is half that, or 4. Area is length × width. The area of this rectangle is 8 × 4, which is nowhere near 128. Eliminate (A) and (B), as both are too small. Try (C). If the length is 16, the width is 8. So, does 128 = 16 × 8? Yes, it does! Since this matches the information in the question, stop here. The correct answer is (C).

2. **B** The question asks which statements must be true. A question with unknown variables indicates a good place to plug in. You need numbers for x and y that will give you a negative product. Try $x = 1$ and $y = -2$. If you plug these into the statements in the Roman numerals, you find that (I) is false, but (II) and (III) are true. You can eliminate any answer choice that contains (I). This leaves (B) and (D). Now try different numbers to see if you can eliminate another choice. If you try $x = -1$ and $y = 2$, you find that (II) is false and (III) is still true. The correct answer is (B).

3. **D** The question asks for the value of x. This is a specific amount, and there are numbers in the answer choices, so plug in the answers, starting with (B). If $x = 16$, the left side of the equation is $\frac{\sqrt{16}}{2} = \frac{4}{2} = 2$. Does that equal $2\sqrt{2}$? No—it's too small. Choice (C) seems tough to work with, so try (D) next. If it is too big, (C) is your answer. For (D), $x = 32$, and the left side of the equation becomes $\frac{\sqrt{32}}{2} = \frac{\sqrt{16 \times 2}}{2} = \frac{4\sqrt{2}}{2} = 2\sqrt{2}$. It's a match. The correct answer is (D).

4. **B** The question asks for the possible solutions to an equation. Since the question asks for a specific value and the answers contain numbers in increasing order, plug in the answers. Write the answers on the scratch paper, label them as "x," and start with a number that appears more than once in the answers, such as 2. Plug $x = 2$ and $k = 3$ into the equation to get $\sqrt{2(2)-3} = 3-2$, which becomes $\sqrt{4-3} = 1$, then $\sqrt{1} = 1$, and finally $1 = 1$. This is true, so eliminate (A) and (D) because they do not include 2. Try 6 next, and plug $x = 6$ and $k = 3$ into the equation to get $\sqrt{2(6)-3} = 3-6$, which becomes $\sqrt{12-3} = -3$, then $\sqrt{9} = -3$, and finally $3 = -3$. (On the Digital SAT, the square root of a number is always positive.) This is not true, so eliminate (C). The correct answer is (B).

5. **C** The question asks for the number of napkins that can be folded in y hours. The two variables tell you this is a great place to plug in. Pick numbers that make the math easy. You can try $x = 30$ and $y = 2$. So in 2 hours there are 4 periods of 30 minutes each: 12 × 4 = 48. Alex can fold 48 napkins in 2 hours, so 48 is your target. Plug the values for x and y into the answer choices to see which one matches the target. Only (C) works, so the correct answer is (C).

6. **A** The question asks for the greatest possible number of 20-ounce boxes. Because this is a specific amount and there are numbers in the answer choices, this is a perfect opportunity to use PITA. Start with (C). If there are twenty-five 20-ounce boxes, then there are twenty-five 8-ounce boxes because a total of 50 boxes was purchased. In this case, the twenty-five 20-ounce boxes weigh 500 ounces, and the twenty-five 8-ounce boxes weigh 200 ounces; the total is 700 ounces. This is too big because the question says the total weight was less than 600. If (C) is too big, (D) must also be too big; eliminate both answers. If you try (B), the total weight is 604 ounces, which is still too big. Thus, the correct answer is (A).

7. **A** The question asks for a percentage. No specific values are given, so plug in. Since *percent* means "out of 100," plug in 100 for the total number of students to make the math easy. Next, work the steps of the question one at a time. The question states that *55% of the students sing in the choir*, so 55 of the 100 students sing in the choir. Read carefully: the next step refers to *those who do not sing in the choir.* If 55 sing in the choir, $100 - 55 = 45$ do not sing in the choir. Take 80%, or $\frac{80}{100}$, of those 45 students to get $\frac{80}{100}(45) = 36$ students who play in the band. That leaves $100 - 55 - 36 = 9$ students who participate in a musical activity other than choir or band. As a result of plugging in 100, there is no need to do math to convert to a percentage: 9 out of 100 is 9%. The correct answer is (A).

8. **D** The question asks for the value of a constant in a quadratic equation. One way to solve the question is to work with the discriminant, which you learned about in Chapter 21. However, the built-in calculator or a personal graphing calculator, combined with plugging in the answers, will get the question right faster. Start with (C), and plug in 2 for a. The equation becomes $2x^2 - 12x + 12 = 0$. Enter the left side of the equation into the built-in calculator. There are two dots where the graph intersects the x-axis, which means the quadratic has two solutions. Eliminate (C). It might not be obvious whether a bigger or smaller number is needed, but it won't take long to try other numbers. Try (B) and replace 2 with –2 in the equation. The calculator shows that the quadratic again has two solutions; eliminate (B). Try (D) and replace –2 with 3. The quadratic now has one solution at (2, 0). The correct answer is (D).

9. **B** The question asks for the number of gallons of premium gasoline that were sold. When asked for a specific value, try plugging in the answers. Label them as gallons of premium and start with the value in (B). If 75 gallons of premium were sold, the station would make 75($2.79) = $209.25 for those sales. A total of 550 gallons was sold, so the station would have sold 550 – 75 = 475 gallons of regular gasoline. The sales for the regular gasoline would be 475($2.39) = $1,135.25. The total sales for both types of gasoline would be $209.25 + $1,135.25 = $1,344.50. That matches the information in the question, so the correct answer is (B).

10. **C** The question asks for the relationship between two values in an equation. It will help to understand what the parts of the equation represent, so label parts of the equation and rewrite it. The question states that C represents the number of right answers, W represents the number of wrong answers, and 400 represents the total number of points. Rewrite the equation as 25(number of right answers) – 20(number of wrong answers) = (total number of points). Thus, 25 and –20 must represent the number of points earned for each right and wrong answer, respectively. To determine how much more a right answer is worth than a wrong answer, subtract the values to get 25 – (–20) = 45. The correct answer is (C).

Summary

- When an algebra question asks for a specific amount and has numbers in the answer choices, plug each of the answer choices into the problem until you find one that works.
- If you start with one of the middle numbers, you may be able to cut your work. The answer choices will be in order, so if your number is too high or too low, you'll know what to eliminate.
- When the question has variables in the answer choices, you can often plug in your own amounts for the unknowns and do arithmetic instead of algebra.
- When you plug in, use "good" numbers—ones that are simple to work with and that make the problem easier to manipulate: 2, 5, 10, or 100 are generally easy numbers to use.
- On meaning in context questions, label the parts of the equation with information from the question, and eliminate answers that don't match the labels.
- Plugging In can also be used on meaning in context questions. If labeling the answers and using Process of Elimination isn't enough to answer the question, plug your own amounts into the equation so you can start to see what is going on.

Chapter 23
Functions and Graphs

The Digital SAT includes a large number of questions about functions, either by themselves or connected to a graph. Some of these questions can get quite complicated, but the same basic concepts apply no matter what. This chapter will give you the tools you need to work on questions about functions and understand how functions and graphs are connected.

CALL ON THE CALCULATOR

A complete understanding of a graphing calculator can make a significant difference in how long it takes to answer questions about the graphs of functions. Try solving the examples with the built-in calculator or your own to discover how powerful it can be. Some questions cannot be solved by the graphing calculator, however, so it's also important to understand the concepts covered in this chapter.

FUNCTION FUNDAMENTALS

Think of a **function** as just a machine for producing ordered pairs. You put in one number and the machine spits out another. Think of these as the input and the output. An input value, x, gets put into the function machine, f, and an output value, y, comes out of the function machine. The most common function is an $f(x)$ function. A simple way to keep functions straight is to remember that $f(x) = y$.

Let's look at a question.

1 Mark for Review

If $f(x) = x^3 - 4x + 8$, what is the value of $f(5)$?

Ⓐ 67

Ⓑ 97

Ⓒ 113

Ⓓ 147

What's This?

Anytime you see the notation *f*(*x*), know that *f* isn't a variable; it's the name of the function. When you say it out loud, it's "*f* of *x*." Though *f*(*x*) is the most common way to show that an equation is a mathematic function, any letter can be used. So you may see *g*(*x*) or *h*(*d*). Know that you're still dealing with a function.

Here's How to Crack It

The question asks for the value of $f(5)$ for the given function. Any time you see a number inside the parentheses, such as $f(5)$, plug in that number for x. The question is actually telling you to use Plugging In! Let's do it:

$$f(5) = 5^3 - 4(5) + 8$$
$$f(5) = 125 - 20 + 8$$
$$f(5) = 113$$

The correct answer is (C).

The previous question gave you a number to put into the function, which made it a Plugging In question. If the question gives you information about what comes out of the function and asks what should go in, it's a PITA question!

Here's an example of using PITA on a function question.

2 Mark for Review

For what value of x does $f(x) = 12$ if the function f is defined as $f(x) = \frac{1}{2}x + 2$?

Ⓐ 5

Ⓑ 8

Ⓒ 20

Ⓓ 24

Use PITA!
Don't forget that you can often plug in the answer choices on function questions! Noticing a pattern yet? Just a few easy tricks can unlock a lot of easy points.

Here's How to Crack It

The question asks for the input value of a function that results in a specific output value. The answer choices contain numbers in increasing order, and one of them must be the input that will result in an output of 12. Plug in the answers. Rewrite the answer choices on the scratch paper and label them "x." Next, start with one of the middle numbers. Try (B), 8. Plug $x = 8$ into the function to get $f(8) = \frac{1}{2}(8) + 2$, or $f(8) = 4 + 2$, and finally $f(8) = 6$. This does not match the output value of 12, so eliminate (B). The result was too small, so try a larger number and plug in $x = 20$. The function becomes $f(20) = \frac{1}{2}(20) + 2$, or $f(20) = 10 + 2$, and finally $f(20) = 12$. This matches the output value of 12, so stop here. The correct answer is (C).

In this case, it would have been possible to set the function equal to 12 and solve for x. However, solving will be difficult on more complicated problems, and it's easy to make mistakes with algebra. PITA is always a good idea when a question gives the output of a function and asks for the input.

Now that you know the basics of functions on the Digital SAT, try the next one.

3 Mark for Review

If $f(x) = x^2 + 2$, which of the following could be a value of $f(x)$?

Ⓐ –1

Ⓑ 0

Ⓒ 1

Ⓓ 2

Here's How to Crack It

The question asks for a possible value of the function. Therefore, the question is asking which of these values could be spit out of the $f(x)$ machine. Think about what is going in. No matter what you put in as a value for x, the value of x^2 has to be positive or zero. So, the lowest possible value of $x^2 + 2$ is 2. The correct answer is (D).

Note that you could also approach this question by plugging in the answers. If you plugged in 1 for $f(x)$, for instance, you would get $1 = x^2 + 2$, which becomes $x^2 = -1$, which is impossible.

Sometimes you'll get more complicated questions. As long as you know that when you put in x, your function will spit out another number, you'll be fine. Now try another one.

4 Mark for Review

What is the value of c if $g(x) = 4x^2 - 6$ and $g(x - c) = 4x^2 + 40x + 94$?

Ⓐ –40

Ⓑ –5

Ⓒ 5

Ⓓ 40

Here's How to Crack It

The question asks for the value of c. In function notation, the number inside the parentheses is the x-value that goes into the function. This question might seem complicated, but look beyond the math and use your Princeton Review Digital SAT knowledge. The question asks for a specific value and has numbers in the answers, so try PITA! Label the answer choices as "c" and start in the middle with (C), 5. Plug $c = 5$ into the question, and the value to put into the function becomes $x - 5$.

$$g(x - 5) = 4(x - 5)^2 - 6$$

FOIL the quadratic to get

$$g(x - 5) = 4(x^2 - 10x + 25) - 6$$

Distribute and combine like terms to get

$$g(x - 5) = 4x^2 - 40x + 100 - 6$$
$$g(x - 5) = 4x^2 - 40x + 94$$

Set the results equal to the quadratic given in the question.

$$4x^2 - 40x + 94 = 4x^2 + 40x + 94$$

This is not true, so eliminate (C). The middle term has the right coefficient but the wrong sign, so try (B), –5. The function becomes

$$g(x + 5) = 4(x + 5)^2 - 6$$

Carry out the same steps as before to get

$$g(x + 5) = 4(x^2 + 10x + 25) - 6$$
$$g(x + 5) = 4x^2 + 40x + 100 - 6$$
$$g(x + 5) = 4x^2 + 40x + 94$$

This is equal to the quadratic given in the question, so –5 is the value of c. The correct answer is (B).

Sometimes you may see a word problem that describes a function and then asks you to "build a function" that describes the real-world situation presented in the question. Take the following question, for example.

5 Mark for Review

Rock climbing routes are rated on a numbered scale with the highest number representing the most difficult route. Sally tried a range of shoe sizes on each of several routes of varying difficulty and found that when she wore smaller shoes, she could climb routes of greater difficulty. If D represents the difficulty rating of a route Sally successfully climbed and s represents the size of the shoes she wore on such a route, then which of the following could express D as a function of s?

Ⓐ $D(s) = s^2$

Ⓑ $D(s) = \sqrt{s}$

Ⓒ $D(s) = s - 3.5$

Ⓓ $D(s) = \frac{45}{s}$

Here's How to Crack It

The question asks for a function that best represents a situation. Start by thinking about the relationship described in the question: the smaller the shoes, the greater the difficulty. This is an inverse relationship. So, look for an inverse function. Only (D) expresses this type of relationship because a greater value of s leads to a smaller value of D.

If you aren't sure, try plugging in numbers to try it out. Plug in $s = 8$ and then $s = 10$ to see if the result for D is smaller when you use a larger shoe size. Since only (D) results in a smaller difficulty for a larger shoe size, the correct answer is (D).

One way the test-writers will make functions more complicated is to use percentages. Use your knowledge of function basics from this chapter and of percentages from earlier in this book to work through these questions.

Try this example.

6 Mark for Review

For every increase in the value of x by 1 in function z, the value of $z(x)$ increases by 25%. Which of the following functions defines z if $z(1) = 12.5$?

(A) $z(x) = 10(1.25)^x$

(B) $z(x) = 1.25(10)^x$

(C) $z(x) = 0.75(10)^x$

(D) $z(x) = 10(0.75)^x$

Here's How to Crack It

The question asks for the equation that defines a function. Recall that, in function notation, the number inside the parentheses is the x-value that goes into the function, or the input, and the value that comes out of the function is the y-value, or the output. The question provides a pair of input and output values by stating that $z(1) = 12.5$. Plug $x = 1$ into the answer choices and eliminate answers that do not result in $z(1) = 12.5$. These are the results:

A) $z(1) = 10(1.25)^1$	$z(1) = 10(1.25)$	$z(1) = 12.5$	Keep (A).
B) $z(1) = 1.25(10)^1$	$z(1) = 1.25(10)$	$z(1) = 12.5$	Keep (B).
C) $z(1) = 0.75(10)^1$	$z(1) = 0.75(10)$	$z(1) = 7.5$	Eliminate (C).
D) $z(1) = 10(0.75)^1$	$z(1) = 10(0.75)$	$z(1) = 7.5$	Eliminate (D).

Two answers worked, so try a different value. The question states that *for every increase in the value of x by 1 in function z, the value of z(x) increases by 25%*. Increase the input value by 1 to get $x = 1 + 1 = 2$. When $x = 1$, $z(x) = 12.5$, so when $x = 2$, $z(x)$ will increase by 25%. Take the value of $z(1)$, which is 12.5, and add 25% of it. *Percent* means out of 100, so translate 25% as $\frac{25}{100}$. Thus, $z(2) = 12.5 + \left(\frac{25}{100}\right)(12.5)$, or $z(2) = 15.625$. The other option is to use the built-in calculator, which automatically translates the % symbol and adds the word "of" to multiply the percent by the next number you enter. Either way, the target value for $z(2)$ is 15.625. Plug $x = 2$ into the remaining answer choices:

A) $z(2) = 10(1.25)^2$	$z(2) = 10(1.5625)$	$z(2) = 15.625$	Keep (A).
B) $z(2) = 1.25(10)^2$	$z(2) = 1.25(100)$	$z(2) = 125$	Eliminate (B).

Only one answer remains, so it must be correct. If the functions in the answer choices look familiar, that's because they are in the form of the growth and decay formula you learned about in Chapter 21: *final amount* = *original amount* $(1 \pm rate)^{number\ of\ changes}$. In correct answer (A), $z(x)$ is the *final amount*, 10 is the *original amount*, 0.25 is the *rate*, and x is the number of changes. But don't worry if you didn't catch that: plugging in values from the question was all you needed to do to get this one right. The correct answer is (A).

Functions and Tables

There is one more way the test-writers will test you on input and output values in a function, and that's by putting the values into a table. Stick to the basics of functions and look for chances to plug in.

Take a look at the following example.

7 Mark for Review

x	$f(x)$
1	8
2	17
3	26
4	35

Linear function f is represented in the table above, which shows four values of x and their corresponding values of $f(x)$. Which of the following functions accurately represents function f?

Ⓐ $f(x) = 8x$

Ⓑ $f(x) = 8x + 8$

Ⓒ $f(x) = 9x - 1$

Ⓓ $f(x) = 9x + 8$

Here's How to Crack It

The question asks for the function that represents values given in a table. Apply the function basics: x is the input, and $f(x)$, which is equivalent to y, is the output of the function. The table shows pairs of values for x and $f(x)$, and the correct function must work for every pair of values. Plug in values from the table and eliminate functions that don't work. Plug in $x = 1$ and $f(x) = 8$ to get the following results:

A) $8 = 8(1)$, or $8 = 8$ — True, so keep (A).
B) $8 = 8(1) + 8$, or $8 = 16$ — Not true; eliminate (B).
C) $8 = 9(1) - 1$, or $8 = 8$ — True, so keep (C).
D) $8 = 9(1) + 8$, or $8 = 17$ — Not true; eliminate (D).

Two answers worked for the first pair of input and output values, so try a second pair from the table. Plug $x = 2$ and $y = 17$ into the remaining answers to get these results:

A) $17 = 8(2)$, or $17 = 16$ — Not true; eliminate (A).
C) $17 = 9(2) - 1$, or $17 = 17$ — True, so keep (C).

The only answer that worked both times must be correct, so don't spend time trying the other two points. The correct answer is (C).

What's the Point?

Why did math folks come up with functions? To graph them, of course! When you put in a value for x, and your machine (or function) spits out another number, that's your y. You now have an ordered pair. Functions are just another way to express graphs. Knowing the connection between functions and graphs is useful, because you will most likely see questions involving graphs on the Digital SAT.

THE COORDINATE PLANE

A **coordinate plane,** or the ***xy*-plane,** is made up of two number lines that intersect at a right angle. The horizontal number line is called the ***x*-axis,** and the vertical number line is the ***y*-axis.**

The four areas formed by the intersection of the axes are called **quadrants.** The location of any point can be described with a pair of numbers (x, y), just the way you would describe a point on a map: (0, 0) are the coordinates of the intersection of the two axes (also called the **origin**); (1, 2) are the coordinates of the point one space to the right and two spaces up; (–1, 5) are the coordinates of the point one space to the left and five spaces up; (–4, –2) are the coordinates of the point four spaces to the left and two spaces down. All of these points are located on the following figure.

Quadrants
A coordinate plane has four distinct areas known as quadrants. The quadrants are numbered counterclockwise, starting from the top right. They help determine generally whether *x* and *y* are positive or negative. Sometimes knowing what quadrant a point is in and what that means is all you need to find the answer.

Ways to Remember
Having trouble remembering that the *x*-coordinate comes before the *y*-coordinate in an ordered pair? Just remember the phrase "*x* before *y*, walk before you fly." The letter *x* also comes before *y* in the dictionary.

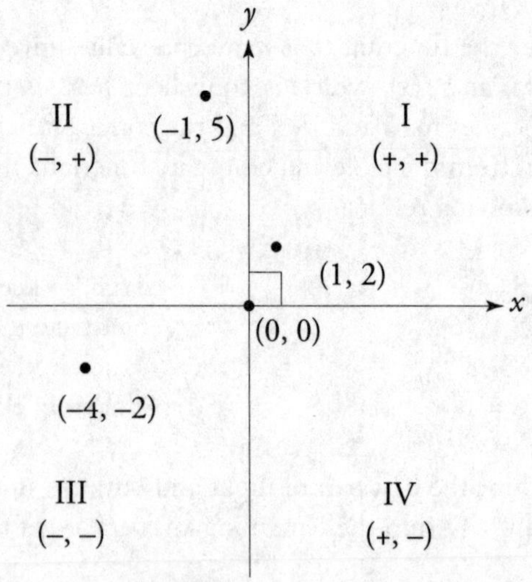

Some of the questions on the Digital SAT may require you to know certain properties of lines on the *xy*-plane. Let's talk about them.

POINTS ON A LINE

You may be asked if a point is on a line or on the graph of any other equation. Just plug the coordinates of the point into the equation of the line to determine if that point makes the equation a true statement.

8 Mark for Review

In the *xy*-plane, which of the following ordered pairs is a point on the line $y = 2x - 6$?

Ⓐ (6, 7)

Ⓑ (7, 7)

Ⓒ (7, 8)

Ⓓ (8, 7)

Here's How to Crack It

The question asks for a point that is on the given line. Plug in the answers, starting with (B). The (x, y) point is (7, 7), so plug in 7 for x and 7 for y. The equation becomes $7 = 2(7) - 6$ or $7 = 8$. This isn't true, so eliminate (B). The result was very close to a true statement, and the point in (C) has the same x-coordinate and a larger y-coordinate, so try that next. Because $8 = 2(7) - 6$, the correct answer is (C).

SLOPE

You always read a graph from left to right. As you read the graph, how much the line goes up or down is known as the slope. **Slope** is the rate of change of a line and is commonly known as "rise over run." It's denoted by the letter m. Essentially, it's the change in the y-coordinates over the change in the x-coordinates and can be found with the following formula:

$$m = \frac{(y_2 - y_1)}{(x_2 - x_1)}$$

This formula uses the points (x_1, y_1) and (x_2, y_2). For example, if you have the points (2, 3) and (7, 4), the slope of the line created by these points would be

$$m = \frac{(4 - 3)}{(7 - 2)}$$

So the slope of a line with points (2, 3) and (7, 4) would be $\frac{1}{5}$, which means that every time you go up 1 unit, you travel to the right 5 units.

EQUATIONS OF A LINE

Slope-Intercept Form

The equation of a line can take multiple forms. The most common of these is known as the **slope-intercept form.** If you know the slope and the y-intercept, you can create the equation of a given line. A slope-intercept equation takes the form $y = mx + b$, where m is the slope and b is the ***y*-intercept** (the point where the function crosses the y-axis).

Let's say that you know that a certain line has a slope of 5 $\left(\text{which is the same as } \frac{5}{1}\right)$ and a y-intercept of 3. The equation of the line would be $y = 5x + 3$. You could graph this line simply by looking at this form of the equation. First, draw the y-intercept, (0, 3). Next, plug in a number for x and solve for y to get a coordinate pair of a point on the line. Then connect the point you just found with the y-intercept you already drew, and voilà, you have a line. If you want more points, you can create a table such as the following:

x	y
–2	–7
–1	–2
0	3
1	8

Take a look at the finished product:

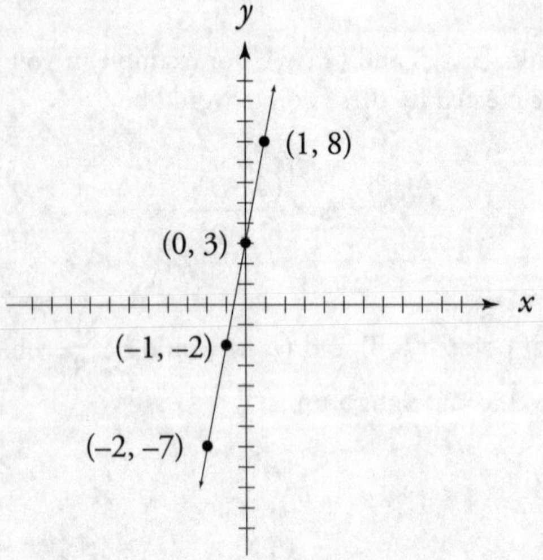

One way the Digital SAT can test your understanding of lines is to show you a graph and ask you which equation describes that graph.

Here's an example.

9 Mark for Review

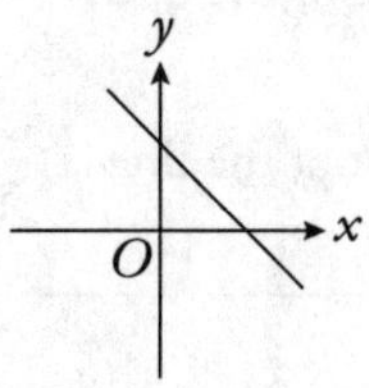

Which of the following could be the equation of the line represented in the graph above?

Ⓐ $y = -2x - 1$

Ⓑ $y = -2x + 4$

Ⓒ $y = 2x - 4$

Ⓓ $y = 2x + 4$

Here's How to Crack It

The question asks for the equation of a line based on the graph. Remember that the equation of a line is $y = mx + b$, where m is the slope and b is the y-intercept. Look at the graph and think about what the equation should look like. Since the line is sloping downward, it should have a negative slope, so you can eliminate (C) and (D). Next, since the line has a positive y-intercept, you can eliminate (A). The correct answer is (B).

Standard Form

Another way the equation of a line can be written is the **standard form** of $Ax + By = C$, where A, B, and C are constants and A and B do not equal zero. The test-writers will sometimes present equations in this form in the hopes that you will waste time putting it in slope-intercept form. If you know what to look for, the standard form can be just as useful as the slope-intercept form.

In standard form $Ax + By = C$:

- the slope of the line is $-\frac{A}{B}$
- the y-intercept of the line is $\frac{C}{B}$
- the x-intercept of the line is $\frac{C}{A}$

The equation $y = 5x + 3$ in the previous example would be $-5x + y = 3$ when written in the standard form. Using the information above, you can see that:

$$\text{slope} = -\left(\frac{-5}{1}\right) = 5$$

$$y\text{-intercept} = \frac{3}{1} = 3$$

$$x\text{-intercept} = \frac{3}{-5} = -\frac{3}{5}$$

The answers for the slope and the y-intercept were the same as when the slope-intercept form was used. Depending on the form of the equation in the question or in the answers, knowing these line equation facts can help save time on the test.

Let's look at how this may be tested.

10 Mark for Review

The graph of which of the following equations is parallel to the line with equation $y = -\frac{1}{3}x - \frac{1}{6}$?

Ⓐ $x - \frac{1}{3}y = 3$

Ⓑ $x - 3y = 2$

Ⓒ $x + 6y = 4$

Ⓓ $x + 3y = 5$

Here's How to Crack It

The question asks for the equation of a line that has a slope parallel to the slope of the line given. In the form $y = mx + b$, m represents the slope. The equation in the question is in that form, so the slope is $-\frac{1}{3}$. Parallel lines have equal slopes, so all you need to do now is find the answer choice that also has a slope of $-\frac{1}{3}$.

One way to do that would be to rewrite each answer in the $y = mx + b$ form. However, notice that the equations in the answer choices are in the $Ax + By = C$ form, and in that form the slope is equal to $-\frac{A}{B}$. Find the slope of each answer choice, and eliminate the ones that are not $-\frac{1}{3}$. The slope of the line in (A) is $-\frac{1}{-\frac{1}{3}} = 3$. This is not the correct slope, so eliminate (A). The slope of the line in (B) is $-\frac{1}{-3} = \frac{1}{3}$. This is also the wrong slope, so eliminate (B). The slope of the line in (C) is $-\frac{1}{6}$, which is also the wrong slope, so eliminate (C). The slope of the line in (D) is $-\frac{1}{3}$. This is the same slope as the line given in the question. The correct answer is (D).

PARALLEL AND PERPENDICULAR LINES

So now you know that **parallel lines** have the same slope. Whenever the Digital SAT brings up **perpendicular lines,** just remember that a perpendicular line has a slope that is the *negative reciprocal* of the other line's slope. For instance, if the slope of a line is 3, then the slope of a line perpendicular to it would be $-\frac{1}{3}$. Combine this with the skills you've already learned to work on a question about perpendicular lines.

Parallel vs. Perpendicular
Parallel lines have the same slope and never intersect. Perpendicular lines have slopes that are negative reciprocals and intersect at a right angle.

Here's an example.

11 Mark for Review

Which of the following is the graph of a line perpendicular to the line defined by the equation $2x + 5y = 10$?

Ⓐ
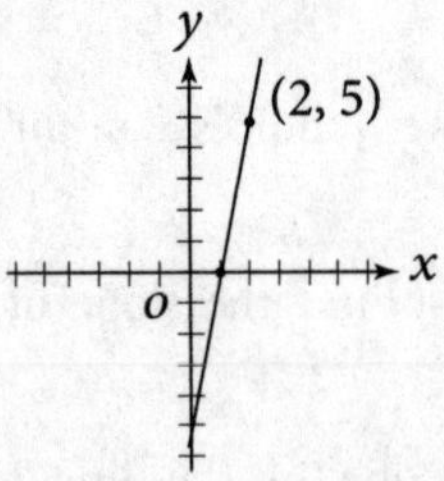

Ⓑ
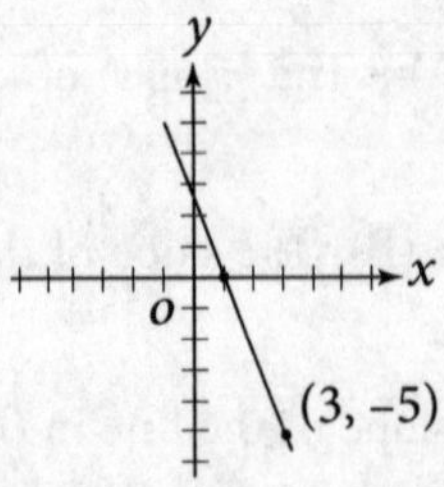

Ⓒ
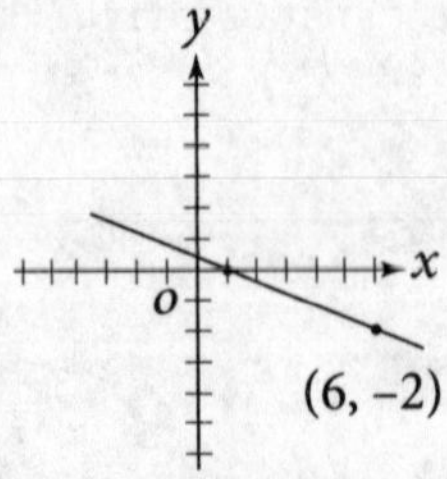

Ⓓ
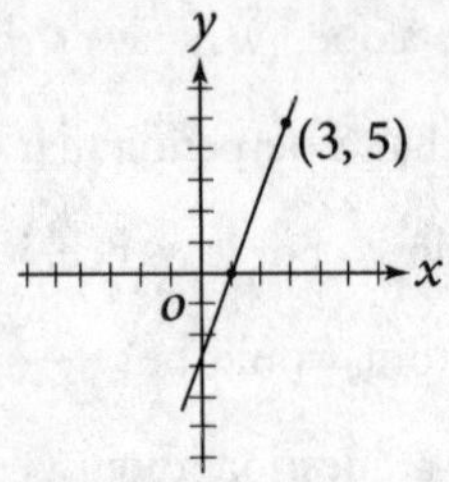

Here's How to Crack It

The question asks for a line perpendicular to the line $2x + 5y = 10$. Therefore, you need to find the slope of the line and then take the negative reciprocal to find the slope of the perpendicular line. You can convert the equation into the $y = mx + b$ format in order to find the slope, or simply remember that when an equation is presented in the form $Ax + By = C$, the slope is equal to $-\frac{A}{B}$. So the slope of this line is $-\frac{2}{5}$, and the slope of a perpendicular line would be $\frac{5}{2}$.

Look at the answer choices for one with a positive (upward) slope. Choices (B) and (C) slope downward, so eliminate them. Next, use points in the graph to find the slope of each answer. Eliminate (A); it has points at (1, 0) and (2, 5), for a slope of 5—too steep. The only remaining choice is (D), so the correct answer is (D).

TWO EQUATIONS WITH INFINITELY MANY SOLUTIONS

In the previous chapters on algebra, we discussed equations with one or multiple solutions. Now imagine an equation in which any value of *x* would create a viable solution to the equation.

$$x + 3 = x + 3$$

In this case, it is fairly obvious that any number you choose to put in for *x* will create a true equation. But what does it mean when two lines have infinitely many solutions? Let's look at an example.

To Infinity...and Beyond!
When given two equations with infinitely many solutions, find a way to make them equal. The equations represent the same line.

12 Mark for Review

$$gx - hy = 78$$
$$4x + 3y = 13$$

In the system of equations above, *g* and *h* are constants. If the system has infinitely many solutions, what is the value of *gh*?

Ⓐ –432

Ⓑ –6

Ⓒ 6

Ⓓ 432

Here's How to Crack It

The question asks for the value of gh, where g and h are coefficients in the system of equations. This question may have you scratching your head and moving on to the next question, but explore what you can do to solve this before you decide it's not worth your time. You may be surprised by how easy it is to solve a problem like this.

When they say that these equations have infinitely many solutions, what they are really saying is that these are the same equation, or that one equation is a multiple of the other equation. In other words, these two equations represent the same line. With that in mind, try to determine what needs to be done to make these equations equal. Since the right side of the equation is dealing with only a constant, first determine what you would need to do to make 13 equal to 78.

In this case, you need to multiply 13 by 6. Since you are working with equations, you need to do the same thing to both sides of the equation in order for the equation to remain equal.

$$6(4x + 3y) = 6 \times 13$$

$$24x + 18y = 78$$

Since both equations are now equal to 78, you can set them equal to each other, giving you this equation:

$$24x + 18y = gx - hy$$

You may know that when you have equations with the same variables on each side, the coefficients on those variables must be equal, so you can deduce that $g = 24$ and $h = -18$. (Be cautious when you evaluate this equation. The test-writers are being sneaky by using addition in one equation and subtraction in another.) Therefore, gh equals $24 \times -18 = -432$. The correct answer is (A).

TWO EQUATIONS WITH NO SOLUTIONS

You saw above that a system of equations can have infinitely many solutions. When solving equations, you likely assume, as most people do, that there will be at least one solution to the equation, but that is not always the case. Look at the following example.

$$3x - 6 = 3x + 7$$

If you solve this equation, you will find that $-6 = 7$. Since -6 can never equal 7, there is no value of x that can be put into this equation to make it true. In this case, the equation has no solutions.

What does it mean if two equations of lines have no solutions? Here's one to try.

There's Just No Solution
When given two equations with no solutions, find a way to compare slopes. The equations represent parallel lines.

13 Mark for Review

Which of the following accurately represents the set of solutions for the lines $6x + 12y = -24$ and $y = -\frac{1}{2}x + 2$?

Ⓐ (0, –4)

Ⓑ (0, 4)

Ⓒ There are no solutions.

Ⓓ There are infinitely many solutions.

Here's How to Crack It

The question asks for the solution to the system of equations. If the lines intersect, this will be the point of intersection. The answers in (C) and (D), though, suggest that the lines may be the same or parallel. Rather than plugging in the points in (A) and (B), look for a way to compare slopes. Start by putting the first line into $y = mx + b$ form: $12y = -6x - 24$. Divide the whole equation by 12, so $y = -\frac{1}{2}x - 2$. Since these lines have the same slope but different *y*-intercepts, the lines are parallel, and they will never intersect. Therefore, the correct answer is (C).

If two lines had different slopes, the lines would intersect at a single point such as (A) or (B). If the equations were identical, then they would be the same line and therefore have infinitely many solutions.

POINTS OF INTERSECTION

Earlier in this book you learned how to find the solution to a system of equations. There are several ways to do this, including stacking up the equations and adding or subtracting, setting them equal, or even plugging in the answers. The Digital SAT may also ask about the intersection of the graphs of two equations in the *xy*-plane, which is a similar idea.

Let's try one.

14 Mark for Review

In the *xy*-plane, which of the following is a point of intersection between the graphs of $y = x + 2$ and $y = x^2 + x - 2$?

Ⓐ (0, −2)

Ⓑ (0, 2)

Ⓒ (1, 0)

Ⓓ (2, 4)

Here's How to Crack It

The question asks for the point of intersection for two equations. This is a point that is on the graphs of both equations. Therefore, the point would work if plugged into the equation of the line and the equation of the parabola.

Here's how you would apply PITA in a point of intersection question.

So, use PITA by testing the answer choices: start with one of the answers in the middle and plug the point into each equation to see if it is true. The correct point of intersection will work in both functions. Try (C) in the first equation: does 0 = (1) + 2? No. So, (C) is not the answer. Try (D) in the first equation: does 4 = (2) + 2? Yes. So, try (D) in the second equation: does 4 = (2)2 + 2 – 2? Yes. Since (2, 4) works in both equations, the correct answer is (D).

CALL ON THE CALCUATOR

It's good to know the concepts and math behind the graphs of lines and the way they're tested on the Digital SAT. It's also good to know how to use the built-in graphing calculator or your own that you bring with you on test day. Go back to some of the previous examples and try them again using a graphing calculator (if you didn't use it the first time). You might be surprised by how easy some of them are to answer.

The rest of this chapter will deal with graphs of parabolas and circles instead of straight lines. The graphing calculator is extremely useful on many questions like this, and we'll show you how to take advantage of it.

GRAPHING FUNCTIONS

One type of function question you might be asked is how the graph of a function would shift if you added a value to it.

Here is a quick guide for the graph of $f(x) = x^2$, as seen below:

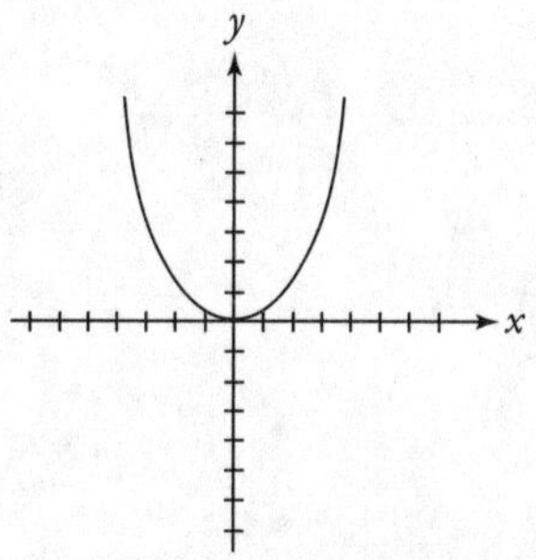

For $f(x) + c$, where c is a constant, the graph will shift up c units, as shown in the figure below:

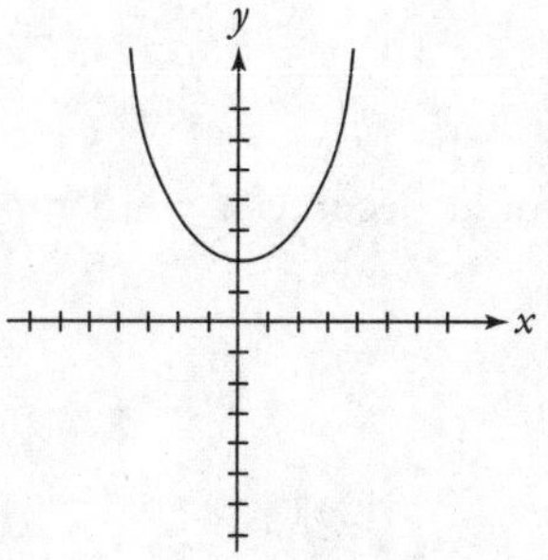

y = f(x)

Sometimes, instead of seeing the typical $y = mx + b$ equation, or something similar, you'll see $f(x) = mx + b$. Look familiar? Graphs are just another way to show information from a function. Functions show information algebraically and graphs show functions geometrically (as pictured).

Here's an example. The function $f(x) = 3x - 2$ is shown graphically as the following:

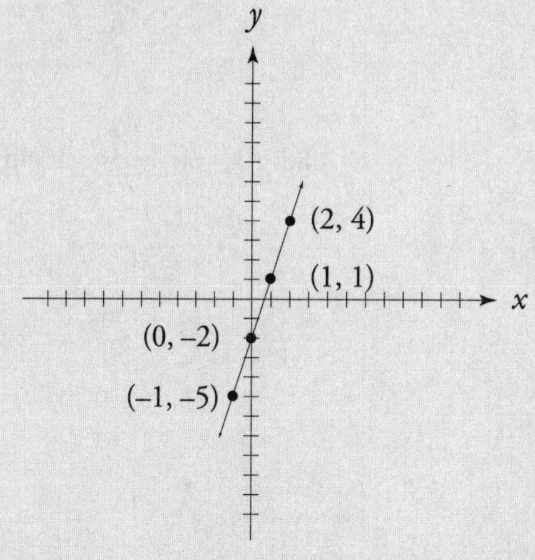

The reason the Digital SAT includes function questions is to test whether you can figure out the relationship between a function and its graph. To tackle these questions, you need to know that the independent variable, the x, is on the x-axis, and the dependent variable, the $f(x)$, is on the y-axis. For example, if you see a function of $f(x) = 7$, then you need to understand that this is a graph of a horizontal line where $y = 7$.

Conversely, $f(x) - c$ will shift the graph down by c units:

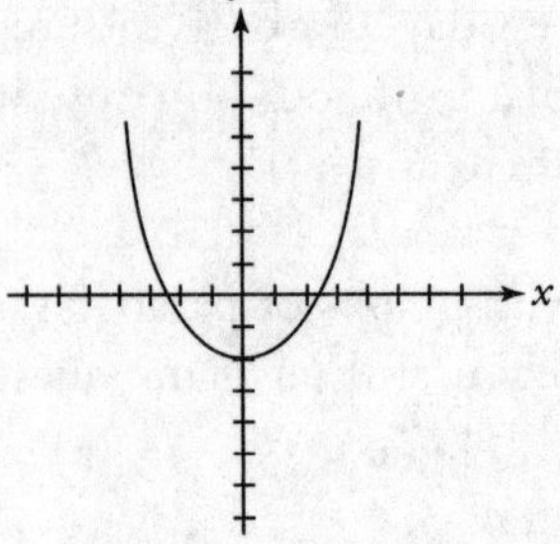

For $f(x + c)$, the graph will shift c units to the left:

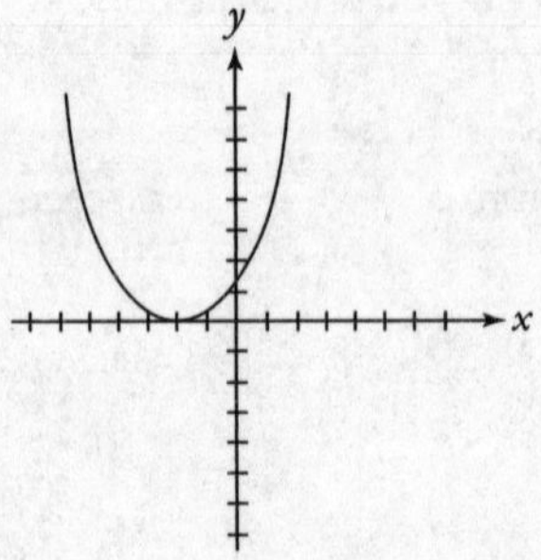

For $f(x - c)$, the graph will shift to the right by c units:

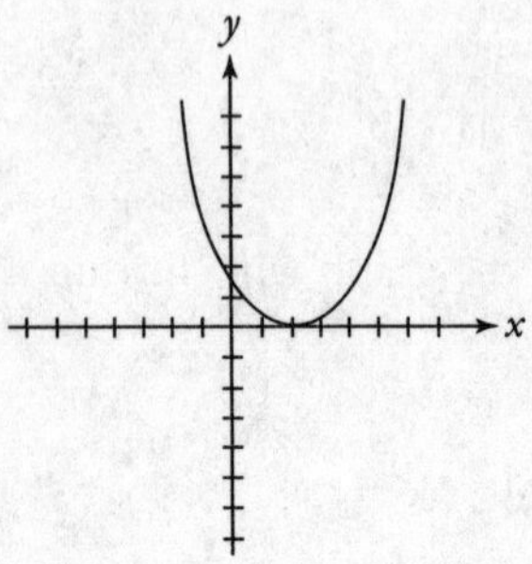

You may have realized how easy these questions would become if you simply put them into your graphing calculator.

You can also plug in points to find the correct graph.

You have several options for dealing with questions like this. You can know the four rules for transforming graphs, you can plug in points to find the correct graph, or you can use a graphing calculator. The built-in calculator can graph the equation even if the test-writers give you an equation in an unusual form.

Try the next one using the built-in graphing calculator or your own.

15 Mark for Review

Function f can be graphed in the xy-plane by translating function g down 3 units. Function g is defined by $g(x) = -2x^3 + 4x^2 - x + 2$. What is the value of $f(1)$?

Watch Us Crack It
Watch the step-by-step video explanation of how to answer this question in your Student Tools.

Here's How to Crack It

The question asks for the value of a function. Start by graphing the equation of $g(x)$. In the built-in calculator, enter $g(x) = -2x^3 + 4x^2 - x + 2$ into the first entry field and you will see the graph in the graph display. The question asks about $f(1)$, so find the point where $x = 1$ on the graph of $g(x)$. You might need to scroll and zoom to see 1 on the x-axis, and use the mouse pointer to find the y-value when $x = 1$. The point is at (1, 3). The question states that the graph of function f is the graph of function g translated down 3 units. Count 3 units down from the point at (1, 3) in the graph of $g(x)$ to get to a point at (1, 0). At this point, $x = 1$ and $y = 0$. Since $f(x) = y$, the value of $f(1)$ is 0. The correct answer is 0.

EQUATIONS OF A PARABOLA

Standard Form

The Digital SAT will ask questions using three different forms of the equation for a parabola.

> The standard form of a parabola equation is
>
> $$y = ax^2 + bx + c$$

In the standard form of a parabola, the value of a tells whether a parabola opens upward or downward (if a is positive, the parabola opens upward, and if a is negative, the parabola opens downward).

Factored Form

We looked at equations for parabolas in Chapter 21 when we solved quadratics. The factored form of a quadratic equation reveals the roots of the parabola. These are also the solutions of x. Given a question about roots or solutions, it can be helpful to know the relationship between the equation and the graph of the parabola in the xy-plane.

> The factored form of a parabola equation is
>
> $$y = a(x - r_1)(x - r_2)$$
>
> In the factored form, r_1 and r_2 are the roots or x-intercepts of the parabola.

For the next question, the equation is $y = x^2 - 4x - 12$. If you factored this, you'd get $y = (x + 2)(x - 6)$, and the roots would be at $x = -2$ and $x = 6$. You can see that those are the exact points on the graph that the parabola crosses the x-axis.

Vertex Form

The vertex form of a parabola equation is

$$y = a(x - h)^2 + k$$

In the vertex form, the point (h, k) is the vertex of the parabola.

In vertex form, the value of a still indicates which way the parabola opens. The most useful feature of vertex form is that it shows the vertex of the parabola, which is the minimum value of y when $a > 0$ or the maximum value of y when $a < 0$. When the equation is not in vertex form, you'll have to do some work to find the vertex.

Here's a typical question about the vertex of a parabola.

16 Mark for Review

The function g is defined by $g(x) = -x^2 + 4x + 12$. For what value of x does $g(x)$ reach its maximum?

Here's How to Crack It

The question asks for the value when a quadratic function reaches its maximum. A parabola reaches its minimum or maximum value at its vertex, so find the x-coordinate of the vertex. The simplest method is to enter the equation into the built-in calculator, then scroll and zoom as needed to find the vertex. The vertex is at (2, 16), so the value of the x-coordinate is 2.

There is also a way to find the x-coordinate using algebra. In vertex form, the vertex is at (h, k). When a quadratic is in standard form, $ax^2 + bx + c$, use the formula $h = -\frac{b}{2a}$ to find the x-coordinate of the vertex. The equation in this question is in standard form, so $a = -1$, $b = 4$, and $c = 12$. The formula becomes $h = -\frac{4}{2(-1)}$, or $h = -\frac{4}{-2}$, and then $h = 2$. You don't need this formula to answer this question, but if you needed to solve for the y-coordinate of the vertex, you could plug $x = 2$ back into the equation to get $-(2)^2 + 4(2) + 12 = -4 + 8 + 12 = 16$. This is the vertex of (2, 16) that you found using the calculator.

Using either method, the correct answer is 2.

In the chapter on algebra, we showed you how the Digital SAT asks questions about the number of solutions to a system of linear equations or a quadratic. Review that to know the rules and how to use the discriminant. However, the calculator provides additional options, and some of the other skills you've learned in this book apply to questions about graphing too.

Think about using a calculator and apply what you've learned so far to the following question.

---

17 Mark for Review

$$\frac{y}{3} = -\frac{7}{2}x$$
$$y = ax^2 + 12.25$$

In the system of equations above, *a* is a constant. If the system of equations has exactly one solution, what is the value of *a*?

Ⓐ −2.25

Ⓑ −1.5

Ⓒ 1.5

Ⓓ 2.25

Here's How to Crack It

The question asks for the value of a constant in a system of equations. The question asks for a specific value, and the answers contain numbers in increasing order, so plug in the answers. Yes, PITA can work on graphing questions, too! Start with an answer in the middle. Try (C), 1.5. Plug $a = 1.5$ into the second equation to get $y = (1.5)(x^2) + 12.25$. Next, enter both equations in the entry fields of the built-in graphing calculator and look at the results in the graph display. Zoom out enough to see both the parabola and the line clearly in the graph display (expanding the calculator window also helps). If you click one of the equations, several gray dots will appear on the graph. One shows the vertex of the parabola, and the other two show where the line intersects the parabola.

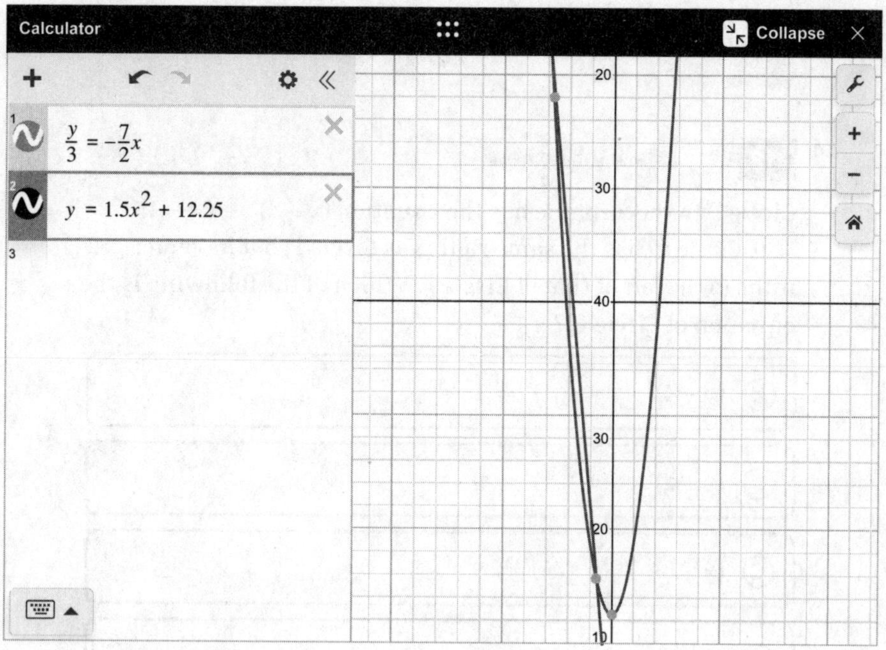

The question states that the *system of equations has exactly one solution*, not two, so eliminate (C). Next, try (D), 2.25. Keep the two equations you already entered and change 1.5 to 2.25 in the second equation. Click on one of the equations to see two gray dots: one is the vertex and the other is the single point where the line intersects the graph. The system now has exactly one solution, and the correct answer is (D).

EQUATION OF A CIRCLE

The Digital SAT will also ask questions about the equation of a circle in the *xy*-plane.

> The equation of a circle is
>
> $$(x - h)^2 + (y - k)^2 = r^2$$
>
> In the circle equation, the center of the circle is the point (h, k), and the radius of the circle is r.

Let's look at a question that tests the use of the circle equation.

18 Mark for Review

Circle P in the xy-plane has the equation $(x - 4)^2 + (y + 1)^2 = 9$. Circle Q has the same radius as Circle P, but its center is 2 units to the left of that of Circle P. Which of the following is the equation of Circle Q?

(A) $(x - 4)^2 + (y + 1)^2 = 1$

(B) $(x - 2)^2 + (y + 1)^2 = 9$

(C) $(x - 6)^2 + (y + 1)^2 = 9$

(D) $(x - 4)^2 + (y + 3)^2 = 9$

Here's How to Crack It

The question asks for an equation that represents a graph. The equation of a circle in standard form is $(x - h)^2 + (y - k)^2 = r^2$, where (h, k) is the center and r is the radius. Since the equation of Circle P is $(x - 4)^2 + (y + 1)^2 = 9$, the center is at (4, –1) and $r^2 = 9$, so $r = 3$. The question states that *Circle Q has the same radius as Circle P*, so the right side of the equation of Circle Q should also be 3^2, or 9; eliminate (A) because it has an incorrect value for r^2. The center of Circle Q is 2 units to the left of the center of Circle P. Two units to the left of (4, –1) is (2, –1), so the equation of Circle Q is $(x - 2)^2 + (y + 1)^2 = 9$. The correct answer is (B).

On the last question, you could have graphed the original circle and the circles in the answers. That would be time-consuming, though, and it was easy to find the center given the equation in standard form. Some circle questions are better cracked using a graphing calculator, either the built-in calculator or your own. Try using a calculator to answer this question.

19 Mark for Review

What is the radius of a circle graphed in the xy-plane and given by the equation $3x^2 + 15x + 3y^2 - 3y = 28.5$?

Ⓐ 3

Ⓑ 4

Ⓒ $\sqrt{35}$

Ⓓ $\sqrt{48}$

Here's How to Crack It

The question asks for the radius of a circle given an equation for its graph. The equation is not given in standard form, so you cannot simply look at the equation and determine the radius. One approach is to graph the equation. Using the built-in calculator, enter the equation as given; the calculator will graph the circle correctly even though the equation isn't in standard form. Click in the entry field or on the circle to see several gray dots.

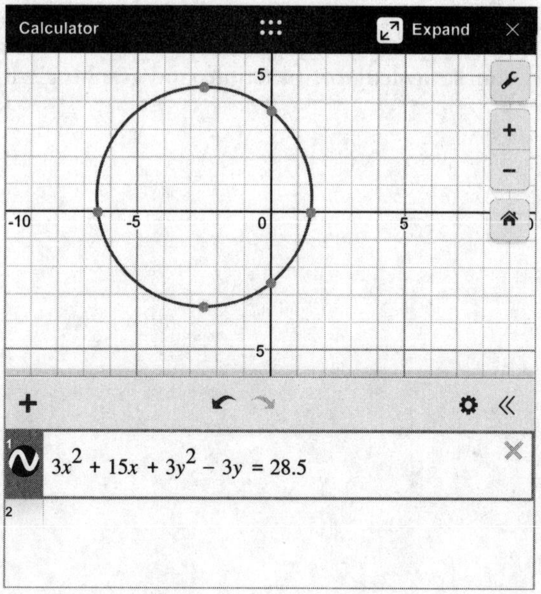

Click the dots at the maximum and minimum y-values to find the two ends of the diameter. The maximum y-value is at (–2.5, 4.5), and the minimum y-value is at (–2.5, –3.5). Because these points have the same x-coordinate, the distance between them is the diameter of the circle. Find the difference to get a diameter of 4.5 – (–3.5) = 8. The radius of a circle is half the diameter, so the radius is 4.

The other way to solve for the radius is to convert the equation to standard form. The equation in standard form of a circle in the xy-plane is

$$(x - h)^2 + (y - k)^2 = r^2$$

where (h, k) is the center of the circle and r is the radius. The equation given in the question is not in standard form. To put it into standard form, complete the squares. Start by dividing the entire equation by 3 to remove the coefficients on the x^2 and y^2 terms. This leaves

$$x^2 + 5x + y^2 - y = 9.5$$

Next, take half the coefficient on the x term, or 2.5, square it to get 6.25, and add 6.25 to both sides. Now the equation is

$$x^2 + 5x + 6.25 + y^2 - y = 15.75$$

Do the same with the coefficient on the y term to get

$$x^2 + 5x + 6.25 + y^2 - y + 0.25 = 16$$

The standard form equation for this circle is thus

$$(x + 2.5)^2 + (y - 0.5)^2 = 16$$

The question didn't ask for the center of the circle, so focus on the radius. If $r^2 = 16$, then $r = 4$.

Using a graphing calculator or completing the square, the correct answer is (B).

Got all of that? Now test your knowledge of functions and graphing with the following drills.

Functions and Graphs Drill

Use your new knowledge of functions, graphs, and coordinate geometry to complete the questions. Answers and explanations can be found starting on page 492.

1 Mark for Review

Function f is defined by $f(x) = x^2 - c$, where c is a constant. If $f(-2) = 6$, what is the value of c?

Ⓐ -10

Ⓑ -2

Ⓒ 0

Ⓓ 2

2 Mark for Review

A farming crew harvests 100 hectares a day on a wheat farm. If the crew maintains this rate, which of the following functions represents the number of hectares, h, the crew can harvest in d days?

Ⓐ $h(d) = d + 100$

Ⓑ $h(d) = d - 100$

Ⓒ $h(d) = 100d$

Ⓓ $h(d) = \frac{d}{100}$

3 Mark for Review

x	y
-3	-7
-1	-3
2	3

Based on the chart above, which of the following could express the relationship between x and y?

Ⓐ $y = x - 4$

Ⓑ $y = 2x - 1$

Ⓒ $y = 2x + 2$

Ⓓ $y = 3x - 3$

4 Mark for Review

Line l contains points (3, 2) and (4, 5). If line m is perpendicular to line l, which of the following could be the equation of line m?

Ⓐ $-5x + y = \frac{1}{3}$

Ⓑ $x + 3y = 15$

Ⓒ $x + 5y = 15$

Ⓓ $3x + y = 5$

5 Mark for Review

If $f(x) = 2x^2 + 4$ for all real numbers x, what is the value of $f(3) + 3f(5)$?

6 Mark for Review

The variable c represents a positive constant in the exponential function $f(x) = \frac{1}{3}c^x$. What is the value of $f(3)$ if $f(4) = 27$?

7 Mark for Review

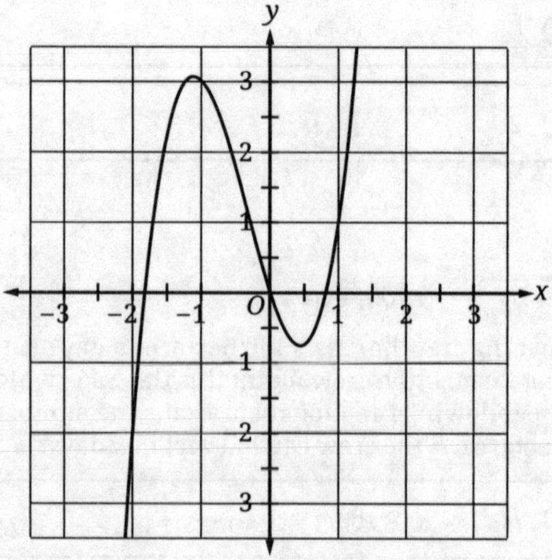

The graph of $y = g(x)$ in the xy-plane is shown above. The function g is defined by $g(x) = ax^3 + bx^2 - cx$, where a, b, and c are constants. For how many values of x does $g(x) = 0$?

Ⓐ Zero

Ⓑ One

Ⓒ Two

Ⓓ Three

8 Mark for Review

The acceleration of a ball rolling down a ramp can be estimated using the function $s(t) = 5t$, where s represents the speed of the ball and t represents time. Given this relationship, which of the following tables contains 4 values of t and the corresponding values of s?

Ⓐ

t	s
1	5
2	10
3	15
4	20

Ⓑ

t	s
1	5
2	10
3	30
4	120

Ⓒ

t	s
1	5
2	25
3	125
4	625

Ⓓ

t	s
5	1
10	2
15	3
20	4

9 Mark for Review

The graph of line l in the xy-plane passes through the points (2, 5) and (4, 11). The graph of line m has a slope of -2 and an x-intercept of 2. If point (x, y) is the point of intersection of lines l and m, what is the value of y?

Ⓐ $\frac{3}{5}$

Ⓑ $\frac{4}{5}$

Ⓒ 1

Ⓓ 2

10 Mark for Review

The movement of a roller coaster cart as it completes one ride can be modeled by the equation $y = -0.05(x - 55.5)^2 + 154$, which shows the cart's height above the ground y, in feet, x seconds after the ride starts, where $0 < x \leq 111$. Which of the following statements best describes the meaning of the vertex of the graph of the equation in the xy-plane?

Ⓐ The cart reached a maximum height of 154 feet above the ground.

Ⓑ The cart reached a maximum height of 55.5 feet above the ground.

Ⓒ The cart's final height was 154 feet above the ground.

Ⓓ The cart's final height was 55.5 feet above the ground.

FUNCTIONS AND GRAPHS DRILL ANSWERS AND EXPLANATIONS

1. **B** The question asks for the value of c. Start by plugging in what you know into the given function. If $f(x) = x^2 - c$, and $f(-2) = 6$, then plug in -2 for x in the function: $f(-2) = (-2)^2 - c$. Solve and replace $f(-2)$ with 6: $6 = 4 - c$; $2 = -c$; and $c = -2$. If you picked (A), you forgot that $(-2)^2$ is positive 4. The correct answer is (B).

2. **C** The question asks for a function that represents a specific situation. There are variables in the answer choices, and the question asks about the relationship between the number of hectares and the number of days, so plug in. Make $d = 2$. If the crew harvests 100 hectares in 1 day, it will harvest twice as many hectares, 200, in 2 days. Now plug $d = 2$ and $h(d) = 200$ into the answer choices and eliminate any that don't work. Choice (A) becomes $200 = 2 + 100$, or $200 = 102$. This is not true, so eliminate (A). Choice (B) becomes $200 = 2 - 100$, or $200 = -98$; eliminate (B). Choice (C) becomes $200 = 100(2)$, or $200 = 200$; this is true, so keep (C) but check (D) just in case. Choice (D) becomes $200 = \frac{2}{100}$; eliminate (D). The correct answer is (C).

3. **B** The question asks for the equation that best models pairs of values given in a table. Plug in the values from the chart. Use the pair $(-3, -7)$ from the top of the chart and eliminate answers that are not true. Choice (A) becomes $-7 = -3 - 4$, which is true. Keep it. Keep (B): $-7 = 2(-3) - 1$ is true. Get rid of (C), which becomes $-7 = 2(-3) + 2$: -7 does not equal -4. Get rid of (D): $-7 = 3(-3) - 3$, and -7 does not equal -12. Now use another pair just to test (A) and (B). Using $(-1, -3)$, (A) gives $-3 = -1 - 4$, which is not true, so eliminate it. The correct answer is (B).

4. **B** The question asks for the equation of line m. First, find the slope of line l by using the slope formula: $\frac{y_2 - y_1}{x_2 - x_1} = \frac{5-2}{4-3} = \frac{3}{1}$. A line perpendicular to line l must have a slope that is the negative reciprocal of l's slope. So, its slope should be $-\frac{1}{3}$. In the standard form of a line $Ax + By = C$, the slope is $-\frac{A}{B}$. Only (B) has a slope of $-\frac{1}{3}$. If you didn't remember the rule about the slope of perpendicular lines in standard form, you could have converted the answers to slope-intercept form and sketched out each of the lines to look for the answer that looked perpendicular to l. The correct answer is (B).

5. **184** The question asks for the value of expression that contains two functions. In function notation, the number inside the parentheses is the x-value that goes into the function, or the input, and the value that comes out of the function is the y-value, or the output. When there is a number in front of the function, the output value is multiplied by that number. Plug $x = 3$ into the function to get $f(3) = 2(3)^2 + 4$, then $f(3) = 2(9) + 4$. This becomes $f(3) = 18 + 4$, and then $f(3) = 22$. Plug $x = 5$ into the function to get $f(5) = 2(5)^2 + 4$, then $f(5) = 2(25) + 4$, then $f(5) = 50 + 4$, and then $f(5) = 54$. Multiply

this output by 3 to get (3)(54) = 162. Finally, add the values of $f(3)$ and $3f(5)$ to get 22 + 162 = 184. The correct answer is 184.

6. **9** The question asks for the value of a function. In function notation, $f(x) = y$. The number inside the parentheses is the x-value that goes into the function, or the input, and the value that comes out of the function is the y-value, or the output. According to the question, $f(4) = 27$, so when the input is 4, the output is 27. Plug in $f(x) = 27$ and $x = 4$, and solve for c. The function becomes $27 = \frac{1}{3}c^4$. Multiply both sides of the equation by 3 to get $81 = c^4$. Take the fourth root of both sides of the equation to get $c = 3$. With the built-in calculator, enter $81^{\frac{1}{4}}$ or use the $\sqrt[x]{}$ button under the Functions menu to take the fourth root of 81. The question asks for the value of $f(3)$, so plug $x = 3$ and $c = 3$ into the function, and solve for $f(3)$. The function becomes $f(3) = \frac{1}{3}(3^3)$, then $f(3) = \frac{1}{3}(27)$, which becomes $f(3) = 9$. The correct answer is 9.

7. **D** The question asks for the number of times the value of a function is 0. In function notation, $f(x) = y$. The number inside the parentheses is the x-value that goes into the function, or the input, and the value that comes out of the function is the y-value, or the output. When $g(x) = 0$, the y-value on the graph is 0, so this question is asking for the number of x-intercepts. Look at the graph to see that it crosses the x-axis 3 times, with points at approximately (–1.8, 0), (0, 0), and (0.8, 0). Thus, there are 3 times when $g(x) = 0$. The correct answer is (D).

8. **A** The question asks for correct values in a function. In function notation, the number inside the parentheses is the x-value that goes into the function, or the input, and the value that comes out of the function is the y-value, or the output. In this scenario, t is the input and s is the output. When given a function and asked for the table of values, plug values from the answer choices into the function and eliminate answers that don't work. Start with $t = 2$. Plug $t = 2$ into the function to get $s(2) = 5(2)$, or $s(2) = 10$. Eliminate (C) because it has an incorrect value of s when t is 2. Plug $t = 3$ into the function to get $s(3) = 5(3)$, or $s(3) = 15$. Eliminate (B) because it has an incorrect value of s when t is 3. Next, try a value for t that is in (D) but not (A). Plug $t = 5$ into the function to get $s(5) = 5(5)$, or $s(5) = 25$. Eliminate (D) because it has an incorrect value of s when t is 5. The correct answer is (A).

9. **D** The question asks for the value of y. First, find the slope of line l by using the slope formula: $\frac{y_2 - y_1}{x_2 - x_1} = \frac{11-5}{4-2} = \frac{6}{2} = 3$. Plug this slope and one of the points on line l into the slope-intercept form $y = mx + b$ to solve for b, giving you the full equation of the line. If you use the point (2, 5), you get $5 = 3(2) + b$ or $5 = 6 + b$, so $b = -1$. Therefore, the equation for line l is $y = 3x - 1$. For line m, the slope is given as –2, and the x-intercept is 2. Be very careful not to jump to the conclusion that the equation of line m is $y = -2x + 2$. In the form $y = mx + b$, the b is the y-intercept, not the

x-intercept. The *x*-intercept is where $y = 0$, so you know that (2, 0) is a point on line *m*. Use this point and the slope to find the equation of line *m* in the same way you did for line *l*: $0 = -2(2) + b$, so $b = 4$ and the equation is $y = -2x + 4$. Now set the *x* parts of the equations equal to find the point of intersection. If $3x - 1 = -2x + 4$, then $5x = 5$ and $x = 1$. Again, be careful! The question asked for the value of *y*. Plug $x = 1$ into one of the line equations to find *y*. For line *l*, the equation becomes $y = 3(1) - 1 = 3 - 1 = 2$. The correct answer is (D).

10. **A** The question asks about the graph of the data representing a certain situation. Start by reading the final question, which asks for the meaning of the vertex of the graph. The function is a quadratic in vertex form, $y = a(x - h)^2 + k$, in which the vertex is at (h, k). Since $a = -0.05$, the parabola opens downward, and the vertex of the parabola is at (55.5, 154). Entering the equation into a graphing calculator is a good way to visualize all of this information. Next, label parts of the equation given. The question states that *y* is the height above the ground, in feet, and *x* is the number of seconds after the ride starts. The greatest height is at the vertex, and the *y*-value of the vertex is 154, so it is the maximum height. The correct answer is (A).

Summary

- Given a function, you put an x-value in and get an $f(x)$ or y-value out.
- Look for ways to use Plugging In and PITA on function questions.
- For questions about the graphs of functions, remember that $f(x) = y$.
- If the graph contains a labeled point or the question gives you a point, plug it into the equations in the answers and eliminate any that aren't true.
- The equation of a line can take two forms. In either form, (x, y) is a point on the line.
    - In slope-intercept form, $y = mx + b$, the slope is m and the y-intercept is b.
    - In standard form, $Ax + By = C$, the slope is $-\frac{A}{B}$ and the y-intercept is $\frac{C}{B}$.
- Given two points on a line, (x_1, y_1) and (x_2, y_2), the slope is $\frac{(y_2 - y_1)}{(x_2 - x_1)}$.
- Two linear equations with infinitely many solutions represent the same line.
- Parallel lines have the same slopes and no points of intersection.
- Perpendicular lines have slopes that are negative reciprocals and intersect at a right angle.
- To find a point of intersection, plug the point into both equations to see if it works, or graph the lines on your calculator when it is allowed.
- The roots of a function, also known as solutions, zeroes, or x-intercepts, are the points where the graph crosses the x-axis and where $y = 0$.
- Graphs of functions can be moved up or down if a number is added to or subtracted from the function, respectively. They move left if a number is added inside the parentheses of the function or move right if a number is subtracted inside the parentheses.

- The standard form of a parabola is $y = ax^2 + bx + c$, where c is the y-intercept. If a is positive, the parabola opens up, and if a is negative, it opens down.
- The factored form of a parabola equation is $y = a(x - r_1)(x - r_2)$, where r_1 and r_2 are the roots or x-intercepts of the parabola.
- The vertex form of a parabola equation is $y = a(x - h)^2 + k$, where (h, k) is the vertex. To get a parabola in the standard form into vertex form, complete the square.
- The standard form of a circle equation is $(x - h)^2 + (y - k)^2 = r^2$, where (h, k) is the center and r is the radius. To get a circle equation into the standard form, complete the square for both the x-terms and the y-terms.
- A graphing calculator can make an enormous difference on questions about graphs. Practice with the calculator you plan to use on test day—either the built-in calculator or your own—to learn all of the tricks and feel comfortable with using it during the test.

Chapter 24
Advanced Arithmetic

The Digital SAT includes questions about what the test-writers call Problem Solving and Data Analysis. Many of these questions test concepts you learned a few years ago, such as averages and proportions. More difficult questions will build on these basic concepts by requiring you to use charts and data or to combine multiple techniques. In this chapter, we will review the arithmetic and statistical concepts you'll need to know for the Digital SAT.

CALL ON THE CALCULATOR

While you work through the topics and examples in this chapter, don't forget to use the built-in calculator or your own. Make sure to review the Calculator Guide in your Student Tools so you can take advantage of this tool. Many of the examples in this chapter will show you how to do the question by hand because that can help make the concept clearer, but a calculator will help you do some questions very quickly while avoiding calculation errors. Even scary-sounding topics like margin of error come down to the basics of addition, subtraction, multiplication, and division, and that's what calculators do best!

RATIOS AND PROPORTIONS

A Ratio Is a Comparison

Many students get extremely nervous when they are asked to work with ratios. But there's no need to be nervous. A **ratio** is a comparison between the quantities of ingredients you have in a mixture, be it a class full of people or a bowl of cake batter. Ratios can be written to look like fractions—don't get them confused.

The ratio of x to y can be expressed in the following three ways:

1. $\frac{x}{y}$
2. the ratio of x to y
3. $x{:}y$

Ratios vs. Fractions
Keep in mind that a ratio compares part of something to another part. A fraction compares part of something to the whole thing.

Ratio: $\frac{\text{part}}{\text{part}}$

Fraction: $\frac{\text{part}}{\text{whole}}$

Part, Part, Whole

Ratios are a lot like fractions. In fact, anything you can do to a fraction (convert it to a decimal or percentage, reduce it, and so on), you can do to a ratio. The difference is that a fraction gives you a part (the top number) over a whole (the bottom number), while a ratio typically gives you two parts (boys to girls, cars to trucks, sugar to flour), and it is your job to come up with the whole. For example, if there is one cup of sugar for every two cups of flour in a recipe, that's three cups of stuff. The ratio of sugar to flour is 1:2. Add the parts to get the whole.

Ratio to Real

If a class contains 3 students and the ratio of boys to girls in that class is 2:1, how many boys and how many girls are there in the class? Of course, there are 2 boys and 1 girl.

Now, suppose a class contains 24 students and the ratio of boys to girls is still 2:1. How many boys and how many girls are there in the class? This is a little harder, but the answer is easy to find if you think about it. There are 16 boys and 8 girls.

How did we get the answer? We added up the number of "parts" in the ratio (2 parts boys plus 1 part girls, or 3 parts all together) and divided it into the total number of students. In other words, we divided 24 by 3. This told us that the class contained 3 equal parts of 8 students each. From the given ratio (2:1), we knew that two of these parts consisted of boys and one of them consisted of girls.

The test-writers will often combine ratios with diagrams or data from charts and graphs. Don't let them intimidate you with these: just work in bite-sized pieces and write down the part-to-part relationships that you need to solve the question.

Try this example.

1 Mark for Review

A lapping slurry contains microbeads suspended in a solution and is used to polish a silicon wafer by abrasion of the surface. The distribution of the particle size, in micrometers, is shown below.

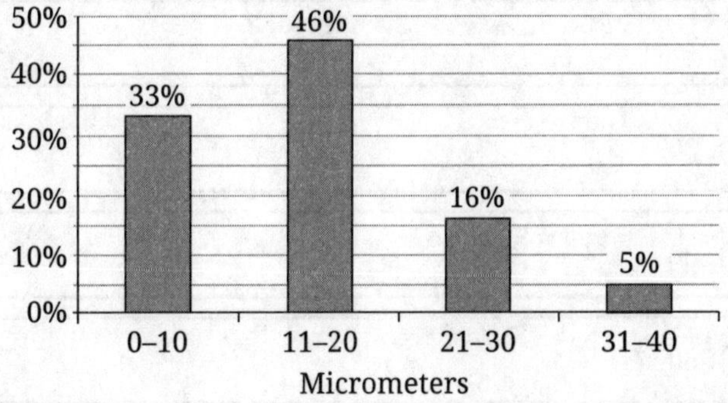

Which of the following is closest to the ratio of the number of 11–20 micrometer microbeads to the number of 31–40 micrometer microbeads?

Ⓐ 1:9

Ⓑ 2:1

Ⓒ 3:1

Ⓓ 9:1

Here's How to Crack It

The question asks for a ratio based on data from a graph. To find the ratio of 11–20 micrometer microbeads to 31–40 micrometer microbeads, read carefully, look up the right information in the graph, and set up the part-to-part relationship. The 11–20 micrometer microbeads make up 46% of the total, and the 31–40 micrometer microbeads make up 5% of the total. Plug in 100 for the total to get actual numbers of 46 and 5, respectively. That is a ratio of 46:5. Because the question is asking for the closest ratio, round the numbers to get a ratio of 45:5, which reduces to 9:1. Notice that (A) has the right numbers in the wrong order; always read carefully and use your scratch paper to avoid this mistake. The correct answer is (D).

Proportions Are Equal Ratios

Some Digital SAT math questions will contain two proportional, or equal, ratios from which one piece of information is missing.

Here's an example.

2 Mark for Review

If 2 packages contain a total of 12 doughnuts, how many doughnuts are there in 5 packages?

Ⓐ 24

Ⓑ 30

Ⓒ 36

Ⓓ 60

Here's How to Crack It

The question asks for the number of doughnuts in 5 packages. This question simply describes two equal ratios, one of which is missing a single piece of information. Here's the given information represented as two equal ratios:

$$\frac{2\text{ (packages)}}{12\text{ (doughnuts)}} = \frac{5\text{ (packages)}}{x\text{ (doughnuts)}}$$

Because ratios can be written so they look like fractions, you can treat them exactly like fractions. To find the answer, all you have to do is solve for x. Start by cross-multiplying:

$$\frac{2}{12} \times \frac{5}{x}$$

$$\text{so, } 2x = 60$$

$$x = 30$$

The correct answer is (B).

Proportions: Advanced Principles

Many proportion questions will also involve unit conversion. Be sure to pay attention to the units and have the same units in both numerators and the same units in both denominators.

Let's look at an example.

3 Mark for Review

Gary is using a 3D printer to create a miniature version of himself. The scale of the miniature is 0.4 inches to 1 foot of Gary's actual height. If Gary is 5 feet and 9 inches tall, what will be the height of his 3D-printed miniature?
(12 inches = 1 foot)

(A) 2.0 inches

(B) 2.3 inches

(C) 2.6 inches

(D) 2.9 inches

Here's How to Crack It

The question asks for the height of the 3D miniature. The scale of the 3D printer is in inches and feet—0.4 inches on the miniature for every 1 foot in real life. Start by converting every measurement to inches. There are 12 inches in each foot, so the scale will be 0.4 inches = 12 inches in real life. Now convert Gary's height into inches. Begin by setting up a proportion to find out how many inches are in 5 feet.

$$\frac{12 \text{ inches}}{1 \text{ foot}} = \frac{x \text{ inches}}{5 \text{ feet}}$$

Cross-multiply to find that 5 feet equals 60 inches. Gary is 5 feet and 9 inches tall, so he is 60 + 9 = 69 inches tall. Now set up a proportion with the scale of the miniature and Gary's height in inches.

$$\frac{0.4 \text{ inches}}{12 \text{ inches}} = \frac{x \text{ inches}}{69 \text{ inches}}$$

Cross-multiply to get $12x = 27.6$, and then divide both sides by 12 to find that $x = 2.3$ inches. The correct answer is (B).

Now try a question that requires converting the units of both parts of a rate.

4 Mark for Review

A car is traveling on the highway at a speed of 65 miles per hour. Which of the following is the best approximation of the car's speed, in feet per second? (1 mile = 5,280 feet)

(A) 95

(B) 190

(C) 5,720

(D) 343,200

Here's How to Crack It

The question asks for a rate in different units. Take it one piece at a time to avoid getting confused. Start by converting miles to feet. The question states that *1 mile = 5,280 feet*, so set up a proportion to determine how many feet are in 65 miles, being sure to match up units. The proportion is $\frac{1 \text{ mile}}{5{,}280 \text{ feet}} = \frac{65 \text{ miles}}{x \text{ feet}}$. Cross-multiply to get $(5{,}280)(65) = x$, or $x = 343{,}200$ feet per hour. This is answer choice (D), but you're only halfway done with the conversion. Eliminate trap answer (D).

Next, convert hours to seconds. There are 60 minutes in 1 hour and 60 seconds in 1 minute, so there are $(60)(60) = 3{,}600$ seconds in 1 hour. Thus, a rate of $\frac{343{,}200 \text{ feet}}{1 \text{ hour}}$ is the same as a rate of $\frac{343{,}200 \text{ feet}}{3{,}600 \text{ seconds}}$. Reduce the fraction to get a rate of $95.\overline{3}$ feet per second. The question asks for the *best approximation of the car's speed*, and the closest answer is 95. The correct answer is (A).

PERCENTAGES

Percentages Are Fractions

There should be nothing frightening about a percentage. It's just a convenient way of expressing a fraction with a denominator of 100.

Percent means "per 100" or "out of 100." If there are 100 questions on your math test and you answer 50 of them, you will have answered 50 out of 100, or $\frac{50}{100}$, or 50 percent. To think of it another way:

$$\frac{\text{part}}{\text{whole}} = \frac{x}{100} = x \text{ percent}$$

Memorize These Percentage-Decimal-Fraction Equivalents

These show up all the time, so go ahead and memorize them.

$0.01 = \frac{1}{100} = 1$ percent

$0.1 = \frac{1}{10} = 10$ percent

$0.2 = \frac{1}{5} = 20$ percent

$0.25 = \frac{1}{4} = 25$ percent

$0.5 = \frac{1}{2} = 50$ percent

$0.75 = \frac{3}{4} = 75$ percent

Converting Percentages to Fractions

To convert a percentage to a fraction, simply put the percentage over 100 and reduce:

$$80 \text{ percent} = \frac{80}{100} = \frac{8}{10} = \frac{4}{5}$$

Converting Fractions to Percentages

Because a percentage is just another way to express a fraction, you shouldn't be surprised to see how easy it is to convert a fraction to a percentage. To do so, simply use a calculator to divide the top of the fraction by the bottom of the fraction, and then multiply the result by 100. Here's an example:

Problem: Express $\frac{3}{4}$ as a percentage.

Solution: $\frac{3}{4} = 0.75 \times 100 = 75$ percent.

Converting fractions to percentages is easy with the built-in calculator or your own. In fact, a calculator is going to be the fastest and most accurate way to answer most questions about percentages.

Converting Percentages to Decimals

To convert a percentage to a decimal, simply move the decimal point *two places to the left*. For example, 25 percent can be expressed as the decimal 0.25; 50 percent is the same as 0.50 or 0.5; 100 percent is the same as 1.00 or 1.

Call on the Calculator

Review the first two sections of the Digital SAT Calculator Guide in your Student Tools to remember how to work with fractions, decimals, and percentages using the calculator. If you're planning to use your own calculator, make sure you know how to use it to make these conversions.

Converting Decimals to Percentages

To convert a decimal to a percentage, just do the opposite of what you did in the preceding section. All you have to do is move the decimal point *two places to the right*. Thus, 0.5 = 50 percent; 0.375 = 37.5 percent; 2 = 200 percent.

The following drill will give you practice working with fractions, decimals, and percentages.

FRACTIONS, DECIMALS, AND PERCENTS EXERCISE

Fill in the missing information in the following table. Answers can be found on page 532.

	Fraction	Decimal	Percent
	$\frac{1}{5}$	0.2	20%
1.	$\frac{1}{2}$		
2.		3.0	
3.			0.5%
4.	$\frac{1}{3}$		

Translation, Please!

Word problems can be translated into arithmetic symbols. Learning how to translate from English to math will help you immensely on the Digital SAT Math section. We covered some of this already, but as a review, here are some of the most common terms you will see in word problems and their math symbol equivalents:

Word	**Symbol**
is, are, costs	=
greater than, more than	+
fewer than, less than	–
of	× (multiply)
percent	÷ 100
what	*n* (variable)

Do You Speak Math?

Problem: What number is 5 more than 10 percent of 20?

Students often make careless errors on questions like this because they aren't sure how to translate the words they are reading into math. You won't make mistakes if you take the words slowly, one at a time, and translate each one into a mathematical symbol. Use the chart above to write this question in math. *What number* means "variable," so you can write that as n (or x or whatever letter works for you). *Is* means "equals," so now you have $n =$. Next you are given the number 5, so write that in your equation and you get $n = 5$. *More than* translates to +, and *10 percent* is $\frac{10}{100}$. That gives you $n = 5 + \frac{10}{100}$. Finally, *of 20* means multiply by 20, so now you have the equation:

$$n = 5 + \frac{10}{100}(20)$$

$$n = 5 + 2$$

$$n = 7$$

You will see the words *of, is, product, sum,* and *what* pop up a lot in math questions on the Digital SAT. Don't let these words fool you because they all translate into simple math functions. Memorize all of these terms and their math equivalents. It will save you time on the test and make your life with the Digital SAT much less unpleasant.

What Percent of What Percent of What?

On more challenging Digital SAT questions, you may be asked to determine the effect of a series of percentage increases or decreases. The key point to remember on such questions is that each successive increase or decrease is performed on the result of the previous one.

Here's an example.

5 Mark for Review

A business paid \$300 to rent a piece of office equipment for one year. The rent was then increased by 10% each year thereafter. How much will the company pay for the first three years it rents the equipment?

(A) \$920

(B) \$960

(C) \$990

(D) \$993

Bite-Sized Pieces
Always handle percentage problems using Bite-Sized Pieces: one piece at a time.

Here's How to Crack It

The question asks for the cost of the equipment over three years. This question is a great place to use the Bite-Sized Pieces strategy. You know that the business paid \$300 to rent the piece of office equipment for the first year. Then, you were told that the rent increases by 10 percent for each year thereafter. That's a sure sign that you're going to need the rent for the second year, so go ahead and calculate it. For the second year, the rent is $300+\left(\frac{10}{100}\times 300\right)=330$.

Now, the question tells you that the business rents the equipment for three years. So, you need to do the calculation one more time. At this point, you might want to set up a chart to help keep track of the information.

Year 1: \$300

Year 2: $300+\left(\frac{10}{100}\times 300\right)=\$330$

Year 3: $330+\left(\frac{10}{100}\times 330\right)=\$363$

To find the answer, all you need to do is add up the costs for each of the three years.

Year 1: $300
Year 2: $330
Year 3: $363
$993

The correct answer is (D).

What Percent of What Percent of . . . Yikes!

Sometimes you may find successive percentage questions in which you aren't given actual numbers to work with. In such cases, you need to plug in some numbers.

Here's an example.

6 Mark for Review

A number is increased by 25 percent and then decreased by 20 percent. The result is what percent of the original number?

(A) 80

(B) 100

(C) 105

(D) 120

Plugging Away at Relationships
Questions dealing with percents, fractions, and other ways of expressing relationships among numbers are great chances to plug in!

Here's How to Crack It

The question asks for the result of a percent increase and a percent decrease on an original number. You aren't given a particular number to work with in this question—just "a number." Rather than trying to deal with the problem in the abstract, you should immediately plug in a number to work with. What number would be easiest to work with in a percentage question? Why, 100, of course.

1. 25 percent of 100 is 25, so 100 increased by 25 percent is 125.
2. Now you have to decrease 125 by 20 percent; 20 percent of 125 is 25, so 125 decreased by 20 percent is 100.
3. 100 (the result) is 100 percent of 100 (the number you plugged in). The correct answer is (B).

Remember, never try to solve a percentage problem by writing an equation if you can plug in numbers instead. Using Plugging In on percentage questions is faster, easier, and more accurate. Why work through long, arduous equations if you don't have to?

AVERAGES

What Is an Average?

The **average,** also called the **arithmetic mean,** of a set of *n* numbers is simply the sum of all the numbers divided by *n*. In other words, if you want to find the average of three numbers, add them up and divide by 3. For example, the average of 3, 7, and 8 is $\frac{(3+7+8)}{3}$, which equals $\frac{18}{3}$, or 6.

That was an easy example, but average questions on the Digital SAT won't always have clear solutions. That is, you won't always be given the information for averages in a way that is easy to work with. For that reason, use the formula $T = AN$, in which T is the *total*, A is the *average*, and N is the *number of things*. The total is the sum of all the numbers you're averaging, and the number of things is the number of elements you're averaging. Plug in the information you've been given, and then you can solve the equation for the quantity that you don't know.

Here's what the formula looks like using the simple average example we just gave you.

$$T = AN$$

$$3 + 7 + 8 = (A)(3)$$

$$18 = (A)(3)$$

$$A = 6$$

Here's another simple example:

Problem: If the mean of three test scores is 70, what is the total of all three test scores?

Solution: Just put the average (70) and the number of things (3 tests) into the formula to get $T = (70)(3)$. Then multiply to find the total, which is 210.

Total
When calculating averages and means, always find the total. It's the one piece of information that the Digital SAT loves to withhold.

Mark It!
Make sure you're using the formula $T = AN$ each time you see the word *mean* or *average* in a question.

Averages: Advanced Principles

To solve most difficult average questions, all you have to do is use the formula more than once. Most of the time you will use it to find the total of the number being averaged. Here's an example.

7 Mark for Review

Maria has taken four chemistry tests and has a mean score of 80. If she scores a 90 on her fifth chemistry test, what is her mean for these five tests?

Ⓐ 80

Ⓑ 81

Ⓒ 82

Ⓓ 84

Here's How to Crack It

The question asks for the mean score Maria received on all 5 tests. Start by writing out $T = AN$ and filling in what you know. You can put 80 in for the average and 4 in for the number of things to get $T = (80)(4)$. You can calculate that Maria has gotten 320 total points on her first four tests.

Now, since the question mentions another average, write the formula again and fill in the new information. This time, there are five tests, making the formula $T = (A)(5)$. The question asks for the average, so you also need to find the total. The total for all five tests is the total from the first four tests plus the score from the fifth test: $320 + 90 = 410$. Put that into the formula to get $410 = (A)(5)$ and divide to find the average: 82. The correct answer is (C).

Averages, and many other arithmetic topics, may be tested using charts and data. To find the numbers to average, look them up on the graphic provided and watch out for mismatched units.

8 Mark for Review

Charge No.	Battery Life
1	1:11
2	1:05
3	0:59
4	0:55
5	0:55
6	0:54
7	0:54

A toy drone is opened and charged to full battery life. The table above shows the duration of the battery life in hours and minutes between charges. What is the mean battery life for the first five charges?

Ⓐ 55 minutes

Ⓑ 58 minutes

Ⓒ 1 hour and 1 minute

Ⓓ 1 hour and 5 minutes

Here's How to Crack It

The question asks for the mean battery life for the first 5 charges. To find the average, add up the battery life values for the first 5 charges and divide by 5. Make sure that you convert the battery charge time for charges 1 and 2 into minutes before calculating: 1:11 = 60 + 11 = 71 minutes, and 1:05 = 60 + 5 = 65 minutes. The average is equal to $\frac{71+65+59+55+55}{5} = \frac{305}{5} = 61$ minutes, which is equal to 1 hour and 1 minute. The correct answer is (C).

Call on the Calculator
The built-in calculator can give you an average at the click of a button. Read the section on the scientific calculator in the Digital SAT Calculator Guide in your Student Tools to review how to find that button in the Functions menu and how to use it to work with averages.

Don't forget that you can also plug in when answering average questions.

9 Mark for Review

The mean of a list of 5 numbers is n. When an additional number is added to the list, the mean of all 6 numbers is $n + 3$. Which of the following is the value, in terms of n, of the number added to the list?

(A) $6n + 18$

(B) $5n$

(C) $n + 18$

(D) $n + 6$

Here's How to Crack It

The question asks for the value of a number added to the list. There are variables in the answers, so plug in for the value of n, which is the average. If $n = 20$, then you can use the average formula to find the total of the five numbers on the list.

$$T = AN$$

$$T = (20)(5)$$

$$T = 100$$

A number is added and there is a new average, so it's time to write out the formula again. For this one, you know that there are 6 numbers and that their average is $n + 3 = 20 + 3 = 23$.

$$T = AN$$

$$T = (23)(6)$$

$$T = 138$$

Since the difference in the two totals was caused by the addition of the sixth number, the sixth number must be 138 – 100 = 38. That's the target, so be sure to circle it. Now check the answer choices. Choice (A) becomes 6(20) + 18 = 120 + 18 = 138. This does not match the target, so eliminate it. The value with (A) was much too large, so (B) will also be large. Try (C) and (D) next: (C) becomes 20 + 18 = 38, and (D) becomes 20 + 6 = 26. Only (C) matches the target, so the correct answer is (C).

On the Digital SAT, you'll also need to know four other statistical topics: *median, mode, range,* and *standard deviation.* These topics have pretty straightforward definitions. One way the Digital SAT will complicate the issue is by presenting the data in a chart or graph, making it harder to see the numbers you are working with.

WHAT IS A MEDIAN?

The **median** of a list of numbers is the number that is exactly in the middle of the list when the list is arranged from smallest to largest, as on a number line. For example, in the group 3, 6, 6, 6, 6, 7, 8, 9, 10, 10, 11, the median is 7. Five numbers come before 7 in the list, and 5 come after. Remember it this way: median sounds like *middle.*

Let's see how this idea might be tested.

Missing the Middle?
To find the median of a set containing an even number of items, take the average of the two middle numbers.

10 Mark for Review

Milligrams of Gold					
	1	2	3	4	5
Limestone	0.45	0.58	0.55	0.42	0.41
Granite	0.94	0.87	0.82	0.55	0.73
Gneiss	0.38	0.60	0.37	0.40	0.34

Five samples of each of three different rock types were collected on a hiking trip in Colorado. Each sample was analyzed for its gold content. The milligrams of gold found in each sample are presented in the table above. How much larger is the median of the amount of gold in the granite samples than that of the limestone samples?

Ⓐ 0.00

Ⓑ 0.37

Ⓒ 0.45

Ⓓ 0.55

Here's How to Crack It

The question asks for a comparison of the medians of data for limestone and granite. Start by putting the gold weights for limestone in order to get

0.41, 0.42, 0.45, 0.55, 0.58

The median for limestone is the middle number: 0.45 mg.

Next, place the gold weights for granite in order to get

0.55, 0.73, 0.82, 0.87, 0.94

The median for granite is 0.82.

Therefore, the difference between the median amount of gold in the granite and limestone samples is 0.82 – 0.45 = 0.37. The correct answer is (B).

WHAT IS A MODE?

The **mode** of a group of numbers is the number in the list that appears most often. In the list 3, 4, 4, 5, 7, 7, 8, 8, 8, 9, 10, the mode is 8, because it appears three times while no other number in the group appears more than twice. Remember it this way: *mode* sounds like "most."

Because mode by itself is pretty easy to figure out, questions will usually combine mode with other concepts like mean, median, or range.

WHAT IS A RANGE?

The **range** of a list of numbers is the difference between the greatest number in the list and the least number in the list. For the list 4, 5, 5, 6, 7, 8, 9, 10, 20, the greatest number is 20 and the least is 4, so the range is 20 – 4 = 16.

11 Mark for Review

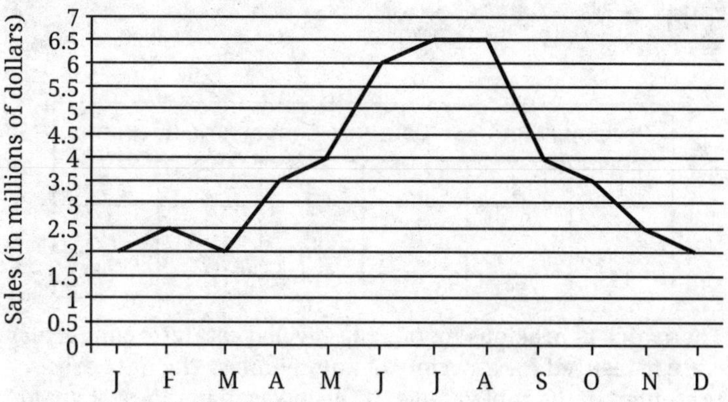

The forecasted monthly sales of a type of sunscreen are presented in the figure above. Which of the following best describes the range of monthly sales, in millions of dollars, throughout the year shown?

Ⓐ 2.5

Ⓑ 3.5

Ⓒ 4.0

Ⓓ 4.5

Here's How to Crack It

The question asks for the range in monthly sales based on the graph. The range of a set of values is the difference between the greatest and the smallest value. The lowest monthly sales number for the sunscreen can be found where the line dips closest to the bottom of the graph. This happens in both January and March, when the forecasted sales are 2 million. Make sure to read the units carefully. The highest point is where the line goes closest to the top of the graph. This happens in July and August, when the forecasted monthly sales are 6.5 million. Therefore, the range is 6.5 million – 2 million = 4.5 million. The correct answer is (D).

The Digital SAT might even have a question that tests more than one of these statistical concepts at the same time. Take it one step at a time and use POE when you can.

12 Mark for Review

Precious Metals in Catalytic Converters, in grams					
1	2	2	3	4	6
6	6	9	9	10	10
11	13	14	14	15	17

The grams of precious metals in recycled catalytic converters were measured for a variety of automobiles. The data are presented in the table above. If the lowest data point, 1 gram, and highest data point, 17 grams, are removed from the set, which of the following quantities would change the most?

Ⓐ Mode

Ⓑ Mean

Ⓒ Range

Ⓓ Median

Here's How to Crack It

The question asks for the measure of the data that will change the most if two specific data points are removed. Start by evaluating the easier answer choices and save mean for last. The mode of the current list is 6, and removing 1 and 17 from the list won't change that. Eliminate (A). The range is the difference between the smallest number and the largest number on the list. Right now, the range is $17 - 1 = 16$. If those extremes are removed from the list, the new range is $15 - 2 = 13$, and the range changed by 3 units. Keep (C) for now. The median is the middle number in the list, or the average of the middle two numbers. Currently, both middle numbers are 9, so the median is 9. This won't change if 1 and 17 are removed, so eliminate (D). The mean of a list is not likely to change dramatically with the removal of the numbers at the extremes, so (C) is likely correct. To actually evaluate the mean, you need to add up all the numbers on the list and divide by the number of items in the list. For the current list, the total is 152 for the 18 items, so the average is $8.\overline{44}$. To find the new total if 1 and 17 are removed, don't re-add everything; just subtract 18 from the previous total. The new list will have only 16 items, so the new average is 8.375. This is only slightly different than the previous mean, so eliminate (B). The correct answer is (C).

WHAT IS A MARGIN OF ERROR?

Some questions will test **margin of error**, which is a range of percentages rather than numbers. A margin of error gives a range for random sampling errors in a survey or poll. It indicates how much the results might change if the poll were repeated or if the entire population were asked instead of a random sample. For example, if a survey shows that 70% of randomly sampled test-takers prefer the Digital SAT to the paper-and-pencil SAT, and there is a margin of error of ±5%, that means it is highly likely that between 65% and 75% of all test-takers prefer the Digital SAT.

Let's look at an example of how this can be tested.

13 Mark for Review

A summer beach volleyball league has 750 players in it. At the start of the season, 150 of the players are randomly chosen and polled on whether games will be played while it is raining or if the games should be canceled. The results of the poll show that 42 of the polled players would prefer to play in the rain. The margin of error on the poll is ±4%. What is the range of players in the entire league that would be expected to prefer to play volleyball in the rain rather than cancel the game?

Ⓐ 24–32

Ⓑ 39–48

Ⓒ 150–195

Ⓓ 180–240

Here's How to Crack It

The question asks for the range of players that would prefer to play in the rain. The first step is to determine the percent of polled players that wanted to play in the rain.

$$\frac{42}{150} = 0.28 \text{ or } 28\%$$

Now apply this percent to the entire population of the league. Since 28% of the polled players wanted to play in the rain, 28% of all players should want to play in the rain.

$$\frac{28}{100} \times 750 = 210$$

The only range that contains this value is (D), so that is the correct answer. To actually calculate the margin of error, add and subtract 4% to the actual percent of 28% to get a range of 24–32% of the total.

24% of 750 = 180

32% of 750 = 240

Therefore, the entire range is 180 to 240. The correct answer is (D).

WHAT IS A FREQUENCY TABLE?

Another way the Digital SAT tests statistical concepts is by using a **frequency table**. This is just what it sounds like: a table to show how frequently something happens. One column shows the numbers of something, like ages or scores on a test, and the other column shows how often that thing occurs. If you wanted to show, for example, how many meetings each member of a 15-person club attended, you could use the table below.

Meeting Attendance for this Cool Club I'm In

Meetings attended	Frequency
1	2
2	1
3	1
4	3
5	5
6	3

Frequency tables give you ways to find the mean, median, and mode of a list of numbers without needing to write out the whole list, so the test-writers will often combine those concepts with frequency tables in the same question.

Try out an example of this below.

14 Mark for Review

Number of Ice Cream Scoops for Customers at an Ice Cream Parlor

Number of Ice Cream Scoops	Frequency
8	1
5	2
4	2
3	7
2	6
1	6

The distribution of ice cream scoops for 24 customers at an ice cream parlor is displayed in the table above. Which of the following orders the median, mode, and range correctly?

Ⓐ mode < median < range

Ⓑ median < mode < range

Ⓒ median < range < mode

Ⓓ range < median < mode

Here's How to Crack It

The question asks for the correct order of the median, mode, and range of the data from least to greatest. Start with the mode, which is easy to determine from the table. Since the greatest number in the Frequency column is 7, the corresponding number of scoops is the mode. Thus, the mode is 3.

The range is also easy to determine from the table because the range of a list of numbers is the difference between the greatest number and the least number. The greatest number of ice cream scoops is 8 and the least number of ice cream scoops is 1, so the range is 8 – 1 = 7. The mode of 3 is less than the range of 7. Eliminate (C) and (D) because they have the range as less than the mode.

Next, find the median, which is the middle number of an ordered list. You could write out all 24 numbers in this list and count up to the middle number(s), but there's a better way. When a list has an even number of terms, the median is the average of the two middle terms. Since $\frac{24}{2} = 12$, the median is the average of the 12th and 13th terms. To confirm this, notice that there are 12 – 1 = 11 terms to the left of the 12th term and 24 – 13 = 11 terms to the right of the 13th term. Now, use the frequency table to find the 12th and 13th terms. The table shows that 6 customers chose 1 scoop, and 6 customers chose 2 scoops, so the 12th term is 2. The next 7 customers chose 3 scoops, so the 13th term is 3. The average of 2 and 3 is $\frac{2+3}{2} = 2.5$. Thus, the median is 2.5. This is less than 3, so the median is less than the mode. Eliminate (A) because it has the mode as less than the median. The correct answer is (B).

WHAT IS STANDARD DEVIATION?

In real-world applications, **standard deviation** is a measure of how numbers are distributed around the mean, and the calculations can get complicated. But Digital SAT math is not the real world! Think of standard deviation as similar to range in that it shows the spread of a group of numbers. When the numbers are more spread out around the mean, the standard deviation is greater. When the numbers are clumped closer together around the mean, the standard deviation is smaller.

Take a look at the example on the next page of how a Digital SAT question might combine standard deviation with another statistical concept you already know.

15 Mark for Review

Data Set 1	Data Set 2
6	4
4	3
3	7
8	8
4	2
6	5
5	6

The table above shows two sets of data. Of the following statements comparing Data Set 1 to Data Set 2, which is true?

(A) The standard deviations are the same, and the medians are the same.

(B) The standard deviations are the same, and the medians are different.

(C) The standard deviations are different, and the medians are the same.

(D) The standard deviations are different, and the medians are different.

Here's How to Crack It

The question asks which statement is true about the medians and standard deviations of two data sets. Start by finding the median of each data set, recalling that the median of a group of numbers is the middle number when all values are arranged in order. Start by putting the lists in order. Data Set 1 is 3, 4, 4, 5, 6, 6, 8, and Data Set 2 is 2, 3, 4, 5, 6, 7, 8. Both Data Set 1 and Data Set 2 have 7 numbers, so the median will be the fourth number. The median of Data Set 1 is 5, and the median of Data Set 2 is 5. The medians are the same, so eliminate (B) and (D).

Standard deviation is a measure of the spread of a group of numbers. In Data Set 1, the numbers are clustered toward the middle. In Data Set 2, each number appears once and the numbers are evenly spread throughout the list. Thus, Data Set 1 has a smaller standard deviation than does Data Set 2. Eliminate (A), which says the standard deviations are the same. The correct answer is (C).

PROBABILITY

Probability is a mathematical expression of the likelihood of an event. The basis of probability is simple. The likelihood of any event is discussed in terms of all of the possible outcomes. To express the probability of a given event, *x*, you would count the number of possible outcomes, count the number of outcomes that give you what you want, and arrange them in a fraction, like this:

$$\text{Probability of } x = \frac{\text{number of outcomes that give you what you want}}{\text{total number of possible outcomes}}$$

Every probability is a fraction. The largest a probability can be is 1; a probability of 1 indicates total certainty. The smallest a probability can be is 0, meaning that it's something that cannot happen. Furthermore, you can find the probability that something WILL NOT happen by subtracting the probability that it WILL happen from 1. For example, if the meteorologist tells you that there is a 0.3 probability of rain today, then there must be a 0.7 probability that it won't rain, because $1 - 0.3 = 0.7$. Figuring out the probability of any single event is usually simple. When you flip a coin, for example, there are only two possible outcomes, heads and tails; the probability of getting heads is therefore 1 out of 2, or $\frac{1}{2}$. When you roll a die, there are six possible outcomes, 1 through 6; the odds of getting a 4 are therefore $\frac{1}{6}$. The odds of getting an even result when rolling a die are $\frac{1}{2}$ because there are 3 even results in 6 possible outcomes.

Here's an example of a probability question.

16 Mark for Review

A bag contains 7 blue marbles and 14 marbles that are not blue. If one marble is drawn at random from the bag, what is the probability that the marble is blue?

Ⓐ $\frac{1}{3}$

Ⓑ $\frac{1}{2}$

Ⓒ $\frac{2}{3}$

Ⓓ $\frac{3}{7}$

Here's How to Crack It

The question asks for the probability that a selected marble is blue. To make the probability, find the number of blue marbles and the total number of marbles. Here, there are 21 marbles in the bag, 7 of which are blue. The probability that a marble chosen at random would be blue is therefore $\frac{7}{21}$, or $\frac{1}{3}$. The correct answer is (A).

Let's look at a probability question based on a chart. Again, getting to the correct answer involves reading the chart carefully to find the right numbers to use.

17 Mark for Review

The table below shows the distribution of 300 high school students signing up for elective classes.

	Culinary Arts	World Literature	Computer Coding	Total
Freshmen	18	22	38	78
Sophomores	24	21	15	60
Juniors	30	9	18	57
Seniors	37	38	30	105
Total	109	90	101	300

If one of the students is randomly selected, what is the probability of selecting a student who is a junior taking culinary arts? (Express your answer as a decimal or fraction, not as a percent.)

See Chapter 26 for more about fill-in questions.

Here's How to Crack It

The question asks for a probability based on data in a table. Probability is defined as $\frac{\text{\# of outcomes that give you what you want}}{\text{total \# of possible outcomes}}$. Read the table carefully to find the numbers to make the probability. There are 300 total students, so that is the *total # of possible outcomes*. Of these 300 students, 30 are juniors taking culinary arts, so that is the *# of outcomes that give you what you want*. Therefore, the probability that a student chosen at random is a junior taking culinary arts is $\frac{30}{300}$. This answer cannot be entered into the fill-in box, which only accepts 5 characters when the answer is positive. All equivalent answers that fit will be accepted, so reduce the fraction or convert it to a decimal. The correct answer is $\frac{3}{30}$, $\frac{1}{10}$, 0.1, or another equivalent form.

RATES

Rate is a concept related to averages. Cars travel at an average speed. Work gets done at an average rate. Because the ideas are similar, the formulas you can use for rate problems are similar to the one for averages you learned about earlier. These formulas are $D = RT$ for distance and $W = RT$ for work.

Here's a simple example:

Problem: If a fisherman can tie 9 flies for fly fishing in an hour and a half, how long does it take him to tie one fly, in minutes?

Solution: First, convert the hour and a half to 90 minutes so your units are consistent. Then, fill in the formula with the work or amount done (9 flies) and the time (90 minutes).

$$W = RT$$

$$9 = (R)(90)$$

Divide 9 by 90 to get $R = \frac{1}{10}$, so the rate is one fly every 10 minutes.

You have already seen that rate questions often involve proportions or unit conversion. As always, write down everything and label it carefully to avoid performing the wrong arithmetic operations.

IS THERE SCIENCE ON THE DIGITAL SAT?

No, there isn't, but the test-writers like to make it look like there is. Some questions will use scientific topics and other "real-world" contexts to make things look more complicated. Don't worry about memorizing data about rock types or knowing what a lapping slurry is; just focus on the math.

Take a look at this next example.

18 Mark for Review

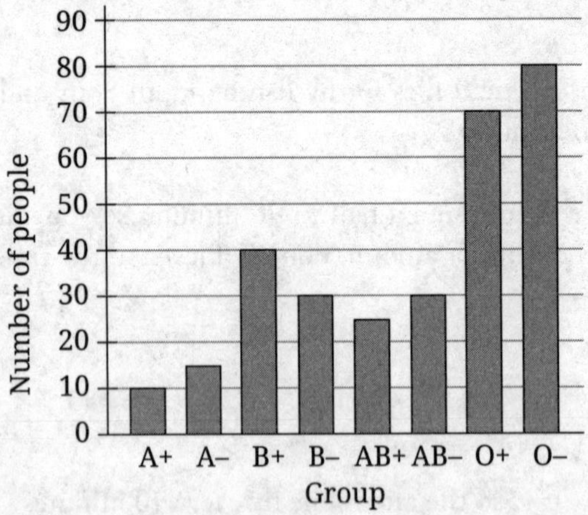

A study about changes in blood type phenotypes after bone marrow transplants recorded the blood types of 300 people before they underwent a bone marrow transplant. How many more people in the study had blood type B– than blood type A+?

Here's How to Crack It

The question asks for the difference between two values based on a graph. Read the graph carefully and look up the necessary values. Find the bar on the graph for blood type B–, then look at the vertical axis to find the number of people with that blood type. The bar goes up to the line at 30, so 30 people have blood type B–. Do the same thing for A+ to see that 10 people have blood type A+. Translate *how many more* as subtraction to get 30 – 10 = 20. The correct answer is 20.

You may also be asked to graph the data presented in a table. Your knowledge of positive and negative relationships will help—you can eliminate things with the wrong relationship.

19 Mark for Review

Temperature in °C (t)	Vapor Pressure in kPa (p)
10	4
20	9
30	37
40	66
50	100

A student conducting experiments in class noticed that the temperature of a given liquid affected the vapor pressure of the liquid, as shown in the table above. Which of the following graphs best represents the relationship between the temperature, t, and the vapor pressure, p, as indicated by the table?

(A)

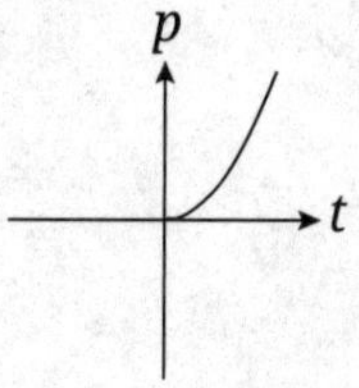

(B)

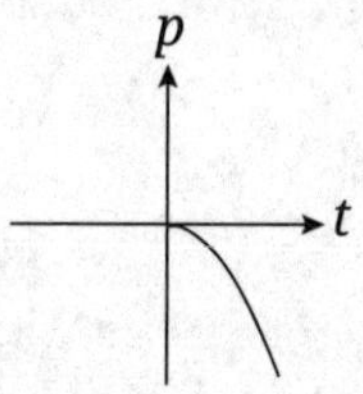

(C)

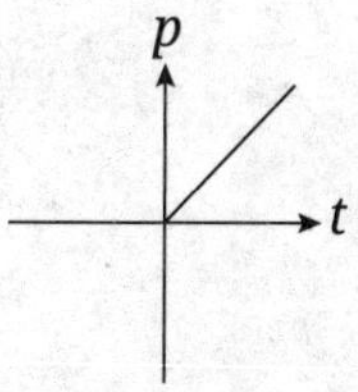

(D)

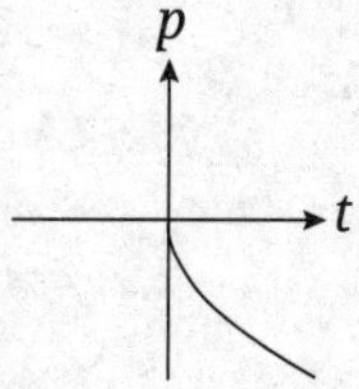

Here's How to Crack It

The question asks for the graph that shows the relationship between temperature and vapor pressure. Notice that the vapor pressure increases as the temperature increases. The line or curve of best fit will go up as you follow the graph from left to right, so eliminate (B) and (D). To determine if the correct graph is (A) or (C), try roughly plotting the data points, and then look at your graph. Notice that the vapor pressure does not increase by the same number for each 10-degree temperature increase. This is an exponential increase, not a linear increase. Therefore, the graph will be curved. Eliminate (C). The correct answer is (A).

Advanced Arithmetic Drill

Work these questions using the advanced arithmetic techniques covered in this chapter. Answers and explanations can be found starting on page 532.

1 Mark for Review

The volume of a water tank decreased by a total of 144 liters over the course of 9 days. What was the rate, in liters per day, at which the volume decreased?

Ⓐ 16

Ⓑ 135

Ⓒ 153

Ⓓ 1,296

2 Mark for Review

Number	Frequency
1	3
2	1
3	2
4	4

Which of the following lists of data is represented by the frequency table shown above?

Ⓐ 1, 1, 2, 2, 2, 3, 4, 4, 4, 4

Ⓑ 1, 1, 1, 2, 3, 3, 4, 4, 4, 4

Ⓒ 1, 2, 2, 3, 3, 3, 4, 4, 4, 4

Ⓓ 2, 3, 6, 16

3 Mark for Review

Steve ran a 12-mile race at an average speed of 8 miles per hour. If Adam ran the same race at an average speed of 6 miles per hour, how many minutes longer did Adam take to complete the race than did Steve?

Ⓐ 12

Ⓑ 16

Ⓒ 24

Ⓓ 30

4 Mark for Review

The amount of time that Amy walks is directly proportional to the distance that she walks. If she walks a distance of 2.5 miles in 50 minutes, how many miles will she walk in 2 hours?

Ⓐ 4.5

Ⓑ 5

Ⓒ 6

Ⓓ 6.5

5 Mark for Review

A total of 140,000 votes was cast for two candidates, Candidate A and Candidate B. If Candidate A won by a ratio of 4 to 3, how many votes were cast for Candidate B?

Ⓐ 30,000

Ⓑ 40,000

Ⓒ 60,000

Ⓓ 80,000

6 Mark for Review

A random sample of students at a local school was surveyed to determine the proportion of students with brown hair. Out of the 200 students sampled, 70 had brown hair. The margin of error of the survey was 6%. Which of the following is the most reasonable conclusion about the percentage of students with brown hair?

Ⓐ No less than 29% of the students have brown hair.

Ⓑ Between 29% and 41% of the students have brown hair.

Ⓒ Exactly 35% of the students have brown hair.

Ⓓ No more than 41% of the students have brown hair.

7 Mark for Review

29, 32, 31, 29, 24, 25, 26

The data set shown above contains 7 integer values. If an 8th integer between 20 and 50 is added to the data set, the new mean will be 2 more than the current mean. What is the value of the 8th integer added to the data set?

______

8 Mark for Review

Of all the houses in a certain neighborhood, 80% have garages. Of those houses with garages, 60% have two-car garages. If there are 56 houses with garages that are <u>not</u> two-car garages, how many houses are there in the neighborhood?

Ⓐ 93

Ⓑ 117

Ⓒ 156

Ⓓ 175

9 Mark for Review

Data Set R

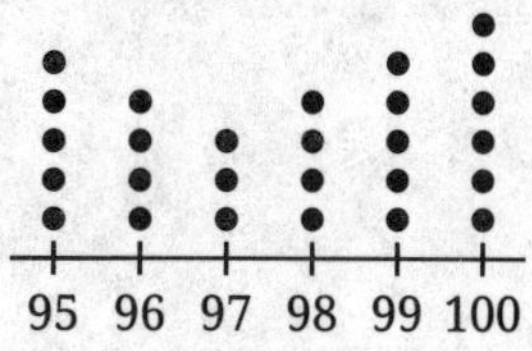

Data set R is represented by the dot plot above. Data set Q is created by subtracting 35 from each of the values in data set R. Which of the following statements correctly compares the standard deviations of data sets R and Q?

Ⓐ There is not enough information to compare these standard deviations.

Ⓑ The standard deviation of data set R is greater than the standard deviation of data set Q.

Ⓒ The standard deviation of data set R is less than the standard deviation of data set Q.

Ⓓ The standard deviation of data set R is equal to the standard deviation of data set Q.

10 Mark for Review

On Tuesday, a watchmaker made 4 more watches than he made on Monday. If he made 16% more watches on Tuesday than on Monday, how many watches did he make on Tuesday?

Ⓐ 20

Ⓑ 21

Ⓒ 25

Ⓓ 29

ANSWERS TO FRACTIONS, DECIMALS, AND PERCENTS EXERCISE

1. $\frac{1}{2}$ 0.5 50%
2. $\frac{3}{1}$ 3.0 300%
3. $\frac{1}{200}$ 0.005 0.5%
4. $\frac{1}{3}$ $0.333\overline{3}$ $33\frac{1}{3}\%$

ADVANCED ARITHMETIC DRILL ANSWERS AND EXPLANATIONS

1. **A** The question asks for a rate. Begin by reading the question to find information about the rate. The question states that the volume *decreased by a total of 144 liters over the course of 9 days* and asks for the rate of decrease in *liters per day*. Divide the number of liters by the number of days to get $\frac{144 \text{ liters}}{9 \text{ days}} = \frac{16 \text{ liters}}{1 \text{ day}}$. The rate is 16 liters per day. The correct answer is (A).

2. **B** The question asks for the list of numbers that correctly represents a frequency table. A frequency table has two columns: the left-hand column contains the values, and the right-hand column contains the number of times each value occurs, or its frequency. Work in bite-sized pieces and eliminate answer choices that do not match the data. According to the table, the number 1 has a frequency of 3, so the number 1 should be in the list 3 times. Eliminate (A), (C), and (D) because they do not have the number 1 in the list 3 times. Choice (B) shows the correct frequency for each value. The correct answer is (B).

3. **D** The question asks for the difference in minutes between Steve's time and Adam's time. Use the formula $D = RT$ to calculate the time for each runner. Steve runs 12 miles at 8 miles per hour, so the formula becomes $12 = (8)(T)$. To find Steve's time, divide his distance by his rate, which means that he runs for $1\frac{1}{2}$ hours (or 1.5 if you're using your calculator). Adam runs the same 12 miles at 6 miles per hour, so the formula becomes $12 = (6)(T)$. This means that Adam runs for 2 hours. Adam takes one-half hour longer to complete the race, and one-half hour is 30 minutes. The correct answer is (D).

4. **C** The question asks for the distance Amy can walk in two hours if she walks at a given rate. Since you know the time that Amy walked and the distance she walked are directly proportional, you can set up a proportion to show her distance ÷ time. The time it took her to walk 2.5 miles is given in minutes and the requested time is in hours, so match the units in the proportion by putting 120(60 × 2) minutes in the second half of the ratio: $\frac{2.5}{50} = \frac{x}{120}$. To solve, cross-multiply, and you'll get $50x = 2.5 \times 120$; $50x = 300$; $x = 6$ miles. The correct answer is (C).

5. **C** The question asks for the number of votes Candidate B received. You know the ratio for the votes is 4 for Candidate A to every 3 for Candidate B, so the proportion of votes Candidate B received is 3 out of every 7 or $\frac{3}{7}$ of the total votes. There were 140,000 votes all together, so Candidate B received $\frac{3}{7}(140{,}000) = 60{,}000$ votes. The correct answer is (C).

6. **B** The question asks for a reasonable conclusion based on survey results and a margin of error. Work in bite-sized pieces and eliminate after each piece. Start by determining the percent of surveyed students with brown hair by dividing the number of students with brown hair by the total number of students and multiplying by 100: $\frac{70}{200} \times 100 = 35\%$. A margin of error expresses the amount of random sampling error in a survey's results. Eliminate (C) because it is only the result, 35%, not a range above and below the result. The margin of error is 6%, meaning that results within a range of 6% above and 6% below the estimate are reasonable. The study found that 35% of students have brown hair, so the reasonable results for this study are between 29% and 41%. Eliminate (A) because it only addresses the lower limit. Keep (B) because it addresses both the lower limit and the upper limit. Eliminate (D) because it only addresses the upper limit. The correct answer is (B).

7. **44** The question asks for a value given information about the mean of a data set. For averages, use the formula $T = AN$, in which T is the *Total*, A is the *Average*, and N is the *Number of things*. Start by finding the average of the seven integers given in the question. There are 7 values, so $N = 7$. Find the *Total* by adding the seven integers to get $T = 29 + 32 + 31 + 29 + 24 + 25 + 26 = 196$. The average formula becomes $196 = (A)(7)$. Divide both sides of the equation by 7 to get $A = 28$. The question states that, after an eighth integer is added to the data set, *the new average will be 2 more than the current average.* Since the current average is 28, the new average will be $28 + 2 = 30$. There are now 8 integers in the data set, so plug $N = 8$ and $A = 30$ into the data set to get $T = (30)(8) = 240$. The question asks for the value of the eighth integer, so subtract the *Total* of the 7 integers from the *Total* of the 8 integers to get $240 - 196 = 44$ as the value of the eighth integer. The correct answer is 44.

8. **D** The question asks for the number of houses in the neighborhood. Start by figuring out what percent of the houses do not have two-car garages. Since 60% of the houses with garages have two-car garages, 40% of the houses with garages do not have two-car garages. In other words, 40% of 80% of the houses do not have two-car garages. Translate that into math to get $\frac{40}{100} \times \frac{80}{100} = 0.32$, or 32% of the houses. The question states that 56 houses do not have two-car garages, which means 32% of the houses equals 56. Translating into math gives $\frac{32}{100} \times x = 56$. Solve for x, and you'll get 175. Another great option for questions that ask for something specific like number of houses is plugging in the answers. Either way, the correct answer is (D).

9. **D** The question asks for a comparison of the standard deviations of two data sets. Standard deviation is a measure of the spread of a group of numbers. A group of numbers close together has a small standard deviation, whereas a group of numbers spread out has a large standard deviation. Subtracting 35 from each number will change the values in the data set but will not change how they are distributed. The dot plot of data set Q will look the same as the dot plot of data set R except for the values along the bottom of the dot plot. Because the shape of the dot plot remains the same, so does the standard deviation, and the two data sets have the same standard deviation. The correct answer is (D).

10. **D** The question asks for the number of watches a watchmaker made on Tuesday. This is a specific amount, and there are numbers in the answer choices, so plug in the answers. Start with (B). If the watchmaker made 21 watches on Tuesday, then he must have made 17 watches on Monday. You know that he should have made 16% more watches on Tuesday than on Monday, so use the percent change formula $\left(\frac{\text{difference}}{\text{original}} \times 100\right)$ to see if you get 16%: $\frac{4}{17} \times 100 = 23.5\%$, which is too big. Eliminate (B). You want the 4 watches to be a smaller percent of the total, so you need a bigger total. Try a bigger answer choice, like (D). If he made 29 watches on Tuesday, then he made 25 watches on Monday. Now the percent change is $\frac{4}{25} = 0.16 = 16\%$, which is exactly what you want. The correct answer is (D).

Summary

- A ratio can be expressed as a fraction, but ratios are not fractions. A ratio compares parts to parts; a fraction compares a part to the whole.
- Set up proportions in the form $\frac{x_1}{y_1} = \frac{x_2}{y_2}$.
- A percentage is just a convenient way of expressing a fraction with a denominator of 100.
- To convert a percentage to a fraction, put the percentage over 100 and reduce.
- To convert a fraction to a percentage, use your calculator to divide the top of the fraction by the bottom of the fraction. Then multiply the result by 100.
- To convert a percentage to a decimal, move the decimal point two places to the left. To convert a decimal to a percentage, move the decimal point two places to the right.
- In questions that require you to find a series of percentage increases or decreases, remember that each successive increase or decrease is performed on the result of the previous one.
- If you need to find the percent increase or decrease, use $\% \text{ change} = \frac{\text{difference}}{\text{original}} \times 100$.
- To find the mean, or average, of several values, add up the values and divide the total by the number of values.
- Use the formula $T = AN$ to solve questions involving means, or averages. The key to most average questions is finding the total.
- The median of a group of numbers is the number that is exactly in the middle of the group when the group is arranged from smallest to largest, as on a number line. If there is an even number of numbers, the median is the average of the two middle numbers.
- The mode of a group of numbers is the number in the group that appears most often.
- The range of a group of numbers is the difference between the greatest number in the group and the least number.

- Standard deviation is a measure of the spread, or distribution, of a group of numbers. More spread out means a large standard deviation, and more clustered together means a small standard deviation.
- Margin of error is the range above and below the value predicted by a survey within which the actual value is likely to be.
- Probability is expressed as a fraction:
  - $\text{Probability} = \dfrac{\text{number of outcomes that give you what you want}}{\text{total number of possible outcomes}}$
- On questions about rates, use the formulas $D = RT$ and $W = RT$. Be careful with the units—the Digital SAT will often require you to do a unit conversion such as minutes to hours or inches to feet.

Chapter 25
Geometry and Trigonometry

The final math topics that are tested regularly on the Digital SAT are geometry and trigonometry. There will be 5–7 questions total on these topics, split between the two modules. These questions cover topics such as lines and angles, triangles, circles, and trig functions. This chapter covers each of those topics and more, and provides a step-by-step walkthrough for each type of question.

GEOMETRY ON THE DIGITAL SAT

Several geometry questions will test your knowledge of basic geometry rules, including formulas. Never fear! There is a reference sheet in the testing app that you can open at any time by clicking on the word Reference in the upper right corner of the screen. It saves time to know these facts and formulas ahead of time, but use the reference sheet to check or to look things up that you don't already know.

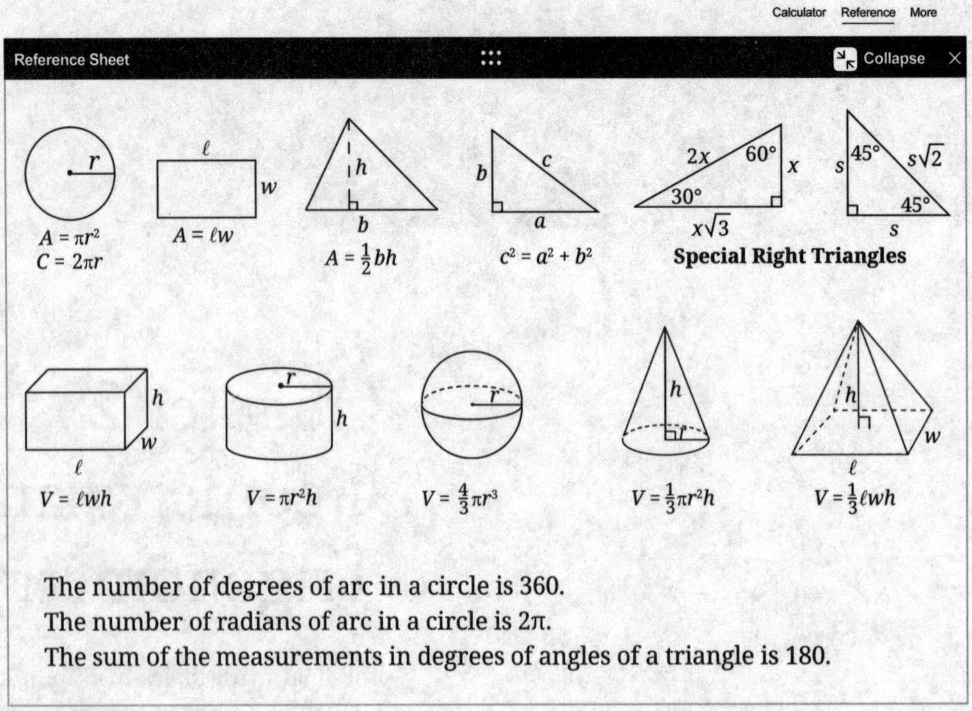

This reference sheet contains *some* of what you'll need to tackle geometry on the Digital SAT. In this chapter, we'll cover a basic approach for geometry questions and other information you'll need to know to handle geometry and trig questions on the Digital SAT.

Geometry: Basic Approach

For the handful of geometry questions that appear on the Digital SAT, we recommend the following step-by-step approach:

1. **Draw a figure** on your scratch paper. If the question contains the note "Figure not drawn to scale," draw the figure using information in the question.
2. **Label the figure** with any information given in the question. Sometimes you can plug in for parts of the figure as well.
3. **Write down formulas** that you might need for the question.
4. **Ballpark** if you're stuck or running short on time.

These four steps, combined with the techniques you've learned in the rest of this book and the geometry concepts this chapter will cover, will enable you to tackle any geometry question you might run across on the Digital SAT.

Before we dive in to the nitty-gritty, let's try a question using this approach.

1 Mark for Review

In triangle ABC, angle $B = 60°$ and AC is perpendicular to BC. If $AB = x$, what is the area of triangle ABC, in terms of x?

Ⓐ $\frac{x^2\sqrt{3}}{8}$

Ⓑ $\frac{x^2\sqrt{3}}{4}$

Ⓒ $\frac{x^2\sqrt{3}}{2}$

Ⓓ $x^2\sqrt{3}$

Here's How to Crack It

The question asks for the area of the triangle. Follow the steps outlined on the previous page. Start by drawing the figure. If AC is perpendicular to BC, then triangle ABC is a right triangle with the right angle at point C:

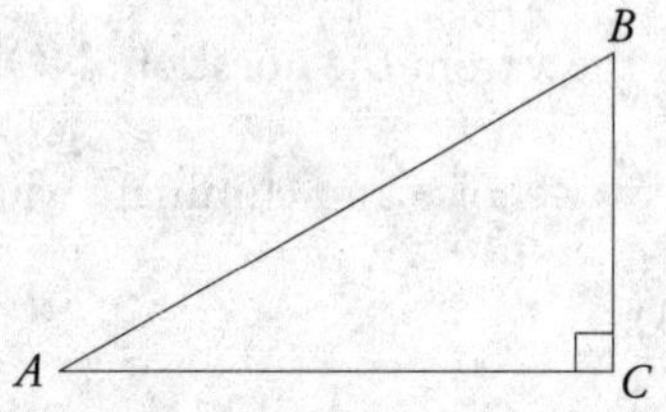

The next step is to label what you know. Angle $B = 60°$ can go right into the figure. Because $AB = x$, you can plug in for x; make $x = 4$. Label this information in the figure:

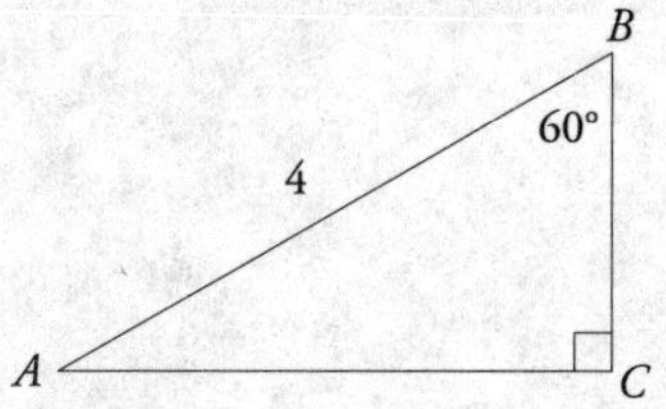

Next, figure out what other information you know. Because there are 180° in a triangle, angle $A = 180 - 90 - 60 = 30°$. This is a 30°-60°-90° special right triangle, which you are given information about in the reference sheet. Based on the figure given in the box, the hypotenuse is equal to $2x$. (Note that this is a different x from the one you plugged in for; the test-writers are trying to confuse you.) So, if the hypotenuse is 4, $x = \frac{4}{2} = 2$; this is the side opposite the 30° angle, BC. The remaining side, AC, is $x\sqrt{3}$, which is $2\sqrt{3}$. Label this information in your figure:

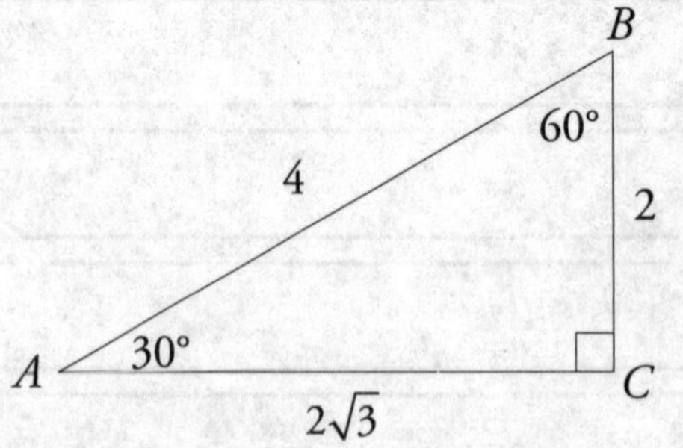

Now write down the formula you need. The question is asking for the area, so use the area of a triangle formula from the reference sheet: $A = \frac{1}{2}bh$. Fill in what you know. Because this is a right triangle, you can use the two legs of the triangle as the base and the height. Make $b = 2\sqrt{3}$ and $h = 2$ in the equation and solve: $A = \frac{1}{2}(2\sqrt{3})(2) = 2\sqrt{3}$. This is your target; circle it. Now plug in $x = 4$ (that's the x from the question, NOT the x from the information in the reference sheet!) into each answer choice and eliminate what doesn't equal $2\sqrt{3}$. Only (A) works, so the correct answer is (A).

Now that we've covered how to approach geometry questions, let's look more closely at some of the geometry concepts you'll need for these questions.

LINES AND ANGLES

Here are the basic rules you need to know for questions about lines and angles on the Digital SAT.

1. **A circle contains 360 degrees.**

   Every circle contains 360 degrees. Each degree is $\frac{1}{360}$ of the total distance around the outside of the circle. It doesn't matter whether the circle is large or small; it still has exactly 360 degrees.

2. **When you think about angles, remember circles.**

   An angle is formed when two line segments extend from a common point. If you think of the point as the center of a circle, the measure of the angle is the number of degrees enclosed by the lines when they pass through the edge of the circle. Once again, the size of the circle doesn't matter; neither does the length of the lines. Refer to the following figure.

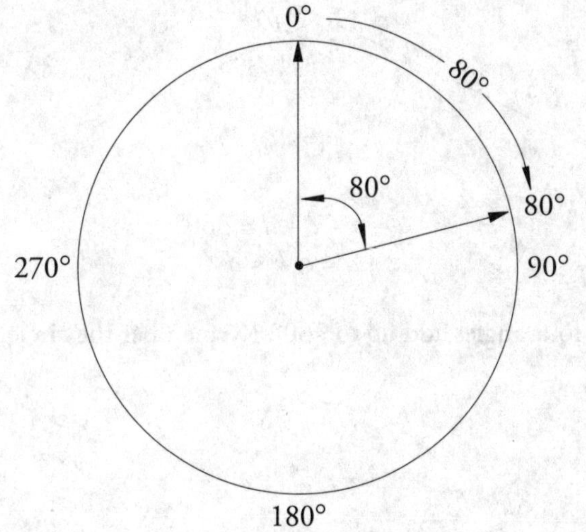

3. **A line is a 180° angle.**

   You probably don't think of a line as an angle, but it is one. Think of it as a flat angle. The following drawings should help:

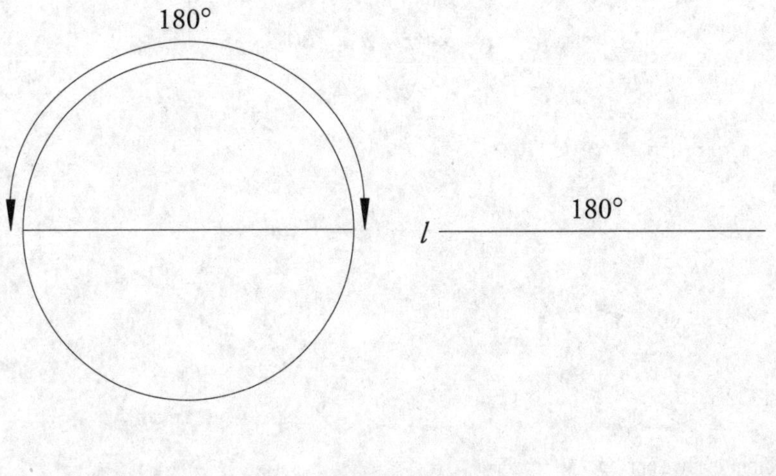

4. **When two lines intersect, four angles are formed.**
The following figure should make this clear. The four angles are indicated by letters.

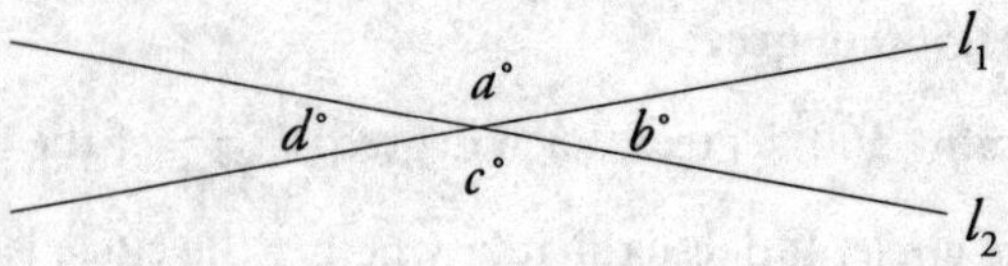

5. **When two lines intersect, the angles opposite each other will have the same measures.**
Such angles are called **vertical angles.** In the following figure, angles *a* and *c* are equal; so are angles *b* and *d*.

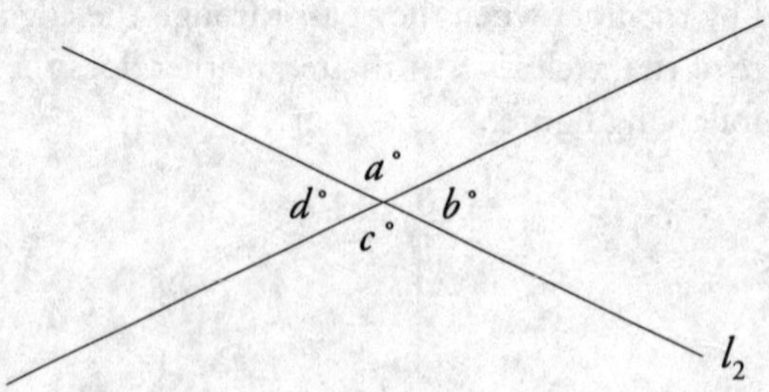

$$a + b + c + d = 360°$$
$$a = c,\ b = d$$

The measures of these four angles add up to 360°. (Remember the circle.)

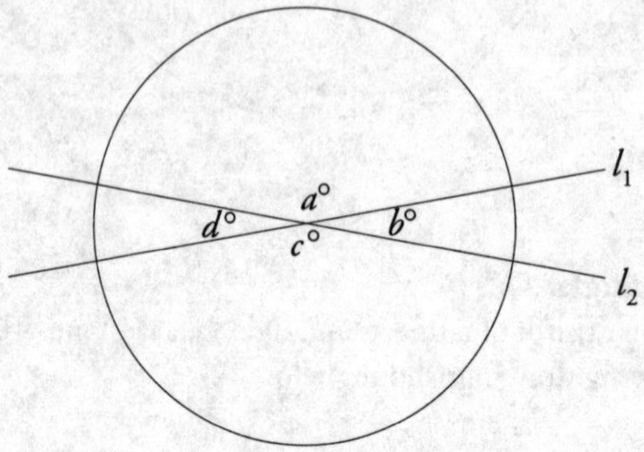

$$a + b + c + d = 360°$$

It doesn't matter how many lines you intersect through a single point. The total measure of all the angles formed will still be 360°.

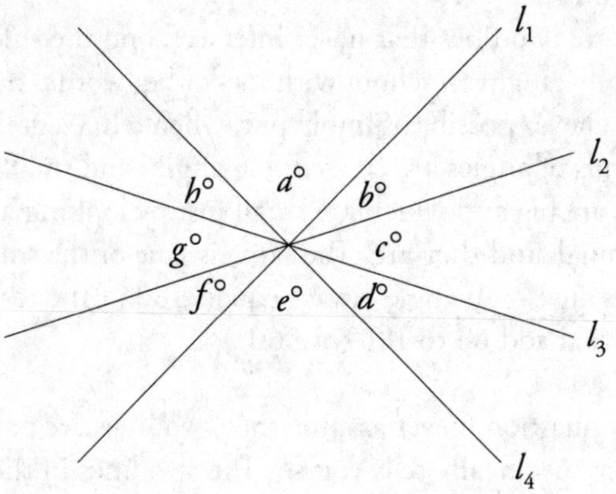

$$a + b + c + d + e + f + g + h = 360°$$
$$a = e,\ b = f,\ c = g,\ d = h$$

Perpendicular:
Meeting at right (90°) angles

6. **If two lines are perpendicular to each other, each of the four angles formed is 90°.**
A 90° angle is called a **right angle.**

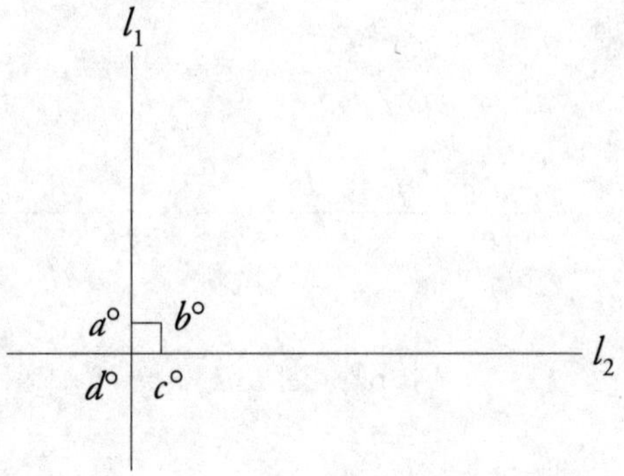

Angles *a, b, c,* and *d* all equal 90°.

The little box at the intersection of the two lines is the symbol for a right angle. If the lines are not perpendicular to each other, then none of the angles will be right angles. Don't assume that an angle is a right angle unless you are specifically told that it is a right angle, either in the question or with the right angle symbol.

Flip and Negate
If two lines are perpendicular, then their slopes are negative reciprocals; i.e., if l_1 has a slope of 2 and l_2 is perpendicular to l_1, then l_2 must have a slope of $-\frac{1}{2}$.

7. **When two parallel lines are cut by a third line, all of the small angles are equal, all of the big angles are equal, and the sum of any big angle and any small angle is 180°.**

Parallel lines are two lines that never intersect, and the rules about parallel lines are usually taught in school with lots of big words. But we like to avoid big words whenever possible. Simply put, when a line cuts through two parallel lines, two kinds of angles are created: big angles and small angles. You can tell which angles are big and which are small just by looking at them. All the big angles look equal, and they are. The same is true of the small angles. Lastly, any big angle plus any small angle always equals 180°. (The test-writers like rules about angles that add up to 180° or 360°.)

Parallel Lines
Parallel lines have the same slope.

In any geometry question, never assume that two lines are parallel unless the question or figure specifically tells you so. The two lines in the following figure are parallel. Angle *a* is a big angle, and it has the same measure as angles *c*, *e*, and *g*, which are also big angles. Angle *b* is a small angle, and it has the same measure as angles *d*, *f*, and *h*, which are also small angles.

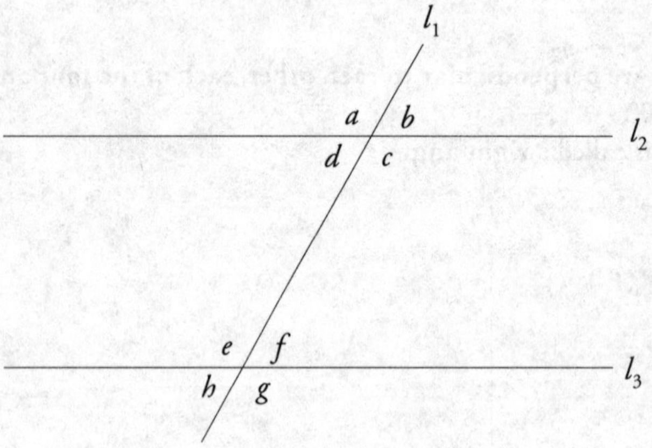

l_2 is parallel to l_3
$a = c = e = g$
$b = d = f = h$

You should be able to see that the degree measures of angles *a*, *b*, *c*, and *d* add up to 360°. So do those of angles *e*, *f*, *g*, and *h*. If you have trouble seeing it, draw a circle around the angles. What is the degree measure of a circle? Also, the sum of any small angle (such as *d*) and any big angle (such as *g*) is 180°.

Let's see how these concepts might be tested on the Digital SAT.

2 Mark for Review

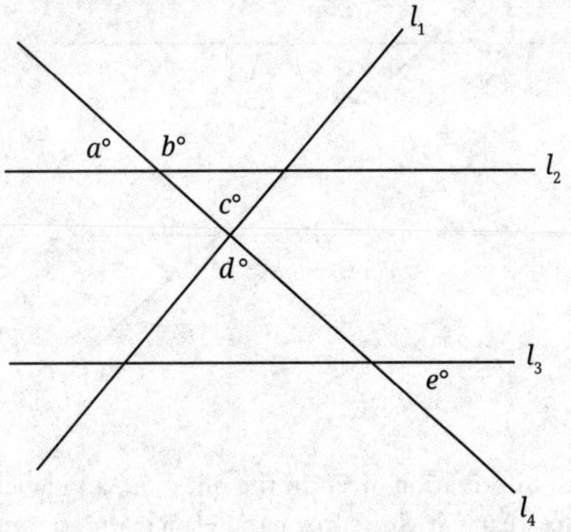

Note: Figure not drawn to scale.

In the figure above, l_2 is parallel to l_3. If $b = 130$, what is the value of e?

Ⓐ 40

Ⓑ 50

Ⓒ 90

Ⓓ 130

Here's How to Crack It

The question asks for the value of an angle on a figure. Use the Geometry Basic Approach. Start by redrawing the figure on your scratch paper. This figure has a lot going on, so only draw the parts you need and add more later if necessary. Angle e is between lines 3 and 4, and line 2 is parallel to line 3. That all seems important, so include it in your figure.

The drawing should look something like this:

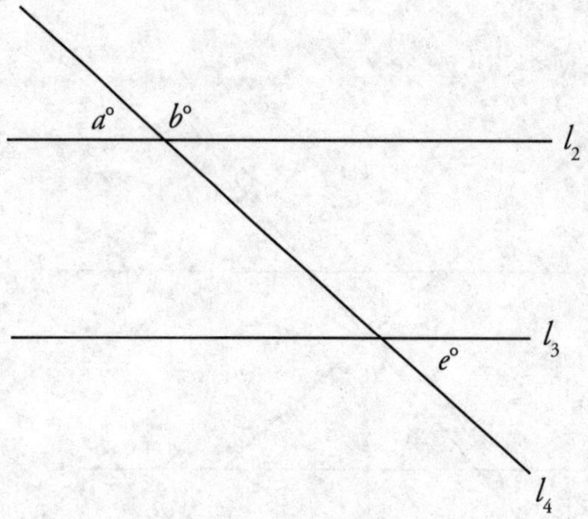

Next, label the figure with information given in the question, and label angle b as 130°. When a geometry question states that two lines are parallel, it's almost certainly testing the rules about angles. Recall that when two parallel lines are cut by a third line, two kinds of angles are created: big and small. All of the small angles are equal to each other, all of the big angles are equal to each other, and any small angle + any big angle = 180°. Angle b is a big angle and angle e is a small angle, so $b + e = 180$. Plug in the measure of angle b to get $130 + e = 180$. Subtract 130 from both sides of the equation to get $e = 50$. The correct answer is (B).

TRIANGLES

Here are some basic triangle rules you'll need to know for the Digital SAT.

1. **Every triangle contains 180°.**
   The word *triangle* means "three angles," and every triangle contains three interior angles. The measure of these three angles always adds up to exactly 180°. You don't need to know why this is true or how to prove it. You just need to know it. And we mean *know* it.

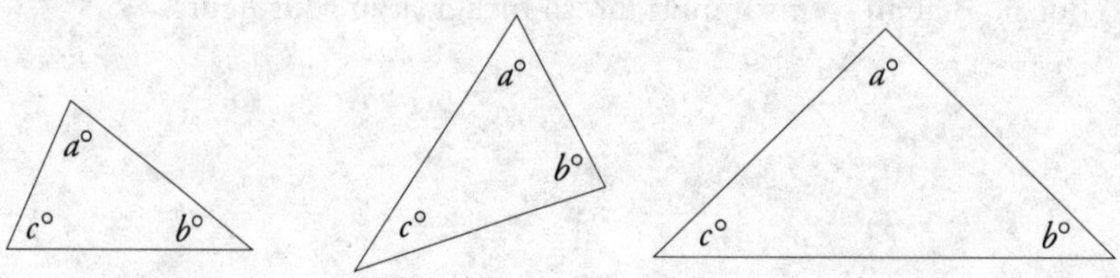

$a + b + c = 180°$ $a + b + c = 180°$ $a + b + c = 180°$

2. **An isosceles triangle is one in which two of the sides are equal in length.** The angles opposite those equal sides are also equal because angles opposite equal sides are also equal.

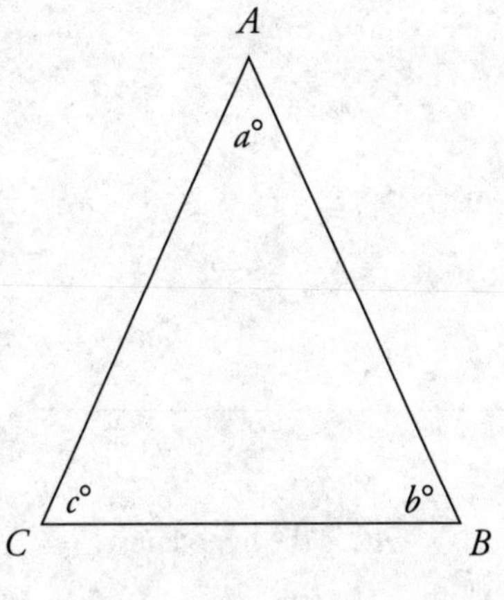

$AB = AC \quad AB \neq BC$

$c = b \quad c \neq a$

3. **An equilateral triangle is one in which all three sides are equal in length.** Because the angles opposite equal sides are also equal, all three angles in an equilateral triangle are equal too. (Their measures are always 60° each.)

Equilateral Triangles
An equilateral triangle is also isosceles.

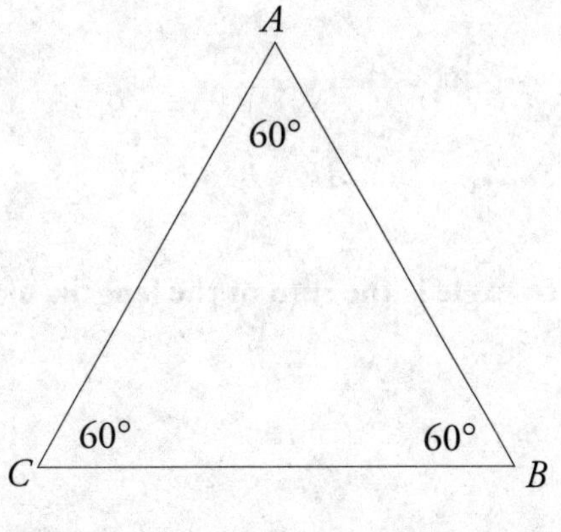

$AB = BC = AC$

4. A right triangle is a triangle in which one of the angles is a right angle (90°).

The longest side of a right triangle, which is always opposite the 90° angle, is called the **hypotenuse.** The other two sides are called **legs.**

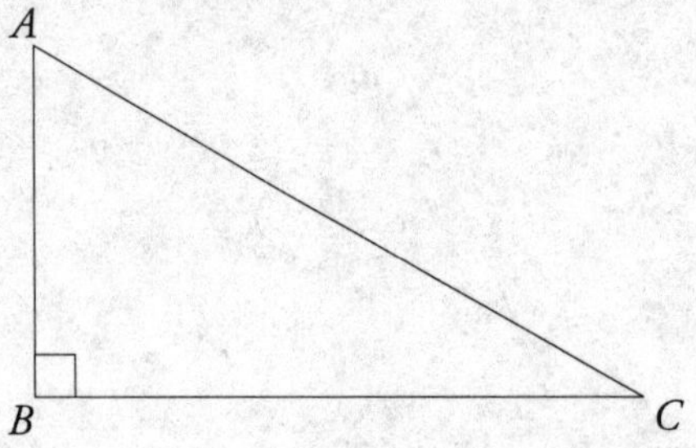

AC is the hypotenuse.

Some right triangles are also **isosceles.** The angles in an isosceles right triangle always measure 45°, 45°, and 90°.

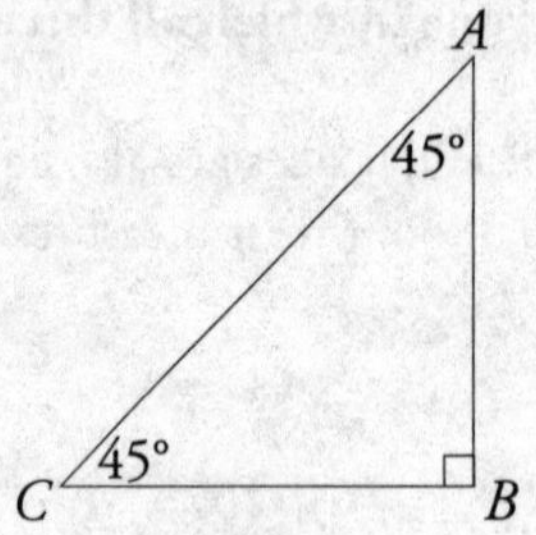

$AB = BC$

5. The perimeter of a triangle is the sum of the lengths of its sides.

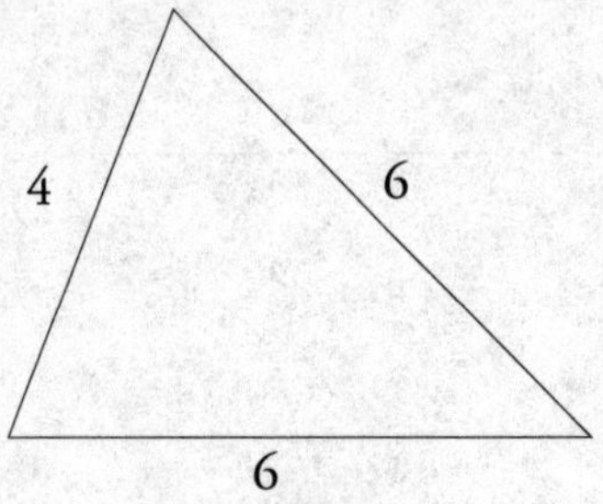

perimeter = 4 + 6 + 6 = 16

6. The area of a triangle is $\frac{1}{2}$ (base × height).

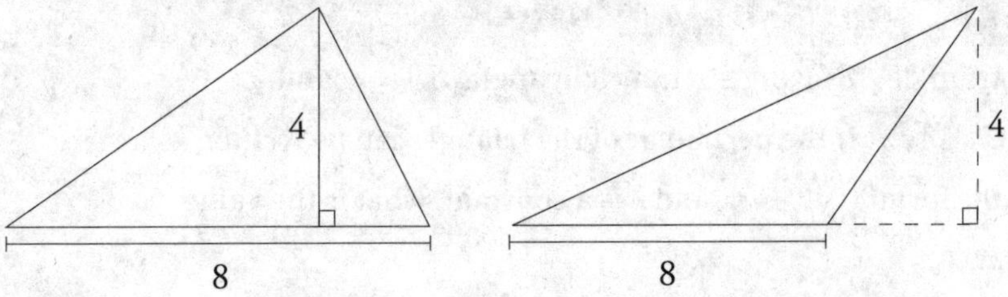

area = $\frac{1}{2}(8 \times 4) = 16$ area = $\frac{1}{2}(8 \times 4) = 16$

In or Out
The height can be found with a line dropped inside or outside the triangle—just as long as it's perpendicular to the base.

Pythagorean Theorem

The **Pythagorean Theorem** states that in a right triangle, the square of the hypotenuse equals the sum of the squares of the other two sides. As mentioned earlier, the hypotenuse is the longest side of a right triangle; it's the side opposite the right angle. The square of the hypotenuse is its length squared. Applying the Pythagorean Theorem to the following drawing, we find that $a^2 + b^2 = c^2$.

Pythagorean Theorem
$a^2 + b^2 = c^2$, where c is the hypotenuse of a right triangle. Learn it; love it.

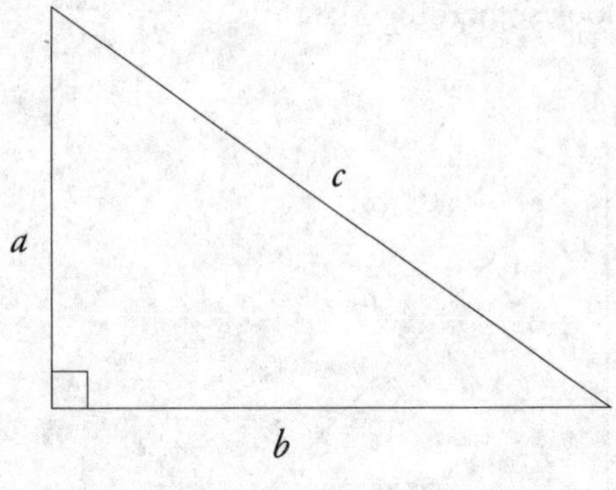

If you forget the Pythagorean Theorem, you can always look it up on the reference sheet.

3 Mark for Review

In triangle ABC, angle B is a right angle, $AB = 4$, and $AC = 4\sqrt{2}$. If the perimeter of the triangle can be written in the form $4\left(\sqrt{2} + a\right)$, and a is a constant, what is the value of a?

Here's How to Crack It

The question asks for the value of a constant given information about a triangle. Use the Geometry Basic Approach. Start by drawing a right triangle on your scratch paper and put the right angle symbol at B. Next, label the figure with information from the question. Label side AB as 4 and side AC as $4\sqrt{2}$. Notice that side AC is opposite the right angle, so it is the hypotenuse. The drawing should look something like this:

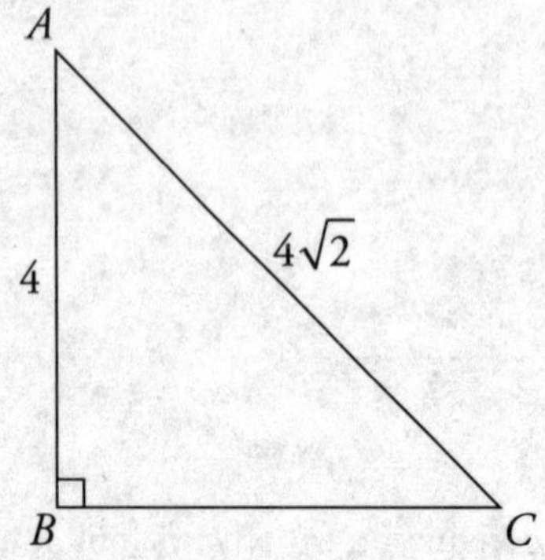

To find the length of the third side, use the Pythagorean Theorem: $a^2 + b^2 = c^2$. Plug in the known values to get $4^2 + b^2 = \left(4\sqrt{2}\right)^2$. Square the numbers to get $16 + b^2 = 32$, then subtract 16 from both sides of the equation to get $b^2 = 16$. Take the square root of both sides of the equation to get $b = 4$. Label side BC as 4. This happens to be an isosceles right triangle, which is one of the triangles on the reference sheet. If you catch that, you might be able to find the length of the third side faster, but using the Pythagorean Theorem works well, too.

The perimeter of a geometric shape is the sum of the lengths of the sides, so $P = 4 + 4 + 4\sqrt{2}$, or $P = 8 + 4\sqrt{2}$. Set this equal to the different form of the perimeter given in the question to get $8 + 4\sqrt{2} = 4\left(\sqrt{2} + a\right)$. Distribute on the right side of the equation to get $8 + 4\sqrt{2} = 4\sqrt{2} + 4a$. Subtract $4\sqrt{2}$ from both sides of the equation to get $8 = 4a$. Divide both sides of the equation by 4 to get $2 = a$. The correct answer is 2.

TRIGONOMETRY

SOHCAHTOA

Trigonometry will appear on the Digital SAT Math section. But fear not! Many trigonometry questions you will see mostly require you to know the basic definitions of the three main trigonometric functions. **SOHCAHTOA** is a way to remember the three functions.

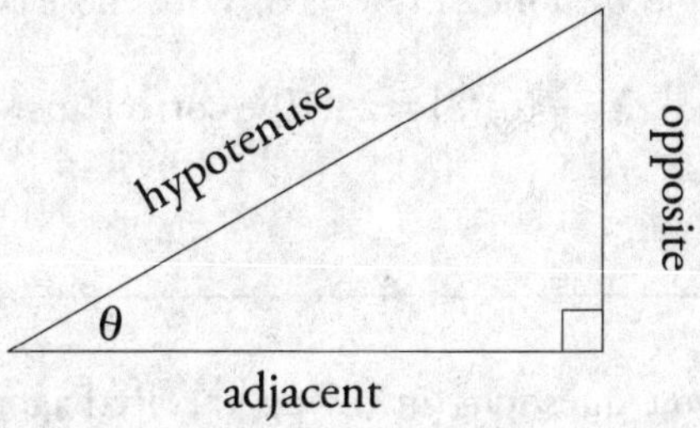

$$\text{sine } \theta = \frac{\text{opposite}}{\text{hypotenuse}} \qquad \text{cosine } \theta = \frac{\text{adjacent}}{\text{hypotenuse}} \qquad \text{tangent } \theta = \frac{\text{opposite}}{\text{adjacent}}$$

Check out this next example.

4 Mark for Review

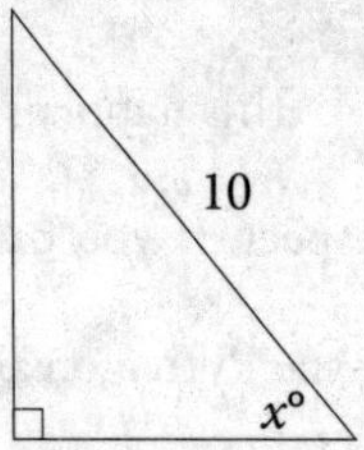

In the triangle above, $\sin x = 0.8$ and $\cos x = 0.6$. What is the area of the triangle?

(A) 0.48

(B) 4.8

(C) 24

(D) 48

Here's How to Crack It

The question asks for the area of the triangle. Use the definitions of sine and cosine to find the two legs of the triangle. Sine is $\frac{\text{opposite}}{\text{hypotenuse}}$, so if $\sin x = 0.8$, then $0.8 = \frac{\text{opposite}}{10}$. Multiply both sides by 10 and you find the side opposite the angle with measure $x°$ is 8. Similarly, cosine is $\frac{\text{adjacent}}{\text{hypotenuse}}$, so if $\cos x = 0.6$, then $0.6 = \frac{\text{adjacent}}{10}$. Multiply both sides by 10 to determine that the side adjacent to the angle with measure $x°$ is 6. With those two sides, find the area. The formula for area is $A = \frac{1}{2}bh$, so $A = \frac{1}{2}(6)(8) = 24$. The correct answer is (C).

The test-writers love to ask you questions involving the Pythagorean Theorem along with SOHCAHTOA. See the following question.

5 Mark for Review

In triangle ABC, AC is perpendicular to BC and $\cos(B) = \frac{12}{13}$.

What is the value of $\tan(B)$?

Ⓐ $\frac{5}{13}$

Ⓑ $\frac{5}{12}$

Ⓒ $\frac{12}{13}$

Ⓓ $\frac{12}{5}$

Here's How to Crack It

The question asks for the value of the tangent of an angle. Use the Geometry Basic Approach: start by drawing triangle ABC.

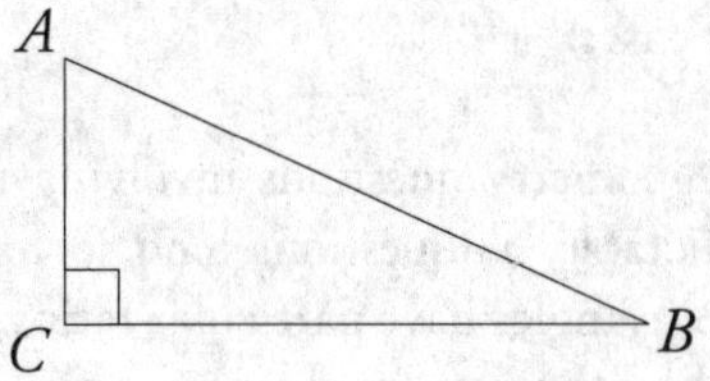

Next, label what you can. You don't know the actual side lengths, but because $\cos(B) = \frac{12}{13}$, you do know the relationship between the side adjacent to angle B and the hypotenuse. You can plug in for this relationship: make BC (the side adjacent to the angle) 12 and AB (the hypotenuse) 13:

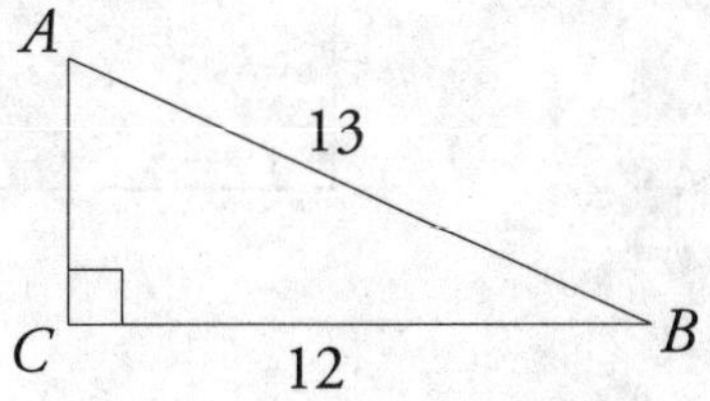

You need to find tan (B), which means you need $\frac{\text{opposite}}{\text{adjacent}}$. You already know the adjacent side is 12, but you still need the side opposite, AC. Use the Pythagorean Theorem to find the missing side:

$$a^2 + b^2 = c^2$$
$$12^2 + b^2 = 13^2$$
$$144 + b^2 = 169$$
$$b^2 = 25$$
$$b = 5$$

Therefore, $AC = 5$, and tan $(B) = \frac{5}{12}$, so the correct answer is (B).

Special Right Triangles

Both of the previous questions you worked also used special right triangles. While in the last question we used the Pythagorean Theorem to find the missing side, if you memorize these special triangles, you can avoid using the Pythagorean Theorem in a lot of cases.

When it comes to geometry questions involving right triangles, the Digital SAT is often fairly predictable, as questions tend to focus on certain relationships. In these questions, the triangles have particular ratios. There are two different types of special right triangles. The first involves the ratio of sides, and the second involves the ratio of angles.

The most common special right triangles with side ratios are known as **Pythagorean triples.** Here are the test-writers' favorites:

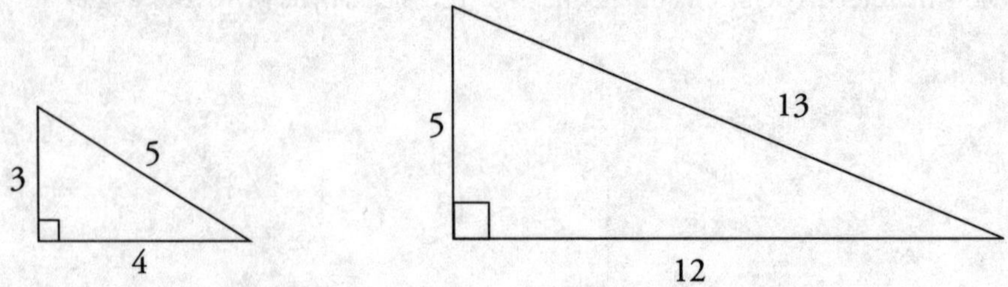

If you memorize these two sets of Pythagorean triples (3-4-5 and 5-12-13), you'll often be able to find the answer without using the Pythagorean Theorem. If you're given a right triangle with a side of 3 and a hypotenuse of 5, you know right away that the other side has to be 4. Likewise, if you see a right triangle with sides of 5 and 12, you know the hypotenuse must be 13.

Your Friend the Rectangle

Be on the lookout for questions in which the application of the Pythagorean Theorem is not obvious. For example, every rectangle contains two right triangles. That means that if you know the length and width of the rectangle, you also know the length of the diagonal, which is the hypotenuse of both triangles.

Relax; It's Just a Ratio

A 3-4-5 triangle may be hiding, disguised as 6-8-10 or 18-24-30. It's all the same ratio, though, so be on the lookout.

The test-writers also like to use right triangles with sides that are simply multiples of the common Pythagorean triples. For example, you might see a 6-8-10 or a 10-24-26 triangle. These sides are simply the sides of the 3-4-5 and 5-12-13 triangles multiplied by 2.

There are two types of special right triangles that have a specific ratio of angles. They are the **30°-60°-90° triangle** and the **45°-45°-90° triangle.** The sides of these triangles always have the same fixed ratio to each other. The ratios are as follows:

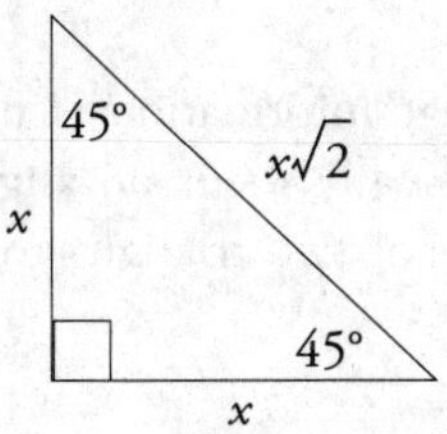

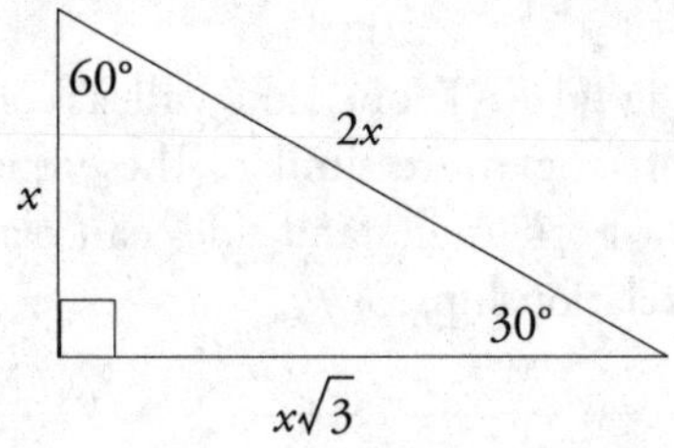

Don't Forget the Reference Sheet!
The relationships of the sides of special right triangles can be found in the reference sheet in the testing app, so you don't necessarily need to memorize them. However, you should be able to recognize them.

Let's talk about a 45°-45°-90° triangle first. Did you notice that this is also an isosceles right triangle? The legs will always be the same length. And the hypotenuse will always be the length of one leg times $\sqrt{2}$. Its ratio of side to side to hypotenuse is always 1:1: $\sqrt{2}$. For example, if you have a 45°-45°-90° triangle with a leg length of 3, then the second leg length will also be 3 and the hypotenuse will be $3\sqrt{2}$.

Now let's talk about a 30°-60°-90° triangle. The ratio of shorter leg to longer leg to hypotenuse is always 1: $\sqrt{3}$:2. For example, if the shorter leg of a 30°-60°-90° triangle is 5, then the longer leg would be $5\sqrt{3}$ and the hypotenuse would be 10.

Similar and Congruent Triangles

Similar triangles have the same shape, but they are not necessarily the same size. Having the same shape means that the angles of the triangles are identical and that the corresponding sides have the same ratio. Look at the following two similar triangles:

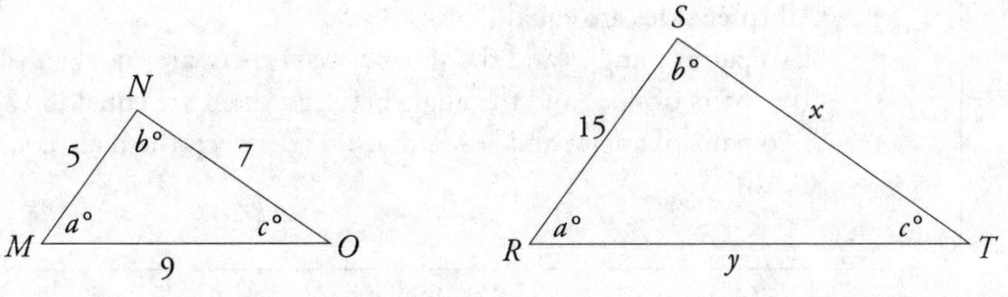

These two triangles both have the same set of angles, but they aren't the same size. Whenever this is true, the sides of one triangle are proportional to those of the other. Notice that sides *NO* and *ST* are both opposite the angle that is *a*°. These are called corresponding sides, because they correspond to the same angle. So the lengths of $\overline{NO}$ and $\overline{ST}$ are proportional to each other.

In order to figure out the lengths of the other sides, set up a proportion: $\frac{MN}{RS} = \frac{NO}{ST}$. Now fill in the information that you know: $\frac{5}{15} = \frac{7}{x}$. Cross-multiply and you find that $x = 21$. You could also figure out the length of y: $\frac{NO}{ST} = \frac{MO}{RT}$. Therefore, $\frac{7}{21} = \frac{9}{y}$, and $y = 27$. Whenever you have to deal with sides of similar triangles, just set up a proportion.

Once in a while, a Digital SAT question will ask about what information is necessary in determining that two triangles are similar. These questions usually focus on angles, but it's important to know how both angles and sides can play a role. For two triangles to be similar, you need one of these relationships:

> Two triangles are <u>similar</u> when at least **one** of the following is true:
>
> - All three angles of the triangles are congruent (AAA).
> - Pairs of sides of the triangles are in proportion, and the angle in between those sides is congruent (SAS).
> - All three sides of one triangle are in proportion to the corresponding three sides of the other triangle (SSS).

In the previous example, there was enough information about triangles *MNO* and *RST* to use the AAA rule but not the SAS rule or the SSS rule.

Similar or Congruent?
All congruent triangles are similar.

Not all similar triangles are congruent.

AAA proves that triangles are similar but not necessarily congruent.

You might also be asked about the information needed to prove that two triangles are congruent. Here are the rules for that:

> Two triangles are <u>congruent</u> when at least **one** of the following is true:
>
> - All three sides are equal (SSS).
> - Two pairs of angles and the side between them are equal (ASA).
> - Two pairs of sides and the angle between them are equal (SAS).
> - Two pairs of angles and a side that *isn't* between them are equal (AAS).

That's a lot, isn't it? The good news is that these topics aren't tested very often, so if they aren't in your POOD, you'll be okay. Here's a question that will help you review these concepts.

6 Mark for Review

In triangles PQR and WXY, angles Q and X each measure $101°$ and angles R and Y each measure $37°$. This information is sufficient to prove which of the following?

I. Triangles PQR and WXY are similar.
II. Triangles PQR and WXY are congruent.

(A) Neither I nor II

(B) I only

(C) II only

(D) I and II

Here's How to Crack It

The question asks what can be proven about two triangles using the given information. Eliminate (C) immediately because it is impossible for a triangle to be congruent without also being similar. The information in the question is about angles only, and at least one pair of corresponding sides must be the same length for triangles to be congruent. There is not sufficient information to determine whether the triangles are congruent; eliminate (D). Since all triangles have 180 degrees and the triangles have two equal angles, the third angles must also equal each other. All three angles are congruent, which matches the AAA rule for similar triangles, so the information is sufficient to prove that the triangles are similar; eliminate (A). The correct answer is (B).

Similar Triangles and Trig

Finally, there's a special relationship between similar triangles and trigonometry. Side lengths in similar triangles are proportional, and the trigonometric functions give the proportions of the sides of a triangle. Therefore, if two triangles are similar, the corresponding trigonometric functions are equal! Let's look at how this might work in a question.

7 Mark for Review

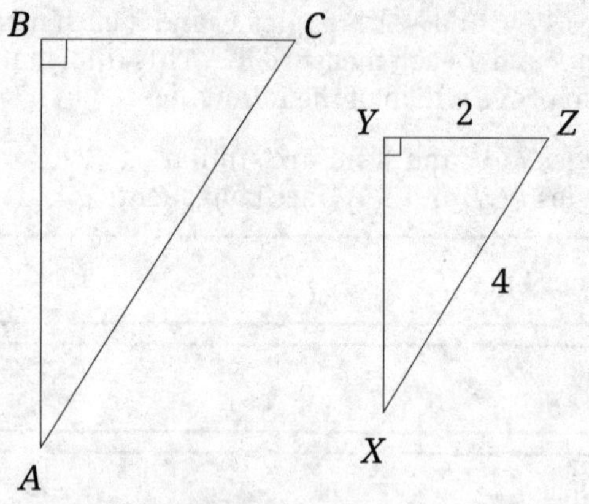

In the figure above, triangle ABC is similar to triangle XYZ. What is the value of cos(A)?

(A) $\frac{1}{2}$

(B) $\frac{\sqrt{3}}{2}$

(C) $\sqrt{3}$

(D) 2

Here's How to Crack It

The question asks for the value of cos (A) but gives measurements on triangle XYZ. Because the two triangles are similar, the value of corresponding trigonometric functions will be equal. Therefore, cos (A) = cos (X). The value of cos X is $\frac{\text{adjacent}}{\text{hypotenuse}}$ or $\frac{XY}{XZ}$. You could use the Pythagorean Theorem to find XY, but it's easier to use the special right triangle discussed earlier. Because the hypotenuse is twice one of the legs, you know this is a 30°-60°-90° triangle. YZ is the shortest side (x), so XY is $x\sqrt{3}$ or $2\sqrt{3}$. Therefore, cos (X) = $\frac{2\sqrt{3}}{4}$, which reduces to $\frac{\sqrt{3}}{2}$. Because cos (X) = cos (A), cos (A) also equals $\frac{\sqrt{3}}{2}$. The correct answer is (B).

CIRCLES

Here are the rules you'll need in order to tackle circle questions on the Digital SAT.

1. **The circumference of a circle is $2\pi r$ or πd, where r is the radius of the circle and d is the diameter.**
This information is in the reference sheet, so don't stress over memorizing these formulas. You will always be able to open the reference sheet in the testing app if you forget them. Just keep in mind that the diameter is always twice the length of the radius (and that the radius is half the diameter).

A Few Formulas
Area = πr^2
Circumference = $2\pi r$ or πd
Diameter = $2r$

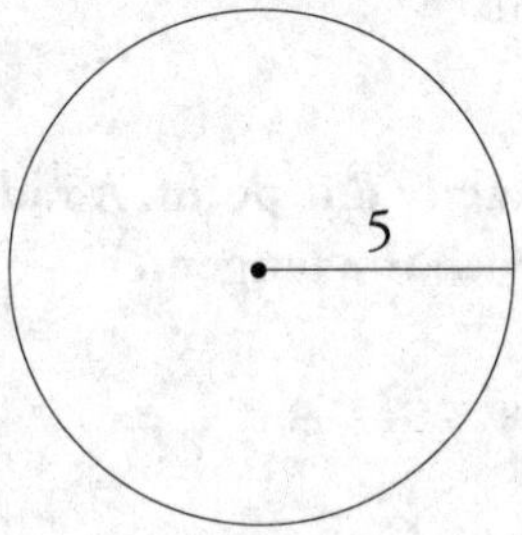

circumference = $2 \times \pi \times 5 = 10\pi$

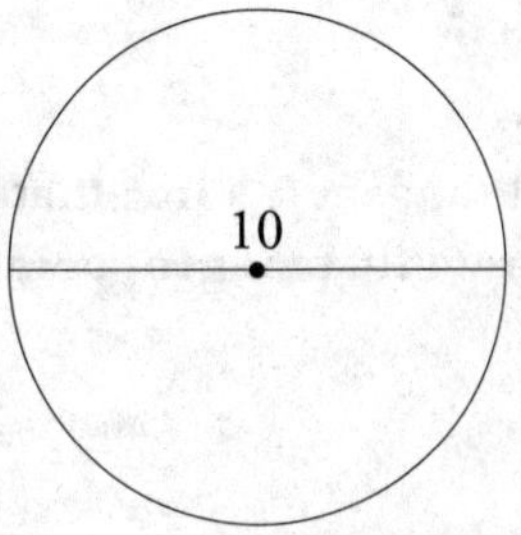

circumference = 10π

In math class you probably learned that π = 3.14 (or even 3.14159). On the Digital SAT, $\pi = 3^+$ (a little more than 3) is a good enough approximation. Even with a calculator, using π = 3 will give you all the information you need to solve difficult Digital SAT multiple-choice geometry questions.

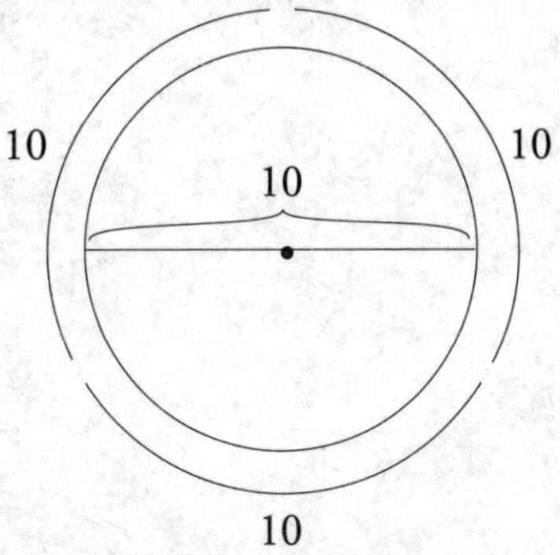

circumference = about 30

Leave That π Alone!
Most of the time, you won't multiply π out in circle questions. Because the answer choices will usually be in terms of π (6π instead of 18.849...), you can save yourself some trouble by leaving your work in terms of π.

2. **The area of a circle is πr^2, where r is the radius of the circle.**

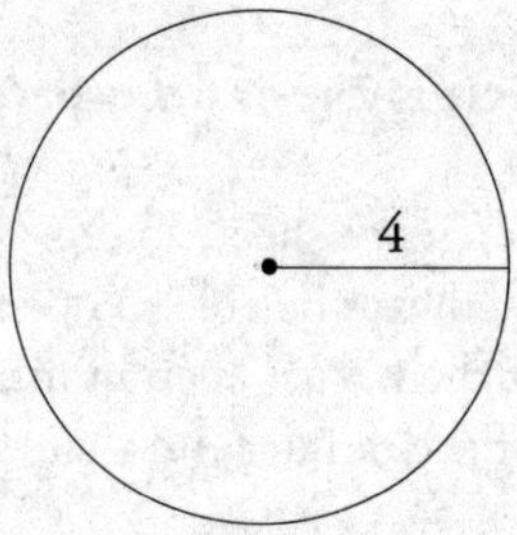

area = $\pi(4)^2 = 16\pi$

3. **A tangent is a line that touches a circle at exactly one point. A radius drawn from that tangent point forms a 90° angle with the tangent.**

Circles Have Names?
If a question refers to Circle R, it means that the center of the circle is point *R*.

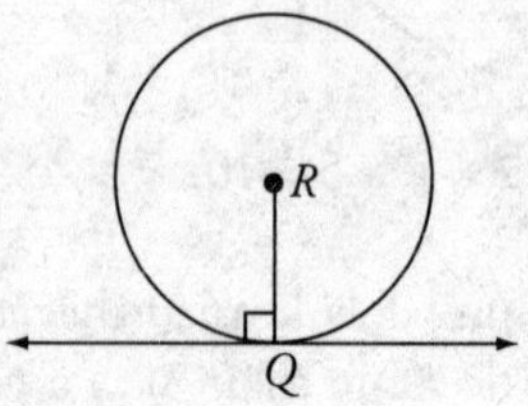

Let's see how these rules can show up on the Digital SAT.

8 Mark for Review

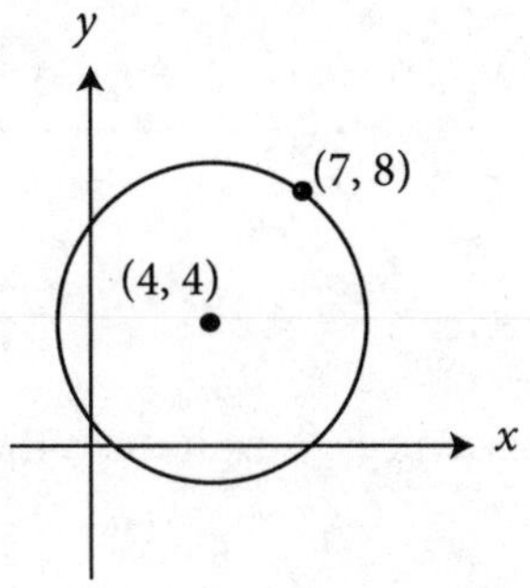

The circle defined by the equation $(x - 4)^2 + (y - 4)^2 = 25$ has its center at point (4, 4) and includes point (7, 8) on the circle. This is shown in the figure above. What is the area of the circle shown?

Ⓐ 5π

Ⓑ 10π

Ⓒ 16π

Ⓓ 25π

Here's How to Crack It

The question asks for the area of the circle, so write down the formula for area of a circle: $A = \pi r^2$. That means you need to determine the radius of the circle. If you remember the circle formula from Chapter 23, you simply need to recall that $r^2 = 25$ and multiply by π to find the area. If not, you can find the distance between (4, 4) and (7, 8) by drawing a right triangle. The triangle is a 3-4-5 right triangle, so the distance between (4, 4) and (7, 8) (and thus the radius) is 5. If the radius is 5, then the area is $\pi(5)^2$, or 25π. The correct answer is (D).

Converting Degrees to Radians

Some geometry questions will ask you to convert an angle measurement from degrees to radians. While this may sound scary, doing this conversion only requires that you remember that $180° = \pi$ radians. Use this relationship, which is included on the reference sheet, to set up a proportion and convert the units.

9 Mark for Review

An angle in a circle measures $\frac{\pi}{6}$ radians. What is the measure of the angle in degrees?

Here's How to Crack It

The question asks for the measure of an angle in degrees. Use the relationship between radians and degrees to set up a proportion. If $180° = \pi$ radians, the proportion will look like this:

$$\frac{180°}{\pi \text{ radians}} = \frac{x°}{\frac{\pi}{6} \text{ radians}}$$

Cross-multiply to get $(\pi)(x) = (180)\left(\frac{\pi}{6}\right)$. Simplify the right side of the equation to get $\pi x = 30\pi$, then divide both sides of the equation by π to get $x = 30$. The correct answer is 30.

30

Arcs and Sectors

Many circle questions on the Digital SAT will not ask about the whole circle. Rather, you'll be asked about arcs or sectors. Both arcs and sectors are portions of a circle: arcs are portions of the circumference, and sectors are portions of the area. Luckily, both arcs and sectors have the same relationship with the circle, based on the central angle (the angle at the center of the circle that creates the arc or sector):

$$\frac{\text{part}}{\text{whole}} = \frac{\text{central angle}}{360°} = \frac{\text{arc length}}{2\pi r} = \frac{\text{sector area}}{\pi r^2}$$

Note that these relationships are all proportions. Arcs and sectors are proportional to the circumference and area, respectively, as the central angle is to 360°.

Questions sometimes refer to "minor" or "major" arcs or sectors. A minor arc or sector is one that has a central angle of less than 180°, whereas a major arc or sector has a central angle greater than 180° (in other words, it goes the long way around the circle). Let's see how arcs and sectors might show up in a question.

10 Mark for Review

Points A and B lie on circle O (not shown). $AO = 3$ and angle $O = 120°$. What is the area of minor sector AOB?

(A) $\frac{\pi}{3}$

(B) π

(C) 3π

(D) 9π

Here's How to Crack It

The question asks for the area of minor sector AOB in circle O. Because O is the name of the circle, it's also the center of the circle, so AO is the radius. Angle O is the central angle of sector AOB, so you have all the pieces you need to find the sector. Put them into a proportion:

$$\frac{120°}{360°} = \frac{x}{\pi(3)^2}$$

Cross-multiply to get $360x = 1{,}080\pi$ (remember to not multiply out π). Divide both sides by 360, and you get $x = 3\pi$. The correct answer is (C).

Relationship Between Arc and Angle in Radians

Sometimes you'll be asked for an arc length, but you'll be given the angle in radians instead of degrees. Fear not! Rather than making the question more complicated, the test-writers have actually given you a gift! All you need to do is memorize this formula:

$$s = r\theta$$

In this formula, s is the arc length, r is the radius, and θ is the central angle in radians. If you know this formula, these questions will be a snap!

When an arc measure is given in degrees, it's even simpler: the arc is the same number of degrees as the angle that defines it.

Little Boxes
Here's a progression of quadrilaterals from least specific to most specific:
quadrilateral is any 4-sided figure
↓
parallelogram is a quadrilateral in which opposite sides are parallel
↓
rectangle is a parallelogram in which all angles = 90°
↓
square is a rectangle in which all sides are equal

RECTANGLES AND SQUARES

Here are some rules you'll need to know about rectangles and squares:

1. **The perimeter of a rectangle is the sum of the lengths of its sides.** Just add them up.

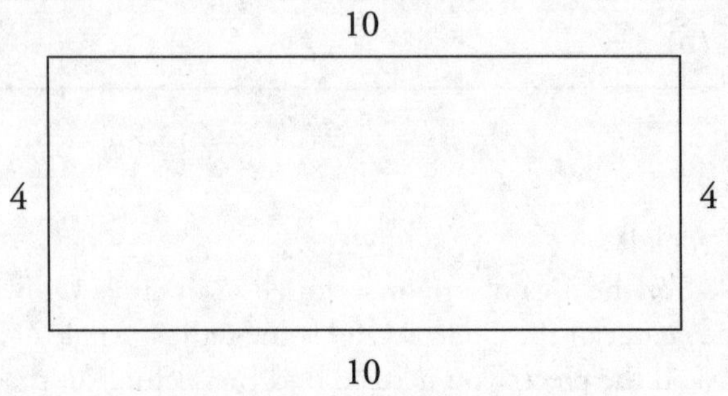

perimeter = 10 + 4 + 10 + 4 = 28

2. **The area of a rectangle is length × width.**
   The area of the preceding rectangle, therefore, is 10 × 4, or 40.

3. **A square is a rectangle whose four sides are all equal in length.**
   The perimeter of a square, therefore, is four times the length of any side. The area is the length of any side squared.

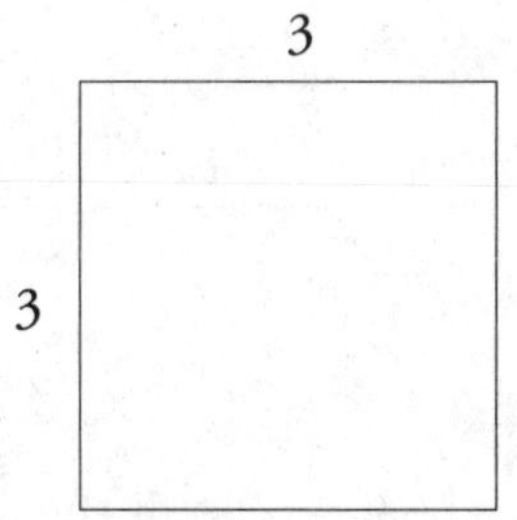

perimeter = 4(3) = 12
area = $3^2 = 9$

4. **In rectangles and squares all angles are 90° angles.**
   It can't be a square or a rectangle unless all angles are 90°.

Let's check out an example.

11 Mark for Review

If the perimeter of a square is 28, what is the length of the diagonal of the square?

Ⓐ $2\sqrt{14}$

Ⓑ $7\sqrt{2}$

Ⓒ $7\sqrt{3}$

Ⓓ 14

Here's How to Crack It

The question asks for the diagonal of a square based on its perimeter. The perimeter of a square is $4s$. So, $28 = 4s$. Divide by 4 to find $s = 7$. The diagonal of a square divides the square into two 45°-45°-90° triangles, with sides in the ratio of $x{:}x{:}x\sqrt{2}$. If the side is 7, the diagonal is $7\sqrt{2}$. The correct answer is (B).

VOLUME

Volume questions on the Digital SAT can seem intimidating at times. The test-writers love to give you questions featuring unusual shapes such as pyramids and spheres. Luckily, the reference sheet in the testing app contains all the formulas you will ever need for volume questions on the Digital SAT. Simply apply the Basic Approach for geometry using the given formulas and you'll be in good shape (pun entirely intended)!

Let's look at an example.

12 Mark for Review

A sphere has a volume of 36π. What is the surface area of the sphere? (The surface area of a sphere is given by the formula $A = 4\pi r^2$.)

Ⓐ 3π

Ⓑ 9π

Ⓒ 27π

Ⓓ 36π

Here's How to Crack It

The question asks for the surface area of a sphere given its volume. Start by writing down the formula for volume of a sphere from the reference sheet: $V = \frac{4}{3}\pi r^3$. Put what you know into the equation: $36\pi = \frac{4}{3}\pi r^3$. From this you can solve for r. Divide both sides by π to get $36 = \frac{4}{3}r^3$. Multiply both sides by 3 to clear the fraction: $36(3) = 4r^3$. Note we left 36 as 36, because the next step is to divide both sides by 4, and 36 divided by 4 is 9, so $9(3) = r^3$ or $27 = r^3$. Take the cube root of both sides to get $r = 3$. Now that you have the radius, use the formula provided to find the surface area: $A = 4\pi(3)^2$, which comes out to 36π. The correct answer is (D).

BALLPARKING

You may be thinking, "Wait a second, isn't there an easier way?" By now, you should know that of course there is, and we're going to show you. On many Digital SAT geometry questions, you won't have to calculate an exact answer. Instead, you can estimate an answer choice. We call this **Ballparking,** a strategy mentioned earlier in this book.

> **Rocket Science?**
> The SAT is a college admissions test, not an exercise in precision. Because approximately 33 of its 44 Math questions are multiple-choice, you can afford to approximate numbers like π, $\sqrt{2}$, and $\sqrt{3}$ (3+, 1.4, and 1.7+, respectively).

Ballparking is extremely useful on Digital SAT geometry questions. At the very least, it will help you avoid careless mistakes by immediately eliminating answers that could not possibly be correct. On many questions, Ballparking will allow you to find the answer without even working out the problem at all.

For example, on many Digital SAT geometry questions, you will be presented with a drawing in which some information is given and you will be asked to find some of the information that is missing. In most such questions, you're expected to apply some formula or perform some calculation, often an algebraic one. But look at the drawing and make a rough estimate of the answer (based on the given information) before you try to work it out. You might be able to eliminate an answer choice or two or even narrow it down to one.

The basic principles you just learned (such as the number of degrees in a triangle and the fact that $\pi \approx 3$) will be enormously helpful to you in Ballparking on the Digital SAT.

Even though many geometric figures are marked with a note that they are not drawn to scale, you will also find it very helpful if you have a good sense of how large certain common angles are. Study the following examples.

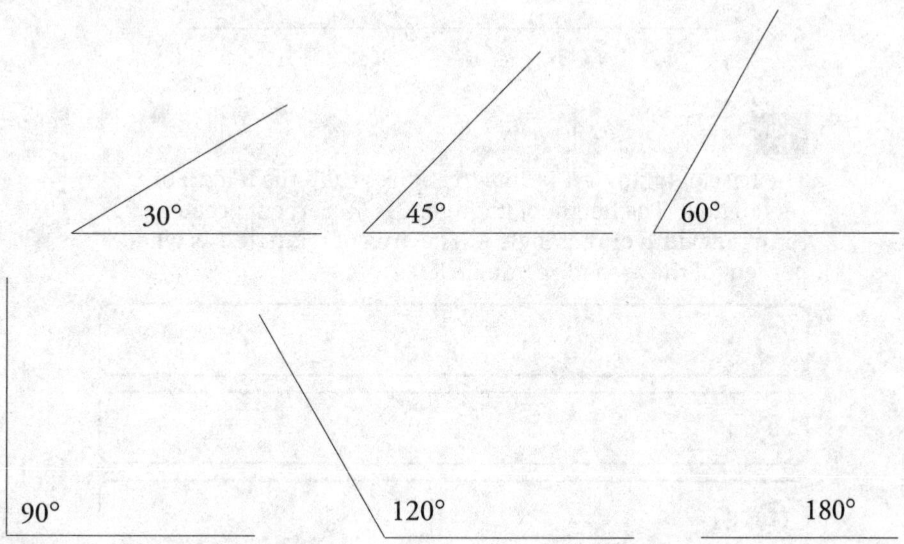

How High Is the Ceiling?

If your friend stood next to a wall in your living room and asked you how high the ceiling was, what would you do? Would you get out your trigonometry textbook and try to triangulate using the shadow cast by your pal? Of course not. You'd look at your friend and think something like this: "Dave's about 6 feet tall. The ceiling's a couple of feet higher than he is. It must be about 8 feet high."

Your Ballpark answer wouldn't be exact, but it would be close. If someone later claimed that the ceiling in the living room was 15 feet high, you'd be able to tell her with confidence that she was mistaken.

The Correct Choice
Remember that the Digital SAT is a mostly multiple-choice test. This means that you don't always have to come up with an answer; you just have to identify the correct one from among the four choices provided.

You'll be able to do the same thing on the Digital SAT. If line segment *A* has a length of π and line segment *B* is exactly half as long, then the length of line segment *B* is a little more than 1.5. All such questions are ideal for Ballparking.

PLUGGING IN

As you learned already, Plugging In is a powerful technique for solving Digital SAT algebra questions. It is also very useful on geometry problems. For some questions, you will be able to plug in values for missing information and then use the results either to find the answer directly or to eliminate answers that cannot be correct.

Here's an example.

13 Mark for Review

The base of triangle T is 40 percent less than the length of rectangle R. The height of triangle T is 50 percent greater than the width of rectangle R. The area of triangle T is what percent of the area of rectangle R?

Ⓐ 10

Ⓑ 45

Ⓒ 90

Ⓓ 110

Watch Us Crack It
Watch the step-by-step video explanation of how to answer this question in your Student Tools.

Here's How to Crack It

The question asks for the relationship between the areas of triangle T and rectangle R. This is a challenging question. Don't worry—you'll still be able to find the right answer by sketching and plugging in.

When plugging in, always use numbers that are easy to work with. Say the length of the rectangle is 10; that means that the base of the triangle, which is 40 percent smaller, is 6. If you plug 4 in for the width of rectangle R, the height of triangle T is 6. You should come up with two sketches that look like this:

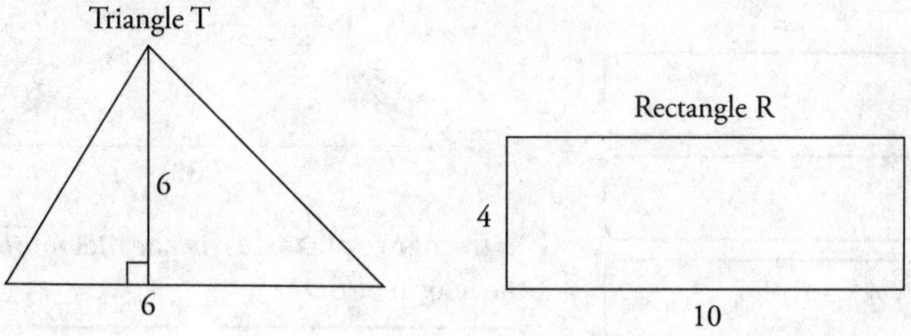

T has an area of $\frac{1}{2}bh$, or 18. R has an area of 40. Now set up the translation: $18 = \frac{x}{100}(40)$, where x represents what percent the triangle is of the rectangle.

Solve for x and you get 45. The correct answer is (B).

Drill 1: Geometry

Answers and explanations can be found starting on page 574.

1 Mark for Review

If a rectangular swimming pool has a volume of 16,500 cubic feet, a uniform depth of 10 feet, and a length of 75 feet, what is the width of the pool, in feet?

Ⓐ 22

Ⓑ 26

Ⓒ 32

Ⓓ 110

2 Mark for Review

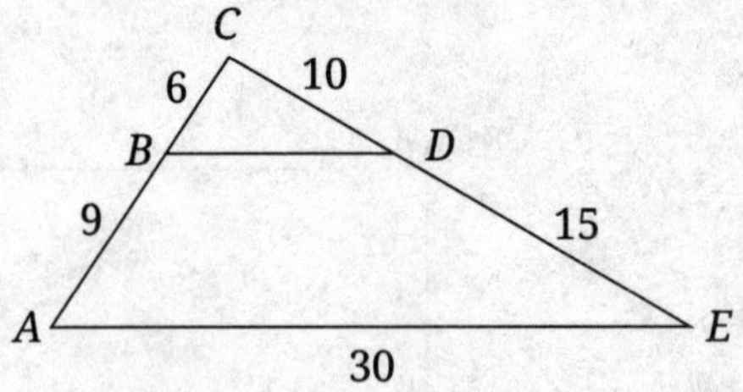

In the figure above, $\overline{AE}$ is parallel to $\overline{BD}$. what is the length of $\overline{BD}$?

Ⓐ 8

Ⓑ 9

Ⓒ 12

Ⓓ 15

3 Mark for Review

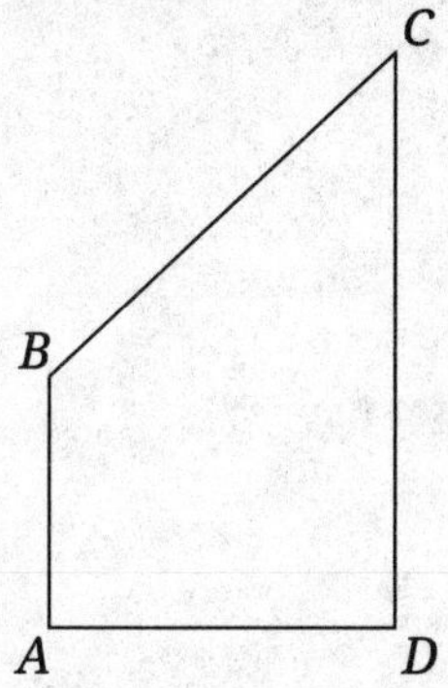

In the quadrilateral above, the ratio of side length $\overline{AD}$ to $\overline{BC}$ is 5 to 7. If the length of $\overline{AD}$ is decreased by 1, how must the length of $\overline{BC}$ change to maintain this ratio?

(A) It must decrease by 1 unit.

(B) It must increase by 1 unit.

(C) It must decrease by 1.4 units.

(D) It must increase by 1.4 units.

4 Mark for Review

Cube X has a side length 22 times the side length of cube Y. How many times greater is the volume of cube X than that of cube Y?

____

5 Mark for Review

In right triangle ABC, angle A is a right angle, $AB = x$, and $BC = y$. The value of AC can be represented by which of the following expressions?

(A) $\sqrt{y-x}$

(B) $\sqrt{y^2-x^2}$

(C) $\sqrt{x^2+y^2}$

(D) $y-x$

6 Mark for Review

A pyramid has a height of 4 centimeters (cm) and a regular hexagonal base with an area of 15 cm^2. If the pyramid has a mass of 21.129 grams (g), what is the density of the pyramid in $\frac{g}{cm^3}$?

(A) 1.06

(B) 1.18

(C) 2.09

(D) 6.51

Drill 2: Trigonometry

Answers and explanations can be found on page 576.

1 Mark for Review

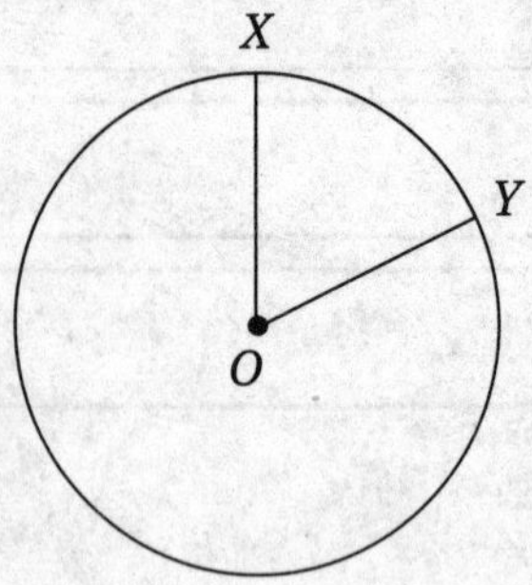

In the figure above, circle O has a radius of 8, and angle XOY measures $\frac{5}{16}\pi$ radians. What is the measure of minor arc XY?

Ⓐ $\frac{5}{16}\pi$

Ⓑ $\frac{5}{2}\pi$

Ⓒ 5π

Ⓓ 16π

2 Mark for Review

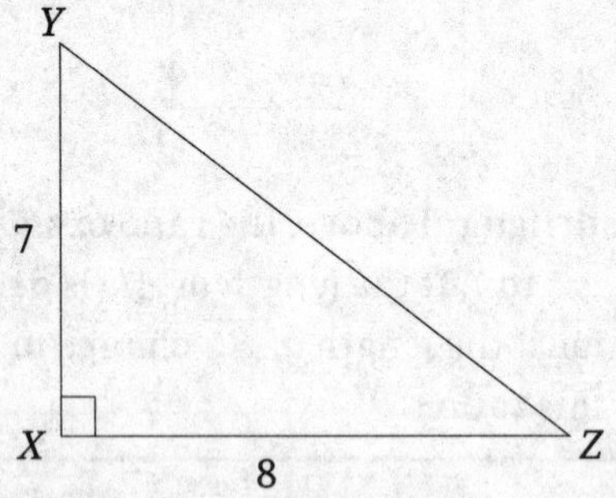

What is the value of $\tan(Z)$?

Ⓐ $\frac{7\sqrt{115}}{115}$

Ⓑ $\frac{8\sqrt{115}}{115}$

Ⓒ $\frac{7}{8}$

Ⓓ $\frac{8}{7}$

3 Mark for Review

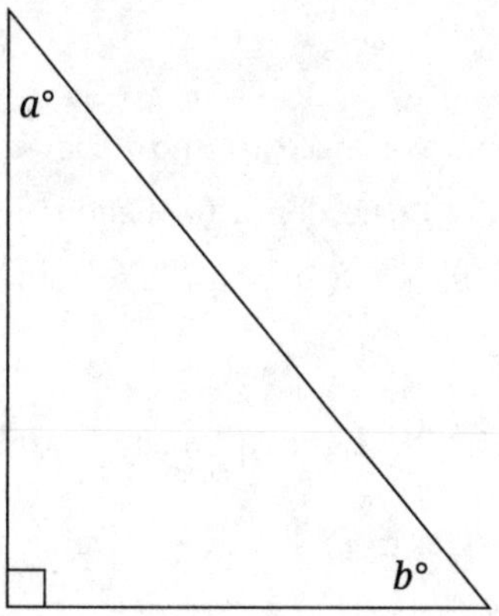

In the figure above, $\sin a = x$. What is the value of $\cos b$?

Ⓐ x

Ⓑ $\frac{1}{x}$

Ⓒ $|1 - x|$

Ⓓ $\frac{90 - x}{90}$

4 Mark for Review

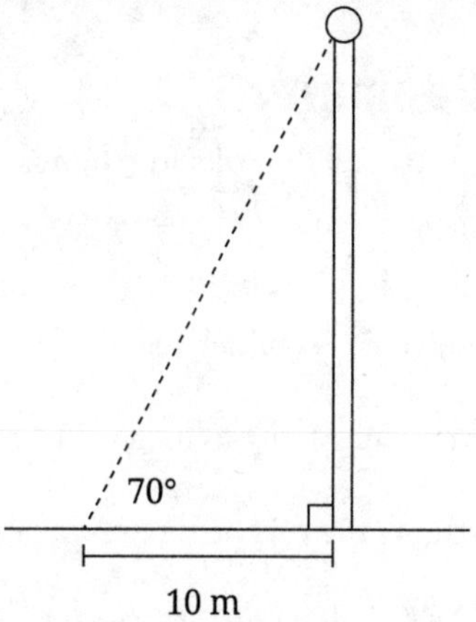

Martin wants to know how tall a certain flagpole is. Martin walks 10 meters from the flagpole, lies on the ground, and measures an angle of 70° from the ground to the base of the ball at the top of the flagpole. Approximately how tall, in meters, is the flagpole from the ground to the base of the ball at the top of the flagpole?

Ⓐ 3 meters

Ⓑ 9 meters

Ⓒ 27 meters

Ⓓ 29 meters

DRILL 1 AND DRILL 2 ANSWERS AND EXPLANATIONS

Drill 1: Geometry

1. **A** The question asks for the width of the pool. For this question, you need to know that volume equals *length* × *width* × *height*. You know that the volume is 16,500, the depth (or height) is 10, and the length is 75. Just put those numbers into the formula: $16{,}500 = 75 \times w \times 10$. Use your calculator to solve for w, which equals 22. The correct answer is (A).

2. **C** The question asks for a value in a geometric figure. Use the Geometry Basic Approach. Start by redrawing the figure on the scratch paper. Split the figure into two triangles to make things clearer: triangle *ACE* and triangle *BCD*. Next, label the figure with the given information. The only new information is that $\overline{AE}$ is parallel to $\overline{BD}$. Use the knowledge that parallel lines cut by a third line create big and small angles, and label angles *A* and *B* as congruent and angles *D* and *E* as congruent. Triangles *ACE* and *BCD* have the same angle *C*, which means they have three congruent angles and are similar triangles. The sides of similar triangles have an equivalent ratio, so set up a proportion. First, add *CD* to *DE* to get the length of *CE*: $10 + 15 = 25$. Now use the ratio of *CD* to *CE* to find the ratio of *BD* to *AE*. The proportion is $\frac{10}{25} = \frac{x}{30}$. Cross-multiply to get $(25)(x) = (10)(30)$, which becomes $25x = 300$. Divide both sides of the equation by 25 to get $x = 12$. The correct answer is (C).

3. **C** The question asks for the change in a value given a proportion. Use the Geometry Basic Approach. Start by redrawing the figure on the scratch paper. Next, label the figure with information from the question. Since no specific numbers are given, only a ratio, plug in. Label *AD* as 5 and *BC* as 7. Draw the figure a second time and label it based on the change described in the question. Since *AD* is decreased by 1, label *AD* on the second figure as 4. Since *AD* decreased and the ratio stays the same, *BC* must also decrease. Eliminate (B) and (D) because they would both make *BC* longer. To find the new length of *BC*, set up a proportion for $\frac{AD}{BC}: \frac{5}{7} = \frac{4}{x}$. Cross-multiply to get $(7)(4) = (5)(x)$, which becomes $28 = 5x$. Divide both sides of the equation by 5 to get $x = 5.6$. Since the original length of *BC* was 7, the change is $7 - 5.6 = 1.4$. Eliminate (A) because it gives the wrong value for the decrease. The correct answer is (C).

4. **10648** The question asks for the relationship between the volumes of two geometric figures. Use the Geometry Basic Approach. Draw two cubes—or at least two squares to represent one face of each cube—on the scratch paper. Next, label the figure with the given information. No specific values are given, so plug in and label the side length of cube Y as 2. Since the side length of cube X is 22 times that of cube Y, label the side length of cube X as 44. The reference sheet doesn't give the formula for the volume of a cube, but it does give the volume of a rectangular solid: $V = lwh$. All three sides of a cube are the same length, so the formula becomes $V = s^3$. Plug in the two side lengths to determine the volume of each cube. The volume of cube Y becomes $V = 2^3$, or $V = 8$. The volume of cube X becomes $V = 44^3$, or $V = 85{,}184$. To answer the final question, divide the volume of cube X by the volume of cube Y to get $\frac{85{,}184}{8} = 10{,}648$. Leave out the comma when entering the answer in the fill-in box. The correct answer is 10648.

5. **B** The question asks for an expression that represents a value in a geometric figure. Use the Geometry Basic Approach. Start by drawing a triangle on the scratch paper with a right angle at *A*. Next, label the figure with the information given. No specific values are given, so plug in. To make things easier, use one of the Pythagorean triples and make it a 3-4-5 right triangle. The drawing should look something like this:

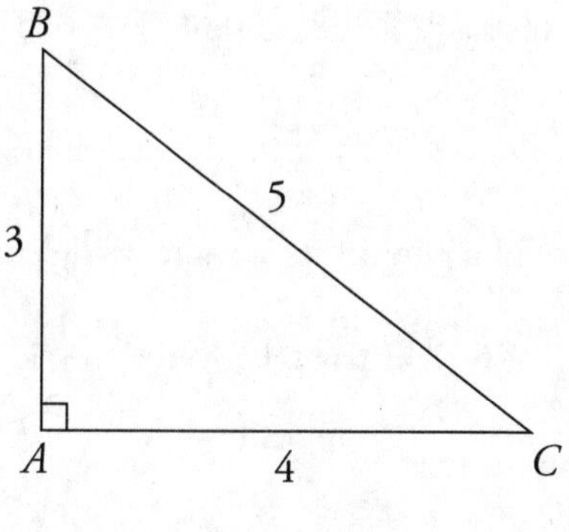

Write down $x = 3$ and $y = 5$ to keep track of which variable has which value. The question asks for *AC*, which is 4. This is the target value; write it down and circle it. Now plug $x = 3$ and $y = 5$ into the answer choices and eliminate any that do not match the target value. Choice (A) becomes $\sqrt{5-3} = \sqrt{2}$. This does not match the target value of 4, so eliminate (A). Choice (B) becomes $\sqrt{5^2 - 3^2} = \sqrt{25-9} = \sqrt{16} = 4$. This matches the target, so keep (B), but check the remaining answers just in case. Choice (C) becomes $\sqrt{3^2 + 5^2} = \sqrt{9+25} = \sqrt{36} = 6$; eliminate (C). Choice (D) becomes $5 - 3 = 2$; eliminate (D). The correct answer is (B).

6. **A** The question asks for the density of a geometric figure. Start by determining the volume of the pyramid. Look up the formula for the volume of a right regular pyramid in the reference sheet and write it down: $V = \frac{1}{3}lwh$. The base of a pyramid is the length times the width—or the area of the base—and the area of the base is given as 15 cm^2, so plug in 15 cm^2 for lw. Also plug in 4 cm for h. The formula becomes $V = \frac{1}{3}(15\text{ cm}^2)(4\text{ cm})$, or V = 20 cm^3. Next, use the units to figure out how to solve for the density. Since density is in $\frac{\text{g}}{\text{cm}^3}$, the mass is in g, and the volume is in cm^3, density must be mass divided by volume. This happens to be the formula for density, which can be written as $D = \frac{m}{V}$. Plug in m = 21.129 and V = 20 to get $D = \frac{21.129}{20}$, or D = 1.05645. This rounds to 1.06, which is an answer choice. The correct answer is (A).

Drill 2: Trigonometry

1. **B** The question asks for the measure of minor arc XY. Since the question gives you the measure of the central angle in radians, you can use the formula $s = r\theta$ to find the arc length: $s = (8)\left(\frac{5}{16}\pi\right) = \frac{40}{16}\pi$, which reduces to $\frac{5}{2}\pi$. The correct answer is (B).

2. **C** The question asks for the tangent of an angle, which is defined as $\frac{\text{opposite}}{\text{adjacent}}$. The side opposite angle Z is 7, and the side adjacent to this angle Z is 8, so tan(Z) = $\frac{7}{8}$. The correct answer is (C).

3. **A** The question asks for the value of cos b. You can plug in when you're dealing with a geometry question with unknowns. When you're plugging in for a right triangle, use one of the special right triangles to make your life easier. Use a 3-4-5 right triangle. Make the side opposite a 3, the side adjacent to a 4, and the hypotenuse 5. Because sine is $\frac{\text{opposite}}{\text{hypotenuse}}$, $\sin a = \frac{3}{5}$, so $x = \frac{3}{5}$. Cosine is $\frac{\text{adjacent}}{\text{hypotenuse}}$, so $\cos b = \frac{3}{5}$. This is your target; circle it. Make $x = \frac{3}{5}$ in each answer choice and look for the answer that equals $\frac{3}{5}$. Only (A) works, so the correct answer is (A).

4. **C** The question asks how tall the flagpole is. Use SOHCAHTOA and your calculator to find the height of the flagpole. From the 70° angle, you know the adjacent side of the triangle, and you want to find the opposite side, so you need to use tangent. Tangent $= \frac{\text{opposite}}{\text{adjacent}}$, so tan 70° $= \frac{x}{10\text{m}}$, where x is the height of the flagpole up to the ball. Isolate x by multiplying both sides by 10: 10 tan 70° = x. Use your calculator to find that 10 tan 70° = 27.47, which is closest to 27. The correct answer is (C).

Summary

- **Degrees and angles**
  - A circle contains 360°.
  - When you think about angles, remember circles.
  - A line is a 180° angle.
  - When two lines intersect, four angles are formed; the sum of their measures is 360°.
  - When two parallel lines are cut by a third line, the small angles are equal, the big angles are equal, and the sum of a big angle and a small angle is 180°.

- **Triangles**
  - Every triangle contains 180°.
  - An isosceles triangle is one in which two of the sides are equal in length, and the two angles opposite the equal sides are equal in measure.
  - An equilateral triangle is one in which all three sides are equal in length, and all three angles are equal in measure (60°).
  - The area of a triangle is $\frac{1}{2}bh$.
  - The height of a triangle must form a right angle with the base.
  - The Pythagorean Theorem states that in a right triangle, the square of the hypotenuse equals the sum of the squares of the two legs. Remember the test-writers' favorite Pythagorean triples (3-4-5 and 5-12-13).
  - Remember the other special right triangles: 45°-45°-90° and 30°-60°-90°.
  - Similar triangles have the same angles, and their lengths are in proportion.
  - Congruent triangles have the same angles and their side lengths are exactly the same.
  - For trigonometry questions, remember SOHCAHTOA:
    - $\sin\theta = \frac{\text{opposite}}{\text{hypotenuse}}$
    - $\cos\theta = \frac{\text{adjacent}}{\text{hypotenuse}}$
    - $\tan\theta = \frac{\text{opposite}}{\text{adjacent}}$

- **Circles**
  - The circumference of a circle is $2\pi r$ or πd, where r is the radius of the circle and d is the diameter.
  - The area of a circle is πr^2, where r is the radius of the circle.
  - A tangent touches a circle at one point; any radius that touches that tangent forms a 90° angle with the tangent.
  - Arcs are proportional to the circumference based on the central angle: $\dfrac{\text{central angle}}{360°} = \dfrac{\text{arc length}}{2\pi r}$.
  - Sectors are proportional to the area based on the central angle: $\dfrac{\text{central angle}}{360°} = \dfrac{\text{sector area}}{\pi r^2}$.
  - If the central angle is given in radians, the measure of the arc is given by $s = r\theta$.
- **Rectangles and squares**
  - The perimeter of a rectangle is the sum of the lengths of its sides.
  - The area of a rectangle is *length* × *width*.
  - A square is a rectangle whose four sides are all equal in length.
  - The volume of a rectangular solid is *length* × *width* × *height*. The formulas to compute the volumes of other three-dimensional figures are supplied in the reference sheet that can be opened at any time in the testing app.
- When you encounter a geometry question on the Digital SAT, ballpark the answer before trying to work it out.
- Always draw the figure on your scratch paper.
- When information is missing from a diagram, ballpark or plug in.

Chapter 26
Fill-Ins

On the Digital SAT, approximately 11 of the 44 Math questions will require you to produce your own answer. Although the format of these questions is different from that of the multiple-choice questions, the mathematical concepts tested aren't all that different. In this chapter, we'll show you how to apply what you have learned in the previous chapters to answering fill-in questions.

WHAT IS A FILL-IN?

Both Math modules on the Digital SAT have several questions without answer choices. The exact breakdown per module varies, but you can expect to see about 11 total questions in this format. The test-writers call these Student-Produced Response questions, but we're going to keep things simple and call them fill-ins.

Different Format, Same Content
Fill-in questions test the same math topics as multiple-choice questions:

- Algebra
- Advanced Math
- Problem Solving and Data Analysis
- Geometry and Trig

Despite the different format, many of the techniques that you've learned so far still apply to fill-in questions. You can't use Process of Elimination or PITA, of course, but you can still use Plugging In, Bite-Sized Pieces, and other great techniques. Your calculator will still help you out on many of these questions, as well.

The only difficulty with fill-ins is getting used to the way in which you are asked to answer the question. For each fill-in question, you will have a box like this:

To enter your answer, click inside the box and start typing. The numbers you enter will automatically appear left to right, and the testing app will show a preview of your answer so you can make sure it looks right.

THE INSTRUCTIONS

The fill-in instructions will appear on the left side of the screen for every fill-in question. There are buttons in the middle of the screen that look like this:

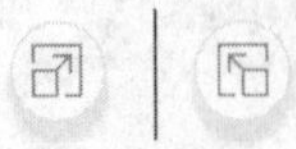

You can use the buttons to make the instructions on the left and the question on the right take up more or less of the screen. The instructions and examples in the testing app look like those on the next page.

Student-produced response questions

- If you find **more than one correct answer**, enter only one answer.
- You can enter up to 5 characters for a **positive** answer and up to 6 characters (including the negative sign) for a **negative** answer.
- If your answer is a **fraction** that doesn't fit in the provided space, enter the decimal equivalent.
- If your answer is a **decimal** that doesn't fit in the provided space, enter it by truncating or rounding at the fourth digit.
- If your answer is a **mixed number** (such as $3\frac{1}{2}$), enter it as an improper fraction (7/2) or its decimal equivalent (3.5).
- Don't enter **symbols** such as a percent sign, comma, or dollar sign.

Examples

Answer	Acceptable ways to enter answer	Unacceptable: will NOT receive credit
3.5	3.5 3.50 7/2	31/2 3 1/2
$\frac{2}{3}$	2/3 .6666 .6667 0.666 0.667	0.66 .66 0.67 .67
$-\frac{1}{3}$	–1/3 –.3333 -0.333	–.33 –0.33

Fill the Space
Know what you can and can't enter into the fill-in box:

- 5 characters for a positive answer
- 6 characters for a negative answer
- Don't enter extra zeros if the answer is short
- Do enter as much of a long decimal as will fit
- Don't enter a fraction that doesn't fit
- Do enter reduced fractions that fit

You don't want to have to spend time rereading the instructions every time, so make sure you know them well. Here is all the information you need to know about entering a fill-in answer:

1. There is space to enter 5 characters if the answer is positive and 6 characters—including the negative sign—if the answer is negative.
2. You do not need to type the comma for numbers longer than three digits, such as 4,200. In fact, the testing app will not allow it.
3. The testing app also will not allow symbols such as %, $, or π. Square roots, units, and variables cannot be entered.
4. You can enter your answer as either a fraction or a decimal. For example, .5, 0.5, and 1/2 are all acceptable answers. Use the forward slash for fractions.
5. If your answer is a fraction, it must fit within the space. Do not try to enter something like $\frac{200}{500}$ as a fraction: either reduce it or convert it to a decimal. Entering 20/50, 2/5, .4, and 0.4 would all count as the correct answer.
6. Fractions do not need to be in the lowest reduced form. As long as it fits, it's fine.
7. You cannot fill in mixed numbers. Convert all mixed numbers to improper fractions or decimals. If your answer is $2\frac{1}{2}$, you must convert it to 5/2 or 2.5. If you enter 21/2, the testing app will read your answer as $\frac{21}{2}$.
8. If your answer is a decimal that will not fit in the space provided, either enter as many digits as will fit or round the last digit. The fraction $-\frac{2}{3}$ can be entered in decimal form as –0.666, –0.667, –.6666, or –.6667.
9. Some questions will have more than one right answer. Any correct answer you enter will count as correct; do not try to enter multiple answers.

FILL-INS: A TEST DRIVE

To get a feel for this format, let's work through two examples. As you will see, fill-in questions are just regular Digital SAT Math questions.

1 Mark for Review

If $a + 2 = 6$ and $b + 3 = 21$, what is the value of $\frac{b}{a}$?

Here's How to Crack It

The question asks for the value of $\frac{b}{a}$. You need to solve the first equation for a and the second equation for b. Start with the first equation, and solve for a. By subtracting 2 from both sides of the equation, you should see that $a = 4$.

Now move to the second equation, and solve for b. By subtracting 3 from both sides of the second equation, you should see that $b = 18$.

The question asked you to find the value of $\frac{b}{a}$. That's easy. The value of b is 18, and the value of a is 4. Therefore, the value of $\frac{b}{a}$ is $\frac{18}{4}$.

That's an odd-looking fraction. How in the world do you fill it in? Ask yourself this question: "Does $\frac{18}{4}$ fit?" Yes! Fill in $\frac{18}{4}$.

18/4

Your math teacher wouldn't like it, but the scoring computer will. You shouldn't waste time reducing $\frac{18}{4}$ to a prettier fraction or converting it to a decimal. Spend that time on another question instead. The fewer steps you take, the less likely you will be to make a careless mistake.

2 Mark for Review

The radius of circle O is 212 times the radius of circle P. If the area of circle O is t times the area of circle P, what is the value of t?

Here's How to Crack It

The question asks for the relationship between the areas of two geometric figures. It doesn't matter that this is a fill-in instead of a multiple-choice question: you still start with the Geometry Basic Approach. Draw two circles on your scratch paper. Next, label the figure. Mark the center of one circle as O and the center of the other as P, and draw in the radius of each circle. The question doesn't give you any numbers for the radius or area of circle P, so plug in. Make the radius 2 and label that on the figure. Finally, write down formulas. The area of a circle is given by $A = \pi r^2$. Plug in $r = 2$ to get $A = \pi(2)^2$, or $A = 4\pi$ for circle P.

The question states that *the radius of circle O is 212 times the radius of circle P*, so multiply 2 by 212 to get $r = (2)(212) = 424$. Label the radius of circle O as 424. Plug $r = 424$ into the area formula to get $A = \pi(424)^2$, or $A = 179{,}776\pi$. To solve for t, divide the area of circle O by the area of circle P to get $t = \frac{179{,}776\pi}{4\pi}$, or $t = 44{,}944$. This is a big number! However, it's still only 5 characters long, so it will fit in the fill-in box. The fill-in box doesn't accept commas, so don't worry about that. The correct answer is 44944.

44944

MORE POOD

The fill-in questions are mixed in with the multiple-choice questions, and both math modules have an approximate order of difficulty. More important than the question order is your Personal Order of Difficulty (POOD), a strategy that encourages you to focus on the questions you know how to answer first. Don't spend too much time on a question you are unsure about, no matter which format it is.

Keep in mind, of course, that many of the math techniques that you've learned are still very effective on fill-in questions. The Geometry Basic Approach and Plugging In both worked well on the previous question. If you're able to plug in or take an educated guess, go ahead and fill in that answer. As always, there's no penalty for getting it wrong.

Here's another fill-in question that you can answer by using a technique you've learned before.

3 Mark for Review

Town A has 2,200 residents. The mean age of the residents of Town A is 34. Town B has 3,680 residents with a mean age of 40. What is the mean age of the residents of Town A and Town B combined?

Here's How to Crack It

The question asks for a mean, or average. Work the question in bite-sized pieces and start with Town A. For averages, use the formula $T = AN$, in which T is the *Total*, A is the *Average*, and N is the *Number of things*. The question states that *Town A has 2,200 residents*, so that is the *Number of things*. The question also states that the *mean age of the residents of Town A is 34*, so that is the *Average*. Plug these numbers into the average formula to get $T = (34)(2,200)$, or $T = 74,800$. Do the same thing for Town B: the *Number of things* is 3,680 residents, and the *Average* is the mean age of 40, so the formula becomes $T = (40)(3,680)$, or $T = 147,200$.

Next, add the two totals to get $74,800 + 147,200 = 222,000$. This is the *Total* for the two towns combined. The *Number of things* for the two towns combined is $2,200 + 3,680 = 5,880$ residents. Use the average formula one more time to get $222,000 = (A)(5,880)$. Divide both sides of the equation by 5,880 to get $37.7551020408 = A$.

There clearly isn't room to enter this answer in the fill-in box, so either cut it off or round when you run out of room. You can enter 37.75 or 37.76 and get the question right. Don't round too much, though: if you enter 37.8, you'll get the question wrong. Enter the full five characters to get credit for a positive answer. The correct answer is 37.75 or 37.76.

37.75 **or** 37.76

Careless Mistakes

On fill-in questions, you obviously can't use POE to get rid of bad answer choices, and Plugging In the Answers won't work either. In order to earn points on fill-in questions, you're going to have to find the answer yourself, as well as be extremely careful when you enter your answers in the fill-in box. If you need to, double-check your work to make sure you have solved correctly. If you suspect that the question is a difficult one and you get an answer too easily, you may have made a careless mistake or fallen into a trap.

Try the example below with this in mind.

4 Mark for Review

A teacher is grading two assignments that each had to be a specific length: research papers and short stories. Each research paper has 5 more pages than each short story. How many pages are in a research paper if 7 research papers and 5 short stories have a total of 275 pages?

Here's How to Crack It

The question asks for the number of pages in a research paper given other information about two assignments. Use another skill from earlier in this book and translate English to math in bite-sized pieces. The question states that *each research paper has 5 more pages than each short story.* Let r represent the number of pages in a research paper. The word *has* translates to =. The phrase *5 more than* translates to 5 +. Finally, let s represent the number of pages in a short story. The sentence, therefore, translates to $r = 5 + s$. Do the same thing with the information that *7 research papers and 5 short stories have a total of 275 pages.* Use r and s again for the number of pages in a research paper and a short story, respectively. Translate *and* as + and *have a total of* as =, and the sentence translates to $7r + 5s = 275$. You now have two equations with the same two variables:

$$r = 5 + s$$

$$7r + 5s = 275$$

Substitute $5 + s$ for r in the second equation to get

$$7(5 + s) + 5s = 275$$

Distribute the 7.

$$35 + 7s + 5s = 275$$

Combine like terms on the left side, then subtract 35 from both sides.

$$12s = 240$$

Isolate s.

$$s = 20$$

It's tempting to fill in 20 and call it a day, but always read the final question! The question asks for the number of pages in a research paper, not in a short story. Plug 20 for s into the first equation to solve for r.

$$r = 5 + 20 = 25$$

Thus, $r = 25$, so fill in that value. The correct answer is 25.

25

MULTIPLE CORRECT ANSWERS

As you've already seen, some fill-in questions will have more than one possible correct answer. It won't matter which correct answer you enter as long as it really is correct. This happens frequently when the answer is a fraction or a decimal. It can also happen when there is more than one solution to an equation.

Let's look at one of those.

5 Mark for Review

What is one possible solution to the equation $|a + 3| = 7$?

Here's How to Crack It

The question asks for a possible solution to an equation with an absolute value. With an absolute value, the value inside the absolute value bars can be either positive or negative. Set $a + 3$ equal to both 7 and –7, and solve both equations. When $a + 3 = 7$, subtract 3 from both sides of the equation to get $a = 4$. When $a + 3 = -7$, subtract 3 from both sides of the equation to get $a = -10$. Enter either 4 or –10 and you'll get the question right.

In this case, that was more work than you needed to do. The question asked for *one possible solution*, so you could have stopped after finding one value. However, questions about absolute value might ask for a specific solution—either the positive solution or the negative solution—so always read the final question (RTFQ) to make sure you don't enter a value that isn't correct.

4 **or** –10

Fill-In Drill

Answers and explanations can be found starting on page 591.

1 Mark for Review

If $a^b = 4$, and $3b = 2$, what is the value of a?

2 Mark for Review

If $4x + 2y = 24$ and $\frac{7y}{2x} = 7$, what is the value of x?

3 Mark for Review

$$n = 12(2)^{\frac{t}{3}}$$

The number of mice in a certain colony is shown by the formula above, such that n is the number of mice and t is the time, in months, since the start of the colony. If 2 years have passed since the start of the colony, how many mice does the colony contain now?

4 Mark for Review

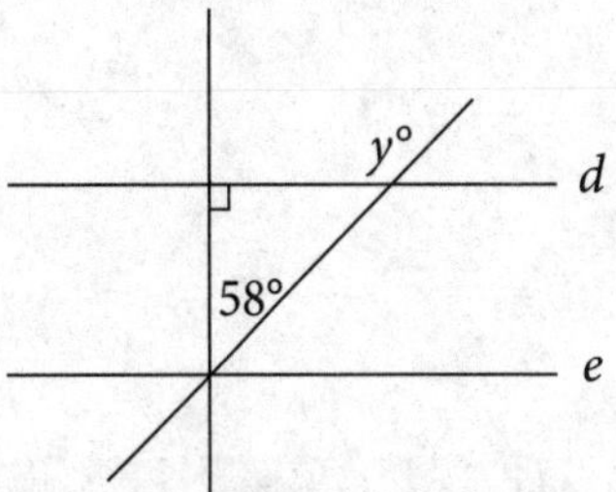

In the figure above, if d is parallel to e, what is the value of y?

5 Mark for Review

The function g is defined by $g(x) = -(x - 3)(x + 11)$. For what value of x is the value of $g(x)$ at its maximum?

6 Mark for Review

If line m is defined by the equation $-3x = -2y - 12$ and line n is parallel to line m, what is the slope of line n?

7 Mark for Review

If Alexandra pays \$56.65 for a table, and this amount includes a tax of 3% on the price of the table, what is the amount, in dollars, that she pays in tax?

8 Mark for Review

In triangle ABC, where angle A is a right angle, $\sin(C)$ is $\frac{13}{85}$. What is the value of $\tan(B)$?

9 Mark for Review

The kinetic energy (KE) of a ball in motion is given by the equation $KE = \frac{1}{2}mv^2$, where m is the mass of the ball in kilograms (kg) and v is the velocity in meters per second $\left(\frac{\text{m}}{\text{s}}\right)$. A ball with a mass of 5 kg and a kinetic energy of 18.225 kg$\left(\frac{\text{m}^2}{\text{s}^2}\right)$ is to be rolled along the ground. What is the velocity of the ball in meters per second, assuming there is no friction?

10 Mark for Review

$$x(mx + 42) + 18 = 0$$

If the equation above has exactly two real solutions and m is an integer constant, what is the greatest possible value of m?

FILL-IN DRILL ANSWERS AND EXPLANATIONS

1. **8** The question asks for the value of a. Using $3b = 2$, solve for b by dividing both sides by 3 to get $b = \frac{2}{3}$. That means $a^{\frac{2}{3}} = 4$. Fractional exponents tell you to use the denominator as the root and use the numerator as a regular exponent. So, $\sqrt[3]{a^2} = 4$. First, cube both sides to find $a^2 = 4^3 = 64$. Next, take the square root of both sides to find $a = 8$. The correct answer is 8.

2. **3** The question asks for the value of x in a system of equations. To solve for one variable, find a way to make the other variable disappear when stacking and adding the equations. Start by dividing both sides of the first equation by 2 to get $2x + y = 12$. Multiply both sides of the second equation by $2x$ to get $7y = 14x$, and then subtract $7y$ from both sides of the equation to get $0 = 14x - 7y$. Now divide both sides of the equation by 7 to get $0 = 2x - y$. The y-terms in the two equations now have the same coefficient with opposite signs, so stack and add the equations.

$$\begin{array}{r} 2x + y = 12 \\ +\ \underline{2x - y = 0} \\ 4x \qquad = 12 \end{array}$$

   Divide both sides of the resulting equation by 4 to get $x = 3$. The correct answer is 3.

3. **3072** The question asks for a value in an equation and gives conflicting units. The question states that t is in months and asks about years. There are 12 months in 1 year, so there are (12)(2) = 24 months in 2 years. Thus, $t = 24$. Plug this value into the given equation to get $n = 12(2)^{\frac{24}{3}}$, which becomes $n = 12(2)^8$. Use a calculator to get $n = 12(256)$, or $n = 3{,}072$. Leave out the comma when entering the answer in the fill-in box. The correct answer is 3072.

4. **148** The question asks for the measure of an angle on a figure. Use the Geometry Basic Approach. Start by redrawing the figure on the scratch paper, including the labels. There is a triangle in the middle of the figure, and all triangles contain 180°. Right angles are 90°, so the third angle measures 180° – 90° – 58° = 32°. That angle and angle y make up a straight line, and there are 180° in a line, so $32° + y° = 180°$. Subtract 32° from both sides of the equation to get $y° = 148°$. The fill-in box does not allow degree signs, so leave it out. The correct answer is 148.

5. **–4** The question asks for the value when a quadratic function reaches its maximum. A parabola reaches its minimum or maximum value at its vertex, so find the x-coordinate of the vertex. One method is to enter the equation into a graphing calculator, then scroll and zoom as needed to find the vertex. The vertex is at (–4, 49), so the value of the x-coordinate is –4. Another way to solve is to recognize that the vertex of a parabola is on the axis of symmetry, which is the midpoint between the two x-intercepts. Find the x-intercepts by setting each factor equal to 0 and solving. When $x - 3 = 0$, $x = 3$. When

$x + 11 = 0$, $x = -11$. The x-coordinate of the midpoint is the average of the two x-intercepts, which is $\frac{3+(-11)}{2} = \frac{-8}{2} = -4$. Using either method, the correct answer is –4.

6. **$\frac{3}{2}$ or 1.5**

The question asks for the slope of a line. The question states that line m and line n are parallel, which means they have the same slope but different y-intercepts. The question gives the equation of line m, so find the slope of that line. Rearrange the equation so it is in slope-intercept form, $y = mx + b$, in which m is the slope and b is the y-intercept. Add $2y$ to both sides of the equation to get $-3x + 2y = -12$, then add $3x$ to both sides of the equation to get $2y = 3x - 12$. Finally, divide both sides of the equation by 2 to get $y = \frac{3}{2}x - 6$. The slope of line m is $\frac{3}{2}$, so the slope of line n is also $\frac{3}{2}$. The answer can be entered as a fraction or in decimal form, which is 1.5. The correct answer is $\frac{3}{2}$ or 1.5.

7. **1.65** The question asks for a value given a specific situation. Translate the information in bite-sized pieces. The question states that *Alexandra pays \$56.65 for a table,* which includes *a tax of 3% on the price of the table.* The unknown is the price of the table before tax, so make that x. *Percent* means out of 100, so translate 3% as $\frac{3}{100}$. The tax is added to the cost before tax, so add those two values and set them equal to the total cost of \$56.65. The equation becomes $x + \left(\frac{3}{100}\right)x = \$56.65$. Simplify the left side of the equation to get $x + 0.03x = \$56.65$, and then $1.03x = \$56.65$. Divide both sides of the equation by 1.03 to get $x = \$55.00$. This is the cost before tax. The question asks for the amount of tax, *in dollars*, so subtract the cost before tax from the final cost to get \$56.65 – \$55.00 = \$1.65. The fill-in box does not allow dollar signs, so leave it out. The correct answer is 1.65.

8. **$\frac{84}{13}$ or 6.461 or 6.462**

The question asks for the value of a trigonometric function. Use the Geometry Basic Approach. Begin by drawing a right triangle. Next, label the vertices and label the right angle as angle A. The drawing should look something like this:

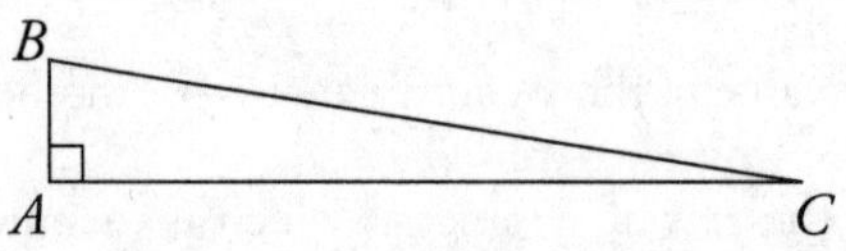

Next, write out SOHCAHTOA to remember the trig functions. The SOH part defines the sine as $\frac{\text{opposite}}{\text{hypotenuse}}$, and the question states that $\sin(C) = \frac{13}{85}$. Label the side opposite angle *C*, which is $\overline{AB}$, as 13 and the hypotenuse, which is $\overline{BC}$, as 85. To find the length of the third side, use the Pythagorean Theorem: $a^2 + b^2 = c^2$. Plug in the known values to get $13^2 + b^2 = 85^2$. Square the numbers to get $169 + b^2 = 7{,}225$, then subtract 169 from both sides of the equation to get $b^2 = 7{,}056$. Take the square root of both sides of the equation to get $b = 84$. With all three side lengths labeled, the drawing looks like this:

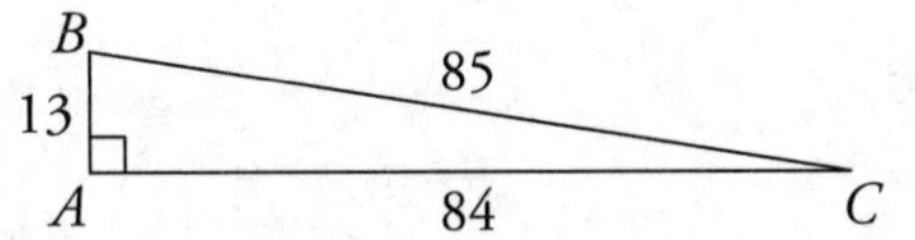

To find tan(*B*), use SOHCAHTOA again. The TOA part defines the tangent as $\frac{\text{opposite}}{\text{adjacent}}$. The side opposite angle *B* is 84, and the side adjacent to angle *B* is 13, so $\tan(B) = \frac{84}{13}$. The answer can also be entered in the fill-in box as a decimal. In this case, $\frac{84}{13} = 6.\overline{461538}$, which is too long. Either stop when there's no more room and enter 6.461 or round the last digit and enter 6.462. The correct answer is $\frac{84}{13}$ or equivalent forms.

9. **2.7** The question asks for a value given an equation. Plug in the values given in the question and solve for the other value. The question states that the ball has a mass of 5 kg, and that *m* represents mass, so plug in $m = 5$. The question also states that the kinetic energy is 18.225, and that *KE* represents kinetic energy, so plug in $KE = 18.225$. The equation becomes $18.225 = \frac{1}{2}(5)(v)^2$. Multiply both sides of the equation by 2 to get $36.45 = (5)(v)^2$. Divide both sides of the equation by 5 to get $7.29 = v^2$, then take the square root of both sides of the equation to get $2.7 = v$. The correct answer is 2.7.

10. **24** The question asks for the value of a constant in a quadratic equation. Start by distributing the *x* on the left side of the equation to get $mx^2 + 42x + 18 = 0$. The question states that the system *has exactly two real solutions.* To determine the number of solutions to a quadratic, use the discriminant. The discriminant is the part of the quadratic formula under the square root sign, and it can be written as $D = b^2 - 4ac$. When the discriminant is positive, the quadratic has exactly two real solutions; when the discriminant is 0, the quadratic has exactly one real solution; and when the discriminant is negative, the quadratic has no real solutions. Since this quadratic has exactly two real solutions, the discriminant must be positive.

The quadratic is now in standard form, $ax^2 + bx + c = 0$, so $a = m$, $b = 42$, and $c = 18$. Plug these into the discriminant formula to get $D = 42^2 - 4(m)(18)$, which becomes $D = 1{,}764 - 72m$. In order for D to be positive, the result must be greater than 0, so write the inequality $1{,}764 - 72m > 0$. Add $72m$ to both sides of the inequality to get $1{,}764 > 72m$, and then divide both sides of the inequality by 72 to get $24.5 > m$. The question states that m is an integer, so the greatest possible value of m is 24. The correct answer is 24.

Summary

- Both of the Math modules on the Digital SAT contain several questions without answer choices. The test-writers call these questions "student-produced responses." We call them fill-ins because you have to fill in your own answer.
- Despite their format, fill-ins are really just like other Math questions on the Digital SAT, and many of the same techniques that you have learned still apply.
- The fill-in questions and multiple-choice questions are mixed together in a loose order of difficulty. Use your knowledge of your own strengths and weaknesses to decide which ones to tackle first and which ones, if any, to skip.
- The fill-in format increases the likelihood of careless errors. Know the instructions and check your work carefully.
- Just like the rest of the Digital SAT, there is no guessing penalty for fill-ins, so you should always fill in an answer, even if it's a guess.
- Enter only one answer even if the question has multiple possible answers. It doesn't matter which answer you enter, as long as it's one of the possible answers.
- Enter up to 5 characters when the answer is positive. Enter up to 6 characters, including the negative sign, when the answer is negative.
- The characters that can be entered are the digits 0–9, the negative sign, the forward slash (/) for fractions, and the decimal point. Special characters such as % or π cannot be entered.
- If the answer to a fill-in question contains a fraction or decimal, you can enter the answer in either form. Use whichever form is easier and less likely to cause mistakes.
- If your answer is a fraction that doesn't fit in the space, either reduce the fraction or convert it to a decimal.

- If a fraction fits in the space, you don't have to reduce the fraction before entering it.
- Do not enter mixed numbers. Convert mixed numbers to fractions or decimals before entering your answer.
- If your answer is a long or repeating decimal, fill up all of the space. Either keep entering digits until the space is full or round the last digit that will fit.

Part IV
Taking the Digital SAT

THE DIGITAL SAT IS A WEEK AWAY—WHAT SHOULD YOU DO?

First of all, you should practice the techniques we've taught you on any practice test you take. If you haven't done so already, take and score one or more of the practice tests in this book and online. You can also download a practice test from College Board's website, satsuite.collegeboard.org/digital/digital-practice-preparation.

If you want more practice, pick up a copy of our very own *645+ Practice Questions for the Digital SAT* at your local bookstore or through our website at PrincetonReview.com/bookstore.

Perfect Your Skills
In addition to taking the practice tests in this book, you should register your book (See "Get More (Free) Content" on pages xiv–xv) to gain access to your Student Tools for even more practice, as well as other fantastic resources to enhance your prep.

Getting Psyched

The Digital SAT is a big deal, but don't let it scare you. Sometimes students get so nervous about doing well that they worry they will freeze up on the test and ruin their scores. The best thing to do is to think of the Digital SAT as a game. It's a game you can get better at, and beating the test can be fun. When you go into the test center, just think about the advantage you have because you know how to plug in when you see variables in the answer choices.

The best way to keep from getting nervous is to build confidence in yourself and in your ability to remember and use our techniques. When you take practice tests, time yourself exactly as you will be timed on the real Digital SAT. Develop a sense of how long 35 minutes is, for example, and how much time you can afford to spend on cracking difficult questions. If you know ahead of time what to expect, you won't be as nervous.

Of course, taking a real Digital SAT is much more nerve-racking than taking a practice test. Prepare yourself ahead of time for the fact that 35 minutes will seem to go by a lot faster on a real Digital SAT than it did on your practice tests.

It's all right to be nervous; the point of being prepared is to keep from panicking.

Veg Out
Although preparation is key to doing well on the test, you shouldn't exhaust yourself trying to cram information into your head. Take some breaks between study sessions to relax, unwind, and rest your mind.

Should You Sleep for 36 Hours?

Some guidance counselors tell their students to get a lot of sleep the night before the Digital SAT. This probably isn't a good idea. If you aren't used to sleeping 12 hours a night, doing so will just make you groggy for the test. The same goes for going out all night: tired people are not good test-takers.

A much better idea is to get up early each morning for the entire week before the test and do your homework before school. This will get your brain accustomed to functioning at that hour of the morning. You want to be sharp at test time.

Before dinner the night before the test, spend an hour or so reviewing or doing a few practice problems. The goal here is to brush up on the material, not to exhaust yourself by over-cramming.

Furthermore...

Here are a few pointers for test day and beyond:

1. Eat a good breakfast before the test—your brain needs energy.

2. Work out a few Digital SAT questions on the morning of the test to help dust off any cobwebs in your head and get you to start thinking analytically.

3. Arrive at the test center early. Everyone is headed to the same place at the same time.

4. You must take acceptable identification to the test center on the day of the test. Acceptable identification must include a recognizable photograph and your name. Acceptable forms of ID include your driver's license, a school ID with a photo, or a valid passport. If you don't have an official piece of ID with your signature and your photo, you can have your school make an ID for you using a Student ID form provided by College Board. Complete instructions for making such an ID are found on College Board's website. According to College Board, the following forms of ID are *unacceptable:* a birth certificate, a credit card, or a Social Security card. Make sure you read all of the rules in the Student Registration Booklet because conflicts with the College Board are just not worth the headache. Your only concern on the day of the test should be doing well on the Digital SAT. To avoid hassles and unnecessary stress, make *absolutely certain* that you take your admissions ticket and your ID with you on the day of the test.

5. If you are taking the Digital SAT on your own laptop or tablet, you will need to bring it to the testing center. Make sure it is fully charged, and bring a charging cable—but there's no guarantee you'll have access to an outlet. If you are using a device from the testing center or from College Board, leave your smart devices at home. Cell phones are permitted as long as they are put away and turned off, but we recommend leaving them at home or in a car, if at all possible, because if your phone somehow makes a noise or you touch or look at it by accident, you could have your test canceled.

6. The only outside tool you are allowed to use on the test is a calculator. The Digital SAT has a built-in calculator for all Math questions, but you may be more comfortable with your own calculator. If so, make sure it is on the approved calculator list and has fresh batteries before the test.

7. Some proctors allow students to bring food into the test room; others don't. Take a snack like a banana, which is sure to give you an energy boost. Save it until your break and eat it outside the test room.

1. Eat Breakfast
You'll work better on a satisfied stomach.
2. Try Some Questions
Get your mind moving.
3. Show Up Early
Leave time for traffic.
4. Take Your ID
A driver's license, a passport, or a school photo ID will do.

5. No Extra Technology
Only bring a laptop or tablet if you need it for testing. Don't wear a smartwatch, and leave your phone at home or in the car if possible!

6. Remember Supplies
Bring your calculator if you plan to use it, and bring extra batteries just in case.

7. Take Fruit or Other Energy Food
Grapes or oranges can give you an energy boost if you need it.

8. Your Desk...
should be comfortable and suited to your needs.

9. Your Testing App...
should be functioning properly, but ask for tech help if needed.

10. Click Carefully
Make sure to select the correct answer to each question after doing your work. Enter answers to student-produced response questions and verify correct entry with the answer preview.

11. We're Here for You
The Princeton Review is proud to advise students who feel their exam was not administered properly.

8. You are going to be sitting in the same place for a little over two hours, so make sure your desk isn't broken or unusually uncomfortable. If you are left-handed, ask for a left-handed desk. (The center may not have one, but it won't hurt to ask.) If the Sun is in your eyes, ask to move. If the room is too dark, ask someone to turn on the lights. Don't hesitate to speak up.

9. Make sure to follow all directions from College Board about how to be ready to go at testing time. You will have to ensure that your device has the testing application and that you can access the test. Tech help will be available if you need it.

10. Make sure to click on an answer for every question. Use the module Review tool at any time during the module and again at the end of the module to see which questions remain marked, unanswered, or both.

11. You deserve to take your Digital SAT under good conditions. While you are testing, if there is an issue that can be addressed immediately (the high school band is practicing outside the window or your chair is wobbly), see if you can get the proctor to fix the situation. If not, you can report the conditions to College Board, but do all you can to ensure good testing conditions while at the testing center.

This test is challenging, but you've put in the time and effort to succeed.

You've got this!

Part V
Practice Test 2

Practice Test 2

The Digital SAT will be administered on a computer or tablet, so it is best if you take your practice tests in the online Student Tools for this book. However, if you are unable to test on a computer or if you have accommodations and will take the official test on paper, you may take Test 2 on paper in this book instead. Both sets of instructions are below.

To Test Online:

Register your book according to the instructions on pages xiv–xv. In your Student Tools, you will be able to access the tests associated with this book: both the two printed in this book and the additional online-only tests. Taking these online adaptive tests is a great way to prepare for taking the actual Digital SAT.

The Digital SAT has only two modules in each section, not three like the test printed in this book. The second module you get in each section will be determined by your performance on the first module in that section. The online tests follow this structure, and once you finish the test, you will get an estimated score based on the modules you saw and the questions you got right.

To Test on Paper:

For both RW and Math, the following test contains a standard first module and two options for the second module, one easier and one harder. You should take the appropriate second module based on your performance in the first module, as detailed below, but you can feel free to use the other module for extra practice later.

In order to navigate the practice test in this book, take the following steps. To record your answers, you can either indicate them as described in the directions for print tests included with each module or by entering them onto the answer sheet on pages 663–664.

- ☐ Take Reading and Writing (RW) Module 1, allowing yourself 32 minutes to complete it.
- ☐ Go to the answer key starting on page 666 and determine the number of questions you got correct in RW Module 1.
- ☐ If you get fewer than 15 questions correct, take RW Module 2 – Easier, which starts on page 617. If you get 15 or more questions correct, take RW Module 2 – Harder, which starts on page 627.
- ☐ Whichever RW Module 2 you take, start it immediately and allow yourself 32 minutes to complete it.
- ☐ Take a 10-minute break between RW Module 2 and Math Module 1.
- ☐ Take Math Module 1, allowing yourself 35 minutes to complete it.
- ☐ Go to the answer key starting on page 668 and determine the number of questions you got correct in Math Module 1.
- ☐ If you get fewer than 14 questions correct, take Math Module 2 – Easier, which starts on page 646. If you get 14 or more questions correct, take Math Module 2 – Harder, which starts on page 654.
- ☐ Whichever Math Module you take, start it immediately and allow yourself 35 minutes to complete it.
- ☐ After you finish the test, check your answers to RW Module 2 and Math Module 2.
- ☐ Only after you complete the entire test should you read the explanations for the questions, which start on page 670 and are also available online.
- ☐ Go to your online Student Tools to see the latest information about scoring and to get your estimated score.

SAT Prep Test 2—Reading and Writing
Module 1

Turn to Section 1 of your answer sheet (p. 663) to answer the questions in this section.

DIRECTIONS

The questions in this section address a number of important reading and writing skills. Each question includes one or more passages, which may include a table or graph. Read each passage and question carefully, and then choose the best answer to the question based on the passage(s).

All questions in the section are multiple-choice with four answer choices. Each question has a single best answer.

1 Mark for Review

The Chilean volcano Calabozos is located in ______ area. Therefore, the risk of loss of human life in the event of an eruption is minimal.

Which choice completes the text with the most logical and precise word or phrase?

Ⓐ a hazardous

Ⓑ an active

Ⓒ a mountainous

Ⓓ a remote

2 Mark for Review

Contemporaries of American modernist poet H.D. focused only on her important contributions to the Imagist movement in the 1920s, taking ______ view of her work. However, she wrote in a variety of forms and genres, from short, lyrical works to complex, book-length poems.

Which choice completes the text with the most logical and precise word or phrase?

Ⓐ an expansive

Ⓑ a limited

Ⓒ an imaginative

Ⓓ a complicated

CONTINUE

3 Mark for Review

Since the 1950s, scientists have known that rapid eye movement, or REM, occurs when someone is sleeping. Previous studies attempting to determine the meaning of these eye movements have been unsuccessful in part because these studies relied on human subjects recalling the content of their dreams. A recent study by physiologists Yuta Senzai and Massimo Scanziani has avoided this issue by studying dreaming mice instead. Their results suggest that REM is correlated to changes in direction during the dream.

Which choice best describes the function of the second sentence in the overall structure of the text?

Ⓐ It names a problem in the approach taken by Senzai and Scanziani.

Ⓑ It introduces the difficulty that the study by Senzai and Scanziani was designed to bypass.

Ⓒ It presents the findings of studies done prior to the study by Senzai and Scanziani.

Ⓓ It clarifies how others studying REM sleep interpret the study by Senzai and Scanziani.

4 Mark for Review

Electroreception is the ability of an animal to sense the flow of electricity around it by using specialized organs known as electroreceptors. Most species known to use electroreception are fish, including many sharks, elephant fishes, and eels. However, electroreception is not limited to fish. Monotremes, a group of mammals that includes the platypus and some echidnas, have electroreceptors on or near their mouths to help locate prey. There is also some evidence that bees can detect static electricity on flowers.

Which choice best describes the function of the third sentence in the overall structure of the text?

Ⓐ It generalizes the phenomenon discussed beyond fishes.

Ⓑ It offers another explanation of electroreception that is different from the explanation of how electroreception is used by fishes.

Ⓒ It provides more examples of animals with electroreception.

Ⓓ It explains how electroreception evolved in monotremes and bees.

CONTINUE

5 Mark for Review

Text 1

An animal is said to have a theory of mind when it is able to act according to the mental states of other individuals. Psychologists David Premack and Guy Woodruff studied whether chimpanzees have such a theory of mind. They showed videos of human actors struggling with various problems. The chimpanzees were able to select photographs that showed the best tool to solve each actor's problem.

Text 2

Biologist Daniel J. Povinelli and psychologists Kurt E. Nelson and Sarah T. Boysen have argued that previous research into whether chimpanzees have a theory of mind have not adequately addressed alternative explanations for the chimpanzees' behaviors. Specifically, it may be the case that chimpanzees are following learned behaviors in a known environment, rather than applying a theory of mind in a novel situation.

Based on the texts, how would Povinelli, Nelson, and Boysen (Text 2) most likely respond to Premack and Woodruff (Text 1)?

Ⓐ They would argue that nonhuman primates other than chimpanzees, such as baboons and gorillas, may also have a theory of mind.

Ⓑ They would argue that the chimpanzees would be able to solve the problems themselves without referencing the photographs by struggling with the situation themselves and eventually determining the correct solution.

Ⓒ They would encourage Premack and Woodruff to show the same videos and photographs to other nonhuman primates and compare the other nonhuman primates' reactions to the chimpanzees' reactions.

Ⓓ They would suggest that placing the chimpanzee subjects in novel environments, such as rooms distinct from the chimpanzees' regular enclosures, may help better ascertain whether chimpanzees have a theory of mind.

6 Mark for Review

The following text is from Oscar Wilde's 1890 novel *The Picture of Dorian Gray*. Dorian is seeing his portrait, painted by Basil Hallward, for the first time.

> Dorian made no answer, but passed listlessly in front of his picture and turned towards it. When he saw it he drew back, and his cheeks flushed for a moment with pleasure. A look of joy came into his eyes, as if he had recognized himself for the first time. He stood there motionless and in wonder, dimly conscious that Hallward was speaking to him, but not catching the meaning of his words. The sense of his own beauty came on him like a revelation. He had never felt it before.

According to the text, what is true about Dorian?

Ⓐ Dorian is distracted by the beauty of the painting.

Ⓑ Dorian believes that what Hallward is saying is unimportant.

Ⓒ Dorian does not recognize his own image.

Ⓓ Dorian is prone to embarrassment.

CONTINUE

7 Mark for Review

The following text is from Frederick Marryat's 1847 novel *The Children of the New Forest*.

> The old forester lay awake the whole of this night, reflecting how he should act relative to the children; he felt the great responsibility that he had incurred, and was alarmed when he considered what might be the consequences if his days were shortened. What would become of them—living in so sequestered a spot that few knew even of its existence—totally shut out from the world, and left to their own resources?

Based on the text, what is true about the children?

Ⓐ They are isolated from people other than the old forester.

Ⓑ They are completely unable to take care of themselves.

Ⓒ The old forester is resentful of having to take care of them.

Ⓓ They attempt to help the old forester with his responsibilities.

8 Mark for Review

The following text is Baron George Gordon Byron's poem "Answer to ______'s Professions of Affection," written around 1814. The poem is addressed to an unknown person.

> In hearts like thine ne'er may I hold a place
> Till I renounce all sense, all shame, all grace—
> That seat,—like seats, the bane of Freedom's realm,
> But dear to those presiding at the helm—
> Is basely purchased, not with gold alone;
> Add Conscience, too, this bargain is your own—
> 'Tis thine to offer with corrupting art
> The rotten borough of the human heart.

What is the main idea of the text?

Ⓐ The speaker is expressing disapproval towards the unknown person.

Ⓑ The speaker is unimportant to the unknown person.

Ⓒ The speaker is thinking of purchasing a seat.

Ⓓ The speaker holds a place in the heart of the unknown person.

CONTINUE

9 Mark for Review

Sepsis is a life-threatening condition caused by the body's response to an infection. These infections are typically bacterial but may be fungal, parasitic, or viral. The body's response to these infections leads to increased inflammation and organ damage. This damage, in turn, results in a weakened immune system, which increases the likelihood of reinfection. In a recent study, a team of doctors and pharmacologists led by Shubham Soni claims that administering ketone esters can reduce inflammation and immune system weakening caused by sepsis.

Which finding from the team led by Soni, if true, would most directly support its claim?

Ⓐ Patients with sepsis who were administered ketone esters had fewer signs of inflammation and less organ damage than those administered standard antibiotics.

Ⓑ When administered, ketone esters are known to increase blood ketone levels, which in turn are a source of energy for the brain.

Ⓒ Both those patients administered ketone esters and those administered standard antibiotics did not have reduced inflammation when treated with medication intended to reduce fever.

Ⓓ Those sepsis patients administered ketone esters had reduced inflammation but greater organ damage than those administered standard antibiotics.

10 Mark for Review

Horses' Responses to Novel Objects Based on Number of Handlers

	Only One Handler	Multiple Handlers
No reluctance	45%	25%
Mild reluctance	42%	49%
Strong reluctance	13%	26%

Horses have been domesticated for thousands of years. Therefore, they show great sensitivity to the emotions of humans. Biologist Océane Liehrmann from the University of Turku, Finland, led a team of researchers in a study of horses to determine the effect of the number of handlers (either only one person or multiple people) on the horses' responses to a novel object. The researchers determined that horses with only one handler were less reluctant to interact with the novel object than were horses with multiple handlers. For example, 45% of horses with only one handler had no reluctance when interacting with a novel object while ______

Which choice most effectively uses data from the table to complete the example?

Ⓐ 13% of horses with only one handler had strong reluctance.

Ⓑ 25% of horses with multiple handlers had no reluctance.

Ⓒ 26% of horses with multiple handlers had strong reluctance.

Ⓓ 42% of horses with only one handler had mild reluctance.

CONTINUE

11 Mark for Review

Indian Lok Sabha Results by Percentage of Seats Won, 1999–2019

Party	1999	2004	2009	2014	2019
Bharatiya Janata Party	33%	25%	21%	52%	56%
Indian National Congress	21%	27%	38%	8%	10%
Communist Party of India (Marxist)	6%	8%	4%	7%	4%
Other	40%	40%	37%	33%	30%

India is the largest democracy in the world, with over 614 million people voting in the 2019 election for the Lok Sabha, the parliament of the federal government. In the early years of Indian independence, from the first election in 1951–52 through the eighth Lok Sabha in 1984, each election resulted in one party winning the majority of seats. However, starting with the 1989 election, the party with the largest number of seats failed to win more than half of the total seats. This trend was eventually broken by the Bharatiya Janata Party, which ______

Which choice most effectively uses data from the graph to illustrate the claim?

(A) went from holding the second most seats among the top 3 parties in parliament in 2004 and 2009 to holding a majority of seats in 2014 and 2019.

(B) reached its highest percentage of seats the same year that the Indian National Congress had its lowest percentage of seats over the same time period.

(C) won a lower percentage of seats in the 2009 election than in the 2004 election.

(D) had a lower percentage of seats than the Indian National Congress in 2004 but a higher percentage of seats than the Indian National Congress in 1999.

CONTINUE

12 Mark for Review

Changes in Indicators of Fatty Liver Disease in Vitamin B12 and Placebo Groups

Indicator	Vitamin B12 Group	Control Group
steatosis values (dB/cm/MHz)	–0.41	–0.30
fibrosis values (kPa)	–0.35	0.10
fasting blood glucose (mg/dl)	–5.00	–1.50
fasting serum insulin (μU/ml)	–1.46	–0.21
homeostasis model assessment of insulin resistance (HOMA-IR)	–0.23	0.06

Fatty liver disease (FLD) occurs when excess fat builds up in the liver. While there are often few or no symptoms of FLD, if left untreated, it can lead to cirrhosis or liver cancer. Because FLD is often asymptomatic, doctors and researchers rely on indicators such as steatosis (retention of fat in the liver), fibrosis (scarring), blood glucose (sugar), serum insulin, and insulin resistance to measure and track the development of FLD. A group of researchers led by radiologist Hamid Reza Talari hypothesized that those who take vitamin B12 would experience improvements in fibrosis and insulin resistance when compared to a control group over the same time period.

Which choice best describes data from the table that support the researchers' hypothesis?

Ⓐ Those in the control group had decreases in their steatosis values and fasting blood glucose but had increases in fibrosis values and HOMA-IR.

Ⓑ Those in the vitamin B12 group had decreases in fibrosis values and HOMA-IR levels, whereas those in the control group had increases in these same values.

Ⓒ Both those in the vitamin B12 group and the control group had decreases in their steatosis values.

Ⓓ Those in the control group had a decrease in their fasting blood glucose, but those in the vitamin B12 group had an increase in their fasting blood glucose.

CONTINUE

13 Mark for Review

Mean Levels of Carbon Monoxide (ppm), November 18–26, 1966

City	Day of the Month of November								
	18	19	20	21	22	23	24	25	26
Newark, NJ	16	14	15	21	23	28	32	27	21
New York, NY	4	3	1	2	3	6	7	13	8
Philadelphia, PA	6	0	0	0	1	6	9	10	6
Washington, D.C.	4	2	3	0	0	0	0	0	0

The air pollution produced in an area is only one factor in that area's air quality. Weather patterns, in particular wind and the movement of air masses, can affect the concentration of pollutants such as carbon monoxide. During a smog event that occurred in the northeastern United States in November 1966, levels of carbon monoxide were recorded in Newark, New Jersey, the origin of the smog event, as well as neighboring city New York, NY, and more distant cities such as Philadelphia, PA, and Washington, D.C. The localized nature of weather patterns during this event can be seen by comparing Newark, NJ, and New York, NY, with ______

Which choice most effectively uses data from the table to complete the statement?

(A) Washington, D.C., on the 18th and the 19th.

(B) Philadelphia, PA, on the 23rd and the 25th

(C) Philadelphia, PA, on the 24th and the 26th.

(D) Washington, D.C., on the 23rd and the 24th.

14 Mark for Review

Neurons respond to stimuli from sensory organs or other neurons. Learning occurs when neurons change how they respond to stimuli based on previous experience, which is a property of memory. Electrical engineers seek to replicate similar processes in their development of computer memory. Recently, research by electrical engineer Mohammad Samizadeh Nikoo has demonstrated that vanadium dioxide (VO_2) has a similar memory property to that of neurons, suggesting that ______

Which choice most logically completes the text?

(A) VO_2 could be used in the development of computer memory.

(B) neurons use VO_2 when forming memories.

(C) VO_2 can learn to respond to stimuli from sensory organs.

(D) electrical engineers can now use neurons to develop computer memory.

CONTINUE

15 Mark for Review

Uruguayan-Spanish author Carmen Posadas has written the children's books *Juego de Niños* (*Child's Play*) and *La Cinta Roja* (*The Red Ribbon*). Currently, ______ available in over fifty countries and thirty languages.

Which choice completes the text so that it conforms to the conventions of Standard English?

Ⓐ some are

Ⓑ this is

Ⓒ they are

Ⓓ it is

16 Mark for Review

During a meeting, a group of twelve young deaf people shared their feelings of isolation and their desire for support. In 1988, the group worked together to form Action Deaf Youth, an ______ provides services and programs for deaf children and youth throughout Northern Ireland.

Which choice completes the text so that it conforms to the conventions of Standard English?

Ⓐ organization, that

Ⓑ organization

Ⓒ organization that

Ⓓ organization,

17 Mark for Review

In 1986, after a 56-day expedition, Ann Bancroft became the first woman to reach the North Pole. Her experience as a physical education teacher and her leadership of the first all-female team to cross the ice to the South ______ her to create a foundation that supports girls in pursuing their dreams.

Which choice completes the text so that it conforms to the conventions of Standard English?

Ⓐ Pole to inspire

Ⓑ Pole that inspired

Ⓒ Pole, inspiring

Ⓓ Pole inspired

18 Mark for Review

American artist Simone Leigh creates art in various mediums, including sculptures, video, and ______ the themes and images in her artwork, Leigh has emphasized that Black women are her primary audience and that they would be familiar with the allusions in her work.

Which choice completes the text so that it conforms to the conventions of Standard English?

Ⓐ performance. Discussing

Ⓑ performance discussing

Ⓒ performance and discussing

Ⓓ performance, discussing

CONTINUE

19 Mark for Review

Japanese origamist Akira Yoshizawa is considered the grandmaster of origami, creating more than 50,000 models as well as wet-folding, the most well-known of his invented techniques. ______ dampening the paper before folding, leading to origami models with rounder and more sculpted looks.

Which choice completes the text so that it conforms to the conventions of Standard English?

Ⓐ It involves

Ⓑ They involve

Ⓒ One involves

Ⓓ These involve

20 Mark for Review

Chinese artist Xu Bing is known for his art installations that showcase his printmaking skills and his creative use of languages and texts. His 1991 installation *A Book from the Sky*, for example, consists of volumes and scrolls printed with characters he invented, while his 2004 installation *The Glassy Surface of a* ______ uses the text of Henry David Thoreau's *Walden* to create the illusion of a lake.

Which choice completes the text so that it conforms to the conventions of Standard English?

Ⓐ *Lake*:

Ⓑ *Lake*

Ⓒ *Lake*,

Ⓓ *Lake*—

21 Mark for Review

Developed along with the swing style of jazz music in the 1920s, swing dance is a group of social dances that once comprised hundreds of styles. Not all of the styles survived beyond that time ______ the dances that are still popular today include Lindy Hop, Balboa, Collegiate Shag, and Charleston.

Which choice completes the text so that it conforms to the conventions of Standard English?

Ⓐ period; however,

Ⓑ period, however;

Ⓒ period, however,

Ⓓ period, however

22 Mark for Review

Evolutionary biologist Jonathan Calede may have discovered the oldest amphibious beaver species in the world. Calede first compared measurements of the beaver's ankle to those of almost 350 other rodent species to learn more about how it moved. ______ Calede dated the species to approximately 30 million years ago based on its location between rock and ash layers.

Which choice completes the text with the most logical transition?

Ⓐ For example,

Ⓑ In conclusion,

Ⓒ Next,

Ⓓ In fact,

CONTINUE

23 Mark for Review

Male and female American citizens had starkly different roles during World War II. Men served as soldiers or took part in the workforce to create weapons and other wartime materials. ______ women were responsible for maintaining the home and supporting the men. Some women also ventured into the workforce for the first time, and the famous "We Can Do It" poster featuring "Rosie the Riveter" was created to motivate women to pursue this new role.

Which choice completes the text with the most logical transition?

Ⓐ Besides,

Ⓑ Instead,

Ⓒ Likewise,

Ⓓ Meanwhile,

24 Mark for Review

While treatment for hearing loss is typically associated with the ears, some patients with damaged ear structures are not able to use traditional cochlear implants. ______ researchers are working to develop hearing aids anchored to patients' bones in order to combat hearing loss through vibrations in the skull.

Which choice completes the text with the most logical transition?

Ⓐ Secondly,

Ⓑ In addition,

Ⓒ Finally,

Ⓓ Hence,

25 Mark for Review

Korean artist Anicka Yi uses a unique process and materials to generate her art installations. Her materials are often perishable and biological, such as soap and flowers, and are not traditionally used for artwork. ______ Yi spends almost as much time transforming these substances into completely new materials as she does creating the actual art pieces.

Which choice completes the text with the most logical transition?

Ⓐ Meanwhile,

Ⓑ Instead,

Ⓒ In fact,

Ⓓ To conclude,

CONTINUE

26 Mark for Review

While researching a topic, a student has taken the following notes:

- A writing system for expressing numbers is a numeral system.
- Two examples of numeral systems from history are Babylonian cuneiform numerals and Roman numerals.
- The Babylonian cuneiform numeral system is a base-60 system and lacks a zero digit.
- It's a positional numeral system in which the position of a digit affects its value.
- The Roman numeral system is a base-10 system and lacks a zero digit.
- It's a non-positional numeral system in which the position of a digit does not affect its value.

The student wants to emphasize a difference between the two numeral systems. Which choice most effectively uses relevant information from the notes to accomplish this goal?

Ⓐ Babylonian cuneiform numerals and Roman numerals are two writing systems for expressing numbers.

Ⓑ The Roman numeral system is a base-10 non-positional system that lacks a zero digit.

Ⓒ One system for expressing numbers is Babylonian cuneiform; however, another one is the Roman numeral system.

Ⓓ The Babylonian cuneiform numeral system is base-60 and positional, while the Roman numeral system is base-10 and non-positional.

27 Mark for Review

While researching a topic, a student has taken the following notes:

- Archaeologists studied the burial of an individual at the Newen Antug site in Argentinian Patagonia.
- The individual was buried in a wooden structure over 800 years ago.
- An analysis of the structure revealed that it was carved from a tree with excellent buoyancy.
- The wooden structure was a canoe, suggesting that canoes were used as coffins at that time.

The student wants to present the Newen Antug study and its conclusions. Which choice most effectively uses relevant information from the notes to accomplish this goal?

Ⓐ The burial site of an individual over 800 years ago was found at the Newen Antug site in Argentinian Patagonia.

Ⓑ Archaeologists studied the burial site of an individual who was buried at the Newen Antug site over 800 years ago.

Ⓒ An analysis of a burial site at the Newen Antug site in Argentinian Patagonia provided evidence that canoes were used as coffins over 800 years ago.

Ⓓ As part of a study of a burial site at the Newen Antug site in Argentinian Patagonia, a wooden structure buried with an individual was analyzed.

YIELD

Once you've finished (or run out of time for) this section, use the answer key to determine how many questions you got right. If you got fewer than 15 questions right, move on to Module 2—Easier, otherwise move on to Module 2—Harder.

SAT Prep Test 2—Reading and Writing

Module 2—Easier

Turn to Section 1 of your answer sheet (p. 663) to answer the questions in this section.

DIRECTIONS

The questions in this section address a number of important reading and writing skills. Each question includes one or more passages, which may include a table or graph. Read each passage and question carefully, and then choose the best answer to the question based on the passage(s).

All questions in the section are multiple-choice with four answer choices. Each question has a single best answer.

1 Mark for Review

Shakespeare intentionally provided no stage directions for his play *Macbeth* regarding whether to have Banquo's ghost physically present on stage or simply to have Macbeth react fearfully to something invisible, thus providing future directors with the ______ to indulge their own artistic interpretations.

Which choice completes the text with the most logical and precise word or phrase?

(A) confusion

(B) dedication

(C) instruction

(D) liberty

2 Mark for Review

German-Dutch paleontologist Ralph von Koenigswald was the first to discover the fossilized remains of *Gigantopithecus blacki*, a gargantuan ape believed to have lived during the Pleistocene Epoch. Because the fossils were exclusively found in caves in southern China, many experts believe that the species was ______ that region—that is, anyone claiming to have found remains of *Gigantopithecus* elsewhere would be mistaken.

Which choice completes the text with the most logical and precise word or phrase?

(A) restricted to

(B) eliminated from

(C) common in

(D) unknown to

CONTINUE

3 Mark for Review

Computer scientist Ray Kurzweil ______ that although artificial intelligence will not displace human beings, it will undoubtedly become smarter than people within this generation. This possibility has been the domain of science fiction writers for decades, whose works explore the ramifications of just such a future.

Which choice completes the text with the most logical and precise word or phrase?

Ⓐ proves

Ⓑ requires

Ⓒ predicts

Ⓓ denies

4 Mark for Review

In psychology, it's critical not to generalize from the results of studies in which the subjects are not representative of the larger population. The infamous Stanford Prison Experiment ______ this principle: the participants, whose behavior supposedly demonstrated the "human" tendency towards alarming aggression in authoritarian situations, were a handful of male college-age individuals from the same private university in California rather than a diverse sampling of subjects.

Which choice completes the text with the most logical and precise word or phrase?

Ⓐ illustrates

Ⓑ refutes

Ⓒ supersedes

Ⓓ critiques

5 Mark for Review

Neurologists know that prosopagnosia—the ______ to recognize faces—involves a specific lesion in the brain and can be caused by disease or head injury. However, prominent author Dr. Oliver Sacks believes that this "face blindness" also has a definite genetic component.

Which choice completes the text with the most logical and precise word or phrase?

Ⓐ capability

Ⓑ incapacity

Ⓒ tendency

Ⓓ reluctance

6 Mark for Review

The shark's competitive advantage in the oceanic ecosystem is principally due to electroreception, or the ability to detect electrical impulses. Marine biologists believe that this heightened ______ to electrical stimuli allows the shark to easily find its prey, for as fish swim through water, their movement produces minute electrical signals.

Which choice completes the text with the most logical and precise word or phrase?

Ⓐ allergy

Ⓑ sensitivity

Ⓒ indifference

Ⓓ aversion

CONTINUE

7 Mark for Review

The Voynich manuscript was written on vellum dating from the fifteenth century in a script that is not found in any other source. Since cryptographers have yet to demonstrably decipher any portion of the text, the meaning and purpose of the Voynich manuscript remain ______.

Which choice completes the text with the most logical and precise word or phrase?

(A) enigmatic

(B) venerable

(C) multifarious

(D) coherent

8 Mark for Review

It is commonly believed that, in the complex ecosystem of the Nile River in Africa, the crocodile and the Egyptian plover bird have formed an ______ relationship: the crocodile opens its mouth and keeps it open while the bird instinctively eats the food particles remaining in the crocodile's teeth, thus nourishing the bird while simultaneously promoting the crocodile's dental health.

Which choice completes the text with the most logical and precise word or phrase?

(A) interdependent

(B) inexplicable

(C) enthralling

(D) inarticulate

9 Mark for Review

The following text is from Herman Melville's 1924 short novel *Billy Budd* and pertains to Edward Vere, the captain of the ship on which Billy is sailing.

> Captain the Honorable Edward Fairfax Vere, to give his full title, was a bachelor of forty or thereabouts, a sailor of distinction even in a time prolific of renowned seamen. Though allied to the higher nobility, his advancement had not been altogether owing to influences connected with that circumstance. He had seen much service, been in various engagements, always acquitting himself as an officer mindful of the welfare of his men, but never tolerating an infraction of discipline; thoroughly versed in the science of his profession, and intrepid to the verge of temerity, though never injudiciously so.

According to the text, what is true of Captain Vere?

(A) He dislikes many of the men who serve under him.

(B) He is proud of his aristocratic background.

(C) He is a capable and evenhanded naval officer.

(D) He prefers navy life to life outside the navy.

CONTINUE

10 Mark for Review

I Remember, I Remember is an 1844 poem by Thomas Hood. The poem conveys the speaker's sadness that his life as an adult does not compare favorably to his childhood: ______

Which quotation from the poem most effectively illustrates the claim?

Ⓐ "The lilacs where the robin built, / And where my brother set / The laburnum on his birthday,— / The tree is living yet!"

Ⓑ "I remember, I remember, / The house where I was born, / The little window where the sun / Came peeping in at morn."

Ⓒ "I remember, I remember, / The roses, red and white, / The vi'lets, and the lily-cups, / Those flowers made of light!"

Ⓓ "It was a childish ignorance,/ But now 'tis little joy / To know I'm farther off from heav'n / Than when I was a boy."

11 Mark for Review

Dracula is an 1897 novel by Bram Stoker. In the story, English lawyer Jonathan Harker has traveled to Transylvania to conduct business with Count Dracula at his castle. In his journal, Harker conveys his belief that he has become Dracula's prisoner: ______

Which quotation from Jonathan Harker's journal most effectively illustrates the claim?

Ⓐ "What manner of man is this, or what manner of creature, is it in the semblance of man? I feel the dread of this horrible place overpowering me."

Ⓑ "My lamp seemed to be of little effect in the brilliant moonlight, but I was glad to have it with me, for there was a dread loneliness in the place which chilled my heart and made my nerves tremble."

Ⓒ "I start at my own shadow, and am full of all sorts of horrible imaginings. God knows that there is ground for my terrible fear in this accursed place!"

Ⓓ "I rushed up and down the stairs, trying every door and peering out of every window I could find, but after a little the conviction of my helplessness overpowered all other feelings."

CONTINUE

12 Mark for Review

"In Flanders Fields" is a 1915 poem written by Lieutenant-Colonel John McCrae, a Canadian military officer who died three years later in World War I. The poem is meant to be a plea towards others to join the war effort, as is evident by the following lines: ______

Which quotation from "In Flanders Fields" most effectively illustrates the claim?

Ⓐ "Loved and were loved and now we lie / In Flanders fields"

Ⓑ "In Flanders fields the poppies blow / Between the crosses row on row"

Ⓒ "To you from failing hands we throw / The torch; be yours to hold it high"

Ⓓ "We are the dead. Short days ago / We lived, felt dawn, saw sunset glow"

13 Mark for Review

The curator of a museum claims that a dress in his possession was worn by the wife of one of Lincoln's generals at the presidential inauguration in 1865. Radiocarbon dating, which dates organic material with an error range of about thirty years in either direction, was performed on the sleeves of the dress, revealing that they date back to the 1975–2005 period. If both the curator's claim and the radiocarbon dating analysis are correct, that would suggest that ______

Which choice most logically completes the text?

Ⓐ the dress was made sometime between 1835 and 1895 and then damaged sometime after 1975.

Ⓑ vintage dresses are more commonly recovered from the late twentieth and early twenty-first centuries than from the mid-nineteenth century.

Ⓒ over one hundred years after the dress was made, its sleeves were replaced.

Ⓓ the dress was made from material different from that used for most dresses in the nineteenth century.

CONTINUE

14 Mark for Review

In the early 1900s, paleontologists largely believed that there were no undocumented prehistoric aquatic species that had survived to the present day because it would be impossible for such a species to have enough animals to sustain a breeding population while escaping detection in the modern era. However, a coelacanth, a large lobe-finned fish universally believed by scientists to have gone extinct sixty-six million years ago, was found off the coast of South Africa as recently as 1938. This event may suggest that ______

Which choice most logically completes the text?

Ⓐ fewer coelacanths are required to sustain a breeding population than was previously thought.

Ⓑ it is possible for a prehistoric species to go undiscovered for longer than expected.

Ⓒ the scientists who determined that the coelacanth was extinct ignored critical evidence.

Ⓓ the same environmental conditions that eliminated the dinosaurs nearly killed off the coelacanths.

15 Mark for Review

The *door-in-the-face* technique involves initially making an outrageous or unappealing request or offer, which the other person is highly likely to refuse, then following up with a more reasonable one. The subject is more likely to look favorably upon this second request or offer because it seems acceptable compared to the initial proposition. So, if an employee wants the best raise in annual salary from her boss that she can get, she might succeed by asking for a ______

Which choice most logically completes the text?

Ⓐ 50% raise, then asking for a 5% raise.

Ⓑ 3% raise, then asking for a 2% raise.

Ⓒ 10% raise, then asking for a 50% raise.

Ⓓ 3% raise, then asking for a 3% raise again.

CONTINUE

16 Mark for Review

The North American Free Trade Agreement (NAFTA) was an agreement among the United States, Canada, and Mexico that was in effect between 1994 and 2020. During this time, the number of manufacturing jobs in the United States and Canada declined, but the total number of manufacturing jobs in the countries covered by NAFTA increased. This suggests that, between 1994 and 2020, ______

Which choice most logically completes the text?

Ⓐ the number of manufacturing jobs in Mexico increased by a greater amount than the combined decreases in the United States and Canada.

Ⓑ NAFTA made it more difficult for manufacturers to establish factories in the United States and Canada.

Ⓒ the cost of manufacturing goods in the area covered by NAFTA decreased.

Ⓓ complex goods, such as automobiles and electronics, were increasingly manufactured in the United States, Canada, and Mexico.

17 Mark for Review

American chef Alice Waters is well-known for opening the restaurant Chez Panisse, which ______ the farm-to-table movement by serving local and seasonal food.

Which choice completes the text so that it conforms to the conventions of Standard English?

Ⓐ originating

Ⓑ to originate

Ⓒ having originated

Ⓓ originated

18 Mark for Review

American activists Dolores Huerta and Cesar Chavez founded the National Farm Workers Association in 1962 to defend the rights of farm workers through nonviolent organizing tactics, such as marches and boycotts. ______ organization merged with the Agricultural Workers Organizing Committee, led by Larry Itliong, to form United Farm Workers, a labor union that advocates on behalf of farm workers across the U.S.

Which choice completes the text so that it conforms to the conventions of Standard English?

Ⓐ Its

Ⓑ Their

Ⓒ It's

Ⓓ They're

CONTINUE

19 Mark for Review

Researchers at the University of York found that people who are highly individualistic feel less connected to the natural world and engage in fewer activities to improve the environment; however, engaging with nature through activities such as walking and bird-watching can reconnect ______ to the natural world and encourage environmentally-friendly behaviors.

Which choice completes the text so that it conforms to the conventions of Standard English?

(A) it

(B) you

(C) one

(D) them

20 Mark for Review

National flags are designed to best represent and symbolize the individual ______ when countries share a history or culture, their flags are designed to look similar, thus creating a flag family that shares colors, shapes, or other elements.

Which choice completes the text so that it conforms to the conventions of Standard English?

(A) country but

(B) country,

(C) country

(D) country, but

21 Mark for Review

Scientists at the University of Illinois and the University of Lancaster observed that plants under very bright sunlight enter a protective mode for several minutes, during which they stop photosynthesizing and growing. If the crops were genetically modified to have a shorter time in protective mode, ______ The scientists resolved to find out.

Which choice completes the text so that it conforms to the conventions of Standard English?

(A) could the crop yield increase?

(B) the crop yield could increase?

(C) the crop yield could increase.

(D) could the crop yield increase.

22 Mark for Review

Take Our Daughters and Sons to Work Day originally started as a day focused on engaging girls with the workforce, Take Our Daughters to Work Day. On the national day, the fourth Tuesday in April, parents and caregivers go to work with their children; shadowing their parents or caregivers ______ children real-world experience and ideas for potential future careers.

Which choice completes the text so that it conforms to the conventions of Standard English?

(A) offer

(B) have offered

(C) are offering

(D) offers

CONTINUE

23 Mark for Review

In order to allow olive ridley turtles to lay eggs on Versova Beach in Mumbai, community activist Afroz Shah organized a large group of volunteers to remove over 11 million pounds of trash. The beach now allows community members to connect with the natural world and ______ a healthy habitat for olive ridley turtles to use after a twenty-year absence.

Which choice completes the text so that it conforms to the conventions of Standard English?

Ⓐ provided

Ⓑ providing

Ⓒ provides

Ⓓ provide

24 Mark for Review

Yoga is an ancient discipline from India that aims to combine physical fitness with mental and spiritual control and calm and has expanded to become popular with many different cultures. ______ yoga is shifting into different forms to allow a wider range of people to participate. For example, accessible yoga provides opportunities for those with physical disabilities to access the health and mental benefits of the practice.

Which choice completes the text with the most logical transition?

Ⓐ Nevertheless,

Ⓑ Similarly,

Ⓒ Thus,

Ⓓ Currently,

25 Mark for Review

Scientists often disagree about what traits to use to place newly discovered species in the tree of life and debate different ways to organize evolutionary relationships. *Chimerarachne yingi*, ______ is an extinct arachnid species that is sometimes placed near modern spiders based on its acquisition of silk-spinning organs or near other arachnids based on its loss of a tail.

Which choice completes the text with the most logical transition?

Ⓐ as a result,

Ⓑ in comparison,

Ⓒ for example,

Ⓓ still,

26 Mark for Review

In 2011, a seismometer detected seismic activity from a magnitude 8.9 earthquake and automatically cut the power to all 30 bullet trains in Japan, potentially avoiding mass architectural damage to the tracks. ______ the cut to the power prevented citizens from being caught in a dangerous location during the earthquake and allowed riders to seek shelter.

Which choice completes the text with the most logical transition?

Ⓐ In addition,

Ⓑ In comparison,

Ⓒ For example,

Ⓓ Specifically,

CONTINUE

27 Mark for Review

While researching a topic, a student has taken the following notes:

- The Endangered Species Act (ESA) was enacted in 1973 to recover species and prevent extinction.
- A species is listed under the ESA when it's determined that the species needs protection and delisted when the population has recovered.
- Only 54 of the over 1,000 listed species have been delisted from the ESA, raising concerns about the effectiveness of the ESA.
- Erich Eberhard, David Wilcove, and Andrew Dobson conducted an analysis of population trends of species listed under the ESA.
- They found that most species had to wait multiple years before being listed and by then their populations were already so low that recovery was much more difficult.

The student wants to make a generalization about the kind of study conducted by Eberhard, Wilcove, and Dobson. Which choice most effectively uses relevant information from the notes to accomplish this goal?

Ⓐ Scientists have analyzed population trends to find out the impact of legal protections in the realm of conservation.

Ⓑ Species listed under the ESA have low population levels when they are listed.

Ⓒ Only 54 once-listed species have been delisted; many more species have not recovered and are still listed.

Ⓓ Based on an analysis of population trends, Eberhard, Wilcove, and Dobson found that species listed under the ESA have very small populations when listed.

STOP

If you finish before time is called, you may check your work on this module only.
Do not turn to any other module in the test.

SAT Prep Test 2—Reading and Writing

Module 2—Harder

Turn to Section 1 of your answer sheet (p. 663) to answer the questions in this section.

DIRECTIONS

The questions in this section address a number of important reading and writing skills. Each question includes one or more passages, which may include a table or graph. Read each passage and question carefully, and then choose the best answer to the question based on the passage(s).

All questions in the section are multiple-choice with four answer choices. Each question has a single best answer.

1 Mark for Review

Dutch philosopher Baruch Spinoza argued as part of his rejection of dualism that all things, living or not, have the inclination to continue to exist and enhance themselves, a property he named "conatus." All things, he believed, had the tendency to ______ and would only cease to be if acted upon by outside forces.

Which choice completes the text with the most logical and precise word or phrase?

Ⓐ deteriorate

Ⓑ perish

Ⓒ persevere

Ⓓ disappear

2 Mark for Review

Many species demonstrate rescue behavior, a behavior in which an individual will help another in distress without any obvious benefit to the helper. In fact, this behavior ______ a recent study of Australian magpies when some birds in the study helped other birds remove the trackers that researchers had placed upon them, making it more difficult for the researchers to obtain data.

Which choice completes the text with the most logical and precise word or phrase?

Ⓐ aided

Ⓑ impeded

Ⓒ clarified

Ⓓ exposed

CONTINUE

3 Mark for Review

Dutch artist M.C. Escher's work uses ______ to engage viewers by employing mathematical and intuitive processes to create images of objects that at first appear normal but on closer inspection are, in fact, impossible.

Which choice completes the text with the most logical and precise word or phrase?

Ⓐ geometry

Ⓑ beauty

Ⓒ paradox

Ⓓ color

4 Mark for Review

Typically, pure water is not considered particularly ______, but a team of scientists led by Richard Zare has discovered how microdroplets of water can turn into caustic hydrogen peroxide. When microdroplets of water hit a solid surface, an electric charge jumps between the water and the solid, producing hydroxyl radicals that, in turn, combine with remaining oxygen to form hydrogen peroxide.

Which choice completes the text with the most logical and precise word or phrase?

Ⓐ viable

Ⓑ contaminated

Ⓒ common

Ⓓ reactive

5 Mark for Review

The Beat Generation, a literary subculture movement featured in works such as Allen Ginsberg's *Howl* (1956) and William S. Burroughs's *Naked Lunch* (1959), was characterized by its ______ the traditional values of the 1950s. The movement's central message of nonconformity would be criticized by American literary critic Manuel Luis Martinez, who believed that the Beat Generation's lack of attention to the politics of individualism undermined the movement's goals.

Which choice completes the text with the most logical and precise word or phrase?

Ⓐ dissension from

Ⓑ gratitude towards

Ⓒ adherence to

Ⓓ deference to

6 Mark for Review

The possibility of recycling used car tires as building materials is ______ indeed: the disposal of used tires is a major environmental problem, so potentially reusing them would be beneficial. Furthermore, initial studies have shown that walls made of used tires and dirt are more structurally robust than those made of concrete.

Which choice completes the text with the most logical and precise word or phrase?

Ⓐ derivative

Ⓑ ludicrous

Ⓒ auspicious

Ⓓ innovative

CONTINUE

7 Mark for Review

The Voynich manuscript was written on vellum dating from the fifteenth century in a script that is not found in any other source. Since cryptographers have yet to demonstrably decipher any portion of the text, the meaning and purpose of the Voynich manuscript remain ______.

Which choice completes the text with the most logical and precise word or phrase?

Ⓐ enigmatic

Ⓑ venerable

Ⓒ multifarious

Ⓓ coherent

8 Mark for Review

Astronautics owes much to the ______ contributions of Charles E. Whitsett. His ground-breaking development of the manned maneuvering unit enabled the first spacewalks in which astronauts were not tethered to a spacecraft.

Which choice completes the text with the most logical and precise word or phrase?

Ⓐ dubious

Ⓑ futile

Ⓒ galvanizing

Ⓓ avant-garde

9 Mark for Review

The following text is adapted from Charles Dickens's 1859 novel *A Tale of Two Cities*. Mr. Lorry, traveling to France on business, is delivering some news to Miss Manette, the daughter of one of his friends.

> "Miss Manette, I am a man of business. I have a business charge to acquit myself of. In your reception of it, don't heed me any more than if I was a speaking machine—truly, I am not much else. I will, with your leave, relate to you, miss, the story of one of our customers."
>
> "Story!"
>
> He seemed wilfully to mistake the word she had repeated, when he added, in a hurry, "Yes, customers; in the banking business we usually call our connection our customers. He was a French gentleman; a scientific gentleman; a man of great acquirements—a Doctor."

Based on the text, how does Mr. Lorry interact with Miss Manette?

Ⓐ Although he claims to be uninterested in the news, he makes purposeful decisions during his conversation with Miss Manette.

Ⓑ Although he is a professional, he misunderstands Miss Manette's interjection.

Ⓒ Although he acts as if the news has no importance to him, he cannot keep the details of the story accurate.

Ⓓ Although he is unthinkingly following directions, he is flustered by Miss Manette's rudeness.

CONTINUE

10 Mark for Review

Nisga'a poet Jordan Abel addresses the experiences of Indigenous people as European settlers and their descendants took over North America. Abel's first book of poetry, *The Place of Scraps* (2014), uses *Totem Poles*, a 1929 book by anthropologist Marius Barbeau, as source material. Abel claims that his use of Barbeau's text shows how anthropological texts can be used to portray Indigenous people differently based on the author.

Which finding, if true, would most directly support Abel's claim?

Ⓐ Abel intersperses Barbeau's text with images of Indigenous people and personal anecdotes written in the third person.

Ⓑ Abel explains that Barbeau presented two chiefs feuding over constructing the largest pole as unreasonable, yet other anthropologists claim that such arguments between chiefs of Indigenous tribes were important political exchanges.

Ⓒ *The Place of Scraps* won the Dorothy Livesay Poetry Prize and was a finalist for the Gerald Lampert Award.

Ⓓ Before Abel wrote *The Place of Scraps*, other Indigenous writers had used texts from anthropologists in their works.

11 Mark for Review

In Japan, adults may be legally adopted into a family. The practice may have started as early as the 13th century CE, but widespread adult adoption dates from the Tokugawa shogunate, a military government which began around 1600 CE. During this time, members of the ruling class would adopt competent adult males, who would then ensure that the family's political and business interests would be sustained. While adult adoption remains a way for individuals to improve their economic and social status, the practice has its detractors as well, with some researchers arguing that it can lead to issues with the adoptee developing a firm sense of identity in his or her new environment.

Which of the following best illustrates the researchers' claim?

Ⓐ Adult adoptees are entitled to an inheritance from their adoptive families, strengthening the ties between them, which further encourages the adult adoptee to work to enhance the new family's prosperity.

Ⓑ While most adult adoptees typically report improved financial status after adoption, many of those same adoptees also experience higher-than-normal rates of depression and anxiety.

Ⓒ Elsewhere in East Asia, such as in China and Korea, families have a traditional obligation to adopt blood relatives who lack more closely-related living kin, but adoptions in Japan are almost exclusively between those with no blood relations.

Ⓓ Families with ancestors who were adult adoptees do not distinguish between those ancestors who were members of the family by birth and those who were adopted into the family.

CONTINUE

12 Mark for Review

Neurologists have hypothesized that tau protein, the mutation of which is known to cause Alzheimer's disease, is key to controlling glutamate receptors, which are involved in the production of memories. Tau protein does not directly affect glutamate receptors but does inhibit NSF, an enzyme found in the brain.

Which finding, if true, would most directly support the neurologists' hypothesis?

Ⓐ Other studies have shown that an excess of NSF has been shown to lead to abnormal glutamate receptor behavior.

Ⓑ Patients with Alzheimer's disease have been found to have an excess of NSF in their brains during autopsies.

Ⓒ Neurologists do not yet know what causes mutations of tau protein; one hypothesis is that disease leads to these mutations.

Ⓓ Other types of dementia are not caused by mutations in tau protein but rather physical damage to the brain.

13 Mark for Review

From 1634 to 1637 CE, tulips in the Dutch Republic sold for extraordinarily high prices, sometimes as much as 10 times the annual wage of a skilled worker, in a phenomenon known as tulip mania. Some economists, such as Charles Kindleberger, argue that tulip mania was the first speculative bubble in history, during which the prices of a commodity (in this case tulip bulbs) do not follow the typical rules of economics. Others, such as Peter Garber, believe that tulip mania is explainable by fundamental economic concepts such as supply and demand.

Which finding, if true, would most directly support Garber's argument?

Ⓐ Tulips during this period were very rare, and demand for tulips was fueled in part by the ability to reproduce and sell bulbs, enabling some purchasers to make profits.

Ⓑ Some common bulbs, such as the Witte Croonen bulb, saw price increases as dramatic as those of rare bulbs.

Ⓒ The prices of tulip bulbs were much higher than could be supported by the banking system in place in 17th century Europe.

Ⓓ The tulip mania led to an increase of the supply of gold coins in the Dutch Republic.

CONTINUE

14 Mark for Review

The use of pesticides in agriculture poses risks to both humans and the environment, so finding alternative methods of pest control is an important area of research. The use of ants to control pests in China goes back to at least the 4th century CE, and farmers in places such as Kenya, Ghana, and Canada have also used ants to control various organisms. Entomologist Diego Anjos and others have identified several positive effects (services) of ants, such as reducing both the abundance of non-honeydew-producing species and plant damage. However, ants also have negative effects, such as increasing the abundance of honeydew-producing species and spreading pathogens, suggesting that ______

Which choice most logically completes the text?

Ⓐ ants may have unintended environmental consequences when used to control pests in certain circumstances.

Ⓑ other species may also be effective in providing services to farmers.

Ⓒ ants as pest control provide numerous services without serious ramifications.

Ⓓ scientists do not yet know whether using ants to control organisms is a net positive in any situation.

15 Mark for Review

Among many animals, such as mice, fruit flies, and humans, each odor that an animal can smell is detected by a particular kind of sensory neuron that has a particular kind of receptor; eliminating that receptor through illness or genetic manipulation results in the inability to smell that odor. A team led by neurobiologist Margo Herre tested whether mosquitoes modified to lack the receptor for smelling blood would be unable to find humans. These mosquitoes were still able to find humans, suggesting that ______

Which choice most logically completes the text?

Ⓐ mosquitoes without damage to their odor receptors are more capable of finding humans than those with damage.

Ⓑ like mice, fruit flies, and humans, individual mosquitoes with damage to particular receptors will be unable to detect certain odors.

Ⓒ researchers cannot assume that mosquitoes have the same correlation between receptors and the ability to sense certain odors that mice, fruit flies, and humans have.

Ⓓ researchers can assume that interfering with mosquitoes' odor receptors is a potential way to prevent mosquitoes from feeding on humans.

CONTINUE

16 Mark for Review

The North American Free Trade Agreement (NAFTA) was an agreement among the United States, Canada, and Mexico that was in effect between 1994 and 2020. During this time, the number of manufacturing jobs in the United States and Canada declined, but the total number of manufacturing jobs in the countries covered by NAFTA increased. This suggests that, between 1994 and 2020, ______

Which choice most logically completes the text?

Ⓐ the number of manufacturing jobs in Mexico increased by a greater amount than the combined decreases in the United States and Canada.

Ⓑ NAFTA made it more difficult for manufacturers to establish factories in the United States and Canada.

Ⓒ the cost of manufacturing goods in the area covered by NAFTA decreased.

Ⓓ complex goods, such as automobiles and electronics, were increasingly manufactured in the United States, Canada, and Mexico.

17 Mark for Review

Researchers studying the recent eruption of Hunga Tonga–Hunga Ha'apai, a submarine volcano located near the islands of Tonga in the South Pacific, found that the volcanic cloud, compared to those of other eruptions, ______ the highest ever recorded.

Which choice completes the text so that it conforms to the conventions of Standard English?

Ⓐ have been

Ⓑ are

Ⓒ was

Ⓓ were

18 Mark for Review

Connectomes, extensive maps of neural connections in the brain, reveal that each person has a distinct pattern of connections known as a functional fingerprint. In a 2017 study, behavioral ______ found that about one-third of the functional fingerprint is unique to an individual and that other parts are inherited.

Which choice completes the text so that it conforms to the conventions of Standard English?

Ⓐ neuroscientist, Damien Fair,

Ⓑ neuroscientist Damien Fair

Ⓒ neuroscientist Damien Fair,

Ⓓ neuroscientist, Damien Fair

CONTINUE

19 Mark for Review

Throughout her career, Muscogee Nation member and poet Joy Harjo has edited multiple anthologies that have highlighted Native voices in the U.S. For example, a map showcasing 47 Native Nations poets ______ her signature project during her time as the U.S. Poet Laureate.

Which choice completes the text so that it conforms to the conventions of Standard English?

Ⓐ was

Ⓑ are

Ⓒ have been

Ⓓ were

20 Mark for Review

When bees pollinate flowers, they may be exposed to insecticides, potentially affecting their nervous systems. Recently, Dr. Rachel Parkinson of the University of Oxford added the common ______ to a sucralose solution to examine the insecticide's impact on honeybees' ability to walk in a straight line.

Which choice completes the text so that it conforms to the conventions of Standard English?

Ⓐ insecticide sulfoxaflor

Ⓑ insecticide, sulfoxaflor,

Ⓒ insecticide sulfoxaflor,

Ⓓ insecticide, sulfoxaflor

21 Mark for Review

In 1946, Juliet Rice Wichman acquired 1,000 acres on Kaua'i, one of the Hawaiian islands, to transform the land into a garden by removing grazing cattle and restoring terraces to grow taro. Wichman's work to preserve the culture of Kaua'i wasn't ______ as the first director of the Kaua'i Museum, she oversaw exhibits celebrating the history, culture, and art of Native Hawaiians.

Which choice completes the text so that it conforms to the conventions of Standard English?

Ⓐ finished though

Ⓑ finished. Though,

Ⓒ finished, though,

Ⓓ finished, though:

22 Mark for Review

Researchers studying bacteria have solved a 50-year mystery of how bacteria are able to move using appendages that are made of a single ______ the subunits of the protein can exist in 11 different shapes, allowing the appendages to "supercoil" into corkscrews that the bacteria use to propel themselves.

Which choice completes the text so that it conforms to the conventions of Standard English?

Ⓐ protein

Ⓑ protein while

Ⓒ protein,

Ⓓ protein:

CONTINUE

23 Mark for Review

Fault tree analysis was originally used in engineering to enhance safety practices in high-risk fields, such as nuclear power and pharmaceuticals, but other fields are experimenting with ways to utilize this process to benefit their work. ______ fault tree analysis is also being used in low-risk fields, such as social services and software engineering.

Which choice completes the text with the most logical transition?

Ⓐ Increasingly,

Ⓑ Nevertheless,

Ⓒ Therefore,

Ⓓ In addition,

24 Mark for Review

When Monika Sosnowska began her career in Amsterdam as a painter, she never expected to branch out into other media. ______ she had primarily worked on canvas, but she quickly found her works evolving to include the three-dimensional space around her.

Which choice completes the text with the most logical transition?

Ⓐ Instead,

Ⓑ Consequently,

Ⓒ Previously,

Ⓓ Similarly,

25 Mark for Review

Fish sometimes appear in otherwise uninhabited bodies of water, seemingly emerging out of nowhere. Some scientists believe that the fish are carried to these locations in the beaks or talons of birds. ______ new research suggests that the fish eggs enter a state of hibernation and are actually eaten by birds and excreted out into the bodies of water.

Which choice completes the text with the most logical transition?

Ⓐ For instance,

Ⓑ Next,

Ⓒ Likewise,

Ⓓ Alternatively,

CONTINUE

26 Mark for Review

While researching a topic, a student has taken the following notes:

- To restore oyster reefs in Australia, limestone boulders are submerged to provide habitats, but baby oysters need help finding the boulders.
- A team from University of Adelaide looked into using sound as a way to encourage the baby oysters to attach to the boulders.
- The research team recorded sounds at the healthy Port Noarlunga Reef to play near the submerged boulders.
- Boulders in the area with the soundscape attracted around 17,000 more oysters per square meter compared to boulders without the soundscape.
- Soundscapes can indicate a healthy place for baby oysters to grow and can be a cost-effective way to restore oyster reefs.

The student wants to emphasize the aim of the research study. Which choice most effectively uses relevant information from the notes to accomplish this goal?

Ⓐ Researchers obtained a soundscape at Port Noarlunga Reef to help in the restoration of oyster reefs in Australia.

Ⓑ Researchers now know that the soundscape of a healthy marine ecosystem can attract baby oysters to attach to submerged limestone boulders.

Ⓒ After they measured the number of oysters attracted to boulders in the soundscape area compared to no soundscape, researchers determined that the soundscape attracted more baby oysters.

Ⓓ Researchers wanted to know whether a soundscape of a healthy marine ecosystem could encourage baby oysters to attach to submerged limestone boulders.

27 Mark for Review

While researching a topic, a student has taken the following notes:

- Neanderthals are an extinct species of humans who died out about 40,000 years ago and are the closest evolutionary relatives of present-day humans.
- Studying the genomes of Neanderthals provides insight into human evolution.
- Professor Svante Pääbo is a Swedish geneticist and the director of the Department of Genetics at the Max Planck Institute for Evolutionary Anthropology.
- His landmark study presented the first draft sequence of the Neanderthal genome.
- Laurits Skov of the Max Planck Institute for Evolutionary Anthropology has a doctorate in bioinformatics and studied evolutionary anthropology.
- One of his recent studies revealed the genomes of a family of Neanderthals.

The student wants to emphasize the affiliation and purpose of Pääbo's and Skov's work. Which choice most effectively uses relevant information from the notes to accomplish this goal?

Ⓐ The closest evolutionary relatives of present-day humans, Neanderthals went extinct about 40,000 years ago.

Ⓑ By studying the genomes of Neanderthals, Svante Pääbo and Laurits Skov of the Max Planck Institute for Evolutionary Anthropology provide insight into human evolution.

Ⓒ Svante Pääbo and Laurits Skov study the genome of Neanderthals, an extinct species of humans.

Ⓓ Studies by Svante Pääbo and Laurits Skov reveal information about Neanderthals, who died out about 40,000 years ago.

STOP

If you finish before time is called, you may check your work on this module only.
Do not turn to any other module in the test.

THIS PAGE LEFT INTENTIONALLY BLANK.

SAT Prep Test 2—Math
Module 1

Turn to Section 2 of your answer sheet (p. 664) to answer the questions in this section.

DIRECTIONS

The questions in this section address a number of important math skills.
Use of a calculator is permitted for all questions.

NOTES

Unless otherwise indicated:

- All variables and expressions represent real numbers.
- Figures provided are drawn to scale.
- All figures lie in a plane.
- The domain of a given function f is the set of all real numbers x for which $f(x)$ is a real number.

REFERENCE

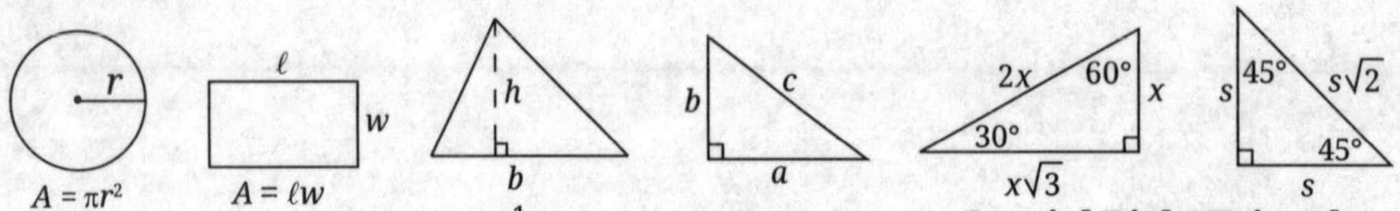

$A = \pi r^2$, $C = 2\pi r$ | $A = \ell w$ | $A = \frac{1}{2}bh$ | $c^2 = a^2 + b^2$ | **Special Right Triangles**

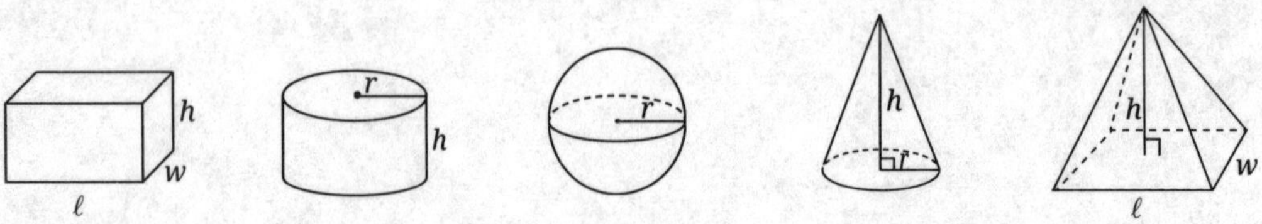

$V = \ell wh$ | $V = \pi r^2 h$ | $V = \frac{4}{3}\pi r^3$ | $V = \frac{1}{3}\pi r^2 h$ | $V = \frac{1}{3}\ell wh$

The number of degrees of arc in a circle is 360.
The number of radians of arc in a circle is 2π.
The sum of the measures in degrees of the angles of a triangle is 180.

CONTINUE

For multiple-choice questions, solve each problem, choose the correct answer from the choices provided, and then circle your answer in this book. Circle only one answer for each question. If you change your mind, completely erase the circle. You will not get credit for questions with more than one answer circled or for questions with no answers circled.

For student-produced response questions, solve each problem and write your answer next to or under the question in the test book as described below.

- Once you've written your answer, circle it clearly. You will not receive credit for anything written outside the circle or for any questions with more than one circled answer.
- If you find **more than one correct answer**, write and circle only one answer.
- Your answer can be up to 5 characters for a **positive** answer and up to 6 characters (including the negative sign) for a **negative** answer, but no more.
- If your answer is a **fraction** that is too long (over 5 characters for positive, 6 characters for negative), write the decimal equivalent.
- If your answer is a **decimal** that is too long (over 5 characters for positive, 6 characters for negative), truncate it or round at the fourth digit.
- If your answer is a **mixed number** (such as $3\frac{1}{2}$), write it as an improper fraction (7/2) or its decimal equivalent (3.5).
- Don't enter **symbols** such as a percent sign, comma, or dollar sign in your circled answer.

CONTINUE

1 Mark for Review

A data set containing only the values 2, 2, 9, 9, 9, 16, 16, 16, 16, 26, 26, and 26 is represented by a frequency table. Which of the following is the correct representation of this data set?

Ⓐ

Number	Frequency
2	4
9	27
16	64
26	78

Ⓑ

Number	Frequency
2	2
9	3
16	4
26	3

Ⓒ

Number	Frequency
2	2
3	9
4	16
3	26

Ⓓ

Number	Frequency
4	2
27	9
64	16
78	26

2 Mark for Review

The expression $x^2 - x - 56$ is equivalent to which of the following?

Ⓐ $(x - 14)(x + 4)$

Ⓑ $(x - 7)(x + 8)$

Ⓒ $(x - 8)(x + 7)$

Ⓓ $(x - 4)(x + 14)$

3 Mark for Review

A carpenter hammers 10 nails per minute and installs 7 screws per minute during a project. Which of the following equations represents the scenario if the carpenter hammers nails for x minutes, installs screws for y minutes, and uses a combined total of 200 nails and screws?

Ⓐ $\frac{1}{10}x + \frac{1}{7}y = 200$

Ⓑ $\frac{1}{10}x + \frac{1}{7}y = 3{,}420$

Ⓒ $10x + 7y = 200$

Ⓓ $10x + 7y = 3{,}420$

CONTINUE

4 Mark for Review

What is the measure of angle F in the triangle DEF, where angle D is $73°$ and angle E is $35°$?

Ⓐ $38°$

Ⓑ $72°$

Ⓒ $108°$

Ⓓ $126°$

5 Mark for Review

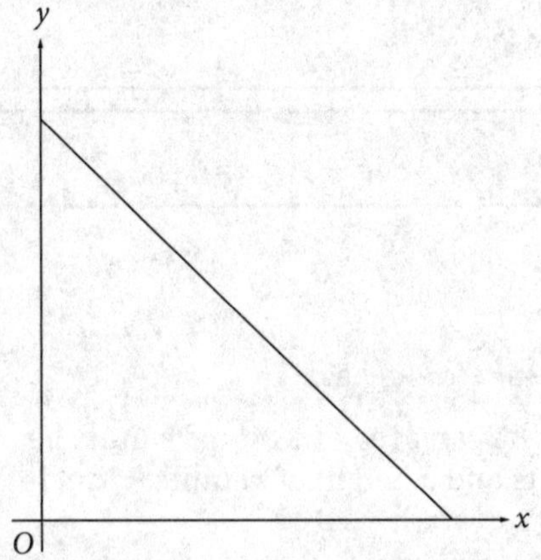

The total amount of plastic remaining to be recycled in a facility over x shifts is represented by the graph above. Which of the following represents the y-intercept of the graph?

Ⓐ The total amount of plastic remaining at any given time

Ⓑ The number of shifts it will take to finish recycling the plastic

Ⓒ The amount of plastic that is recycled per shift

Ⓓ The initial amount of plastic to be recycled

6 Mark for Review

The table below shows the condition and subject type for 200 textbooks at a bookstore.

	Biology	Chemistry	Physics	Anatomy	Total
Used	10	25	30	15	80
New	30	25	10	55	120
Total	40	50	40	70	200

What is the probability that a textbook chosen at random will be a new textbook? (Express your answer as a decimal or fraction, not as a percent.)

______

7 Mark for Review

A random sample of 5,000 students out of 60,000 undergraduate students at a university were surveyed about a potential change to the registration system. According to the survey results, 75% of the respondents did not support the existing registration system, with a 4% margin of error. Which of the following represents a reasonable total number of students who did not support the existing registration system?

Ⓐ 1,250

Ⓑ 3,750

Ⓒ 13,800

Ⓓ 43,800

CONTINUE

8 Mark for Review

What is the negative solution to the equation $\frac{32}{a} = a - 4$?

9 Mark for Review

After a hot air balloon is launched from a plateau 1,000 meters above sea level, it rises at a constant rate of 750 meters per minute. Which of the following best describes the function used to model the balloon's distance above sea level over time?

Ⓐ Increasing linear

Ⓑ Increasing exponential

Ⓒ Decreasing linear

Ⓓ Decreasing exponential

10 Mark for Review

What is the x-intercept of the function $f(x) = (22)^x - 1$ when it is graphed in the xy-plane, where $y = f(x)$?

Ⓐ (–1, 0)

Ⓑ (0, 0)

Ⓒ (21, 0)

Ⓓ (22, 0)

11 Mark for Review

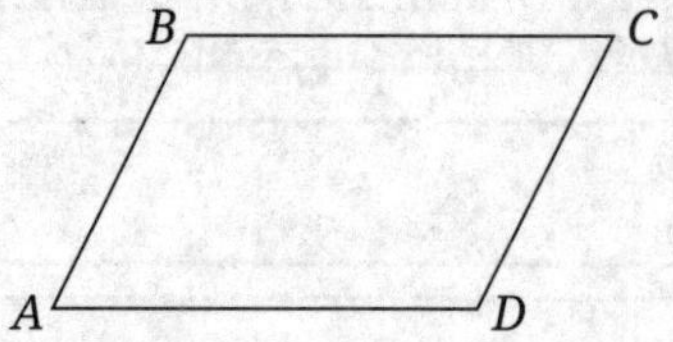

Note: Figure not drawn to scale.

In parallelogram $ABCD$ shown above, the length of $\overline{AB}$ is one-third the length of $\overline{AD}$. The perimeter of the parallelogram is 64. What is the length of $\overline{AB}$?

Ⓐ 8

Ⓑ 16

Ⓒ 24

Ⓓ 32

12 Mark for Review

A triangle with an area of 18 square units has a base of $(m + 5)$ units and a height of m units. What is the value of m?

Ⓐ 4

Ⓑ 9

Ⓒ 13

Ⓓ 36

CONTINUE

13 Mark for Review

Time (seconds)	Number of colonies of yeast
0	5
1	20
2	80
3	320

The table above shows the exponential growth of a type of yeast over time s, in seconds. There are c total yeast colonies on the count plate. What is the equation that represents this relationship, assuming that no yeast was added or removed after counting began?

Ⓐ $c = (1 + 3)^s$

Ⓑ $c = (1 + 5)^s$

Ⓒ $c = 3(1 + 5)^s$

Ⓓ $c = 5(1 + 3)^s$

14 Mark for Review

The equations $12x = y$ and $24x + 7 = 2y$ intersect at how many points when graphed in the xy-plane?

Ⓐ 0

Ⓑ 1

Ⓒ 2

Ⓓ 7

15 Mark for Review

Several tiles labeled with either an A or a B are placed in a bag, and tiles are worth a different point value depending on the label. The equation $15a + 10b = 100$ represents the situation when a of the A tiles and b of the B tiles are drawn from the bag for a total of 100 points. How many points would be earned by drawing one A tile and one B tile from the bag?

16 Mark for Review

The amount of money remaining in a scholarship fund is reduced by one-fourth every year. The amount of money in the fund is represented by d and the number of years by y. If the fund starts with $10,000, which equation below represents this situation after y years?

Ⓐ $d = \frac{1}{4}(10{,}000)^y$

Ⓑ $d = \frac{3}{4}(10{,}000)^y$

Ⓒ $d = 10{,}000\left(\frac{1}{4}\right)^y$

Ⓓ $d = 10{,}000\left(\frac{3}{4}\right)^y$

CONTINUE

17 Mark for Review

What is the diameter, in millimeters (mm), of a cylinder with a volume of 144π mm^3 and a height of 4 mm?

Ⓐ 6

Ⓑ 9

Ⓒ 12

Ⓓ 36

18 Mark for Review

$$4x + 2y = 4$$
$$19x + 10y = 14$$

When graphed in the xy-plane, the linear equations shown above intersect at (a, b). What is the value of a?

Ⓐ −20

Ⓑ −10

Ⓒ 6

Ⓓ 14

19 Mark for Review

The longest side of right triangle ABC is opposite angle B. If $\sin(A) = \frac{9}{41}$, what is the value of $\sin(C)$?

20 Mark for Review

Function g reaches its maximum value when $x = a$. If $g(x) = -6x^2 - 30x - 24$, what is the value of a?

CONTINUE

21 Mark for Review

$$f(x) = -\frac{1}{5}x - 3$$

The linear function $f(x)$, given above, is perpendicular to $g(x)$ when graphed in the xy-plane. If $g(0) = 0$, what is the value of $g(2)$?

22 Mark for Review

$$y = 5kx^2 + 2x + 3$$

$$\frac{y}{10} = -x$$

The given system of equations has exactly one solution. If k is a positive constant, what is the value of k?

YIELD

Once you've finished (or run out of time for) this section, use the answer key to determine how many questions you got right. If you got fewer than 14 questions right, move on to Module 2—Easier, otherwise move on to Module 2—Harder.

SAT Prep Test 2—Math

Module 2—Easier

Turn to Section 2 of your answer sheet (p. 664) to answer the questions in this section.

DIRECTIONS

The questions in this section address a number of important math skills.
Use of a calculator is permitted for all questions.

NOTES

Unless otherwise indicated:

- All variables and expressions represent real numbers.
- Figures provided are drawn to scale.
- All figures lie in a plane.
- The domain of a given function *f* is the set of all real numbers *x* for which *f*(*x*) is a real number.

REFERENCE

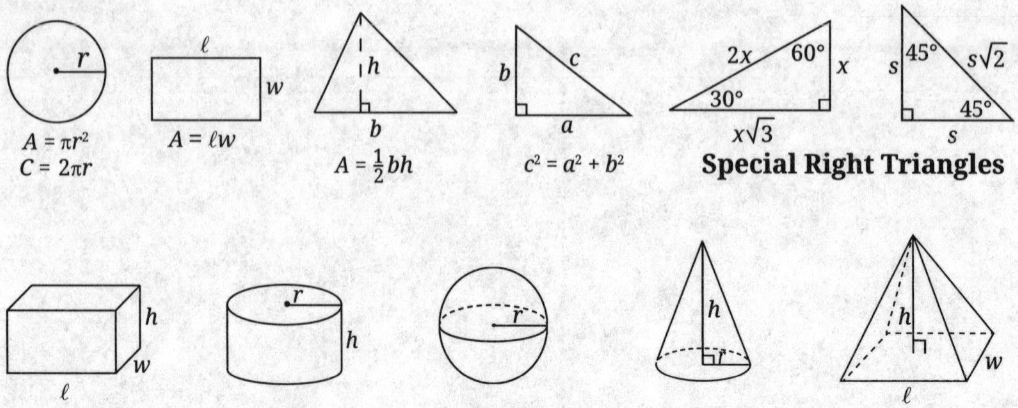

$A = \pi r^2$, $C = 2\pi r$

$A = \ell w$

$A = \frac{1}{2}bh$

$c^2 = a^2 + b^2$

Special Right Triangles

$V = \ell wh$

$V = \pi r^2 h$

$V = \frac{4}{3}\pi r^3$

$V = \frac{1}{3}\pi r^2 h$

$V = \frac{1}{3}\ell wh$

The number of degrees of arc in a circle is 360.
The number of radians of arc in a circle is 2π.
The sum of the measures in degrees of the angles of a triangle is 180.

CONTINUE

For multiple-choice questions, solve each problem, choose the correct answer from the choices provided, and then circle your answer in this book. Circle only one answer for each question. If you change your mind, completely erase the circle. You will not get credit for questions with more than one answer circled or for questions with no answers circled.

For student-produced response questions, solve each problem and write your answer next to or under the question in the test book as described below.

- Once you've written your answer, circle it clearly. You will not receive credit for anything written outside the circle or for any questions with more than one circled answer.
- If you find **more than one correct answer**, write and circle only one answer.
- Your answer can be up to 5 characters for a **positive** answer and up to 6 characters (including the negative sign) for a **negative** answer, but no more.
- If your answer is a **fraction** that is too long (over 5 characters for positive, 6 characters for negative), write the decimal equivalent.
- If your answer is a **decimal** that is too long (over 5 characters for positive, 6 characters for negative), truncate it or round at the fourth digit.
- If your answer is a **mixed number** (such as $3\frac{1}{2}$), write it as an improper fraction (7/2) or its decimal equivalent (3.5).
- Don't enter **symbols** such as a percent sign, comma, or dollar sign in your circled answer.

CONTINUE

1 Mark for Review

33, 34, 38, 41, 43, 44, 47

Which of the following is the median of the given data?

Ⓐ 38

Ⓑ 40

Ⓒ 41

Ⓓ 42

2 Mark for Review

What is the value of the solution to the equation $22 = y - 10$?

3 Mark for Review

A rectangle has a height of 23 inches (in) and a width of 9 in. What is its perimeter, in inches?

Ⓐ 32

Ⓑ 64

Ⓒ 207

Ⓓ 1,024

4 Mark for Review

$15a - (6a - 2a)$

Which of the following expressions is equivalent to the given expression?

Ⓐ $5a$

Ⓑ $7a$

Ⓒ $11a$

Ⓓ $23a$

5 Mark for Review

Which equation represents the relationship between the numbers a and b if a is half of b?

Ⓐ $a = \frac{1}{2}b$

Ⓑ $a = b - 2$

Ⓒ $a = b + 2$

Ⓓ $b = \frac{1}{2}a$

CONTINUE

6 Mark for Review

For all positive values of y, the expression $\frac{3}{y+c}$ is equivalent to $\frac{15}{5y+30}$. What is the value of constant c?

Ⓐ 3

Ⓑ 6

Ⓒ 8

Ⓓ 150

7 Mark for Review

A total of 200 pets were adopted at an event. If 70% of the adopted pets were dogs, how many of the pets were dogs?

8 Mark for Review

James must drive 100 miles before he can take his driver's license test. He knows that when he drives around town running errands, he drives at an average speed of 20 miles per hour. If James maintains this average speed, how many hours must he drive to meet the requirement for his driver's license test?

Ⓐ 5

Ⓑ 20

Ⓒ 80

Ⓓ 100

9 Mark for Review

What is the value of $4y - 16$ if $y - 4 = 11$?

CONTINUE

10 Mark for Review

The function g is defined as $g(x) = x^2 - 1$. What is the value of $g(x)$ when $x = 3$?

Ⓐ 4

Ⓑ 5

Ⓒ 7

Ⓓ 8

11 Mark for Review

The production cost $p(x)$, in dollars, to produce x units of an item when materials cost \$2 per item is given by $p(x) = 2x + 150$. What is the total cost to produce 2,000 units of this item?

Ⓐ \$1,850

Ⓑ \$2,300

Ⓒ \$3,850

Ⓓ \$4,150

12 Mark for Review

The function f is given as $f(x) = \frac{2}{3}x$. When $x = 6$, what is the value of $f(x)$?

Ⓐ 2

Ⓑ 4

Ⓒ 6

Ⓓ 9

13 Mark for Review

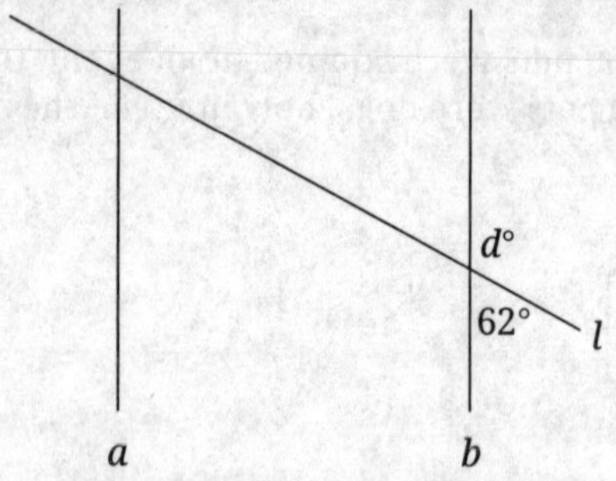

Note: Figure not drawn to scale.

In the given figure, what is the value of d if line a is parallel to line b?

CONTINUE

14 Mark for Review

$$3x - 4y = 17$$

In the xy-plane, the graph of a line with an x-intercept of $(c, 0)$ and a y-intercept of $(0, k)$, where c and k are constants, can be represented by the given equation. What is the value of $\frac{c}{k}$?

Ⓐ $-\frac{4}{3}$

Ⓑ $-\frac{3}{4}$

Ⓒ $\frac{3}{4}$

Ⓓ $\frac{4}{3}$

15 Mark for Review

A postal machine processes mail at a constant rate of 21 pieces of mail per minute. At this rate, how many pieces of mail would the machine process in 7 minutes?

Ⓐ 3

Ⓑ 14

Ⓒ 28

Ⓓ 147

16 Mark for Review

Stella had 211 invitations to send for an event. She has already sent 43 invitations and will send them all if she sends 24 each day for the next d days. Which of the following equations represents this situation?

Ⓐ $24d - 43 = 211$

Ⓑ $24d + 43 = 211$

Ⓒ $43d - 24 = 211$

Ⓓ $43d + 24 = 211$

17 Mark for Review

x	-1	0	1	2
$f(x)$	12	15	18	21

When the linear function $y = f(x)$ is graphed in the xy-plane, the graph contains the corresponding values of x and $f(x)$ shown in the table above. Which of the following could represent the function?

Ⓐ $f(x) = 3x + 12$

Ⓑ $f(x) = 3x + 15$

Ⓒ $f(x) = 15x + 12$

Ⓓ $f(x) = 15x + 15$

CONTINUE

18 Mark for Review

The height of a rocket launched from a rooftop can be modeled by the equation $h = -16s^2 + 64s + 21$, where h is the height of the rocket above the ground, in feet, and s is the number of seconds since the rocket was launched. Which of the following represents the height, in feet, of the rooftop from which the rocket was launched?

Ⓐ 0

Ⓑ 16

Ⓒ 21

Ⓓ 64

19 Mark for Review

Function f is defined by $f(x) = x^3 + 1$. Which of the following tables gives three values of x and their corresponding values of y?

Ⓐ

x	2	3	4
y	3	4	5

Ⓑ

x	2	3	4
y	3	28	64

Ⓒ

x	2	3	4
y	9	10	65

Ⓓ

x	2	3	4
y	9	28	65

20 Mark for Review

If $h(-1) = 3$ and $h(0) = 5$ in linear function h, which of the following is the equation of function h?

Ⓐ $h(x) = 2x + 5$

Ⓑ $h(x) = 2x + 3$

Ⓒ $h(x) = 2x$

Ⓓ $h(x) = 3x + 5$

CONTINUE

21 Mark for Review

Which of the following equations correctly expresses r in terms of p and s if the relationship between the numbers p, r, and s can be expressed as $p = 13r - 6s$?

(A) $r = \frac{-6s - p}{13}$

(B) $r = 13p + 6s$

(C) $r = \frac{1}{13}p + 6s$

(D) $r = \frac{p + 6s}{13}$

22 Mark for Review

Right triangle ABC has sides of the following lengths: $AB = 165$, $BC = 280$, and $AC = 325$. Another triangle, LMN, is similar to ABC such that A corresponds to L and B corresponds to M. What is the value of $\cos(L)$?

(A) $\frac{33}{65}$

(B) $\frac{33}{56}$

(C) $\frac{56}{65}$

(D) $\frac{65}{33}$

STOP

If you finish before time is called, you may check your work on this module only. Do not turn to any other module in the test.

SAT Prep Test 2—Math
Module 2—Harder

Turn to Section 2 of your answer sheet (p. 664) to answer the questions in this section.

DIRECTIONS

The questions in this section address a number of important math skills.
Use of a calculator is permitted for all questions.

NOTES

Unless otherwise indicated:

- All variables and expressions represent real numbers.
- Figures provided are drawn to scale.
- All figures lie in a plane.
- The domain of a given function f is the set of all real numbers x for which $f(x)$ is a real number.

REFERENCE

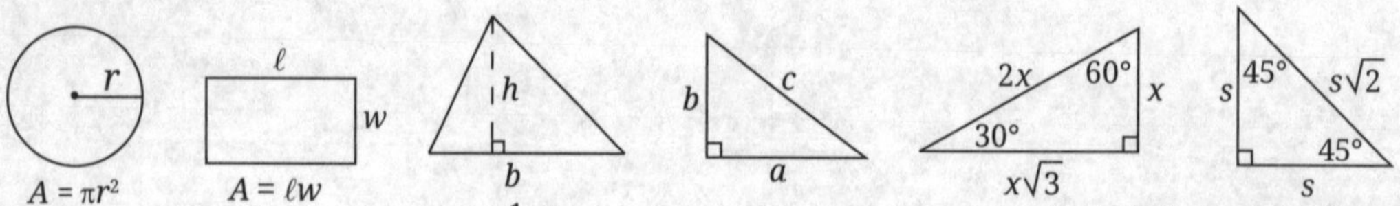

$A = \pi r^2$, $C = 2\pi r$ | $A = \ell w$ | $A = \frac{1}{2}bh$ | $c^2 = a^2 + b^2$ | **Special Right Triangles**

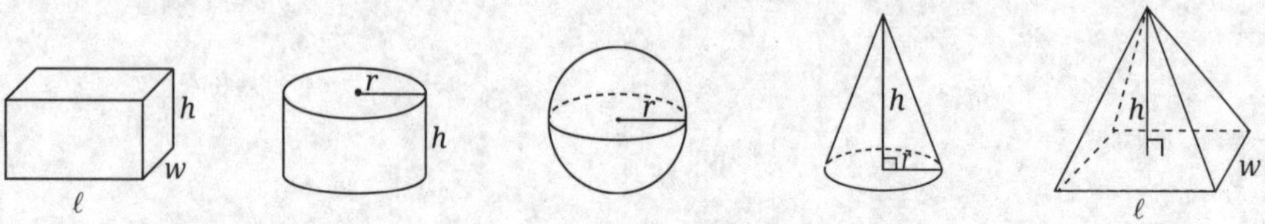

$V = \ell wh$ | $V = \pi r^2 h$ | $V = \frac{4}{3}\pi r^3$ | $V = \frac{1}{3}\pi r^2 h$ | $V = \frac{1}{3}\ell wh$

The number of degrees of arc in a circle is 360.
The number of radians of arc in a circle is 2π.
The sum of the measures in degrees of the angles of a triangle is 180.

CONTINUE

For multiple-choice questions, solve each problem, choose the correct answer from the choices provided, and then circle your answer in this book. Circle only one answer for each question. If you change your mind, completely erase the circle. You will not get credit for questions with more than one answer circled or for questions with no answers circled.

For student-produced response questions, solve each problem and write your answer next to or under the question in the test book as described below.

- Once you've written your answer, circle it clearly. You will not receive credit for anything written outside the circle or for any questions with more than one circled answer.
- If you find **more than one correct answer**, write and circle only one answer.
- Your answer can be up to 5 characters for a **positive** answer and up to 6 characters (including the negative sign) for a **negative** answer, but no more.
- If your answer is a **fraction** that is too long (over 5 characters for positive, 6 characters for negative), write the decimal equivalent.
- If your answer is a **decimal** that is too long (over 5 characters for positive, 6 characters for negative), truncate it or round at the fourth digit.
- If your answer is a **mixed number** (such as $3\frac{1}{2}$), write it as an improper fraction (7/2) or its decimal equivalent (3.5).
- Don't enter **symbols** such as a percent sign, comma, or dollar sign in your circled answer.

CONTINUE

1 Mark for Review

Which of the following is equivalent to $3a^3 - 5a^3 + 6a$?

Ⓐ $-2a^3 + 6a$

Ⓑ $3a^3 + a$

Ⓒ $4a$

Ⓓ $-15a^9 + 6a$

2 Mark for Review

In a shipment of 45,000,000 shirts, 4,950,000 are white. What percentage of the shirts are white shirts?

Ⓐ 11%

Ⓑ 22%

Ⓒ 78%

Ⓓ 89%

3 Mark for Review

If $3(x - 8) - 16 = 8(x + 10) + x$, what is the value of $6x$?

______

4 Mark for Review

$$8(a - 3) - 17 = 9(a - 3)$$

In the given equation, what is the value of $a - 3$?

Ⓐ -20

Ⓑ -17

Ⓒ -14

Ⓓ 3

5 Mark for Review

A school classroom with a total of 4,200 floor tiles is divided into a 30 square-foot lab area and an 80 square-foot seating area. The number of tiles on the entire classroom floor can be represented by the equation $30a + 80b = 4{,}200$. In this context, which of the following does b represent?

Ⓐ The average number of tiles per square foot in the lab area

Ⓑ The total number of tiles in the lab area

Ⓒ The average number of tiles per square foot in the seating area

Ⓓ The total number of tiles in the seating area

CONTINUE

6 Mark for Review

A triangle has a base that is 65% of its height. If the base were decreased by 13 inches, how would the height need to change to keep the same proportions?

Ⓐ It must increase by 13 inches.

Ⓑ It must increase by 20 inches.

Ⓒ It must decrease by 13 inches.

Ⓓ It must decrease by 20 inches.

7 Mark for Review

If $\frac{a}{3} = 10 - 7b$ and $a \neq 0$, which of the following correctly expresses b in terms of a?

Ⓐ $b = \frac{a-21}{30}$

Ⓑ $b = \frac{30-a}{21}$

Ⓒ $b = 10 + \frac{a}{3}$

Ⓓ $b = 10 + \frac{3}{a}$

8 Mark for Review

For all positive values of y, the expression $\frac{3}{y+c}$ is equivalent to $\frac{15}{5y+30}$. What is the value of constant c?

Ⓐ 3

Ⓑ 6

Ⓒ 8

Ⓓ 150

9 Mark for Review

In the xy-plane, the equation $(x-7)^2 + (y+7)^2 = 64$ defines circle O, and the equation $(x-7)^2 + (y+7)^2 = c$ defines circle P. If the two circles have the same center, and the radius of circle P is three less than the radius of circle O, what is the value of constant c?

CONTINUE

10 Mark for Review

A school has received a donation of \$20,000 for the purchase of new laptops. If each laptop costs \$149, no tax is charged, and the laptop manufacturer offers a 7.5% discount on orders of at least 100 laptops, what is the maximum number of laptops the school can purchase with the donation?

(A) 124

(B) 134

(C) 145

(D) 146

11 Mark for Review

$$3x^2 - y - 26 = 0$$
$$y = -3x + 10$$

The point (a, b) is an intersection of the system of equations above when graphed in the xy-plane. What is a possible value of a?

(A) -4

(B) 6

(C) 20

(D) 26

12 Mark for Review

How many values for y satisfy the equation $-6(4y + 2) = 3(4 - 8y)$?

(A) Zero

(B) Exactly one

(C) Exactly two

(D) Infinitely many

13 Mark for Review

A parabola represents the graph of the function f in the xy-plane, where $y = f(x)$. If the vertex of the parabola is $(5, -4)$ and one of the x-intercepts is $(-1.5, 0)$, what is the other x-intercept?

(A) $(-6.5, 0)$

(B) $(1.5, 0)$

(C) $(3.5, 0)$

(D) $(11.5, 0)$

CONTINUE

14 Mark for Review

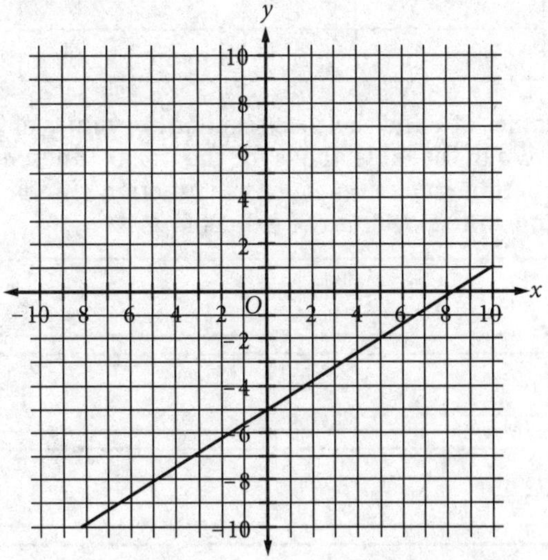

Which equation defines function g, if the graph of $y = g(x) - 10$ is shown above?

Ⓐ $y = \frac{3}{5}x - 15$

Ⓑ $y = \frac{3}{5}x - 5$

Ⓒ $y = \frac{3}{5}x + 5$

Ⓓ $y = \frac{3}{5}x + 10$

15 Mark for Review

If c is a constant in the equation $10x^2 + c = -5x$, and the equation has no real solutions, what is the value of c?

Ⓐ -20

Ⓑ -5

Ⓒ 0

Ⓓ 1

16 Mark for Review

$$3x - 4y = 17$$

In the xy-plane, the graph of a line with an x-intercept of $(c, 0)$ and a y-intercept of $(0, k)$, where c and k are constants, can be represented by the equation above. What is the value of $\frac{c}{k}$?

Ⓐ $-\frac{4}{3}$

Ⓑ $-\frac{3}{4}$

Ⓒ $\frac{3}{4}$

Ⓓ $\frac{4}{3}$

CONTINUE

17 Mark for Review

$$-7 + 2f = cg$$
$$21g + 21 = 6f - 15g$$

If c is a constant, and the system of equations shown above has infinitely many solutions, what is the value of c?

______

18 Mark for Review

Triangle A has angles measuring 30°, 60°, and 90°. What is the perimeter, in centimeters, of this triangle if the smallest side has a length of 15 centimeters?

Ⓐ $15\sqrt{3}$

Ⓑ $15 + 15\sqrt{3}$

Ⓒ $45 + 15\sqrt{3}$

Ⓓ $45\sqrt{3}$

19 Mark for Review

x	2	4	6	8
$g(x)$	46	0	−46	−92

Four values of x and their corresponding values of $g(x)$ are shown in the table above for the linear function g. The equation $g(x) = cx + d$ defines function g, and c and d are constants. What is the value of $c + d$?

Ⓐ −23

Ⓑ 69

Ⓒ 92

Ⓓ 115

20 Mark for Review

114, 109, 106, 111

A data set consists of 5 positive integers greater than 101. What is the value of the smallest integer in the data set if the mean of the entire data set is an integer that is less than the mean of the four integers from the data set shown above?

______

CONTINUE

21 Mark for Review

A teacher awards points to a class based on completed assignments. He gives 5 points per assignment for the first 50 completed assignments and 3 points for each additional completed assignment beyond 50. When $a \geq 50$, which function g gives the total number of points earned by the class for a completed assignments?

Ⓐ $g(a) = 3a + 5$

Ⓑ $g(a) = 3a + 100$

Ⓒ $g(a) = 3a + 250$

Ⓓ $g(a) = 8a - 150$

22 Mark for Review

In triangles ABC and XYZ, $AB = 22$, $XY = 11$, and angles A and X both measure $77°$. Which of the following pieces of information, if any, would be enough to prove that the two triangles are similar to each other?

I. Angle B measures $40°$

II. Angle Y measures $50°$

III. Angle Z measures $63°$

Ⓐ No additional information is necessary.

Ⓑ Angle measures alone do not provide enough information.

Ⓒ I and II together provide enough information.

Ⓓ I and III together provide enough information.

STOP

If you finish before time is called, you may check your work on this module only.
Do not turn to any other module in the test.

SAT Prep, 2025 Edition
Practice Test

The Princeton Review®

YOUR NAME: ____
(Print) Last First M.I.

SIGNATURE: ______________________________ DATE: ___/___/___

HOME ADDRESS: ____
(Print) Number and Street

____
City State Zip Code

PHONE NO.: ____
(Print)

DATE OF BIRTH: ___/___/___
(Print) Month / Day / Year

For both the Reading and Writing and the Math, be sure to only fill in the bubbles for the version of Module 2 that you took. If you took the Easier Module 2, only fill in the answer in the Easier column. If you took the Harder Module 2, only fill in the answers in the Harder column.

Section 1: Module 1 Reading and Writing	Section 1: Module 2 (Easier) Reading and Writing	Section 1: Module 2 (Harder) Reading and Writing
1. (A) (B) (C) (D)	1. (A) (B) (C) (D)	1. (A) (B) (C) (D)
2. (A) (B) (C) (D)	2. (A) (B) (C) (D)	2. (A) (B) (C) (D)
3. (A) (B) (C) (D)	3. (A) (B) (C) (D)	3. (A) (B) (C) (D)
4. (A) (B) (C) (D)	4. (A) (B) (C) (D)	4. (A) (B) (C) (D)
5. (A) (B) (C) (D)	5. (A) (B) (C) (D)	5. (A) (B) (C) (D)
6. (A) (B) (C) (D)	6. (A) (B) (C) (D)	6. (A) (B) (C) (D)
7. (A) (B) (C) (D)	7. (A) (B) (C) (D)	7. (A) (B) (C) (D)
8. (A) (B) (C) (D)	8. (A) (B) (C) (D)	8. (A) (B) (C) (D)
9. (A) (B) (C) (D)	9. (A) (B) (C) (D)	9. (A) (B) (C) (D)
10. (A) (B) (C) (D)	10. (A) (B) (C) (D)	10. (A) (B) (C) (D)
11. (A) (B) (C) (D)	11. (A) (B) (C) (D)	11. (A) (B) (C) (D)
12. (A) (B) (C) (D)	12. (A) (B) (C) (D)	12. (A) (B) (C) (D)
13. (A) (B) (C) (D)	13. (A) (B) (C) (D)	13. (A) (B) (C) (D)
14. (A) (B) (C) (D)	14. (A) (B) (C) (D)	14. (A) (B) (C) (D)
15. (A) (B) (C) (D)	15. (A) (B) (C) (D)	15. (A) (B) (C) (D)
16. (A) (B) (C) (D)	16. (A) (B) (C) (D)	16. (A) (B) (C) (D)
17. (A) (B) (C) (D)	17. (A) (B) (C) (D)	17. (A) (B) (C) (D)
18. (A) (B) (C) (D)	18. (A) (B) (C) (D)	18. (A) (B) (C) (D)
19. (A) (B) (C) (D)	19. (A) (B) (C) (D)	19. (A) (B) (C) (D)
20. (A) (B) (C) (D)	20. (A) (B) (C) (D)	20. (A) (B) (C) (D)
21. (A) (B) (C) (D)	21. (A) (B) (C) (D)	21. (A) (B) (C) (D)
22. (A) (B) (C) (D)	22. (A) (B) (C) (D)	22. (A) (B) (C) (D)
23. (A) (B) (C) (D)	23. (A) (B) (C) (D)	23. (A) (B) (C) (D)
24. (A) (B) (C) (D)	24. (A) (B) (C) (D)	24. (A) (B) (C) (D)
25. (A) (B) (C) (D)	25. (A) (B) (C) (D)	25. (A) (B) (C) (D)
26. (A) (B) (C) (D)	26. (A) (B) (C) (D)	26. (A) (B) (C) (D)
27. (A) (B) (C) (D)	27. (A) (B) (C) (D)	27. (A) (B) (C) (D)

SAT Prep, 2025 Edition
Practice Test

The Princeton Review®

YOUR NAME: ______________________________
(Print) Last First M.I.

SIGNATURE: ______________________________ DATE: ____/____/____

HOME ADDRESS: ______________________________
(Print) Number and Street

____
City State Zip Code

PHONE NO.: ______________________________
(Print)

DATE OF BIRTH: ____/____/____
(Print) Month / Day / Year

For both the Reading and Writing and the Math, be sure to only fill in the bubbles for the version of Module 2 that you took. If you took the Easier Module 2, only fill in the answer in the Easier column. If you took the Harder Module 2, only fill in the answers in the Harder column.

Section 2: Module 1
Math

1. (A) (B) (C) (D)
2. (A) (B) (C) (D)
3. (A) (B) (C) (D)
4. (A) (B) (C) (D)
5. (A) (B) (C) (D)
6. ______________
7. (A) (B) (C) (D)
8. ______________
9. (A) (B) (C) (D)
10. (A) (B) (C) (D)
11. (A) (B) (C) (D)
12. (A) (B) (C) (D)
13. (A) (B) (C) (D)
14. (A) (B) (C) (D)
15. ______________
16. (A) (B) (C) (D)
17. (A) (B) (C) (D)
18. (A) (B) (C) (D)
19. ______________
20. ______________
21. ______________
22. ______________

Section 2: Module 2 (Easier)
Math

1. (A) (B) (C) (D)
2. ______________
3. (A) (B) (C) (D)
4. (A) (B) (C) (D)
5. (A) (B) (C) (D)
6. (A) (B) (C) (D)
7. ______________
8. (A) (B) (C) (D)
9. ______________
10. (A) (B) (C) (D)
11. (A) (B) (C) (D)
12. (A) (B) (C) (D)
13. ______________
14. (A) (B) (C) (D)
15. (A) (B) (C) (D)
16. (A) (B) (C) (D)
17. (A) (B) (C) (D)
18. (A) (B) (C) (D)
19. (A) (B) (C) (D)
20. (A) (B) (C) (D)
21. (A) (B) (C) (D)
22. (A) (B) (C) (D)

Section 2: Module 2 (Harder)
Math

1. (A) (B) (C) (D)
2. (A) (B) (C) (D)
3. ______________
4. (A) (B) (C) (D)
5. (A) (B) (C) (D)
6. (A) (B) (C) (D)
7. (A) (B) (C) (D)
8. (A) (B) (C) (D)
9. ______________
10. (A) (B) (C) (D)
11. (A) (B) (C) (D)
12. (A) (B) (C) (D)
13. (A) (B) (C) (D)
14. (A) (B) (C) (D)
15. (A) (B) (C) (D)
16. (A) (B) (C) (D)
17. ______________
18. (A) (B) (C) (D)
19. (A) (B) (C) (D)
20. ______________
21. (A) (B) (C) (D)
22. (A) (B) (C) (D)

Practice Test 2: Diagnostic Answer Key and Explanations

PRACTICE TEST 2: DIAGNOSTIC ANSWER KEY

Let's take a look at how you did on Practice Test 2. Check your answers and fill in the scorecard below by marking correct answers with a check. Then read the explanations for any questions you got wrong, or you struggled with but got correct. Once you finish working through the scorecard and the explanations, go back to page 10 to review how to make your study plan.

Reading and Writing Comprehension—Module 1							
Q #	Ans.	✔	Chap. # Section	Q #	Ans.	✔	Chap. # Section
1	D		**7,** Vocabulary Questions	15	C		**16,** Pronouns
2	B		**7,** Vocabulary Questions	16	C		**13,** Who or What Are You Talking About?
3	B		**7,** Purpose Questions (Sentence Function)	17	D		**12,** Verb Forms in Complete Sentences
4	A		**7,** Purpose Questions (Sentence Function)	18	A		**14,** How to Connect Independent Clauses
5	D		**7,** Dual Texts Questions	19	A		**16,** Pronouns
6	A		**8,** Retrieval Questions	20	B		**15,** Where Punctuation is Not Needed
7	A		**8,** Retrieval Questions	21	B		**14,** Punctuation with Transitions
8	A		**8,** Main Idea Questions	22	C		**17,** Transition Questions
9	A		**8,** Claims Questions	23	D		**17,** Transition Questions
10	B		**8,** Charts Questions	24	D		**17,** Transition Questions
11	A		**8,** Charts Questions	25	C		**17,** Transition Questions
12	B		**8,** Charts Questions	26	D		**17,** Rhetorical Synthesis Questions
13	D		**8,** Charts Questions	27	C		**17,** Rhetorical Synthesis Questions
14	A		**8,** Conclusions				

Reading and Writing Comprehension—Module 2: Easier							
Q #	Ans.	✔	Chap. # Section	Q #	Ans.	✔	Chap. # Section
1	D		**7,** Vocabulary Questions	15	A		**8,** Conclusions
2	A		**7,** Vocabulary Questions	16	A		**8,** Conclusions
3	C		**7,** Vocabulary Questions	17	D		**12,** Verb Forms in Complete Sentences
4	A		**7,** Vocabulary Questions	18	B		**16,** Pronouns and Apostrophes
5	B		**7,** Vocabulary Questions	19	D		**16,** Pronouns
6	B		**7,** Vocabulary Questions	20	D		**14,** How to Connect Independent Clauses
7	A		**7,** Vocabulary Questions	21	A		**12,** Question or Statement?
8	A		**7,** Vocabulary Questions	22	D		**16,** Verbs
9	C		**8,** Retrieval Questions	23	C		**12,** Verb Forms in Complete Sentences
10	D		**8,** Claims Questions	24	D		**17,** Transition Questions
11	D		**8,** Claims Questions	25	C		**17,** Transition Questions
12	C		**8,** Claims Questions	26	A		**17,** Transition Questions
13	C		**8,** Conclusions	27	A		**17,** Rhetorical Synthesis Questions
14	B		**8,** Conclusions				

Reading and Writing Comprehension—Module 2: Harder							
Q #	**Ans.**	**✔**	**Chap. # Section**	**Q #**	**Ans.**	**✔**	**Chap. # Section**
1	C		**7,** Vocabulary Questions	15	C		**8,** Conclusions
2	B		**7,** Vocabulary Questions	16	A		**8,** Conclusions
3	C		**7,** Vocabulary Questions	17	C		**16,** Verbs
4	D		**7,** Vocabulary Questions	18	B		**13,** Who or What Are You Talking About?
5	A		**7,** Vocabulary Questions	19	A		**16,** Verbs
6	C		**7,** Vocabulary Questions	20	A		**13,** Who or What Are You Talking About?
7	A		**7,** Vocabulary Questions	21	D		**14,** Punctuation with Transitions
8	D		**7,** Vocabulary Questions	22	D		**14,** How to Connect Independent Clauses
9	A		**8,** Retrieval Questions	23	A		**17,** Transition Questions
10	B		**8,** Claims Questions	24	C		**17,** Transition Questions
11	B		**8,** Claims Questions	25	D		**17,** Transition Questions
12	A		**8,** Claims Questions	26	D		**17,** Rhetorical Synthesis Questions
13	A		**8,** Claims Questions	27	B		**17,** Rhetorical Synthesis Questions
14	A		**8,** Conclusions				

Math—Module 1							
Q #	Ans.	✔	Chap. # Section	Q #	Ans.	✔	Chap. # Section
1	B		**24,** What is a Frequency Table?	12	A		**22,** Plug In the Answers (PITA)
2	C		**23,** Equations of a Parabola	13	D		**23,** Function Fundamentals
3	C		**21,** Write Your Own Equations	14	A		**23,** Solving Systems of Equations
4	B		**25,** Triangles	15	25		**22,** Meaning In Context
5	D		**22,** Meaning In Context	16	D		**21,** Growth and Decay
6	$\frac{12}{20}$ or 0.6		**24,** Probability	17	C		**25,** Volume
7	D		**24,** What is Margin of Error?	18	C		**23,** Points of Intersection
8	–4		**21,** Solving Quadratic Equations	19	$\frac{40}{41}$		**25,** Triangles
9	A		**21,** Growth and Decay	20	–2.5		**23,** Equations of a Parabola
10	B		**22,** Plug In the Answers (PITA)	21	10		**23,** Parallel and Perpendicular Lines
11	A		**22,** Plug In the Answers (PITA)	22	2.4		**23,** Points of Intersection

Math—Module 2: Easier							
Q #	Ans.	✔	Chap. # Section	Q #	Ans.	✔	Chap. # Section
1	C		**24,** What is a Median?	12	B		**23,** Function Fundamentals
2	32		**21,** Fundamentals of Digital SAT Algebra	13	118		**25,** Lines and Angles
3	B		**25,** Rectangles and Squares	14	A		**23,** Equations of a Line
4	C		**21,** Fundamentals of Digital SAT Algebra	15	D		**24,** Rates
5	A		**21,** Fundamentals of Digital SAT Algebra	16	B		**21,** Write Your Own Equations
6	B		**21,** Solving Rational Equations	17	B		**23,** Function Fundamentals
7	140		**24,** Percentages	18	C		**23,** Equations of a Parabola
8	A		**24,** Rates	19	D		**23,** Function Fundamentals
9	44		**21,** Solving for Expressions	20	A		**23,** Function Fundamentals
10	D		**23,** Function Fundamentals	21	D		**21,** Fundamentals of Digital SAT Algebra
11	D		**23,** Function Fundamentals	22	A		**25,** Triangles

Math—Module 2: Harder							
Q #	Ans.	✔	Chap. # Section	Q #	Ans.	✔	Chap. # Section
1	A		**21,** Fundamentals of Digital SAT Algebra	12	A		**21,** Fundamentals of Digital SAT Algebra
2	A		**24,** Percentages	13	D		**23,** Equations of a Parabola
3	–120		**21,** Solving for Expressions	14	C		**23,** Graphing Functions
4	B		**21,** Solving for Expressions	15	D		**21,** Solving Quadratic Equations
5	C		**22,** Meaning In Context	16	A		**23,** Equations of a Line
6	D		**24,** Ratios and Proportions	17	12		**21,** Solving Systems of Equations
7	B		**22,** Plugging In Your Own Numbers	18	C		**25,** Triangles
8	B		**21,** Solving Rational Equations	19	B		**23,** Function Fundamentals
9	25		**23,** Equation of a Circle	20	105		**24,** Averages
10	C		**22,** Plug In the Answers (PITA)	21	B		**22,** Plugging In Your Own Numbers
11	A		**23,** Points of Intersection	22	D		**25,** Triangles

PRACTICE TEST 2—READING AND WRITING EXPLANATIONS

Module 1

1. **D** This is a Vocabulary question, as it's asking for a *logical and precise word or phrase.* Read the passage and highlight what can help fill in the blank. The passage states that *the risk of loss of human life in the event of an eruption is minimal,* so the area surrounding Calabozos must not be very inhabited. A good word for the annotation box based on this information would be "isolated."

    - (A) and (B) are wrong because *hazardous* and *active* don't match "isolated."
    - (C) is wrong because *mountainous* is a **Beyond the Text trap**: mountainous regions are often isolated, but the passage does not support that the area surrounding Calabozos has any other mountains besides the volcano itself.
    - (D) is correct because *remote* matches "isolated."

2. **B** This is a Vocabulary question, as it's asking for a *logical and precise word or phrase.* Read the passage and highlight what can help fill in the blank. The passage states that H.D. *wrote in a variety of forms and genres,* yet her contemporaries *focused only on her important contributions to the Imagist movement.* Therefore, a good phrase for the annotation box based on this information would be that the contemporaries' view was "narrow."

    - (A) is wrong because *expansive* is the **Opposite** of "narrow."
    - (B) is correct because *limited* matches "narrow."
    - (C) and (D) are wrong because *imaginative* and *complicated* don't match "narrow."

3. **B** This is a Purpose question, as it's asking for the *function* of a sentence. Read the passage and highlight what can help understand the function of the second sentence. In the second sentence, *Previous studies...have been unsuccessful because these studies relied on human subjects.* In the third sentence, it states that *A recent study by physiologists Yuta Senzai and Massimo Scanziani has avoided this issue by studying dreaming mice instead.* Therefore, the second sentence must be describing an issue that the scientists in the third sentence avoided. Write "explain issue with previous studies" in the annotation box.

    - (A) is wrong because it is the **Opposite** of what the passage supports: *previous studies* ran into a *problem,* but the study by *Yuta Senzai and Massimo Scanziani has avoided this issue.*
    - (B) is correct because it's consistent with the relationship between the second and third sentences.

- (C) is wrong because it is **Half-Right:** the sentence mentions the studies before Senzai and Scanziani's but does not *present the findings* of those studies.
- (D) is wrong because the passage does not discuss anyone interpreting Senzai and Scanziani's study.

4. **A** This is a Purpose question, as it's asking for the *function* of a sentence. Read the passage and highlight what can help understand the function of the third sentence. In the third sentence, it states that *electroreception is not limited to fish.* Write "explain it's not just fish" in the annotation box.
    - (A) is correct because it's consistent with the highlighting and annotation.
    - (B) is wrong because it's **Half-Right:** the fourth sentence explains how monotremes use electroreception, but the earlier sentences do not explain how fish use electroreception, just that they have it.
    - (C) is wrong because it is **Right Answer, Wrong Question:** the fourth and possibly the fifth sentence give more *examples* of animals with electroreception, not the third sentence, which is what the question asks about.
    - (D) is wrong because the passage does not explain *how electroreception evolved* in any of the animals discussed.

5. **D** This is a Dual Texts question, as it asks how the scientists in Text 2 would *most likely respond* to those in Text 1. Read Text 1 and highlight the claim made by Premack and Woodruff regarding a theory of mind: after seeing videos of human actors struggling with various problems, *the chimpanzees were able to select photographs that showed the best tool to solve each actor's problem.* Read Text 2 and highlight Povinelli, Nelson, and Boysen's response to the same idea: *it may be the case that chimpanzees are following learned behaviors in a known environment, rather than applying a theory of mind in a novel situation.* Write in the annotation box for the highlighting in Text 2 that "Text 2 offers an alternate explanation."
    - (A) and (C) are wrong because neither passage discusses any other *nonhuman primates* besides chimpanzees.
    - (B) is wrong because it is **Recycled Language:** it's the human subjects in Text 1 that are described as *struggling* with a problem and Text 2 never suggests that the chimpanzees could solve problems by struggling through the problems on their own.
    - (D) is correct because it would address the scientists in Text 2's main objection to the claim in Text 1: by placing the chimpanzees *in novel environments* that they *would have been unlikely to encounter* previously, Premack and Woodruff could better determine whether the chimpanzees have a theory of mind rather than are just *following learned behaviors in a known environment.*

6. **A** This is a Retrieval question, as it says *According to the text.* Read the passage and highlight what is said about Dorian. The passage mentions that *his cheeks flushed for a moment with pleasure* and *A look of joy came into his eyes* upon seeing his picture. He knows that *Hallward was speaking to him, but* he was *not catching the meaning of his words.* Lastly, *The sense of his own beauty came on him like a revelation.* The correct answer should be consistent with as many of these ideas as possible.

- (A) is correct because it exactly describes what is occurring in the passage. Dorian cannot focus on what Hallward is saying because of the beauty of his own picture.
- (B) is wrong because it is **Extreme Language:** Dorian can't focus on what Hallward is saying, but the passage never goes so far as to state that Dorian thinks it's *unimportant.*
- (C) is wrong because it is the **Opposite** of the passage: not only does Dorian *recognize his own image,* but he is also immensely pleased by it.
- (D) is wrong because nothing about how easily Dorian gets embarrassed is mentioned in the passage.

7. **A** This is a Retrieval question, as it says *Based on the text.* Read the passage and highlight what is said about the children. The passage states that the old forester wondered *What would become of them* (the children)—*living in so sequestered a spot that few even knew of its existence—totally shut out from the world, and left to their own resources?* The correct answer should be as consistent with this description of the children as possible.

- (A) is correct because *isolated from people other than the old forester* is consistent with *totally shut out from the world.*
- (B) is wrong because it is **Extreme Language:** while the forester is worried about what would happen to the children if left alone, the passage does not indicate that the children would be *completely unable* to take care of themselves.
- (C) is wrong because it is the **Opposite** of the forester's feelings towards the children: he feels responsible for them, not *resentful* of them.
- (D) is wrong because it is **Recycled Language:** the answer misuses the word *responsibility* from the passage and never indicates that the children help the forester with his tasks.

8. **A** This is a Main Idea question, as it asks for the *main idea* of the text. Read the passage and highlight the main phrases or lines that all of the other sentences seem to support. The citation states that the author is addressing an unknown person. The opening two lines state that the author will never *hold a place* in this person's (*thine*) heart until the author renounces *all sense, all shame, all grace.* The author also states at the end of the poem that this individual will make an *offer with corrupting*

art / The rotten borough of the human heart. The main idea would be that author's feelings towards this individual in this poem are negative, and the correct answer should be consistent with this.

- (A) is correct because it is consistent with the main idea and *disapproval towards the unknown person* is expressed several times in the poem.
- (B) and (D) are wrong because the poem never states what the unknown person feels towards the author, just what the author feels towards the unknown person. Choice (D) is also **Recycled Language** and warps the meaning of the opening line of the passage.
- (C) is wrong because it is **Recycled Language:** the author is not referring to a literal seat. Rather, the seat is a metaphor for the place the speaker may hold in the unknown person's heart.

9. **A** This is a Claims question, as it asks for what answer would support Soni and his team's claim. Read the passage and highlight the claim made by Soni's team, which is that *administering ketone esters can reduce inflammation and immune system weakening caused by sepsis.*

- (A) is correct because it shows *ketone esters* to be more effective at reducing inflammation and reducing damage to organs (which the passage states are connected to immune system response) than at least one other treatment, *standard antibiotics.*
- (B) is wrong because it does not address the items mentioned in the claim, referencing *blood ketone levels* and *energy* rather than *inflammation* and the *immune system* or *organ damage.*
- (C) is wrong because the passage does not mention *medication intended to reduce fever* or how such medication would affect the performance of *ketone esters.*
- (D) is wrong because it is **Half-Right:** patients treated with *ketone esters* should have *reduced inflammation*, but they should have *less* organ damage, not *greater* organ damage, than those treated with other treatments, such as standard antibiotics.

10. **B** This is a Charts question as it asks about *data from the table* that will complete an example. Read the table first and note the title and terms on the table. Then, read the passage and look for a claim and example that mentions those same terms. The fourth sentence states that *horses with only one handler were less reluctant to interact with the novel object than were horses with multiple handlers.* The example states that *45% of horses with only one handler had no reluctance when interacting with a novel object,* so a good completion of this example would compare that statistic to a statistic regarding *multiple handlers* while remaining consistent with the claim in the fourth sentence.

- (A) and (D) are wrong because they don't mention *multiple handlers,* which are needed to be consistent with the passage's claim.
- (B) is correct because it shows that horses with *multiple handlers* only had *no reluctance* towards interacting with the novel object 25% of the time, whereas horses with only one handler showed no reluctance 45% of the time, making them less reluctant overall as the claim states.

- (C) is wrong because the claim and the first half of the example address no reluctance rather than strong reluctance. It's best to compare two items from the same row or same column to complete comparisons, depending on what the problem is looking for.

11. **A** This is a Charts question as it asks about *data from the table* that will illustrate a claim. Read the table first and note the title and variables. Then, read the passage and look for a claim that mentions those same terms. The fourth sentence states that *starting with the 1989 election, the party which won the largest number of seats failed to win more than half of the total seats.* The final sentence claims that *This trend was eventually broken by the Bharatiya Janata Party.* The correct answer should offer evidence from the table that supports the Bharatiya Janata Party breaking the trend described in the fourth sentence.

    - (A) is correct because it is consistent with the table for those years and shows the Bharatiya Janata Party holding both the largest number of seats *and* a majority of the total seats.
    - (B), (C), and (D) are wrong because none of them mention the Bharatiya Janata Party winning a majority, or *more than half of the total seats,* as stated in the passage.

12. **B** This is a Charts question as it asks about *data from the table* that will support a hypothesis. Read the table first and note the title and terms. Then, read the passage and look for a hypothesis that mentions those same terms. The last sentence states that *A group of researchers...hypothesized that those who take vitamin B12 would experience improvements in fibrosis and insulin resistance when compared to a control group over the same time period.* The correct answer should use data from the table to support this idea.

    - (A) is wrong because it only talks about the control group and not the Vitamin B12 group.
    - (B) is correct because it references both groups and is consistent with the relationship between those groups stated by the claim in the passage.
    - (C) and (D) are wrong because neither mentions the terms *fibrosis* and *insulin resistance* that were referenced by the claim.

13. **D** This is a Charts question as it asks about *data from the table* that will complete a statement. Read the table first and note the title and terms. Then, read the passage and look for a statement that mentions those same terms. The last sentence states that *The localized nature of weather patterns during this event can be seen by comparing Newark, NJ, and New York, NY, with ______.* The correct answer should complete this statement regarding localized weather patterns by showing a difference in mean levels of carbon monoxide in Newark and New York when compared to a more distant city.

    - (A), (B), and (C) are wrong because the mean levels of carbon monoxide shown for Washington, D.C., and Philadelphia, PA, on the dates in each answer are similar or identical to the levels in New York, NY, on those dates. Farther cities from Newark showing similar levels to neighboring cities to Newark would not show the *localized nature of weather patterns during* the smog event.

- (D) is correct because Washington, D.C., shows zero carbon monoxide recorded on those dates, while Newark and New York show positive carbon monoxide level.

14. **A** This is a Conclusions question as it asks for an answer that *logically completes the text.* Read the passage and highlight the main ideas. The passage states that *neurons change how they respond to stimuli based on previous experience* and that *electrical engineers seek to replicate similar processes in their development of computer memory.* Lastly, *electrical engineer Mohammad Samizadeh Nikoo has demonstrated that vanadium dioxide (VO_2) has a similar memory property to that of neurons.* The correct answer should be consistent with these ideas and establish a logical link between them.

    - (A) is correct because it establishes a link between VO_2 from the last sentence and the computer memory that electrical engineers are trying to work on from the second sentence.
    - (B) and (C) are wrong because both are **Recycled Language.** For (B), it's never stated that neurons use VO_2 in any way, just that they have a similar memory property. Choice (C) takes the words *neurons, VO_2,* and *stimuli from sensory organs* and combines them in a way not supported by the passage.
    - (D) is wrong because it uses **Extreme and Recycled Language:** it is VO_2, not neurons, that may be helpful for computer memory. Furthermore, the passage supports this as only a possibility, whereas the answer states that the engineers *can now use* it.

15. **C** In this Rules question, pronouns are changing in the answer choices, so it's testing consistency with pronouns. Find and highlight the word the pronoun refers back to, *books,* which is plural, so a plural pronoun is needed. Write an annotation saying "plural." Eliminate any answer that isn't consistent with *books.*

    - (A) is wrong because *some* doesn't refer back to a specific thing.
    - (B) and (D) are wrong because they are singular.
    - (C) is correct because *they* is plural and is consistent with *books.*

16. **C** In this Rules question, commas and the word *that* are changing in the answers, which suggests that the question is testing the construction of describing phrases. The first part of the sentence says *In 1988, the group worked together to form Action Deaf Youth,* which is an independent clause followed by a comma. Eliminate any answer that isn't consistent with the first part of the sentence.

    - (A) is wrong because a phrase starting with "that" is Specifying and never follows a comma.
    - (B) and (D) are wrong because they both create a run-on sentence.
    - (C) is correct because it creates a Specifying phrase with *that* and no punctuation.

17. **D** In this Rules question, verb forms are changing in the answer choices, so it's testing sentence structure. If the main verb is in the wrong form, the sentence won't be complete. The subject of the sentence is *Her experience*, but there is no main verb, so one is needed. Eliminate any answer that does not produce a complete sentence.

- (A) is wrong because a "to" verb can't be the main verb in a sentence.
- (B) is wrong because it lacks a main verb and thus creates an incomplete sentence.
- (C) is wrong because an *-ing* verb can't be the main verb in a sentence.
- (D) is correct because *inspired* is in the right form to be the main verb and make a complete sentence.

18. **A** In this Rules question, punctuation is changing in the answer choices, so look for independent clauses. The first part of the sentence says *American artist Simone Leigh creates art in various mediums, including sculptures, video, and performance*, which is an independent clause. The second part says *discussing the themes and images in her artwork, Leigh has emphasized that Black women are her primary audience…*, which is also an independent clause. Eliminate any answer that can't correctly connect two independent clauses.

- (A) is correct because a period is appropriately used after an independent clause.
- (B) is wrong because it creates a run-on sentence.
- (C) and (D) are wrong because neither a coordinating conjunction by itself nor a comma by itself can connect two independent clauses.

19. **A** In this Rules question, pronouns are changing in the answer choices, so it's testing consistency with pronouns. Find and highlight the word the pronoun refers back to, *wet-folding*, which is singular, so a singular pronoun is needed. Write an annotation saying "singular." Eliminate any answer that isn't consistent with *wet-folding*.

- (A) is correct because *it* is singular and is consistent with *wet-folding*.
- (B) and (D) are wrong because they are plural.
- (C) is wrong because *one* doesn't refer back to a specific thing.

20. **B** In this Rules question, punctuation is changing in the answer choices. Look for independent clauses. The first part of the sentence says *His 2004 installation The Glassy Surface of a Lake*. The verb (*uses*) comes right after this. A single punctuation mark can't separate a subject and a verb, so eliminate answers with punctuation.

- (A), (C), and (D) are wrong because a single punctuation mark can't come between a subject and a verb.
- (B) is correct because no punctuation should be used here.

21. **B** In this Rules question, punctuation with a transition is changing in the answer choices. The first part of the sentence says *Not all of the styles survived beyond that time.* There is an option to add *however* to this independent clause, and since it is contrasting with the previous idea, eliminate options that don't include *however* in the first part or are incorrectly punctuated.

- (A) is wrong because it doesn't put *however* with the first independent clause.
- (B) is correct because *however* is part of the first independent clause.
- (C) and (D) are wrong because a comma can't be used to connect two independent clauses.

22. **C** This is a transition question, so follow the basic approach. Highlight ideas that relate to each other. The previous sentence says *Calede first compared measurements of the beaver's ankle*, and the next sentence says *Calede dated the species to approximately 30 million years ago.* These ideas are different steps Calede took, so a same-direction transition is needed. Make an annotation that says "agree." Eliminate any answer that doesn't match.

- (A) is wrong because *for example* introduces an example not stated in the passage.
- (B) is wrong because *in conclusion* introduces a conclusion not present in the passage.
- (C) is correct because *next* introduces another step in a sequence.
- (D) is wrong because *in fact* is used to give more detail, which is not present.

23. **D** This is a transition question, so follow the basic approach. Highlight ideas that relate to each other. The previous part of the paragraph says *Male and female American citizens had starkly different roles during World War II* and lists the roles of men, and the sentence in question says *women were responsible for maintaining the home and supporting the men.* These ideas disagree, so an opposite-direction transition is needed. Make an annotation that says "disagree." Eliminate any answer that doesn't match.

- (A) and (C) are wrong because they are same-direction transitions.
- (B) is wrong because *instead* introduces an alternative, but the paragraph discusses the different roles of men and women, not alternative roles for men.
- (D) is correct because *meanwhile* shows that women had different roles during the same time period.

24. **D** This is a transition question, so follow the basic approach. Highlight ideas that relate to each other. The first sentence says *some patients with damaged ear structures are not able to use traditional cochlear implants*, and the next sentence tells what *researchers are working* on as a result of this problem. These ideas agree, so a same-direction transition is needed. Make an annotation that says "agree." Eliminate any answer that doesn't match.

- (A) is wrong because there is no first step in the paragraph.

- (B) is wrong because the last sentence is not an addition to the previous sentence.
- (C) is wrong because *finally* is used to indicate the last step or a conclusion.
- (D) is correct because *hence* suggests that the last sentence is an effect of the previous sentence.

25. **C** This is a transition question, so follow the basic approach. Highlight ideas that relate to each other. The previous sentence says *Her materials are often perishable and biological and are not traditionally used for artwork*, and the next sentence says *Yi spends almost as much time transforming these substances into completely new materials as she does creating the actual art pieces.* These ideas agree, so a same-direction transition is needed. Make an annotation that says "agree." Eliminate any answer that doesn't match.

- (A) and (B) are wrong because they are opposite-direction transitions.
- (C) is correct because *in fact* adds detail to the previous sentence.
- (D) is wrong because the last sentence is not a conclusion.

26. **D** This is a Rhetorical Synthesis question, so follow the basic approach. Highlight the goal(s) stated in the question: *emphasize a difference between the two numeral systems.* Eliminate any answer that doesn't fulfill this purpose.

- (A) is wrong because it states a similarity between the two numeral systems.
- (B) is wrong because it doesn't mention both *numeral systems.*
- (C) is wrong because it doesn't mention a *difference* between the systems.
- (D) is correct because it states differences between the two numeral systems and uses the contrast word *while.*

27. **C** This is a Rhetorical Synthesis question, so follow the basic approach. Highlight the goal(s) stated in the question: *present the Newen Antug study and its conclusions.* Eliminate any answer that doesn't fulfill this purpose.

- (A), (B), and (D) are wrong because they do not include a *conclusion*—what the researchers found.
- (C) is correct because *canoes were used as coffins* is a conclusion.

Module 2—Easier

1. **D** This is a Vocabulary question, as it's asking for a *logical and precise word or phrase.* Read the passage and highlight what can help fill in the blank. The passage states that *Shakespeare intentionally provided no stage directions* as to what should happen in a scene, so it's logical that he meant for *future directors* to use their *own artistic interpretations.* A good word for the annotation box based on this information would be "freedom."

    - (A) and (B) are wrong because *confusion* and *dedication* don't match "freedom."
    - (C) is wrong because it is the **Opposite** of what the passage states—Shakespeare *provided no stage directions.*
    - (D) is correct because *liberty* matches "freedom."

2. **A** This is a Vocabulary question, as it's asking for a *logical and precise word or phrase.* Read the passage and highlight what can help fill in the blank. The passage states that the *fossils were exclusively found in caves in southern China and that anyone claiming to have found the remains of Gigantopithecus elsewhere would be mistaken.* A good phrase for the annotation box based on this information would be "only in" that region.

    - (A) is correct because *restricted to* matches "only in."
    - (B) and (D) are wrong because *eliminated from* and *unknown to* are the **Opposite** of "only in."
    - (C) is wrong because *common in* doesn't match "only in."

3. **C** This is a Vocabulary question, as it's asking for a *logical and precise word or phrase.* Read the passage and highlight what can help fill in the blank. The passage states that *artificial intelligence will not displace human beings* but *will undoubtedly become smarter than people within this generation.* The next sentence calls this *a possibility.* A good word for the annotation box would be that Kurzweil "hypothesizes" what will happen.

    - (A) is wrong because *proves* is **Extreme Language:** it goes too far beyond "hypothesizes."
    - (B) and (D) are wrong because *requires* and *denies* don't match "hypothesizes."
    - (C) is correct because *predicts* matches "hypothesizes."

4. **A** This is a Vocabulary question, as it's asking for a *logical and precise word or phrase.* Read the passage and highlight what can help fill in the blank. The passage states that the Stanford Prison Experiment *supposedly demonstrated* an idea: *supposedly* means that the author does not think the experiment actually demonstrated that idea. The passage also notes that the individuals were of the same background *rather than* representing *a diverse sampling of subjects.* Since all of this supports the point made in the first sentence, a good word or phrase for the annotation box would be "shows" or "is an example of."

    - (A) is correct because *illustrates* matches "shows."
    - (B) and (D) are wrong because *refutes* and *critiques* are the **Opposite** tone of "shows."
    - (C) is wrong because *supersedes,* which means "overrides," doesn't match "shows."

5. **B** This is a Vocabulary question, as it's asking for a *logical and precise word or phrase.* Read the passage and highlight what can help fill in the blank. The passage states that prosopagnosia is also called *"face blindness,"* so a good word for the annotation box would be the "inability" to recognize faces.

    - (A) and (C) are wrong because *capability* and *tendency* are the **Opposite** of "inability."
    - (B) is correct because *incapacity* matches "inability."
    - (D) is wrong because *reluctance* suggests not wanting to do something, which isn't the same as "inability."

6. **B** This is a Vocabulary question, as it's asking for a *logical and precise word or phrase.* Read the passage and highlight what can help fill in the blank. The passage states that the shark has a *competitive advantage…due to electroreception, or ability to detect electrical impulses.* A good phrase for the annotation box based on this information would be "detection ability."

    - (A) and (D) are wrong because *allergy* and *aversion* are the **Opposite** of the shark's "ability" being a *competitive advantage.*
    - (B) is correct because *sensitivity* matches "detection ability."
    - (D) is wrong because *indifference,* which means not having a preference, doesn't match "detection ability."

7. **A** This is a Vocabulary question, as it's asking for a *logical and precise word or phrase.* Read the passage and highlight what can help fill in the blank. The passage states that *cryptographers have yet to demonstrably decipher any portion of the text,* so a good word for the annotation box to describe *the meaning and purpose of the Voynich manuscript* would be "mysterious."

    - (A) is correct because *enigmatic* matches "mysterious."

- (B) and (D) are wrong because *venerable* and *coherent* don't match "mysterious."
- (C) is wrong because it is a **Beyond the Text trap** answer. While *multifarious,* or complex, things can be *mysterious,* the words are not synonyms: mysterious things can be simple and complex things can be quite well known and understood.

8. **A** This is a Vocabulary question, as it's asking for a *logical and precise word or phrase.* Read the passage and highlight what can help fill in the blank. The passage states after the colon that the relationship between the crocodile and bird nourishes *the bird while simultaneously promoting the crocodile's dental health.* A good phrase for the annotation box based on this information would be "mutually beneficial."

    - (A) is correct because *interdependent* matches "mutually beneficial."
    - (B), (C), and (D) are incorrect because *inexplicable* (puzzling), *enthralling* (fascinating), and *inarticulate* (unclear) don't match "mutually beneficial."

9. **C** This is a Retrieval question, as it says *According to the text.* Read the passage and highlight what is said about Captain Vere. The passage states that he is a *sailor of distinction,* was *mindful of the welfare of his men, but never tolerating an infraction of discipline, versed in the science of his profession,* and *intrepid.* The correct answer should be as consistent with these qualities as possible.

    - (A) is wrong because it is the **Opposite** of the passage: Vere is *mindful* of his men's welfare.
    - (B) is wrong because it is **Recycled Language:** this answer misuses *nobility* from the passage, which never states that Vere has an *aristocratic background.*
    - (C) is correct because it is consistent with the Vere's qualities in the passage.
    - (D) is wrong because the passage doesn't state which lifestyle Vere *prefers.*

10. **D** This is a Claims question, as it asks for an illustration of the claim in the question. Read the passage and highlight the claim made, which is that the *poem conveys the speaker's sadness that his life as an adult does not compare favorably to his childhood.*

    - (A), (B), and (C) are wrong because they are all **Half-Right:** each focuses on some element or description from the speaker's childhood but makes no comparisons to the speaker's adult life.
    - (D) is correct because *'tis little joy* is consistent with sadness and *To know I'm farther off from heav'n / Than when I was a boy* is consistent with the speaker's life as an adult not comparing favorably to childhood.

11. **D** This is a Claims question, as it asks for an illustration of the claim in the question. Read the passage and highlight the claim made, which is that *Harker conveys his belief that he has become Dracula's prisoner.*

- (A), (B), and (C) are wrong because while in each of them the speaker expresses negative emotions toward a place *(dread, loneliness, fear)*, none of these answers support the idea that the speaker is *Dracula's prisoner.*
- (D) is correct because the speaker *rushed up and down the stairs, trying every door and peering out of every window* and after this still has a feeling of *helplessness.* This would be the best support toward the idea that the narrator is at least trapped or imprisoned.

12. **C** This is a Claims question, as it asks for an illustration of the claim in the question. Read the passage and highlight the claim made, which states that the *poem is meant to be a plea towards others to join the war effort.*

- (A), (B), and (D) are wrong because none of these answers include any call to an or group to fight or take any action.
- (C) is correct because the answer describes a *torch* that is being thrown to someone from those with *failing hands,* with the hope that the new holder would hold the torch high. These lines best support *a plea towards others* even if they don't directly reference any war effort.

13. **C** This is a Conclusions question as it asks for an answer that *logically completes the text.* Read the passage and highlight the main ideas. The passage states that *The curator of a museum claims* that the dress was worn *at the presidential inauguration in 1865. Radiocarbon dating,* on the other hand, reveals that the *sleeves of the dress...date back to the 1975–2005 period.* If both are assumed to be correct as the passage says, the correct answer to the question must be consistent with both claims.

- (A) is wrong because it is **Recycled Language:** it's applying the *error range of about thirty years* to the year 1865, but the error range is mentioned when discussing radiocarbon dating in a completely separate part of the passage.
- (B) is wrong because it is a **Beyond the Text trap:** as logical as it is that dresses would be recovered more frequently from modern times than from older times, the passage does not state anything to this regard.
- (C) is correct because it shows how both claims could be correct, offering a possible reason for the contradictory statements made by the claims.
- (D) is wrong because the passage never discusses what material was used to make the dress or whether it was different from the materials used for most other dresses.

14. **B** This is a Conclusions question as it asks for an answer that *logically completes the text*. Read the passage and highlight the main ideas. The passage states that *paleontologists largely believed that there were no undocumented prehistoric aquatic species that had survived* to the early 1900s. However, just such a species *was found off the coast of South Africa as recently as 1938*. These two claims indicate that there is indeed at least one undocumented species that survived. The correct answer should be consistent with this idea.

- (A) is wrong because it is **Recycled Language:** this answer mentions *breeding population* from the passage, but no numbers regarding breeding population for the coelacanth are given.
- (B) is correct because the *coelacanth* from the second sentence did indeed go *undiscovered longer than* the 1900's paleontologists expected it would—they had thought there were *no undocumented prehistoric aquatic species* in their era.
- (C) is wrong because the passage never states that the scientists *ignored* any evidence.
- (D) is wrong because it is a **Beyond the Text trap:** it uses outside knowledge of when the dinosaurs went extinct to make an assumption regarding a similar fate for most coelacanths.

15. **A** This is a Conclusions question, as it asks for an answer that *logically completes the text*. Read the passage and highlight the main idea: *The door-in-the-face technique involves initially making an outrageous or unappealing offer, which the other person is likely to refuse, then following up with a more reasonable one.* The concluding sentence to the passage must be consistent with this main idea.

- (A) is correct because the second amount requested is comparatively much smaller than the first.
- (B) is wrong because the first request of 3% is unlikely to be considered *outrageous* when compared to 2%.
- (C) is wrong because according to the door-in-the-face technique in the passage, the more *outrageous* amount should be asked for first.
- (D) is wrong because the two amounts are the same and therefore neither one would be considered *outrageous* compared to the other.

16. **A** This is a Conclusions question, as it asks for an answer that *logically completes the text*. Read the passage and highlight the main ideas. The focus of the passage is on *NAFTA* and its relation to *manufacturing jobs*. During the interval from 1994 to 2020, the second sentence states that *the number of manufacturing jobs in the United States and Canada declined, but the total number of manufacturing jobs in the countries covered by NAFTA increased.* Therefore, a logical conclusion would explain how this might be possible.

- (A) is correct because if an increase in *the number of manufacturing jobs in Mexico*, which is also covered by NAFTA, was greater than the *combined decreases in the United States and Canada*, this would explain the seemingly contradictory data in the second sentence.

- (B), (C), and (D) are wrong because none of them offers a reason as to how the number of manufacturing jobs in the United States and Canada declined, but the total number of manufacturing jobs in all three countries increased.

17. **D** In this Rules question, verb forms are changing in the answer choices, so it's testing sentence structure. If the main verb is in the wrong form, the sentence won't be complete. The subject of the clause is *which*, but the clause has no verb, so the verb in the answers must be the main verb of the clause. Eliminate any answer that does not produce a complete sentence.

    - (A) and (C) are wrong because an *-ing* verb can't be the main verb in a sentence.
    - (B) is wrong because a "to" verb can't be the main verb in a sentence.
    - (D) is correct because it's in the right form to make a complete sentence.

18. **B** In this Rules question, pronouns and apostrophes are changing in the answer choices, so it's testing consistency with pronouns. Find and highlight the word that the pronoun refers back to: *activists*. This is plural, so in order to be consistent, a plural pronoun is needed. Make an annotation saying "plural." Eliminate any answer that isn't consistent with *activists* or is incorrectly punctuated.

    - (A) and (C) are wrong because *its* and *it's* are singular.
    - (B) is correct because *their* is plural and possessive.
    - (D) is wrong because *they're* means "they are."

19. **D** In this Rules question, pronouns are changing in the answer choices, so it's testing consistency with pronouns. Find and highlight the word the pronoun refers back to, *people*, which is plural, so a plural pronoun is needed. Write an annotation saying "plural." Eliminate any answer that isn't consistent with *people*.

    - (A) and (C) are wrong because they are singular.
    - (B) is wrong because *you* is not appropriate to refer to *people* in this context.
    - (D) is correct because *them* is plural and is consistent with *people*.

20. **D** In this Rules question, punctuation is changing in the answer choices, so look for independent clauses. The first part of the sentence says *National flags are designed to best represent and symbolize the individual country*, which is an independent clause. The second part of the sentence says *when countries share a history or culture, their flags are designed to look similar…*, which is also an independent clause. Eliminate any answer that can't correctly connect two independent clauses.

    - (A) and (B) are wrong because neither a comma by itself nor a coordinating conjunction by itself can connect two independent clauses.
    - (C) is wrong because it creates a run-on sentence.

- (D) is correct because a comma + a coordinating conjunction (FANBOYS) can connect two independent clauses.

21. **A** In this Rules question, periods and question marks are changing in the answer choices, so it's testing questions versus statements. The last sentence says *The scientists resolved to find out*, which suggests that the previous sentence was a question. Eliminate answers that aren't correctly written as questions.

    - (A) is correct because it's correctly written as a question.
    - (B) is wrong because it has a question mark but is written as a statement.
    - (C) and (D) are wrong because they are statements.

22. **D** In this Rules question, verbs are changing in the answer choices, so it's testing consistency with verbs. Find and highlight the subject, *shadowing*, which is singular, so a singular verb is needed. Write an annotation saying "singular." Eliminate any answer that is not singular.

    - (A), (B), and (C) are wrong because they are plural.
    - (D) is correct because it's singular.

23. **C** In this Rules question, verbs are changing in the answer choices, so it's testing consistency with verbs. In this case, the verb is part of a list of two things that the beach does, the first of which is *allows community members to connect with the natural world*. Highlight the word *allows*, which the verb in the answer should be consistent with. Eliminate any answer that isn't consistent with *allows*.

    - (A), (B), and (D) are wrong because *provided*, *providing*, and *provide* aren't consistent with *allows*.
    - (C) is correct because *provides* is in the same tense and form as *allows*.

24. **D** This is a transition question, so follow the basic approach. Highlight ideas that relate to each other. The first sentence says *Yoga is an ancient discipline that…has expanded to become popular with many different cultures*, and the next sentence says *yoga is shifting into different forms to allow a wider range of people to participate*. These ideas agree, so a same-direction transition is needed. Make an annotation that says "agree." Eliminate any answer that doesn't match.

    - (A) is wrong because it is an opposite-direction transition.
    - (B) is wrong because the second sentence is not about a separate but similar topic.
    - (C) is wrong because *thus* indicates a conclusion.
    - (D) is correct because *currently* suggests a change, which is consistent with *yoga is shifting*.

25. **C** This is a transition question, so follow the basic approach. Highlight ideas that relate to each other. The first sentence says *Scientists often disagree about what traits to use to place newly discovered species in the tree of life*, and the second sentence describes a species that *is sometimes placed near modern spiders based on its acquisition of silk-spinning organs or near other arachnids based on its loss of a tail.* These ideas agree, so a same-direction transition is needed. Make an annotation that says "agree." Eliminate any answer that doesn't match.

- (A) is wrong because *as a result* suggests a conclusion that is not stated in the passage.
- (B) and (D) are wrong because they are opposite-direction transitions.
- (C) is correct because *Chimerarachne yingi* is an example of the previous sentence.

26. **A** This is a transition question, so follow the basic approach. Highlight ideas that relate to each other. The first sentence says that the seismometer's detection potentially avoided *mass architectural damage*, and the second sentence says *the cut to the power prevented citizens from being caught in a dangerous location during the earthquake and allowed riders to seek shelter.* These ideas agree, so a same-direction transition is needed. Make an annotation that says "agree." Eliminate any answer that doesn't match.

- (A) is correct because allowing *riders to seek shelter* is another way the cut to power was beneficial.
- (B) is wrong because it is an opposite-direction transition.
- (C) and (D) are wrong because the second sentence is an additional point, not an example or specification.

27. **A** This is a Rhetorical Synthesis question, so follow the basic approach. Highlight the goal(s) stated in the question: *make a generalization about the kind of study conducted by Eberhard, Wilcove, and Dobson*. Eliminate any answer that doesn't *make a generalization.*

- (A) is correct because it provides a *generalization about the kind of study* conducted by the scientists: analyzing *population trends to find out the impact of legal protections.*
- (B), (C), and (D) are wrong because they don't provide a *generalization* or a broader way of explaining the type of study.

Module 2—Harder

1. **C** This is a Vocabulary question, as it's asking for a *logical and precise word or phrase.* Read the passage and highlight what can help fill in the blank. The passage states that *all things, living or not, have the inclination to exist and enhance themselves.* A good word or phrase for the annotation box based on this information would be "exist" or "hold on."

    - (A), (B), and (D) are wrong because *deteriorate, perish,* and *disappear* are the **Opposite** of "exist" or "hold on."
    - (C) is correct because *persevere* matches with "exist" or "hold on."

2. **B** This is a Vocabulary question, as it's asking for a *logical and precise word or phrase.* Read the passage and highlight what can help fill in the blank. The passage states that the birds' behavior in the study made it *more difficult for the researchers to obtain data.* A good word for the annotation box based on this information would be "hindered."

    - (A) and (C) are wrong because *aided* and *clarified* are the **Opposite** of "hindered."
    - (B) is correct because *impeded* matches "hindered."
    - (D) is wrong because *exposed* doesn't match "hindered."

3. **C** This is a Vocabulary question, as it's asking for a *logical and precise word or phrase.* Read the passage and highlight what can help fill in the blank. The passage states that the objects that M.C. Escher creates *first appear normal but on closer inspection are, in fact, impossible.* A good phrase for the annotation box based on this information would be "confusing objects."

    - (A), (B), and (D) are wrong because *geometry, beauty,* and *color* don't match "confusing objects."
    - (C) is correct because *paradox* best matches "confusing objects."

4. **D** This is a Vocabulary question, as it's asking for a *logical and precise word or phrase.* Read the passage and highlight what can help fill in the blank. The passage states that *When microdroplets of water hit a solid surface, an electric charge* produces *hydroxyl radicals that in turn combine with remaining oxygen to form hydrogen peroxide.* This information describes a chain of events started by water, so a good phrase for the annotation box would be "likely to trigger something."

    - (A), (B), and (C) are wrong because *viable, contaminated,* and *common* don't match "likely to trigger something."
    - (D) is correct because *reactive* matches "likely to trigger something."

5. **A** This is a Vocabulary question, as it's asking for a *logical and precise word or phrase.* Read the passage and highlight what can help fill in the blank. The passage states that *The Beat Generation* had a *central message of nonconformity,* meaning that they would reject *the traditional values of the 1950s.* A good word for the annotation box based on this information would be "rejection of."

   - (A) is correct because *dissension from* matches "rejection of."
   - (B), (C), and (D) are wrong because *gratitude, adherence,* and *deference* all imply a positive attitude toward or at least an acknowledgment of traditional values, which is the **Opposite** of "rejection of."

6. **C** This is a Vocabulary question, as it's asking for a *logical and precise word or phrase.* Read the passage and highlight what can help fill in the blank. In regard to *recycling used car tires,* the passage states *potentially reusing them would be beneficial* and that *walls made of used tires and dirt* are *structurally robust,* or strong. A good word for the annotation box based on this information would be that the author considers the possibility of recycling used car tires as building materials to be "promising."

   - (A) and (B) are wrong because both *derivative* and *ludicrous* are negative words that are the **Opposite** tone of "promising."
   - (C) is correct because *auspicious* matches with "promising."
   - (D) is wrong because *innovative* is a **Beyond the Text trap** answer: the passage doesn't actually say reusing tires as the passage describes would be a new idea or has not been done before.

7. **A** This is a Vocabulary question, as it's asking for a *logical and precise word or phrase.* Read the passage and highlight what can help fill in the blank. The passage states that *cryptographers have yet to demonstrably decipher any portion of the text,* so a good word for the annotation box to describe *the meaning and purpose of the Voynich manuscript* would be "mysterious."

   - (A) is correct because *enigmatic* matches "mysterious."
   - (B) and (D) are wrong because *venerable* and *coherent* don't match "mysterious."
   - (C) is wrong because it is a **Beyond the Text trap** answer. While *multifarious,* or complex, things can be *mysterious,* the words are not synonyms: mysterious things can be simple, and complex things can be quite well known and understood.

8. **D** This is a Vocabulary question, as it's asking for a *logical and precise word or phrase.* Read the passage and highlight what can help fill in the blank. The passage describes Whitsett's *ground-breaking development* and states that astronautics *owes much to him.* A good word for the annotation box based off this information would be "innovative."

   - (A) and (B) are wrong because *dubious* (doubtful) and *futile* (hopeless) are the **Opposite** tone of "innovative."
   - (C) is wrong because *galvanizing,* which means "stimulating," doesn't match "innovative."

- (D) is correct because *avant-garde* means "pioneering," which matches "innovative."

9. **A** This is a Retrieval question, as it says *Based on the text.* Read the passage and highlight what is said about Mr. Lorry in his interaction with Miss Manette. Mr. Lorry states that he is *a man of business* and *not much else* before telling Miss Manette he wants to tell her a story. After her repetition of the word *story,* the passage states that *He seemed willfully to mistake the word she had repeated* and acts as if she had repeated the word *customers* instead of *story.* The correct answer should be as consistent with these two descriptions of Mr. Lorry as possible.

    - (A) is correct because it is consistent with the description of Mr. Lorry before and after Miss Manette's reply.
    - (B) and (C) are wrong because they are **Half-Right:** In (B), Mr. Lorry does not misunderstand Miss Manette's interjection; he intentionally focuses on a different word. Similarly, in (C), it's never stated that he *cannot keep the details of the story accurate.*
    - (D) is wrong because the passage never indicates that Miss Manette is *rude,* nor does it state that Mr. Lorry is *unthinking* in his actions.

10. **B** This is a Claims question, as it asks what finding would support a claim. Read the passage and highlight the claim made, which is that *Abel claims that his use of Barbeau's text shows how anthropological texts can be used to portray Indigenous people differently based on the author.*

    - (A), (C), and (D) are wrong because they do not contain *different* portrayals of Indigenous peoples.
    - (B) is correct because it focuses on one anthropologist, Marius Barbeau, choosing to portray the chiefs' feud *over constructing the largest pole as unreasonable,* while the *other anthropologists* offer a reason as to why *larger totem poles* may have been culturally important to a tribe.

11. **B** This is a Claims question, as it asks for an illustration of a claim. Read the passage and highlight the claim made, which is that *While adult adoption remains a way for individuals to improve their economic status, the practice has its detractors as well, with some researchers arguing that it can lead to issues with the adoptee developing a firm sense of identity in his or her new environment.* The correct answer should be consistent with this claim and support both the positive and negative viewpoints towards adult adoption.

    - (A) and (D) are wrong because they are **Half-Right:** both express positive opinions toward adult adoptees but fail to account for the negative opinions towards adult adoption stated in the second half of the passage.
    - (B) is correct because it is consistent with both the positive and negative outcomes of adult adoption discussed in the claim.
    - (C) is wrong because the distinction made in the passage is between positive and negative outcomes of adult adoption, not the status of adult adoption in different East Asian countries.

12. **A** This is a Claims question, as it asks for support for a hypothesis. Read the passage and highlight the hypothesis, which states that *tau protein, the mutation of which is known to cause Alzheimer's disease, is key to controlling glutamate receptors.* It's also important to note the last sentence, which clarifies that *Tau protein does not directly affect glutamate receptors but does inhibit NSF.* The correct answer should be consistent with these two sentences.

- (A) is correct because if *an excess of NSF has been shown to lead to abnormal glutamate receptor behavior,* and *tau protein...does inhibit NSF,* this would support the link made between tau proteins and glutamate receptors made in the hypothesis.
- (B) and (D) are wrong because even if true, they either disregard or do not mention *tau protein* and *glutamate receptors,* the main components of the hypothesis.
- (C) is wrong because the hypothesis is not about *what causes mutations of tau protein*, but how tau protein controls glutamate receptors.

13. **A** This is a Claims question, as it asks for support for an argument. Read the passage and highlight Garber's argument, which states that *tulip mania is explainable by fundamental economic concepts such as supply and demand.* The correct answer will be as consistent as possible with this claim.

- (A) is correct because it discusses supply and demand, which is consistent with Garber's claim.
- (B) and (C) are wrong because even though they focus on the price of tulip bulbs, they don't discuss supply and demand.
- (D) is wrong because Garber's argument does not mention any connection between tulip bulbs and the *supply of gold coins in the Dutch republic.*

14. **A** This is a Conclusions question as it asks for an answer that *logically completes the text.* Read the passage and highlight the main ideas. The focus of the passage is on *the use of ants to control pests.* The third sentence identifies *several positive effects*, but the last sentence mentions that *ants also have negative effects.* Therefore, a logical conclusion to the passage should expand upon the negative effects introduced in the final sentence.

- (A) is correct because it references *unintended environmental consequences,* which relate back to the negative effects described in the first half of the last sentence when ants are *used to control pests.*
- (B) and (D) are wrong because they do not focus on *negative effects* that ants may have as pest control.
- (C) is wrong because it is the **Opposite** of what the last sentence states: there are indeed *ramifications*, or negative effects, to using ants as pest control.

15. **C** This is a Conclusions question as it asks for an answer that *logically completes the text.* Read the passage and highlight the main ideas. The focus of the passage is on *a receptor* related to *odor.* The first sentence states that *eliminating that receptor…results in the inability to smell that odor.* The second sentence states that *mosquitoes modified to lack the receptor for smelling blood would be unable to find humans,* but the third sentence says they *were still able to find humans.* Therefore, a logical conclusion to the passage should make some claim about how mosquitoes may be different from other animals.

- (A) is wrong because no comparison between *mosquitoes without damage* and *those with damage* is made in the passage.
- (B) and (D) are wrong because they are the **Opposite** of what is stated in the passage: in both cases, mosquitoes with damage to their odor receptors were still able to find humans, so there is no evidence they could not detect certain odors or would be prevented from feeding.
- (C) is correct because it indicates that mosquitoes may not *have the same correlation between receptors and the ability to sense certain odors* that other animals do.

16. **A** This is a Conclusions question as it asks for an answer that *logically completes the text.* Read the passage and highlight the main ideas. The focus of the passage is on *NAFTA* and its relation to *manufacturing jobs.* During the interval from 1994 to 2020, the second sentence states that *the number of manufacturing jobs in the United States and Canada declined, but the total number of manufacturing jobs in the countries covered by NAFTA increased.* Therefore, a logical conclusion would explain how this might be possible.

- (A) is correct because if an increase in *the number of manufacturing jobs in Mexico,* which is also covered by NAFTA, was greater than the *combined decreases in the United States and Canada,* this would explain the seemingly contradictory data in the second sentence.
- (B), (C), and (D) are wrong because none of them offers a reason as to how the number of manufacturing jobs in the United States and Canada declined, but the total number of manufacturing jobs in all three countries increased.

17. **C** In this Rules question, verbs are changing in the answer choices, so it's testing consistency with verbs. Find and highlight the subject, *cloud,* which is singular, so a singular verb is needed. Write an annotation saying "singular." Eliminate any answer that is not singular.

- (A), (B), and (D) are wrong because they are plural.
- (C) is correct because it's singular.

18. **B** In this Rules question, punctuation is changing in the answer choices. The words *behavioral neuroscientist* are a title for *Damien Fair,* so no punctuation should be used. Eliminate answers that use punctuation.

- (A), (C), and (D) are wrong because a comma isn't used before or after a title.

- (B) is correct because titles before names have no punctuation

19. **A** In this Rules question, verbs are changing in the answer choices, so it's testing consistency with verbs. Find and highlight the subject, *map*, which is singular, so a singular verb is needed. Write an annotation saying "singular." Eliminate any answer that is not singular.

    - (A) is correct because it's singular.
    - (B), (C), and (D) are wrong because they are plural.

20. **A** In this Rules question, punctuation is changing in the answer choices. The words *common insecticide* are a title for *sulfoxaflor*, so no punctuation should be used. Eliminate answers that use punctuation.

    - (A) is correct because titles before names have no punctuation.
    - (B), (C), and (D) are wrong because a comma isn't used before or after a title.

21. **D** In this Rules question, punctuation with a transition is changing in the answer choices. Look for independent clauses. The first part of the sentence says *Wichman's work to preserve the culture of Kaua'i wasn't finished*. There is an option to add *though* to this independent clause, and since it's contrasting with the previous idea, the transition should be added. Eliminate options that don't have *though* in the first part.

    - (A) and (C) are wrong because they create a run-on sentence.
    - (B) is wrong because it puts *Though* with the second independent clause.
    - (D) is correct because *though* is part of the first independent clause.

22. **D** In this Rules question, punctuation is changing in the answer choices, so look for independent clauses. The first part of the sentence says *Researchers studying bacteria have solved a 50-year mystery of how bacteria are able to move using appendages that are made of a single protein*, which is an independent clause. The second part of the sentence says *the subunits of the protein can exist in 11 different shapes…*, which is also an independent clause. Eliminate any answer that can't correctly connect two independent clauses.

    - (A) and (C) are wrong because two independent clauses can't be linked with a comma by itself or with no punctuation at all.
    - (B) is wrong because *while* is used for a contrast or for simultaneous events, which isn't the case here.
    - (D) is correct because a colon can connect two independent clauses and is appropriately used when the second part explains the first.

23. **A** This is a transition question, so follow the basic approach. Highlight ideas that relate to each other. The first part of the sentence says *Fault tree analysis was originally used...in high-risk fields...but other fields are experimenting* with using it, and the second part of the sentence says *fault tree analysis is also being used in low-risk fields*. These ideas agree, so a same-direction transition is needed. Make an annotation that says "agree." Eliminate any answer that doesn't match.

- (A) is correct because *increasingly* supports the change from fault tree analysis's original use to where it is begun to be used.
- (B) is wrong because it is an opposite-direction transition.
- (C) is wrong because the second sentence isn't a conclusion.
- (D) is wrong because the second sentence isn't an additional point.

24. **C** This is a transition question, so follow the basic approach. Highlight ideas that relate to each other. The first part of the sentence says *she had primarily worked on canvas*, and the second part of the sentence says *but she quickly found her works evolving to include the three-dimensional space around her*. These ideas disagree, so an opposite-direction transition is needed. Make an annotation that says "disagree." Eliminate any answer that doesn't match.

- (A) is wrong because *instead* implies that the contrast is between the first and second sentence, but the contrast is between the two parts of the sentence.
- (B) and (D) are wrong because they are same-direction transitions.
- (C) is correct because *previously* is opposite-direction and supports the shift described in the sentence.

25. **D** This is a transition question, so follow the basic approach. Highlight ideas that relate to each other. The previous sentence says *Some scientists believe that the fish are carried to these locations in the beaks or talons of birds*, and this sentence describes what *new research suggests* as a different way the fish travel. These ideas disagree, so an opposite-direction transition is needed. Make an annotation that says "disagree." Eliminate any answer that doesn't match.

- (A), (B), and (C) are wrong because they are same-direction transitions.
- (D) is correct because *alternatively* is an opposite-direction transition.

26. **D** This is a Rhetorical Synthesis question, so follow the basic approach. Highlight the goal(s) stated in the question: *emphasize the aim of the research study*. Eliminate any answer that doesn't fulfill this purpose.

- (A), (B), and (C) are wrong because they don't mention the *aim of the research study*—what researchers wanted to accomplish.
- (D) is correct because it mentions the *aim of the research study* by stating what researchers *wanted to know*.

27. **B** This is a Rhetorical Synthesis question, so follow the basic approach. Highlight the goal(s) stated in the question: *emphasize the affiliation and purpose of Pääbo's and Skov's work*. Eliminate any answer that doesn't fulfill this purpose.

- (A), (C), and (D) are wrong because they don't mention the *affiliation*—the group or institution the scientists are associated with.
- (B) is correct because it states the *affiliation* (*Max Planck Institute for Evolutionary Anthropology*) and *purpose* (*provide insight into human evolution*).

PRACTICE TEST 2—MATH EXPLANATIONS

Module 1

1. **B** The question asks for the frequency table that correctly represents a list of numbers. A frequency table has two columns: the left-hand column contains the values, and the right-hand column contains the number of times each value occurs, or its frequency. Work in bite-sized pieces and eliminate answer choices that do not match the data. The number 2 occurs twice in the list, so its frequency is 2. Eliminate (A) because it shows a frequency of 4 for the number 2. Eliminate (D) because it does not include the number 2 at all. Next, the number 9 occurs three times in the list, so its frequency is 3. Eliminate (C) because it shows the number 3 occurring 9 times instead of the number 9 occurring 3 times. Choice (B) shows the correct frequency for each value. The correct answer is (B).

2. **C** The question asks for an equivalent form of an expression. When given a quadratic in standard form, which is $ax^2 + bx + c$, one approach is to factor it. Find two numbers that multiply to 56 and add to –1. These are –8 and 7, so the factored form of the quadratic is $(x - 8)(x + 7)$, which is (C). When a quadratic is more difficult to factor than this one was, another approach is to use a graphing calculator. Enter the expression given in the question, then enter the expressions from the answer choices one at a time and stop when one of the answers produces the same graph. Using either method, the correct answer is (C).

3. **C** The question asks for an equation that represents a specific situation. Translate the information in bite-sized pieces and eliminate after each piece. One piece of information says that the carpenter *hammers 10 nails per minute*, and another piece says that the carpenter *hammers nails for x minutes*. Multiplying the rate of 10 nails per minute by the number of minutes gives the number of nails:

$\left(\frac{10 \text{ nails}}{1 \text{ minute}}\right)(x \text{ minutes}) = 10x$ nails. Eliminate (A) and (B) because they multiply the number of minutes by $\frac{1}{10}$ instead of by 10. Compare the remaining answer choices. The difference between (C) and (D) is the number on the right side of the equation. Since the carpenter *uses a combined total of 200 nails and screws*, the equation must equal 200. Eliminate (D) because it equals 3,420. The correct answer is (C).

4. **B** The question asks for the value of the measure of an angle on a figure. Use the Geometry Basic Approach. Start by drawing a triangle on the scratch paper. Then label the figure with the given information. Label angle D as 73°, angle E as 35°, and angle F without a number. Since the measures of the angles in a triangle have a sum of 180°, set up the equation $73° + 35° + F = 180°$, which becomes $108° + F = 180°$. Subtract 108° from both sides of the equation to get $F = 72°$. The correct answer is (B).

5. **D** The question asks about a graph representing a certain situation. In a linear graph that represents an amount over time, the y-intercept represents the initial amount. In this case, it represents the amount of plastic remaining to be recycled when $x = 0$. After 0 shifts, no plastic has been recycled yet, so the y-intercept represents the initial amount of plastic to be recycled. The answer is (D).

6. **$\frac{12}{20}$ or 0.6**

The question asks for a probability based on data in a table. Probability is defined as $\frac{\textit{\# of outcomes that fit requirements}}{\textit{total \# of outcomes}}$. Read the table carefully to find the numbers to make the probability. There are 200 total textbooks, so that is the *total # of outcomes.* Of these 200 textbooks, 120 are new textbooks, so that is the *# of outcomes that fit requirements.* Therefore, the probability that a textbook chosen at random is a new textbook is $\frac{120}{200}$. This cannot be entered into the fill-in box, which only accepts 5 characters when the answer is positive. All equivalent answers that fit will be accepted, so reduce the fraction or convert it to a decimal. The correct answer is $\frac{12}{20}$, 0.6, or another equivalent form.

7. **D** The question asks for a reasonable number based on survey results and a margin of error. Work in bite-sized pieces and eliminate after each piece. A margin of error expresses the amount of random sampling error in a survey's results. Start by applying the percent of respondents who did not support the existing registration system to the entire population of undergraduate students. Take 75%

of the entire undergraduate student population to get $\frac{75}{100}(60{,}000) = 45{,}000$ students. Eliminate (A) and (B) because they are not close to this value and do not represent a reasonable number of students who did not support the existing registration system. The margin of error is 4%, meaning that results within a range of 4% above and 4% below the estimate are reasonable. A 4% margin of error will not change the result by very much, and (D) is the only answer choice close to 45,000. To check, calculate the lower limit of the range based on the margin of error, since 43,800 is less than 45,000. To find the lower limit, subtract 4% from 75% to get 71%, then find 71% of the total population to get a lower limit of $\frac{71}{100}(60{,}000) = 42{,}600$. The value in (C) is less than the lower limit, so it is not a reasonable number. Choice (D) contains a value between 42,600 and 45,000, so it is reasonable. The correct answer is (D).

8. **–4** The question asks for a solution to an equation. To begin solving for a, multiply both sides of the equation by a to get $32 = a(a - 4)$. Next, distribute on the right side of the equation to get $32 = a^2 - 4a$. Subtract 32 from both sides of the equation to get $0 = a^2 - 4a - 32$. Now that the equation is a quadratic in standard form, which is $ax^2 + bx + c$, factor it to find the solutions. Find two numbers that multiply to –32 and add to –4. These are 4 and –8, so the factored form of the quadratic is $0 = (a + 4)(a - 8)$. Now set each factor equal to 0 to get two equations: $a + 4 = 0$ and $a - 8 = 0$. Subtract 4 from both sides of the first equation to get $a = -4$. Add 8 to both sides of the second equation to get $a = 8$. Therefore, the negative solution to the given equation is –4. It is also possible to enter the equation into a graphing calculator—using x as the variable—then scroll and zoom as needed to find the x-intercept with a negative value. Using either method, the correct answer is –4.

9. **A** The question asks for a description of a function that models a specific situation. Compare the answer choices. Two choices say the function is increasing, and two say it is decreasing. Since the balloon is rising, its distance above sea level is increasing over time. Eliminate (C) and (D) because they describe a decreasing function. The difference between (A) and (B) is whether the function is linear or exponential. Since the distance above sea level changes by a constant amount during each unit of time, the relationship between the balloon's distance above sea level and time is linear. Eliminate (B) because it describes an exponential function. The correct answer is (A).

10. **B** The question asks for the x-intercept of a function. An x-intercept is a point where $y = 0$. In function notation, $f(x) = y$. The number inside the parentheses is the x-value that goes into the function, or the input, and the value that comes out of the function is the y-value, or the output. Together, they represent points on the graph of the function. The answers are points that could be the x-intercept, so plug in the answers. Start with (A), and plug $x = -1$ and $y = 0$ into the function,

keeping in mind that $f(x) = y$. The equation becomes $0 = (22)^{-1} - 1$. Add 1 to both sides of the equation to get $1 = (22)^{-1}$. Either use a calculator or know how to work with a negative exponent. A negative exponent means to raise the value to the positive exponent and take the reciprocal, so $(22)^{-1}$ becomes $\frac{1}{22^1}$. The equation then becomes $1 = \frac{1}{22^1}$. This is not true, so eliminate (A). Next, try (B) and plug $x = 0$ and $y = 0$ into the function to get $0 = (22)^0 - 1$. Add 1 to both sides of the equation to get $1 = (22)^0$. Any number raised to the power of 0 is 1, so the equation becomes $1 = 1$. This is true, so stop here. The correct answer is (B).

11. **A** The question asks for the length of a side of a geometric figure. Use the Geometry Basic Approach. Start by redrawing the figure on the scratch paper, then label it with information from the question. Since the question asks for a specific value and the answers contain numbers in increasing order, plug in the answers. Write the answers on the scratch paper, label them as "side $\overline{AB}$," and start with a middle number. Try (B) and make $\overline{AB} = 16$. The question states that *the length of $\overline{AB}$ is one-third the length of $\overline{AD}$*. Given this, if $\overline{AB} = 16$, $\overline{AD} = 3(16) = 48$. The perimeter of a geometric shape is the sum of the lengths of the sides, so the perimeter of this figure is $16 + 48 + 16 + 48 = 128$. This does not match the perimeter of 64 given in the question, so eliminate (B). The result was too big, and a longer side length will make the perimeter even bigger, so eliminate (C) and (D) as well. The correct answer is (A).

12. **A** The question asks for a value based on a geometric figure. Use the Geometry Basic Approach. Start by drawing a triangle on the scratch paper, then label the figure with the given information. The question gives the area of the triangle, so write out the formula for the area of a triangle, $A = \frac{1}{2}bh$, and plug in the given area to get $18 = \frac{1}{2}bh$. Since the question asks for a specific value and the answers contain numbers in increasing order, plug in the answers. Write the answers on the scratch paper, label them as "m," and start with a middle number. Try (B), 9. If $m = 9$, the base of the triangle is $9 + 5 = 14$, and the height of the triangle is 9. Plug these numbers into the area formula to get $18 = \frac{1}{2}(14)(9)$. Simplify the right side of the equation to get $18 = 63$. This is not true, so eliminate (B). The result was too big, and a larger value of m will make the area even bigger, so eliminate (C) and (D) as well. The correct answer is (A).

13. **D** The question asks for the equation that represents the relationship between two variables. When given a table of values and asked for the correct equation, plug values from the table into the answer choices to see which one works. According to the table, $s = 2$ when $c = 80$. Choice (A) becomes $80 = (1 + 3)^2$, or $80 = 4^2$, then $80 = 16$. This is not true, so eliminate (A). Choice (B) becomes $80 = (1 + 5)^2$, or $80 = 6^2$, then $80 = 36$; eliminate (B). Choice (C) becomes $80 = 3(1 + 5)^2$, or $80 = 3(6)^2$, then $80 = 3(36)$, then $80 = 108$; eliminate (C). Choice (D) becomes $80 = 5(1 + 3)^2$, or $80 = 5(4)^2$, then $80 = 5(16)$, then $80 = 80$. This is true, so keep (D). The correct answer is (D).

14. **A** The question asks for the number of points of intersection in a system of equations. One method is to use a graphing calculator. Enter both equations into the calculator, then scroll and zoom to see where, if at all, they intersect. The lines appear to be parallel and do not intersect. To solve algebraically, substitute $12x$ for y in the second equation to get $24x + 7 = 2(12x)$. Simplify the right side of the equation to get $24x + 7 = 24x$. Subtract $24x$ from both sides of the equation to get $7 = 0$. This is not true, so the system of equations has no solution. This means the lines are parallel and do not intersect. Using either method, the correct answer is (A).

15. **25** The question asks for a value given a specific situation. Translate the information in bite-sized pieces. The question states that the *equation 15a + 10b = 100 represents the situation when a of the A tiles and b of the B tiles are drawn for a total of 100 points.* Since the sum of $15a$ and $10b$ is the number of points, and a and b are numbers of tiles, 15 and 10 must be the point values of one A tile and one B tile, respectively. To find the number of points earned by drawing 1 of each type of tile, plug in 1 for a and 1 for b to get $15(1) + 10(1) = 15 + 10 = 25$. The correct answer is 25.

16. **D** The question asks for an equation that represents a specific situation. The value of the fund is decreasing by a certain fraction over time, so this question is about exponential decay. Knowing the parts of the growth and decay formula can help with this question. That formula is *final amount* = (*original amount*)(1 ± *rate*)$^{number\ of\ changes}$. In this case, d is the final amount, and the question states that the original amount was \$10,000. Eliminate (A) and (B) because they do not have 10,000 as the original amount in front of the parentheses. Since this situation involves a decrease, the original amount must be multiplied by (1 – *rate*), and the rate here is $\frac{1}{4}$, so the value in parentheses should be $1-\frac{1}{4}$ or $\frac{3}{4}$. Eliminate (C), which does not have this rate. The only remaining answer is (D), and it matches the growth formula. Without this formula, it is still possible to answer this question. Plug in a value of y to see how the fund amount decreases over time. After 1 year, the fund will have $\frac{1}{4}$ less than the initial \$10,000. The value of the account will then be $\$10{,}000-\frac{1}{4}(\$10{,}000)=\$10{,}000-\$2{,}500=\$7{,}500$. After another year, the fund will have

$\frac{1}{4}$ less than \$7,500, so the value will be $\$7{,}500-\frac{1}{4}(\$7{,}500)=\$7{,}500-\$1{,}875=\$5{,}625$. Plug $y = 2$ into the answer choices to see which gives a value of 5,625 for d. Only (D) works. Using either method, the correct answer is (D).

17. **C** The question asks for the measurement of part of a geometric figure. Use the Geometry Basic Approach. Start by drawing a cylinder on the scratch paper, then label the figure with the given information. Look up the formula for the volume of a cylinder on the online reference sheet and write it down: $V = \pi r^2 h$. Plug in the values given in the question for the volume and the height to get $144\pi = \pi r^2(4)$. Divide both sides of the equation by 4π to get $36 = r^2$. Take the square root of both sides of the equation to get $6 = r$. Be careful, and read the final question, which asks for the diameter, not the radius. The diameter of a circle is twice the radius, so $d = 2(6)$, or $d = 12$. The correct answer is (C).

18. **C** The question asks for the value of the x-coordinate of the solution to a system of equations. The quickest method is to enter both equations into a graphing calculator, then scroll and zoom as needed to find the point of intersection. The point is (6, –10), so the x-coordinate, or a, is 6. To solve the system for the x-coordinate algebraically, find a way to make the y-coordinates disappear when stacking and adding the equations. Compare the y-terms: the larger coefficient, 10, is 5 times the smaller one, 2. Multiply the entire first equation by –5 to get the same coefficient with opposite signs on the y terms. The first equation becomes $-5(4x + 2y) = -5(4)$ and then $-20x - 10y = -20$. Now stack and add the two equations.

$$\begin{array}{rcr} -20x - 10y & = & -20 \\ +\ \underline{19x + 10y} & \underline{=} & \underline{14} \\ -x \quad\quad & = & -6 \end{array}$$

Divide both sides of the resulting equation by –1 to get $x = 6$. Using either method, the correct answer is (C).

19. $\frac{40}{41}$ The question asks for the value of a trigonometric function. Use the Geometry Basic Approach. Begin by drawing a triangle and labeling the vertices. The largest angle in a right triangle is the 90° angle, and the largest angle is opposite the longest side, so label angle B as a right angle. The drawing should look something like this:

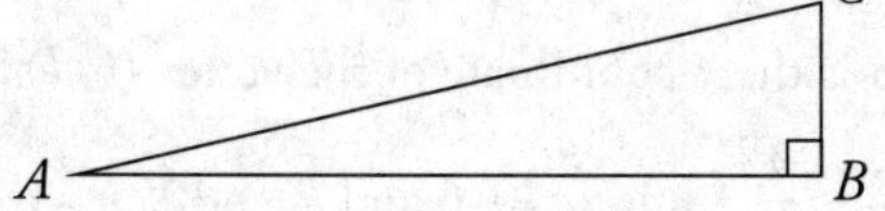

Next, write out SOHCAHTOA to remember the trig functions. The SOH part defines the sine as $\frac{\text{opposite}}{\text{hypotenuse}}$, and the question states that $\sin(A) = \frac{9}{41}$, so label the side opposite angle *A*, which is $\overline{BC}$, as 9 and the hypotenuse, which is $\overline{AC}$, as 41. To find the length of the third side, use Pythagorean Theorem: $a^2 + b^2 = c^2$. Plug in the known values to get $9^2 + b^2 = 41^2$. Square the numbers to get $81 + b^2 = 1{,}681$, then subtract 81 from both sides of the equation to get $b^2 = 1{,}600$. Take the square root of both sides of the equation to get $b = 40$.

With all three side lengths labeled, the drawing looks like this:

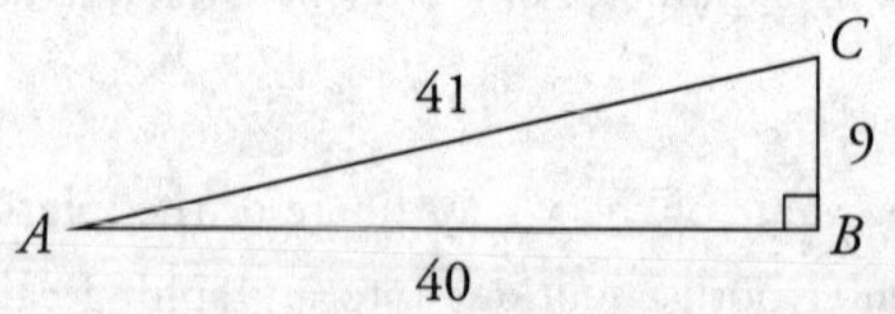

To find sin(*C*), use the SOH part of SOHCAHTOA again. The side opposite angle *C* is 40, and the hypotenuse is 41, so $\sin(C) = \frac{40}{41}$. On fill-in questions, a fractional answer can also be entered as a decimal. When the answer is positive, there is room in the fill-in box for five characters, including the decimal point. In this case $\frac{40}{41} = .\overline{97560}$, which is too long. Either stop when there's no more room and enter .9756, or round the last digit, which in this case is also .9756. It is allowed but not required to put a 0 in front of the decimal point, which would make the answer 0.975 or 0.976, but do not shorten it more than that. The correct answer is $\frac{40}{41}$ or equivalent forms.

20. **–2.5** The question asks for the value when a quadratic function reaches its maximum. A parabola reaches its minimum or maximum value at its vertex, so find the *x*-coordinate of the vertex. One method is to enter the equation into a graphing calculator, then scroll and zoom as needed to find the vertex. The vertex is at (–2.5, 13.5), so the value of the *x*-coordinate is –2.5. To solve algebraically, find the value of *h*, which is the *x*-coordinate of the vertex (*h*, *k*). The equation is in standard form, $ax^2 + bx + c$, in which $h = -\frac{b}{2a}$. Since $a = -6$ and $b = -30$, $h = -\frac{-30}{2(-6)}$. This becomes $h = -\frac{-30}{-12}$, and then $h = -2.5$. Using either method, the correct answer is –2.5.

21. **10** The question asks for the value of a function. The question states that the graph of function f and the graph of function g are perpendicular lines, which means they have slopes that are negative reciprocals of each other. The question gives the equation of line f, so find the slope of that line. This function is in the form $y = mx + b$, in which m is the slope and b is the y-intercept, so the slope of line f is $-\frac{1}{5}$. The negative reciprocal of $-\frac{1}{5}$ is 5, so the slope of line g is 5. In function notation, the number inside the parentheses is the x-value that goes into the function, or the input, and the value that comes out of the function is the y-value, or the output. Together, they represent points on the graph of the function. Thus, if $g(0) = 0$, that means line g contains the point (0, 0). Plug this point into the $y = mx + b$ equation to get $0 = 5(0) + b$, or $0 = b$. Now plug $x = 2$, $m = 5$, and $b = 0$ into $y = mx + b$ to get $y = 5(2) + 0$, or $y = 10$. The correct answer is 10.

22. **2.4** The question asks for a value in a system of equations. Start by simplifying the second equation by multiplying both sides of the equation by 10 to get $y = -10x$. Now that both equations are equal to y, set them equal to each other to get $-10x = 5kx^2 + 2x + 3$. Add $10x$ to both sides of the equation to get $5kx^2 + 12x + 3 = 0$. The question states that the system *has exactly one solution*. To determine the number of solutions to a quadratic, use the discriminant. The discriminant is the part of the quadratic formula under the square root sign, and it can be written as $D = b^2 - 4ac$. When the discriminant is positive, the quadratic has exactly two real solutions; when the discriminant is 0, the quadratic has exactly one real solution; and when the discriminant is negative, the quadratic has no real solutions. Since this quadratic has exactly one real solution, the discriminant must equal 0. The quadratic is now in standard form, $ax^2 + bx + c = 0$, so $a = 5k$, $b = 12$, and $c = 3$. Plug these into the discriminant formula, along with $D = 0$, to get $0 = 12^2 - 4(5k)(3)$, which becomes $0 = 144 - 60k$. Add $60k$ to both sides of the equation to get $144 = 60k$, then divide both sides of the equation by 60 to get $2.4 = k$. The correct answer is 2.4.

Module 2—Easier

1. **C** The question asks for the median of a set of data. The median of a list of numbers is the middle number when the numbers are arranged in order. In lists with an even number of numbers, the median is the average of the two middle numbers. Count to see that there are 7 numbers in the list. Since there is an odd number of numbers, the median is the middle number. Since this list is already in order, cross out one number at a time from each end until only the middle number is left, like so: ~~33~~, ~~34~~, ~~38~~, 41, ~~43~~, ~~44~~, ~~47~~. The middle number is 41, so the median is 41. The correct answer is (C).

2. **32** The question asks for the value of a variable based on an equation. Isolate the variable by moving everything else to the other side of the equation. Since the right side of the equation has –10, add 10 to both sides of the equation. Write this step on the scratch paper like this:

$$\begin{array}{rl} 22 = & y - 10 \\ \underline{+10} & \underline{+10} \\ 32 = & y \end{array}$$

The correct answer is 32.

3. **B** The question asks for the perimeter of a rectangle. Use the Geometry Basic Approach. Start by drawing a rectangle on the scratch paper. Next, label the figure with information from the question. In a rectangle, opposite sides are equal, so this rectangle has two sides that are 23 inches long and two sides that are 9 inches long. The drawing should look something like this:

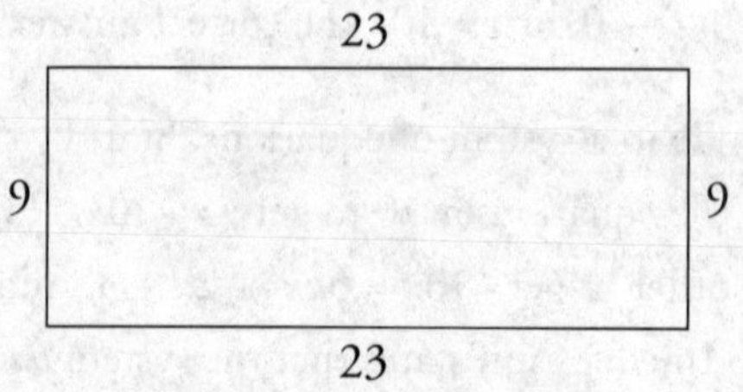

The perimeter of a geometric shape is the sum of the lengths of the sides. Add all four side lengths to get $9 + 23 + 9 + 23 = 64$. The correct answer is (B).

4. **C** The question asks for an equivalent form of an expression. Every term includes the variable *a* multiplied by a different number, called a coefficient. Work with the coefficients, and remember the order of operations, PEMDAS, which stands for Parentheses, Exponents, Multiply, Divide, Add, Subtract. Start inside the parentheses: $6a - 2a = 4a$. The expression becomes $15a - 4a$. Subtract the coefficients to get $15a - 4a = 11a$. The correct answer is (C).

5. **A** The question asks for an equation that represents the relationship between two variables. Translate the English to math in bite-sized pieces. Translate *is* as equals, or =. Translate *half* as $\frac{1}{2}$. Translate *of* as times, or ×. Thus, *a is half of b* translates to $a = \frac{1}{2} \times b$. The multiplication sign is not needed when multiplying a number by a variable, so this can be written as $a = \frac{1}{2}b$. The correct answer is (A).

6. **B** The question asks for the value of a constant given two equivalent expressions. Start by rewriting the expressions with an equals sign between them to get $\frac{3}{y+c}=\frac{15}{5y+30}$. Next, start to solve by cross-multiplying. The equation becomes $(y + c)(15) = (3)(5y + 30)$. Distribute on both sides of the equation to get $15y + 15c = 15y + 90$. Subtract $15y$ from both sides of the equation to get $15c = 90$. Divide both sides of the equation by 15 to get $c = 6$. The correct answer is (B).

7. **140** The question asks for a value based on a percentage. Translate the English to math in bite-sized pieces. *Percent* means out of 100, so translate 70% as $\frac{70}{100}$. Translate *how many* as a variable, such as d for dogs. Translate *of* as times, or ×. Translate *the pets* as 200. The equation becomes $d=\left(\frac{70}{100}\right)(200)$. Solve the equation by hand or on a calculator to get $d = 140$. The correct answer is 140.

8. **A** The question asks for a value given a rate. Begin by reading the question to find information about the rate. The question states that James *drives at an average speed of 20 miles per hour.* Set up a proportion to determine how many hours it will take James to drive 100 miles. The proportion is $\frac{20\text{ miles}}{1\text{ hour}}=\frac{100\text{ miles}}{x\text{ hours}}$. Cross-multiply to get $(1)(100) = (20)(x)$, or $100 = 20x$. Divide both sides of the equation by 20 to get $5 = x$. The correct answer is (A).

9. **44** The question asks for the value of an expression given an equation. When an SAT question asks for the value of an expression, there is usually a straightforward way to solve for the expression without needing to completely isolate the variable. Since $4y$ is four times y and 16 is four times 4, multiply the entire equation by 4 to get $(4)(y - 4) = (4)(11)$. The equation becomes $4y - 16 = 44$. The correct answer is 44.

10. **D** The question asks for the value of a function. In function notation, $f(x) = y$. The number inside the parentheses is the x-value that goes into the function, or the input, and the value that comes out of the function is the y-value, or the output. The question provides an input value, so plug $x = 3$ into the function to get $g(3) = 3^2 - 1$, which becomes $g(3) = 9 - 1$, and then $g(3) = 8$. The correct answer is (D).

11. **D** The question asks for the value of a function. In function notation, $f(x) = y$. The number inside the parentheses is the x-value that goes into the function, or the input, and the value that comes out of the function is the y-value, or the output. The question provides the number of items, which is represented by x, so plug $x = 2{,}000$ into the function to get $p(2{,}000) = 2(2{,}000) + 150$, which becomes $p(2{,}000) = 4{,}000 + 150$, and then $p(2{,}000) = 4{,}150$. The correct answer is (D).

12. **B** The question asks for the value of a function. In function notation, $f(x) = y$. The number inside the parentheses is the x-value that goes into the function, or the input, and the value that comes out of the function is the y-value, or the output. The question provides an input value, so plug $x = 6$ into the function to get $f(6) = \frac{2}{3}(6)$, which becomes $f(6) = 4$. The correct answer is (B).

13. **118** The question asks for the value of an angle on a figure. Use the Geometry Basic Approach. Start by redrawing the figure on the scratch paper, then label the figure with the given information. The fact that two of the lines are parallel will be important on some questions about lines and angles, but here it's unnecessary information. Instead, since d and 62 make up a straight line and there are 180° in a line, $d + 62 = 180$. Subtract 62 from both sides of the equation to get $d = 118$. The correct answer is 118.

14. **A** The question asks for the value of an expression given the equation of a graph in the xy-plane. One method is to use a graphing calculator. Enter the equation of the line, then scroll and zoom as needed to find the intercepts. The x-intercept is at (5.667, 0), and the y-intercept is at (0, –4.25). Thus, $c = 5.667$, $k = -4.25$, and $\frac{c}{k} = \frac{5.667}{-4.25} = -1.33$. This is the same value as $-\frac{4}{3}$, which matches (A). To solve algebraically, plug the given points into the equation of the line. Plug in $x = c$ and $y = 0$ to get $3c - 4(0) = 17$, or $3c = 17$. Divide both sides of the equation by 3 to get $c = \frac{17}{3}$. Next, plug in $x = 0$ and $y = k$ to get $3(0) - 4k = 17$, or $-4k = 17$. Divide both sides of the equation by -4 to get $k = -\frac{17}{4}$. Finally divide c by k to get $\frac{c}{k} = \frac{\frac{17}{3}}{-\frac{17}{4}}$. When dividing fractions, multiply the reciprocal of the fraction in the denominator and the fraction in the numerator. This becomes $\frac{c}{k} = \left(\frac{17}{3}\right)\left(-\frac{4}{17}\right)$, and then $\frac{c}{k} = -\frac{4}{3}$. Using either method, the correct answer is (A).

15. **D** The question asks for a value given a rate. Begin by reading the question to find information about the rate. The question states that the machine *processes mail at a constant rate of 21 pieces of mail per minute.* Set up a proportion to determine how many pieces of mail the machine will process in 7 minutes, being sure to match up units. The proportion is $\frac{\text{21 pieces of mail}}{\text{1 minute}} = \frac{x\text{ pieces of mail}}{\text{7 minutes}}$. Cross-multiply to get $(1)(x) = (21)(7)$, or $x = 147$. The correct answer is (D).

16. **B** The question asks for an equation that represents a specific situation. Translate the information in bite-sized pieces and eliminate after each piece. One piece of information says that Stella will send 24 invitations *each day for the next d days*. Since d represents the number of days, it should be multiplied by 24. Eliminate (C) and (D) because they multiply d by 43 instead of 24. Compare the remaining answer choices. The difference between (A) and (B) is whether 43 is added to $24d$ or subtracted from $24d$. Since Stella *has already sent 43 invitations* and will send a total of 211 invitations, 43 should be added to $24d$ and set equal to 211. Eliminate (A) because it uses subtraction. The correct answer is (B).

17. **B** The question asks for the function that represents values given in a table. In function notation, the number inside the parentheses is the x-value that goes into the function, or the input, and the value that comes out of the function is the y-value, or the output. Together, they represent points on the graph of the function. The table shows pairs of values for x and $f(x)$, and the correct function must work for every point on the graph. Plug in values from the table and eliminate functions that don't work. Try the point (0, 15) and plug $x = 0$ and $f(x) = 15$ into the answer choices. Choice (A) becomes $15 = 3(0) + 12$, or $15 = 12$. This is not true, so eliminate (A). Choice (B) becomes $15 = 3(0) + 15$, or $15 = 15$. This is true, so keep (B), but check the remaining answers just in case. Choice (C) becomes $15 = 15(0) + 12$, or $15 = 12$; eliminate (C). Choice (D) becomes $15 = 15(0) + 15$, or $15 = 15$; keep (D). Two answers worked for the first point, so try a second point from the table and plug $x = 1$ and $f(x) = 18$ into the remaining answers. Choice (B) becomes $18 = 3(1) + 15$, or $18 = 18$; keep (B). Choice (D) becomes $18 = 15(1) + 15$, or $18 = 30$; eliminate (D). The correct answer is (B).

18. **C** The question asks for the term in an equation that represents a specific part of a scenario. The question states that s represents *the number of seconds since the rocket was launched* and asks for the height when the rocket was launched. No time had elapsed at the instant the rocket was launched, so plug $s = 0$ into the equation. The equation becomes $h = -16(0)^2 + 64(0) + 21$. Simplify the right side of the equation to get $h = 0 + 0 + 21$, or $h = 21$. Since the height at the time of 0 seconds is 21 feet, that number represents the initial height, or the height of the rooftop. The correct answer is (C).

19. **D** The question asks for correct values in a function. In function notation, $f(x) = y$. The number inside the parentheses is the x-value that goes into the function, or the input, and the value that comes out of the function is the y-value, or the output. When given a function and asked for the table of values, plug values from the answer choices into the function and eliminate answers that don't work. Start with $x = 2$ because two answers pair it with $y = 3$ and two pair it with $y = 9$, so this will eliminate half of the answer choices. Plug $x = 2$ into the function to get $f(2) = 2^3 + 1$, which becomes $f(2) = 8 + 1$, and then $f(2) = 9$. Eliminate (A) and (B) because they both have $y = 3$ for this x value. The third pair of values is the same in (C) and (D), so try the second pair of values and plug $x = 3$ into the function. The function becomes $f(3) = 3^3 + 1$, then $f(3) = 27 + 1$, and then $f(3) = 28$. Eliminate (C). The correct answer is (D).

20. **A** The question asks for the equation that defines a function. In function notation, the number inside the parentheses is the x-value that goes into the function, or the input, and the value that comes out of the function is the y-value, or the output. The question provides two pairs of input and output values, so plug those into the answer choices and eliminate answers that don't work with both pairs. Start by plugging $x = -1$ and $h(x) = 3$ into the answer choices. Choice (A) becomes $3 = 2(-1) + 5$, then $3 = -2 + 5$, and then $3 = 3$. This is true, so try the second pair of values in (A). Plug in $x = 0$ and $h(x) = 5$ and the function becomes $5 = 2(0) + 5$, then $5 = 0 + 5$, and then $5 = 5$. This is also true. Since both pairs work in the function defined by (A), it is the correct function. The correct answer is (A).

21. **D** The question asks for an equation in terms of a specific variable. The question asks about the relationship among variables and there are variables in the answer choices, so plugging in is a good option. That might get messy with three variables, and all of the answer choices have r by itself, so the other option is to solve for r. To begin to isolate r, add $6s$ to both sides of the equation to get $p + 6s = 13r$. Divide both sides of the equation by 13 to get $\frac{p+6s}{13} = r$. Flip the sides of the equation to get $r = \frac{p+6s}{13}$. The correct answer is (D).

22. **A** The question asks for the value of a trigonometric function. Use the Geometry Basic Approach. Start by drawing two right triangles that are similar to each other, meaning they have the same proportions but are different sizes. Be certain to match up the corresponding angles that are given in the question, and put the longest side opposite the right angle. Then label the sides of triangle *ABC* with the lengths given in the question. The drawing should look something like this:

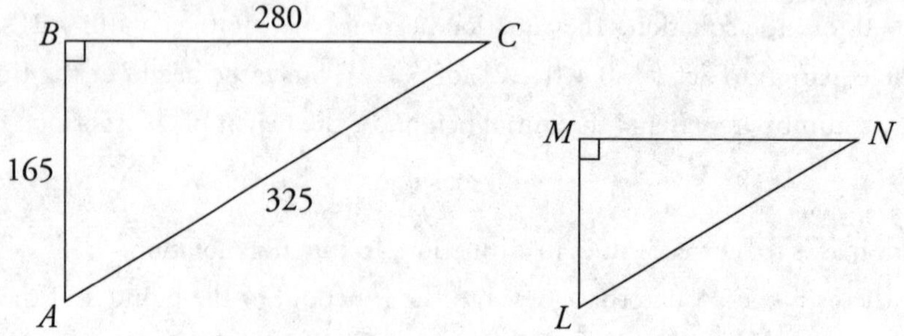

The question asks for the cosine of angle L, which corresponds to angle A. Trig functions are proportional so $\cos(L) = \cos(A)$, and it is possible to answer the question without knowing any of the side lengths of triangle *LMN*. To find $\cos(A)$, use SOHCAHTOA to remember the trig functions and label the sides. The CAH part of the acronym defines the cosine as $\frac{\text{adjacent}}{\text{hypotenuse}}$. The side adjacent to A is 165, and the hypotenuse is 325, so $\cos(A) = \frac{165}{325}$. Since $\cos(L) = \cos(A)$, $\cos(L)$ is also $\frac{165}{325}$. To match the result with an answer choice, either use a calculator to find the decimal equivalent or reduce the fraction. Using a calculator, $\frac{165}{325} \approx 0.5077$ and $\frac{33}{65} \approx 0.5077$. To reduce the fraction, notice that both numbers are multiples of 5, and divide the numerator and denominator by 5 to get $\cos(L) = \frac{33}{65}$. Either way, the correct answer is (A).

Module 2—Harder

1. **A** The question asks for an equivalent form of an expression. Use Bite-Sized Pieces and the Process of Elimination to tackle this question. The only term with a single a is $6a$, so it cannot be combined with any other terms and must appear in the correct answer. Eliminate (B) and (C) because they do not include $6a$. Combine the two terms with a^3 to get $3a^3 - 5a^3 = -2a^3$. Eliminate (D) because it does not include $-2a^3$. The correct answer is (A).

2. **A** The question asks for a percent based on the information provided. Start by ballparking: 10% of 45,000,000 is 4,500,000, so 4,950,000 is a little more than 10%. Eliminate (C) and (D) because they are much too large. Choice (A) is likely correct, but to check, plug in 11%. *Percent* means out of 100, so 11% can be represented as $\frac{11}{100}$. Multiply this by the total number of shirts to get $\frac{11}{100}(45{,}000{,}000) = 4{,}950{,}000$. This matches the number of white shirts given in the question. The correct answer is (A).

3. **–120** The question asks for the value of an expression based on an equation. When a Digital SAT question asks for the value of an expression, there is usually a straightforward way to solve for the expression without needing to completely isolate the variable. Start solving by distributing the numbers outside the parentheses on both sides of the equation. The equation becomes $3x - 24 - 16 = 8x + 80 + x$. Simplify both sides of the equation to get $3x - 40 = 9x + 80$. Subtract $3x$ from both sides of the equation to get $-40 = 6x + 80$, then subtract 80 from both sides of the equation to get $-120 = 6x$. The question asked for the value of $6x$, so stop here. The correct answer is –120.

4. **B** The question asks for the value of an expression based on an equation. When a Digital SAT question asks for the value of an expression, there is usually a straightforward way to solve for the expression without needing to completely isolate the variable. Start by subtracting $8(a - 3)$ from both sides of the equation to get $-17 = 9(a - 3) - 8(a - 3)$. Combine the terms with $(a - 3)$ to get $-17 = (9 - 8)(a - 3)$, which becomes $-17 = 1(a - 3)$, or $-17 = a - 3$. The correct answer is (B).

5. **C** The question asks for the meaning of a constant in context. Start by reading the final question, which asks for the meaning of the constant *b*. Then label the parts of the equation with the information given. The question states that the lab area is 30 square feet, the seating area is 80 square feet, and the total number of floor tiles is 4,200. Rewrite the equation with these labels: (lab area size)(a) + (seating area size)(b) = total tiles. Next, use Process of Elimination to get rid of answer choices that are not consistent with the labels. Since b is multiplied by the size of the seating area, eliminate (A) and (B) because they refer to the lab area, not the seating area. Compare the remaining answer choices. The difference is between the average number of tiles and the total number of tiles. Since b is multiplied by the number of square feet in the seating area, it must represent a value per square foot, not a total value. Keep (C) because it is consistent with this information, and eliminate (D) because it refers to a total number. The correct answer is (C).

6. **D** The question asks for the change in a value given a proportion. Use the Geometry Basic Approach. Start by drawing two triangles, one with a smaller base than the other. The question asks about the height, so draw a line for the height. This figure should look something like this:

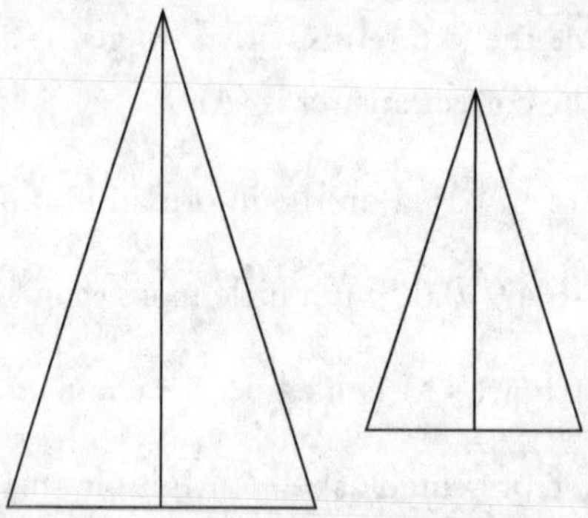

Next, label the figure with the information given. Since no specific numbers are given for the base and the height, plug in. Make the height of the larger triangle 100, so the base would be 65% of 100 or just 65. If the base decreases by 13 inches, the new base would be 65 – 13 = 52 inches.

Label this information on the figure, which now looks like this:

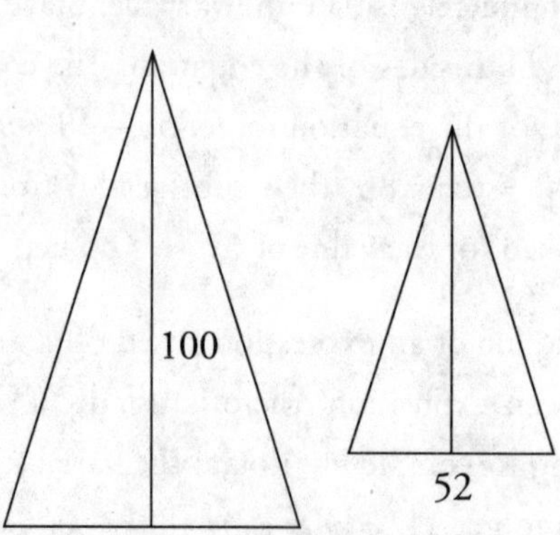

Since the base is smaller and the proportions stay the same, the height must also be smaller. Eliminate (A) and (B) because they would both make the height larger. To find the length of the new height, set up a proportion for $\frac{\text{base}}{\text{height}}:\frac{65}{100}=\frac{52}{x}$. Cross-multiply to get (100)(52) = (65)(x). Simplify both sides of the equation to get 5,200 = 65x. Divide both sides of the equation by 65 to get 80 = x. Since the original height was 100, the change is 100 – 80 = 20. The new height is less than the original height, so it decreased by 20. The correct answer is (D).

7. **B** The question asks for an equation in terms of a specific variable. Since the question is about the relationship between variables and the answers contain variables, plug in. The fraction on the left side of the equation could make the numbers awkward, so start on the right side of the equation and make b = 2. The equation becomes $\frac{a}{3}=10-7(2)$, then $\frac{a}{3}=10-14$, and then $\frac{a}{3}=-4$. Multiply both sides of the equation by 3 to get a = –12. Now plug a = –12 and b = 2 into the answer choices and eliminate any that do not work. Choice (A) becomes $2=\frac{-12-21}{30}$, then $2=-\frac{33}{30}$. This is not true, so eliminate (A). Choice (B) becomes $2=\frac{30-(-12)}{21}$, then $2=\frac{42}{21}$, and then 2 = 2. This is true, so keep (B), but check the remaining answers just in case. Choice (C) becomes $2=10+\frac{-12}{3}$, then 2 = 10 + (–4), and then 2 = 6; eliminate (C). Choice (D) becomes $2=10+\frac{3}{-12}$, then $2=10+\left(-\frac{1}{4}\right)$, and then $2=9\frac{3}{4}$; eliminate (D). The correct answer is (B).

8. **B** The question asks for the value of a constant given two equivalent expressions. Start by rewriting the expressions with an equal sign between them to get $\frac{3}{y+c}=\frac{15}{5y+30}$. Next, start to solve by cross-multiplying. The equation becomes (y + c)(15) = (3)(5y + 30). Distribute on both sides of the equation to get 15y + 15c = 15y + 90. Subtract 15y from both sides of the equation to get 15c = 90. Divide both sides of the equation by 15 to get c = 6. The correct answer is (B).

9. **25** The question asks for the value of a constant, given information about circles in the coordinate plane. The equation of a circle in standard form is $(x-h)^2+(y-k)^2=r^2$, where (h, k) is the center and r is the radius. In the equation given for circle O, r^2 = 64. Take the square root of both sides of the equation to get r = 8. The question states that *the radius of circle P is three less than the radius of circle O,* so the radius of circle P is 8 – 3 = 5. Plug r = 5 into the equation of circle P to get $(x-7)^2+(y+7)^2=5^2$, or $(x-7)^2+(y+7)^2=25$. Thus, c = 25. The correct answer is 25.

10. **C** The question asks for a maximum value given a specific situation. Since the question asks for a specific value and the answers contain numbers in increasing order, plug in the answers. Rewrite the answer choices on the scratch paper and label them "number of laptops." Next, pick a value to start with. Since the question asks for the maximum, start with the largest number, 146. The question states that *each laptop costs $149*, so multiply that by the number of laptops to get (\$149)(146) = \$21,754. The question also states that there is *a 7.5% discount on orders of at least 100 laptops.* Since 146 is more than 100, the discount applies. Take 7.5% of the cost and subtract the result from the cost to get $\$21,754-\left(\frac{7.5}{100}\right)(\$21,754)=\$20,122.45$. This is greater than the donation of \$20,000, so eliminate (D). The result was close, so plug in the next largest value, 145, for the number of laptops. The initial cost becomes (\$149)(145) = \$21,605. Apply the 7.5% discount to get $\$21,605-\left(\frac{7.5}{100}\right)(\$21,605)\approx\$19,984.63$. This is less than the donation of \$20,000, so the school can purchase 145 laptops. The correct answer is (C).

11. **A** The question asks for the value of the x-coordinate of the solution to a system of equations. The quickest method is to enter both equations into a graphing calculator, then scroll and zoom as needed to find the points of intersection. The graph shows two points of intersection: (3, 1) and (–4, 22), so the x-coordinate is either 3 or –4. Only –4 is in an answer choice, so choose (A). To solve the system for the x-coordinate algebraically, substitute $-3x + 10$ for y in the first equation to get $3x^2 - (-3x + 10) - 26 = 0$. Distribute the negative sign to get $3x^2 + 3x - 10 - 26 = 0$, then combine like terms to get $3x^2 + 3x - 36 = 0$. Factor out 3 to get $3(x^2 + x - 12) = 0$. Factor the quadratic to get $3(x + 4)(x - 3) = 0$. Set each factor equal to 0 and solve to get $x = -4$ and $x = 3$. Using either method, the correct answer is (A).

12. **A** The question asks for the number of solutions to an equation. Distribute on both sides of the equation to get $-24y - 12 = 12 - 24y$. Add $24y$ to both sides of the equation to get $-12 = 12$. This is not true, so the equation has no solutions. The correct answer is (A).

13. **D** The question asks for an x-intercept of a parabola. Sketch a graph using the given points, and label those points. The vertex of a parabola is on the axis of symmetry, so the axis of symmetry of this parabola is the line $x = 5$; add this line to the graph. The graph should look something like this:

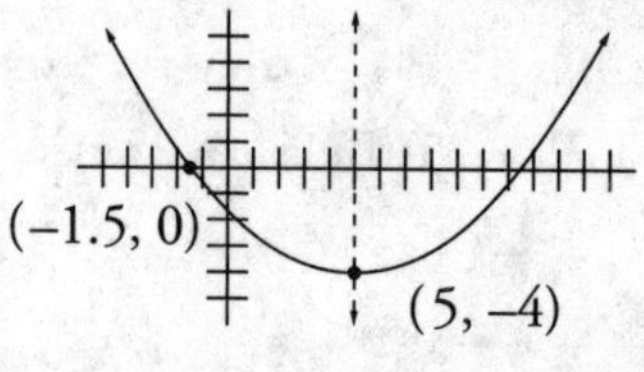

The two x-intercepts are an equal distance from the line of symmetry. The x-coordinate of the given x-intercept is –1.5, so the distance from the line of symmetry is $5 - (-1.5) = 6.5$. The x-coordinate of the other x-intercept is thus $5 + 6.5 = 11.5$. The correct answer is (D).

14. **C** The question asks for an equation that represents a graph. To find the best equation, compare features of the graph to the answer choices. The answer choices all take the form $y = mx + b$, in which m is the slope and b is the y-intercept. All of the answer choices have the same slope, so focus on the y-intercept. The graph shown in the question has been transformed from the graph of function g. Adding or subtracting outside the parentheses shifts the graph up or down. Thus, the given graph of $g(x) - 10$ is shifted 10 units down from the graph of $g(x)$. Undo this by adding 10 to transform the given graph back to $g(x)$. The graph of $g(x) - 10$ has its y-intercept at (0, –5). Move the point up 10 units to get a y-intercept of (0, 5). Eliminate (A), (B), and (D) because the equations have the wrong y-intercept. The correct answer is (C).

15. **D** The question asks for the value of a constant in a quadratic equation. To determine when a quadratic equation has no real solutions, use the discriminant. The discriminant is the part of the quadratic formula under the square root sign and is written as $D = b^2 - 4ac$. When the discriminant is positive, the quadratic has exactly two real solutions; when the discriminant is 0, the quadratic has exactly one real solution; and when the discriminant is negative, the quadratic has no real solutions. Thus, the discriminant of this quadratic must equal a negative number. First, put the quadratic in standard form, which is $ax^2 + bx + c = 0$, by adding $5x$ to both sides of the equation to get $10x^2 + 5x + c = 0$. Now $a = 10$, $b = 5$, and $c = c$. Plug these into the discriminant formula to get $D = (5)^2 - 4(10)(c)$, or $D = 25 - 40c$. Next, plug in the values from the answer choices to see which value of c makes the discriminant negative. Start with a middle answer and try (C), 0. If $c = 0$, the discriminant becomes $D = 25 - 40(0)$, or $D = 25$. This is not negative, so eliminate (C). It might not be clear whether a larger or smaller number is needed, so pick a direction and try (D), 1. If $c = 1$, the discriminant becomes $D = (5)^2 - (4)(10)(1)$, or $D = 25 - 40$, and then $D = -15$. This is negative, so stop here. The correct answer is (D).

16. **A** The question asks for the value of an expression given the equation of a graph in the xy-plane. One method is to use a graphing calculator. Enter the equation of the line, then scroll and zoom as needed to find the intercepts. The x-intercept is at (5.667, 0), and the y-intercept is at (0, –4.25). Thus, $c = 5.667$, $k = -4.25$, and $\frac{c}{k} = \frac{5.667}{-4.25} = -1.33$. This is the same value as $-\frac{4}{3}$, which matches (A). To solve algebraically, plug the given points into the equation of the line. Plug in $x = c$ and $y = 0$ to get $3c - 4(0) = 17$, or $3c = 17$. Divide both sides of the equation by 3 to get $c = \frac{17}{3}$. Next,

plug in $x = 0$ and $y = k$ to get $3(0) - 4k = 17$, or $-4k = 17$. Divide both sides of the equation by -4 to get $k = -\frac{17}{4}$. Finally, divide c by k to get $\frac{c}{k} = \frac{\frac{17}{3}}{-\frac{17}{4}}$. When dividing fractions, multiply the reciprocal of the fraction in the denominator and the fraction in the numerator. This becomes $\frac{c}{k} = \left(\frac{17}{3}\right)\left(-\frac{4}{17}\right)$, and then $\frac{c}{k} = -\frac{4}{3}$. Using either method, the correct answer is (A).

17. **12** The question asks for the value of a constant in a system of equations. When a system of linear equations has infinitely many solutions, the two equations form the same line and are equivalent to each other. Since c is a coefficient of g, look for a way to cancel the f-terms and the constants when stacking and adding the equations. First, put the two equations in the same order by subtracting $21g$ from both sides of the second equation to get $21 = 6f - 36g$, and then subtract $6f$ from both sides of the second equation to get $21 - 6f = -36g$. The f-term and constant of the second equation are both 3 times the equivalent terms in the first equation with opposite signs, so multiply the first equation by 3 to get $-21 + 6f = 3cg$. Now stack and add the equations.

$$\begin{array}{r} -21 + 6f = 3cg \\ +\ \underline{21 - 6f = -36g} \\ 0 + 0 = 3cg - 36g \end{array}$$

Add $36g$ to both sides of the resulting equation to get $36g = 3cg$. Divide both sides of the equation by $3g$ to get $12 = c$. The correct answer is 12.

18. **C** The question asks for the perimeter of a triangle. Use the Geometry Basic Approach. Start by drawing a triangle on the scratch paper with a right angle and one of the remaining angles twice the size of the other. Next, label the figure with the information given, and label the smallest side as 15. The drawing should look something like this:

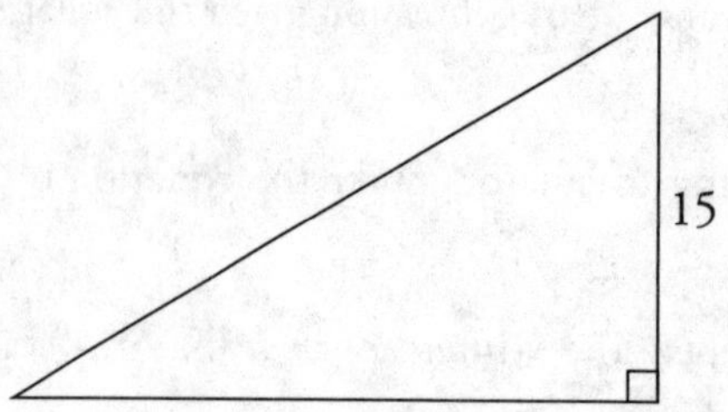

A 30:60:90 triangle is one of the special right triangles that has a specific proportional relationship among the sides. The proportion can be found by clicking open the reference sheet, and it is $x: x\sqrt{3}:2x$. Since the smallest side is 15, $x = 15$. The other sides are $15\sqrt{3}$ and $2(15) = 30$. Label the figure with this information; the figure now looks like this:

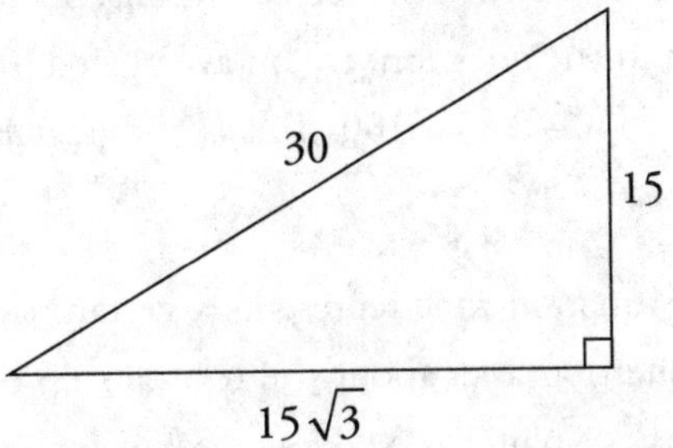

The perimeter of a geometric shape is the sum of the lengths of all of the sides. Add all three side lengths to get $15 + 15\sqrt{3} + 30 = 45 + 15\sqrt{3}$. The correct answer is (C).

19. **B** The question asks for the value of an expression based on information about a function. In function notation, $f(x) = y$. The number inside the parentheses is the x-value that goes into the function, or the input, and the value that comes out of the function is the y-value, or the output. The table gives four pairs of input and output values for the function. To solve for the constants c and d, start by plugging in one of the pairs from the table. Plug $x = 2$ and $g(x) = 46$ into the function to get $46 = 2c + d$. There is no way to solve for $c + d$ using only this equation, so plug in a second pair of values. Plug $x = 4$ and $g(x) = 0$ into the function to get $0 = 4c + d$. There are now two equations with two constants, so find a way to make one of the constants disappear when stacking and adding the equations. Multiply the second equation by –1 to get $0 = -4c - d$.

The d-terms are now the same with opposite signs, so stack and add the two equations.

$$\begin{array}{r} 46 = 2c + d \\ +\ \underline{0 = -4c - d} \\ 46 = -2c \end{array}$$

Divide both sides of the resulting equation by –2 to get $c = -23$. Plug $c = -23$ into the first equation to get $46 = 2(-23) + d$, or $46 = -46 + d$. Add 46 to both sides of the equation to get $92 = d$. Add the values of the two constants to get $c + d = -23 + 92 = 69$. The correct answer is (B).

20. **105** The question asks for a value given information about the mean, or average, of a data set. For averages, use the formula $T = AN$, in which T is the *Total*, A is the *Average*, and N is the *Number of things*. Start by finding the mean of the four integers given in the question. There are 4 values, so $N = 4$. Find the *Total* by adding the four integers to get $T = 114 + 109 + 106 + 111 = 440$. The average formula becomes $440 = (A)(4)$. Divide both sides of the equation by 4 to get $A = 110$. The question asks for the smallest integer that results in the full data set having an average less than

that of the four integers shown, which is 110. Start with the next smallest integer, 109, for the average, and solve for the fifth integer in the data set. The average formula becomes $T = (109)(5)$, so $T = 545$. The total of the first four integers was 440, so the fifth integer is $545 - 440 = 105$. The question also states that *the mean of the entire data set is an integer* and that all of the integers are *greater than 101*, and 105 meets both of these conditions. To see whether a smaller integer meets all of the conditions given in the question, try an average of 108. The *Total* is now $T = (108)(5) = 540$, and the fifth integer is $540 - 440 = 100$. This is not greater than 101, so 100 is too small. The correct answer is 105.

21. **B** The question asks for the function that represents a certain situation. There are variables in the answer choices, and the question asks about the relationship between the number of points and the number of assignments, so plug in. Make $a = 51$ to include the 5-point assignments and at least one 3-point assignment. The first 50 completed assignments earn 5 points each, for a total of $(50)(5) = 250$ points. The additional completed assignment earns 3 points. The total number of points earned for the 51 completed assignments is $250 + 3 = 253$. This is the target value; write it down and circle it. Now plug $a = 51$ into the answer choices and eliminate any that do not match the target value. In function notation, $f(x) = y$. The number inside the parentheses is the x-value that goes into the function, or the input, and the value that comes out of the function is the y-value, or the output. Since $a = 51$, 51 is the input value, and the output value should be 253. Choice (A) becomes $g(51) = 3(51) + 5$, then $g(51) = 153 + 5$, and then $g(51) = 158$. This does not match the target value, so eliminate (A). Choice (B) becomes $g(51) = 3(51) + 100$, then $g(51) = 153 + 100$, and then $g(51) = 253$. This matches the target, so keep (B), but check the remaining answers just in case. Choice (C) becomes $g(51) = 3(51) + 250$, then $g(51) = 153 + 250$, and then $g(51) = 403$; eliminate (C). Choice (D) becomes $g(51) = 8(51) - 150$, then $408 - 150$, and then $g(51) = 258$; eliminate (D). The correct answer is (B).

22. **D** The question asks for information that will provide proof of similar triangles. Use the Geometry Basic Approach. Triangles are similar when they have the same angle measures and proportional side lengths, so draw two triangles on the scratch paper that look similar but are different sizes. Then label the figures with information from the question: label *AB* as 22, *XY* as 11, and angles *A* and *X* as 77°. The drawing should look something like this.

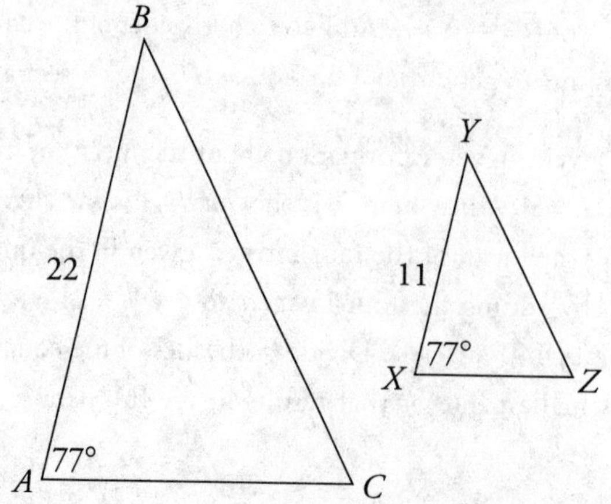

Next, evaluate the Roman numeral statements. They all give information about angles, so focus on the rule that similar triangles have the same three angle measures. The question only provides enough information to know that one angle measure is the same in both triangles, so more information is necessary; eliminate (A). Angle measures alone do provide enough information if all three angles have the same measure, so eliminate (B).

Check the remaining answers one at a time to see whether one shows that all three angles have the same measure. Try (C), and label angle B as 40° and angle Y as 50°. Find the measure of the third angle in each triangle. All triangles contain 180°, so set up equations: $77° + 40° + C° = 180°$, and $77° + 50° + Z° = 180°$. Simplify the first equation to get $117° + C° = 180°$, then subtract 117° from both sides of the equation to get $C = 63°$. Simplify the second equation to get $127° + Z° = 180°$, then subtract 127° from both sides of the equation to get $Z = 53°$.

Label the figures with this information, and they now look like this:

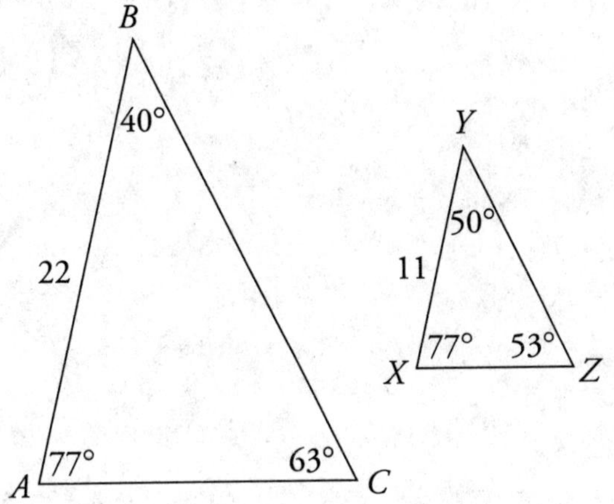

The triangles do not have the same three angle measures, so they are not similar; eliminate (C). Try (D) and follow the same steps. Label angle B as 40° and angle Z as 63°. Angle C is again 63°. Solve for angle Y: $77° + Y° + 63° = 180°$, $140° + Y° = 180°$, and $Y° = 40°$. Label the triangles with this information to see that the triangles now have the same three angle measures. The correct answer is (D).

NOTES

NOTES